D0786492

POLICY AND POLITICS

for Nurses and Other Health Professionals

Advocacy and Action

Edited by:

Donna M. Nickitas, PhD, RN, CNAA, BC
Professor and Graduate Specialty Coordinator
Dual Degree MS/MPA
Hunter College
Hunter-Bellevue School of Nursing
The City University of New York
Deputy Executive Director, Doctor of Nursing Science Program
Graduate Center, The City University of New York
New York, NY
Editor
Nursing Economic$, The Journal for Health Care Leaders
Pitman, NJ

Donna J. Middaugh, PhD, RN
Associate Dean
Coordinator, Nursing Administration Master's Specialty
College of Nursing
University of Arkansas for Medical Sciences
Little Rock, AR

Nancy Aries, PhD
Interim University Dean for Undergraduate Education
City University of New York
New York, NY

JONES AND BARTLETT PUBLISHERS
Sudbury, Massachusetts
BOSTON TORONTO LONDON SINGAPORE

World Headquarters
Jones and Bartlett Publishers
40 Tall Pine Drive
Sudbury, MA 01776
978-443-5000
info@jbpub.com
www.jbpub.com

Jones and Bartlett Publishers Canada
6339 Ormindale Way
Mississauga, Ontario L5V 1J2
Canada

Jones and Bartlett Publishers International
Barb House, Barb Mews
London W6 7PA
United Kingdom

Jones and Bartlett's books and products are available through most bookstores and online booksellers. To contact Jones and Bartlett Publishers directly, call 800-832-0034, fax 978-443-8000, or visit our website, www.jbpub.com.

Substantial discounts on bulk quantities of Jones and Bartlett's publications are available to corporations, professional associations, and other qualified organizations. For details and specific discount information, contact the special sales department at Jones and Bartlett via the above contact information or send an email to specialsales@jbpub.com.

Production Credits

Publisher: Kevin Sullivan
Acquisitions Editor: Amy Sibley
Associate Editor: Patricia Donnelly
Editorial Assistant: Rachel Shuster
Senior Production Editor: Carolyn F. Rogers
Marketing Manager: Rebecca Wasley
Photo and Permissions Associate: Emily Howard
V.P., Manufacturing and Inventory Control: Therese Connell
Composition: Auburn Associates, Inc.
Cover Design: Timothy Dziewit
Cover and Title Page Images: left to right, Courtesy of the National Library of Medicine (taken at the American National Red Cross Hospital No. 1 in Paris, France); © Kim Seidl/ShutterStock, Inc.; © Rmarmion/Dreamstime.com
Printing and Binding: Malloy, Inc.
Cover Printing: Malloy, Inc.

Library of Congress Cataloging-in-Publication Data

Policy and politics for nurses and other health professions : advocacy and action / edited by Donna M. Nickitas, Donna J. Middaugh, Nancy Aries.
p. ; cm.
Includes bibliographical references and index.
ISBN-13: 978-0-7637-5659-8 (pbk.)
ISBN-10: 0-7637-5659-8 (pbk.)
1. Medical policy–United States. 2. Nursing–United States. I. Costello-Nickitas, Donna M. II. Middaugh, Donna J. III. Aries, Nancy.
[DNLM: 1. Health Policy–United States. 2. Health Care Costs–United States. 3. Lobbying–United States. 4. Policy Making–United States. WA 540 AA1 P766 2011]
RA395.A3P587 2011
362.10973--dc22

2010006367

6048

Printed in the United States of America
14 13 12 11 10 9 8 7 6 5 4 3

Dedication

In memory of my parents, John and Anna Costello: Thank you for encouraging me to follow my dream and discover my passion of becoming a registered professional nurse. For my husband, Michael: Thank you for all your patience, love, and guidance on my journey promoting advocacy and action for my patients, students, and colleagues.

Donna M. Costello-Nickitas

I dedicate this book to my husband Robert and our son Robert Guy, who have awakened my soul and are my inspiration in everything I do and every choice I make. They have taught me to love unconditionally, enjoy life and live with purpose. Also, to the memory of my mother, Alpha Duff, a teacher, who taught me to never stop learning. *Ex Deo familia. Ex pertinacia victoria.*

Donna J. Middaugh

To the memory of my father, Leon J. Aries, a surgeon, who taught me that caring for one's patients was the fundamental job of all health professionals.

Nancy Aries

Contents

Foreword

I have been fortunate to have worked in the health field at every professional level through 5 decades. Being a registered nurse has afforded me a unique vantage point and lens to view through the "retrospectoscope" as well as peer into the future. Nurses by their nature and training view their patients, community and even the world with great refractive holistic clarity. Being a nurse first has made me a better physician and surgeon general.

The core values of nursing are with me in all of my endeavors. In fact, I am most proud to always state, "once a nurse, always a nurse"! I have watched nursing evolve from a subservient role where we could not write our nursing notes in the progress notes and our observations and constructive input were not always welcome. Today we have evolved as health leaders, consummate patient advocates, and clinical and administrative experts, and public polls often demonstrate that nurses are among the most trusted professionals.

Our nursing leadership is apparent at all levels of our healthcare systems to include advising on, constructing, and implementing policy. Policy development and execution is complex and multifactorial while being essential to the orderly, efficient, and effective conduct of any organization.

Understanding the process and components of effective policy takes years of training and experience. Nurses are perfectly positioned to assume a growing role in policy by virtue of their training, experience, holistic approach, selfless service, and extraordinary public credibility.

We should require our nurses and all health professionals to be knowledgeable about the intersection of policy and politics and encourage them to take an active role in the policy arena.

Today more than ever we need well-informed nurses and health professionals to guide our nonpartisan discussions about health reform. As nurses, we serve a special interest group, but our special interest group is often the forgotten constituent in the partisan political debate—the patient!

This textbook, *Policy and Politics for Nurses and Other Health Professions*, is a wonderful guide for the novice or the professor and it will serve to improve policy health literacy for all.

Richard H. Carmona, RN, MD, MPH, FACS*
17th Surgeon General of the United States
Distinguished Professor, University of Arizona
Vice Chairman, Canyon Ranch
President, Canyon Ranch Institute
**Inactive*

Preface

Our vision and commitment in writing this book was based on the belief that healthcare policy is centered on the notion that all healthcare professionals regardless of their discipline required a fundamental understanding of the healthcare system. No longer can healthcare professionals be prepared solely for clinical practice. They must ready themselves to engage in the economic, political, and policy debates in the field. This process of engagement requires knowledge about advocacy and action. For meaningful influence to occur, health professionals must stand ready to inform, educate, and advocate to leaders at their own institutions and to the insurance companies, government, health suppliers such as the pharmaceutical industry and other players within the industry on health policy, planning, and management.

The ideas presented in this book offer our combined thoughts about ways for nurses and allied health professionals and other grassroots activists who have an interest in improving healthcare systems and services in local, state, national and global communities to become involved in healthcare advocacy and action. This book offers an interdisciplinary approach to understanding health care, health finance, health professionals, and health policy.

We have sought contributions from a group of diverse experts who recognize the internal and external forces influencing healthcare in America. Our rationale for seeking a transdisciplinary approach was the understanding that no one individual or discipline has a comprehensive understanding of the challenges and complexities confronting the healthcare system and the potential for healthcare reform. These challenges include, but are not limited to, increasing access to care and improving quality by such actions as the reduction of medical errors and the promotion of health and wellness, and last by improving efficiency and reducing costs.

As the nation explores ways to reform the healthcare system, health professionals recognize that our healthcare system is broken and needs complete, comprehensive reform to assure that future generations may enjoy a delivery system that will ensure their health and well-being. With unreliable quality, Americans on average receive only 55% of the recommended care they need for common conditions. An estimated 44,000 to 98,000 people die every year from medical errors. With inconsistent access, there remains 47 million who are uninsured; many uninsured are from working families. Despite healthcare costs that exceed $7,000 for every citizen in this country, the uninsured are 8 times more likely to skip medical care because they cannot afford it.

Every day, healthcare professionals exercise their clinical judgment and leadership skills to make important and much-needed changes that increase access to and improve the quality and affordability of health care. This textbook offers future healthcare practitioners and others who are committed to improving health disparities and healthcare equality, keen insight and understanding that clinical practice is derived from regulation, laws, and policies that are initiated from public policy and politics. This is just the starting point. As educators, and health professionals, we are committed to support nurses and other health professionals to gain leadership expertise as well as executive positions and ensure that they have a place and a voice at decision-making tables. For nurses, in particular, the seat at the table has not always been that easy. They have had less influence on healthcare reform than physicians, institutional providers, government, insurance and pharmaceutical executives and others. We believe that nurses must have increased influence and equity as compared to other important decision makers or revenue generators on national issues relating to influencing health reform. This why we have placed nurses first in the title of the book. However, the lessons from this book are addressed to a broader audience of health professionals because together with nurses they have insights that are not otherwise represented. Given their role as caregivers, they bring a unique perspective to policy-making concerns. Our hope that in the not so distance future, nurses and other health professionals will assume their rightful place at the table and speak with equal voice and influence.

Donna M. Nickitas
Donna J. Middaugh
Nancy Aries

Contributors

Nancy Aries, PhD
Interim University Dean for Undergraduate Education
City University of New York
New York, NY

Steven L. Baumann, PhD, APRN-BC, RN
Professor
Hunter College
The City University of New York
New York, NY

Kunsook Bernstein, PhD, RN, PMHNP-BC, CASAC
Associate Professor
Hunter College
Hunter-Bellevue School of Nursing
The City University of New York
New York, NY

Claudia Beverly, PhD, RN, FAAN
Professor
Director, Hartford Center of Geriatric Nursing Excellence
University of Arkansas for Medical Sciences
Little Rock, AR

Barbara Caress
Director of Strategic Planning & Policy
SEIU Local 32BJ Benefit Funds
New York, NY

Ellen Chesler, PhD
Distinguished Lecturer
Director, Eleanor Roosevelt Initiative at Roosevelt House
Hunter College
The City University of New York
New York, NY

Leah Curtin, ScD(h), MA, RN, FAAN
Executive Editor
Professional Outreach
American Nurse Today
Director
Nurse Manager Bootcamp
Former Editor in Chief, *Journal of Nursing Management*
Cincinnati, OH

Jessie Daniels, PhD
Associate Professor
Hunter College
Community Health, Department of Urban Health
The City University of New York
New York, NY

Donna DuLong, RN, BSN
Professional Research Assistant
College of Nursing
University of Colorado Denver
Denver, CO

Jonathan Engel, PhD
Professor of Public Affairs
School of Public Affairs
Baruch College
The City University of New York
New York, NY

Nancy L. Falk, PhD, MBA, BSN
Adjunct Faculty
College of Health and Human Services
George Mason University

Keville Frederickson, EdD, RN, FAAN
Professor and Director Research and Scholarship
Lehman College
The City University of New York
Director, Doctor of Nursing Science Program
Graduate Center, The City University of New York
New York, NY

Mary Mincer Hansen, PhD, RN
Associate Professor
MPH Program and Global Health Department
Des Moines University
Des Moines, IA

Mary J. Jones, BSEMS, MA
Deputy Director
Iowa Department of Public Health
Division Director
Acute Disease Prevention and Emergency Response Lucas State Office Building
Des Moines, IA

Emma Kontzamanis, RN, MA
Assistant Professor
Department of Nursing
New York City College of Technology
The City University of New York
New York, NY

Eileen Levy, MS, NP
Huntington Hospital
Huntington, NY

Paula A. Lucey, MSN, RN, CNAA
Lamplighter Consulting, LLC
Greenfield, WI

Donna J. Middaugh, PhD, RN
Associate Dean
Coordinator, Nursing Administration Master's Specialty
College of Nursing
University of Arkansas for Medical Sciences
Little Rock, AR

Donna M. Nickitas, PhD, RN, CNAA, BC
Professor and Graduate Specialty Coordinator
Dual Degree MS/MPA
Hunter College
Hunter-Bellevue School of Nursing
The City University of New York
Deputy Executive Director, Doctor of Nursing Science Program
Graduate Center, The City University of New York
New York, NY
Editor
Nursing Economic$, The Journal for Health Care Leaders
Pitman, NJ

Kathleen M. Nokes, PhD, RN, FAAN
Professor
Hunter College
Hunter-Bellevue School of Nursing
The City University of New York
New York, NY

Roby Robertson, PhD
Director and Professor
Institute of Government
University of Arkansas at Little Rock
Little Rock, AR

Carol Roye, EdD, RN
Professor
Hunter College
Hunter-Bellevue School of Nursing
The City University of New York
New York, NY

Joseph Saladino, MSN, RN, NPP
Instructor
Hunter College
Hunter-Bellevue School of Nursing
The City University of New York
New York, NY

Franklin A. Shaffer, EdD, ScD(h), RN, FAAN
Sr. Vice President and Chief Nursing Officer
Cross Country Healthcare, Inc.
Chief Learning Officer
Cross Country University
New York, NY

Diane J. Skiba, PhD, FAAN, FACMI
Professor and Project Director
I-Collaboratory: Partnerships in Learning
College of Nursing
University of Colorado Denver
Aurora, CO

Jonathan Small, BA
College Assistant
Doctor of Nursing Science Program
Graduate Center, The City University of New York
New York, NY

Alison P. Smith, BA, BS, RN
Director
C-Change
Washington, DC

Elizabeth Summy, MSc, CAE
Vice President, Personal Membership Groups
American Hospital Association
Chicago, IL

Pamela Trevino, RN, BSN
Staff Nurse IV
Arkansas Children's Hospital
Little Rock, AR

Ralph J. Vogel, RN, PhD
University of Arkansas for Medical Sciences
College of Nursing
Little Rock, AR

Lametria S. Wafford, RN, BSN, MNSc(C)
Arkansas Children's Hospital
Little Rock, AR

Helen Werner, PhD, RN
Assistant Professor
Hunter College
Hunter-Bellevue School of Nursing
The City University of New York
New York, NY

Section I

Introduction

Chapter 1

To Engage or Not Engage: Choices Confronting Nurses and Other Health Professionals

Nancy Aries

OVERVIEW

Healthcare professionals of the 21st century must understand how the government, together with providers, consumers, and insurers, interacts in the health policy process. This chapter provides a comprehensive overview of the essential elements that drive and shape health policy in America. By understanding the politics of policy making and program implementation, health professionals will be better prepared to advocate for a healthcare system that best meets the population's needs.

OBJECTIVES

- To understand the formal definition of health policy
- To understand the policy-making process, which includes the following:
  - Describing the ways competing concepts of federalism create the structure within which policy is determined
  - Explaining the role of the market and the government in the framing of health policy
  - Identifying the competing interests that shape health policy and the ways these competing interests determine policy outcomes
  - Recognizing the role that implementation plays in the policy process
- To describe the opportunities and constraints that health professionals and their patients face as a result of policy decisions
- To recognize different ways that healthcare advocates can impact policy and programmatic decisions

KEY TERMS

- ❑ Advocacy
- ❑ Federalism
- ❑ Government programs: Taxation, provision or purchase of services, regulation
- ❑ Implementation
- ❑ Policy: Social policy, health policy
- ❑ Policy-making process
- ❑ The role of markets and government
- ❑ Stakeholders and interest groups

Another Text on Health Policy and Politics: Why?

Numerous text books are available that describe the healthcare delivery system in the United States or step back to explain how politics and policy making influence the organization of care delivery. Why are we putting another text on the market that purports to address many of the same questions? Our answer is both simple and complex.

Simply put, we believe that many of these books fail to address the reality of health care as experienced by nurses and other health professionals. Many of the students and practitioners with whom we work are totally absorbed in the day-to-day demands of their jobs. They work hard just to keep up with the needs of patients and their families, health colleagues, physicians, and administrators. Many describe themselves as running up a down escalator that speeds up every time they think that they might make some forward progress. One consequence of this consuming daily struggle is that there is no time or intellectual space to step back and reflect on the larger institutional, social, political, and economic forces that shape their professions and their industry.

The more complex answer is that students often recognize that the hospitals, community-based agencies, and other health facilities that employ them are under severe pressure to cut costs and that they, as front-line workers, bear the brunt of these cost-cutting measures when their organizations are understaffed and the demand for productivity is increasing. If they are going to act to improve this situation, they need to know exactly how the dots that define health policy connect to the dots that define care and treatment. This book is intended to provide an understanding of policy that is rooted in the perspectives of nursing and other health professionals but at the same time helps make students conversant with the politics and economics that generate the rules of the game under which they work with such skill and dedication.

In this book, we want to put the opportunities and constraints that confront our professions in a larger perspective. By developing a more nuanced understanding of the ways policy shapes the organization of the healthcare system, we hope to provide those working in healthcare delivery with the tools that they need to influence these decisions. One book cannot change how we conduct our professional lives, but it can change how we understand our options. This book demonstrates that we have options other than hoping to get by or finding positions where we do not experience the pain of those whose care is compromised. To take no action is to allow decisions to be made by others. Engagement in the policy world can be an effective way to overcome a sense of helplessness about the current state of the healthcare system. By more fully understanding the healthcare system and the levers for change, it becomes possible to influence more actively the direction that the system takes.

This plea for engagement is shaped by our own experiences of the healthcare system. There has not been a time in recent history when the problems of healthcare costs, access, and quality were not serious concerns. In the early 1970s, we achieved greater access to care after the implementation of Medicare and Medicaid, but healthcare costs began to escalate. Access was expanded, but no one was sure how it could be sustained. In the mid 1980s, healthcare expenditures topped 10% of gross domestic product (GDP), and the concept of managed care gained salience as a way to control costs while maintaining quality. Cost control, but not necessarily quality improvement, was achieved, whereas access declined as the number of uninsured increased. In the early 1990s, President Clinton's healthcare reform proposal reached Congress. Through a complicated system labeled managed competition, the plan was purported to increase access, control costs, and improve quality. The bill was defeated. Healthcare costs stayed flat through most of the 1990s, as managed care became the predominant insurance model; however, access became more restricted, and there were growing concerns regarding quality of care.

We cannot continue on our present course. Healthcare expenditures reached $2.3 trillion in 2008, or 16% of GDP. That amounted to $7,681 per person. The health share of the GDP is projected to reach 19.5% by 2017 (National Health Expenditure Data Fact Sheet, 2008). The number of uninsured Americans was nearly 47 million, or 16% of the population in 2005, the latest government data available (DeNavas-Walt et al., 2007). This is an increase of almost nine million people since 2000. The United States probably has one of the most sophisticated healthcare systems—yet it ranked twenty-sixth internationally for mortality of children under 5 years of age (State of the World's Mothers, 2007).

Although it is critical that we describe the ways that health policy has shaped the healthcare system, it is equally important to understand that policy making is an interactive process. In some instances, government dictates the response of providers. In other cases, providers dictate the response of government. Then there is the business sector, insurance companies, public health organizations, professional associations, and advocacy groups. Each one is trying to be heard and push the system to become more responsive in its needs and the needs of its constituents. In this book, we want you to recognize that as health professionals you can play a similar role in this process. You are in a position to advocate for your professions and for the patients that you serve. Your voice can and should be heard. The combination of describing the health system and explaining how complex policy processes shape it and the ways you can become instrumental in that process distinguishes this book.

In order to provide the context for understanding the policy and the policy-making process, this chapter addresses the following issues. In the first section, we define policy and consider how it shapes our experience of the healthcare system. When we are successful in our jobs, it is often because of policies. When we fail, it is often the case that policies have created an environment in which it is difficult to operate. Policy, as will be explained, can have many meanings. In this book, the term policy is used to refer to government programs. The second section highlights the different ways that government policy and programs intervene in the organization and delivery of health services in order to assure greater social equity in the distribution of goods and services. This involves understanding the competing concepts of federalism and the ways that it impacts the development of government programs. After this framework is established, we can consider the actual programmatic tools available to government to achieve its goals. The choice of tools is determined by the balance established between the market and the government in overseeing the organization of healthcare delivery.[1] Although we have a mixed system, each presents a different set of opportunities and constraints for policy makers. Next, we examine the actual process by which government policy is made. This involves understanding which groups have a stake in the development of government programs, how their interests get expressed in the political process, and whose interests are ultimately reflected in the government programs. This chapter does not explain the legislative process. That is better left to a civics text. Rather, it explains how interest groups influence that process in order to achieve what they perceive to be a more favorable outcome. Policy making, however, does not stop with the passage of legislation. Implementation is equally important, although sometimes overlooked. Implementation is also an opportunity to influence how policy is realized on a day-to-day basis. The final section of the chapter brings this discussion back to the nurses and other health professionals for whom this text is written. We reconsider why a better understanding of policy not only impacts our work and the experiences of those seeking health care but also provides a framework for better understanding how to become more effective players within the field.

Health Policy Defined

Policy in the broadest sense is the manifestation of ideology or belief systems about how the world should work (Rushefsky, 2008). For example, as a nation, we have watched our beliefs about foreign relations shift from being highly isolationist to becoming the protector of democratic values. We have strong beliefs about the value of rugged individualism, which is manifest in rags-to-riches stories. One way our beliefs are manifest is in government actions. This means we should be able to analyze government actions in terms of the ways that they are reflective of dominant social values or ideology. The ideological justification for the Iraq War put forward by President Bush was our nation's responsibility to promote democracy. Similarly, the passage of welfare reform in the 1990s can be rooted in a social value of financial independence.

Public policy, the term used to describe government actions, is typically divided into three areas: foreign policy, economic policy, and social policy (Lowi & Ginsberg, 1998). The objective of foreign policy is to defend national sovereignty. Economic policy is designed to promote and regulate markets. Although foreign and economic policy seeks to improve the overall well-being of society by promoting the political and economic well-being of American society, typically policies in these areas do not have equal impact on all sectors of society. Some groups may

[1]The terms "market" and "government" are short-hand expressions to describe the two alternative ways in which society conducts its business. "Market" means reliance on generally voluntary exchanges between private parties. Sometimes these exchanges are mandated and regulated by government, as is the case with mandatory liability insurance to own a motor vehicle. "Government" means reliance on the direct provision of a service by government employees, as is the case with Veterans Affairs hospitals. It is not uncommon to use a combination of markets and government, as is the case with Medicare and Medicaid, where government makes payments to private providers to care for individuals who the government is seeking to service.

benefit, whereas others might find themselves suffering undue consequences. The North American Free Trade Agreement benefited the economy overall, but many persons who held manufacturing jobs found themselves unemployed as production moved from the United States to countries with lower production costs. Social policy often becomes the means by which the unintended consequences of policies that seek to better the overall condition of American society are addressed. Government actions become the means by which we ensure the provision of the basic necessities: food, shelter, health care, and education (Midgley & Livermore, 2008). Social policy is redistributive by its very nature. Its goal is to achieve greater social equity.

Health policy can be located within the larger realm of social policy. Because policy generally is rooted in social values and ideologies, our discussion of health policy begins with the recognition of the values and ideology that are reflected in the organization of the healthcare system. The historic course of American health policy is best described in terms of our shifting beliefs about how access to care is provided. Sometimes we have stridently pursued health care as a right for all. Sometimes we have treated it as a privilege (Knowles, 1977). In fact, these competing values (i.e., a right versus a privilege) are simultaneously and continually at work in the outcomes of our health policy. Therefore, to understand health policy requires that we delve further into explaining how values can shape a complex set of actions.

The American approach to health insurance provides a good illustration of this duality. On one hand, we have a health insurance program that covers practically all Americans over the age of 65 years. One argument underscoring the creation of Medicare was that the older population had worked for the benefit of society and should not risk poverty in old age because of high healthcare costs. For those over 65 years of age, health care was deemed a right. The opposite holds true for the working-age population and their dependents. No universal health insurance program is available to Americans under 65 years of age. Either they can obtain health insurance as a benefit of employment, or they can purchase health insurance out of pocket. Health insurance, however, is costly. The average premium in 2007 was $2,613 for an individual health insurance policy. For those who cannot afford to purchase insurance, there is an array of safety net programs that provide marginal care and have been unable to address the needs of the rising number of uninsured (Center for Policy and Research, 2007). How did this situation come to pass? To get the answer, we need to understand how policy in this area evolved. We begin by understanding the nature of our federal system of policy making.

The Framework for Public Policy Making

Federalism

In order to understand the process of policy formation in the United States, it is necessary to grasp the meaning of federalism in the American context (Bovbjerg et al., 2003). American federalism is a system of governance in which the exercise of sovereign power is split between the 50 states and the national government. Hence, the federal government is limited in its actions in several important ways. First, there is the dual nature of our system of state and federal governance. When the nation was founded, the states ceded certain responsibilities to the federal government but retained others for themselves. In addition, within the federal government, there is a separation of powers among the legislative, executive, and judicial branches. This further constrains the power of the national government by dividing the government against itself. Finally, the Constitution limits government by protecting individual rights that cannot be denied except by extraordinary procedures.

According to the framers of the Constitution, the central government has express powers to levy taxes, declare war, and oversee interstate commerce. All power not expressly delegated to the federal government falls under the jurisdiction of the states. This system of dual federalism provides the context in which the patchwork quilt pattern of health policy exists. Although there is a strong national government, the states were initially more important than the national government in virtually all policies governing the lives of Americans, such as economic regulation, public health, and education. When President Pierce vetoed a law setting aside millions of acres of federal land to benefit the mentally ill, he argued that mental health was a state, not a federal, responsibility (Rothman, 1971).

Despite the fact that social policy relating to individual welfare is a state responsibility, there has been a constant expansion of federal power in this area since the Civil War. By the 1930s, scholars saw such a radical departure in the conduct of federalism that the New Deal has been characterized as a shift from a system of dual federalism to a system of cooperative federalism (Kernell & Jacobson, 2006). This shift was brought on by the severe social hardship of the Great Depression. During this period, the ability of states to protect the well-being of their citizens was diminished, as states had limited ability to raise funds through taxation or deficit financing; therefore, the states turned to the federal government, which initiated and funded many social programs. Using grants-in-aid programs, Congress appropriated money to state and local governments with the condition that the money be spent for particular purposes as defined by Congress. The Maternal and Child Health program, which was created under Title V of the Social Security Act in 1933, is an example of such a grants-in-aid program. This program sought to improve the health of low-income mothers and children. From a policy perspective, cooperative federalism is important because Congress began to set national goals and influence state activity in the realm of social programs.

Federal power increased through the 1960s as opposition grew to the variability in the ways that states implemented social programs. The federal government assumed a larger role in terms of shaping and funding social welfare programs by imposing national standards on the states through regulations and unfunded man-

dates (Conlan, 2006). Typically, the costs of regulatory compliance were not funded by the federal government. Hence, these were labeled as unfunded mandates. States needed to comply with the regulations or risk penalty such as the withholding of grant money. Federal regulatory authority was further advanced by the social movements of the 1960s. Civil rights advocates demanded greater regulation of federal programs in their efforts to achieve racial and social equity. One response of the federal government was to create categorical programs that made program funding directly available to community-based providers (Davis & Schoen, 1978). This meant federal funding bypassed the state governments entirely. The community health centers that were funded by the Office of Economic Opportunity provide an example of a categorically funded program. In this instance, the federal government bypassed the sovereign powers of the state governments and contracted directly with the healthcare providers for specified services.

In the late twentieth century, there was one more shift in the relationship between the federal government and the states. Starting with President Nixon but affirmed during Reagan's presidency, there has been a push to return authority to the states. Called the new federalism, it involves devolution of authority to the states to define social welfare programs that are funded by the federal government (Anton, 1997). The expressed intention is to permit the states to accommodate their diversity better. This is not possible when the federal government attempts to impose a "one size fits all" approach to social programs. The use of block grants is the mechanism by which greater discretion has been given to the states to shape programs to meet their specific needs. The block grants essentially combine funding from several grant-in-aid programs and allowed states to determine how the money will be spent to achieve broad social goals.

The very nature of federalism is that it results in an inherently fragmented system of governance (Steinmo & Watts, 1995). Nowhere is this clearer than in the arenas of social policy and health policy. Laws addressing similar needs are being passed at the federal, state, and local levels. As a result, there is no uniformity in health policy and related health programs. One of the consequences is the fragmentation and duplication of services caused by the different programs that address a particular need. Examples of gaps in services, duplication of services because of the nonalignment of program requirements, are easily recognized by persons serving older persons. An individual seeking long-term care is confronted with myriad programs. These include the Medicare and Medicaid programs as well as social service programs developed under Title XX of the Social Security Act and the Older Americans Act. Individuals must navigate this maze to determine their eligibility for services or providers must try to integrate the various funding streams in order to make available coordinated and comprehensive services for consumers. Although insurance regulation is a seemingly obscure problem, it has negatively impacted the nation's ability to develop a system of national health insurance. States have regulatory authority over insurance, including health insurance, but the Employment Retirement Income Security Act of 1975 supersedes state laws relating to benefit plans. This means businesses that self-insure for employee health as part of their benefits program are exempt from state insurance regulations. The significance of this dual regulatory system is that neither the states nor the federal government can easily mandate employers to offer health benefits because neither governing body has regulatory authority over all businesses in a particular area (Mariner, 1996).

Markets versus Government

Although individual well-being is a state responsibility, we do not depend on the government to provide for our basic needs. We acquire most goods and services, including health care, through the market. Our decisions and choices are influenced by the signals we get from sellers in terms of the prices at which they offer products. An obvious example is the ways in which the cost of gasoline is shifting consumer preferences away from large, fuel-inefficient automobiles toward smaller, fuel-efficient cars. Less obvious, perhaps, but more important are the ways in which the market responds to broader shifts in society. Consider how the housing market is responding to the reality of an aging population. As the population ages, the number of persons looking for housing alternatives that offer service options not readily available in single-family or multiunit dwellings is growing. Companies such as Marriott are entering the senior housing market in response to this demand. These are cases in which consumers influence producers. There are also cases in which business tries to influence consumer behavior. The direct marketing of pharmaceuticals to consumers through television and print advertising is intended to influence consumer perceptions about possible remedies for their health conditions.

A fundamental problem with the market is that it cannot respond adequately to social needs and preferences that cannot be expressed in terms of price. In a market, one only has a "right" to purchase the goods and services that one can afford. Those who cannot afford their desired goods and services are not entitled to them. What if, however, the service is essential to an individual's welfare or the welfare of a society? In these cases, the market is an inadequate distributive mechanism because competition puts those with fewer resources at a disadvantage in terms of accessing health services. Most Americans less than 65 years of age rely on health insurance as the means by which they can afford and therefore access health services; however, a growing number of small businesses have limited their benefit packages, no longer offer health insurance to family members, or have dropped their health insurance plans altogether (Reschovsky et al., 2006). To buy individual insurance policies is extremely expensive, which means the number of uninsured Americans is rising. As this case demonstrates, the market is limited in its ability to assure distributive justice. The market assumes an exchange among equals, but such an exchange is not possible in a society with unequal distribution of income (Arrow, 1963).

The government intervenes in these situations (Lowi & Ginsberg, 1998). The government's role derives from this fundamental tension between the economic organization of the production and the distribution of goods and services. Although the market pulls in the direction of economic inequality, political beliefs demand counterbalance in terms of the distribution of rights and opportunities. The government becomes the arena to address the needs of those persons who cannot provide for themselves through the exchange of goods and services in the market (Arrow, 1974). Through its policies and programs, government mediates the interests of the market and interests that have no expression in the market. It is the mechanism by which a society seeks to achieve greater equality. Its policies and programs are redistributive. By looking at who benefits and who is overlooked, one can see a broader theme about whether we are advancing social justice or reinforcing social inequality.

This tension between the role of the markets and government can be seen in the history of government programs such as Medicare. Medicare is a universal entitlement, which means that a defined population is eligible for care regardless of ability to pay. With few exceptions, a package of health services is available to persons over the age of 65 years. Such programs tend to be more expensive because of their all-inclusive nature, but they also tend to have broader political support because all persons can ultimately expect to benefit from the program (Brown & Sparer, 2003). Medicare benefits have come to be seen as a right, but the right is being questioned as the cost of Medicare continues to increase. In light of what is perceived to be the government's failure to organize care efficiently, proposals seek to balance the market and government as providers of this important benefit (Steuerle & Bovbjerg, 2008). Many alternatives to the existing Medicare program have been proposed, including making Medicare a premium support program rather than a defined set of benefits. This means that individuals would receive a predetermined sum to purchase a basic health plan. The amount might vary by age, gender, or geographic location. Those persons desiring more comprehensive coverage would have to pay an additional out-of-pocket charge.

Alternatively programs may be more selective in the population being served. Medicaid is an example of a selective program, in that it has need-based criteria for eligibility (Brown & Sparer, 2003). Medicaid creates a safety net for those who cannot afford to access health services through the market. Such programs are less expensive because they serve a subset of the population. The benefits are often more redistributive or in the case of Medicaid more comprehensive than the benefits of a universal program such as Medicare. Such selective programs tend to have less political support because they typically serve needy populations whose claim for services is considered questionable and because they often provide a level of service that is greater than can be accessed in the market by persons who are slightly above the cutoff. As a result, they are an easier target for cutbacks because their benefits are not available to the general population.

Governmental Intervention

The government has several tools at its disposal to intervene when the market cannot adequately address a problem (Stone, 2002). Among these are taxation, service provision, and regulation. Most often we think about taxation as the means by which government raises money in order to support its spending. Medicare Part A is financed by payroll taxes to which employers and employees contribute. Taxation, however, can also be used as a way to influence behavior. Many states place a high tax on the sale of cigarettes in order to influence personal choices about cigarette use (DeCicca et al., 2008). Higher cigarette taxes have resulted in lower rates of consumption. The revenues raised in this way can be either targeted for programs to support the desired behavioral change or contribute to the state's general revenues.

Another tool is the use of government revenues to support service provision. In some cases, the government is the actual provider of services. Public hospitals are locally financed institutions that were organized to serve persons who could not afford care. The Veterans Administration is a comprehensive healthcare system provided by the federal government to the men and women who have medical problems related to their injuries after discharge from the service. Both are "socialized" medicine in that the programs are managed and provided by government agencies. Alternatively, the government can purchase services from the private market. Medicaid is an example of such a program. Medicaid enrollees seek services from providers who have contracted with the state government to provide services. These providers bill the government for their services and are reimbursed for the medical care they provide. Such spending is designed to increase access of persons with limited resources to the market. The government can also be a producer and a purchaser of services. This is the case with biomedical research. The National Institutes of Health has a large biomedical research complex that supports numerous researchers. In addition, the National Institutes of Health fund independent researchers at universities and research laboratories across the country.

The purchase of service may also take an indirect form whereby the government subsidizes specific sellers to encourage their participation in markets that might not be competitive based on price. For example, medical education is an extremely costly endeavor (Koenig et al., 2003). Hospitals that train physicians cannot compete on price with nonteaching hospitals given the additional costs incurred for resident and faculty salaries and the additional resources used for each patient seen by a resident. As a result, Medicare funds physician training by funding the salaries of residents and subsidizing the hospitals where residents are trained. Another example is the orphan drug program (Grabowski, 2005). The government subsidizes pharmaceutical companies to develop and produce drugs that are used by a very small number of persons and therefore are unprofitable to develop and produce. Through these types of programs, the government offsets what might be the high cost of services or encourages program expansion in specific areas.

A third programmatic tool is government regulation of the market. Regulations are legal restrictions that aim to produce outcomes that otherwise might not occur. Examples of regulation include the licensure of physicians and other health professionals (Grumbach, 2002). These regulations were adapted in the early twentieth century as a way to protect the public from practitioners who were not deemed qualified to provide care. Through a series of educational and practice requirements and an examination, states regulate who can and cannot provide medical and healthcare services. Another example of government regulation is state-mandated nursing staff to patient ratios for hospital-based care (Conway et al., 2008). These regulations are designed to protect patients by maintaining a minimum number of nurses in a department at any time. These regulations are intended to prevent hospitals from cutting corners financially by understaffing a unit.

The Policy-Making Process

Interest Groups

Federalism creates the structure within which social policy is made. Federalism, however, does not explain what will be the content of a particular program and how programs are changed over time. The substance is determined by those individuals and groups that have interests in the field, and change occurs as the power of these groups to influence outcomes rises and falls (Smith, 1993). The healthcare field is comprised of many players who can be found inside and outside of government. There are physicians, nurses, hospital administrators, insurance companies, and on and on. They represent multiple interests, and each one is trying to influence the direction of government policy. The challenge for policy analysts is to understand how these interests are organized and which ones have the most influence and why.

Because health and health care are fundamental to each of our well-being, it is a sphere of activity that garners everyone's interest even if in passing. Although it is possible to speak generally about the public's interest in health care, there are multiple pressure groups that represent discrete interests in the health sector and that want to influence the outcome (Kernell

& Jacobson, 2006). These groups are generally known and identifiable. They typically work on their own behalf when issues are quite specific. They form coalitions when the issues are more general. These groups must be examined more closely as they shape the content of health policy making.

Figure 1-1 provides a schema for understanding which groups are part of the healthcare field and how their interests can be understood in relation to each other and the field as a whole. Healthcare providers are most central to the discussion of health policy. They are surrounded by persons who use the healthcare system and by three groups that support the operation of the system: payers, the medical supply industry, and knowledge producers. Although there are stronger and weaker ties between each of these groups, their actions have impacts that reverberate throughout the field.

Healthcare providers can broadly be categorized in two groups: clinicians and the organizations where they work. On the clinical side, one can speak about physicians, nurses, and other

Figure 1-1 Health policy field.

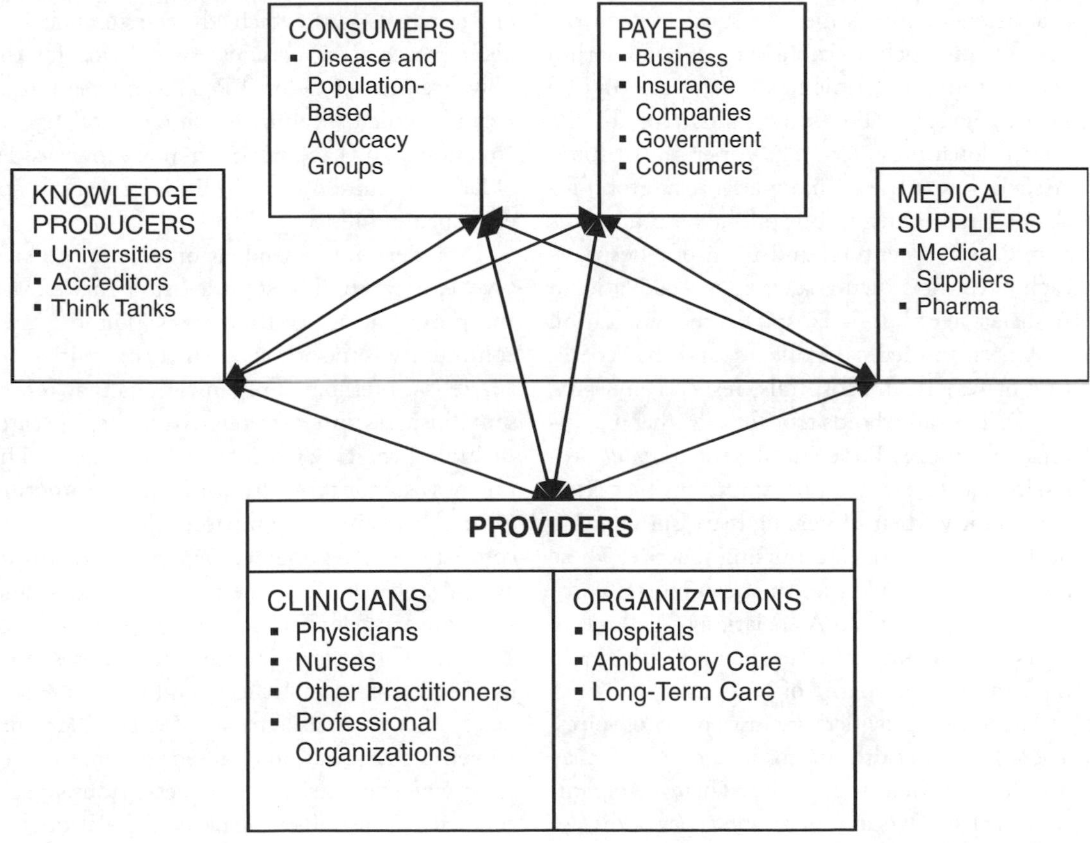

advanced practice providers. On the institutional side, there are hospitals, long-term care organizations, and ambulatory care organizations. Although it is possible to identify broad categories of interest, none of these groups speak with a single voice. Physicians as a group are represented by the American Medical Association (AMA); however, on specific policies, the AMA may avoid the issue because the specialists' point of view differs from the interests of primary care physicians. As a result, there are many physician organizations representing unique sets of interests. For example, the American Board of Internal Medicine represents internists. The American Academy of Family Physicians represents family practice physicians. The American College of Surgeons represents practitioners of this medical specialty, and the list goes on. Such divisions can be found within other groups of clinicians. There are myriad nursing groups. The same holds true for the institutional providers. The American Hospital Association is the primary advocacy group for the hospital industry, but public hospitals, academic health centers, and for-profit hospitals each have their own associations: the National Association of Public Hospitals, the Association of American Medical Colleges, and the Federation of American Hospitals, respectively (Fox, 1986). The same holds true for the other organizational groups. For example, the nursing profession has several lead organizations that often work jointly when addressing issues surrounding health, health care, and nursing practice. These associations include the American Nurses Association, the American Association of Colleges of Nursing, the National League of Nursing, and the American Academy of Nursing.

Healthcare providers are just one set of voices. There are also healthcare consumers. Again, they do not speak in a single voice. There are organizations that advocate for single types of disease such as the American Cancer Association, the American Lung Association, and the National Mental Health Association. This list is also long, with organizations representing persons with specific diseases such as Parkinson's, lupus, arthritis, and autism. In some cases, their concerns are specific to advancing the treatment of the specific illness, and in other cases, their agendas more broadly relate to better financing of a discrete set of services. In addition to disease-specific groups, there are population-based groups that speak on behalf of their membership's need for health services. The largest groups represent women, older persons, and the poor and racial and ethnic minorities. For example, there is the National Organization for Women, which advocates for women's health; the American Association of Retired Persons, which advocates on behalf of older persons; the National Association for the Advancement of Colored People and the Urban League, which speak to the interests of African Americans; and La Raza, which speaks to the issues of Latino groups. Again, the list is long and is not explained in full.

Providers are dependent on revenue to survive. Critical to the system are those that pay for the provision of health services. The business community is the prime purchaser of health care. There is a plethora of organizations that represent business interests relative to health care, including the U.S. Chamber of Commerce. The business sector typically works in conjunction with the insurance companies. The insurance companies are represented by the Health Insurance Association of America. The federal and state governments are also major purchasers of services. The federal government is represented by the Centers for Medicare and Medicaid Services, and organizations such as the National Governors Association represent the interests of state governments. Each of these groups has a concern for the well-being of the population, but each one also has a stake in how health services are financed and reimbursed.

Closely aligned to the clinical providers is what is termed as knowledge producers. The most obvious are the universities and biomedical research organizations. These groups are concerned with advancing the knowledge that underpins medical care and establishing and maintaining standards for medical practice. One of the most central organizations is the American Association of Medical Colleges. Beyond the university, there are think tanks that are concerned with the production and dissemination of knowledge and the associations such as the Institute of Medicine, the PEW Commission, and the Commonwealth Fund, as well as the Joint Commission on the Accreditation of Healthcare Organizations that are concerned with maintaining the standards of medical practice through accreditation, examinations, and licensing.

The last group to consider is the medical supply industry. This sector is assuming a larger role in health policy decisions as technology plays a greater role in the provision of health care. The fastest growing part of this sector is the pharmaceutical industry, which is represented by the Pharmaceutical Research and Manufacturers of America. The growing set of suppliers of medical devises such as stents and medical equipment such as imaging machines should be taken into account also. The American healthcare system is known for its technological know-how. This means that these interests must be considered when decisions are made that impact their use.

Interest Group Power and Influence

Although all groups aim to influence the policy-making process, the power of these groups is not equal. On any given issue, one must understand the constant give and take between the many interests described previously and within the framework of power. It is the interplay between these groups that shape policy (Smith, 1993). Historically, physicians were the dominant group shaping health policy (Morone, 1995). The power of the AMA was legendary, particularly when discussing the possibility of national health insurance. Power was ceded to the medical profession at the turn of the last century (Freidson, 1970; Starr, 1982). Physicians had a claim to technical expertise that justified their control over the organization and delivery of medical services. Second, their professional authority was extended to state-supported control over the healthcare field. Physicians determined the regulation of medicine through state licensing procedures. Finally, physicians actively sought to control health politics. They historically advocated against programs such as national health insurance that were perceived to undermine their authority by increasing the role of the state to regulate the provision of health services. Later they began to advocate for programs that enhanced physician authority such as the Peer Review Organizations (Starr, 1982).

Although nurses and other healthcare providers are a larger group in terms of actual numbers, it is physicians who set the terms of the debate historically. Their expertise was the basis for their having authority over nursing practice (Gordon, 2005). Although nurses have autonomy over their professional scope of practice, they take their directions from doctors for all matters related to direct patient care. Physicians' knowledge base is oriented toward cure, and the healthcare system is directed toward that end (Glouberman & Mintzberg, 2001). Nursing practice is oriented toward care. This function, however, is often secondary in the ways that we organize the healthcare delivery, although there has been a constant call for its centrality to achieving health (Gawande, 2007).

In addition to physicians, the other centers of power until the 1980s were the hospitals and the academic medical centers in particular (Tierney, 1987). The advancement of both groups augmented the work of physicians. Their growing strength can be seen post–World War II when increased pressure was put on the federal government to provide support for health care. The federal government could not intervene directly and support the provision of health services because such proposals were aggressively opposed by physicians as being precursors to socialized medicine. Physicians acceded to government funding of hospital construction and biomedical research spending, which enhanced their ability to practice medicine (Stevens, 1971). The Hill-Burton Act of 1946 made money available to rebuild and expand the deteriorating hospital infrastructure. The federal government also dramatically increased its support for the National Institutes for Health that became the vehicle for funding biomedical research at the universities where doctors trained (Daniels, 1971).

The balance of power between these groups is not constant. A shift began to occur in the 1980s because of a convergence of several factors. Most important was the increasing cost of care. Healthcare expenditures rose from 5.1% of the GDP in 1960 to 9.1% by 1980 (National Health Expenditure Data, 2008). With the country in an economic downturn, the rising healthcare costs put pressure on payer groups to find a solution to the problem. Second, the government was fast becoming one of the largest payers of health services with the growth of the Medicare and Medicaid programs. A third trend was the growing corporatization of the healthcare field (Relman, 1980; Starr, 1982). The growth of for-profit facilities and multifacility corporations were seen as shifting institutional goals away from public benefit toward more narrow concerns for financial profitability. Finally, technology and demographic trends pointed to ever-increasing costs caused by the rate of medical innovation and the aging of the population that would require increased services (Bodenheimer, 2005; Marmor, 2001).

The growing complexity of the healthcare system led to its transformation from what was termed a physician-dominated system to a finance-driven system (Starr, 1982). When the issue was recast as one of constraining costs, professional expertise was no longer the critical skill needed to resolve the problem. Doctors' ability to influence and direct the organization and delivery of care began to give way to the administrators of the system, including third-party payers. These groups were in a better position to control the cost of care by creating the appropriate financial incentives to influence physician practice patterns. By the 1990s, authority over health policy was becoming firmly rooted in the organizations that paid for health services. This includes big business, the insurance companies that are represented by the Health Insurance Association of America, and increasingly the federal and state governments.

The challenge to physician dominance was not limited to the financial sector of the industry. Patients were also advocating for greater autonomy and sovereignty over the decisions that affect their health (Schneider, 1998). They wanted to demystify the role of physicians and enable patients to become active participants in their own care. Patients' loss of trust in the medical profession became manifest in many ways (Mechanic, 1996). Among these was the use of the courts for recourse to care that they found negligent. The number of malpractice suits began rising in the 1980s, which led to a crisis of sorts related to the cost and availability of malpractice insurance (Studdert et al., 2004). What started with protest groups outside of the healthcare system became a legitimate concern within the medical field. In 2003, several physician groups spearheaded by the American Board of Internal Medicine issued a statement on medical professionalism that reaffirmed the importance of the patient/physician relationship being defined by integrity, respect, and compassion (American Board of Internal Medicine, 1994).

Finally, other healthcare practitioners began to challenge physician authority. The healthcare labor force has historically been described as a pyramid with physicians at the apex directing all related medical practice. As the provision of care becomes increasingly complex, alternative practitioners have begun to seek professional status and the right to independent practice. Research demonstrates that they provided care comparable to or of higher quality than their physician counterparts (Cromwell, 1999; Maule, 1994). These practitioners are capable of providing quality care at a lower cost. Thus, they offer a cost effective alternative to physicians. Professional associations of groups such as physical therapists and nurse practitioners are lobbying on a state-by-state basis to change licensing laws so that these clinicians can practice independently and receive direct reimbursement for their services. Such laws create an alternative center of authority.

Agenda Setting and Policy Adoption

Although there are numerous policy advocates with numerous policy alternatives, not all of their ideas can be acted on. Some ideas have a greater chance to succeed than others (Bachrach & Baratz, 1962; Smith, 2002). Why do some ideas take precedence over others in shaping policy? The objective conditions, or what we might term the actual problem, are always a necessary foundation for a social policy idea to succeed, but not a sufficient one. The first step is for an idea to become part of the public agenda. National health insurance is an interesting case study because it has moved on and off the public agenda since the early twentieth century but has never been affirmed as policy despite the fact that there is an actual problem (Cairl & Imershein, 1977; Skocpol, 1995; Steinmo & Watts, 1995). It was last considered in 1993 when Clinton's healthcare proposal was defeated in Congress. Once again, national health insurance has been put on the agenda with the election of Barack Obama as president, but the uncertainty in the economy makes action highly uncertain.

Numerous factors can elevate the status of an issue to the extent that it might be acted on by the government (Peterson, 1993). In some instances, there are triggering events such as Hurricane Katrina. Many public health issues that had been ignored before the hurricane, such as emergency preparedness, were suddenly perceived as needing immediate action (Fee & Brown, 2002). In other instances, interest groups have used the courts to further their policy change agenda. The series of law suits brought against the tobacco companies in the 1990s led these companies to seek a compromise with the government that would provide liability protection in exchange for greater regulation (Pertschuk, 2001). Interest groups found an effective way to use the courts to get their issues on the agenda. Such groups have many tools available to them. They can meet with legislators. They can meet with corporate executives. They can also organize conferences to inform policy makers and the public about a particular issue. Political action is another means to build consensus about the need for action. Whether on the mall or at corporate headquarters, demonstrations are intended to be a show of support for a set of issues and thus pressure legislatures to act. Persons in political power can also put issues on the public agenda. The President sets the agenda each year when he gives the State of the Union address. Legislators also advance particular interests. Harrison Wofford's special Senate run in 1991 for U.S. Senator from Pennsylvania was framed by a single issue, national health insurance. His upset victory was a major impetus for President Clinton to advance healthcare reform as one of his first legislative initiatives following his 1992 election victory.

Although the tactics used by different groups to elevate their issues are important, the fact remains that some groups find themselves struggling to be heard, whereas others have greater access to policy makers and their proposals have greater credibility. This was the case with AIDS during the 1980s (Shilts, 1987). The policies and programs that are most reflective of the strongest interests in the healthcare field have greatest chance of being taken under consideration (Schnattschneider, 1960). These are the groups that hold the most power within society generally and the healthcare field specifically. The healthcare field has been characterized as being comprised of five broad groups of actors, and within each broad group, some players are more powerful than others. Physicians have typically dominated nurses in policy debates. Recently, nurses and other health professionals have found themselves with greater authority and they are leading several of the policy discussions. It is notable that the Obama administration appointed a nurse, Mary Wakefield, to oversee the Health Resources and Services Administration. The business community carries more weight than consumer advocacy groups in regard to policies related to health insurance. The interests of the academic medical centers often outweigh those of community hospitals. These groups' strength is reflected in their ability to organize, the cohesion of their members, their funding, their expertise on the issue, and their legal status (Howlett & Ramesh, 2003).

The culmination of the policy-making process is the adaptation of policy via the legislative process. Elected officials decide the broad outlines of policy when they enact laws. Legislators do not act in isolation. There are many centers of power both inside and outside of government that try to influence the process. As a result, legislators usually seek a middle ground that is responsive to these competing interests (Smith, 2002). When looking for this middle ground, two of the most important issues for having a policy alternative recognized in law are its technical feasibility and its acceptability among different political constituencies (Kingdon, 1995; Tierney, 1987). Legislators are often looking for programs that are small and limited in scope because implementation is not as difficult to achieve and the programs are more likely to succeed. As proposed programs becomes more complex and impact a greater number of groups, developing legislation that is acceptable to all of the parties involved becomes more difficult (Morone, 1995). In these cases, legislators are looking for proposals around which they can build public support. Such proposals have often been termed "safe." This means legislators are seeking to adjust existing programs rather than proposing fundamental change to the status quo (Bachrach & Baratz, 1962).

There are moments of exceptionalism when programs disrupt existing social relations that define the organization and delivery of services. The passage of Medicare and Medicaid in 1965 is the most notable example in the healthcare field. These programs sought to redistribute control over access to healthcare resources (Ball, 1995), but even such major pieces of legislation are rooted in past programs and shaped in response to existing political interests (Vladeck, 1999). Medicare succeeded in making health insurance available to persons over 65 years of age, but the legislation must also be understood as an extension of the existing healthcare system. The hospitals supported Part A because its charges would be determined retrospectively based on actual costs. This meant that hospitals would see a growth in revenue from persons who previously had difficulty paying for hospital care. Physicians and the AMA supported Part B because it was voluntary and did not create a broader precedent for the government provision of care. Along with Medicaid, Congress preserved the principle of a safety net as opposed to the principle of health care as a right. The insurance companies supported Medicare because they would be responsible for claims administration. Also, there was bipartisan support in Congress. For Democrats, Medicare was a social insurance program that provided universal coverage for persons over 65 years of age for hospitalization, a high-cost health service. The Republicans ultimately supported the legislation because it maintained a program of voluntary insurance for physicians' services and therefore did not set a precedent for the socialization of the healthcare system (Marmor, 1973).

Implementation

Although often ignored, policy implementation is a continuation of the politics of policy creation in the administrative arena and cannot be divorced from the policy-making process. Legislation provides the broadest possible outline of a program. The specificity of the law determines the flexibility that the administration has in its implementation (Lowi, 1979). Congress can attempt to be specific in its formulation of programs in order to control the actions of a possibly hostile administration, or Congress can choose to leave the details of implementation to the administering agency. There are advantages and disadvantages to both choices. A bill in which details are clearly specified may encounter difficulty in Congress because groups may oppose the particulars as opposed to the overarching program. Clinton's health insurance plan was a victim to this approach (Brady & Buckley, 1995). A consensus can be more easily built around a law with broad, overarching goals, but few details. In this case, decisions about implementation are left to the administering agencies.

Program implementation is the responsibility of the executive branch and its administrative agencies. At the federal level, the Department of Health and Human Services has responsibility for realizing the legislation's goals through the administration of programs created by Congress (Pressman & Wildavsky, 1973). Implementation can be difficult because the abstract agreements made during the legislative process often fall apart if underlying conflicts have not been resolved. This makes the administrative leadership and organizational capacity of administrative agencies even more important. How an agency chooses to implement the program can have tremendous influence on its outcome (Jacobson & Wasserman, 1999; Morone, 1995; Pressman & Wildavsky, 1973). The leadership of the agency must be in accord with the program's goals so that it does not languish, and the personnel must also have program expertise to implement the program effectively. The State Children's Health Insurance Program, commonly referred to as SCHIP, is a case in point. As power over program implementation devolved back to the states in the late 1980s and early 1990s, there was concern about the capacity of the states to implement such a complex health program. The states, however, have developed capacity in these areas over the past decades, as it was their intent to expand children's access to health care (Kinney & Chang, 2004). They had supportive leadership and developed the internal capacity required to operate the program.

As in the case of the legislation process, administrative agencies do not work in a vacuum. Organized interests that are instrumental in mobilizing and building support for policies throughout the legislative process play a comparable role during its implementation. They work with the administrative agencies to insure that implementation meets their interests by monitoring the process (Pressman & Wildavsky, 1973). The agency staff also develops a stake in the programs that they oversee (Peterson, 1993). As they become expert in a given field, they also become influential in the policy-making process. It is not atypical for government employees to work with advocacy groups and Congressional committees to advance their program's interests. Given their expertise in a given field, the situation exists where professionals move between these sectors—sometimes working for the government and sometimes working in the private or nonprofit sectors.

Healthcare professionals and their patients experience the impact of the implementation process on a daily basis. How patients are recruited to programs such as SCHIP and Part D of Medicare is determined by the regulations of these programs. Which companies have contracts to provide Medicare Managed Care programs is also a result of program guidelines. The same is true for the nurse-to-patient ratios specified in the laws of California or the limit on the hours that medical residents can work in New York State hospitals (which came about in response to a patient's death in a city hospital). These are all examples of programs that were developed by federal and/or state legislatures and implemented by federal and state administering agencies. Although their work is seemingly distant, its impact is immediate in terms of access to quality health care.

What Is at Stake for Nurses and Other Health Professionals?

The work of nurses and other health professionals tends to be highly individualized. By interacting with patients, they see the many problems that result from policy decisions made at a distance. They understand how the loss of healthcare insurance can result in patients deferring care much to their detriment. They understand that the pursuit of quality patient care is dependent on their ability to engage and use nursing resources effectively, which will likely become more challenging as the nursing shortage persists and resources become increasingly limited (Draper, Felland, Liebhaber, & Melichar, 2008).

In many cases, these professionals become the patients' advocates, but historically, they have not played a major role in the initial development of the policies that have such a tremendous subsequent impact on the lives of their patients and on their work. Some have attributed this to the heavy workloads. Others have discussed the educational process that socializes nurses to distance themselves from politics. Still others speak about the difficulty nurses have asserting their professional authority when they find themselves up

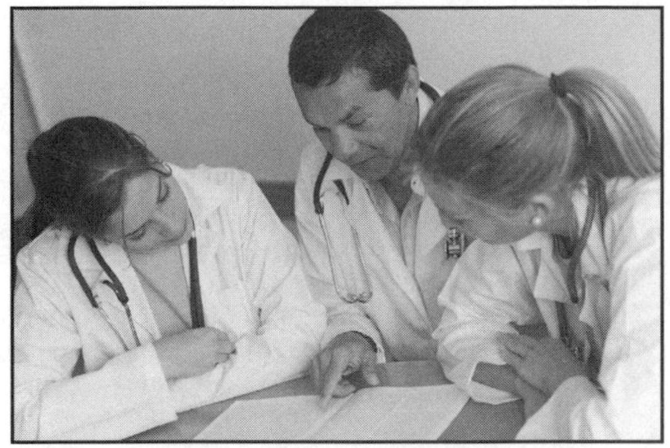

against dominant interests such as physician groups, hospitals, and payers. Regardless of cause, there is now a growing concern that nurses and other health professionals find an even greater voice in the policy-making process (Thomas & While, 2007; Wolf & Greenhouse, 2007).

By understanding the policy-making process and how it has shaped the organization and delivery of health care, it is possible to understand the many ways one can become politically engaged. Since the 1990s, we have looked to the market to bring greater efficiency to the organization and delivery of care. It is the failure of this approach that is reinvigorating interest in the politics of health care. We know that health costs are rising, that the risk of becoming uninsured is increasing, and that the quality can suffer despite the best efforts of healthcare providers. The critical challenge will be determining how health care should be organized and delivered so as to ensure the best possible health outcomes for the population. With the worsening financial situation of the country, the stresses that ordinary Americans will experience will be evidenced in the healthcare arena through even greater numbers of uninsured and even greater numbers of persons who are delaying or foregoing care. Determining what will be the tradeoffs between access, costs, and quality will impact the situation that nurses and other professionals confront every day. Nurses and other healthcare providers need to become one of the dominant voices in the policy-making and policy-implementation process if we are to have a healthcare system that best meets the needs of the people it serves.

References

American Board of Internal Medicine. (1994). Project professionalism medical professionalism in the new millennium: a physician charter. *Annals of Internal Medicine, 136,* 243–246.

Anton, T. (1997). New federalism and intergovernmental fiscal relationships: The implications for health policy. *Journal of Health Politics Policy and Law, 22*(3), 691–720.

Arrow, K. J. (1963). Uncertainty and the welfare economics of medical care. *The American Economic Review, 5*(5), In *Bulletin of the World Health Organization, 82*(2), 141–149.

Arrow, K. J. (1974). *The limits of organization*. New York: W.W. Norton and Co.

Bachrach, P., & Baratz, M. (1962). Two faces of power. *American Political Science Review, 56,* 4632–4642.

Ball, R. (1995). What Medicare's architects had in mind. *Health Affairs, 14*(4), 62–73.

Bodenheimer, T. (2005). High and rising health care costs. Part 2: Technologic innovation. *Annals of Internal Medicine, 142,* 932–937.

Bovbjerg, R., Wiener, J., & Housman, M. (2003). State and federal roles in health care: Rationales for allocating responsibilities. In J. Holahan, A. Weil, & J. Wiener (Eds.), *Federalism and Health Policy* (vol. 3, pp. 25–51). Washington, DC: The Urban Institute Press.

Brady, D. W., & Buckley, K. M. (1995). Health care reform in the 103d Congress: A predictable failure. *Journal of Health Politics Policy and Law, 20,* 447–454.

Brown, L. D., & Sparer, M. S. (2003). Poor program's progress: The unanticipated politics of Medicaid policy. *Health Affairs, 22*(1), 31–44.

Cairl, R., & Imershein, A. (1977). National health insurance policy in the United States: A case of non-decision-making. *International Journal of Health Services,* 7(2), 167–178.

Center for Policy and Research. (2007). *Individual Health Insurance 2006–2007: A Comprehensive Survey of Premiums, Availability, and Benefits.* Retrieved July 1, 2008, from http://www.ahipresearch.org/pdfs/Individual_Market_Survey_December_2007.pdf

Conlan, T. (2006). From cooperative to opportunistic federalism: Reflections on the half-century anniversary of the commission on intergovernmental relations. *Public Administration Review, 66,* 663–676.

Conway, P. H., Tamara Konetzka, R., Zhu, J., Volpp, K. G., & Sochalski, J. (2008). Nurse staffing ratios: Trends and policy implications for hospitalists and the safety net. *Journal of Hospital Medicine, 3*(3), 193–199.

Cromwell, J. (1999). Barriers to achieving a cost-effective workforce mix: Lessons from anesthesiology. *Journal of Health Politics Policy and Law, 24,* 1331–1361.

Daniels, G. H. (1971). *Science in American society: A social history.* New York: Alfred Knopf.

Davis, K., & Schoen, C. (1978). *Health and the war on poverty: A ten year appraisal.* Washington, DC: Brookings Institution.

DeCicca, P., Kenkel, D., Mathios, A., Shin, Y. J., & Lim, J. Y. (2008). Youth smoking, cigarette prices, and anti-smoking sentiment. *Health Economics, 17,* 733–749.

DeNavas-Walt, C., Proctor, B., & Smith, J. (2007). U.S. Census Bureau, *Current population reports, P60-233, Income, Poverty, and Health Insurance Coverage in the United States: 2006.* Retrieved September 26, 2008, from http://www.census.gov/prod/2007pubs/p60-233.pdf

Draper, D., Felland, L., Liebhaber, A., & Melichar, L. (2008). The role of nurses in hospital quality improvement. *Center for Studying Health System Change, 3,* 1–8.

Fee, E., & Brown, T. M. (2002). The unfulfilled promise of public health: Déjà vu all over again. *Health Affairs, 21*(6), 31–43.

Fox, D. (1986). The consequences of consensus: American health policy in the twentieth century. *The Milbank Quarterly, 64,* 176–199.

Freidson, E. (1970). *Profession of medicine: A study of the sociology of applied knowledge.* New York: Dodd, Mead.

Gawande, A. (2007). *Better: A surgeon's notes on performance.* New York: Picador.

Glouberman, S., & Mintzberg, H. (2001). Managing the care of health and the cure of disease: Part I: Differentiation. *Health Care Management Review, 26*(1), 56–69.

Gordon, S. (2005). *Nursing against the odds: How health care cost cutting, media stereotypes, and medical hubris undermine nurses and patient care (the culture and politics of health care work).* Ithaca, NY: Cornell University Press.

Grabowski, H. (2005). Encouraging the development of new vaccines. *Health Affairs, 24*(3), 697–700.

Grumbach, K. (2002). Fighting hand to hand over physician workforce policy: The invisible hand of the market meets the heavy hand of government planning. *Health Affairs, 32*(5), 13–27.

Howlett, M., & Ramesh, M. (2003). *Studying public policy: Policy cycles and policy subsystems.* Toronto, ON: Oxford University Press.

Jacobson, P., & Wasserman, J. (1999, June). The implementation and enforcement of tobacco control laws: Policy implications for activists and the industry. *Journal of Health Politics Policy and Law, 24,* 567–598.

Kernell, S., & Jacobson, G. C. (2006). *The logic of American politics* (3rd ed.). Washington, DC: CQ Press.

Kingdon, J. W. (1995). *Agendas, alternatives, and public policies.* New York: Harper Collins College Publishers.

Kinney, G., & Chang, D. I. (2004). The state children's health insurance program: Successes, shortcomings, and challenges. *Health Affairs, 23*(5), 51–62.

Knowles, J. H. (1977). The responsibility of the individual. In J. H. Knowles (Ed.), *Doing better and feeling worse: Health in the United States.* Cambridge: American Academy of Arts and Sciences.

Koenig, L., Dobson, A., Silver, H., Jonathan, M., Siegel, J. M., Blumenthal, D., & Weissman, J. S. (2003). Estimating the mission-related costs of teaching hospitals. *Health Affairs, 22*(6), 112–122.

Lowi, T. (1979). *The end of liberalism: ideology, policy, and the crisis of public authority* (2nd ed.). New York: Norton.

Lowi, T., & Ginsberg, B. (1998). *American government* (5th ed.). New York: Norton and Co.

Mariner, W. (1996). State regulation of managed care and the employee retirement income security act. *New England Journal of Medicine, 335,* 1986–1990.

Marmor, T. (1973). *The politics of Medicare.* Chicago: Aldine Publishing Co.

Marmor, T. (2001). How not to think about Medicare reform. *Journal of Health Politics, Policy and Law, 26*(1), 107–117.

Maule, W. (1994). Screening for colorectal cancer by nurse endoscopists. *New England Journal of Medicine, 330,* 183–186.

Mechanic, D. (1996). Changing medical organization and the erosion of trust. *The Milbank Quarterly, 74*(2), 171–189.

Midgley, J., & Livermore, M. (Eds.). (2008). *The handbook of social policy* (pp. 3–20). Los Angeles: Sage.

Morone, J. (1995). Elusive community: Democracy, deliberation, and the reconstruction of health policy. In M. Landy & M. Levin (Eds.), *The new politics of public policy* (pp. 180–204). Baltimore, MD: Johns Hopkins University Press.

National Health Expenditure Data. Aggregate, per capita amounts, percent distribution, and average annual percent growth, by source of funds: Selected Calendar Years 1960–2006. Retrieved July14, 2008, from http://www.cms.hhs.gov/NationalHealthExpendData/downloads/tables.pdf

National Health Expenditure Data Fact Sheet. Retrieved September 26, 2008, from http://www.cms.hhs.gov/NationalHealthExpendData/25_NHE_Fact_Sheet.asp#TopOfPage

Pertschuk, M. (2001). *Smoke in their eyes: Lessons in movement leadership from the tobacco wars*. Nashville, TN: Vanderbilt University Press.

Peterson, M. A. (1993). Political Influence in the 1990s: From iron triangles to policy networks. *Journal of Health Politics, Policy and Law, 18,* 395–436.

Pressman, J. L., & Wildavsky, A. (1973). *Implementation*. Berkeley, CA: University of California Press.

Relman, A. S. (1980). The new medical-industrial complex. *New England Journal of Medicine, 303,* 963–970.

Reschovsky, J. D., Strunk, B. C., & Ginsburg, P. (2006). Why employer-sponsored insurance coverage change, 1997–2003. *Health Affairs, 25,* 774–782.

Rothman, D. J. (1971). *The discovery of the asylum: Social order and disorder in the New Republic*. Boston: Little, Brown.

Rushefsky, M. (2008). *Public policy in the United States: At the dawn of the 21st century* (4th ed.). Armonk, NY: M.E. Sharpe.

Schnattschneider, E. E. (1960). *The semisovereign people: A realist's view of democracy in America*. New York: Holt, Rinehart and Winston.

Schneider, C. E. (1998). *The practice of autonomy: Patients, doctors, and medical decisions*. New York: Oxford University Press.

Shilts, R. (1987). *And the band played on: Politics, people and the AIDS epidemic*. New York: St. Martin's Press.

Skocpol, T. (1995). *Boomerang: Clinton's health security effort and the turn against government in US politics*. New York: W.W. Norton.

Smith, M. (1993). *Pressure, power and policy: State autonomy and policy networks in Britain and the United States*. Pittsburgh, PA: University of Pittsburgh Press.

Smith, D. G. (2002). *Entitlement politics: Medicare and Medicaid 1995–2001*. New York: Aldine de Gruyter.

Starr, P. (1982). *The social transformation of American medicine*. New York: Basic Books.

State of the World's Mothers. (2007). *Saving the lives of children under 5.* Retrieved September 26, 2008, from http://www.savethechildren.org.au/australia/publications/mothers_report/mothers_report.html#findings

Steinmo, S., & Watts, J. (1995). It's the institutions, stupid! Why comprehensive national health insurance always fails in America. *Journal of Health Politics, Policy and Law*, *20*, 329–372.

Steuerle, C. E., & Bovbjerg, R. R. (2008). Health and budget reform as handmaidens. *Health Affairs*, *27,* 633–644.

Stevens, R. (1971). *American medicine in the public interest*. New Haven, CT: Yale University Press.

Stone, D. (2002). *Policy paradox: The art of political decision making*. New York: Norton.

Studdert, D. M., Mello, M. M., & Brenna, T. A. (2004). Medical malpractice. *New England Journal of Medicine, 350,* 283–292.

Thomas, P., & While, A. (2007). Should nurses be leaders of integrated health care? *Journal of Nursing Management, 15,* 643–648.

Tierney, J. (1987). Organized interests in health politics and policy-making. *Medical Care Review*, *44*(1), 89–118.

Vladeck, B. (1999). The political economy of Medicare. *Health Affairs*, *18*(1), 22–36.

Wolf, G. A., & Greenhouse, P. K. (2007). Blueprint for design: Creating models that direct change. *Journal of Nursing Administration, 37,* 9381–9387.

Health Status and Access to Care

Chapter 2

Paula Lucey

GOOD HEALTH IS ESSENTIAL TO HAPPINESS AND HAPPINESS IS AN ESSENTIAL TO GOOD CITIZENSHIP.

Charles Horace Mayo (1865–1939), U.S. Physician

OVERVIEW

Health is an essential part of an individual's overall happiness and ability to function within society. The health of an individual, community, or even a population can be affected by a variety of factors. Researchers continue to find new genetic links within our bodies that influence our health. There is increasing data on the ways that individual behavior impacts health outcomes. External environmental conditions such as air pollution, water purity, or exposure to toxins can impact health and well-being and continue to be a subject of investigation. An evolving area of study is the influence of social factors such as housing, employment status, and working conditions on individual and community health. The social determinants of health are the focus of this chapter. Nurses and other public health professionals may be at the cutting edge for recognizing the impact that these factors have on the health of individuals; this puts the profession in an ideal position to work to modify these factors to improve health.

OBJECTIVES

- To understand the formal definition of health
- To understand how theory shapes our understanding of the social determinants of health; specifically to describe life course theory and the theory of vulnerability

(continues)

- To explain the root causes of health disparities, including social attributes and social resources
- To identify health practices and behaviors that influence health outcomes
- To explain how health policy and healthcare programs influence health outcomes

KEY TERMS

- ❑ Health
- ❑ Health disparity
- ❑ Health practices and behaviors
- ❑ Healthcare resources
- ❑ Human capital
- ❑ Life course theory
- ❑ Resource availability
- ❑ Social capital
- ❑ Social determinants of health
- ❑ Theory of vulnerability

Defining Health

Defining health can be difficult. The Institute of Medicine (2001) observed that health is more than the absence of disease and injury. The Institute uses the concept of "positive health" along with four components: a healthy body, high-quality personal relationships, a sense of purpose in life, and resilience to stress, trauma, and change (p. 23). The World Health Organization (World Health Organization & UNICEF, 1978) defines health as physical, mental, and social well-being. It is significant that both of these definitions include the concept of social health as an essential factor. In addition, both definitions take into account the interrelated nature of these factors. For example, a person whose depression may be caused by a social condition such as social isolation or poverty will often suffer from physical manifestations such as fatigue or pain.

Relationship between Biological and Social Factors

Although this chapter is concerned with the social determinants of health, biology is the ultimate cause of health or illness. Illness can be defined as a disturbance in biology. Biology is considered an individual attribute more than a social exposure (Brunner & Marmot, 2006). However, the pathway between the biological and the social is a critical area of continued study given the holistic definition of health provided previously.

For example, neuroendocrine pathways exist for the survival of the individual. They produce the classic fight-or-flight response to stressful situations. While this pathway works well in the acute threat of a danger, it also occurs in other types of occupational or living situations. The classic image of a CEO enduring stress that leads to a heart attack is a familiar one. We are less likely to realize that ongoing stresses such as poverty, chronic unemployment, or lack of social support can also activate the stress pathways. These also result in an individual experiencing increased heart rate, elevated blood pressure, and altered reflexes, as well as other biological responses. While additional studies are needed to define the relationship in greater detail, it does appear that the repeated activation of the fight or flight response may be responsible for social differences in creating variables that are precursors of ill health and disease. The rate of vulnerability to the impact of this stress reaction is individually determined (Brunner & Marmot, 2006). A variety of factors, such as age at time of exposure, duration and intensity of exposure, and individual resilience, may serve to enhance or limit the long-term impact of the stress pathway.

Emergence of Social Causation as a Field of Study

Health inequalities have become more pronounced than they were in the past (Smith, 2003). In Britain, before the 1750s, wealthier groups experienced the same death rate and life expectancy as the overall population. Smith (2003) suggests that many factors contributed to this outcome. Although the aristocracy enjoyed lives of privilege, they lived in close proximity to the lower classes and did not have a higher standard of living in terms of sanitation, nutrition, or medical assistance than the poor. Research and the ability to translate research into action helped create the differential that exists today.

As research developed information about nutrition, sanitation, and medical assistance, the rich were able to make better use of these advances and thus the differentiation in health status began to grow; "the better-off began to dramatically improve their health compared to and sometimes at the expense of the poor" (Smith, 2003, p. xxiii). Current research is looking at these same types of effects, as the poor have less access to digital information and market and social resources than the wealthy.

Although interest in examining the relation between social conditions and individual well-being goes back to the nineteenth century (Marmot, 2004), the Whitehall Study launched this field of investigation. Named for the roadway on which a number of British government offices are located, the hallmark study investigated social determinants of health, specifically the prevalence of cardiorespiratory disease and mortality rates among British male civil servants between the ages of 20 and 64 years. The initial Whitehall I Study, was conducted over a period of 10 years, beginning in 1967 (Marmot et al., 1978). A second phase, the Whitehall II Study, examined the health of 10,308 civil servants aged 35 to 55 years, of whom two thirds were men and one third were women. A long-term follow-up of study subjects from the first two phases remains ongoing (Marmot et al., 1984).

These studies found a strong association between pay grade, which indicates the level of authority in the organization, and mortality rates from a range of causes. Men in the lowest grade (messengers, doorkeepers, etc.) had a three times higher mortality rate than that of men in the highest grade (administrators) (Marmot et al., 1978). This was an early indication of health disparity for individuals based on socioeconomic status.

The initial Whitehall study found that men in lower status positions had a greater propensity for significant risk factors, including obesity, smoking, reduced relaxation time and physical activity, more baseline illness, higher blood pressure, and shorter height. Controlling for these risk factors accounted for no more than 40% of grade differences in cardiovascular disease mortality. Even after these standard risk factors were controlled for, the lowest grade still had a relative risk of 2:1 for cardiovascular disease mortality compared with the highest grade (Marmot et al., 1978).

Among the conclusions drawn from the second phase were that stress caused by the psychosocial work environment factors predicts rates of sickness absenteeism and that enhanced control of task management and support could have beneficial effects, such as increasing productivity and improving employee health and well-being (Marmot et al., 1984). Those persons who had greater control over their work experienced better health. Together, the two Whitehall studies were significant for demonstrating that there were differences in health status within occupation groups. These groundbreaking studies served to intensify the interest in identifying the relationship between social factors and health and were therefore important in the evolution of the field.

The Social Determinants of Health

There are two theoretic constructs, discussed in the following paragraphs, that attempt to model the relation between health and social causation. The explanation of this relationship is important because it shapes how we go about developing interventions that improve health outcomes.

Life Course Theory

The first theory is life course theory. Life course epidemiology is the "study of long-term biological, behavioral, and psychosocial processes that link adult health and disease risk to physical or social exposures acting during gestation, childhood, adolescence, earlier in adult life or across generations" (Kuh & Ben-Sholomo, 2005, p. 3). It suggests that risk factors for adults are a function of biological programming during critical periods of growth and development as early as in utero and/or early infancy. Within this model there are two types of potential exposures. The first is the exposure that occurs at a critical time and has a permanent effect on the fetus or infant. The second is exposure at a critical developmental moment, but the effect remains latent unless or until there is an exposure or triggering event later in life. The triggering event can in fact enhance the impact of the earlier exposure or limit its effect in a positive manner (Kuh & Ben-Sholomo, 2005). The ability to alter these risk factors or prevent exposure during the life course is the key question for researchers, advocates, and policy makers in this area.

There is an alternative approach to life course theory that has greater applicability for the study of social determinants and offers greater hope for improving health. This model hypothesizes that adult chronic disease reflects the cumulative lifetime exposure to damaging physical and social environments. This model allows that the risk factors occur over a life span and form a chain of risk factors that alter the course of a person's health potential. The difference in this model is the fundamental role of time. In this model risks gradually accumulate over the course of life, but it does not discount the increased impact that an exposure can have at a critical time. The accumulation of risk is dependent on the frequency, intensity, and duration of exposure.

Risk factors can be independent or clustered. If they are clustered, they are most likely from a common source. The chain of risk factors is also referred to as the pathway model (Kuh & Ben-Sholomo, 2005). Each exposure in the chain may or may not lead to a subsequent exposure to another risk. Blane (2006) calls this social accumulation. He describes this as the continuation of social circumstances from prenatal care to social conditions in childhood and adolescence and eventually to adult social status. One hypothesis is that the impact on health may come more from a series of relatively minor factors that become a pathway to disadvantage rather than exposure to any one major factor (Blane, 2006).

Consider the cycle of health risks for a child born into poverty. First, the prenatal care of the mother may have been substandard. The mother may have a physically difficult job, and her ability to have a robust nutritional diet may have been compromised. Once born, the child comes into a home that often has potential risks, including lead paint or building materials with formaldehyde. The neighborhood may have an increase in violence. The grocery stores in the neighborhood may have limited healthy choices such as fresh fruit, vegetables, and meat. As the child grows, he or she may attend a stressed and underfunded public school. The child's chances of graduating from an urban public school system can be as low as 40%. If the child does not graduate from high school, his or her occupational choices are limited, and frequently, those jobs offer no health insurance, leading to limited access to health care and preventive services. Although this description is in some ways a worst-case example, it is the real life experience of many people.

The life course theory may be regarded as "combining biological and social elements which interact with each other" (Blane, 2006, p. 55). In a somewhat circular manner, individual biological development takes place within a social context that structures life chances so that advantages and disadvantages of life are available for the individual to enhance or challenge his or her health. As the biological development occurs, resilience or susceptibility to adverse social impact also develops. The life course model offers some optimism in that the course of risk can be altered by attention to its key components. These different possibilities, however, are not mutually exclusive. The root causes of exposure, such as poverty, result in a clustering of the factors. They operate simultaneously, which makes it difficult to identify one tipping point factor. The problems related to differentiation make it difficult to develop a research agenda or programs of social intervention.

Theory of Vulnerability

The theory of vulnerability as posited by Lu Ann Aday (2001) offers a second theoretical framework for the study of the social determinants of disease. Aday argues that both the origins and remedies of vulnerability are rooted in the bonds of human communities (Aday, 2001, p. 1).

This model recognizes two opposing forces: the rights of individuals and the needs of the common good. There is often tension between these two, especially in American society with its fundamental dedication to the individual's rights (Aday, 2001).

A common example that public health officials face daily clearly demonstrates this tension. A person with an infectious disease, such as tuberculosis, refuses to follow isolation protocols and/or take medications. The individual claims that this is a violation of his personal rights, but the common good has to be considered, as this individual's rights could put others at risk for an illness. The theory of vulnerability considers how the mediation of these two different points of view shapes not only our world view but the options available to individuals (Aday, 2001) (Figure 2-1).

Ethical Norms and Values

The different points of view regarding the rights and responsibilities of individuals versus the rights and responsibilities of a community are

Figure 2-1 Model of vulnerability.

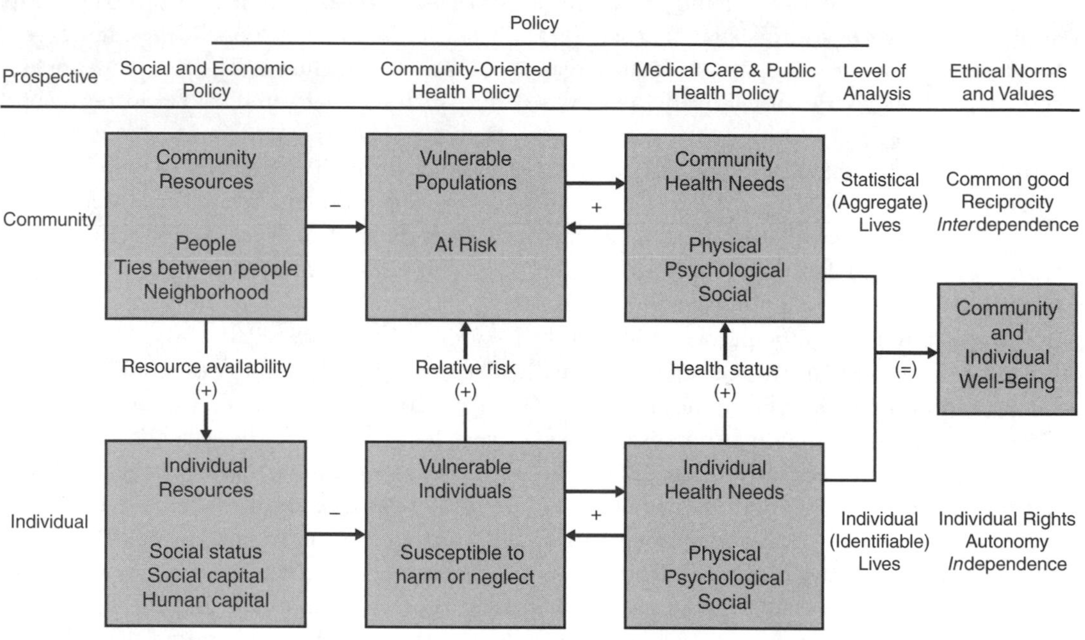

NOTE: A plus sign indicates a direct relationship (the likelihood of outcomes increases as the predictor increases). A minus sign indicates an inverse relationship (the likelihood of outcomes decreases as the predictor increases).

clear when looking at the ethical norms in this model. From the individual perspective, health can be viewed as being the result of personal decisions and choices such as lifestyle. This point of view suggests that resolution to health issues needs to be done at a personal level (Aday, 2001). The key principles from this perspective are independence and autonomy. The key approaches to health would include individual education and personal health coaching.

The community point of view suggests that the health of different groups is a result of different levels of access to resources and opportunities to make positive lifestyle choices. When viewed from this perspective, poor health is a result of failure of the community to create the opportunity for successful health. Looking from this perspective, the key principles would be interrelationships and reciprocity. The approach taken by nurses and other health professionals is to look at community-level interventions, including the use of laws and regulations and market-based goods and services designed to improve the health of the community.

HEALTH STATUS

The World Health Organization's definition of health as physical, mental and social well-being"

(WHO & UNICEF, 1978) can be applied to both individuals and communities.

Indicators of individual health can be measured by the judgment of clinician-specific measurements such as blood pressure and blood testing, self-perception, freedom from pain, or a person's ability to function independently in society. Ironically, a person might perceive him- or herself to be healthy but have undiagnosed high blood pressure. Another individual with significant physical challenges may consider him- or herself to be healthy but be unable to function independently.

Social health is more difficult to define and quantify. From a community perspective, health status is measured in aggregate terms. Common measures include disease prevalence such as cancer rates, causes of death, and rates of health interventions such as childhood immunization. These measures are then correlated to social phenomena such as housing, the location and environmental practices of different industries, levels of community violence, access to healthy food choices, and eligibility and participation in health insurance programs, in order to demonstrate a relationship between social conditions and individual health outcomes. Using findings like these, some communities have developed community-level "report cards" and share the data and actions taken to improve the social health status with the citizens of the community.

Relative Risk

Risk is one of the keys to vulnerability in this model (Aday, 2001). Risk is defined as a "nonzero probability that an individual will become ill within a stated period of time" (Aday, 2001, p. 4). Risk factors refer to attributes or exposures associated with the occurrence of health-related outcomes. Relative risk refers to "the ratio of the risk of poor health among groups that are exposed to the risk factors versus those who are not exposed" (Aday, 2001, p. 4).

The exposure to risk factors for individuals can be the result of individual choice such as smoking or be the result of socioeconomic factors such as hazardous work conditions or lead paint exposure in older housing stock. Community risk factors include water safety and air quality, both of which are susceptible to human interventions. This factor in the vulnerability model is most closely aligned to life course theory, as the exposure to risks increases vulnerability for poor health in both theoretical models.

Resource Availability

The availability of and access to community resources have a significant impact on the level of risk for poor health or opportunity for improved health at the individual level. Resource availability forms the basis of social determinants for health for individuals. For example, a black male without a family who is eating more meals away from home than at home has a higher risk of high blood pressure and diabetes. The issue of resource availability also applies to communities. Crime in a community, for example, can lead to isolation, as individuals are not able to help their neighbors and perhaps even develop a distrust of their neighbors. This component of risk illustrates the interconnection between the individual, social factors, and the community (Aday, 2001) (Figure 2-2).

Access to resources is based on social status. The social status of an individual refers to the position that person occupies in society. This is a function of age, gender, race, and ethnicity as well as socially defined roles/indicators of status such as employment, educational achievement, marriage, and location and type of housing. As a

Figure 2-2 Predictors of populations at risk.

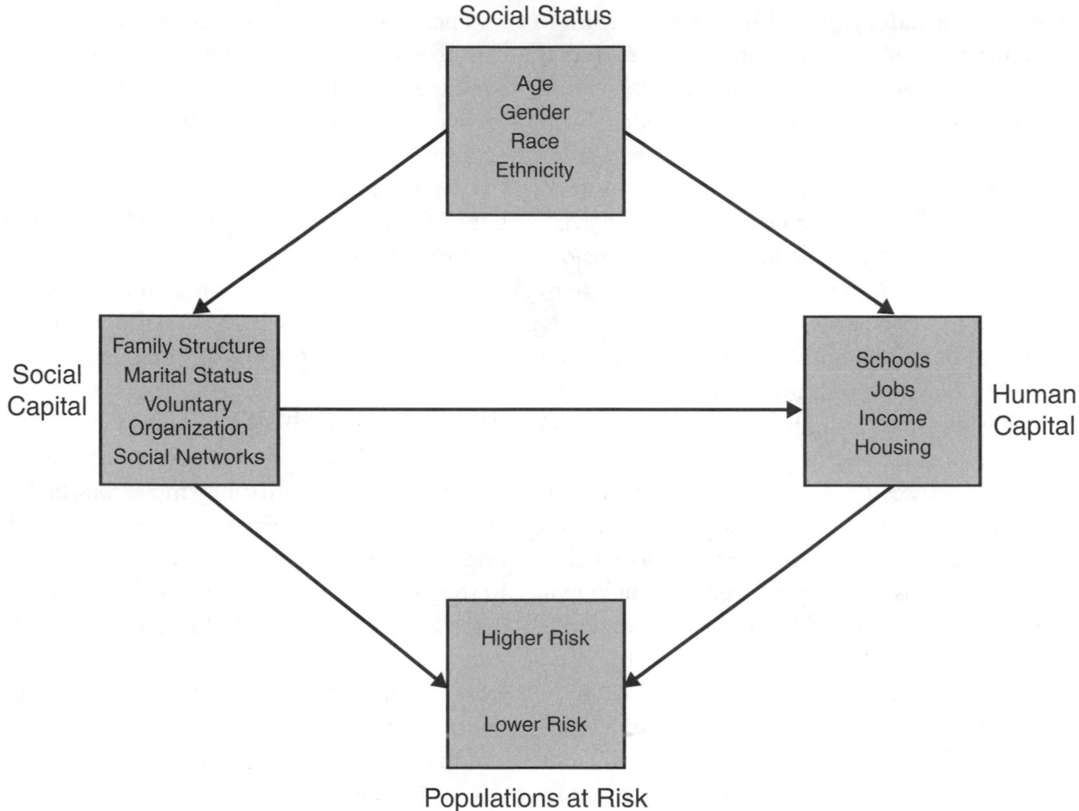

result of this status, rewards and resources become available to individuals (Aday, 2001).

There are three major resources that are awarded based on these factors. The first, social status, confers power and prestige; as was demonstrated in the Whitehall studies, this impacts health. The second is social capital. Social capital refers to the quality and quantity of interpersonal relationships and ties to other people. Networks provide opportunities for individuals to gather social capital in the form of social support, a feeling of belonging, and self-esteem, all of which support better health (Aday, 2001). Although there is evidence that social support leads to better health and that social isolation leads to ill health, the exact mechanism has not been determined (Stansfeld, 2006). The opposite of social inclusion is social exclusion. Social exclusion includes "not only the economic hardship of economic poverty, but also incorporates the notion of the process of marginalization" (Shaw et al., 2006, p. 207). Social exclusion means that the individual or a group of individuals are excluded from the cultural norms and activities of the wider society and as a result are subject to discrimination. Social exclusion establishes a definition of who is included and who is not included in society (Shaw et al., 2006). The last is human capital, which is defined as productivity potential. Human capital refers to "investments in people's skills and capabilities (such as vocational or public education) that enable them to act in new ways, master a skill or enhance their contributions to society" (Aday, 2001, p. 6). The investment that society makes in individuals (for example schooling or access to care) impacts life chances and health. Studies have shown that neighborhoods where the average income is lower have fewer choices in healthy food and even fewer choices in where to shop for food (Lewis et al., 2005). In another example, the inability to receive proper oral health care means uninsured poor individuals have poor or missing teeth; this in turn limits their employment possibilities, as they are not hired for positions with significant interaction with the public (Sered & Fernandopulle, 2005).

These three resources interact with life cycle placement, which can have a dramatic impact on the exposure to risk factors. For example, there is the risk-taking behavior of teens or the physical vulnerability of the elderly. While social status, social capital, and human capital are strong predictors of health outcomes, it is important to recognize differences within groups. Aday (2001) points out that in addition to these factors, cultural norms and beliefs form the fundamental basis of differences in risk levels between individuals and groups.

Policy

Aday suggests that healthcare policy alone will not resolve the challenges in the long term. While it is important that individuals and communities have access to good health care, she concludes that policymakers seeking to resolve these concerns must do so by looking at the elements of a community-based health policy. Vulnerability, or increased risk of poor health outcomes, can be modeled and improved by focusing policy on ethical norms and values, health status, relative risk, and resource availability, as well as the ways they are shaped by the rights and obligations of the individual and the rights and obligations of the community (Aday, 2001).

Social Attributes and Health Disparities

Individual outcomes are a function of our ability to care for our self. Because we are social beings, this ability is determined largely by social characteristics. The reality is that our society ranks, values, and devalues these social characteristics, which in turn leads to health disparities. Health disparities have begun to receive significant attention in the United States. Research is focusing on the disparities of health outcomes between groups based on ethnic group, gender, and other social factors. The Institute of Health (Institute of Medicine, 2003b) has taken a leadership role in calling attention to this phenomenon and calling for systematic changes to decrease vulnerability to health risks.

There is no single definition for the broad issue of health disparities. Healthy People 2010 (U.S. Department of Health and Human Services, 2000) defines health disparities as differences in disease prevalence or treatment by gender, race, ethnicity, educational attainment, income, sexual orientation, or geographic location. The National Institutes of Health takes a broader perspective and looks at differences in diseases, adverse health conditions and outcomes, and access to health care. From that framework, the National Institutes of Health looks to see whether the differences create health outcomes that appear avoidable, unfair, or unacceptable in populations or subgroups related to gender, ethnic, or other social classifications (National Institutes of Health, 2005). This section of the chapter will draw from both frameworks and look at disparities based on social attributes such as culture, race, and gender; the social distribution of resources such as education, income, residential location, occupation; health practices and behaviors; and finally access to and utilization of health resources.

Culture and Its Impact on Health

Looking at social determinants in health requires an understanding of culture. Because the United States is such a complex society that brings together so many different groups of people, it is difficult to talk about a single national character or an understanding of what it means to be an American. Rather, we talk about the many cultures that make up American society. Culture refers to shared values, customs, and beliefs that shape a person's identity as part of a social group. To talk about culture is to talk about individuals who are defined by their ethnic, religious, or even racial identities.

To demonstrate the impact of culture on health, Napoles-Springer et al. (2005) asked 161 participants in three different ethnic groups to identify how their culture affected the quality of their encounters with the medical system. They reported issues such as a lack of sensitivity to alternative medicine valued in their culture and a lack of understanding of the important role of family within their culture. The participants identified various types of discrimination that they had experienced, related to their health insurance status, social class, ethnicity, and age. These all played an adverse role in their perception about the quality of health care. Language issues and immigration status were particularly important to Hispanic participants.

A unique perspective on culture is offered by looking at recent immigrants to the United States. They pose a special case in terms of discrimination and health disparities; immigrants from Mexico, South America, and the Caribbean experience significant health disparities as compared with European Americans. While studies demonstrate that the longer the Latino immigrant is in the United States the worse their health status becomes, Batbum and Baumann (2007) posit that strong community affiliation can offset the negative consequences experienced by these immigrants. Community involves a sense of belonging to a group that is based on knowing one's importance in the group, the emotional connections to the group, and the trust developed among group members. The challenge for immigrants in developing a sense of community in their new homeland has been found to be a protective factor related to health risks.

Public health is especially dependent on knowledge of the culture and the communities in which the health professionals work. In fact, the mission of public health is "to ensure socie-

tal conditions in which people can be healthy" (Cortiss et al., 2007, p. 1023). To meet this mission, public health providers must be aware of the needs of diverse groups and the cultural influences on their health. To be culturally competent, health professionals must know how to assess health issues, including risks and influences, health behaviors, and the ways culture shapes attitudes and practices.

Health Disparities and Race

Racial disparities in health are well documented. For example, Williams and Braboy Jackson (2005) used national longitudinal data to assess health disparities embedded in "larger historical, geographic, sociocultural, economic, and political contexts" (p. 325). They reviewed three examples of racial health disparity in the areas of homicide, heart disease, and cancer. The homicide rate in 2000 for blacks was almost six times greater than for whites. In 1950, there was little difference in cardiac disease rates between the races, but by 2000, the death rate from cardiac causes was 30% higher for blacks than whites. In 1950, whites had a death rate from cancer that was 30% higher than blacks. In the ensuing 50 years, the death rates for whites has stabilized and in some cases decreased, whereas the rate for blacks has increased 40%.

Racial disparities can be viewed in three different ways: racial disparities reflect biological differences; race is a proxy for class, and disparities are really class disparities, not race based; or both race and class create increased health risks independently, and both are factors in creating health disparities.

The theory that racial disparities are biological has its roots in slavery. The widely held belief was that black individuals were inherently inferior mentally (Kawachi et al., 2005) but were well suited for physical work. Although the original "scientific studies" used to support these beliefs "have long been discredited, the tradition of ascribing racial disparities in health to fixed biological traits persists" (Kawachi et al., 2005, p. 344). It is important to challenge such work as in the case of race-based drug promotion (Sankar & Kahn, 2005).

A second way of looking at racial disparities is to treat race as a proxy for class. This tradition of thought seems to be based on two different observations. First, black Americans are overrepresented in economically disadvantaged social groups, and second, adjusting for class greatly reduces the racial differences in health disparities (Kawachi et al., 2005). Unfortunately, information about class indicators, such as income and education, is not often collected; thus, more data are available looking at race and not at class. The authors suggest that looking at racial data and controlling for social economic data should be a part of all health disparity research.

The third and perhaps strongest way to look at disparities is to look at race and class as separate but interactive factors. This allows for such observations as looking at the differences between middle-class whites and middle-class blacks, as well as looking at same-race differences between income groups.

Viewing healthcare disparities in this way allows for a broader approach toward eliminating these disparities. Racism and classism are both significant forces in American society; thus, looking at health disparities separate from race has political implications. Kawachi et al. (2005) suggest that health activities that aim to promote greater racial equality may be more politically acceptable than those that seek to eliminate class differences.

Gender, Sexuality, and Health

Gender and sexuality are another lens through which to consider the social attributes of health. The health needs of women are more complex than those of men given the attention required for their reproductive health. It is also the case that women have a more difficult time seeking health services. They have less access to health insurance through employment, and healthcare providers are less likely to develop services that are responsive to their needs. As a result, it is typical to find disparities in health outcomes when comparing women to men, controlling for other variables (Mitchell & Schlesinger, 2005).

The invisibility of the problem is demonstrated by a survey of public health schools (Cortiss et al., 2007). The researchers evaluated three domains: the overall climate for lesbian, gay, bisexual, and transgender faculty, staff, and students; research activities related to this population; and a review of the curriculum currently presented or planned to be presented related to health issues for this population. Fewer than 50% of the schools reporting noted activities in these areas that were supportive of the lesbian, gay, bisexual, and transgender population.

A study of gender differences in self-reports of experiences with managed care found significant differences between men and women (Mitchell & Schlesinger, 2005). This finding, based on a national survey of 5,000 persons, raises interesting questions for health policy advocates because managed care could be considered an organizational model for healthcare delivery that would be more responsive to women's needs due to the importance placed on primary care providers. Women reported more problems in closed panel plans and plans that used gatekeepers to access specialty care. A related finding is that women reported more problems in states where access to OB/GYNs is regulated.

Interactive Effects and Special Populations

It is often the case that health problems related to the social attributes described are impacted by a person's age. In a comprehensive review of studies on health disparities of minority elderly persons, Byrd et al. (2007) concluded that two population trends are merging into one health issue. America is aging. In 2000, approximately 12% of the population was over the age of 65 years. By the year 2030, this will increase to over 20% of the total population. In addition, the oldest population category, those over 85 years, is expected to grow from 5 to 15 million. At the same time that this change is occurring, the ethnic makeup of America is also changing. Currently, only 20% of the older population is minority; by 2050, that percentage will change to a projected 50%.

Byrd et al. (2007) call attention to these changes to focus on the need to improve the care of older minorities. Minority older persons carry a greater burden of many chronic diseases and have poorer health outcomes. As a result, minority older persons have a higher utilization of healthcare resources, which creates a strain on public funding and family caregivers.

A model that focuses on creating a plan of care that is developed mutually with the patient

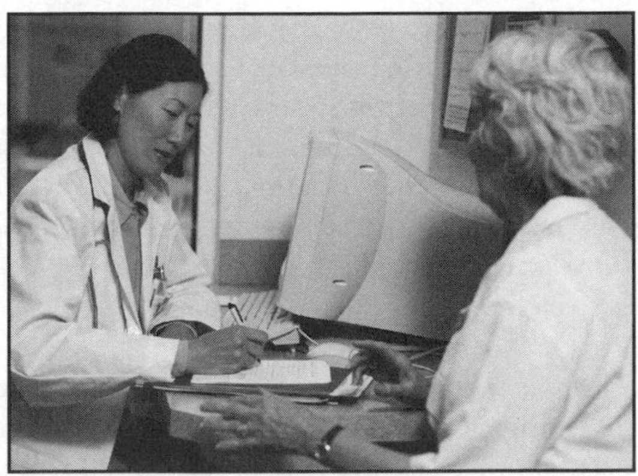

and his or her family and includes the individual's values and culture as cornerstones of the plan is needed. Nurses are in an ideal position to create plans of care that meet these objectives if they are culturally competent.

Care of older persons from diverse ethnic backgrounds is a significant emerging issue in health care. The social determinants of health can have long-term effects, and the cost to care for that impact in the older population will be a burden to the healthcare system and general society for years to come. As shown by life course theory, interceding at any point in the cycle is important, but it must be recognized that each health risk has a compounding effect.

Social Resource Distribution and Health

Social attributes are closely related to human capital or the distribution of social resources such as education, income, occupation, and place of residence.

Education

Education does not correlate directly to health outcomes. However, it is a mediating factor because it has a significant impact on potential life chances such as employment opportunities for individuals. Those who do not graduate high school, for example, have limited work options and frequently end up in jobs with increased physical demands, potential exposure to hazardous materials (such as cleaning fluids or noise pollution in a factory), and limited benefits such as health insurance.

Education level also appears to have a significant impact on negative social behaviors such as homicide rates. Black males who do not graduate from high school have a death by homicide rate that is five times higher compared with black males who do graduate. Compared with white males who graduate, the homicide rate for nongraduate blacks is nine times greater. The mechanism for this not clearly defined, but the disparity is remarkable.

Woolf et al. (2007) found education to be a major driver in the slow decrease in the death rate in the past 100 years, which, with the exception of pandemics, has decreased about 1% annually. This decrease has continued despite the investment of billions into technological advances. Woolf et al. (2007) hypothesized that the return on investment from medical advances is insignificant to the potential decrease in death rates if the level of education was standardized throughout society. In a study of mortality data for the years between 1996 and 2002, they compared the maximum number of deaths averted

by the decrease in the death rate with the number of deaths that could have been averted had all adults had the same mortality rate as those with at least one year of college education. Medical advances averted a maximum of 178,193 deaths within the study period. By correcting disparities in education-associated mortality rates, 1,369,335 lives would have been saved. This is almost a ratio of 8 to 1. A statistical review such as this includes many assumptions. The accuracy of these assumptions represents a limitation to this study; however, Woolf et al. (2007) suggest that even with more reliable data and statistical methods, the precision of the projection might be altered, but the magnitude of the ratio suggests that the overall findings would not be.

Woolf et al. (2007) recognize that the link between mortality and education is complex and compounded by other social issues, including life experiences, race, gender, and income status. The positive impact of education is associated with empowerment of individuals to care for themselves, make better lifestyle choices, and have access to medical care. Education also creates the means to better social conditions, including better housing, safer neighborhoods, and better employment.

Woolf et al. (2007) acknowledge the complexity of creating the social structure to ensure that all members of society receive an adequate education but they suggest that an investment in improving the educational level of individuals may have a greater return than continued investment in medical technology.

Income

Income is closely related to education. The more education a person has, the more likely that person is to have a high-paying job. In 2007, the median income of full-time workers was $41,000. For persons who had not completed high school, the median income was almost $25,000, and for persons with an advanced degree it was just over $75,000 (Witt, 2009). Income is also correlated to health status. Williams and Braboy Jackson (2005) found that Americans with a low socioeconomic status, regardless of race, have levels of illness in their thirties and forties that are not seen in groups with a higher socioeconomic status until 30 years later.

Income rates play an important role in understanding difference in coronary health disease and cancer deaths. For example, death rates are two to three times higher in low income blacks and whites than their higher income peers. Although this information is disheartening, they also found a racial disparity when looking at compatible incomes: Black women have a death rate from heart disease that is 65% higher than white women.

Unfortunately, public health surveillance only includes income data on birth and death certificates. In addition, the United States government does not follow the lead of other Western nations and report health data as a function of income as well as race. Understanding the interrelation between the two issues is important if we are to fully understand health disparities (Kawachi et al., 2005).

Place of Residence

Residential location can be highly correlated to education, income, and occupation. Therefore, neighborhoods will differ on the level of healthiness. Low-income communities often have poor housing stock, which means residents may be exposed to risk factors such as lead paint or asbestos. It is also the case that low-income persons live in more densely populated areas and are at risk of communicable diseases such as tuberculosis. Last, low-income persons may not have access to the same level of goods and services as persons living in higher income neighborhoods. Brown et al. (2007) studied the relation between residence in a socioeconomically depressed neighborhood and the overall quality of life for its residents. The study looked at the health differences for individuals with chronic diseases such as diabetes, asthma, hypertension, and cardiac disease that require self-management to prevent additional complications. Self-management includes diet, exercise, and compliance with medical regimes. They posited that these essential components of care can be challenged by neighborhood factors such as limited access to grocery stores, safe places to exercise, and access to pharmacy and medical services.

To evaluate this relationship (Brown et al., 2007), data were reviewed from 2,536 individuals who had participated in the Los Angeles Family and Neighborhood Survey to correlate the relationship between individual reports of chronic disease, the socioeconomic status of the neighborhood, and self-reported health levels. Those reporting at least one chronic disease were more likely to live in a census track with a lower socioeconomic status and were more likely to report their health to be fair or poor than those without a chronic disease. In addition, they found that health can be related to environmental factors such as access to high-quality food and perceived safety concerns. It is difficult to determine the direction of this relationship. Those with a chronic disease and lower annual income may not be able to afford to live in a neighborhood with a higher socioeconomic status. It may be that the lower education and income lead to the chronic disease.

The authors (Brown et al., 2007) suggest that the findings have implications for the healthcare system. They recommend additional research to determine whether changes in the built environment, such as the addition of more grocery stores or safe access to exercise facilities, could be helpful.

In a community-based participatory research program in Detroit, Schulz et al. (2005) created a model of the impact of neighborhood attributes on diabetes care. The framework they developed looked at fundamental factors, intermediate factors, proximate factors, and outcomes. The fundamental factors were determined to be race-based residential segregation and local economic context. These fundamental factors led to intermediate factors, including stressful life conditions such as financial insecurity and discrimination; built environment issues such as safety to walk for exercise, availability of fresh produce, and location of food stores; social environment, including police capacity to maintain safety, social norms related to dietary practices, and physical activity, workforce conditions, and leisure time activities; and finally, educational opportunities and access to information. These intermediate factors led to the identification of proximate factors of physiologic responses to stress, dietary practices, physical activity, and an overall limited knowledge of relationship between diet, physical activity, and diabetes. This finally led to the outcome of obesity, poor fitness, and diabetes (Schulz et al., 2005).

Based on this model, a two-week training program was developed to assist clients in developing skills needed to advocate and community build. This study (Schulz et al., 2005) demonstrates that by working with a community to analyze the factors impacting the health of a population creative and sustainable solutions can be found.

Occupational Impact

Another important social determinant of health is occupational health hazards and risks. The type of job that a person holds determines the risks to which a person is exposed (Hsin-Chin Tsai & Salazar, 2007). As mentioned before, occupational activities have a direct impact on health in physical demands, access to health services, and exposure to hazards.

Occupational risk has been associated with five different risk factors: physical, chemical, biological, enviromechanical, and psychosocial. Physical includes agents that cause trauma, such as burns and cuts. Chemical injuries arise from exposure to toxic or irritating solutions or gases such as fumes from cleaning solutions. Biological hazards rise from contact with organisms that cause harm to human health, such as biomedical waste. Enviromechanical hazards include injuries caused by poor equipment, slippery floors, second-hand smoke, and so forth. In addition, this may include injuries that occur from activities related to the job, such as heavy lifting. Finally, psychosocial hazards include stress and emotional strain from the pace of activity and interaction with the public.

Practically all of these hazards can be found in what might be considered an ordinary workplace, such as a restaurant. In a study of Chinese restaurant workers, Hsin-Chin Tsai & Salazar (2007) identified exposure to all forms of risk with the exception of biological ones. Psychosocial hazards were the most frequently mentioned. The volume of business was a source of stress, and the workers experienced the stress of communication with customers in English, when it is not their primary language. Physical hazards were second most prevalent, with kitchen workers identifying the extreme temperatures from hot oils and steam in the kitchen. This was followed by mechanical and chemical hazards. The authors recommend that public health workers and restaurant owners work together to identify hazards and determine how best to decrease the risk. They also suggest that the unique nature of being an immigrant might be addressed by community groups or associations. "Disentangling the relative importance of the complex causal processes that to disparities in disease is challenging" (Williams & Braboy Jackson, 2005, p. 330). Often social programs are developed to address one of the factors without understanding that any one factor is only part of the overall picture. They suggest that only by addressing the conditions that cause the disparities will any real improvement be seen in the resultant health outcomes.

Health Practices and Behaviors

Health practices and behaviors are another area of focus in looking for causes of health disparities (Williams & Braboy Jackson, 2005). Health practices such as diet, exercise, tobacco use, and alcohol abuse have all been shown to have significant impact on chronic disease development and management, including diabetes, heart disease, and cancer. These health behaviors are strongly patterned by the social environment of individuals. Williams and Braboy Jackson (2005) found that those with a lower socioeconomic status were least likely to change health behaviors to healthier ones. The authors attribute this to a lack of health information and decreased resources to assist the individual to make changes. The realities of a life in poverty must also be considered. Individuals in poverty work hard to meet the basics of life, including food and shelter. The complexity of keeping the basic needs met leads to limited time for exercise or attending health education sessions. One of the frustrating realities is that food that is healthier tends to be more expensive and more time consuming to prepare. Consider the cost of a gallon of milk versus a gallon of soda. Milk can be two to three times more expensive.

Recently, a parish nurse reported that a church with prominently black members experienced the death of a pastor's wife from cardiac issues. The "church ladies" prepared a meal for the wake that included fried chicken, vegetables swimming in butter, and heavy whipping cream on a high-calorie dessert. The nurse began to work slowly with the "church ladies" and was able to improve the church meal menus. Of greater importance, however, was that the "ladies" were informal leaders of the church and able to influence others to improve their home cooking choices. This kind of grassroots health education is an example of health practices and an approach to making changes (Butler County Nurse Parish Project, 2009).

Health-Seeking Behaviors

In an attempt to understand medical care-seeking behaviors of people with low incomes, eight focus groups were interviewed about their use of primary and emergency care (Wetta-Hall et al., 2005). Thirty-five participants between the ages of 18 and 64 years, with no current health insurance and a recent emergency department visit, were recruited to participate in the study. The focus groups included two Spanish-speaking groups. The demographics of the participants relate to other factors in the Aday model. Forty percent of the participants had a high school level of education or less, and 60% were single, separated, divorced, or widowed. Both of these factors are described in the model as increasing the risk of vulnerability (Aday, 2001).

This study identified some key barriers to access to primary care. The first was cost. Participants reported that they did not have money to pay for an office visit and that physicians frequently required payment at the time of service. A related issue was unpaid balances on previous medical care, which again made the individual an unwelcome client (Sered & Fernandopulle, 2005). Other social attributes resulted in barriers to care. These included the lack of a consistent caregiver, lack of transportation, no availability of office hours when the individuals were off of work, and cultural issues such as language, health literacy, and a generalized feeling of being disrespected (Wetta-Hall et al., 2005).

Trust in Resources

Even if resources exist, access to those resources may be impaired by a lack of trust. Trust is a significant factor in developing a therapeutic doctor–patient relationship. Trust in a physician is defined as a "belief that the physician will act in your best interest and arises from the perception of the physician's values and competence" (Armstrong et al., 2007, p. 1283). These authors point to a high positive correlation between trust and compliance with medical treatment plans.

Health-related trust, in general, has decreased related to managed care and for-profit health organizations. The trust between blacks and their healthcare providers may have special stresses related to the history of slave experimentation and the Tuskegee Syphilis Study (Armstrong et al., 2007).

One of the theories related to the root causes of health disparities is that some individuals do not seek medical care for a variety of reasons, including the fear of discrimination. The 1998–1999 Community Tracking Study, conducted by the Center for Health Care Change, tried to determine whether discrimination is a factor in compliance with medical treatment plans. The Tracking Study surveyed 32,047 participants in 60 different communities to evaluate reported levels of trust between different racial and ethnic groups. The survey included four different items related to trust. The four items were scored together to get a composite score. This study found that racial and ethnic factors created a difference in the level of trust in their physicians on a simple analysis (Armstrong et al., 2007). Both blacks and Hispanics reported lower levels of trust than their white counterparts; however, looking at multivariate analysis, the results are more complex. The level of that distrust varies in relation to geographic location, socioeconomic status, and gender.

The authors suggest that the geographic variants may relate to a number of community factors, including access to both primary and secondary care, the racial or ethnic makeup of the providers in the community, and the underlying race relationships in the region. They also suggest that gender may influence the level of interaction with physicians. The results show that women have a higher level of trust than do men. The authors suggest that the degree of involvement with health decision making may make women, who are most likely to be in that role, more trusting of their chosen physician.

Communication

One of the key components of trust is communication. Patient–provider communication is an essential component of good health care (Clemans-Cope & Kenney, 2007). Much has been written about medical literacy. If there is not good communication in all forms, verbal and nonverbal, then medical diagnosis, treatment plans, and outcomes can be altered. The healthcare provider may miss important data to consider in the development of a diagnosis or treatment plan, and the patient may not appreciate the treatment plan or be able to understand and follow directions.

Clemans-Cope and Kenney (2007) used data mining of an existing survey to determine a relationship between reports of communication problems between patients and health providers and two different variables, primary language and public insurance. The data were collected in both English and Spanish. About one third of those with a Spanish interview and low-income children who in some cases were covered by public insurance reported poor communication with a healthcare provider (Clemans-Cope & Kenney, 2007). The source of care was also identified as a variable. Those who used public clinics or hospital outpatient clinics were 9.5% more likely to report poor communications.

This study points (Clemans-Cope & Kenney, 2007) to the need for healthcare providers to continue to improve communication skills and to ensure that adequate translation services are available. This level of service is especially needed by those clinics serving low-income children covered by public insurance; however, the expense of this affects the very healthcare providers who can least afford to meet the need.

In a study completed in Baltimore, Maryland, the impact of perceived discrimination on compliance with medical treatment plans was reviewed (Casagrande et al., 2007). The study had 1,408 adult study participants (59.8% black and 40.7% white). The survey was developed to determine whether the participants had ever perceived discrimination from a healthcare provider. Discrimination could be related to many factors, including race, but also social status, insurance status, and even weight. Then the participants were interviewed about their healthcare-seeking behavior (Casagrande et al., 2007). The blacks and whites who reported feelings of discrimination were 1.2 to 2 times more likely to also report delays in seeking medical care and noncompliance with medical treatment plans. The noncompliance with medical treatment plans creates a situation that compounds any preexisting health disparities. This also has the potential for creating a situation of circular feedback loops, with medical providers having poor compliance experiences with minorities and then treating minorities differently based on their experiences. The study relied on self-report for both variables, which is a limitation because the perception of discrimination is difficult to validate (Casagrande et al., 2007).

Health Resources and Health Disparities

The last section of this chapter considers how social attributes and resources interact with access to healthcare resources. Access to health care is one resource that contributes to healthcare risk, according to the theory of vulnerability (Aday, 2001). Primary care is provided by a consistent provider, which includes management of acute and chronic illness, screening for disease, and prevention. This is the gold standard of care. Lack of such a regular source of care is associated with an increased reliance on emergency department services (Wetta-Hall et al., 2005). Individuals living on low incomes often encounter barriers to receiving primary care. Life course theory posits that limited access to health services adds to the stress of daily life. It is stress reactions that are the main pathway to poor health (Kuh & Ben-Sholomo, 2005).

Unfortunately, emergency departments have become the source of primary care for the uninsured (Siegel, 2004; Wetta-Hall et al., 2005). The Institute of Medicine reports that a lack of primary care providers and overuse of emergency departments are impediments to the health of uninsured individuals. The lack of a consistent provider, including the establishment of a therapeutic relationship, lack of screening and preventive care, and lack of chronic disease management are a few of the problems seen when an emergency department is used as a source of medical care (Institute of Medicine, 2001; Wetta-Hall et al., 2005). One recent study sought to understand more about this situation. In a series of focus groups, 35 participants shared their perspectives related to their emergency department use (Wetta-Hall et al., 2005). Participants sought emergency department care for illnesses that they perceived as urgent, either because the symptoms could no longer be ignored or had begun to interfere with activities of daily living such as employment or child care. Generally, some self-care had been tried without success; however, the medical issues that brought the individual to the emergency department often could have been resolved with a visit to a primary care provider (Wetta-Hall et al., 2005). The other situation is that a medical issue that had been ignored for some period of time had become a crisis situation or was the result of a more serious disease with a delay in diagnosis. In both situations, the emergency department is not the place to obtain the medical care needed; a primary care provider is the more appropriate place to go.

Absent good primary care, a strong link exists between access to care and deaths from diseases such as cancer. Those with limited access to care have less screening and diagnostic services, which may delay diagnosis of conditions and have an adverse effect on the outcome of treatment. It has long been determined that early diagnosis and initial treatment has a significant impact on the outcome of cancer care. Those with limited access to health care do not have the needed screening services such as mammograms or colonoscopy examinations. A weaker link can be found in a study such as Williams and Braboy Jackson (2005), where socioeconomic status was shown to contribute to the homicide disparity, as access to emergency services to save injured individuals or even access to prehospital services such as paramedics is limited in some neighborhoods, and the nature of the care has been shown by the Institute of Medicine to be different.

The public safety net has been challenged to meet the needs of those who have limited access to care (Staff, 2005). In addition to the 46 million uninsured, 41 million people, including 6 million disabled, received services from the federal–state Medicaid program. Many Americans think that all uninsured, poor individuals can received Medicaid The individuals who meet the income criteria for Medicaid must also be disabled or in a family with children. Childless adults, regardless of low income, are not eligible for Medicaid services. Community-level programs have been developed using four major approaches. Many communities have more than one model in place or have a single model that uses components from all prototypes.

Safety Net Hospitals

Public hospitals have been the traditional place for care for those underserved and uninsured. Safety net hospitals have been defined in a variety of ways, but share the common characteristic of providing significant levels of care to clients on government programs, as well as providing more than their market share of uncompensated care (Bazzoli et al., 2005). Many are owned and operated by a local government; they are frequently in urban settings and are often associated with an academic medical center. Reviewing the status of these hospitals, Bazzoli et al. (2005) found that the level of uncompensated care remained high, and as a result, these hospitals were struggling to survive and had to consider reductions in their level of commitment unless additional support was given to the clients they serve.

These traditional cornerstones of the safety net have been under stress and strain for the past decade (Institute of Medicine, 2003a). Unfortunately, these traditional cornerstones of the public safety net, are declining at a rate faster than private hospital closures (Mantone, 2005). Between 1996 and 2002, the number of urban public hospitals fell from 217 to 168, a 22.5% decrease. Private hospitals also experienced some closures, but the rate of closure is much slower. During the same time period, the number of urban private hospitals decreased from 1,419 to 1,316, a 7% decrease.

Charity or Discount Services Model

In addition to public hospitals, nonprofit hospitals have a mission to provide services to the underserved. This mission was reinforced by legislation. More recently, efforts have been made to move charity care outside of the hospital by matching the uninsured with available charity or discounted services. Programs can be modest, such as those to aid clients with applications to prescription assistance programs, or they can be extensive, such as Project Access.

Project Access started in North Carolina. This program recruited community physician volunteers, each of whom agreed to care for a set number of uninsured. The program then determined eligibility and managed the assignment of clients to the care providers within the agreed-on number of clients. This model also arranged discounted rates for hospitalizations and diagnostic work (Andulis & Gusmano, 2000).

Within this prototype are many hospital-based programs that extend charity care to eligible clients. Also in this prototype is the outright support for free or reduced-fee clinics. The sustainability of this model is dependent on ongoing charitable contributions and availability of free or discounted services. This model is not always well accepted by some clients who are reluctant to be the recipient of charity until there is no other option. The care provided within the model tends to be episodic.

Government-Subsidized Employer-Based Insurance

Third, there is government-subsidized health insurance, or what is called multishare or three share, health plans. These programs fill a gap between safety net programs and commercial insurance for the working poor. Many of these individuals are not eligible for traditional safety net programs such as Medicaid or local General Assistance Medical Programs (GAMP) because of levels of income or family status. They are also not likely to be eligible for charity-based programs. The basic premise is that eligible businesses are able to enroll into the program. The eligible businesses are generally small businesses with low-income employees. The business is frequently service-oriented and is unable to afford to offer any healthcare benefit to its employees (Woodbury, 2007).

Although businesses typically split the cost of an insurance product between the business and the employee in various proportions, the multishare programs split the cost between the business, the employee, and a community health partner, typically a government source. The multishare plans are designed to provide affordable employee health insurance to small businesses that cannot afford to purchase health insurance. At the same time they attempt to prevent "crowd out" or the decision of businesses to drop a program and move into three share as a cost-saving measure. These are businesses that would otherwise not offer a health benefit. A few of the businesses in some of the early programs have used three share as a means of support while in a startup phase and have eventually transitioned to an insurance product.

The program in Muskegon County, Michigan, is one of the first programs of this nature. The program considers itself community access program with a goal of increasing access to primary care for its residents (Woodbury, 2007). The Muskegon program covers approximately 1,500 individuals annually. They have between 350 to 400 businesses enrolled annually. The average business has four employees.

The premiums for the benefit in Muskegon are divided between the employer (30%), employee (30%), and the public funds (40%). In 2007, the employer and employee share was $46 per month, which was affordable for both groups. The total cost per member was $156 per month. The program has case management and proudly shares that from 1999 to 2007 the monthly cost had risen from $38 to $46. Vondie Woodbury, the executive director of the Muskegon program, calls this "a remarkably cost effective alternative for small businesses employing workers who might otherwise be uninsured" (2007).

The Muskegon plan design is quite comprehensive. It includes standard benefits such as inpatient care, primary care, specialist care, medications, emergency room and urgent care, hospice, and durable medical equipment. It is a county-based program and does not cover any services provided outside of the county. While in Muskegon, the health plan does the contracting and reimbursement for the services; the more typical approach is to contract with an insurance company to offer a specific policy at a specific rate.

The experience in Michigan, which has at least four counties using this funding approach, is typical of other models of care for the uninsured. The clients initially have some pent-up demand and have had fewer preventive and screening services, and when they are diagnosed with serious illnesses, comorbidities exist. The rate of chronic diseases has also been found to be higher, which is consistent with clients coming from poverty or near poverty (Woodbury, 2007).

The dignity of the clients is maintained, as the clients have an insurance card. The businesses have some economic support for their business development within the community. The sustainability of this model depends on the public support for the third share.

Public–Private Partnerships

The last model is dependent on partnership with providers to discount services and the government to support such programs. In this model, a public agency determines eligibility for low-income uninsured and purchases healthcare services for the eligible residents. The programs have a modified managed-care approach to maximize the funds and have generally had an interest in focusing on primary care (Lucey, 2001). For the clients, the majority of these programs provide a medical home and an ongoing relationship with a provider. The health outcomes of having a medical home are well documented as having positive effects on compliance with medical treatment plans and preventive services (Institute of Medicine, 2003b). The sustainability of these programs is dependent on the ongoing funding of the program, which is in competition with the multiple other demands for public funds. In Denver, the public hospital has continued and has been supported by the development of an extensive network of both public and private primary care clinics (Institute of Medicine, 2001). This hybrid uses the public hospital but purchases services for the community for outpatient care.

In Milwaukee, after 135 years of operation, a decision was made to close the county-owned and -operated public hospital in 1995 and to create a community-based safety net program to assist the residents of Milwaukee County without health insurance. The resulting initiative, the General Assistance Medical Program (GAMP) was developed consistent with the Aday model to attempt to not only provide care but to decrease vulnerability for its clients. The model in Milwaukee has been used in Hillsborough County, which includes Tampa, Florida, and in Boston, Massachusetts until recent state changes in state law. Many policy analysts consider GAMP to be a potential model for national health care reform (Andulis & Gusmano, 2000; Bovbjerg et al., 2000; Swoope, 2001).

Social Change, Public Policy, and Advocacy

This chapter demonstrates the complex set of interactions that impact a person's health and well-being. These range from attributes such as race to factors that explain socioeconomic status, to health behaviors and ultimately access to care (Aday, 2001). At the bottom line, improving health calls for changes both in individual behavior and the social environments within which individuals live. This complexity is summarized by William Frist, who is a physician and United States senator and as such offers a unique perspective of health care. As a policy maker, he writes that the need to define the problems related to health disparities must be clear so that effective solutions can be crafted (Frist, 2005).

His perspective is that health disparities are a symptom of the challenges of the overall health system (Frist, 2005). Working to solve the issue of health disparities may be a key towards solving some of the pervasive quality issues in the healthcare system.

In the article written by Frist, he begins by reviewing studies related to race, ethnicity and socioeconomic status. Some of the key findings are related to the "troubling" health outcomes (p. 445). The overall mortality of African Americans and American Indians/Alaska Natives is double the mortality rate of other population groups. In addition, eight times as many blacks as whites have AIDS. Related to socioeconomic status (SES), the Senator reviews research that finds that those with low SES have poor access to care, riskier behavior, fewer community resources and as a result have higher mortality (Frist, 2005).

In terms of health policy, Frist argues that public solutions might best come from the local level, not the federal level (Frist, 2005). He reasons that health care is primarily delivered locally, and thus, the capability of healthcare providers and healthcare facilities has a direct impact on disparities from a geographic perspective. The community can best understand local health behaviors and cultural traditions that may also be part of these differences. This confirms some of the findings in other studies (Armstrong et al., 2007).

The Senator also reasons that the solutions to health disparities need to be patient-centered care (Frist, 2005). First, he suggests that patients must take accountability for their own health. As a policy maker, the author suggests that policies need to be in place that promote personal responsibility. Second, communication is necessary between providers and patients. Policy actions are suggested to increase health literacy and encourage providers to learn additional languages. Finally, all care and communication must be taken within the context of culture. Improving the overall quality of healthcare delivery will also have a marked impact toward elimination of disparities. By improving quality, the author points out the need to increase information technology, supportive data collection, and increase the diversity of the healthcare work force (Frist, 2005). Unfortunately, Frist's model for change does not consider the social changes that may be required to achieve equal and improved health outcomes that are emphasized by policy analysts such as Aday (2001) and Woolf et al. (2007).

The relationship between health and health disparities is a complex issue with many confounding factors; however, clearly, the factors that contribute to socioeconomic status such as education, location of residence, language, and others have a significant impact on the health of individuals and contribute to the development of health disparities for groups of individuals. As the challenges to health are likely socially based, the potential for finding solutions is also likely to be within the arena of social change.

Nurses and public health professionals have always recognized the need to look at clients and communities from a holistic perspective. This tradition provides and sustains a framework that all professionals can apply when approaching these complex issues.

References

Aday, L. (2001). *At risk in America*. San Francisco: Jossey-Bass.

Andulis, D., & Gusmano, M. (2000). *Community initiatives for the uninsured: How far can innovative partnerships take us?* New York: The New York Academy of Medicine, Office of Urban Populations.

Armstrong, K., Ravenell, K., McMurphy, S., & Putt, M. (2007). Racial/ethnic differences in physician distrust in the United States. *American Journal of Public Health, 97*(7), 1283–1289.

Batbum, M. E., & Baumann, L. (2007). A sense of community among immigrant Latinas. *Community Health, 30*(3), 167–177.

Bazzoli, G. J., Kang, R., Hasnain-Wynia, R., & Lindrooth, R. C. (2005). An update on safety-net hospitals: Coping with the late 1990s and early 2000s. *Health Affairs, 24*(4), 1047–1056.

Blane, D. (2006). The life course, the social gradient and health. In Marmot, M. & Wilkinson, R. G. (Eds.), *The social determinants of health* (2nd ed., pp. 54–77). Oxford: Oxford University Press.

Bovbjerg, R., Marsteller, J., & Ullman, F. (2000). *Health care for the poor and uninsured after a public hospital's closure or conversion.* Washington, DC: The Urban Institute.

Brown, A. F., Ang, A., & Pebley, A. R. (2007). The relationship between neighborhood characteristics and self-rated health for adults with chronic conditions. *American Journal of Public Health, 97*(5), 926–932.

Brunner, E., & Marmot, M. (2006). Social organization, stress and health. In Marmot, M. & Wilkinson, R. G. (Eds.), *Social determinants of health* (2nd ed., pp. 6–30). Oxford: Oxford University Press.

Butler County Nurse Parish Project. Retrieved December 23, 2009, from http://www.raconline.org/success/success_details.php?success_id=522

Byrd, L., Fletcher, A., & Menifield, C. (2007). Disparities in health care: Minority elders at risk. *ABNF Journal, 18*(2), 51–55.

Casagrande, S. S., Gary, T. L., LaVeist, T. A., Gaskin, D. J., & Copper, L. (2007). Perceived discrimination and adherence to medical care in a racially integrated community. *Journal of General Internal Medicine, 22*(3), 389–395.

Clemans-Cope, L., & Kenney, G. (2007). Low income parents' reports of communication problems with health care providers: Effects of language and insurance. *Public Health Reports, 122*(2), 206–216.

Cortiss, H., Shankie, M., & Mover, M. (2007). Research curricula and resources related to lesbian, gay, bisexual and transgender health in U.S. public schools of public health. *American Journal of Public Health, 97*(4), 1023–1026.

Frist, W. (2005). Overcoming disparities in U.S. health care. *Health Affairs, 24*(2), 445–451.

Hsin-Chin Tsai, J., & Salazar, M. K. (2007). Occupational hazards and risks faced by Chinese immigrant restaurant workers. *Community Health, 30*(25), S71–S79.

Institute of Medicine. (2001). *Health and behavior: The interplay between biological, behavioral and social influences.* Washington, DC: National Academies Press.

Institute of Medicine. (2003a). *A shared destiny: The effect on the community of uninsurance.* Washington, DC: National Academies Press.

Institute of Medicine. (2003b). *Unequal treatment: Confronting racial and ethnic disparities in healthcare.* Washington, DC: National Academies Press.

Kawachi, I., Daniels, N., & Robinson, D. E. (2005). Health disparities by race and class: Why both matter. *Health Affairs, 24*(2), 343–352.

Kuh, D., & Ben-Sholomo, Y. (2005). Introduction. In D. Kuh & Y. Ben-Sholomo (Eds.), *A life course approach to chronic disease epidemiology* (2nd ed., pp. 3–14). Oxford: Oxford University Press.

Lewis, L. B., Skone, D. C., Nascimento, L. M., Diamant, A. L., Guiyard, J. J., & Yancy, A. (2005). African Americans' access to healthy food options in south Los Angeles restaurants. *American Journal of Public Health, 95*(4), 668–673.

Lucey, P. (2001). An access program for the medically indigent individuals. *Nursing Economics, 19*(1), 12–16.

Mantone, J. (2005). Safety net shifts. *Modern Healthcare, 34*(35), 24.

Marmot, M. (2004). Creating healthier societies. *Bulletin of the World Health Organization, 82*(5), 320.

Marmot, M., Rose, G., Shipley, M. J., & Hamilton, P. J. (1978). Employment grade and coronary heart disease in British civil servants. *Journal of Epidemiology and Community Health, 32*, 244–249.

Marmot, M., Shipley, M. J., & Rose, G. (1984). Inequalities in death: Specific explanations of a general pattern. *Lancet, 1*, 1003–1006.

Mitchell, S., & Schlesinger, M. (2005). Managed care and gender disparities in problematic health care experiences. *Health Services Research, 40*(5 Pt 1):1489–1513.

Napoles-Springer, A. M., Santoyo, J., Houston, K., Perez-Stable, E., & Steward, A. (2005). Patients' perceptions of cultural factors affecting the quality of their medical encounters. *Health Expectations, 8*, 4–17.

National Institutes of Health. (2005). Strategic research plan to reduce and ultimately eliminate health disparities.

Sankar, P., & Kahn, J. (2005). BiDil: Race medicine or race marketing. *Health Affairs, Web Exclusive.* W5, 455–463.

Schulz, A. J., Zenk, S., Odoms-Young, A., Holis-Neely, T., Nwankwo, R., Lockett, M., et al. (2005). Healthy eating and exercising to reduce diabetes: Exploring the potential of social determinants of health frameworks within the context of community-based participatory diabetes prevention. *American Journal of Public Health, 95*(4), 645–651.

Sered, S. S., & Fernandopulle, R. (2005). *Uninsured in America: Life and death in the land of opportunity*. Berkeley: University of California Press.

Shaw, M., Dorling, D., & Smith, G. D. (2006). Poverty, social exclusion, and minorities. In M. Marmot & R. G. Wilkinson (Eds.), *The social determinants of health* (2nd ed., pp. 196–223). Oxford: Oxford University Press.

Siegel, B. (2004). The emergency department: Rethinking the safety net for the safety net. *Health Affairs,* 146–148.

Smith, G. D. (Ed.). (2003). *Health inequalities*. Bristal, UK: The Policy Press.

Staff. (2005). The uninsured: You can make a difference. *Journal of Family Medicine, 54*(11), 943–945.

Stansfeld, S. (2006). Social support and social cohesion. In M. Marmot & R. G. Wilkinson (Eds.), *The social determinants of health* (2nd ed., pp. 148–171). Oxford: Oxford University Press.

Swoope, C. (2001). Rising from a hospital's ruins. *Governing Magazine, 14*(12), 39–43.

U.S. Department of Health and Human Services. (2000). Healthy people 2010: Understanding and improving health (2nd ed.). Washington, DC: Government Printing Office.

Wetta-Hall, R., Ablah, E., Dismuke, S., Molgaard, C., Fredrickson, D., & Berry, M. (2005). Emergency department use by people on low income. *Emergency Nurse, 13*(3), 12–18.

Williams, D., & Braboy Jackson, P. (2005). Social sources of racial disparities in health. *Health Affairs, 24*(2), 325–334.

Witt, J. (2009). Education pays: Income by education level (2009 update). Retrieved December 27, 2009 from http://soc101.wordpress.com/2009/02/10/education-pays-income-by-education-level-2009-update/

Woodbury, V. (2007). Personal communication. November 2, 2007.

Woolf, S., Johnson, R., Phillips, R., & Philipsen, M. (2007). Giving everyone the health of the educated: An examination of whether social change would save more lives than medical advances. *American Journal of Public Health, 97*(4), 679–683.

World Health Organization & UNICEF. (1978). *Declaration of alma-ata.*

Section II

The Health Labor Force: Understanding the Distribution of Power and Influence

Chapter 3

Physicians

Nancy Aries and Barbara Caress

AS WILLIAM OSLER SAID—OR IS SAID TO HAVE SAID—
"ASK NOT WHAT DISEASE THE PERSON HAS,
BUT RATHER WHAT PERSON THE DISEASE HAS."

Anne Fadiman, The Spirit Catches You and You Fall Down

OVERVIEW

When medicine works, it can be very good, but when it fails, it can be very bad. The challenge of this chapter is to describe more fully how physicians function within the larger arena of the health-care system in order to understand what factors reinforce the practice of medicine, thus leading to the best possible result. The first part of this chapter overviews data concerning who become physicians, what their areas of medical expertise are, where they practice, and how they are paid. By having a better understanding of the medical profession, we can then look in more detail at the problems associated with medical practice and how to assure that physicians provide the best possible care. Next, we consider the concept of medical professionalism and the interrelated questions of medical error and physician accountability. The final section examines efforts being made to overcome the structural and organizational barriers to good quality of care.

OBJECTIVES

- To understand both the centrality and limits of physicians in defining how the health system functions
- To appreciate the changes in physician practice in the late twentieth and early twenty-first century and how they impact access, quality, and cost of care

(continues)

- To understand how the organization of the healthcare system influences physician behavior and vice versa
- To recognize that the intent of healthcare reform is not only to increase access to health care and control healthcare costs but also to influence physician practice in order to improve the quality of care

KEY TERMS

- ❑ Medical error
- ❑ Medical professionalism
- ❑ Physician payment
- ❑ Physician practice patterns
- ❑ Physician supply

Cystic fibrosis is a genetic disease that is characterized by the body's inability to manage chloride, a chemical needed to turn food into energy. The result is a thickening of body secretions or mucus, which prevents the body from absorbing food. Untreated, a child with cystic fibrosis will fail to grow. Ultimately, the secretions block the passageways in the lungs, leading to death. Although there is no cure for cystic fibrosis, the treatment protocols are well documented and standardized. Patients receive nutrients and follow strict diets to ensure their growth. They have medicated nebulizers and are percussed (thumped on the chest) twice a day to break up and expel mucus. Close monitoring by physicians and other health professionals to assure adherence can mean that a person with cystic fibrosis will live well beyond childhood.

Warren Warwick was Director of the Fairview-University Children's Hospital's cystic fibrosis center in Minneapolis for almost 40 years. This treatment center has some of the best outcomes in terms of patient longevity in the United States. Given the standardization of the treatment protocol, the range of outcomes cannot be explained by chance. Warwick attributes his program's success to his following the advice of Leroy Matthews MD: "You do whatever you can to keep your patients' lungs as open as possible" (Gawande, 2005).

Atul Gawande (2005) described Warwick's appointment with Janelle, a 17 year old with cystic fibrosis. Janelle's lung capacity had dropped from better than 100% to 90% in a little over 3 months. This is not a bad level of functioning for a 17 year old. It is a higher level of functioning than many other persons her age. Dr. Warwick, however, was not satisfied. With time and patience, he was able to get Janelle talking about the changes in her life that led her to stop taking medications and being percussed every day. She had a boyfriend and was not spending as much time at home. Having no adverse signs of the disease, although she was failing to comply with the medical regimen, reinforced her sense that she was not doing tremendous harm to herself. Dr. Warwick continued to talk to Janelle about the kinds of accommodations they could jointly make to increase Janelle's compliance. They needed to find a strategy that was acceptable to her and Dr. Warwick in terms of compliance and medical outcomes. Gawande concluded that flexibility and the pursuit of new ways to achieve better functioning of the lungs resulted in excellence.

Janelle's story stands in sharp contrast to Lia Lee's (Fadiman, 1997). Lia is a young Hmong woman who was diagnosed with epilepsy before her first birthday. Lia's family had recently immigrated to the United States. They barely spoke English and were unfamiliar with Western medical practice. Lia's condition, however, was tremendously tenuous. Given the difficulty that the doctors had controlling the disease, her medication regimen was complex and constantly changing. Her parents' failure to adhere to the regimen led one physician to report her family to Child Protective Services. As a result, Lia was removed from her home and placed in foster care. Although the foster family was loving and made sure that Lia followed the prescribed medical regimen, the placement was exceptionally stressful for Lia. She was returned home with the parents' agreement to comply with the doctors' orders, but her condition continued to deteriorate. She continued to have seizures until one seizure, a grand mal, did not stop. Lia was taken to the hospital, where doctors found her to be in septic shock. The doctors were able to stop the seizures and cure the sepsis, but Lia was brain dead. She now lives at home, comatose.

Although Lia's story can be told as a story of medical noncompliance, that is too simple an explanation for her brain death. Lia's parents, recently arrived Hmong refugees, spoke practically no English. The first times they took Lia to the emergency department there were no interpreters who spoke Hmong; thus, her condition was misdiagnosed. A correct diagnosis was made only when Lia arrived at the emergency room during an epileptic seizure. With only limited means of communication, there was no way to bridge what the doctors understood to be a disease that was best managed with anticonvulsant medications and her parents' belief that Lia's soul had left her body and needed to be brought back. Each acted in good faith. Each cared for Lia's well-being. Lia's medications were changed 23 times over 4 years in an attempt to stabilize her condition. The Lee's engaged shamen to treat her soul, which they thought was being hurt by all of her medications. The divide between the two resulted in what her doctors considered her death on the night she had her grand mal seizure. In retrospect, everyone involved agreed that adherence to what was perceived as the best possible treatment regimen for epilepsy most likely resulted in a worse outcome than would have happened if the doctors and Lia's parents jointly devised a plan that would accommodate the cultural divide between the Lees' and the physicians' understanding of health and disease.

These two stories have so many similarities, yet they describe such different perceptions of what comprises good care. In both cases, the care of the children was managed by physicians. In addition to the physicians, these were diseases that required a team of caregivers who could work together to assure compliance. The physicians based the children's care on evidence about which treatments resulted in the best possible outcomes. Both children's conditions were extremely complex, and any backsliding in treatment could result in a worsening of the condition.

However, there are also differences that can be found between these stories. The first is the episodic versus chronic approach to the treatment of complex conditions. Implicit in the telling of these two stories is the episodic nature of Lia's care. She was seen in the emergency department by different doctors who in some cases had not even read her medical record. In contrast, Janelle's care was managed by a team that was informed about all aspects of the progression of the disease and her psychosocial condition. The second is the need for patients and parents to be an integral part of the care process. This was true in the treatment of Janelle's cystic fibrosis. It was not the case for Lia, whose parents, Foua and Nao Kao, were treated dismissively throughout most of the course of her treatment. The last, and most subtle, is the changing nature of the physicians' role as a caregiver. In Janelle's case, the physician is truly part of a team where the role of other clinical professionals and nonprofessional caregivers is augmented. To keep Janelle's lungs at such a high level of functioning required more than her periodic visits with Dr. Warwick. What is not related in the telling of her story is the importance of nutritionists, physical therapists, respiratory therapists, social workers, and nurses to support her and her family at all times during her treatment.

In this chapter, we examine the role of physicians in this system of care that is capable of providing high-quality care as epitomized by Janelle's experience and is also capable of providing cutting-edge treatment that fails to meet the patient's needs, as is the case of Lia. To do so, the chapter is organized in three parts. We begin by explaining who makes up the physician labor force, where physicians practice, and how they are paid. In the second part, we review the literature on medical errors, as it provides a window for understanding how the organization of medical practice can undermine the best intents of those who practice medicine. Finally, we consider a number of initiatives that are designed to address the structural limits of physician practice.

Who Are the Doctors? Physician Supply

There are approximately 1 million physicians in the United States. Is this enough to meet health-care needs in the United States? How many physicians are enough? The answer depends on how the delivery of health care is organized and the services available to prevent, treat, and ameliorate health conditions. If all primary care is to be provided by a physician, then we need a higher ratio of physicians to population than if primary care is provided by nurse practitioners and other physician extenders. Likewise, with advances in medical technology, there is greater demand for health services. For the last 40 years, there has been a steady growth not only in the number of physicians but also in physician to population ratios (Goodman & Fisher, 2008).

Starting in the 1950s, the demand for medical services increased for three interrelated reasons. First, more patients had access to employer-based health insurance and could afford to purchase services. Between 1940 and 1950, the number of Americans with such coverage grew from 21 to 142 million (Pentecost, 2007). In addition, in 1965, the Democratic-controlled Congress was finally able to fulfill part of the promise made 30 years earlier by Franklin Roosevelt with Lyndon Johnson's signing of the act that created Medicare to cover the older population and Medicaid to cover the poor (Marmor, 1973). Finally, technological innovation began to quicken, which directly impacted the possibilities of medicine and the array of services that patients could receive (Stockburger, 2004). As a result, by 1970, the Carnegie Commission called for expanding the supply of doctors by 50%. The commission proposed that the number of students educated at each school and the number of medical schools be increased (Knowles, 1970).

Government intervention made both of these possible. Many states funded the building of new medical schools. As Table 3-1 indicates, the number of physicians increased from 142 per 100,000 in population to 293 by 2005 and the number of medical schools from 79 to 125. In addition, the Medicare program made funds available to pay for graduate medical education. This helped increase the number of clinicians available to train new physicians (Ludmerer, 1999). It got to the point where more residency slots were available than there were American trained physicians to fill them. These slots started to be filled by international medical graduates (IMGs) (Mullan, 1997).

Even with the dramatic growth of the medical profession, a 2005 study of the Council on Graduate Medical Education (COGME) concluded that we face an impending shortage of physicians. In order to meet the demand that will be created by population growth and an aging population, we need to train an additional 3,000 doctors per year (COGME, 2005). COGME's estimates are based on the assumption of the status quo in terms of the present organization of medical care delivery. Thus, current rates of utilization are used to project future demand. This assumption must be explored as the outcome of care is impacted by the composition and utilization of the labor force.

Race and Gender

Despite the fact that the number of minorities in the general population is increasing more rapidly than the number of whites in the population, the percentage of minority physicians is still exceedingly low (Cohen et al., 2002). In the early 1970s, the percentage of minority physicians increased from about 3% to 8% of all physicians. It reached its height of about 14% in the mid 1990s but has decreased slightly since then. When broken out by racial and ethnic group, Asians have seen the greatest increase in number and percentage but still do not have parity in terms of the population. Blacks and Hispanics still struggle to see substantial growth in their numbers. Black enrollment peaked at 9% in 1995, and Hispanic enrollment peaked at just over 7% in 1996.

Although an argument could be made that the percentage of minority physicians in the labor force should be equal to the percentage of minorities in the population on the grounds of

Table 3-1 PHYSICIAN SUPPLY AND NUMBER OF MEDICAL SCHOOLS, 1950–2005

Year	Number of Physicians	Physicians per 100,000 Population	Number of Medical Schools	Number of Medical Graduates
1950	219,997	142	79	5,553
1960	260,484	142	86	7,081
1970	334,028	160	103	8,367
1980	467,679	202	126	15,113
1990	631,830	249	126	15,398
2000	813,770	291	125	15,712
2005	844,464	293	125	15,761

Sources: http://bhpr.hrsa.gov/healthworkforce/reports/factbook02/FB201.htm, http://bhpr.hrsa.gov/healthworkforce/reports/factbook02/FB109.htm, http://www.cogme.gov/16.pdf, and http://www.aamc.org/data/facts/2008/gradraceeth0208.htm.

social equity, this is not the sole basis for concern about the low percentage of minorities trained as physicians. Minority physicians help increase access to health services. Black and Hispanic physicians are more likely to practice in those minority communities that are otherwise underserved (Komaromy et al., 1996). Minority physicians also help advance cultural competence and reduce cultural barriers to care in medical practice and research by advancing issues that are not always seen by the white majority.

Women have fared much better than have underrepresented minorities (see Table 3-2). In 1970, there were just over 25,000 women physicians. By 2004, women comprised almost 30% of the physician labor force (Statistical Abstract of the United States, 2004). The dramatic increase in the number of women is best understood by examining medical school enrollments where women now make up almost 50% of the entering classes. Although women are achieving equity in terms of their numbers, women's participation in the physician labor force is important because women are more likely than men to engage in primary care practice (American Medical Association, 2008). Primary care is singled out as an area of medical practice where there are severe physician shortages. In 2000, 55% of women were primary care physicians.

IMGs

The supply of physicians is augmented by the growing number of physicians who are trained in countries outside of the United States and Canada. The increase in the number and per-

Table 3-2 WOMEN'S AND MINORITY PARTICIPATION IN MEDICAL SCHOOL

Academic Year	Medical School First Year Enrollment	Female First Year Enrollment		Minority First Year Enrollment (Underrepresented Minorities)	
	Number	Number	Percentage	Number	Percentage
1970–1971	11,348	1,256	11.1	808	7.1
1980–1981	17,186	4,966	28.9	1,548	9.0
1990–1991	16,876	6,550	38.8	1,470	8.7
2000–2001	16,699	7,659	45.9	1,739	10.4

Underrepresented minority: African Americans, Latinos/Hispanics, and Native Americans.

Sources: http://www.aamc.org/data/facts/2008/women-count.htm (Retrieved April 18, 2009), http://books.nap.edu/openbook.php?record_id=729&page=178 (Retrieved April 18, 2009), and http://content.nejm.org/cgi/content/full/331/7/472?ijkey=c0848499053c965546e68195c4d8d158ef09434c&keytype2=tf_ipsecsha and http://www.aamc.org/data/facts/archive/famg72001a.htm (Retrieved April 18, 2009).

centage of IMGs is in part due to the fact that the population of the United States has grown more rapidly than has the number of medical school graduates. IMGs now comprise about a quarter of practicing physicians in the country. It is estimated that slightly more than 10% of the IMGs are American citizens who study abroad. The rest are foreign nationals who choose to move to the United States to practice medicine with the dominant sending countries being India, the Philippines, Mexico, and Korea. The IMGs such as underrepresented minorities and women play an important role, as they tend to be primary care physicians who often practice in underserved areas (Hart et al., 2007).

What Do Physicians Do? Physician Practice Patterns

Specialization

It is important to understand how the organization of medical practice directly impacts access and cost of care. The more specialized the practice of medicine, the more difficult it is to obtain cost effective primary care (Goodman & Fisher, 2008). There is also research indicating that the greater the supply of primary care physicians the better the patient outcomes (Starfield et al., 2005). Over the past 40 years, however, there has been an overall decline in the percentage of physicians going into primary care. The growth of managed care in the 1990s heightened concern over the decreasing percentage of primary care physicians because managed care relied more heavily on generalists than did private medical practice (Wennberg et al., 1993). Federal and state policies designed to increase the number of primary care physicians resulted in a slight increase in their numbers during the 1990s. By 2000, the percentage of primary care physicians had increased to 38%. This has now leveled off as the demand for primary care physicians ironically is less than is the demand for specialists (Salsberg & Forte, 2002).

The underlying issue is how best to provide integrated and continuous care such as Janelle receives for her cystic fibrosis. The prevailing belief is that a primary care physician is more able to manage a patient's care than is a specialist who treats a specific condition. There are two models worth considering that sought to advance this organizational premise. In the 1960s, a new specialty in family practice medicine was developed. The intent was to provide advanced training for physicians who were interested in providing primary care but felt that a one-year internship did not adequately train them for the complexity of medicine. Although family practice has shown some traction, the number of physicians currently choosing this residency option is declining (Colwill et al., 2008). Alternatively, there are those who argue that this is not a problem of merely increasing the supply of physicians and potentially the supply of primary care physicians. Rather, the problem is seen as being structural. The healthcare delivery system is highly fragmented, and this mitigates against the type of coordination that is held out as an ideal. The current articulation of this concept is that patients need a medical home where every effort can be made to provide continuous and coordinated care (Berenson et al., 2008). Medical or healthcare homes improve health outcomes and lower costs of care by creating a long-term, stable, and trusting relationship between the patient and his or her healthcare provider and that provider's team. Medical homes are designed to guide patients through the complex healthcare system. A medical home seeks to integrate patients as active participants in their own health and well-being (Nickitas, 2009). Janelle's care takes place in such a medical home.

Where Do Physicians Practice?

Geographic Distribution

The growing physician supply has not resulted in the equalization in the distribution of physicians across geographic areas. The Bureau of Health Professions estimated that 20% of the population lives in an area that carries the designation of medically underserved based on the availability of primary care physicians (Rosenbaum et al. 2009). Physicians prefer to practice in urban and suburban communities, leaving inner cities and rural communities underserved. It is ironic that Harlem, a neighborhood in Northern Manhattan in New York City, is designated as medically underserved when there are two academic medical centers nearby (HANYS, 2009).

Rural and inner-city communities find it hard to attract physicians for several reasons. First, rural and inner-city practices tend to be primary care practices. There are fewer opportunities to practice the type of medicine for which physicians were trained during their residencies and fellowships. Second, although just about everyone needs primary care, specialists need a certain population density to constitute a full panel. Third, there is an income differential between primary care physicians and specialists. Primary care physicians have lower incomes than do specialists. Furthermore, the incomes of physicians practicing in medically underserved communities are lower still than the incomes of physicians who care for urban, middle-income patients (Schroeder, 1992). The same issues related to the content of practice and income can be applied to physicians who choose to work in public health programs.

In the 1960s and 1970s, it was assumed that government programs such as the National Health Service Corps would incentivize physicians to practice in medically underserved areas. By creating loan forgiveness programs for doctors who practiced in rural areas and later medically underserved areas, it was hypothesized that some physicians would choose to remain in these communities long term. Although successful in recruiting physicians to rural and inner-city neighborhoods, the program was largely disassembled during the Reagan administration (Sardell, 1988). In the 1980s and 1990s, with the growth of managed care, it was assumed that market forces would affect physicians' choices related to specialization and geographic location. Faced with the possibility of closed physician panels, economic theory suggested that physicians would opt to practice in geographic areas where there were physician shortages. This did not prove to be the case. The rate of increase of physicians practicing in areas with high physician population ratios is occurring more rapidly than in underserved areas (Goodman, 2004).

Organizational Setting

Physicians are best described as independent entrepreneurs. Historically, they worked alone or in partnership with another physician. Physicians saw patients either in their offices or through home visits. Technological advances required more sophisticated delivery sites. Services such as X-rays, surgery, and pathology were best provided in larger spaces where conditions could be monitored. Physicians in most cases chose not to own hospitals or become hospital employees (Starr, 1982). Rather, they developed collaborative relations whereby they received privileges to admit and treat patients at a particular hospital with the understanding that they would maintain the integrity of the medical services through an autonomous committee structure.

Two interrelated changes have impacted this organizational model. The first is the growth of group practice. Multispecialty group practices such as the Mayo Clinic provide a rational organizational model because they can assure the coordination of complex patient care. Group practice, however, was not always supported by the medical profession. The American Medical Association feared that such practices would undermine physician autonomy by imposing hierarchical control over physicians (Starr, 1982). Resistance to group practice lessened in the 1990s with the growth of managed care. These plans depended on a primary care gatekeeper who would be responsible for the management of a patient's care. With patient access to specialists controlled by primary care physicians, specialists needed to become part of a group practice. By 1995, only 41% of physicians practiced solo or in partnership with another physician (Tu & Ginsburg, 2006). As the reliance on gatekeeping lessened in the late 1990s, there was decreased pressure on physicians particularly specialists to join multispecialty group plans; however, the trend for physicians to join group practices continues with physicians increasingly becoming part of single specialty groups (Casalino et al., 2004).

The second change to affect physicians' relations with hospitals is financial. The incentive structure of physician payment has led to the situation in which physicians find themselves in competitive relations with hospitals as opposed to collaborative ones (Berenson et al., 2007). With the increased ability to provide services in ambulatory care settings, physicians do not need to rely as heavily on hospitals either for access to equipment or access to the ability to provide complex patient care. As a result, the diagnosis and treatment of patients are moving out of the hospital into ambulatory settings. This results in hospitals competing with physicians for patients.

It is also the case that hospitals employ physicians. For the most part, these physicians work at academic medical centers. An academic medical center is an enterprise responsible for providing state-of-the-art health services, educating healthcare practitioners, and undertaking research to advance health and well-being. To accomplish these goals, an academic medical center usually includes a medical school and an affiliated hospital. The physicians who practice in academic medical centers typically hold faculty appointments at the medical school and in that role have teaching responsibilities. They are members of faculty practice plans, care for patients at the affiliated hospital and are typically engaged in research. There is also a growing trend for community hospitals to employ physicians (Casalino et al., 2008). These hospitals are seeking to ward off the competition and stabilize the provision of services. Physicians in their employ are making lifestyle choices to have more regular work hours and greater job security.

Two groups of physicians do not show up in those percentages. A small number of physicians are engaged in public health activities. These physicians are typically employed in federal and state public health programs and are responsible for assuring the health of populations. The physician who is probably best known in this regard is C. Everett Koop. Koop was the Surgeon General of the United States during the Reagan administration. He is remembered for his work in the area of smoking control. By reiterating the connection between tobacco use and lung cancer and affirming the consequences of second-hand smoke, his efforts led to the requirement of health warning labels on cigarettes and supported the work of the antismoking movement (C. Everett Koop Papers, 2009).

A small number of physicians also work in clinics that are organized to provide services to persons who cannot readily access the private practices of physicians described previously here. In some instances, the physicians who have worked at these clinics are full time. In other instances, they work at these clinics on a part-time basis. The clinics may be operated as part of an academic medical center. They may be operated by a public health department. They may also be operated by a community group. In the 1960s, community-based organizations opened neighborhood health centers to meet the needs of persons residing in underserved communities. These community health centers have often been pointed to as a model for quality healthcare delivery as they incorporate not only medical care but also social services at the same site (Sardell, 1988). The community health centers have often provided the kind of medical home that patients in private settings hope to attain.

How Are Physicians Paid?

Physician Income

Physicians have the highest median income of all occupational groups in the United States. This does not seem intuitively obvious when one thinks about corporate executives whose salaries soared into the tens of millions of dollars, but in 1999, physicians, surgeons, and dentists were the only occupational groups to have median incomes above $100,000 (U.S. Census Bureau, 2004). It is also the case that physicians are among the occupation groups with the most dissimilar earnings. Although physicians' reported median was $120,000, the median for men was 63% greater than for women ($140,000 versus $88,000). A 2007 survey of physician income by specialty found that geriatricians had the lowest average income of $177,392, and orthopedic surgeons of the spine reported average incomes of $579,400 (American Medical Group Association, 2007). Physicians in the United States are also the most highly paid group of medical practitioners in the world. On average, U.S. physicians earn three times what their counterparts do who work in countries that belong to the Organization for Economic Co-operation and Development (Bodenheimer, 2005).

Physician Payment

Physicians derive their income from several sources. The most common way in which physicians are paid is fee-for-service. In its simplest form, this means that patients pay physicians for the services that they receive. The concept of fee-for-service is complex because physicians do not charge or receive the same payment from all patients for the same service. Physicians may set their charges based on the patients' ability to pay. For their older patients, they usually accept the fee established by the Medicare fee schedule. If physicians participate in a managed care panel or in a preferred provider organization, they agree to accept a discounted fee for their services. It is assumed that access to a patient population offsets the possible loss of revenue from the discount. Managed care organizations and preferred provider organizations are not the only payers with fee schedules. The Medicaid program also has a fee schedule that is substantially below what physicians charge for services to private patients.

A small but growing percentage of physicians is salaried. Physicians who work for the government in departments such as Public Health or the Veterans Administration have always been paid an annual salary. Among the first practicing physicians who were salaried were doctors who worked for health maintenance organizations. These precursors to managed care organizations employed a group of physicians to assume contractual responsibility for assuring the delivery of a range of services, including hospitalization and ambulatory care, for its members. A growing number of physicians are employed by medical schools and hospitals in addition to interns and residents. Historically, hospitals have given physicians privileges to practice medicine in hospitals. Physicians bill their patients separately from the hospital for the services they render. This means that a patient who has been hospitalized receives multiple bills—one from the hospital and one from each of the physicians who provided medical services. It is now the case that many hospitals employ physicians. There is a new class of physicians called hospitalists who are hospital employees charged with managing inpatient care. Rather than following a patient based on disease, they work in the hospital to assure the management of complex cases (Wachter & Goldman, 2002).

In reality, most physicians' incomes come from hybrid arrangements. Medical school faculty members provide one of the best examples. The physicians receive a base salary from the medical school. This salary ostensibly covers the cost of their teaching and other service to the school. In addition, faculty members derive income from the revenues they generate by participating in practice plans at the hospital. Although the payment for their services goes to the medical center, physicians receive some portion of the fee. Another example includes physicians in private practice who derive the better part of their incomes from fee-for-service practice. These same physicians might also cover clinic sessions at an emergency room or neighborhood health center. The physician would be paid a fixed amount for the session even though the patients would be charged on a fee-for-service basis.

The Impact of Financial Arrangements on Physician Practice and Physician Income

Physician income has become a major policy issue because physicians purportedly control close to 70% of healthcare costs. The ways physicians are reimbursed influences the ways that they practice medicine (Hillman et al., 1989); therefore, there is a quest to advance a payment scheme that incentivizes physicians to act in ways that are both economic and assure quality patient care. Many factors can influence physicians' judgments about patient care plans. Two related to physician payment are related to the payment mechanism and ownership of equipment and facilities. Patient mix is one factor that impacts physician practice under fee-for-service medicine (Town et al., 2004). If physicians see a large number of private pay patients or patients who have indemnity plans, the incentive may be to overtreat. The same physicians may be incentivized to undertreat patients who are covered by managed care companies given the discounted fee. As for physician ownership of equipment and organizations such as laboratories and rehabilitation centers, physicians who own their own equipment such as X-ray machines and EKG machines were more apt to use this equipment during a routine office visit than are their counterparts who do not own such equipment (Schroeder & Showstack, 1978). A similar dynamic exists where physicians have an ownership stake in ancillary services such as hospitals and laboratories (Stensland & Winter, 2006).

The structure of payment not only affects the ways in which physicians provide services, it also impacts physician compensation. The ways services are identified on bills can impact on the total charges to a patient. This concern for billing became pronounced in the 1980s after implementation of Diagnosis-Related Groups (DRGs)[1] (Newcomer et al., 1985). If hospitals did not have accurate medical records from which to derive patients' diagnoses, they risked receiving a lower payment. A variant is the practice of unbundling of services. Rather than providing patients with an all-inclusive bill, physicians have discovered that by billing for each component part of a visit they receive a higher rate of pay for the same level of service. The last way that financial structures can influence physician pay is through the substitution of services. Physicians' direct patient treatment by deciding what diagnostic tests, what treatments, and what follow-up care will be prescribed. Often the more expensive alternative is chosen despite the lack of evidence associated with its efficacy (Kassirer, 2005).

Physician Payment Reform

Ultimately what has evolved is a cat and mouse system of financial reward for physicians. The largest payers of health services such as the government and private insurance companies are looking at payment methods that will encourage physicians to provide cost-effective care. In return, physicians are looking for ways to manipulate the payment system in order to protect and increase their incomes. We know that physician income has not kept pace with the rate of inflation, despite their being one of the best paid professional groups. The decline in physician income is attributed to the failure of fees from Medicare and private health insurance to keep pace with inflation (Tu & Ginsburg, 2006). There is an assumed association between this finding and the fact that the percentage of physicians who provide charity care has declined from 76% to 68% between 1996 and 1997 and 2004 and 2005 (Cunningham & Hadley, 2008). With the number of uninsured Americans increasing, this is cause for concern as to the availability of physicians to serve them.

There is agreement about the need to reform physician payment but no agreement about the best methods (Mechanic & Altman, 2009). Early efforts such as Relative Value Scales did not have the intended consequences of rewarding primary and chronic care (Bodenheimer et al., 2007).[2] A range of options are currently being considered. Keeping closest to the status quo would be the recalibration of fee-for-service medicine so as to minimize the types of financial incentives that currently exist to overtreat or undertreat patients depending on the reimbursement. Similarly, the use of global payments would build on the model of capitated payments used by managed care organizations. To overcome the incentive to undertreat, payment would be linked to performance measures. A third alternative is to bundle physician payments based on an episode of care. The last alternative that is receiving a great deal of attention is pay for performance, a system of

---

[1] A diagnosis-related group is a system of payment for hospital inpatient services based on predetermined rates per discharge for approximately 500 groupings. The system was developed for Medicare and has been in use since 1983. A Medicare recipient is assigned to a payment group depending on principal diagnosis. Other criteria include the patient's age, sex, secondary diagnoses, procedures performed, discharge status, complications, and comorbidity.

[2] Relative Value Scales are a system of physician payment developed by Medicare based on the value of a medical service relative to other medical services.

payment that rewards physicians and providers for meeting performance measures (Werner & Dudley, 2009). Although there are several hundred pay for performance programs in existence, it is a complicated system because there are few good outcome measures to use and it is not clear how much of a physician's pay therefore should be related to performance or improvement.

Physician Accountability

Having overviewed the medical profession, we need to consider what mechanisms are in place to assure that physicians are providing their patients the best care possible. Historically, physicians have been responsible for regulating the practice of their colleagues (Freidson, 1970). Their expertise is in part the basis of their autonomy to define both the content of their work and the ways in which the practice of health care is organized. Physicians, for example, not only set the standards of care for persons with cardiac disease, but they also determine who will provide the care and in what setting. As a result of their powers to determine what and how care will be provided, physicians control both the supply and demand for health services. Their power, however, is moderated by their fiduciary relationship to their patients—meaning that they are obligated to do everything in their power to assure the well-being of their patients.

Self-regulation is carried out in multiple ways. The first point of control is over the system of medical education. Physicians are responsible for all facets of this endeavor. They determine the size and composition of medical school classes, and they control decisions related to medical school's curriculum (Ludmerer, 1999). Medical education is just the beginning of the accountability structure.

A second point of control is the regulation of physicians by the government (Field, 2007). The government is concerned with the public's safety; therefore, the right to practice medicine is limited to only those persons who have demonstrated a mastery of the field. All physicians are required to pass national boards and licensure examinations that fall under the auspices of state governments. In addition, states want to guarantee that physicians keep up with the field and have set standards for continuing medical education. Authority over the government regulation of physician practice assumes tremendous involvement of the medical profession. The standards used by the state are standards set by the profession, implemented by the profession, and overseen by physicians. Likewise, the professional review boards that evaluate physicians for malpractice fall under the auspices of physicians who are employees of the states.

Finally, hospitals in which physicians' practices also have a stake at assuring that the physicians with hospital privileges are held to the highest standards of practice. Institutional providers also defer oversight of physicians to the profession. To accomplish this end, hospitals tend to use three mechanisms. All physicians' credentials are reviewed and presented to the hospitals' boards of trustees before their being awarded hospital privileges. Each hospital also maintains medical boards that review all deaths that occur in the hospital. This is an opportunity for physicians to determine whether a physician's practice did not adhere to accepted standards of care. Beginning in the 1980s under pressure from the government, hospitals instituted the practice of utilization review to assess physician practice relative to their peers.

Medical Errors

Theoretically, a system of self-governance such as utilization review should lead to high quality care. A review of the literature on medical errors indicates that this is not necessarily the case. Complications are a natural result of medical practice that intervenes in complex human processes and mistakes are the normal consequence of human activity. The challenge is to describe complications that are preventable—to understand the causes of medical error and document its prevalence.

The Institute of Medicine (2000) defines medical error as "the failure to complete a planned action as intended or the use of a wrong plan to achieve an aim." An adverse event is defined as "an injury caused by medical management rather than by the underlying disease or condition of the patient." The types of medical errors include the following:

- Diagnostic error, such as misdiagnosis leading to an incorrect choice of therapy, failure to use an indicated diagnostic test, misinterpretation of test results, and failure to act on abnormal results
- Equipment failure, such as a defibrillator, whose valves are easily dislodged or bumped, causing increased doses of medication over too short of a period
- Infections, such as nosocomial and postsurgical wound infections
- Blood transfusion-related injuries, such as giving a patient the blood of the incorrect type
- Misinterpretation of other medical orders, such as failing to give a patient a salt-free meal, as ordered by a physician

Frequency of Medical Errors

Although dramatic malpractice awards capture the headlines, medical errors and complications are far more systematic. The November 1999 report of the Institute of Medicine, entitled *To Err Is Human: Building A Safer Health System*, indicated that as many as 44,000 to 98,000 people die in hospitals each year as the result of medical errors. Even using the lower estimate, this would make medical errors the eighth leading cause of death in this country—higher than motor vehicle accidents (43,458), breast cancer (42,297), or AIDS (16,516). About 7,000 people per year are estimated to die from medication errors alone (Agency for Healthcare Research and Quality, 2000).

Causes of Medical Error

Observers and scholars have offered an array of explanations of why preventable mistakes happen. These range from malfeasance resulting from personal impairment or greed to systematic critique of the way U.S. medical professionals are trained and health care is organized.

Impaired Providers

The simplest explanation for medical mistakes is impaired providers. Physicians, nurses, and other practitioners are no less likely to have substance abuse problems than other Americans. Recent estimates are that during their practice lifetimes 8% to 12% of physicians will experience a substance-related problem:

- 138,000 will have an alcohol-related disorder
- 49,000 will have a drug-related disorder

Substance abuse is the most common reason for disciplinary action by state medical and nursing boards. Like physicians, nurses report significant levels of substance abuse. A 1998 survey of RNs found that 3.6% used marijuana and/or cocaine, 5.6% abused prescription drugs, and 16.0% reported binge drinking (Trinkoff & Stor, 1998).

Another source of impaired judgment is more subtle—the effect of industry–physician relationships. Under the headline "Doctors Reap Millions for Anemia Drugs," the *New York Times* reported how drug companies paid physicians to prescribe expensive anemia drugs. "Critics, including prominent cancer and kidney doctors, say the payments give physicians an incentive to prescribe the medicines at levels that might increase patients' risks of heart attacks or strokes" (Berenson & Pollack, 2007). The prescription drug industry spent $20 billion on direct marketing to physicians in 2007. In fact, 94% of all practicing physicians received some gift from the medical device, biological, or pharmaceutical industry (Wazana, 2000).

System-Induced Errors

Much more complicated than errors made by impaired physicians are errors that occur as a part of the usual practice of medicine. Take, for example, New Yorker author Atul Gawande's report on himself. He describes what happened when, as a surgical resident, he treated a semicomatose car crash victim. She was having difficulty breathing, and Dr. Gawande intubated her; however, he missed the mark, and the woman's oxygen level fell dangerously. Instead of assisting her breathing, his actions actually blocked her airways. At this point, an experienced anesthesiologist arrived and managed to slip a tube through the vocal cords and reestablish oxygen flow to the heart. The woman recovered and was discharged several days later. According to Gawande, the root cause of his error was inexperience. As Gawande commented, "Mistakes do happen. We think of them as aberrant. They are anything but." Could it have been prevented? Yes, with fundamental change in the way surgical residents are trained and emergency care is delivered, it could have been prevented—possible but extremely difficult to achieve (Gawande, 1999).

Other critics make an even more profound critique. Errors occur according to Gawande's New Yorker colleague Dr. Jerome Groopman (2007) because there is a flaw that undermines much of contemporary medicine (Groopman, 2007).

> *Why do we as physicians miss the correct diagnosis? It turns out that the mistakes are rarely due to technical factors, like the laboratory mixing up the blood specimen of one patient and reporting another's result. Nor is misdiagnosis usually due to a doctor's lack of knowledge about what later is found to be the underlying disease.*

As we saw with the case of Lia Lee, cultural differences complicate medical care and can lead to tragic error. In Lia's case, many of the problems occurred because Lia's family did not speak English; however, in the case of Willie Ramirez, fluency in English was not the problem. The meaning of words, however, in different cultures was. Willie Ramirez was 18 years old. He collapsed outside of his girlfriend's house after complaining of a severe headache and was taken to the hospital. His family and friends reported to the doctors in the emergency room that Willie was "intoxicado." The physician understood this to mean that Willie had overdosed. To Cubans, however, the word is all encompassing. If they had pursued his case further and called in a neurosurgeon, they would have found that Willie was having a brain hemorrhage. He would not have become a quadriplegic (Price-Wise, 2008).

Medical Errors and Malpractice

Mr. Ramirez was awarded $71 million to pay for full-time medical care for the rest of his life and to compensate him for the severe avoidable injury. Whether this is an excessive settlement is unknown, but many Americans blame malpractice legal actions for rising healthcare costs. According to a 2006 Kaiser Family Foundation Survey, 58% cite malpractice lawsuits as a "very important" cause of medical care inflation (Kaiser Family Foundation, 2006); however, a study of the relationship between malpractice awards and medical error conducted by physicians at the Harvard School of Public Health found that "the vast majority of expenditures go toward litigation over errors and payment of them." They reviewed a random sample of 1,457 closed malpractice cases and found that most payments were associated with errors. They estimated that claims not involving errors accounted for only 13% to 16% of the total cost of malpractice payments (Thomas et al., 2000).

Medical Errors, Physician Practice, and the Barriers to Quality Care

By examining the problem of medical errors, one gets a window on the problems that flow from the system of care as currently organized. First, there is an overreliance on the "biomedical" or "physician-oriented" model of care (Mishler, 1981). Although many people seek care on an annual basis and hope to prevent disease through immunization or early detection, the overall system is designed to address illness. Little effort goes into prevention, which is considered a matter of public health or into the management of chronic conditions such as heart disease and diabetes.

The second consequence that follows from the first is that there is a mismatch between patient need and physician supply. As we have already demonstrated, the physician work force is highly specialized and locates in urban areas. Specialization is potentially highly fragmented and expensive care. Underrepresented communities, including both racial and ethnic minorities and those with low socioeconomic status, have more difficulty getting care due to the specialization of physicians and their choice to practice in middle class or wealthy urban/suburban settings—class matters. The lack of access contributes to tremendous disparities in health outcomes. Persons from higher socioeconomic classes have better outcomes than do persons from lower socioeconomic classes.

The third consequence is the inconsistent quality of care. Inconsistent quality results first from the effects of inequitable distribution of physicians by geographic location and specialty. Inconsistent quality is further affected by the organizations where physicians work. Health outcomes are better in settings that have high volume and good oversight. When New York State began to publish the data on outcomes for cardiac catheterization and bypass surgery, it was assumed that the data would be used by patients to select a physician and hospital that were known to have better outcomes. It was found that hospitals used the data to improve how care was organized to assure better outcomes (Chassin, 2002).

Overcoming the Barriers to Quality Care

With growing recognition of medical errors and unequal access to care with resulting inequitable outcomes have come increased efforts to overcome the historic, structural, and organizational barriers to good quality care. The medical profession has become increasingly concerned that it has not adequately held itself to professional standards (Rothman, 2000). The growing reliance on the market as a mechanism to support the healthcare industry (and sustain high physician incomes) is thought to shorten contact between patient and doctor. This perception is not supported by study. In fact, the opposite has been found to be the case (Commonwealth Fund, 2006); however, the perception is evidence of a system that is no longer grounded on patient trust and physician integrity. Rather, it is based on the premise that patients are independent consumers who are not dependent on physicians (Mechanic, 1996; Robinson, 1997).

In 2002, several societies representing internal medicine physicians published a physician charter that asserted three principles that underpin the doctor–patient relationship (ABIM Foundation, ACP-ASIM Foundation, and European Federation of Internal Medicine, 2002). The first was the primacy of patient welfare. This commitment calls on physicians to uphold the patients' interests. Second is the principle of patient autonomy. The doctor–patient relationship is being redefined as consultative. They have the expertise to share with their patients, but their patients have concerns that extend beyond the biomedical and may influence the course of medical care that they seek. The last is the principle of social justice. The charter asserts that physicians must "promote justice in the healthcare system," including the fair distribution of healthcare resources. Physicians should work actively to eliminate discrimination in health care, whether based on race, gender, socioeconomic status, ethnicity, religion, or any other social category.

Doctors are also moving to reform the education system and the overall organization of care. There is growing interest in the ways professionalism can be taught and modeled (Branch et al., 2001; Kao, 2003). It is also the case that physicians are increasingly coming to understand and value the importance of their being part of a medical team. Medical care is too complex to be provided by a single person. It takes a team with broad-ranging expertise to provide necessary treatment (O'Malley et al., 2009). Only a team can assure the continuity of care within a care setting such as a hospital and across care settings. What is being described is the importance of a patient having a medical home where there are high levels of coordination between all of the providers who will interact with that patient (Enthoven et al., 2007).

Institutional providers have begun to look for ways to provide their own oversight of physicians. Since the 1980s, hospitals have been increasingly concerned about physician practice patterns. As hospitals are pressured to control costs, they look at ways to influence what care physicians provide and whether there were ways this could be accomplished without compromising quality. The movement to influence physician practice began with utilization review where hospitals hoped to bring greater standardization of physician practice. Hospitals have also sought to create greater alignment of physician and hospital interests through the creation of physician hospital organizations and now through the practice of hiring of hospitalists. Now there is a movement for more evidence-based practice. Organizations like Leapfrog, an employer-based group, seek to improve quality of health care, making data available about hospital care and working to develop incentives to reward quality care (The Leapfrog Group, 2009).

The government has also sought greater accountability from physicians. With the recognition that physician financial interests could be in conflict with patient interests and leveraging its huge financial interest, the government has imposed regulations around self-dealing (Mitchell, 2007). Physicians cannot be reimbursed by Medicare and Medicaid for the treatment of patients who are being referred to facilities that are owned by a physician. Likewise, the government has begun to impose minimum practices standards to prevent physicians from potentially jeopardizing patient well-being. In addition, there is greater pressure for mistake reporting and suspension of licensure in cases of malpractice.

There is also a growing movement for private payer regulation of physician practice that has been motivated by the desire to control costs but now recognizes the delicate relationship between cost and quality. This began practically 25 years ago with such practices as the requirement that patients receive a second opinion before embarking on an expensive medical procedure. These efforts did not achieve their desired end of controlling costs or limiting unnecessary care. Physicians were reticent to make judgments about their colleagues. This led insurers to implement programs requiring prior authorization by the insurers before treatment occurred. What followed was the utilization of physician panels by managed care organizations to control physician practice. This was more complicated to implement than originally assumed. Efforts to create limited pools led to challenges by patients and doctors related to freedom of choice, but it was harder to have a panel of "any willing provider" adhere to fixed practice guidelines. Efforts to shift financial risk onto doctors also had limited success in terms of shifting physician practice. The evolution of payer regulation has now taken the form of pay for performance and performance networks. Under pay for performance, physician reimbursement will be linked to patient outcomes. Performance networks seek a similar end in terms of rewarding healthcare networks that achieve high quality of care at lower costs through the redesign of the ways health care is delivered (Pham et al., 2007).

Conclusion: Choices and Interests

This chapter asks questions about the ways physicians influence the provision of health care and patients' outcomes. The answer in a nutshell: It depends. It depends on who becomes a physician, how they are trained, where they practice, how they are paid, and what exactly they do. The analytic challenge is in understanding and interpreting all of these combinations and their permutations.

Do physicians matter as much today as they did during the mid- to late-twentieth century? Yes, physicians still drive much of the organization and delivery of health care. Our system of care is defined by physician expertise and as a result is heavily biased toward the type of care most physicians are trained to provide—curative care. Given their dominance over the healthcare professions, physicians have been given the legal authority to assure the standard of care. However, due to the complexity of care and the greater need for care coordination, the balance of power is shifting toward a transdisciplinary approach where the patient is the center. This requires shared power among all health providers with the patient choice for treatment, first and foremost. One of the main points made in this chapter is that lapses and compromises in how this is being done are excellent windows into how our health system functions.

How should the job done by physicians be changed in our twenty-first century environment? The policy lessons to be derived from this chapter go back to the place where we started—that decisions have winners and losers. In this case, highly specialized care has produced enormous advances in medicine's effectiveness. At the same time, it has limited access to low-income and minority populations and rural populations; however, policy is negotiated, and the pressure now is to create a more equitable system. Health reform will succeed if it helps to create a system that can assure the type and quality that Janelle receives for her treatment of cystic fibrosis. Such care is highly dependent on involving patients and their families and on involving the team of providers who all hold a piece to understanding the complexity of what is needed. It requires physicians to willingly engage in this process, which an increasing number of physicians are ready to do.

References

ABIM Foundation, ACP-ASIM Foundation, and European Federation of Internal Medicine. (2002). Medical professionalism in the new millennium: A physician charter. *Annals of Internal Medicine, 136*(3), 243–246.

Agency for Healthcare Research and Quality. (2000). *Medical errors: The scope of the problem.* Fact sheet, Publication No. AHRQ 00-P037. Rockville, MD: Agency for Healthcare Research and Quality. Retrieved from http://www.ahrq.gov/qual/errback.htm

American Medical Association. (2008). *Physicians in primary care and subspecialties.* Retrieved July 27, 2008, from http://www.ama-assn.org/ama/pub/category/2687.html

American Medical Group Association. (2007). *Medical group compensation & financial survey.* Retrieved July 30, 2008, from http://www.cejkasearch.com/compensation/amga_physician_compensation_survey.htm

Berenson, R. A., Ginsburg, P. B., & May, J. H. (2007). Hospital–physicians relations: Cooperation, competition, or separation? *Health Affairs, 26*(1), w31–w43.

Berenson, R. A., Hammons, T., Gans, D. N., Zuckerman, S., Merrell, K., Underwood, W. S., & Williams, A. F. (2008). A house is not a home: Keeping patients at the center of practice redesign. *Health Affairs, 27*(5), 1219–1230.

Berenson, R. A., & Pollack, A. (2007, May 9). Doctors reap millions for anemia drugs. *New York Times.* Retrieved February 16, 2010, from http://www.nytimes.com/2007/05/09business/09anemia.html

Bodenheimer, T. (2005). High and rising health care costs. Part 3: The role of health care providers. *Annals of Internal Medicine, 142*(12), 996–1002.

Bodenheimer, T., Berenson, R. A., & Rudolph, P. (2007). The primary care-specialty income gap: Why it matters. *Annals of Internal Medicine, 146*(4), 301–306.

Branch, W., Kern, D., Haidet, P., Weissman, P., Gracey, C. F., Mitchell, G. et al. (2001). Teaching the human dimensions of care in clinical settings. *Journal of the American Medical Association, 286*(9), 1067–1074.

Casalino, L. P., November, E. A., Berenson, R. A., & Pham, H. H. (2008). Hospital-physician relations: Two tracks and the decline of the voluntary medical staff model. *Health Affairs*, 27, 1305–1314.

Casalino, L. P., Pham, H., & Bazzoli, G. (2004). Growth of single-specialty medical groups. *Health Affairs, 23*(2), 82. Retrieved July 31, 2008, from http://content.healthaffairs.org/cgi/reprint/23/2/82?maxtoshow=&HITS=10&hits=10&RESULTFORMAT=&author1=casalino&andorexactfulltext=and&searchid=1&FIRSTINDEX=0&resourcetype=HWCIT

CDC/National Center for Health Statistics. (2009). *Health, United States, 2008.* Washington, DC: U.S. Government Printing Office.

C. Everett Koop Papers. (2009). Retrieved March 14, 2009, from http://profiles.nlm.nih.gov/QQ/Views/Exhibit/narrative/tobacco.html

Chassin, M. (2002). Achieving and sustaining improved quality: Lessons from New York State and cardiac surgery. *Health Affairs, 21*(4), 40–51.

Cohen, J. J., Gabriel, B. A., & Charles, T. (2002). The case for diversity in the health care workforce. *Health Affairs, 21*(5), 90–102. Retrieved July 27, 2008, from http://content.healthaffairs.org/cgi/reprint/21/5/90

Colwill, J. M., Cultice, J. M., & Kruse, R. L. (2008). Will generalist physician supply meet demands of an increasing and aging population? *Health Affairs, 27*(3), w232–w241. Retrieved April 22, 2009, from http://content.healthaffairs.org/cgi/content/full/27/3/w232?maxtoshow=&HITS=10&hits=10&RESULTFORMAT=&fulltext=physician+supply+region&andorexactfulltext=and&searchid=1&FIRSTINDEX=0&resourcetype=HWCIT

Commonwealth Fund. (2006). *Time spent with physician. Performance snapshot.* Retrieved August 22, 2009, from http://www.commonwealthfund.org/Content/Performance-Snapshots/Responsiveness-of-the-Health-System/Time-Spent-with-Physician.aspx

Council on Graduate Medical Education. (2005, January). *Physician workforce policy guidelines for the United States: 2000–2020.* USDHHS, HRSA. Retrieved April 18, 2009, from http://www.cogme.gov/16.pdf

Cunningham, P. J., & Hadley, J. (2008). Effects of changes in incomes and practice circumstances on physicians' decisions to treat charity and Medicaid patients. *The Milbank Quarterly, 86,* 1. Retrieved August 29, 2009, from http://www.milbank.org/860103.html

Enthoven, A. C., Crosson, F. J., Stephen, M., & Shortell, S. M. (2007). Redefining health care: Medical homes or archipelagos to navigate? *Health Affairs, 26*(5), 1366–1372.

Fadiman, A. (1997). *The spirit catches you and you fall down: A Hmong child, her American doctors, and the collision of two cultures.* New York: Farrar, Straus and Giroux.

Field, R. I. (2007). *Health care regulation in America: Complexity, confrontation and compromise.* New York: Oxford University Press.

Freidson, E. (1970). *Profession of medicine: A study of the sociology of applied knowledge*. New York: Dodd, Mead.

Gawande, A. (1999, February 1). Annals of Medicine, "When doctors make mistakes." *The New Yorker*, p. 40.

Gawande, A. (2005, November 14). Annals of Medicine, "The malpractice mess: Who pays the price when patients sue doctors." *The New Yorker*. Retrieved August 22, 2009, from http://www.newyorker.com/archive/2005/11/14/051114fa_fact_gawande

Goodman, D. C. (2004). Trends: Twenty-year trends in regional variations in the U.S. physician workforce. *Health Affairs*, Web Exclusive. Retrieved August 23, 2009, from http://content.healthaffairs.org/cgi/content/full/hlthaff.var.90/DC2?maxtoshow=&HITS=10&hits=10&RESULTFORMAT=&author1=Goodman&fulltext=trends&andorexactfulltext=and&searchid=1&FIRSTINDEX=0&resourcetype=HWCIT

Goodman, D., & Fisher, E. S. (2008). Physician workforce crisis? Wrong diagnosis, wrong prescription. *New England Journal of Medicine, 358,* 16. Retrieved April 22, 2009, from http://content.nejm.org/cgi/content/full/358/16/1658

Groopman, J. (2007, March 19). The mistakes doctors make: Errors in thinking too often lead to wrong diagnosis. *Boston Globe.* Retrieved August 22, 2009, from http://www.boston.com/news/globe/health_science/articles/2007/03/19/the_mistakes_doctors_make

HANYS. (2009). *Expanding access, improving outcomes: The essential role of primary care*. New York: Albany. Retrieved April 22, 2009, from http://www.hanys.org/communications/publications/2009/the_essential_role_of_primary_care.pdf

Hart, L. G., Skillman, S. M., Fordyce, M., Thompson, M., Hagopian, A., & Konrad, T. R. (2007). International medical graduate physicians in the United States: Changes since 1981. *Health Affairs, 26*(4), 1159–1169.

Hillman, A. L., Pauly, M. V., & Kerstein, J. J. (1989). How do financial incentives affect physicians' clinical decisions and the financial performance of health maintenance organizations? *New England Journal of Medicine, 321,* 86–92.

Institute of Medicine Committee on Quality of Health Care in America. (2000). *To err is human: Building a safer health system*. Washington, DC: National Academies Press.

Kaiser Family Foundation. (2006). *Public opinion on the medical malpractice debate.* Retrieved August 22, 2009, from http://www.kff.org/spotlight/malpractice/index.cfm

Kao, A. (2003). Teaching and evaluating students' professionalism in US medical schools, 2002–2003. *Journal of the American Medical Association, 290*(9), 1151–1152.

Kassirer, J. P. (2005). *On the take: How medicine's complicity with big business can endanger your health.* New York: Oxford University Press.

Knowles, J. H. (1970). *Higher education and the nation's health.* Berkeley, CA: Carnegie Commission on the Future of Higher Education.

Komaromy, M., Grumbach, K., Drake, M., Vranizan, K., Lurie, N., Keane, D., & Bindman, A. B. (1996, May 16). The role of black and Hispanic physicians in providing health care for underserved populations. *New England Journal of Medicine, 334*(20), 1305–1310.

The Leapfrog Group. (2009). Retrieved on April 30, 2009, from http://www.leapfroggroup.org/about_us/how_leapfrog_works

Ludmerer, K. M. (1999). *Learning to heal: The development of American medical education*. New York: Oxford University Press.

Marmor, T. (1973). *The politics of Medicare*. Chicago: Aldine Publishing Co.

Mechanic, D. (1996). Changing medical organization and the erosion of trust. *The Milbank Quarterly, 74*(2), 171–189.

Mechanic, R. E., & Altman, S. H. (2009). Payment reform options: Episode payment is a good place to start. *Health Affairs, 28*(2), w262–w271.

Mishler, E. G. (1981). Viewpoint: critical perspectives on the biomedical model. In E. G. Mishler, L. R. Amara-Singham, S. T. Hauser, R. Liem, S. D. Osherson, & N. E. Waxler (Eds.), *Social contexts of health, illness, and patient care*. New York: Cambridge University Press.

Mitchell, J. M. (2007). The prevalence of physician self-referral arrangements after Stark II: The evidence from advanced diagnostic imaging. *Health Affairs, 26*(3), w415–w424.

Mullan, F. (1997). The National Health Service Corps and inner-city hospitals. *New England Journal of Medicine, 336*(22), 1601–1603.

Newcomer, R., Wood, J., & Sankar, A. (1985). Medicare prospective payment: anticipated effect on hospitals, other community agencies, and families. *Journal of Health Politics, Policy and Law, 10*(2), 275–282.

Nickitas, D. M. (2009). Moral courage or moral imperative: Which is it? *Nursing Economics, 27*(6), 361–362.

O'Malley, A. S., Tynan, A., Cohen, G., Kemper, N. M., & Davis, M. M. (2009). Coordination of care by primary care practices: Strategies, lessons and implications.

Research Brief No. 12, Center for Studying Health System Change. Retrieved April 30, 2009, from http://www.hschange.org/CONTENT/1058/?words=

Pentecost, M. (2007, Spring). The future of employer-based health insurance. *Permanente Journal, 11*(2). Retrieved August 22, 2009, from http://xnet.kp.org/permanentejournal/spring07/future.html

Pham, H. H., Ginsburg, P. B., McKenzie, K., & Milstein, A. (2007). Redesigning care delivery in response to a high-performance network: The Virginia Mason Medical Center. *Health Affairs, 26*(4), w532–w544 (Published online 10 July, 2007). Retrieved February 28, 2009, from http://content.healthaffairs.org/cgi/content/full/26/4/w532

Price-Wise, G. (2008, November 19). Language, culture, and medical tragedy: The case of Willie Ramirez. *Health Affairs Blog.* Retrieved September 1, 2009, from http://healthaffairs.org/blog/2008/11/19/language-culture-and-medical-tragedy-the-case-of-willie-ramirez

Robinson, J. C. (1997). Apotheosis of the health care consumer. *Health Affairs, 16*(6), 254–255.

Rosenbaum, S., Jones, E., Shin, P., & Ku, L. (2009). National health reform: How will medically underserved communities fare. Retrieved December 20, 2009, from http://www.gwumc.edu/sphhs/departments/healthpolicy/dhp_publications/pub_uploads/dhpPublication_5046C2DE-5056-9D20-3D2A570F2CF3F8B0.pdf

Rothman, D. T. (2000). Medical professionalism: Focusing on the real issues. *New England Journal of Medicine, 342*, 1284. Retrieved September 10, 2009, from http://content.nejm.org/cgi/content/full/342/17/1284

Salsberg, E. S., & Forte, G. J. (2002). Trends in the physician workforce, 1980–2000. *Health Affairs, 21*(5), 165. Retrieved April 29, 2009, from http://content.healthaffairs.org/cgi/content/full/21/5/165#R31

Sardell, A. (1988). *The U.S. experiment in social medicine: The community health center program, 1965–1986.* Pittsburgh, PA: University of Pittsburgh Press.

Schroeder, S. A. (1992). Physician supply and the U.S. medical marketplace? *Health Affairs, 11*(1), 235–243. Retrieved August 23, 2009, from http://content.healthaffairs.org/cgi/reprint/11/1/235?maxtoshow=&HITS=10&hits=10&RESULTFORMAT=&fulltext=generalist+and+specialist&andorexactfulltext=and&searchid=1&FIRSTINDEX=20&resourcetype=HWCIT

Schroeder, S. A., & Showstack, J. A. (1978). Financial incentives to perform medical procedures and laboratory tests: illustrative models of office practice. *Medical Care, 16,* 289–298.

Starfield, B., Shi, L., Grover, A., & Macinko, J. (2005, March 15). The effects of specialist supply on populations' health: Assessing the evidence. *Health Affairs, Web Exclusive*. Retrieved December 10, 2009, from http://healthaff.highwire.org/cgi/reprint/hlthaff.w5.97v1.pdf

Starr, P. (1982). *The social transformation of American medicine*. New York: Basic Books.

Statistical Abstract of the United States. (2004). *Section 12 labor force, employment, and earnings.* Retrieved July 30, 2008, from http://www.census.gov/prod/2004pubs/04statab/labor.pdf

Stensland, J., & Winter, A. (2006). Do physician-owned cardiac hospitals increase utilization? Physician-ownership has primarily affected where people get cardiac surgery, not who gets the surgery. *Health Affairs, 25*(1), 119–129.

Stockburger, W. T. (2004). CT imaging, then and now: A 30-year review of the economics of computed tomography. *Radiol Management, 26*(6), 20–22, 24–27; quiz 28–30.

Thomas, E. J., Studdert, D. M., Burstin, H. R., Orav, E. J., Zeena, T., Williams, E. J., et al. (2000). Incidence and types of adverse events and negligent care in Utah and Colorado. *Medical Care, 38*(3), 261–271.

Town, R., Wholey, D. R., Kralewski, J., & Dowd, B. (2004, September 1). Assessing the influence of incentives on physicians and medical groups. *Medical Care Research Review, 61*(3 Suppl), 80S–118S.

Trinkoff, A. M., & Stor, C. L. (1998). Substance use among nurses: Differences between specialties. *American Journal of Public Health, 88*(4), 581–585.

Tu, H. T., & Ginsburg, P. B. (2006, June). Losing ground: Physician income, 1995–2003. *Tracking Report No. 15.* Retrieved July 31, 2008, from http://www.hschange.com/CONTENT/851/#ib5

U.S. Census Bureau. (2004). *Evidence from Census 2000 about earnings by detailed occupation for men and women.* Retrieved July 30, 2008, from http://www.census.gov/prod/2004pubs/censr-15.pdf

Wachter, R. M., & Goldman, L. (2002). The hospitalist movement 5 years later. *Journal of the American Medical Association, 287*(4), 487–494.

Wazana, A. (2000). Physicians and the pharmaceutical industry: Is a gift ever just a gift? *Journal of the American Medical Association, 283*(3), 373–380.

Wennberg, J. E., Goodman, D. C., Nease, R. F., & Keller, R. B. (1993). Finding equilibrium in US physician supply. *Health Affairs, 12*(2), 89–103.

Werner, R. M., & Dudley, R. A. (2009). Making the "pay" matter in pay-for-performance: Implications for payment strategies. *Health Affairs, 28*(5), 1498–1508.

Chapter 4

Nurses

Donna M. Nickitas

IMAGINE A WORLD WITHOUT NURSES. THINK OF A WORLD WITHOUT PERSONS WHO KNOW WHAT NURSES KNOW; WHO BELIEVE WHAT NURSES BELIEVE; WHO DO WHAT NURSES DO; WHO HAVE THE EFFECT THAT NURSES HAVE ON THE HEALTH OF INDIVIDUALS, FAMILIES, AND THE NATION; WHO ENJOY THE TRUST THAT NURSES ENJOY FROM THE AMERICAN PEOPLE. IMAGINE A WORLD LIKE THAT, A WORLD WITHOUT NURSES.

Greta Styles, 2005

OVERVIEW

Nursing is the largest segment of the healthcare workforce in the United States and the professionals who spend the most time providing direct care to patients. There are almost 3 million registered nurses (RNs) nationwide (Buerhaus, Donelan, DesRoches, & Hess, 2009). More than 587,000 new nursing positions will be created through 2016 (a 23.5% increase), making nursing the nation's top profession in terms of job growth (Bureau of Labor Statistics, 2006). Nurses are indispensable to a patient's overall quality of health, safety, and satisfaction with care delivery.

As hospitals begin to submit new data to the Centers of Medicare and Medicaid Services on patient satisfaction, nursing will be the most important factor in how patients rate their hospital experience and whether they would recommend their hospital to a family member or friend (Centers for Medicare and Medicaid Services, 2006). In fact, several studies have demonstrated a relationship between patient satisfaction and nurse-staffing levels, a higher proportion of RN skill mix, RN–physician collaboration, and nurses' work environment (Bolton et al., 2003; Larrabee et al., 2004; McGillis Hall et al., 2003; Seago et al., 2006; Sovie & Jawad, 2001; Tervo-Heikkinen et al., 2008; Vahey et al., 2004). Today's healthcare environment is exceedingly complex and requires that nurses be exceptionally prepared to provide quality health care that leads to excellent patient care outcomes; therefore, policy makers and healthcare stakeholders must be informed about the education–quality relationship of nurses and how the nursing profession adds value to the overall healthcare delivery system.

OBJECTIVES

- To explain the critical role nurses play in ensuring high quality patient care
- To examine issues confronting the nursing workforce
- To identify the challenges and opportunities for addressing the nation's shortage of nurses and nurse faculty
- To describe various approaches and solutions to the nursing shortage
- To discuss how health care and policy stakeholders can address and remove the barriers experienced by nurses to improve healthcare quality and patient safety

KEY TERMS

- ❏ Advanced practice registered nurses
- ❏ Certification
- ❏ Licensed practical nurses
- ❏ Licensure
- ❏ Nurse workforce
- ❏ Nursing education
- ❏ Registered nurses

Not an Equal Profession

Origins of the Nursing Profession

From its beginning, nursing was defined as having "charge of the personal health of somebody . . . and what nursing has to do . . . is to put the patient in the best condition for nature to act upon him" (Nightingale, 1860, p. 126). This early definition of nursing was written by Florence Nightingale and included many of the concepts still considered important today; this was remarkable considering how undeveloped professional nursing was in the mid to late 1800s. Nightingale was strategic in her thinking about the importance of the observational skills of the nurse and the impact of the environment on health. She clearly recognized health promotion and health maintenance as important responsibilities of nursing.

Until the late nineteenth century, nursing was seen as common employment for women and nurses were viewed as second-class citizens with ill moral and poor character. To overcome the negative societal views of nursing and to improve the qualities of potential nurse recruits, efforts were made to establish proper preparation for nurses. A physician, Ann Preston, organized in 1861 the first training program for nurses in the United States at Philadelphia's Woman's Hospital. This training program was opened to women "who wished greater proficiency in their domestic responsibilities" (Stevens, 1989, p. 17).

The choice to use hospitals as the site for training nurses expanded rapidly in the late 1800s as hundreds of new hospitals built under the aegis of religious orders, ethnic groups, industrialists, and elite groups of civic-minded individuals were looking for efficient ways to staff their wards. Because student nurses were a constantly renewable source of low-cost workers to staff the wards, even some of the smallest hospitals maintained nursing schools (Stevens, 1989). Hospital nursing school programs, therefore, were primarily sequences of on-the-job training rather than academic courses.

World War I had a profound effect on the nursing profession. Before the war, nursing was divided into three domains—public health, private duty, and hospital. Public health nursing was the elite pursuit and was recognized as instrumental in the campaign against infectious diseases such as tuberculosis and in promoting population health such as infant welfare. By 1920, over 70% of nurses worked in private duty; with about half working in patients' homes and half working for private patients in hospitals. Hospital nurses were primarily those in training. The war emphasized the drama and effectiveness of hospitals, and it soon codified the hospital as the center of nursing education in the increasingly specialized acute-care medical environment. The war experience established nurses as dedicated associates in hospital science. Nursing leaders promoted the idea of upgrading nursing through high-quality hospital nursing schools, preferably associated with universities. The choice to idealize the role of the nurse as dedicated and deferential to the physician specialist in the hospital marginalized the independent role of the nurse in social medicine and public health. The social medicine and public health aspects of nursing were subjugated to the image of nursing as a symbol of patriotism, national sacrifice, and efficiency.

As World War II brought increased funding for the educational preparation of nurses, nurses began to specialize during the 1950s. Because of the short supply of nurses after World War II, hospitals began to group the least physiologically stable patients in one nursing unit for intensive care, where the more competent nurses cared for the sickest patients. This arrangement did not lower the need for nurses but instead created the need for critical care nurse specialty as the need for staff nurses continued to grow. To increase manpower, Congress passed the Nurse Training Act of 1964, the Health Manpower Act of 1968, and the Nurse Training Act of 1971 added substantially to the federal support of nursing education (Lamm, 1996). Nevertheless, state funding provided the largest support for nursing schools, 80% of which are in colleges and universities.

Definition and Scope of Nursing Practice

The definitions of nursing in the early twentieth century focused on nursing functions and were holistic. Virginia Henderson wrote one of the most widely accepted definitions of nursing of this era: "Nursing may be defined as that service to an individual that helps him to attain or maintain a healthy state of mind or body" (Harmer & Henderson, 1939, p. 2). She later refined her definition into one that is perhaps the best known in the world because of its adoption by the International Council of Nurses (Henderson, 1960, p. 3):

> *The unique function of the nurse is to assist the individual, sick or well, in the performance of those activities contributing to health or its recovery (or to a peaceful death) that he would perform unaided if he had the necessary strength, will or knowledge. And to do this in such a way as to help him gain independence as rapidly as possible.*

In 1952, Hildegard Peplau added an important dimension to the definition of nursing by defining it in interpersonal terms. Peplau stated that "the goals of nursing are currently in transition; it's major concerns fifty years ago had to do with getting sick people well; today, nursing is more concerned with ways for helping people to stay well" (1992, p. 6). Nursing theory development during the 1950s and 1960s continued to refine the definition of nursing.

In the contemporary sphere of nursing, the current definition emerges from the 2003 edition of American Nurses Association's (ANA) Nursing's Social Policy Statement (ANA, 2003, p. 6):

> *Nursing is the protection, promotion, and optimization of health and abilities, prevention of illness and injury, alleviation of suffering through the diagnosis and treatment of human response, and advocacy in the care of individuals, families, communities, and populations.*

This definition of nursing provides a framework for nursing practice and curriculum development, as well as the boundaries, functions, and purpose of the profession. A clear understanding of the boundaries of nursing is needed as more allied health professions and unlicensed assistive personnel are added to the patient care arena. Policy makers need to understand the role of nursing to make the best decisions on healthcare policy.

Nursing Regulation

Nursing regulation is provided by governmental oversight through administrative and legislative bodies within each state of the union. Nursing as a health profession must be regulated, as it may pose risk of harm to the public if practiced by someone who is unprepared and incompetent. As a rule, the public may not have sufficient information and experience to identify an unqualified healthcare provider and is vulnerable to unsafe and incompetent practitioners; therefore, in order to protect the public's health and interest, each state established its own Board of Nursing, which is responsible for the regulation of nursing practice including the scope of practice. The Board of Nursing is authorized to enforce the Nurse Practice Act and develop administrative rules/regulations and other responsibilities per the Nurse Practice Act. The definition in the Nurse Practice Act constitutes the legal definition of nursing in that state. In 2007, the Council of State Boards of Nursing Delegate Assembly developed guiding principles of Nursing Regulation (see Table 4-1).

LICENSURE

State boards of nursing regulate nursing practice, including the scope of nursing practice. In each state, the model nurse practice act describes the scope of practice for RNs, licensed practical/vocational nurses, and advanced practice nurses (APRNs). Licensure is one type of regulation. It is the process by which boards of nursing grant permission to an individual to engage in nursing practice after determining that the applicant has attained the competency necessary to perform a unique scope of practice safely

Table 4-1 Guiding Principles of Nursing Regulation

Protection of the public	• Nursing regulation exists to protect the health, safety, and welfare of the public in their receipt of nursing services. • Involvement of nurses in nursing regulation is critical to public protection.
Competence of all practitioners regulated by the board of nursing	• Nursing regulation is responsible for upholding licensure requirements for competence of the various levels of nursing practice. • Competence is assessed at initial licensure/entry and during the career life of all practitioners.
Due process and ethical decision making	• Nursing regulation ensures due process rights for practitioners. • Boards of nursing hold practitioners accountable for conduct based on legal, ethical and professional standards.
Shared accountability	• Nursing regulation requires shared accountability for enhancing safe patient care.
Strategic collaboration	• Nursing regulation requires collaboration with individuals and agencies in the interest of public protection, patient safety, and the education of nurses.
Evidence-based regulation	• Nursing regulation uses evidence-based standards of practice, advances in technology, and demographic and social research in its mission to protect the public.
Response to the marketplace and healthcare environment	• Nursing regulation requires timely and thoughtful responsiveness to the evolving marketplace. • Scope of practice clarity and congruence with the community needs for nursing care are essential.
Globalization of nursing	• Nursing regulation occurs at the state level and concurrently works to standardize regulations and access to licensure. • Nursing regulation requires fair and ethical practices and policies to address the social, political, and fiscal challenges of globalization.

Source: NCSBN, 2010.

(National Council of State Boards of Nursing, 2009). Licensure is necessary when the regulated activities are complex; it requires specialized knowledge and skill and independent decision making. National Council of State Board of Nursing describes the intent of Licensure as including the following elements:

1. A specified scope of practice may only be performed legally by licensed individuals
2. Title protection
3. Authority to take disciplinary action should the licensee violate the laws or rules in order to assure that the public is protected

In 2009, the National Council of State Boards of Nursing unveiled a new Web site with nurse licensure verification tools called Nursys.com. This new and improved verification process will make nurse license verification quicker, easier, and free of charge to employers and the general public. The search allows for the identification of nurse's name, jurisdiction, license type, license number(s), license status(es), and expiration dates, as made available by the board of nursing for all licenses held, and any discipline against the license. Additionally, Nursys.com will allow nurses to verify their license(s) from Nursys licensure participating board of nursing when applying for endorsement into another state by using the online Nurse Licensure Verification application. By completing the Nursys verification process for $30.00 per license type, per state board of nursing where the nurse is applying, verification is available immediately to the endorsing board of nursing.

CERTIFICATION

Certification is another type of credential that affords title protection and recognition of accomplishment but does not include a legal scope of practice. The federal government has used the term certification to define the credentialing process by which a nongovernmental agency or association recognizes individuals who have met specified requirements. Many state boards of nursing use professional certification as one requirement toward granting authority for an individual who obtained advanced or specialized training in an area of practice such as RNs. Some state government agencies have also used the term certification for governmental credentialing. Confusion may occur because regulatory agencies and professional membership associations may use the same term in a different context. Certification is the regulating process under which a state or voluntary professional organization, such as a national board, attests to the educational achievements and performance abilities of persons in a healthcare field of practice. This certification provides practitioners with an additional sense of personal and professional accomplishment beyond an academic degree and licensure.

It is a much less restrictive regulation than licensing. Certification allows the public, employers, and third-party payers to determine which practitioners are appropriately qualified in their specialty or occupation.

Certification generally has no provision for regulating impaired or misbehaving practitioners other than putting them on probation or dropping them from certification. Unlike licensure, certification has no legal basis for preventing an impaired or professionally delinquent individual from practicing (National Council of State Boards of Nursing, 2009).

Impact of Lack of Professional Status

Lack of Recognition

From the very beginning and early in its history, the nursing profession struggled with the challenge of being recognized as a valuable contributor to health care in settings such as hospitals, nursing homes, schools, health departments, and industry. In part, much of this lack of recognition was because nursing was and still is a female profession, with only 5.7% being represented by men (HRSA, 2004). While the increases in enrollments is a positive indicator, the representation of men in nursing education programs remains low. Men accounted for 8.8% of all baccalaureate graduates, 10.6% of master's, and 4% of doctoral program graduates in the fall of 2004 (NACNEP, 2008).

As a female-dominated profession, society viewed caring by nurses as natural to their gender role and not within the confines of a "professional role requiring education and licensure like that of law and medicine." This is evidenced in the education of nurses. During the latter part of the 19th century, much of nursing education and preparation was hospital-based apprenticeships. Nurses learned by doing and were dominated by hospital administrators and the medical profession who were university trained. They were expected to carry out the orders of physicians. With this subservient position, along with the increasing demands of hospitals, nurses became quickly discouraged and turned to collective bargaining and union representation for expanded access to decision making, higher wages, and improved job security.

With hospital training programs now accounting for less than 5% of new graduates, nurses have been able to professionalize their educational preparation (Aiken et al., 2009). From hospital training in the early nineteenth century to university-based schools of nursing in the beginning of the twentieth century to the present and the emergence of associate's degree programs of the mid-twentieth century, nursing slowly began to lift the quality and quantity of a workforce. These varying levels of preparation and differentiation of basic nursing practices have been the basis for a wage issue. Additionally, other health professionals and nurses themselves need to be fully recognized as a profession; a lack of recognition discourages students from choosing this profession or pursuing a higher nursing degree and also discourages many practicing nurses. Only 60% of the nurse workforce enters practice with less than a baccalaureate degree in nursing. Most recent statistics (U.S. Department of Health and Human Services, 2004) reveal that about 20.7% of those initially educated in associate degree programs and 30.2% of those prepared in diploma programs had obtained post-RN nursing or related degrees.

Lack of Autonomy

Nurses are essential to the healthcare system, serving on the front lines at the bedside and in the boardroom. They must articulate in a clear and succinct way the reasons that nursing matters to the overall health and well-being of the nation, and nurses must be involved in health policy and reform. Having a strong executive leadership and hospital administration serves an important function to empower nurses at all levels of the hospital; however, full recognition of nursing as a profession requires nurses themselves to take initiatives to negotiate that kind of dramatic shift to break the stigma under physicians and hospital administrators. To claim leadership, nurses have strategized about the need to extend their education level from the lowest level of education admitted for licensure to the highest level, such as master's or doctoral level. It is argued that the highest level of education will gradually raise the image of nursing as a profession and also better prepare nurses in this highly complex and evolving healthcare environment. With a higher education, nurses increase their capacity beyond patient care but also raise their standard to qualify to teach as well as to conduct healthcare services and related research. Expanding nursing research promotes leadership in giving the nursing profession a voice to exercise knowledge in patient care and general public health issues.

Physically Challenging

Since the mid 1980s, minimizing inpatient hospital stays has been increasingly emphasized with the commitment toward reduction in hospital length of stay and continued hospital downsizing; however, because hospitals now treat much sicker patients than before, more nurses are needed per unit, and their work has become more intensive. In fact, the current shortage has burdened the nurse workforce with extended work hours and shifts and exacerbated occupational injuries and related disabilities. Nelson and Baptiste (2004) have identified that patient handling and movement tasks are physically demanding, performed under unfavorable conditions, and are often unpredictable in nature. Caring for today's patient, regardless of setting, offers multiple challenges, including variations in size, physical disabilities, cognitive function, level of cooperation, and fluctuations in condition, all of which caused greater risk for nursing personnel.

It is estimated that each year 12% of nursing personnel will consider a job transfer to decrease risk, and another 12% to 18% will actually leave the nursing profession because of chronic back pain (Moses, 1992; Owen, 1989). The cost of work-related musculoskeletal disorders in nursing is quite expensive and includes indirect costs associated with temporary hires for replacement personnel, overtime to absorb the duties of an injured worker, legal fees; time-loss costs for claim processing and witnesses; decreased output after a traumatic event; and training for temporary and/or replacement personnel (Charney et al., 1991; U.S. Department of Labor, Occupational Safety and Health Administration, 2002).

The physical difficulty of high-risk patient handling tasks varies by clinical setting. It is critical to understand the specific high-risk tasks in each setting, as solutions must be specifically applied to address each high-risk task identified. Nurses must gain additional and extended education in evidence-based solutions for high-risk patients handling tasks in complex medical and patient care settings. Various types of interventions are being implemented in an attempt to reduce high-risk patient handling tasks. An ergonomic approach has been used, with supporting evidence for solutions proven to be effective. In 2004, the American Nurses Association (ANA) developed a program, called "Handle with Care," that supports safe practices for patient handling. The ANA recently issued a position statement supporting actions and policies that result in the elimination of manual patient lifting to promote a safe environment of care for nurses and patients (ANA, 2003). An effective approach is to educate and train nursing staff on the use of patient handling equipment, emphasizing proper body mechanics, and including evidence-based solutions, such as (1) the use of patient handling equipment/devices, (2) patient care ergonomic assessment protocols, (3) no-lift policies, and (4) patient lift teams. There are remarkable growth and new opportunities, as well as burdens, for nursing employment. The challenge is to promote a safe environment of care for nurses and patients that reduces the risk and physical demands on nurses, ensuring greater coordination and continuity of care.

Alternative Career Choices

As the need of medical care grows more complex, the career pathway of nursing has evolved into five major occupations.

Registered Professional Nurses

Registered nurses (RNs) are typically prepared for professional practice through different levels of nursing education. To achieve the RN title, an individual must graduate from a state-approved school of nursing—a 4-year university program, a 2-year associate's degree program, or a 3-year diploma program—and pass a state RN licensing examination called the National Council Licensure Examination for Registered Nurses. The 4-year university-based Bachelor of Science in Nursing (BSN) degree provides the nursing theory, sciences, humanities, and behavioral science preparation necessary for the full scope of professional nursing responsibilities. It also provides the knowledge base necessary for advanced education in specialized clinical practice, research, or primary health care. A 2-year program granting an associate's degree in nursing (ADN) prepares individuals for a defined technical scope of practice. Set in the framework of general education, the clinical and classroom components prepare ADN nurses for nursing roles that require nursing theory and technical proficiency. Many RNs whose first degree is an ADN return to school during their working life to earn a bachelor's degree or higher. In 2006, many students find the ADN program to be longer than 2 years, often 3 years or more. In 2005, associate's degree programs were 58.9% of all U.S. basic programs. A diploma is usually associated with a hospital; the diploma in nursing program combines classroom and clinical instruction and is usually complete in 3 years. Although once a common educational route for RNs, diploma programs have diminished steadily—to 4% of all basic RN education. Driven by the need for more baccalaureate-level nurses because of the growing complexity of healthcare delivery, the percentage of RNs with BSN degrees grew from 22% in 1980 to 34% in 2004 (HRSA, 2007); however, the majority of RNs continue to enter nursing from community colleges.

Licensed Practical Nurses

A licensed practical nurse (LPN) works under the direct supervision of an RN or physician. The 1-year LPN training is offered at about 1,100 state-approved technical or vocational schools or community or junior colleges. Programs include both classroom study and supervised clinical practice, and LPNs must pass a national licensing examination like RNs. Twenty-eight percent of the over 700,000 LPNs work in hospitals; however, the reduction in inpatient days and the substitution of unlicensed personnel have decreased the number of LPNs in hospitals by almost 10,000 per year. Although the employment in hospitals has been decreasing since 2002, the demand for LPNs in the other work settings, however, is increasing. Nursing homes employ 26% of the LPNs, and another 12% are employed in physician offices and clinics; the remainder works in home health care, residential care facilities, schools, and government agencies.

Advanced Practice Registered Nurses

Advanced Practice Registered Nurses (APRNs) have expanded in numbers and responsibilities and capabilities that have developed over the past several decades. APRNs are highly valued and are an integral part of the healthcare system. They include certified nurse practitioners, certified nurse–midwives, clinical nurse specialists (CNS), and certified registered nurse anesthetists (CRNAs):

1. Nurse practitioners deliver front-line primary and acute care in community clinics, schools, hospitals, and other settings, and perform such services as diagnosing and treating common acute illnesses and injuries, providing immunizations, conducting physical exams, and managing

Figure 4-1 Enrollments in basic RN programs by program type: 1981 to 1994 and 2003 to 2007.

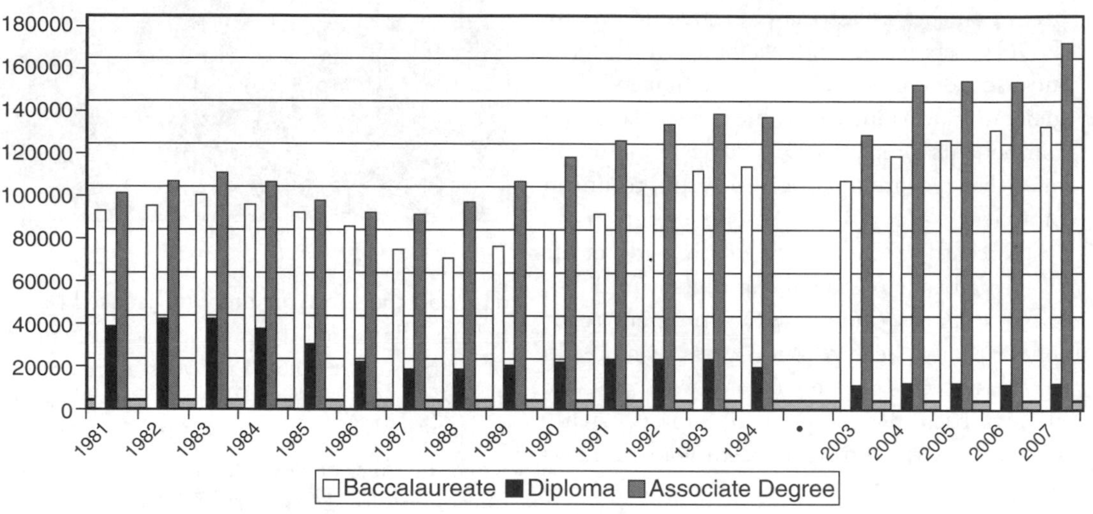

Source: National League for Nursing.

high blood pressure, diabetes, and other chronic problems

2. Certified nurse–midwives provide prenatal and gynecological care to normal healthy women, deliver babies in hospitals, private homes, and birthing centers, and continue with follow-up postpartum care
3. Clinical nurse specialists provide care in a range of specialty areas, such as cardiac, oncology, neonatal, pediatric, and obstetric/gynecological nursing
4. Certified registered nurse anesthetists administer more than 65% of all anesthetics given to patients each year and are the sole providers of anesthesia in approximately one third of U.S. hospitals

Each APRN has a unique history and context. Title distinguishes one's academic achievement as well as the profession level of one's practice. Although education, accreditation, and certification are necessary components of an overall approach to preparing an APRN for practice, the licensing boards governed by state regulations and statutes are responsible for setting practice within a given state. Currently, there is no uniform model of regulation of APRNs across the states. Each state independently determines the APRN legal scope of practice, the roles that are recognized, the criteria for entry into advanced practice, and the certification examinations accepted for entry-level competence assessment. Many licensing exams, such as those for RN, CNS, and CNL, offer a license title without distinguishing those who have graduated from a diploma program versus those who graduated from a BSN or doctorate program. Additionally, an individual who receives a degree such as the Doctor of Nursing Practice (DNP) is prohibited from using the term "doctor" as a title according to American Medical Association resolution passed in 2008. The lack of differentiation of license or title of those with higher degrees is a great obstacle to nurses in finding their own identity in this profession. Also, because of this there is a significant barrier for APRNs to move easily from state to state and has decreased access to care for patients.

To remedy APRN regulation, the APRN Joint Dialogue Group Report (2008) has produced the Consensus Model for APRN Regulation: Licensure, Accreditation, Certification & Education, which is a document that establishes a set of standards to protect the public, improve mobility, and improve access to safe and quality for APRN care (APRN Joint Dialogue Group Report, 2008). This report includes a definition of the APRN Regulatory Model, as well as a definition of the APRN; a definition of broad-based APRN education; a model for regulation to ensure APRN education and certification as a valid and reliable process, that is based on nationally recognized and accepted standards; uniform recommendations for licensing bodies across states; a process and characteristics for recognizing a new APRN role; and a definition of an APRN specialty that allows for the profession to meet future patient and nursing needs.

The work of the Joint Dialogue Group in conjunction with all organizations representing APRN licensure, accreditation, certification, and education to advance a regulatory model is an ongoing collaborative process that is fluid and dynamic. As health care evolves and new standards and needs emerge, the APRN Regulatory Model will advance accordingly to allow APRNs to care for patients in a safe environment to the full potential of their nursing knowledge and skill.

Specialization and the Evolution of Nursing Roles: Clinical Nurse Specialists and Clinical Nurse Leaders

The increasing specialization of nurses is demonstrated in the evolving role of clinical nurse specialists and clinical nurse leaders. Just as the role of nurse practitioners evolved over several decades to meet demands for increased access to primary health care, the role of the CNS was developed in response to the specialized nursing care needs of increasingly complex medical need. Like a physician specialist, CNSs are advanced practice specialists with in-depth knowledge and skills that make them valuable adjunct practitioners in specialized clinical settings. In today's healthcare system, nurses are critical caregivers who have a profound effect on the lives of patients and their families. They play an essential role in the quality of care patients receive; CNSs play a unique role in the delivery of high-quality nursing care. In addition to direct patient care, CNSs also engage in teaching, mentoring, consulting, research, management, and systems improvement. Able to adapt their practice across settings, these clinicians greatly influence outcomes by providing expert consultation to all care providers and by implementing improvements in healthcare delivery systems. Furthermore, the growing body of research on CNS outcomes shows a strong correlation between CNS inter- [illegible]ost-effective patient care. [illegible]irectly linked to reduc- [illegible]d lengths of stay, reduced frequency of emergency room visits, improved pain management practices, increased patient satisfaction with nursing care, and fewer complications in hospitalized patients (Fulton & Baldwin, 2004). Unfortunately, the constraining forces of today's practice environment of mounting financial pressure, limited nursing resources, changing technology along with greater patient acuity, and shorter lengths of stay have tested the very core of the profession's values and contributions to quality care.

CNSs play an important role in the provision of nursing care that does not duplicate the emerging role of the clinical nurse leader (CNL). In terms of focus, CNLs are educated as generalists, whereas CNSs are prepared for specialty practice. The CNL is a new nursing role that is being developed by the American Association of Colleges of Nursing (AACN) in collaboration with leaders from the practice arena. The CNL is a master's-prepared generalist who puts evidence-based practice into action and serves as a central liaison between the patient and all other healthcare providers. To support this effort, the AACN has launched a national pilot project involving more than 90 education–practice partnerships. Partners are working to develop master's degree programs to prepare CNLs, integrate this clinician into the healthcare system, and evaluate outcomes. To understand the role of CNLs, it is important to differentiate the duties of CNLs versus CNSs. CNLs operate primarily on the clinical microsystem level, involving small, functional front-line units unlike CNSs engaging not only within the microsystem but also at the systems levels within three spheres of influence: client, personnel, and organizational systems. The CNL coordinates and implements client care, whereas the CNS designs and evaluates patient-specific and population-based programs. The CNL evaluates and implements evidence-based practice, whereas the CNS has the added responsibility of generating new evidence. The CNS and CNL roles are distinct and complementary (Spross et al., 2004). The AACN envisions that these clinicians will work collaboratively to ensure that patients receive the best care possible. Nurses are needed both at the point of care and in advanced practice roles to deliver care that is growing intensely more complicated.

Current State of the Profession

Nurses play a critical role in ensuring high-quality, patient-centered care, and a significant role in the healthcare reform process. The Institute of Medicine (2003) report *Keeping Patients Safe: Transforming the Work Environment of Nurses* found that nurses are indispensable to patient safety and healthcare quality. The value and importance of nursing to improve the quality, value, and equality of care; address healthcare costs and spending; strengthen the public health system; address the social determinants of health; and prevent disease and promote healthier lifestyles are fully realized. The critical issue is to have the supply of qualified nurses be adequate to meet the demand for their services.

Supply

The supply of nurses is determined by multiple factors. This chapter will consider two of the most important drivers of nursing supply: the availability of educational opportunities and the wages commanded by nurses in the field. According to new survey data released by the AACN, less than half of all qualified applicants to entry-level baccalaureate nursing programs were admitted and enrolled last year despite calls to increase the number of well-educated RNs in the U.S. workforce. The American Association of Colleges of Nursing (AACN) survey data from 2008 to 2009 shows that enrollment in entry-level baccalaureate nursing programs increased by 3.5%. This is the ninth consecutive year of enrollment growth for nursing schools. However, the shortage of faculty, insufficient clinical education sites, and budget cuts continue to act as barriers to future growth in undergraduate education (American Association of Colleges of Nursing, 2009).

Although interest in nursing careers is high, the latest data show that almost 50,000 qualified applicants to professional nursing programs were turned away in 2008, including nearly 6,000 applicants to master's and doctoral degree programs (NLN, 2006). More than 70% of nursing schools responding to the survey pointed to faculty shortages as a reason for not accepting all qualified applicants into nursing programs. Nursing faculty shortage has led to expanding nursing school enrollments. During the 2009 current academic year, there were 814 faculty vacancies at 449 nursing schools across the country, with most of those vacancies in doctoral-level positions. The faculty shortage promises to worsen as faculty age continues to climb. For 2007 to 2008, the average ages of doctoral-prepared nurse faculty holding the ranks of professor, associate professor, and assistant professor were 59.1, 56.1, and 51.7 years, respectively (AACN, 2008). According to Berlin and Sechrist (2002), the average age of nurse faculty at retirement is 62.5 years.

Although the percentage of those entering a university program for graduate-level education who have a BSN degree is rising, nurses with graduate education will likely not choose a faculty position that combines teaching and research. Most clinical care and administration roles offer a higher and more competitive salary than academic positions while still affording opportunities to teach and carry out research. Solutions to the nurse shortage crisis focus on recruiting and training more students to choose nursing as a career but neglect to raise the education level of the current nursing workforce or to promote the teaching faculty position. In the academic institution, raising faculty salaries and using new teaching models such as distance learning and simulation are common strategies to attract more faculty members or use fewer faculty in the existing program. Nonetheless, the true solution may rely on education policy to realign the workforce educational composition to the real demand of nursing with graduate-level education. Again, preliminary data from AACN's fall 2009 survey show that enrollment in master's and doctoral degree nursing programs increased significantly. Nursing schools with master's programs reported a 9.6% increase in enrollment (409 schools reporting) and a 10.5% increase in graduations (380 schools reporting). In doctoral nursing programs, overall enrollment is up by 20.5% (154 schools reporting), and graduations increased by 1.9% (92 schools reporting) from 2008 to 2009. Doctor of Nursing Practice (DNP) programs account for the largest share of the growth in this student population, with a 40.9% increase in enrollments reported this year (85 schools reporting). In 2009, the number of students enrolled in research-focused doctoral programs (i.e., PhD or DNSc) increased by 4.1% according to preliminary estimates.

A second factor is wages. Wages are a way to attract nurses to the field and retain them once they are in practice. RNs are among the highest paying occupations; registered nursing continues as the top occupation in terms of the largest job growth from 2006 to 2016 (Dohm & Shniper, 2007). This job projection growth suggests that more than 587,000 new jobs will be created through 2016. Nearly 57% of RNs worked in general and medical and surgical hospitals, where RN salaries averaged $60,970 per year. In 2006, there were 2.4 million nurses in the workforce, comprising the largest segment of professionals (28%) working in the healthcare industry (Bureau of Labor Statistics, 2007; Mee, 2006). Despite the wage having a positive influence on the RNs supply, there is still a shortage of nurses. Hospitals continue to be the largest single employer for nurses who are the primary providers of patient care; however, in 2004, 56.2% of nurses were employed in hospitals, down from 66% in 1980. As health care has moved out of the hospital to other care settings, including private practices, health maintenance organizations, public health agencies, primary care clinics, home health care, nursing homes, outpatient surgicenters, nursing-school–operated nursing centers, insurance and managed care companies, schools, mental health agencies, hospice, the military, industry, nursing education, and healthcare research, nurses will seek employment in these diverse settings (HRSA, 2007). The long-term supply of RNs relies on the student pool that is currently enrolled or interested in the nursing education programs. Economic factors such as tuition requirement and financial aid availability, duration of the academic program, wages of the markets upon graduation, and number of nursing education programs in the nation will also influence an individual's decision to become a nurse.

Demand

Buerhaus et al. (2008) project a shortage of 500,000 nurses by 2020. As health care continues to shift from acute-care hospitals to a more community-based primary care and other outpatient sites and because of the rising complexity of acute care, the demand for RNs in hospitals will continue to climb by 36% by 2020 (National Advisory Council on Nursing Education and Practice, 1996). Nurses as front-line caregivers provide ongoing vigilance so as to reduce bad things from happening to patients such as medication errors, patient falls, and pressure ulcers. The shortage of RNs, in combination with an increased workload, poses a threat to quality of care. Increases in RN staffing are associated with reductions in hospital-related mortality and a failure to rescue as well as reduce lengths of stays, according to a meta-analysis of existing studies (Agency for Healthcare, Research and Quality, 2007). In a 2002 study reported in the *Journal of the American Medical Association*, University of Pennsylvania researchers reported that patients who have common surgeries in hospitals with the worst nurse staffing levels have up to a 31% increased chance of dying (Aiken et al., 2002). A higher proportion of nursing care provided by RNs and a greater number of hours of care by RNs per day are associated with better outcomes for hospitalized patients, according to a study published in the *New England Journal of Medicine* in 2002 (Needleman et al., 2002). Similarly, a 2003 study found that surgical patients had a "substantial survival advantage" if treated in hospitals with higher proportions of nurses with a BSN or higher degree. Every 10% increase in proportion of BSN nurses in hospitals had a resulting 4% decrease in risk of death (Aiken et al., 2003, 2008). Over the past 5 years, estimates put the RN vacancy rate in hospitals from 8.1% to 13% (American Hospital Association, 2002, 2007). Of the total licensed RN population in March 2004, an overwhelming majority, 83.2%, were employed in nursing, and only 16.8% were not (HRSA, 2007). The average age of the RN is climbing. In March 2004, it was 46.8 years of age, and the percentage of nurses under 30 years old was 8% (HRSA, 2007). By 2010, approximately 40% of the nursing workforce will be over 50 years old (Robert Wood Johnson Foundation, 2006). Americans are aware of the nursing shortage and believe that the availability of nurses is a critical factor in the quality of hospital care (Harvard School of Public Health, 2005).

Policy as a Tool to Influence Nursing Professionalism and Nursing Supply

Healthcare policy, whether it is created through governmental actions, institutional decision making, or organizational standards, creates a framework that can facilitate or impede the delivery of healthcare services. Thus, engagement in the process of policy development is central to creating a healthcare system that meets the needs of its constituents. Political activism and a commitment to policy development are central elements of professional nursing practice; therefore, professional nursing as well as master and doctoral prepared graduates must assume a broad leadership role on behalf of the public as well as the nursing profession (Ehrenreich, 2002). Health policy influences multiple care delivery issues, including health disparities, cultural sensitivity, ethics, the internationalization of healthcare concerns, access to care, quality of care, healthcare financing, and issues of equity and social justice in the delivery of health care. Nurses must stand ready to design, implement, and advocate for healthcare policy that addresses issues of social justice and equity in health care. The nurses can become potent influencers in policy formation. They have the capacity to analyze the policy process and the ability to engage in politically competent action. This capacity included the ability to engage proactively in the development and implementation of health policy at all levels, including institutional, local, state, regional, federal, and international levels. Professional nurses must be seen as leaders in the practice arena and provide a critical interface between practice, research, and policy.

Preparing nurses with the essential competencies to assume a leadership role in the development of health policy requires opportunities to contrast the major contextual factors and policy triggers that influence health policy making at the various levels. For example, nurses can

1. Critically analyze health policy proposals, health policies, and related issues from the perspective of consumers, nursing, other health professions, and other stakeholders in policy and public forums
2. Demonstrate leadership in the development and implementation of institutional, local, state, federal, and/or international health policy
3. Influence policy makers through active participation on committees, boards, or task forces at the institutional, local, state, regional, national, and/or international levels to improve healthcare delivery and outcomes
4. Educate others, including policy makers at all levels, regarding nursing, health policy, and patient care outcomes
5. Advocate for the nursing profession within the policy and healthcare communities
6. Develop, evaluate, and provide leadership for healthcare policy that shapes healthcare financing, regulation, and delivery
7. Advocate for social justice, equity, and ethical policies within all healthcare arenas

The goal is to create a healthcare delivery system that ensures high-quality care at the exact time when the patient needs it. Nurses are creating model programs in acute care, primary care, and public health settings that are improving the health status of individuals while reducing costs (Hassmiller, 2009). These programs promote the goals that policy makers seek for health reform, including expanding access, improving quality and safety, and reducing costs (Robert Wood Johnson Foundation, 2009). They address problems related to both the supply and demand for nursing services.

Legal Remedies (California and Regulation of Patient Loads)

One of the legal remedies being pursued to address the nursing shortage is legislating nurse–patient staffing ratios. On one hand, this would maintain quality at the bedside by ensuring an adequate number of nurses are on duty.

On the other hand, such a policy can have unintended consequences because it does not address the fact that there is not an adequate number of nurses to fill all of the jobs being posted. As a result, a study in the February 10, 2009 issue of *Health Affairs* finds that wages for RNs working in California cities increased after the 2004 passage of legislation mandating nurse-to-patient ratios. Supported by the U.S. Department of Health and Human Services Agency for Healthcare Research and Quality, a researcher from the University of North Carolina School of Nursing and colleagues analyzed data culled from four surveys to assess changes between 2000 and 2006 in nurse wages in California and in other metropolitan cities across the nation. The researchers learned that California RNs experienced wage growth that was between 5% and 12% higher than nurses working in other states, a finding that calls into question California policymakers' assumptions that implementing the nurse staffing requirements would not yield large wage increases for RNs. According to the data, work hours for California RNs increased by an average of 1.4 hours per week, suggesting that the increased wages could be due to additional work hours for RNs, especially if the additional hours generated an overtime-pay premium. Based on the findings, the study authors suggest that states considering such requirements first examine other employment opportunities for RNs and the specific demographic characteristics of their local nursing workforce. Noting, meanwhile, that little evidence suggests that the staffing requirements improved care quality, the researchers urge policymakers to balance the costs of potential wage increases resulting from such legislation and the societal benefit of potentially improved quality of care.

Despite such findings, Rep. Jan Schakowsky (D-Ill.) has introduced legislation that would amend the Public Health Service Act to mandate national inpatient nurse-to-patient staffing ratios, American Hospital Association *News Now* reports. Under the Nurse Staffing Standards for Patient Safety and Quality Care Act of 2009, hospitals would be required to implement staffing plans that adhere to minimum direct care nurse-to-patient ratios and adjust nurse staffing levels based on patient acuity and additional factors within 2 years of the bill's enactment (American Hospital Association *News Now*, 2009). The Nurse Staffing Standards for Patient Safety and Quality Care Act of 2009 has not given enough evidence showing that quality care will be ensured by imposing mandatory nurse staffing ratios. Most importantly, the bill may not have taken account of more significant variables, such as the patient's needs and the complexity of the patient's condition, education and experience level of nurses, the availability of support services, the environment in which the care is delivered, and so forth. Mandated nurse–patient ratios are based on a simple head count rather than patient needs. Peter Buerhaus, RN, PhD, FAAN, states that the bill is indeed counterproductive to building constructive relationships between nursing staff and hospital. The imposition reduces flexibility of hospitals to adjust changing demands in providing patient care. He also noted that "maintaining and strengthening a flexible approach to nurse staffing, not imposing mandatory nurse staffing ratios, is the key to the long-term survival, advancement and prosperity of the nursing profession" (Buerhaus, 2009a).

Educational Remedies (Increase Number of Schools and Accelerated Programs)

To meet the more complex demands of today's healthcare environment, the National Advisory Council on Nurse Education and Practice has recommended that at least two thirds of the basic nurse workforce hold baccalaureate or higher degrees in nursing by 2010. Aware of the need, RNs are seeking the BSN degree in increasing numbers. In 1980, almost 55% of employed RNs held a hospital diploma as their highest educational credential; 22% held a bachelor's degree and 18% an associate's degree. By 2004, a diploma was the highest educational credential for only 17.5% of RNs, whereas the number with bachelor's degrees as their highest education had climbed to 34.2%, with 33.7% holding an associate's degree as their top academic preparation. In 2007, 14,946 RNs with diplomas or associate's degrees graduated from BSN programs (AACN, 2008). In the 2007 to 2008 academic year, 190,483 completed applications were received for entry-level baccalaureate nursing programs, with 122,001 meeting admission criteria and 80,616 applications accepted. These data translate into an acceptance rate of 42.3%. For a graphic showing a five-trend in applications received, see http://www.aacn.nche.edu/Media/pdf/EnrollChanges.pdf.

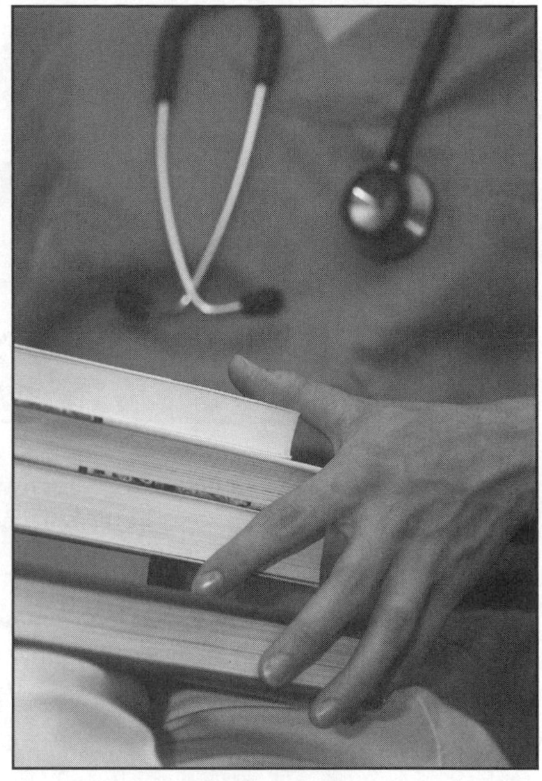

According to the Annual Survey of Schools of Nursing Academic Year 2006–2007: Executive Summary for the National League of Nursing, annual admissions to nursing education programs rose by 12.3% compared with only 7.6% during the prior academic year. The greatest increase was in ADN programs, which admitted 12.3% more new students than last year. Diploma admissions were down slightly (4.2%). Baccalaureate admissions continued to grow, albeit at a slower rate than in recent years. The rate of growth was 5.6% in 2006–2007. The national ranks of prelicensure nursing students expanded by almost 20,000, or 6.7%, between 2006 and 2007; almost 18,000 of those were enrolled in ADN programs. Although enrollment levels in BSN programs were relatively flat during this period, there was a substantial rise in associate's degree enrollments, which increased from about 153,000 in 2006 to 170,651 in 2007.

In 2004, 13% of the nation's RNs held either a master's or doctoral degree as their highest educational preparation. The current demand for master's- and doctoral-prepared nurses for advanced practice, clinical specialties, teaching, and research roles far outstrips the supply. The focus must remain on four key areas, including establishing strategic partnerships and resource alignment, formulating policy and regulation, increasing faculty capacity and diversity, and redesigning educational curricula. Despite the increased interest in nursing programs, limited clinical placements for students and a dearth of nurse educators to teach courses are making it difficult for many schools to expand enrollment in their programs. Increasing enrollment in

baccalaureate nursing programs is a critical first step to correcting an imbalance in the nursing student population and reversing our nation's diminishing supply of nurse educators. In almost all jurisdictions, nursing faculty must possess a graduate degree in order to assume a full-time teaching role. Because the overwhelming majority of nurses with master's and doctoral degrees began their education in baccalaureate programs, efforts to alleviate the faculty shortage must focus on expanding enrollments in 4-year nursing programs. The AACN survey found that total enrollment in all nursing programs leading to the baccalaureate degree is 201,407, an increase from 192,698 in 2007. Within this universe, 145,845 students are enrolled in entry-level baccalaureate nursing programs. In graduate programs, 69,565 students are enrolled in master's programs, and 7,391 are enrolled in doctoral nursing programs. Although the overall number of nursing students in doctoral programs has increased by 20.9% from 2007 to 2008, enrollment growth has been limited to DNP programs. In research-focused doctoral programs (i.e., PhD, DNSc), enrollments increased by only 0.1%, or 3 students, last year, with the total student population reaching 3,976. The number of enrollees in DNP programs nearly doubled during that same timeframe, with the student population growing from 1,874 to 3,415 students (82.2%). In terms of doctoral program graduates, 555 students graduated from research-focused programs in 2008, and 361 graduated from DNP programs.

Accelerated nursing programs continue to be an important pathway into nursing for individuals with degrees in other fields who are looking to change careers. Last year, 13 new accelerated baccalaureate programs were launched, bringing the nationwide total to 218 programs. Currently, 11,018 students are enrolled in these programs, up from 9,938 in 2007, and the number of graduates has climbed to 6,870 graduates in 2008. In the 57 accelerated master's degree programs now available, 4,577 students are enrolled, and 1,177 students graduated last year (see http://www.aacn.nche.edu/Media/FactSheets/AcceleratedProg.htm).

Professional Remedies (Change Status of Nurses)

The role of nursing leadership is fundamental to overturning the misconception that nurses act as subordinates in providing patient care. This misconception is based on the tradition of the nurses' role in "taking physician orders." This traditional view of nursing has not been overturned completely in the public eye because of a lack of nursing leadership. Recruitment efforts focus mainly on the role of nurses helping sick patients, assisting the physician, and bringing direct care to patients, but nothing is mentioned about the role of nursing as a leadership profession to improve our healthcare administration, to develop healthcare policy, and to influence medical practice. To change the general opinion of nursing, nurses must understand the multiple career choices that they have and the meaning of their education.

Nursing is no longer a profession that merely follows physician orders but rather has nurses on the front line participating in initiatives to lead healthcare reform and are suggesting ways to improve access, cost, and quality. For example, APNs have developed initiatives around new infrastructure care models that focus on primary care, chronic care management, care coordination, and wellness. These include the Transitional Model of Care (TCM) designed by Mary Naylor, RN, PhD, RN, Robert Wood Johnson Foundation's Interdisciplinary Nursing Quality Research Initiative director and a professor at the University of Pennsylvania School of Nursing. Under this model, APRNs serve as the primary care coordinators to help older patients avoid hospitalizations and promote longer term positive health outcomes. The nurse meets with a hospitalized patient to coordinate service, evaluate medications, and establish a postdischarge plan of care that meets with patient and caregiver's goals. Within a day of being released from the hospital, the nurse visits the patient's home. The Transition Care Model focuses on continuity, evidence-based practice, coordination across the board, and improved outcomes. In this model, a transitional care nurse, who is an APN, is assigned to a patient upon admission into the hospital. This nurse immediately conducts an in-depth assessment of patient's and family's goals and begins communication and collaboration with the patient's care providers, including their primary care physician. Additionally, this nurse visits the patient daily while he or she is admitted and develops an appropriate evidence-based transition care plan with the rest of the care team. Upon discharge, the nurse will work with the patient to implement the care plan, reassess the patient, and collaborate with the patient's other caregivers. This model has been shown to increase patient satisfaction and improve patient physical function and quality of life (Naylor, 2009). In clinical trials sponsored by the National Institutes of Health (NIH), readmission within 6 weeks was reduced by 57% (Naylor et al., 1994), and readmission within 6 months was reduced by 50% (Naylor, et al., 1999). Six- and 12-month costs were reduced by 58% and 39% respectively (Naylor, et al., 1999, & Naylor et al., 2004).

Another example of expert care coordination and meeting the needs of special populations, is that of Ruth Watson Lubic, PhD, CNM. She has founded certified birth centers, the Maternity Center Association in New York City, and the Family Health and Childbirthing Center in Washington, DC. These programs offer prenatal and labor and delivery care for women who are at low pregnancy risk. The care provided at these birth centers has demonstrated significant cost savings for childbearing women, reduced the Cesarean rate in 2005 compared with the rest of the city (15% versus 28%), and significantly lowered the rates of premature and low-birth rate babies, resulting in $1.2 million in cost savings. If this nurse-driven innovation was converted to a nationwide model, the potential savings could be almost $13 billion for Medicaid-funded deliveries.

Finally, the newest model of care on the healthcare landscape will be funded by the federal government. President Obama has pledged $8.6 billion over 20 years for the Nurse-Family Partnership. This partnership pairs a nurse with a low-income, first-time mother. Over 2 decades, the program has shown significantly better pregnancy outcomes, reductions in high-risk and subsequent pregnancies, fewer injuries among children, reduced child abuse, and fewer language delays among children. The program has generated a $5.70 return for every dollar invested and a net benefit to society of $17,000 to $34,000 per family served.

Institutional Remedies (Recruitment from Overseas)

Healthcare providers have sought their own solution to the shortage of nurses by recruiting nurses from abroad. The growth of foreign-born RNs averaged 6% per year compared with 1.5% among all of the RNs between 1994 and 2001. Nonetheless, the growth of foreign-born RNs doubled to 12.5% in 2002. Overall, the growth of employing foreign-born RNs accounts for more than one third of the total growth of total RN employment in the United States since 2002 (Buerhaus et al., 2003).

The major factor that impacts the inflow of foreign-born or foreign-educated RNs is the availability of the employment-based visa. American Hospital Association *News Now* reports that legislation, which was introduced by Representative Robert Wexler (D-FL), would set aside as many as 20,000 employment-based visas for foreign-educated RNs and physical therapists in each year of the next 3 years. There is currently a long waiting list for employment-based visas for internationally educated nurses. Most of these foreign nurses will eventually gain permanent residency by applying after several years through the hospital where they are employed. Because the recruitment of these foreign nurses is usually conducted at less developed countries, the possibility of residing in the United States permanently with an income higher than they earn in their own country is a very attractive offer.

Although some hospitals may find it may be faster to employ already educated RNs from other countries than to wait for the increase of enrollment and graduation in the U.S. nursing programs (Zachary, 2001), internationally educated RNs may create a liability for the quality and safety of patient care. Some internationally educated RNs have difficulty with communication because of the language or culture differences, and this communication causes lapses in patient safety and quality of care. There is also a gap as well in comparative assessments on care outcomes and safety between those who are United States educated compared with those who are internationally educated. Thus, more research is needed to investigate those relationships. The demand for foreign-educated RNs will likely continue or increase; interventions developed to improve communication skills among all nurses across borders are necessary.

Increasing foreign labor in nursing may have a long-term effect on our immigration policy, the wages of future nurses, and the labor composition for RNs. Importing more foreign-born or foreign-educated nurses will increase our long-term domestic nursing supply; however, we likely shift our shortage problem to another part of the world, thus affecting their quality of care by depleting their nursing staffs. The potential problem or benefit is still unknown; the best solution to solve our nursing shortage might be to break current domestic barriers that prevent men or underrepresented races, such as Hispanics, from entering the field.

Summary

Contemporary nursing practice requires that nurses are well prepared to engage healthcare consumers, their families, and others about nursing contributions to health care. Every patient care encounter is an opportunity for nurses to demonstrate their critical thinking, compassion, and professional expertise. These encounters allow the public to understand better "just how nurses save lives, alleviate suffering and even keep down healthcare cost" (Buresh & Gordon, 2006, p. 21). Nurses have a professional obligation to articulate how intellectually demanding and complex nursing care is and to demonstrate the ways in which they have developed and implemented innovative models of care that promote the goals of health reform: expanding access, improving quality and safety, and reducing costs. By providing thoughtful insight and compassion about nursing, the public gains an accurate image of nurses. It is only through compelling and complete descriptions of the work that nurses do that others come to value and appreciate that work. Changing the status of nursing means making nursing more visible to the public and policy makers. It requires that nurses inform and educate policy makers and leaders of healthcare delivery organizations about how patient-centered, safe, and efficient care contributes to slowing the rate of total healthcare expenditures. Nurse leaders must take responsibility to educate nurse clinicians to take advantage of changes in payment policies by making sure that the contributions of nurses are visible. This requires using pay-for-performance measures and bundling of hospital payments to patient-centered practices of its nursing staff. By linking hospital performance to nurse performance, nurses demonstrate increased understanding of the economic implications of their clinical and administrative practice.

The time has come to recognize fully nursing's social relevance as the nation addresses healthcare reform legislation and increased attention on the future of nursing is addressed by the Institute of Medicine, in collaboration with the Robert Wood Johnson Foundation (2009). The economic, political, and social forces behind healthcare reform favor the interests and advancement of the nursing profession. Buerhaus (2009b) suggests that nurses must intensify efforts to "increase the capacity of nursing education programs so that the aging RNs who will retire from the workforce during 2015–2020 can (a) be replaced, and (b) the total supply of RNs can be increased to meet the increasing demand for health care" (p. 249). This increased effort will mean a commitment to a better prepared workforce where nursing education curricula place greater emphasis on evidence-based nursing practice and where quality, safety, geriatrics, chronic conditions, and nursing care extend beyond the acute hospital setting into nonacute care settings.

With the adoption of information technologies, the expanded use of models of care delivery, increased quality care provided by APRNs, and a better prepared nursing workforce, society will benefit from increased nurse autonomy, productivity, and satisfaction.

References

Agency for Healthcare, Research, & Quality. (2007). *Nurse staffing and quality of patient care.* Retrieved July 30, 2009, from http://www.ahrq.gov/downloads/pub/evidence/pdf/nursestaff/nursestaff.pdf

Aiken, L., Clarke, S., & Sloan, D. (2002). Hospital staffing, organization, and quality of care: Cross-national findings. *Nursing Outlook, 50*(5), 187–194.

Aiken, L., Clarke, S. Cheung, R., Sloane, D., & Sibler, J. (2003). Educational levels of hospital nurses and surgical mortality. *JAMA, 290*(12), 1617–1623.

Aiken, L. H., Clarke, S. P., Sloane, D. M., Lake, E. T., & Cheney, T. (2008). Effects of hospital care environments on patient mortality and nurse outcomes. *Journal of Nursing Administration, 38*(5), 220–226.

Aiken, L. H., Cheung, R., & Olds, D. (2009). Education policy initiatives to address the nurse shortage. *Health Affairs, 28*(4), w646–w656.

American Association of Colleges of Nursing. (2009). *28th annual survey of institutions with baccalaureate and higher degree nursing programs.* Retrieved January 15, 2010, from http://www.aacn.nche.edu/IDS/datarep.htm

American Association of Colleges of Nursing (AACN). (2009, September). *Nursing shortage fact sheet.* Retrieved January 15, 2010, from http://www.aacn.nche.edu/Media/FactSheets/NursingShortage.htm

American Hospital Association. (2002). *Health and hospital trends: The 2002 survey.* Retrieved July 30, 2009, from http://www.aha.org/aha/research-and-trends/health-and-hospital-trends/2003-or-earlier.html

American Hospital Association. (2007). *Health and hospital trends: The 2007 survey.* Retrieved July 30, 2009, from http://www.aha.org/aha/research-and-trends/health-and-hospital-trends/2007.html

American Hospital Association *News Now*. (2009). *Bill would establish nursing staff ratios.* Retrieved July 30, 2009, from http://www.ahanews.com/ahanews_app/jsp/display.jsp?dcrpath=AHANEWS/AHANewsNowArticle/data/ann_050709_staffing&domain=AHANEWS

American Nurses Association. (2003). *Nursing's social policy statement* (2nd ed.). Washington, DC: Nursesbooks.org.

American Nurses Association. (2004). *Nursing: Scope & standards of practice.* Washington, DC: American Nurses Association.

APRN Joint Dialogue Group Report. (2008). *Consensus model for APRN regulation: Licensure, accreditation, certification & education.* Retrieved January 14, 2010, from http://www.aacn.nche.edu/education/pdf/APRNReport.pdf

Berlin, L. E., & Sechrist, K. R. (2002). The shortage of doctorally prepared nursing faculty: A dire situation. *Nursing Outlook, 50*(2), 50–56.

Bolton, L. B., Aydin, C. E., Donaldson, N., Brown, D. S., Nelson, M., & Harms, D. (2003). Nurse staffing and patient perceptions of nursing care. *Journal of Nursing Administration, 33*(11), 607–614.

Buerhaus, P., Donelan, K., DesRoches, C., & Hess, R. (2009). Still making progress to improve the hospital workplace environment? Results from the 2008 national survey of registered nurses. *Nursing Economics, 27*(5), 289–301.

Buerhaus, P. (2009a). Can nursing profession win the game. *Nursing Economics, 27*(4), 247–250.

Buerhaus, P. (2009b, March/April). Avoiding mandatory hospital nurse staffing ratios: An economic commentary. *Nursing Outlook, 57,* 107–112.

Buerhaus, P., Staiger, D., & Auerbach, D. (2003). Is the current shortage of hospital nurses ending? Emerging trends in employment and earnings of registered nurses. *Health Affairs, 22*(6), 191–198.

Buerhaus, P., Staiger, D. O., & Auerbach, D. (2008). *The future of the nursing workforce.* Boston: Jones and Bartlett.

Bureau of Labor Statistics, U.S. Department of Labor. *Occupational outlook handbook, 2006–2007 edition, registered nurses.* Retrieved April 18, 2009, from www.bls.gov/oco/oco83.htm

Bureau of Labor Statistics, U.S. Department of Labor. *Occupational outlook handbook, 2004–2005 edition, licensed practical and licensed vocational nurses.* Retrieved April 18, 2009, from http://www.bls.gov/oco/ocos102.htm

Buresh, P., & Gordon, S. (2006). *Find from silence to voice.* New York: Cornell University Press.

Centers for Medicare and Medicaid Services. (2006). Medicare Program; Hospital Outpatient Prospective Payment System and CY 2007 Payment Rates; CY 2007 Update to the Ambulatory Surgical Center Covered Procedures List; Medicare Administrative Contractors; and Reporting Hospital Quality Data for FY 2008 Inpatient Prospective Payment System Annual Payment Update Program—HCAHPS Survey, SCIP, and Mortality. *Federal Register, 71*(226), 67960–68401.

Charney, W., Zimmerman, K., & Walara, E. (1991). The lifting team: A design method to reduce lost time back injury in nursing. *AAOHN Journal, 39*(5), 231–234.

Dohm, A., & Shniper, L. (2007). *Occupational employment projections to 2016.* Washington, DC: U.S. Department of Labor, Bureau of Labor Statistics.

Ehrenreich, J. H. (2002). *A guide for humanitarian, health care, and human rights workers.* New York: State University of New York.

Friese, C., Aiken, L. H. (2008). Failure to rescue in the surgical oncology population. *Oncology Nursing Forum, 35*(5), 779–785.

Fulton, J. S., & Baldwin, K. (2004, January/February). An annotated bibliography reflecting CNS practice and outcomes. *Clinical Nurse Specialist, 18*(1), 21–39.

Harmer, B., & Henderson, V. (1939). *Textbook of the principles and practice of nursing 1939* (4th ed.). New York: Macmillan.

Harvard School of Public Health. (2005). *Americans' view of nursing care.* Retrieved July 30, 2009, from http://www.rwjf.org/files/publications/other/Research_Highlight_2_0604.pdf

Hassmiller, S. (2009). *Six questions on health reform with Susan Hassmiller, The Robert Wood Johnson Foundation.* Retrieved May 13, 2009, from http://www.rwjf.org/pr/product.jsp?id=41749

Health Resources and Services Administration (HRSA). Bureau of Health Professions. National Center for Health Workforce Analysis. (2004). *Projected supply, demand, and shortages of registered nurses: 2000–2020.* Retrieved April 20, 2009, from http://www.ahcancal.org/research_data/staffing/Documents/Registered_Nurse_Supply_Demand.pdf

Henderson, V. (1960). *Basic principles of nursing care.* Geneva: International Council of Nurses.

Institute of Medicine. (2003). *Keeping patients safe: transforming the work environment of nurses.* Washington, DC: National Academies Press.

Lamm, R. D. (1996). The coming dislocation in the health professions. *Healthcare Forum Journal, 39*(1), 58–62.

Larrabee, J. H., Ostrow, C. L., Withrow, M. L., Janney, M. A., Hobbs, Jr., G. R., & Burantet, C. (2004). Predictors of patient satisfaction with inpatient hospital nursing care. *Research in Nursing and Health, 27*(4), 254–268.

Mark, B., Harless, D., & Spetz, J. (2009). California's minimum-nurse-staffing legislation and nurses' wages. *Health Affairs, 28*(2), (Web exclusive, February 10, 2009), W326–W334.

McGillis Hall, L., Doran, D., Baker, G.R., Pink, G. H., Sidani, S., O'Brien-Pallas, L., & Donner, G. J. (2003). Nurse staffing models as predictors of patient outcomes. *Medical Care, 41*(9), 1096–1109.

Mee, C. (2006). Nursing 2006 salary survey. *Nursing, 36*(10), 46–51.

Moses, E. B. (Ed.). (1992). *The registered nurse population: Findings from the national sample survey of registered nurses.* Washington, DC: U.S. Department of Health and Human Services, U.S. Public Health Service, Division of Nursing.

National Advisory Council on Nurse Education and Practice. (2008). *Meeting the challenges facing the nurse workforce in a changing health care environment of the new millennium. The sixth annual report to the Secretary of the Department of Health and Human Services and the US Congress.* Retrieved March 11, 2009, from ftp://ftp.hrsa.gov/bhpr/nursing/sixth.pdf

National Advisory Council on Nursing Education and Practice. (1996). *First report to the Secretary of the Department of Health and Human Services on the basic registered nurses workforce.* Rockville, MD: U.S. Department of Health and Human Services (DHHS), HRSA, Bureau of Health Professions, Division of Nursing; November 2001. Retrieved March 11, 2009, from bhpr.hrsa.gov/nursing/nacnep/firstreport.htm

National Council of State Boards of Nursing. (2009). Nursing initiatives. Retrieved July 30, 2009, from https://www.ncsbn.org/1623.htm

National League for Nursing. (2006). *Nursing data review, academic year 2004–2005, baccalaureate, associate degree, and diploma programs.* New York: Author.

National League of Nursing. (2007) *Annual survey of schools of nursing, academic year 2006–2007: Executive summary.* Retrieved July 30, 2009, from http://www.nln.org/research/slides/exec_summary.htm

Naylor, M. D., Brooten, D., Jones, R., Lavizzo-Mourey, R., Mezey, M., & Pauly, M. (1994). Comprehensive discharge planning for the hospitalized elderly: A randomized clinical trial. *Annals of Internal Medicine, 120*(12), 999–1006.

Naylor, M. D., Brooten, D., Campbell, R., Jacobsen, B., Mezey, M., Pauly, M., & Schwartz, J. S. (1999). Comprehensive discharge planning and home follow-up of hospitalized elders: A randomized controlled trial. *Journal of the American Medical Association, 28*(7), 613–620.

Naylor, M. D., Brooten, D. A., Campbell, R. L., Maislin, G., McCauley, K. M., & Schwartz, J. S. (2004). Transitional care of older adults hospitalized with heart failure: A randomized clinical trial. *Journal of the American Geriatrics Society, 52*(5), 675–684.

Needleman, J., Buerhaus, P., Mattke, S., Stewart, M., & Zelevinsky, K. (2002). Nurse-staffing levels and the quality of care in hospitals. *New England Journal of Medicine, 346*(22), 1715–1722.

Nelson, A., & Baptiste, A. (September 30, 2004). Evidence-based practices for safe patient handling and movement. *Online Journal of Issues in Nursing. 9*(3). Retrieved March 11, 2009, from www.nursingworld.org/MainMenuCategories/ANAMarketplace/ANAPeriodicals/OJIN/TableofContents/Volume92004/No3Sept04/EvidenceBasedPractices.aspx

Nightingale, F. (1860). *Notes on nursing: What it is and what it is not.* New York: Dover Publications.

Owen, B. (1989). The magnitude of low-back problems in nursing. *Western Journal of Nursing Research, 11,* 234–242.

Peplau, H. E. (1992). *Interpersonal relations in nursing.* New York: Springer.

Robert Wood Johnson Foundation. (2006). *Wisdom at work.* Retrieved July 30, 2009, from http://www.rwjf.org/files/publications/other/wisdomatwork.pdf

Robert Wood Johnson Foundation. (2009, March). *Charting nursing's future: Nursing's prescription for a reformed health system.* Princeton, NJ: Robert Wood Johnson Foundation.

Seago, J. A., Williamson, A., & Atwood, C. (2006). Longitudinal analyses of nurse staffing and patient outcomes: more about failure to rescue. *Journal of Nursing Administration, 36*(1), 13–21.

Sovie, M. D., & Jawad, A. F. (2001). Hospital restructuring and its impact on outcomes: Nursing staff regulations are premature. *Journal of Nursing Administration, 31*(12), 588–600.

Spross, J., Hamric, A., Hall, G., Minarik, P., Sparacino, P., & Stanley, J. (2004, December). *Working statement comparing the clinical nurse leader and clinical nurse specialist roles: Similarities, differences and complementarities.* Washington, DC: American Association of Colleges of Nursing.

Stevens, R. (1989). *In sickness and in wealth: American hospitals in the twentieth century* (p. 17). New York: Basic Books.

Tervo-Heikkinen, T., Kvist, T., Partanen, P., Vehviläinen-Julkunen, K., & Aalto, P. (2008). Patient satisfaction as a positive nursing outcome. *Journal of Nursing Care Quality, 23*(1), 58–65.

U.S. Bureau of Labor Statistics. (2007, May). *Occupational employment and wages for 2006.* Retrieved May 13, 2009, from http://stats.bls.gov/oco/ocos083.htm

U.S. Department of Health and Human Services. Health Resources and Services Administration. (2005, March). *The registered nurse population. National sample survey of registered nurses.* Rockville, MD: Author.

U.S. Department of Health and Human Services. Health Resources and Services Administration. (2004). *Registered nurses in the U.S. The registered nurse population: Findings from the national sample survey of registered nurses.* Retrieved from http://bhpr.hrsa.gov/healthworkforce/reports/nursing/samplesurvey00/chapter2.htm

U.S. Department of Labor. Bureau of Labor Statistics. (2005). *Occupational employment and wages.* Retrieved May 2005, from http://www.bls.gov

U.S. Department of Labor. Bureau of Labor Statistics. (2006). *Occupational employment and wages.* Retrieved June 2009, from http://www.bls.gov

U.S. Department of Labor, Occupational Safety and Health Administration. (2002). *Ergonomics guidelines for nursing homes.* Retrieved July 22, 2009, from http://www.osha.gov/ergonomics/guidelines/nursing%20home/final_nh_guidelines.html

Vahey, D. C., Aiken, L. H., Sloane, D. M., Clarke, S. P., & Vargas, D. (2004). Nurse burnout and patient satisfaction. *Medical Care, 42*(2 Suppl), II57–II66.

Zachary, G. (2001, May 24). Labor movement: Shortage of nurses hits hardest where they are needed the most. *The Wall Street Journal*, pp. A1, A12.

CASE STUDY

Retaining the Wisdom of Aging Nurse Faculty: Shaping Policy to Meet Workforce Needs

Nancy L. Falk

The United States healthcare system faces multiple human resource challenges that impact access to quality care. Without question, nurse and nurse faculty shortages are among the greatest trials faced by the healthcare system and care recipients today. By 2016, over 1 million new and replacement nurses will be essential to care for an aging population (Dohm & Shniper, 2007).

The nursing shortage has received substantial attention in recent years, and recruitment efforts have revitalized attraction of students to the nursing profession (Buerhaus et al., 2009). This renewed interest has provided a boost to staffing levels; nevertheless, many nursing programs are unable to enroll the desired number of students because of a shortage of nurse educators in colleges and universities nationwide. In 2006–2007 alone, 30,709 qualified applications were denied admission to nursing programs largely because of the nurse faculty shortage (Fang et al., 2008a).

The shortage of faculty has two dimensions. The first concerns the recruitment and retention of highly educated faculty into nursing programs. There are many reasons why this is proving difficult, not least of which concerns pay (Dohm & Shniper, 2007). The problem that will be addressed in this case is the aging of the current faculty. Their impending retirements have the potential to further exasperate the problem if ways are not found to retain their wisdom. As will be pointed out, the faculty shortages present schools of nursing with new opportunities.

Nurse Faculty Shortage: A Convergence of Demographic, Economic, and Human Resource Factors

The advancing age of the nurse faculty workforce is a key factor in the educator shortage. The average faculty member in nursing education is over 50 years of age (Fang et al., 2008b), and nursing faculty retire on average at around 62.5 years of age (Berlin & Sechrist, 2002). By 2019, 75% of nursing faculty will be eligible for retirement (National League for Nursing, 2005).

Although eligible for retirement, aging faculty may be reticent to leave the workforce due to the demographics and economics of the situation. With the average lifespan in the United States increasing (Arias, 2007), the amount of time between retirement and end of life increases. Nursing faculty, retirees, and their families face a host of challenges typical of the later stages of a career, namely unanticipated expenses related to child care, college education, health, and older care responsibilities. In addition, there may be a potential shortfall in retirement savings due to the economic downturn in 2008, retiree benefit cuts by employers such as the shifting from defined benefit to defined contribution pension plans (McDonnell, 2008), which has the potential to impact educators and their spouses negatively. Remaining in the workforce on a part-time or full-time basis is an important option to these persons, and nursing programs must gain a greater understanding of the retirement timeline of aging faculty members and identify new and creative solutions to retain aging faculty should they desire to continue working on a part-time or full-time basis.

Retaining the Wisdom of Aging Nurse Faculty

Aging nurse faculty members provide essential services and are highly valued by nursing education programs nationwide. They serve in all capacities and often in leadership positions. These faculty can be found as deans and administrators, teachers, student advisors, researchers, healthcare providers, leaders, mentors, role models, consultants, and committee leaders and members and in many different community service roles (Falk, 2008). Aging faculty members offer a wealth of experience, in addition to institutional, industry, and job-related knowledge. In his extensive work on lost knowledge, Delong (2004) affirms the critical nature of retaining such knowledge and expertise within organizations.

The retirement of nursing faculty can cause two critical problems for nursing schools. In these economic times, vital positions are at risk of remaining vacant. Educator positions might remain open as institutions compete for the limited number of available replacement faculty. Even if filled, the retirement of faculty means the loss of critical program knowledge. Individuals with less knowledge about the institution, its culture, and students might occupy open faculty positions.

Public Policy and Aging Nurse Faculty

Public policy, as instituted by federal, state, and local legislation, regulations, and court rulings, directly affects our choice to retire or continue working. For instance, legislative changes were made to the Age Discrimination in Employment Act in 1986 to forbid mandatory retirement based on age for employees across most sectors and jobs (National Research Council, 1991). The changes included exemptions for employees 70 years of age and older with unlimited tenure contracts within higher education (National Research Council, 1991). In 1994, the mandatory retirement provisions were eliminated within higher education. This policy change opened the door for faculty members to extend their academic careers.

Still other public and social policy measures impact human resource actions and employee retirement decisions. It is uncertain how changes to Medicare might impact retirement decisions. Many aging and older workers are covered by employment-based health insurance plans while Medicare serves as a secondary payer. Changes to Medicare regulations could result in increased employer healthcare costs, thereby discouraging the employment and retention of older workers (Chaikind, 2008). Inversely, changes could encourage workers to stay in their positions if their employer-based insurance offers a richer package of services or until such time as they are eligible for Medicare. Human resources must ensure that current healthcare benefits support continued employment for this group of aging workers.

Legislative and public policy efforts also have the potential to determine the number of nurse educators available to meet workforce needs. From 2007 to 2008, for instance, in the 110th United States Congress, the American Association of Colleges of Nursing supported close to 20 federal legislative efforts aimed at providing support and funding for nursing education nationwide (American Association of Colleges of Nursing, 2008a). Similar legislative efforts are being made at the state level (American Association of Colleges of Nursing, 2008b). As the nursing education community continues to face staffing challenges, it is in the best interest of society to understand policy and make changes that will increase the number of nurse educators available to academia. When possible, policies must be modified to retain aging faculty and the wisdom they bring.

Organizational Policy: A Collaborative Effort

Organizational policy is a key consideration for institutions seeking to support continued employment of aging nurse faculty. Organizational policies must be developed and implemented in light of local, state, and national public and social policy. Leaders of administrative and academic units must make it their aim to understand public policy changes and adjust organizational policies accordingly.

Formal organizational policies have a direct bearing on the opportunity for continued employment of aging nurse faculty. Those academic institutions desiring to have a positive influence on organizational culture and norms must foster attitudes, perceptions, experiences, and policies that would support a multigenerational nurse educator workforce. Sometimes perceptions of aging and older workers will stand in the way of their gainful employment. Aging workers are perceived by some as unskilled, inflexible, less productive, slower in movement and cognitive ability, more expensive to employ, and less willing or able to learn new skills—particularly where new technology and teaching modes are concerned. Conversely, aging workers are also viewed as wise, committed, dependable, conscientious, and possessing a strong work ethic. In some instances, perceptions are reality. In other situations, perceptions are based on myths and misconceptions often attributed to older individuals and our aging population. In all circumstances, efforts must be made to avoid human resource decision making based on myths and misconceptions, particularly as we strive to maintain and enhance the well-being of nursing programs. Age stereotyping and discrimination serve as barriers to employment and must be eliminated (Hedge, 2008). In order to eliminate such barriers, human resource programs should incorporate guidelines into their handbooks and educational materials that would facilitate an understanding of the differences between generations within the workforce (Cook-Ross Inc., 2004).

Carefully crafted human resource strategies and planning will enhance and support employability of aging nurse faculty members. Human resources benefits and pay guidelines should be analyzed and modified to be consistent with workforce demands and needs. Financial incentives can provide an opportunity for continued employment of those individuals who bring unique and highly valued skills to the workforce. Such investments will support retention of aging faculty who may be difficult to replace.

It is also important that human resources departments have open discussions about retirement and transition planning that will encourage faculty and nursing programs to work collaboratively in planning for retirement. Retirement workshops must go beyond a mere discussion of pension options and traditional retirement. Aging sandwich generation caregivers struggle to balance work and family responsibilities. Research shows that aging workers benefit from eldercare support programs (Centers for Medicare and Medicaid Services, 2004) and workshops on flexible work options strengthen collaborative efforts as faculty transition to retirement.

Simultaneously, colleges and universities should highlight the importance of retaining aging workers and encourage valued faculty to stay current and stay employed within academic nursing programs. This will require that nursing programs institute initiatives—including managerial and supervisory training—that support lifelong learning as critical to the success of nursing programs nationwide. Nurse educators need to stay up to date on clinical skills, technology, and teaching modalities. By supporting a philosophy of lifelong learning, programs will ensure that faculty skills and abilities are up to date and beneficial to students and nursing programs alike.

Formal policies within nursing programs and colleges and universities must be developed and redesigned to promote a multigenerational approach to workforce and human resources challenges. Aging workers tend to seek flexibility (Pitt-Catsouphes et al., 2007) through phased retirement (Brown, 2005; Chen & Scott, 2006), bridge jobs (Cahill et al., 2006), and other creative options that meet both employer and aging worker needs. Alternative work options and flexible scheduling will make it possible for deans and administrators to capitalize on faculty strengths and match the wisdom and skills of aging faculty members to nursing program needs. In some instances, academic institutions offer formal phased retirement or other flexible programs. Informal arrangements have been made between aging faculty and administrators who recognize the need for nursing education to offer opportunities so that valued aging nurse faculty might be retained. New work-design and job role solutions will serve to address the current demographic changes affecting academic programs. Creative options include, but are not limited to, in-home technical support to assist faculty with the nuts and bolts of teaching online (sometimes from their place of retirement), computer hardware and software support to facilitate part-time online teaching during retirement transitions and beyond, and flexible work options. Research and other responsibilities, for example, are sometimes phased out so that faculty can continue in other valuable roles such as teaching. Such flexible options are of interest to a growing number of workers but are not as widespread as desired (Georgetown University Law Center: Workplace Flexibility 2010, 2006).

Last, nursing programs have the opportunity to be at the forefront of helping aging employees remain in the workforce even while facing significant health challenges. To the extent possible, nursing programs can foster healthy aging. This can be accomplished by broadening the base of knowledge and understanding on well-being and safety in the nursing program environment. Healthy ergonomic solutions are particularly germane to the well-being of aging workers (Boyce, 2008). Increasingly, organizations are offering workspace solutions and software options that support continued employment of aging faculty. By way of example, voice recognition software is a helpful tool that allows aging workers with arthritic conditions to continue working by reducing the stress and strain on joints due to excessive keyboarding. Today, employers adapt working environments by providing wheelchair accessible lecterns for faculty members with mobility challenges.

Additional Policy Considerations for Deans, Administrators, and Faculty

Deans, administrators, and faculty can actively influence policy and political agendas at the federal, state, and local levels by removing barriers to extending the academic working life of aging nurse faculty. To enhance their effectiveness, nursing education leaders must keep abreast of public policy debates pertaining to the tax implications of continued employment and/or retirement, potential social security modifications, changes in pension plans and pension benefits, and elimination of barriers to continued employment.

Nursing education leaders should seek to raise awareness among university presidents and leaders regarding the importance of nursing as a political priority. They should identify and cultivate high-level nursing advocates within academic institutions and health systems. In support of these efforts, nursing program data collection efforts should be developed and implemented to aid understanding and inform quality-oriented human resource decision making.

Additionally, nursing education leaders should seek to work together with home state and national associations to present a collaborative face for nursing education. Together, the educational and practice communities should seek fiscal appropriations that help to ensure adequate staffing and hiring, thereby reducing overall tensions and pressures on faculty and staff.

Nursing programs and the nursing education community can present a strong, unified voice to influence public policy. Such an approach will yield positive outcomes in support of nursing education in general and retaining the wisdom of aging nurse faculty in particular.

Web Resources

AARP SmartBrief—Twice-monthly e-mail news briefing for employers about the changing workforce: http://www.smartbrief.com/aarp/index.jsp

American Association of Colleges of Nursing—Government Affairs: http://www.aacn.nche.edu/Government/about.htm

KaiserEdu.org—Issue Module: Addressing the Nursing Shortage: http://www.kaiseredu.org/topics_im.asp?imID=1&parentID=61&id=138

National Advisory Council on Nursing Education and Practice: www.bhpr.hrsa.gov/nursing/nacnep.htm

National League for Nursing, Nursing Shortage Information: http://www.nln.org/aboutnln/shortage_info.htm

Robert Wood Johnson Foundation, Wisdom at Work: The Importance of the Older and Experienced Nurse in the Workplace: http://www.rwjf.org/pr/product.jsp?id=15867

U.S. Government Accountability Office, Highlights of GAO Forum: Engaging and Retaining Older Workers: http://www.gao.gov/products/GAO-07-438SP

References

American Association of Colleges of Nursing. (2008a). *AACN supported legislation in the 110th Congress.* Retrieved October 29, 2008, from http://www.aacn.nche.edu/Government/SupportedLegislation.htm

American Association of Colleges of Nursing. (2008b). *State nursing workforce reports.* Retrieved October 29, 2008, from http://www.aacn.nche.edu/media/NsgWrkFrcReps.htm

American Association of Colleges of Nursing. (2009). *Percentage change in enrollments in entry-level baccalaureate nursing programs: 1994–2009.* Retrieved February 7, 2010, from http://www.aacn.nche.edu/Media/pdf/EnrollChanges.pdf

Arias, E. (2007). *United States life tables, 2004.* Atlanta, GA: Centers for Disease Control and Prevention.

Berlin, L. E., & Sechrist, K. R. (2002). The shortage of doctorally prepared nursing faculty: A dire situation. *Nursing Outlook, 50*(2), 50–56.

Boyce, R. W. (2008). An ergonomic approach to the aging workforce utilizing this valuable resource to best advantage by integrating ergonomics, health promotion and employee assistance programs. *Journal of Workplace Behavioral Health, 23*(1/2), 179–199.

Brown, S. K. (2005). *Attitudes of individuals 50 and older toward phased retirement.* Washington, DC: AARP.

Buerhaus, P. I., Staiger, D., & Auerbach, D. I. (2009). *The future of the nursing workforce in the United States: Data, trends, and implications.* Sudbury, MA: Jones and Bartlett Publishers.

Cahill, K. E., Giandrea, M. D., & Quinn, J. F. (2006). Retirement patterns from career employment. *The Gerontologist, 46*(4), 514.

Centers for Medicare and Medicaid Services. (2004). *When employees become caregivers* (No. CMS-11035). Washington, DC: Author.

Chaikind, H. (2008). *Medicare secondary payer: Coordination of benefits (report for Congress).* Washington, DC: Congressional Research Service.

Chen, Y.-P., & Scott, J. C. (2006). *Phased retirement: Who opts for it and toward what end?* Washington, DC: AARP Public Policy Institute.

Cook-Ross Inc. (2004). *Managing a multigenerational workforce: The diversity manager's toolkit.* Silver Spring, MD: Author.

Delong, D. (2004). *Lost knowledge: Confronting the threat of an aging workforce.* New York: Oxford University Press.

Dohm, A., & Shniper, L. (2007). *Occupational employment projections to 2016.* Washington, DC: U.S. Department of Labor, Bureau of Labor Statistics.

Falk, N. L. (2008). *Retaining the wisdom: Deans' reflections on extending the academic working life of aging nurse faculty.* Unpublished Dissertation, George Mason University, Fairfax, VA.

Fang, D., Htut, A., & Bednash, G. D. (2008a). *2007–2008 enrollment and graduations in baccalaureate and graduate programs in nursing.* Washington, DC: American Association of Colleges of Nursing.

Fang, D., Htut, A., & Bednash, G. D. (2008b). *2007–2008 salaries of instructional and administrative nursing faculty in baccalaureate and graduate programs in nursing.* Washington, DC: American Association of Colleges of Nursing.

Georgetown University Law Center. (2006). *Flexible work arrangements: The overview memo* (pp. 1–9). Washington, DC: Author.

Hedge, J. W. (2008). Strategic human resource management and the older worker. *Journal of Workplace Behavioral Health, 23*(1/2), 109–123.

McDonnell, K. (2008). *Retirement annuity and employment-based pension income, among individuals age 50 and over* (Vol. 29, pp. 2–7). Washington, DC: Employee Benefit Research Institute.

National Council of State Boards of Nursing. (2010). *Guiding principles.* Retrieved February 8, 2010, from https://www.ncsbn.org/1325.htm

National League for Nursing. (2005). Position statement: Transforming nursing education. *Nursing Education Perspectives, 26,* 195–197.

National Research Council. (1991). *Ending mandatory retirement for tenured faculty: The consequences for higher education* (report to the U.S. Equal Employment Opportunity Commission, No. 0309044987). Washington, DC: National Academies Press.

Pitt-Catsouphes, M., Smyer, M., Matz-Costa, C., & Kane, K. (2007). *The national study report: Phase II of the National Study of Business Strategy and Workforce Development.* Boston: The Center on Aging & Work/Workplace Flexibility at Boston College.

Chapter 5

Allied and Other Health Professions

Donna M. Nickitas

OVERVIEW

During the twenty-first century, the aging of the population, the shifting nature of diseases, new and advanced technology, the driving need for healthcare reform, and economic factors have significantly changed the demand for care services provided by different types of allied and other health personnel (McLaughlin, 1994). This demand has made it necessary to modify the roles and scope of practice of many healthcare workers to keep pace with changing service patterns. Unfortunately, there is no single body in the United States responsible for making data-based demand/supply projections and policy decisions; therefore, at the moment, these important issues are to be addressed, if only in piecemeal, by a number of interested bodies.

Federal and state governments, educational institutions, professional organizations, insurers, and provider institutions have separate and often conflicting interests in the healthcare workforce education and training, regulation, financing, entry-level preparation, and scope of practice. The various levels at which policy decisions are made and the disparate interests that influence those decisions present major barriers to ensuring an efficient and rational healthcare workforce in the United States. It is precisely these policies and the lack of a coordinated approach that supported the production of an enormous number of health professionals to serve the healthcare system of the late twentieth century. This chapter will review the fragmentation of the allied and other health professional workforce and some policy options available to ensure better coordination and ultimately better care.

OBJECTIVES

- To describe the factors driving the demand for allied and other health professionals
- To identify the diverse types of health services professionals and their training, practice requirements, and practice settings
- To understand the role of allied and other health providers in healthcare delivery

KEY TERMS

- ❑ Allied health professional
- ❑ Alternative medicine practitioners
- ❑ Certification
- ❑ Licensure
- ❑ Non-physician clinicians
- ❑ Support services personnel
- ❑ Technologist and technician
- ❑ Therapeutic science practitioners
- ❑ Work force projection

The Healthcare Labor Force

This nation is confronting an ever rising demand for health services nationally. Two of the most critical factors are an aging population and advances in the treatment of acute and life-threatening conditions. Both result in an increasing survival of people with chronic illness or disabilities. In addition, there are a growing number of patients with deteriorating mental capacities, cardiac conditions, cancer, stroke, head and spinal cord injuries, neonatal deficits, and congenital disorders. These also significantly increase the demand for services and for workers who provide and support prolonged medical treatment, rehabilitation, and nursing home or custodial care. These factors will drive the demand for health services; however, it is often difficult to predict healthcare employment accurately because many factors influence the demand for and use of services (e.g., the nation's economy, reimbursement policies, geographic variation in the organization of health services, and the availability of healthcare workers). In this chapter, we will consider the demand for support personnel who are referred to as allied and other health professionals and advance a more detailed explanation of the occupations that make up this all important segment of the healthcare labor force.

The Demand for Healthcare Workers

At this time, health care is the fastest growing employment sector in the United States. In 2008, health care provided 14.3 million jobs for wage and salary workers, and it will continue to generate 3.2 million new wage and salary jobs between 2008 and 2018, more than any other industry, largely in response to rapid growth in the elderly population (Bureau of Labor Statistics, 2010a). Between 1999 and 2009, healthcare jobs in the United States grew by more than 27%, including a 33% increase in ambulatory care jobs. Despite the economic downturn and subsequent general job loss in the last two years, healthcare employment continues to grow, adding one million jobs between 2006 and 2009 (Bureau of Labor Statistics, 2010a). Between 2006 and 2016, more than half of the top 30 occupations projected to grow the fastest in the U.S. are health occupations. Seventeen of the 30 occupations projected to grow the fastest between 2006 and 2016 are health occupations.

The 14 million healthcare workers are employed in over 200 occupations and professions. One in every 10 jobs in the United States is projected to be in the health sector by 2016. Between 2006 and 2016, nearly 5.5 million health workers will be needed to fill new jobs and to replace workers who leave their jobs across all employment sectors. It is important to understand the reasons for this job growth, where it will occur, and what types of jobs will be involved.

Many factors influence the increase in jobs in the health sector and the location of these jobs. These include population growth; the increasing percentage of older adults in the population who require more ambulatory and inpatient services; the settings and types of health services provided; and healthcare utilization patterns. The most influential factor will be the increase in older adults in proportion of the population as a result of increased life expectancy. This older age group will grow faster than the total population between 2008 and 2018 and will have a higher incidence of injury and illness and often take longer to heal (2010a). Therefore, this will create an increase for health care, especially in employment settings specializing in gerontology care for the elderly. Additionally, employment in home health care and nursing and residential care will increase as advances in medical technology improve the survival rate for severely ill and injured patients, but create a need for extensive therapy and nursing care.

As a result, the growth in the healthcare labor force will take place in the areas of outpatient services and home health care. At the present time, about 40% of healthcare professionals are employed in hospitals; another 21% are in nursing and residential care facilities; and 16% are in offices of physicians (Bureau of Labor Statistics, 2010a). This will not be the case for long. Employment in health practitioners' offices is expected to grow by slightly more than 24% between 2006 and 2016. This translates into more than 850,000 new jobs, or more than one third of the total projected growth in health sector employment (Bureau of Labor Statistics, 2007). Between 2008 and 2018, total employment of home health aides is projected to increase by 50%, medical assistants by 34%, physical therapist assistants by 33%, and physician assistants by 39% (Bureau of Labor Statistics, 2010a, 2010b).

Allied and Other Health Professionals

In the early part of the twentieth century, the healthcare provider workforce consisted of physicians, nurses, pharmacists, and optometrists. There was minimal support staff to support these practitioners as healthcare provision was a singular venture. As knowledge in health sciences expanded, technology began to play a major role in the diagnosis and treatment of illness. The growth in technology and specialized interventions subsequently placed greater demands on the time physicians and nurses spent with their patients. With the standardization of procedures, it became possible to train other professionals who could serve as adjuncts to, or as substitutes for, physicians and nurses. These professionals received specialized training, and their clinical interventions were meant to complement the work of physicians and nurses. They are referred to as allied health professionals. In addition, the management of these personnel required a more complex organizational infrastructure.

As the industry continues to change, making use of new technology, expanding in some sectors and contracting in others, additional health personnel will appear. The personnel of the future will be required to possess even more specialized knowledge and more sophisticated skills. The increased specialization of the health workforce is a double-edged sword. On one hand, specialization increases our capacity to provide highly complex services. On the other hand, specialization reduces the flexibility of providers to develop more efficient staffing patterns. It may also be the case that specialization among the workforce will increase personnel costs as additional employees are required to perform specific tasks. But specialization also makes the substitution of lower paid, less skilled workers which should result in lower costs.

The myriad health professional jobs need to be more fully explained in order to appreciate the opportunities and constraints on developing policies in this area that will improve quality and control costs. For the purposes of this chapter, the occupations that are considered allied and other health professionals will be broken into four groups. There are allied health professionals, which include technologists/technicians, and therapists including behavioral therapists. In addition, there are support services personnel. These persons do not have direct patient contact but support the efforts of the allied health workers. The third major group is clinicians who are sometimes referred to as non-physician clinicians. In most cases, these practitioners have the authority to treat patients independent of physician orders. Last, we will consider the growing field of alternative medicine.

Credentialing and Regulating Health Professionals

Government regulation of the health professions is necessary to protect the public from incompetent and unethical practitioners. Because each state assumes and exercises most of that responsibility for itself, how healthcare professions are regulated and the manner in which regulation is carried out vary from state to state. About 50 health professions are regulated throughout the United States. Regulatory restrictions limit healthcare service agencies in how they may use personnel and limit their ability to be innovative or change ways to provide patient care. Similarly, regulatory restrictions influence educational programs to focus curricula on what has been prescribed by regulatory boards and their related accrediting bodies, even when those practice patterns have been replaced by more advanced procedures. Many states have taken steps to revise their credentialing systems to provide greater flexibility and responsiveness to fast-changing healthcare technology (Collier, 2008).

The healthcare professions have been regulated by one of three procedures: state licensure, state or national certification, or state or national registration. In licensure, the state law defines the scope of practice to be regulated and the educational and testing requirements that must be met to engage in that practice. Licensure, the most restrictive of the three types of regulation, is intended to restrict entry or practice in certain occupations and to prevent the use of professional titles by those without predetermined qualifications. Most licensure boards are composed primarily of practitioners whose concern is for setting standards and assessing competence for initial entrance into the field. Except by requiring attendance at continuing education courses, licensure boards have done very little about ensuring continuing competence, dealing with impaired practitioners, or disciplining wayward members of their professions; however, they do have the power to censure, warn members, or even revoke licenses.

Certification is the regulating process under which a state or voluntary professional organization, such as a national board, attests to the educational achievements and performance abilities of persons in a healthcare field of practice. When applied to such fields as psychology and social work, certification does not make it illegal for unqualified individuals to engage in activities within the scope of practice in those fields as long as they do not claim or use the titles of certified psychologist or social worker.

Certification allows the public, employers, and third-party payers to determine which practitioners are appropriately qualified in their specialty or occupation.

Unlike licensure, certification has no legal basis for preventing an impaired or professionally delinquent individual from practicing. It is a weakness of certification that it is left to third-party payers or employers to insist on only certified practitioners.

Registration began as a mechanism to facilitate contacts and relationships among members of a profession and potential employers or the public. It is the least rigorous of regulatory processes, ranging from simple listings or registries of persons offering a service, such as private duty nurses, to national registration programs of professional or occupational groups that require educational and testing qualifications. Collier (2008) notes that "regulation of the health system consists of both governmental and voluntary processes. While healthcare reimbursement is heavily influenced by governmental action, the regulation of health personnel, even for licensure, is essentially a quasi-voluntary process controlled by the professions being regulated" (p. 16).

Career Advancement in Allied Health

The entry-level degree for practice in the allied health fields ranges from the certificate or associate's degree in some disciplines to the bachelor's degree in others and the master's or doctoral degree in still others. Two-year programs that offer associate's degrees or certificates produce allied health personnel who, for the most part, perform under the supervision of those with more advanced training. Because the allied health fields offer so diverse an array of programs, the opportunity for career advancement through educational "laddering" is probably without equal.

It is commonplace for graduates of allied health programs to practice for a period of time and then advance their careers by entering higher level programs and achieving more advanced degrees. For example, it is not unusual for occupational therapists or physical therapists with bachelor's degrees to pursue master's degrees and doctorates in related fields and then become researchers, university faculty, and more advanced clinical practitioners. Sultz (1987) suggests that allied health practitioners are uniquely positioned to achieve career goals at the highest level of their competence.

Allied Health Professionals

An allied health professional is someone who has received a certificate; an associate's, bachelor's, or master's degree; doctoral level preparation; or postbaccalaureate training in a science related to health care and has responsibility for the delivery of health or related services. These services may include those associated with the identification, evaluation, and prevention of diseases and disorders, dietary and nutritional services, rehabilitation, or health system management. Allied health professionals constitute approximately 60% of the U.S. healthcare workforce. Allied health professionals can be divided into two broad categories: technicians and technologists and therapists who are formally referred to as therapeutic science practitioners.

Educational requirements for allied health professionals range from certificates gained in postsecondary educational programs to postgraduate degrees for some professions. Typically, technicians and assistants receive less than 2 years of postsecondary education and are trained to perform procedures. Assistants and technicians require supervision from therapists or technologists to ensure that care plan evaluation occurs as part of the treatment process. This group includes physical therapy assistants, certified occupational therapy assistants, medical laboratory technicians, radiologic technicians, and respiratory therapy technicians. Technologists and therapists receive more advanced training. They learn how to evaluate patients, diagnose problems, and develop treatment plans. They must also have the training to evaluate the appropriateness and the potential side effects of therapy treatments. Education at the technologist or therapist level includes skill development in teaching procedural skills to technicians.

Certain healthcare workers are not required to be licensed, and they usually learn their skills on the job; however, their roles are generally limited to assisting other professionals in the provision of services. Examples include dietetic assistants, who assist dietitians or dietetic technicians in the provision of nutritional care; electroencephalogram technologists or technicians, who operate electroencephalographs; electrocardiogram technicians, who operate electrocardiographs; paraoptometrics, including optometric technicians and assistants, who perform basic tasks related to vision care; health educators, who provide individuals and groups with facts on health, illness, and prevention to improve individual and community health behaviors; psychiatric/mental health technicians, who provide care to patients with mental illness or developmental disabilities; and sanitarians, who collect samples for laboratory analysis and inspect facilities for compliance with public health laws and regulations. Increasingly, these practitioners seek their credentials through certifications, registrations, and training programs.

Technicians/Assistants and Technologists

There are a rapidly growing number of technicians and technologists, including such major categories as cardiovascular technicians and technologists, clinical laboratory technicians, emergency medical technicians, health information technicians, nuclear medicine technologists, cytotechnologists, histologic technicians and technologists, surgical technologists, occupational safety and health technicians, pharmacy technicians, and many more. The following overview is to provide a broad description of several representative disciplines for allied health professions.

LABORATORY TECHNOLOGISTS AND TECHNICIANS

Clinical laboratory technologists and technicians have a critically important role in the diagnosis of disease, monitoring of physiologic function and the effectiveness of intervention, and application of highly technical procedures. Technologists, also known as clinical laboratory scientists or medical technologists, usually have a bachelor's degree in one of the life sciences. Clinical laboratory technicians, also known as medical technicians or medical laboratory technicians, generally need an associate's degree or a certificate.

Among their roles, clinical laboratory personnel analyze body fluids, tissues, and cells, checking for bacteria and other microorganisms; analyze chemical content; test drug levels in blood to monitor the effectiveness of treatment; and match blood for transfusion.

The National Accrediting Agency for Clinical Laboratory Sciences accredits 467 programs for clinical laboratory technologists and technicians. Employed graduates of those programs number over 300,000. More than 50% of those employed work in hospitals. Most of the others work in physician offices or diagnostic laboratories. The Bureau of Labor Statistics (2010c) reports that a faster than average employment growth is expected because of population growth and development of new laboratory tests.

Radiologic Technology

A radiologic technologist works under the supervision of a radiologist, a physician who specializes in the use and interpretation of radiographs. The radiologic technologist will use radiographs, fluoroscopic equipment, and high-tech imaging machines such as ultrasonography, computed tomography, magnetic resonance imaging, and positron emission tomography units to produce films that allow physicians to study the internal organs and bones of their patients. Formal training programs in radiography range in length from 1 to 4 years and lead to a certificate, associate's degree, or bachelor's degree. Two-year associate's degrees are most prevalent. The Joint Review Committee on Education in Radiology has accredited over 600 formal programs in 2003, as reported by the Bureau of Labor Statistics (2010d).

Technological advances and the growth and aging of the nation's population continue to increase the demand for diagnostic imaging. As a result, the vacancy rate for radiologic technologists is the highest in any field of health care. The U.S. Department of Labor predicts that employment opportunities for radiologic technologists will grow faster than the average for all healthcare occupations through 2014 (Bureau of Labor Statistics, 2010d).

Nuclear Medicine Technology

Nuclear medicine technologists use diagnostic imaging techniques to detect and map radioactive drugs in the human body. They administer radioactive pharmaceuticals to patients and then monitor the characteristics and functions of tissues or organs in which they localize. Abnormal areas show higher or lower concentrations of radioactivity than normal ones do.

Nuclear medicine technologists are prepared in 1-year certificate programs offered by hospitals to those who are already radiologic technologists, medical technologists, or registered nurses or to those who are enrolled in 2- to 4-year nuclear medicine technology programs offered in university schools of allied health. Nuclear medicine technologists must meet the minimum federal standards on the administration of radioactive drugs and the operation of radiation detection equipment. In addition, about half of all states require technologists to be licensed. These technologists also may obtain voluntary professional certification or registration, as reported by the Bureau of Labor Statistics (2010e).

Therapists or Therapeutic Science Practitioners

Practitioners of the therapeutic sciences are essential to the treatment and rehabilitation of patients with diseases and injuries of all kinds. Physical therapists, occupational therapists, speech pathology and audiology therapists, radiation therapists, and respiratory therapists are only some of the allied health disciplines within this field of therapeutic science practitioners.

Physical Therapy

Physical therapists provide services that help restore function, improve mobility, relieve pain, and prevent or limit physical disabilities of patients suffering from injuries or disease. They restore, maintain, and promote overall fitness and health. They review patients' medical histories and measure patients' strength, range of motion, balance, coordination, muscle performance, and motor function. They then develop and implement treatment plans that include exercises to develop flexibility, strength, and endurance. They also may give patients exercises to do at home.

Physical therapists may also use electrical stimulation, hot or cold compresses, and ultrasound to relieve pain and reduce swelling. They also teach patients to use assistive and adaptive devices, such as crutches, prostheses, and wheelchairs. Physical therapists supervise physical therapy assistants to aid them in meeting the needs of an increasing number of patients (American Physical Therapy Association, 1998). Physical therapy assistants earn associate's degrees and take a national certifying examination.

Physical therapists often consult and practice with physicians, dentists, nurses, educators, social workers, and occupational or speech therapists. They may practice as generalists or specialize in areas such as pediatrics, geriatrics, orthopedics, sports medicine, neurology, or cardiopulmonary physical therapy.

The physical therapy profession has developed the Doctor of Physical Therapy as the first professional degree. Persons who pursue a physical therapy degree may choose between a master's and Doctor of Physical Therapy. The rationale behind the change from a baccalaureate in favor of a master's or first professional degree is an increasing need for greater breadth and depth of practice skills, as well as the needs for patients to access the physical therapist directly without a physician referral. Employment opportunities have grown rapidly in the physical therapy field, and the demand now exceeds the supply. Physical therapists have demonstrated their value in the rehabilitation of injured, diseased, or otherwise debilitated patients and are in increasing demand as the population ages (Bureau of Labor Statistics, 2010f).

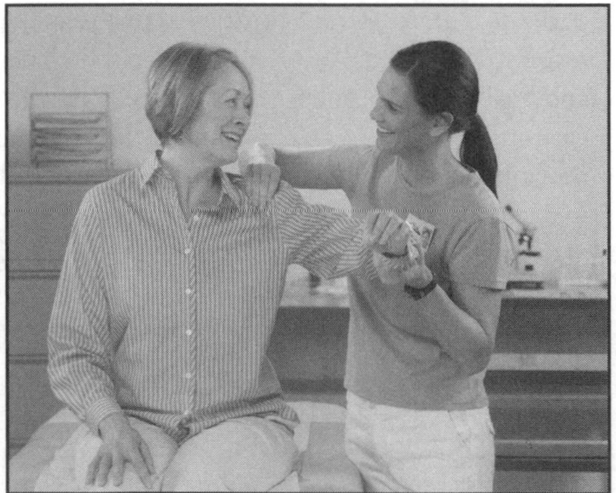

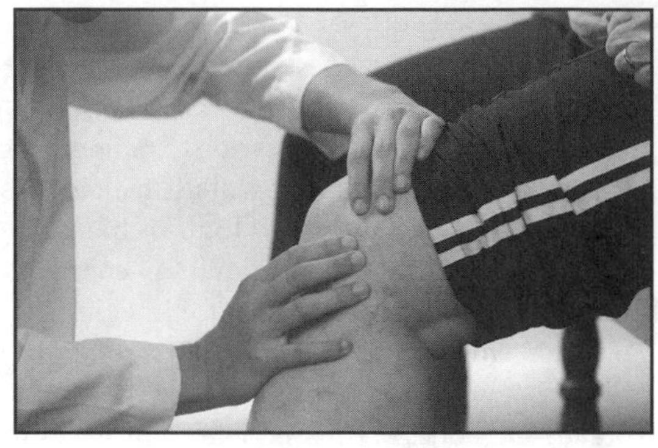

Occupational Therapy

Occupational therapists assist patients in recovering from accidents, injuries, or diseases to improve their ability to perform tasks in their daily living and working environments. A wide range of patients work with occupational therapists, including those with irreversible physical disabilities and those with mental disabilities or disorders. Occupational therapists assist patients in caring for their daily needs such as dressing, cooking, and eating. They also use physical exercises and other activities to increase strength and dexterity, visual acuity, and hand–eye coordination. Occupational therapists instruct in the use of adaptive equipment such as wheelchairs, splints, and aids for eating and dressing. They may also design or make special equipment needed at home or at work. Therapists may collaborate with clients and employers to modify work environments so that clients can maintain employment.

A bachelor's degree in occupational therapy was the minimum requirement for entry into this field, but beginning in 2007, a master's degree or higher is now required.

Most occupational therapists are employed by hospitals, but many also work in offices, nursing homes, community mental health centers, adult day care programs, rehabilitation centers, and residential care facilities. Private practice is currently the fastest growing sector of this profession. As the population ages and patients with critical problems survive more frequently, the demand for occupational therapists will continue to increase (Bureau of Labor Statistics, 2010g).

Speech-Language Pathology

Speech-language pathologists, sometimes called speech therapists, treat patients with speech problems, swallowing, and other disorders in hospitals, schools, clinics, and private practice. About one half of all speech pathologists are employed in the education system—from preschools to universities.

About 233 colleges and universities offer graduate programs in speech-language pathology. A master's degree is the standard practice requirement. Speech-language pathologists use written and oral tests and special instruments to diagnose the nature of the impairment and develop an individualized plan of care. They may teach the use of alternative communication methods, including automated devices and sign language.

The number of speech-language pathologists, now numbering about 130,000, is expected to grow rapidly as the population ages. Older age groups are prone to medical conditions that result in speech, language, and swallowing problems (Bureau of Labor Statistics, 2010h).

Physician Assistant

The emergence of physician assistants (PAs) closely parallels the creation of nurse practitioners in the United States. In the 1960s, there was a shortage of healthcare providers. Duke University initiated the first PA program in 1961. It was a new provider model designed to benefit from the experience and expertise of the many hospital corpsmen and medics that were discharged from the armed forces. As the flow of returning corpsmen and medics tapered, individuals without prior healthcare training were accepted into PA programs. The Medex program, which began at the University of Washington and was later adopted at a number of other universities, is well known. It was designed to train general assistants to family medicine physicians and internists.

Today there are at least 135 education programs for PAs. Sixty eight offer a master's degree, and the rest offer a bachelor or associate's degree. Most PAs have at least a bachelor's degree (American Academy of Physician Assistants, 2010). PAs provide healthcare services under the supervision of a physician. Unlike medical assistants who perform routine clinical and clerical tasks, PAs are formally trained to provide diagnostic, preventive, and therapeutic healthcare services as delegated by the physician. PAs take medical histories, order and interpret laboratory tests and X-rays, make diagnoses, and prescribe medications as allowed in 47 states and the District of Columbia (Bureau of Labor Statistics, 2010i).

Many PAs are employed in specialties such as internal medicine, pediatrics, family medicine, orthopedics, and emergency medicine. Others specialize in surgery and may provide preoperative and postoperative care and act as first or second assistants during major surgery.

The U.S. Department of Labor projects a significant increase in the employment of PAs because of an expected expansion of the healthcare industry and an emphasis on cost containment.

Behavioral Scientists

Behavioral scientists are crucial in the social, psychological, and community and patient educational activities related to health maintenance, prevention of disease, and accommodation of patients to disability. They include professionals in social work, health education, community mental health, alcoholism and drug abuse services, and other health and human service areas.

SOCIAL WORK

Social workers counsel patients and families and assist them in addressing the personal, economic, and social problems associated with illness and disability. They arrange for community-based services as necessary to meet patient needs after discharge from a health facility. A bachelor's degree is required from an accredited college program; however, a master's degree from an accredited graduate school of social work is often the standard requirement for employment.

Social workers provide social services in hospitals and other health-related settings that interact with managed care organizations that strive to contain costs. Medical and public health social workers provide patients and families with psychosocial support in cases of acute, chronic, or terminal illnesses. Mental health and substance abuse social workers assess and treat persons with mental illness or those who abuse alcohol, tobacco, or other drugs.

The most recent tally by the Council on Social Work Education listed 435 bachelor's programs, 149 master's in social work degree programs, and 78 doctoral programs. Employment of social workers is expected to grow faster than the average of other occupations, especially for those with backgrounds in gerontology and substance abuse treatment (Bureau of Labor Statistics, 2010j).

REHABILITATION COUNSELOR

A rehabilitation counselor gives personalized counseling, emotional support, and rehabilitation therapy to patients limited by physical or emotional disabilities. Patients may be recovering from illness or injury, may have psychiatric problems, or may have intellectual deficits. After an injury or illness is stabilized, the rehabilitation counselor will test the patient's motor ability, skill level, interests, and psychologic makeup and develop an appropriate training or retraining plan. The goal of rehabilitation is to maximize the patient's ability to function in society.

A master's degree is often required to be licensed or certified as a rehabilitation counselor. The Commission on Rehabilitation Counselor Certification offers voluntary certification. The need for rehabilitation counselors is expected to grow as the population ages and medical technology saves more lives. In addition, legislation requiring equal employment rights for persons with disabilities will increase the demand for counselors to prepare such people for employment (Bureau of Labor Statistics, 2010k).

Support Services Personnel

Support services are necessary for the highly complex and sophisticated system of health care to function. Specialists who provide services frequently work behind the scenes, performing administrative and management duties and often working closely with the actual providers of healthcare services. Health information administrators, dental laboratory technologists, electroencephalographic technologists, food service administrators, surgical technologists, and environmental health technologists are some of the allied health professionals in this category, and they serve to illustrate the diverse nature of the required support disciplines in allied health.

Health Information Administrators

Health information administrators are responsible for the activities and functions of the medical records departments of hospitals, skilled nursing facilities, managed care organizations, rehabilitation centers, ambulatory care facilities, and a number of other healthcare operations. They are accountable for planning and maintaining an information system that permits patient data to be received, recorded, stored, and retrieved easily to assist in diagnosis and treatment. These data may also be used to track disease patterns, provide information for medical research, assist staff in evaluating the quality of patient care, and verify insurance claims. Health information administrators supervise the staff in the medical records department and are responsible for the confidentiality of all of the information within their departments.

A bachelor's degree in health information administration is the entry-level credential. The Council of Certification of the American Health Information Management Association gives a national accreditation examination for Registered Health Information Administrator. Currently, there are over 50 programs preparing health information administrators and over 150 programs training medical records and health information technologists/technicians. The U.S. Department of Labor estimates a 49% increase in the employment of these health information personnel by 2010 (Bureau of Labor Statistics, 2010l).

Other Clinical Health Professionals or Non-Physician Clinicians

This group of health professionals is distinguished from other groups of therapists and behavioral health scientists because they have achieved the legal right to practice independent of physicians' orders. The one exception is pharmacists. They are identified with this group because their history is one of independent practice. It is the professional stature of this group that is being sought by other allied health professionals through increased education and legal advocacy.

Pharmacists

The traditional role of pharmacists has been to dispense medicines prescribed by physicians, dentists, and podiatrists and to provide consultation on the proper selection and use of medicines. All states require a license to practice pharmacy. The licensure requirements include graduation from an accredited pharmacy program that awards a Bachelor of Pharmacy or Doctor of Pharmacy (PharmD) degree, successful completion of a state board examination, and practical experience or completion of a supervised internship (Stanfield, 1995, pp. 142–147). After 2005, the bachelor's degree was phased out, and a PharmD requiring 6 years of postsecondary education became the standard. The median annual earnings of pharmacists in 2004 were $84,900 (Bureau of Labor Statistics, 2010m).

Although most pharmacists are generalists, dispensing drugs and advising providers and patients, some become specialists. Pharmacotherapists specialize in drug therapy and work closely with physicians. Nutrition-support pharmacists determine and prepare drugs needed for nutritional therapy. Radiopharmacists or nuclear pharmacists produce radioactive drugs used for patient diagnosis and therapy.

Most pharmacists hold salaried positions and work in community pharmacies that are independently owned or are part of a national drugstore, grocery store, or department store chain. Pharmacists are also employed by hospitals, managed care organizations, home health agencies, clinics, government health services organizations, and pharmaceutical manufacturers.

The role of pharmacists has expanded over the last 2 decades from primarily preparing and dispensing prescriptions to include drug product education and serving as experts on specific drugs, drug interactions, and generic drug substitution. Pharmacists play a critical role in promoting rational drug use and effective drug management (Passmore & Kailis, 1994). Under the Omnibus Budget Reconciliation Act of 1990, pharmacists are required to give consumers information about drugs and their potential misuse. This educating and counseling role of pharmacists is broadly referred to as pharmaceutical care. The American Council on Pharmaceutical Education (1992) defined pharmaceutical care as

> *A mode of pharmacy practice in which the pharmacist takes an active role on behalf of patients, by assisting prescribers in appropriate drug choices, by effecting distribution of medications to patients, and by assuming direct responsibilities collaboratively with other health care professionals and with patients to achieve the desired therapeutic outcome.*

This concept entails a high level of drug knowledge, clinical skill, and independent judgment and requires that pharmacists share with other health professionals the responsibility for optimizing the outcome of patients' drug therapy, including health status, quality of life, and satisfaction (Helper & Strand, 1990; Schwartz, 1994; Strand et al., 1991). Pharmacists inform physicians of patient compliance, achievement of therapeutic outcome, and potential drug interactions (Marcrom et al., 1992). Pharmacists are essential in identifying and preventing potential drug-related problems and resolving actual drug-related problems (Morley & Strand, 1989).

Another area in which pharmacists are receiving broadened clinical involvement is referred to as "disease management." In about half the states, pharmacists now have the authority to initiate or modify drug treatment, as long as they have collaborative agreements with physicians. For example, a stroke patient who needs blood thinning medication might walk into the drugstore for an assessment and walk out with a different dosage. Most other states are weighing giving pharmacists similar authority. Other areas in which pharmacists are expected to play an expanded role include management of diabetes, asthma, high cholesterol, and hypertension (Berner, 1999).

Optometrists

Optometrists provide vision care, such as examination, diagnosis, and correction of vision problems. They must be licensed to practice. The licensure requirements include the possession of a Doctor of Optometry degree and passing a written and clinical state board examination. Most optometrists work in solo or group practices. Some work for the government, managed care organizations, optical stores, or vision care centers as salaried employees.

Psychologists

Psychologists provide patients with mental health care. They must be licensed or certified to practice. The ultimate recognition is the diplomate in psychology, which requires a Doctor of Philosophy or Doctor of Psychology degree, a minimum of 5 years of postdoctoral experience, and the successful completion of an examination by the American Board of Examiners in Professional Psychology. Stanfield (1995) notes that psychologists may specialize in several areas, such as clinical, counseling, developmental, educational, engineering, personnel, experimental, industrial, psychometric, rehabilitation, school, and social domains.

Podiatrists

Podiatrists treat patients with diseases or deformities of the feet, including performing surgical operations, prescribing medications and corrective devices, and administering physiotherapy. They must be licensed to practice. Requirements for licensure include completion of an accredited program that awards a Doctor of Podiatric Medicine degree and passing a national examination by the National Board of Podiatry.

Chiropractors

Chiropractors provide treatment to patients through chiropractic (done by hand) manipulation, physiotherapy, and dietary counseling. They typically help patients with neurological, muscular, and vascular disturbances. Chiropractic care is based on the belief that the body is a self-healing organism. Chiropractors do not prescribe drugs or perform surgery. Chiropractors must be licensed to practice. Requirements for licensure include completing an accredited program that awards a 4-year Doctor of Chiropractic degree and passing an examination by the state chiropractic board.

Alternative Medicine Practitioners

Across the country, and notably on the West Coast and in the Midwest, there is widespread interest in complementary and alternative medicine (CAM). CAM is defined as "a group of diverse medical and healthcare systems, practices, and products that are not presently considered to be part of conventional medicine" (National Center for Complementary and Alternative Medicine [NCCAM], 2009). Complementary medicine and alternative medicine differ from each other. Complementary medicine is used together with conventional medicine. Alternative medicine is used in place of conventional medicine (National Center for Complementary and Alternative Medicine, 2004).

In 1992, with one third of Americans resorting to alternative medical therapies at the time, the National Institutes of Health created an Office of Alternative Medicine to examine whether alternative therapies work. The more perplexing question of how they work was to be investigated later. In 1998, when more than 40% of Americans reported the use of alternative or complementary therapies, the Office of Alternative Medicine was elevated to the National Center for Complementary and Alternative Medicine, and its mandate expanded.

A 2004 press release from the National Center provided the findings of a 2002 national health interview survey that queried respondents about 27 types of complementary and alternative treatments—10 requiring the services of a provider, such as an acupuncturist or chiropractor, and 17 nonprovider types, such as herbs, megavitamins, and special diets. The survey found that the U.S. public spent $36 billion to $47 billion that year on CAM therapies. Of that amount, $12 to $20 billion was spent out of pocket to professional CAM providers; $5 billion was spent on herbal products alone.

The Center is also engaged in the first international study of traditional medicines, including ancient Chinese and American Indian methods. Traditional Chinese medicine (TCM), which encompasses many different practices, is rooted in the ancient philosophy of Taoism and dates back more than 5,000 years. TCM is widely used in the United States. It is estimated that in 1997 some 10,000 practitioners served more than 1 million patients. According to the 2007 National Health Interview Survey, which included questions on the use of various CAM therapies, an estimated 3.1 million U.S. adults had used acupuncture in the previous year. In addition, according to this same survey, approximately 17% of adults use natural products, including herbs, making it the most commonly used therapy. In another survey, more than one third of the patients at six large acupuncture clinics said they also received Chinese herbal treatments at the clinics (U.S. National Institutes of Health, Center for Complementary and Alternative Medicine, 2009).

Because estimates of alternative treatment use by cancer patients range from a low of 9% to as high as 50%, the American Cancer Society has a Committee on Unproven Methods of Cancer Treatment that maintains a list of 23 questionable cancer treatment modalities. The use of alternative therapies by cancer patients is usually with family and physician knowledge. McGinnis (1991) reports about 50% of the patients using unproven therapies continue following conventional treatment as well.

Many alternative therapies involve lifestyle programs, such as macrobiotics, natural food diets, yoga, and other stress-reducing techniques. Others focus on mind–body techniques, including biofeedback, visualization, music therapy, and prayer. Still others are traditional practices of other cultures—acupuncture, homeopathy, and microdose pharmacology.

Along with alternative techniques comes a new class of alternative practitioners. To name a few, there are certified triage practitioners, who rock and cradle the patient's body for relaxation and mental clarity; doctors of naturopathy (NDs), who use natural healing methods that include diet, herbal medicine, and homeopathy and who use deep massage to restore the body's natural alignment; and registered polarity practitioners, who use touch and advice on diet, self-awareness, and exercise to balance energy flow. In spite of the fact that medical societies strongly oppose naturopathy, considering the practice "unscientific" and "irrational," naturopathic doctors have made great strides in the last few years. Although they do not have medical degrees and are trained in loosely monitored schools, they are able to generate strong public support within state legislatures. Twelve states already license naturopaths, and seven more are contemplating licensing legislation. Petersen (2002) notes that several of these states allow naturopaths to prescribe conventional drugs, deliver babies, and perform minor surgery.

The gains of naturopaths and other alternative practitioners reflect the public's frustration with much of conventional medicine, high drug prices, and media reports of disproved treatments. The interest of insurance companies in alternative forms of medicine is also important. Insurers say that when traditional medicine is ineffective and an alternative form of therapy, such as acupuncture for a condition such as chronic pain, costs less and satisfies the patient, they will pay for it. Rubenstein (2004) reports several states now require insurance companies to cover naturopathic procedures and others, such as acupuncture.

Power and Influence

Allied and other health professionals can improve access to quality health care, including the use of and reimbursement for qualified health professionals through the power of influence. This influence is accomplished through the education of consumers, policy makers, funding agencies, and physicians about the scope of practice, education and training, credentialing, and qualifications of health professionals. Allied health professionals must work to influence legislation and regulation, which will promote access of patients to the services of trained and qualified healthcare professionals. This begins by first defining and describing for legislators and regulators this definition (http://www.healthpronet.org/docs/allied_health_fact_sheet.pdf):

> *Allied health professionals are health care providers with formal education and clinically training who are credentialed through certification, registration and/or licensure to deliver health services. These professionals, working with physicians and other members of the healthcare team, provide services to identify, evaluate, treat and prevent diseases and disorder.*
>
> ***Allied Health Professionals . . .***
>
> 1. *Decrease cost and improve quality of patient care*
> 2. *Comprise the majority of the healthcare work force*
> 3. *Include more than 85 distinct occupations, exclusive of physicians and nurses*
> 4. *Include over 6 million providers of the 11 million healthcare workforce*
> 5. *Typically attend 2 or 4 year educational programs in community and senior colleges*
> 6. *Are educated in over 1,000 programs in the U.S., which are staffed by 3,000 allied health faculty, and enroll over 30,000 students annually (www.healthpronet.org)*
>
> *Allied health professionals are expert in a multitude of therapeutic, diagnostic, and preventive health interventions and function in several diverse settings including disease prevention and control, dietary and nutritional services, mental and physical health promotion, rehabilitation, and health systems management.*

Expanded Role for Policy Makers

To meet the ever growing demand for improving access to healthcare services, Collier (2007) asks what should be the appropriate mix of health professionals and workers in a particular setting. This is an essential question because health care is delivered by many kinds of allied health professionals with differing levels of education and training. This question is addressed in the recent report issued by the Association of Academic Health (2008). This report addresses the need for a policy-making framework that calls for making the U.S. health workforce a priority domestic policy issue and addressing health workforce issues immediately to avert crises in national workforce capacity and infrastructure to meet rapidly evolving national health workforce needs. Policy makers and stakeholders must work toward the development of an integrated, comprehensive national health workforce policy that recognizes and compensates for the inherent weaknesses and vulnerabilities of the current decentralized system.

The development of an integrated, comprehensive, national health workforce policy requires the creation of a national health workforce planning body that engages diverse federal, state, public, and private stakeholders. These stakeholders would articulate a national workforce agenda that promotes harmonization in public and private standards, requirements, and prevailing practices across jurisdictions; addresses access to the health professions and the ability of educational institutions to respond to economic, social, and environmental factors that impact the workforce; and identifies and addresses unintended adverse policy interactions.

Policy makers at every level of government, insurers, educators, providers, and consumers have a vested interest in the issues that pertain to the healthcare workforce. To create a coherent health workforce policy means moving beyond a century-old policy that has been characterized by a decentralized and distributed approach for workforce regulation and oversight. In the past, policy makers have had difficulty sustaining planning initiatives that were potentially significant in scope and impact, and their tendency to fund crisis responses (rather than long-term strategic investments) has contributed to the inadequacy of current health workforce infrastructure. A broader, more integrated strategic vision for health workforce policy making and planning is needed if complex and urgent health workforce issues are to be addressed effectively. Without a mechanism to coordinate policy making and planning across myriad public and private entities with overlapping roles and responsibilities, the health workforce will continue to be plagued by the problems that arise from fragmented and inconsistent policy making.

Professional Association

This collaboration should begin with the individual allied health professional organizations. For these groups to have a significant impact, they must be aligned with a professional organization that represents beyond their individual specialty association. One group that can unite the separate associations of allied professionals is the Health Professions Network (HPN), which is a voluntary, national group representing over 75 organizations of allied healthcare providers, educators, and accreditors interested in interdisciplinary discussion and collaboration. The HPN focuses on communication, consensus, and advocacy on behalf of allied health professionals.

The philosophy of HPN is to foster collaboration and provide networking and educational opportunities. For example, a very successful collaborative initiative began in 1998 when HPN, the Association of Schools of Allied Health Professions, and the National Network of Health Career Programs in Two-Year Colleges established the Coalition for Allied Health Leadership, which is supported in part by a grant from the Health Resources and Services Administration. The innovative program recruits individuals from each member organization to participate in a collaborative effort designed to familiarize future leaders in the allied health fields with how Capitol Hill works.

The HPN also initiated a campaign to promote Allied Health Week (November 3–7), which includes an allied health awareness effort geared toward students in grades kindergarten through 12. The network also has formed ongoing collaborative relationships with the American Medical Association and the American Hospital Association. The HPN is forging inroads in the political arena by nominating members to sit on several review committees. The network is monitoring several important pieces of healthcare legislation in various stages of development. The HPN promotes the awareness of allied health professions or contributes to the future workforce.

Summary

Health services professionals in the United States constitute the largest labor force. Their development is influenced by demographic trends, advances in research and technology, disease and illness trends, and the changing environment of healthcare financing and delivery. Physicians play a leading role in the delivery of health services. The inconsistency between supply and demand largely contributes to provider surplus in certain metropolitan and suburban areas and to shortages in rural and inner-city areas. Various policies and programs have been used or proposed to address both physician imbalance and maldistribution, including regulation of healthcare professions, reimbursement initiatives targeting suitable incentives, targeted programs for underserved areas, changes in medical school curricula, changes in the financing of medical training, and a more rational referral system.

Other health and allied professionals contribute significantly to the delivery of health care. These professionals require different levels of training and work in a variety of healthcare settings as complements to, or substitutes for, physicians. Health services administrators face new challenges in the leadership of healthcare organizations. These challenges call for some reforms in the educational programs designed to prepare adequately trained managers for the various sectors of the healthcare industry.

References

American Academy of Physician Assistants. (2010). *PA fact sheet.* Arlington, VA. Retrieved January 15, 2010, from http://www.aapa.org/about-aapa/history

American Association of Colleges of Osteopathic Medicine. (2010). *What is osteopathic medicine?* Retrieved January 14, 2010, from http://publish.aacom.org/ABOUT/OSTEOMED/Pages/default.aspx

American Association of Nurse Practitioners. (2010). *About NPs.* Retrieved January 15, 2010, from http://www.aanp.org/AANPCMS2/AboutAANP/About+NPs.htm

American Council on Pharmaceutical Education. (1992). *The proposed revision of accreditation standards and guidelines.* Chicago: National Association of Boards on Pharmacy.

American Physical Therapy Association. (1998, November 10). Pew Commission urges increased action to cut US physician supply. *PT Bulletin,* 10.

Association of Academic Health. (2008). *Out of order, out of time: The state of the nation's health workforce.* Retrieved February 18, 2009, from http://www.aahcdc.org/policy/AAHC_OutofTime_4WEB.pdf

Berner, R. (1999, January 28). Pharmacists start to vie for a broader range of powers. *The Wall Street Journal,* B1.

Bureau of Labor Statistics, U.S. Department of Labor. *Career Guide to Industries, 2010-11 Edition* (a), Healthcare. Washington, DC: Author. Retrieved January 15, 2010, from http://www.bls.gov/oco/cg/cgs035.htm

Bureau of Labor Statistics, U.S. Department of Labor. *Occupational Outlook Handbook, 2010-11 Edition* (b). Washington, DC: Author. Retrieved January 15, 2010, from http://www.bls.gov/oco/home.htm

Bureau of Labor Statistics, U.S. Department of Labor. *Occupational Outlook Handbook, 2010-11 Edition* (c), Clinical Laboratory Technologists and Technicians. Washington, DC: Author. Retrieved January 15, 2010, from http://www.bls.gov/oco/ocos096.htm

Bureau of Labor Statistics, U.S. Department of Labor. *Occupational Outlook Handbook, 2010-11 Edition* (d), Radiation Therapists. Washington, DC: Author. Retrieved January 15, 2010, from http://www.bls.gov/oco/ocos299.htm

Bureau of Labor Statistics, U.S. Department of Labor. *Occupational Outlook Handbook, 2010-11 Edition* (e), Nuclear Medicine Technologists. Washington, DC: Author. Retrieved January 15, 2010, from http://www.bls.gov/oco/ocos104.htm

Bureau of Labor Statistics, U.S. Department of Labor. *Occupational Outlook Handbook, 2010-11 Edition* (f), Physical Therapists. Washington, DC: Author. Retrieved January 15, 2010, from http://www.bls.gov/oco/ocos167.htm

Bureau of Labor Statistics, U.S. Department of Labor. *Occupational Outlook Handbook, 2010-11 Edition* (g), Occupational Therapists. Washington, DC: Author. Retrieved January 15, 2010, from http://www.bls.gov/oco/ocos078.htm

Bureau of Labor Statistics, U.S. Department of Labor. *Occupational Outlook Handbook, 2010-11 Edition* (h), Speech-Language Pathologists. Washington, DC: Author. Retrieved January 15, 2010, from http://www.bls.gov/oco/ocos099.htm

Bureau of Labor Statistics, U.S. Department of Labor. *Occupational Outlook Handbook, 2010-11 Edition* (i), Physician Assistants. Washington, DC: Author. Retrieved January 15, 2010, from http://www.bls.gov/oco/ocos081.htm

Bureau of Labor Statistics, U.S. Department of Labor. *Occupational Outlook Handbook, 2010-11 Edition* (j), Social Workers. Washington, DC: Author. Retrieved January 15, 2010, from http://www.bls.gov/oco/ocos060.htm

Bureau of Labor Statistics, U.S. Department of Labor. *Occupational Outlook Handbook, 2010-11 Edition* (k), Counselors. Washington, DC: Author. Retrieved January 15, 2010, from http://www.bls.gov/OCO/ocos067.htm

Bureau of Labor Statistics, U.S. Department of Labor. *Occupational Outlook Handbook, 2010-11 Edition* (l), Health Information Administrators. Washington, DC: Author. Retrieved January 15, 2010, from http://www.bls.gov/oco/ocoS103.htm

Bureau of Labor Statistics, U.S. Department of Labor. *Occupational Outlook Handbook, 2010-11 Edition* (m), Pharmacists. Washington, DC: Author. Retrieved January 15, 2010, from http://www.bls.gov/oco/ocos079.htm

Collier, S. N. (2008). Changes in the health workforce: Trends, issues and credentialing. (preprint, *From Education to Regulation: Dynamic Challenges for the Health Workforce*). Washington, DC: Association of Academic Health Centers.

Collier, S. (November, 2007). The cost-quality conundrum and its effect on the allied health workforce. *Trends.* Washington, DC: Association of Schools of Allied Health Professions.

Helper, C., & Strand, L. (1990). Opportunities and responsibilities in pharmaceutical care. *American Journal of Hospital Pharmacy, 47*(3), 533–543.

Marcrom, R. E., Horton, R. M., & Shepherd, M. D. (1992). Create value-added services to meet patient needs. *American Pharmacy, S32*(7), 48–57.

Martiniano, R. (2008, May). *Health care employment projections: An analysis of Bureau of Labor Statistics occupational projections, 2006–2016.* Rensselaer, NY: Center for Health Workforce Studies, School of Public Health, SUNY Albany.

Martiniano, R. (2009, February 15). *Health care employment projections: An analysis of Bureau of Labor Statistics Occupational Projections, 2006–2016.* Rensselaer, NY: Center for Health Workforce Studies, School of Public Health, SUNY Albany. Retrieved February 15, 2009.

McGinnis, L. S. (1991). Alternative therapies, 1990: An overview. *Cancer, 67,* 1788–1792.

McLaughlin, C. J. (1994). Health work force issues and policy-making roles. In P. F. Larson, M. Osterweis, & E. R. Rubin (Eds.). *Health work force issues for the 21st century* (pp. 1–3). Washington, DC: Association of Academic Health Centers.

Morley, P., & Strand, L. (1989). Critical reflections of therapeutic drug monitoring. *Journal of Clinical Pharmacy, 2*(3), 327–334.

National Center for Complementary and Alternative Medicine, National Institutes of Health. *What is complementary and alternative medicine?* Retrieved January 15, 2010, from http://nccam.nih.gov/health/whatiscam/#sup1

National Center for Complementary and Alternative Medicine, National Institutes of Health. Press Release. (2004). *More than one-third of U.S. adults use complementary and alternative medicine.* Retrieved from http://nccam.nih.gov/news/2004/052704.htm

Passmore, P., & Kailis, S. (1994). In pursuit of rational drug use and effective drug management: Clinic and public health viewpoint. *Asia-Pacific Journal of Public Health,* 7(4), 236–241.

Petersen, A. (2002, August 22). States grant herb doctors new powers. *Wall Street Journal,* D1.

Rubenstein, S. (2004, August 22). Alternative health plans widen. *Wall Street Journal,* D7.

Schwartz, M. (1994). Creating pharmacy's future. *American Pharmacy, NS34,* 44–45, 59.

Stanfield, P. S. (1995). *Introduction to the health professions* (2nd ed.). Sudbury, MA: Jones and Bartlett.

Strand, L. M., Cipolle, R. J., Morley, P. C., & Perrier, D. G. (1991). Levels of pharmaceutical care: A needs-based approach. *American Journal of Hospital Pharmacy, 48*(3), 547–550.

Sultz, H. A. (1987). *Allied health personnel: Consultant report to the Labor-Health Industry Task Force on Health Personnel.* Albany, NY: New York State Department of Health.

U.S. National Institutes of Health, National Center for Complementary and Alternative Medicine. (2009). *Traditional Chinese medicine: An introduction.* Retrieved January 15, 2010, from http://nccam.nih.gov/health/whatiscam/chinesemed.htm

Section III

Healthcare Providers: Understanding How Power, Markets, and Government Impact the Organization and Delivery of Care

Hospitals: The Power of Institutional Interests

Chapter 6

Nancy Aries
and
Barbara Caress

OVERVIEW

This chapter discusses the critical role of hospitals in the delivery of health care. Hospitals are viewed as the hub of the healthcare system, accounting for more than one third of personal healthcare expenditures. They are often viewed as neutral territories in the provision of care. Here we argue that, they are institutional players with their own set of interests in the policy debate. In this chapter, we outline the ways that this occurs and the impact that it has on the provision of comprehensive and continuous care.

OBJECTIVES

- To understand the transformation of hospitals from social welfare providers to acute-care facilities
- To identify how hospitals became the hub of the healthcare delivery system and their continuing centrality despite competing pressures
- To recognize how different types of hospitals (e.g., academic medical centers, community hospitals, public hospitals, and for-profit hospitals) will fare in this economic political environment

KEY TERMS

- ❑ Academic medical center
- ❑ Diagnostic-related group
- ❑ For-profit or proprietary hospital
- ❑ Length of stay and admissions
- ❑ Nonfederal or community hospital
- ❑ Nonprofit or voluntary hospital
- ❑ Public hospital
- ❑ Retrospective and prospective payment

Hospitals as the Hub of the Healthcare Delivery System

Historically, one can argue that hospitals provide an excellent example of the market and its irrationality in organizing the provision of health services. U.S. hospitals are not part of a singular healthcare system like the hospitals in Canada or any other industrial nation. Rather, they are independent institutions. If they functioned like Adam Smith's invisible hand, each hospital would work independently, but together they would provide Americans with access to medical care. The difficulty with this laissez faire approach to hospital-based care is that institutions acting in their own best interests are not always acting in the best interests of the community. Although a hospital might serve a particular constituency and fight for its own survival, such actions might jeopardize the survival of other hospitals in the area and access of other populations to hospital care. For example, the expansion of the for-profits in smaller communities has resulted in the closing of public hospitals. Unlike the for-profits that seek to maximize their revenue, the mission of public hospitals is to treat all regardless of ability to pay (Seay & Vladeck, 1988).

Over the past three decades, there has been growing pressure to rationalize the delivery of health services to make them more effective and more efficient. An organizing idea of rationalization is the creation of linked integrated healthcare delivery systems composed of complimentary facilities. In such a model, the role of the hospital would vary depending on the community. The development of integrated care systems would rationalize what is now a system of independent operators. Although many efforts have been made to rationalize the organization and financing of care, hospitals have responded to the changing environment in order to maintain their independence and the centrality of their position in the delivery of health services.

History of Hospitals

Before the Civil War, there were a handful of hospitals, including Philadelphia General, Massachusetts General, and New York Hospital. Often they were founded at the urging of doctors as workshops to study and train physicians. They were endowed by city elites. They were supported by the public because they were places that cared for persons who had no family system to care for them (Starr, 1982).

As cities grew in numbers and size after the Civil War, the number of hospitals increased dramatically. Given the social stresses due to immigration, industrialization, and urbanization, hospitals were critical to urban stability, but there was a new wave of hospitals that were built to respond to the defined needs of specific communities. They were a principal tool whereby community elites organized assistance to the poor and dislocated. The names of the hospitals told of their affiliation: Mount Sinai, Lutheran, St. Luke's, Methodist, and St. Vincent's. The goal was not just medical cure. The goal was to provide assistance in whatever form it was needed (Starr, 1982). In 1920, the second Hospital Cen-

sus identified 5,700 institutions, practically the same number as today.

The modern U.S. hospital industry was born between the 1860s and the 1920s as these hospitals underwent a transformation from social welfare institutions to institutions that provide acute medical care. Rather than serving the generic needs of the community, the mission of the hospital became one of curing the acute problems of the sick. The change in the purpose was related to the rise of the biomedical sciences. For the first time, physicians could provide services that could positively impact the health of their patients. Patients who would benefit from medical intervention began to be treated in hospitals, whereas the chronic or social problems such as alcoholism or old age that were not responsive to medical intervention were moved into the realm of social services. Many medical services could no longer be provided in a patient's home. They required a centralized location where sterile conditions could be assured and where equipment such as X-ray machines and pathology laboratories could be located. The complexity of its new tasks called for more complex organizational structures and more complex staffing functions. By 1920, for example, the transformation of the hospital was achieved in Philadelphia when three distinct institutions formed out of Philadelphia General Hospital: an acute-care hospital, an asylum, and an almshouse (Rosenberg, 1982).

Beyond the growth of the hospital, two other transformations took place. First, the hospital changed from an institution operated as charity into one run as a business. Costlier ventures to operate because of technological requirements and changing standards of cleanliness they could no longer be supported through philanthropy alone. Hospitals needed new sources of revenue. Hospitals began charging for services and opening their doors to private practitioners who had access to potentially paying middle-class patients. Once opened and dependent on private physicians, control passed from the boards of trustees drawn from among elite members of the community to physicians who controlled admissions (the most important source of revenue) and ultimately mission (Rosner, 1982). As the hospitals grew in number and size, the role and influence of physicians also grew. One organized agent of the physician community, the American College of Surgeons, sought to standardize hospital services. The College surveyed all hospitals to determine whether (1) physicians were licensed, (2) the medical staff met monthly, (3) there were accurate patient records, and (4) there were diagnostic and therapeutic facilities under competent supervision (Stevens, 1989).

By the late 1930s, the hospital had become the hub of healthcare delivery system. It was the locus of both patient care and medical training. Centralizing care in increasingly complex institutions was the most important manifestation of the transformation of U.S. health care in the 20th century. Hospital care defined medical care as the treatment of injury and disease, not prevention and comfort, and physicians were its heart and soul. Since that time, the hospitals have fought to maintain their hegemony in this tremendously complex system.

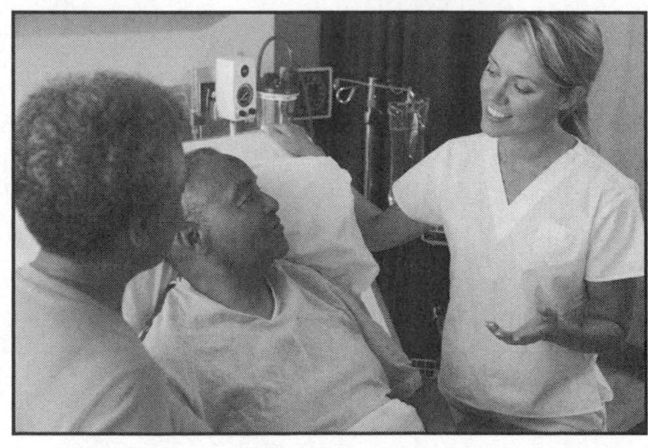

Baseline Information

There were approximately 6,500 hospitals at the peak, and there are now 5,815 hospitals. Of these, 4,897 are community hospitals. A community hospital is broadly defined as a nonfederal, short-term, general, and other hospital whose services are available to the public. This definition excludes hospital units in institutions that are not available to the public such as prisons. The average length of stay (LOS) in a community hospital must be less than 30 days. Discussions about hospitals typically refer to community hospitals. There are 918 noncommunity hospitals. Noncommunity hospitals include federal and long-term institutions. Federal hospitals refer to Veterans Administration hospitals and the United States Public Health Service hospitals and Marine hospitals. Long-term general hospitals refer to psychiatric hospitals, tuberculosis and other respiratory disease hospitals, institutions for the mentally retarded, alcohol and chemical dependency hospitals, and units in short-term institutions. The defining characteristic is an LOS that is greater than 30 days.

Tables 6-1 and 6-2 provide more detailed information about community hospitals. The number of community hospitals is declining. The hospitals that are closing include rural hospitals and urban hospitals that are financially distressed because they serve a patient population with limited ability to pay. The decreased number of beds results from decreased admissions and the decreased average LOS. With a growing and aging population, the number of surgical operations is increasing, as is the number of births—two of the primary services that

Table 6-1 COMMUNITY HOSPITALS: 1982, 1993, 1998, AND 2007

	1982	1993	1998	2007
Community hospitals	5,801	5,261	5,057	4,897
Beds	1,012,000	919,000	853,287	800,892
Beds/hospital	174	175	167	163
Admissions	36,379,000	30,748,000	31,576,960	35,345,986
Daily census	762,000	592,000	525,000	533,250
LOS	7.6	7.0	6.0	5.5
Inpatient days	278,406,000*	215,889,000	191,430,450	194,549,348
Surgical operations	19,236,000	22,806,000	25,329,319	27,355,964
Bassinets	77,000	66,000	62,156	57,546
Births	3,465,000	3,870,000	3,726,233	4,077,962
Occupancy rate (%)	75.3	64.4	62.5	66.6
Outpatient visits	202,768,000*	366,885,000	474,193,468	603,300,374

**1981*

Sources: American Hospital Association, 2002, 2008.

Table 6-2 COMMUNITY HOSPITALS AND AVERAGE NUMBER OF BEDS: 1982, 1993, 1998, AND 2007

Beds	1982	1993	1998	2007
6–24	235	227	293	360
25–49	980	894	900	1,076
50–99	1,440	1,181	1,085	971
100–199	1,380	1,337	1,304	1,083
200–299	738	730	644	613
300–399	426	402	352	343
400–499	273	205	183	191
500+	332	285	254	260

Sources: American Hospital Association, 2002, 2008.

filled the beds in mid-century U.S. hospitals; thus, one might expect increased demand for inpatient admissions. Nevertheless, as can be seen in Table 6-1, the number of hospital beds fell by 200,000 between 1982 and 2007, and there was no change in the number of admissions. During the same 25-year period, the number of outpatient encounters increased 300%.

Table 6-2, which displays the U.S. hospital complement based on the average number of beds, is important because it shows that the typical community hospital is quite small—averaging between 50 and 200 beds. These are not large institutions endowed with facilities to provide the complexity of services required to provide, for example, many of the surgeries indicated in Table 6-1. It also stands in sharp contrast to a city like New York where practically every hospital has more than 200 beds (New York State Department of Health, 2009). The larger hospitals tend to be the academic medical centers that train physicians and care for people with complex medical and social problems. These hospitals find themselves in competition with the smaller community hospitals. One dominates in terms of numbers and the other in terms of prestige.

Hospital costs comprise the largest single portion of spending in the healthcare sector. In 2008, hospital spending was $718 billion or 37% of personal healthcare spending. The relative percentage of health spending on hospitals rose dramatically between 1960 and 1980 and was almost 50% of personal healthcare spending in 1980. Cost-control efforts on the part of the government and private health insurance companies have managed to bring these costs down, and hospital spending is just slightly lower as a percentage of all healthcare spending than it was in 1960. The source of payment has also changed considerably over the last 50 years. In 2008, public funds accounted for almost 57% of hospital costs. When all public sources are combined, government is the largest single payer of hospital costs. This is a direct result of the passage of Medicare and Medicaid in 1965. The federal share of hospital expenditures increased from 17% in 1960 to 46% in 2008. The second largest source of funds is private. As government funding increased, there was a decline in consumer payments from 56% to almost 40%. This decline was also marked by the decline in out-of-pocket payments to hospitals. Between 1960 and 2008, these decreased from 20% to less than 4% of hospital expenditures. These costs were shifted to the federal government (see Table 6-3).

Distribution of Hospitals by Ownership

There are three types of community hospital systems that each grew up to serve a specific need. These can be distinguished by ownership type. Nonprofit hospitals include both the community-based hospitals and the academic health centers. Public hospitals are state and locally owned hospitals, and there are privately owned or for-profit hospitals (Starr, 1982). Table 6-4 indicates that there have not been great changes in the organization of hospitals based on their numbers or the percentage of beds. This has remained fairly constant despite the fears in the 1980s that the for-profit hospitals might come to dominate the delivery of hospital care. The unique mission of the hospitals based on ownership has been a major issue of concern. Although a distinction between the three in terms of mission should be clear, the drive to make health care more market driven, which would mean that each hospital's survival would be dependent on its maintaining financial viability, is making hospitals converge in terms of strategy (Stevens, 1989). The result of this convergence is that many nonprofit community hospitals are being challenged legally to their right to maintain their tax-exempt status for failing to provide community benefit (Gray & Schlesinger, 2009). The public hospitals provide the highest percentage of uncompensated care, but these hospitals are finding it difficult to meet the challenge of serving the uninsured (National Association of Public Hospitals and Health Systems, 2009). The for-profit hospitals remain in the best fiscal position as they serve only patients who are able to pay and provide only those services that are profitable.

Challenges Facing the Community Hospitals

The pressures that hospitals have experienced since the 1980s are in part related to the increased efforts to control healthcare costs that are becoming an increasing share of domestic spending and in part a result of rapidly changing knowledge about how to manage and treat disease. In addition, there is a growing interest in rationalizing the organization of health care into integrated systems of care that will improve the quality of care.

Excess Capacity

Hospitals have been forced to deal with surplus inpatient capacity because of declining admissions and decreased LOS. The decline in admissions is a result of many factors. First, there has been an improvement in the nation's health. The incidence of breast cancer in women under 65 years, for example, is declining. The same is true for coronary disease, cardiovascular disease, and pneumonia. In addition, there are the growing alternatives to hospitalization. It is now the case that myriad surgeries and diagnostic and other procedures can be done in ambulatory settings. Ambulatory surgery centers, diagnostic imaging, and radiological centers are being opened throughout the country (Mitchell, 2007).

Table 6-3 NATIONAL HEALTH EXPENDITURES BY HOSPITALS AND PHYSICIANS AND BY SOURCE OF FUNDS: 1960, 1970, 1980, 1990, 2000, AND 2008

Levels in $ Millions	1960	1970	1980	1990	2000	2008
National health expenditures	27,487	74,857	253,389	714,148	1,352,855	2,338,747
Population	186	210	230	254	283	305
Personal health care	23,320	62,943	214,784	607,542	1,139,192	1,952,255
Hospital care	9,179	27,589	101,008	251,570	416,864	718,360
Private funds	5,301	12,357	47,444	119,607	179,669	309,310
Consumer payments	5,189	11,462	42,366	109,181	157,769	282,209
Out-of-pocket payments	1,904	2,491	5,406	11,319	13,651	23,197
Private health insurance	3,284	8,971	36,960	97,862	144,118	259,013
Other private funds	113	895	5,078	10,426	21,900	27,101
Public funds	3,878	15,233	53,564	131,963	237,196	409,050
Federal funds	1,552	9,961	40,537	101,690	191,866	330,701
State and local funds	2,326	5,272	13,027	30,273	45,330	78,349
Physician and clinical services	5,353	13,981	47,074	157,548	288,621	496,165
Hospital care as percentage of personal health care (%)	39.4	43.8	47.0	41.4	36.6	36.8
Contribution of source						
Private funds (%)	57.8	44.8	47.0	47.5	43.1	43.1
Consumer payments (%)	56.5	41.5	41.9	43.4	37.8	39.3
Out-of-pocket payments (%)	20.7	9.0	5.4	4.5	3.3	3.2
Private health insurance (%)	35.8	32.5	36.6	38.9	34.6	36.1
Other private funds (%)	1.2	3.2	5.0	4.1	5.3	3.8
Public funds (%)	42.2	55.2	53.0	52.5	56.9	56.9
Federal funds (%)	16.9	36.1	40.1	40.4	46.0	46.0
State and local funds (%)	25.3	19.1	12.9	12.0	10.9	10.9

Source: CMS, 2010.

Table 6-4 COMMUNITY HOSPITALS BY OWNERSHIP TYPE

	Nonprofit Hospitals	% Beds	Public State/Local Hospitals	% Beds	For-Profit Hospitals	% Beds	Total Number of Hospitals	Total Number of Beds
1970	3,386		1,704		769		5,859	
1980	3,339	70	1,835	21	730	9	5,904	988,000
1985	3,364	71	1,615	19	805	10	5,784	1,003,000
1987	3,289	80	1,542	21	828	13	5,659	840,000
1998	3,000	70	1,260	17	771	13	5,057	840,000
2007	2,913	69	1,111	16	873	14	4,897	801,000

Sources: American Hospital Association, 2002, 2008.

In addition, the growth of managed care has negatively affected the use of hospital services, as the incentives are to keep patients out of the hospital. The first studies of the health maintenance organizations found that hospital admissions decreased by as much as 40% (Luft, 1981). In addition, financial incentives such as the increased burden of cost sharing has impacted hospital admissions. The Rand health insurance experiment study showed that a 25% coinsurance can decrease the probability of hospital admissions by up to 3% (Gruber, 2006). More recently, the pressures of managed care show up in heavily discounted rates (Tompkins et al., 2006).

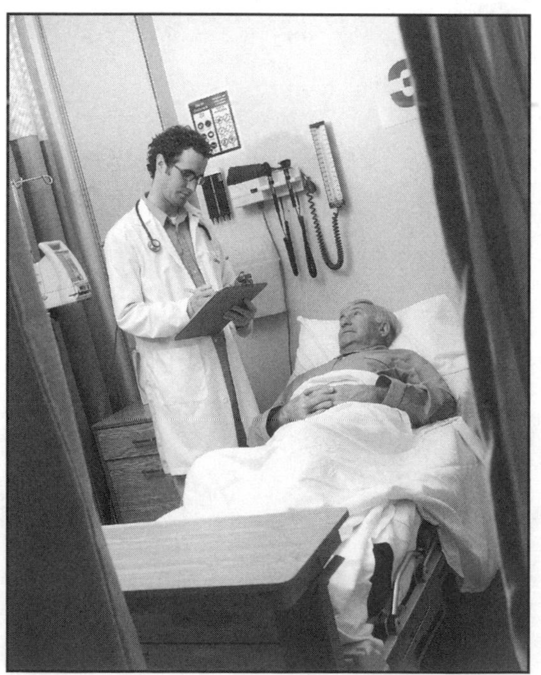

The issue of excess capacity is further aggravated by the variation in medical practice patterns. There is tremendous variation in the number of beds and the number of inpatient days per 100,000 persons across the country (see Figure 6-1). In areas where there are fewer beds and fewer inpatient days, there is excess hospital capacity; however, in areas where there are more beds and inpatient days per 100,000, there is less excess capacity. To reduce further the need for beds would require an acceptance of practice standards in line with those of lower end users (Duke, 1996).

Also, reductions in LOS, which began dropping in 1982, picked up steam with the implemen-

Figure 6-1 Hospital beds per 1,000 population, 2007.

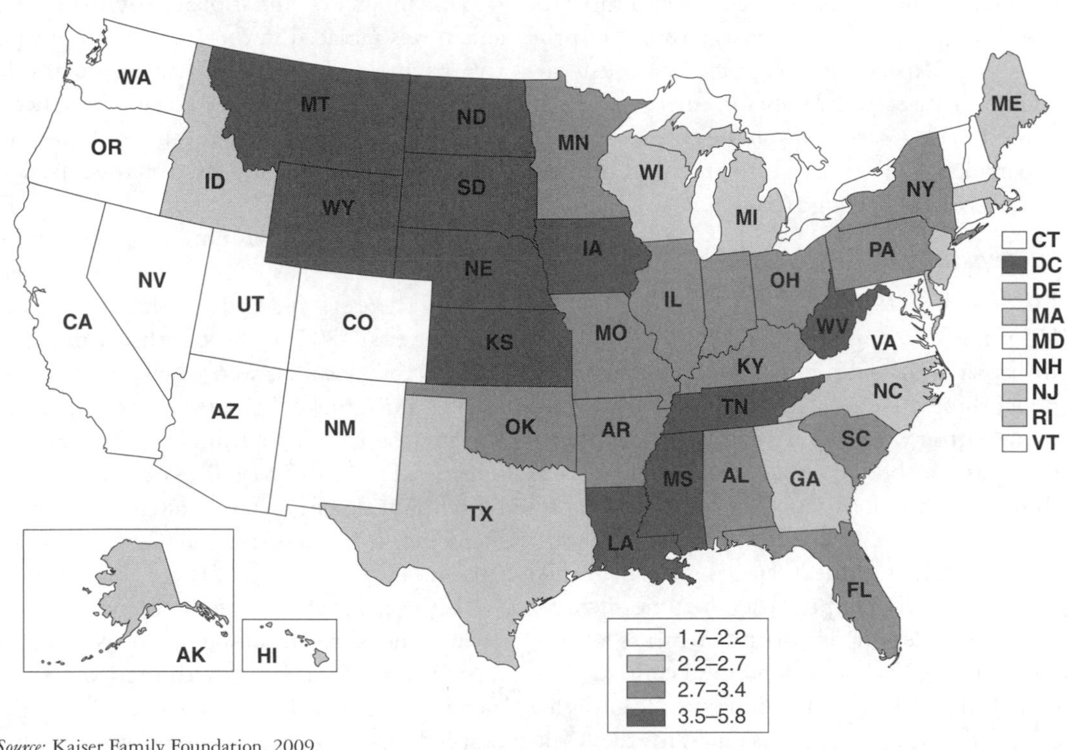

Source: Kaiser Family Foundation, 2009.

tation of hospital payment based on diagnosis-related groups (DRGs).[1] Technological advances and a changed understanding about the management of illness laid the ground work for the decline. DRGs reinforced the incentive to discharge patients more quickly. Hospitals suddenly found themselves penalized financially for failing to discharge patients. Bed rest was no longer considered a treatment modality (Stoeckle, 1995). Between 1975 and 1985, the average LOS in the United States decreased 7.8% from 7.7 to 7.1 days. By 1998, LOS had declined to 6.0 days per admission. The most recent data (2007) show an average inpatient stay of 5.5 days (American Hospital Association, 2008).

The changes in the last 25 years have changed the policy conversation, and the question is now being raised as to whether hospital capacity is in balance or at its limits. To a large extent, hospitals have met the challenge of managing capacity in the areas of medical surgical beds. Where capacity seems to be stretched is in the area of

[1]Diagnosis-related group is a system of payment for hospital inpatient services based on predetermined rates per discharge for approximately 500 groupings. It was developed for Medicare and has been in use since 1983. A Medicare recipient is assigned to a payment group depending on principal diagnosis. Other criteria include the patient's age, sex, secondary diagnoses, procedures performed, discharge status, complications, and comorbidities.

emergency departments. Many hospitals have experienced an increased demand for their services by the uninsured. This population also turns to the emergency departments as a source of primary care. Expanding emergency department capacity to meet the needs for emergency care while moving patients who use the emergency departments to primary care providers has become a major challenge (Bazzoli et al., 2003).

Increasingly Competitive Financial Environment

Hospital financing has gone through three distinct phases. Initially, hospitals were financed by philanthropy. These were the days when the hospital matron would sit with wealthy trustees to negotiate a budget that they would fund through annual donations (Rosner, 1982). By the early decades of the 20th century, hospitals needed more income than a few benefactors could regularly supply. They became increasingly dependent upon patient payments for service. The 1920s boom in hospital construction ended abruptly as the country fell into the depths of the Great Depression. With the stock market crash of 1929 and ensuing financial calamity, hospital revenues fell dramatically. One response was the organization of Blue Cross as a way to guarantee that patients could pay for their care. At its origin, Blue Cross offered the teachers of Dallas 21 days of care for $6 a year. Blue Cross began as a wholly owned subsidiary of the hospital's trade group, the American Hospital Association. It remained so until the early 1970s when the Congress forced American Hospital Association to divest (Law, 1986).

Blue Cross funded hospitals retrospectively. Put simply, there was an annual reckoning. At the end of the year, Blue Cross would pay its share of hospital costs. If 50% of the patients were Blue Cross subscribers, Blue Cross would pay half of the hospitals' annual expenses. Medicare was established in 1965 with a similar reimbursement scheme.

This inherently inflationary payment mechanism was replaced in the 1980s with prospective payment. In this third phase of hospital financing, led by the introduction of Medicare's Prospective Payment System in 1983, hospitals were paid a fixed amount based on the type of illness and type of patient—known as DRGs. The theory was that such a reimbursement system would encourage hospitals to operate more efficiently. There is some evidence that this did happen (Lee et al., 2003). On the other hand, critics charged that hospitals were discharging patients "sicker and quicker" (Newcomer et al., 1985). Private insurers adopted similar reimbursement schemes. By the early 1990s, virtually all hospital reimbursement systems contained some element of the prospective payment, case-based system.

With each payment iteration reimbursement became more specific and more focused. Hospitals finance offices grew with each wave of financing change. The first source of modern hospital financing, philanthropy, provided institutional support with which the hospital's small administration staff was expected to operate the facility. Blue Cross and other retrospective payers arrived on the scene and covered the costs associated with a specific share of the hospital's patients. Currently, prospective payment is specific payment for a specific patient. The range of services that could be undertaken by the hospitals becomes narrower.

It is now the case that many payers are not paying their full costs. With the growth of managed care and the threat by insurers to not contract with a particular hospital, hospitals have had to provide steep discounts in exchange for guaranteed patient share. It is also the case that the public payers, Medicaid and Medicare, often reimburse hospitals less than full cost. Medicare pays only 91 cents for each dollar spent caring for a Medicare patient. The funding shortfall for hospital care exceeds $18 billion per year. Hospitals receive an average of 86 cents for each dollar spent caring for Medicaid patients, resulting in annual funding shortfall of nearly $11 billion (AHA Resource Center, 2008). Hospitals are cost shifting onto a smaller base. Those hospitals with biggest proportion of paying patients are the most viable economically. Those with the largest percentage of uninsured patients are most vulnerable (Tompkins et al., 2006).

The other area where financial stress can be seen is in access to capital (Robinson, 2002). Hospitals were encouraged to debt finance, as all interest and depreciation expenses were treated as allowable costs and could be built into their hospital payments from public and private insurance companies. Without adequate capital, hospitals cannot replace or modernize outdated facilities, respond to changing demand such as the growth of outpatient surgery, or add new technology/equipment. Getting capital is sometimes difficult. For-profit hospitals have greater access to capital, as they can sell stocks and bonds in the public markets. Nonprofit and public hospitals finance most capital needs through tax-exempt revenue bonds. Multihospital systems with substantial assets and cash flow have an easier time gaining access to capital markets than free-standing hospitals. Those in the worse position are inner-city hospitals. Competition for scarce resources reinforces the situation whereby the strongest and best financed hospitals get stronger and the weak get weaker.

Hospital Response

At the same time as economic power shifted from hospitals and doctors to those who pay for services, hospitals found themselves in an increasingly competitive environment (Starr, 1982). With excess capacity in the system, hospitals compete among themselves for control of doctor referrals and patients. The strategies they have chosen to respond to these stresses resulted in institutional isomorphism (DiMaggio & Powell, 1983). In short, many nonprofit and public hospitals developed strategies based on the behavior of for-profit hospitals because they appeared to have created the optimal organizational and financial models for institutional viability. The for-profit model was perceived to have financial and organizational advantages (Stevens, 1989). In the 1960s, only 13% of hospitals were for-profit institutions. Ten years later, the for-profits had grown to 15% of hospitals. The growth of for-profit hospital chains was attributed to Medicare's highly profitable, retrospective, cost-based system of reimbursement (Starr, 1982). There was tremendous consolidation among the for-profit hospitals. By 1985, the four largest investor-owned hospitals corporations owned or managed over 500 community hospitals, more than 50% of the for-profit beds.

Many nonprofits decided to follow suit. With the tremendous uncertainty regarding financing arrangements, the growing alternatives to hospitalization, and increased competition for a smaller patient base, hospitals sought to create certainty through vertical and horizontal integration. These forms of consolidation were a way to strengthen the hospitals' finances by insuring patient flow within a defined group of institutions (Cuellar & Gertler, 2003). These arrangements go from joint purchasing to shared services to full asset mergers.

Strengthening Internal Operations

The growth of managed care, capitation, and other payment arrangements that fix the amount of reimbursement has pressured many hospitals to operate more efficiently. This has been achieved through cost-control efforts in three areas: First, hospitals have sought to operate more efficiently and to create economies of scale. For example, rather than allowing departments to decide what equipment to purchase, these decisions are being made centrally so that the hospital can negotiate for the best price possible given the size of the order. In some cases, hospitals are joining purchasing cooperatives in order to achieve even better price points. The second strategy is to slow expense growth in labor costs. Reengineering studies have examined staffing patterns with the intent of achieving greater budgetary efficiencies. The last set of internal cost control measures looks to the standardization of practice (Stevens, 1989). Utilization review, for example, tries to bring practice standards to bear on patient care and thus reduce the outliers.

Beyond strategies to increase operational efficiencies, hospitals have looked to increase their admissions and thus occupancy rates. More than $90 of every $100 of hospital revenue comes directly from providing medical care services to patients. Patients are the source of revenue, and physicians are the vehicle that delivers patients to the hospital. Hospitals are almost wholly dependent on the physicians who admit patients. Early on, hospitals sought to improve amenities available to admitting physicians. Very quickly, hospitals sought to assure an increased number of admissions by increasing the number of physicians with admitting privileges and strengthening relations with those who already admit. This has been accomplished using a variety of contractual arrangements. One example is a physician hospital organization whereby physicians agree to admit their patients into a given hospital in return for certain financial and organizational arrangements. Physicians, however, found that they could provide many of these services in ambulatory settings and went into competition with hospitals. The hospital response was to employ physicians on staff rather than have loose affiliations with these physicians. Hospitals have also tried to market their services directly to women, bypassing physicians by offering state-of-the-art reproductive and maternity programs. Women typically make decisions for their family about where they will receive health services. The choice of strategy depends on the local market (Berenson et al., 2007).

Diversification of Services/Horizontal and Vertical Integration

Another survival strategy is to diversify the scope of services. Hospitals have done this in part to respond to competition from alternative care systems (freestanding ambulatory surgery centers, nuclear magnetic resonance centers, health maintenance organizations, and hospice). This effort has helped to create profit centers within the hospital (laundry, sports medicine). More important, this strategy has developed a system of one-stop-shop, which is also considered a means to improve the experience of care while potentially controlling the costs (Berwick et al., 2008). Diversification has kept hospitals central to the organization of care as they provide a full spectrum of services, and it creates a protective shield of invincibility.

Diversification and integration of services are achieved by expanding hospitals' outpatient ca-

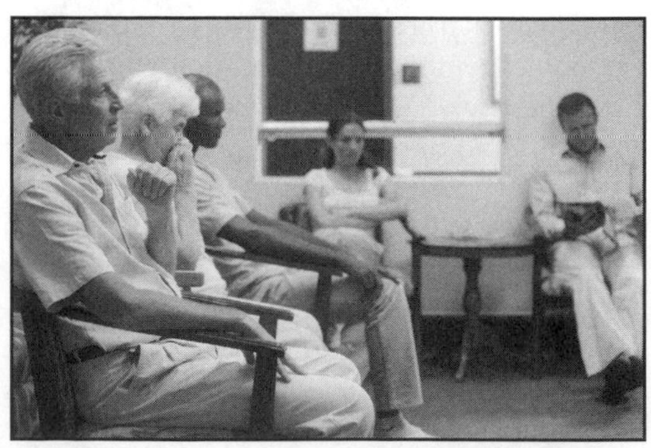

pacity to compete with freestanding ambulatory centers and by expanding rehabilitation and long-term care to compete with the long-term care system. As the population has grown and new medical treatments have been invented, the number of surgeries, deliveries, and outpatient visits has increased. In 2007, 67% of surgeries were performed on an outpatient basis (Cullen et al., 2009). Hospitals garnered half of these procedures. The remainder is performed in freestanding surgery centers and doctor offices. In addition, hospitals have expanded the number and variety of outpatient services such as physical and psychological rehabilitative services. Hospitals have also extended services into the community through home health care. Over 40% of hospitals maintain their own home health services. Rather than contracting in size, a number of hospitals have grown in the last two decades, but not in their traditional areas of service. They have grown in associated outpatient and community- and home-based services (Cuellar & Gertler, 2003).

Winners and Losers in This Competitive Environment

The crux of the problem confronting hospitals today is that they are being squeezed by a changing healthcare environment. More and more care has been moved out of the hospital into alternative settings—from subacute care nursing homes to surgicenters to a vastly expanded scope of services provided at home. Specialty drugs, quick-acting anesthesia, noninvasive surgical techniques, and high-technology diagnostic services have reduced the need for an inpatient stay or significantly shortened its length. Hospitals must compete for the same scarce resources: paying patients and profitable services. Each hospital is working to secure its place in the market. These strategies described above sound relatively benign; however, even adoption of all of these strategies does not guarantee that every hospital will be a winner. Some hospitals will do better in the market than others; some will survive, and others will close (Tompkins et al., 2006). We need to look at who wins and who loses in this environment and how it affects access to hospital care. What might be rational in the free market is not necessarily a rational response to the population's health needs. Allowing the market to solve the problem of too many hospitals and too many beds may further exacerbate the problem of inequitable distribution of healthcare resources.

Academic Medical Centers

Academic medical centers are a small subset of the nonprofit hospital. They are complex organizations that include a medical school, one or more teaching hospitals, and at least one additional health professional program such as nursing, dentistry, or veterinary medicine. Teaching hospitals are more costly to operate than other community hospitals. They are staffed both as educational institutions and as acute-care facilities. Medical personnel are trained using an apprenticeship model. Thus, students work alongside fully trained staff in the provision of patient care. The teaching function requires additional time and resources. Because of the perceived quality difference, higher costs have been deemed acceptable. In addition, academic medical centers care for vulnerable populations and sicker patients, as they have the greatest expertise to undertake this function. Academic medical centers are also the focal point for a great deal of biomedical research. Although biomedical research tends to be funded by the government, research grants do not cover the full costs involved.

Historically, the costs of teaching, research, and patient care are bundled into academic medical centers reimbursement rates from commercial insurers and government. In essence, paying patients subsidized the additional costs of education and the uninsured, but payers, whether government or private, have balked at paying for more care than they are directly responsible for providing and at paying for care when the quality has been called into question (Fisher et al., 2004). Increasingly, academic medical centers are losing money because educational costs are not included in private insurers' reimbursement rates. In addition, the discounts demanded by managed care companies combined with the lower rates paid by Medicare and Medicaid mean that these hospitals are struggling to make ends meet. The payers of health care objected to the use of a private good (patient care) to subsidize the cost of public goods (medical education, research, and charity care) (Blumenthal & Meyer, 1996).

Like all hospitals, the academic medical centers need to reduce overhead. In part, they are employing total quality management techniques to shorten LOS. The hospitals, however, have to walk a fine line in this regard because shortened lengths of stay make comprehensive teaching more difficult, as medical students, interns, and residents need to have experience with patients throughout the entire cycle of care. More recently, academic medical centers have tried to increase clinical productivity and hold down physician compensation (Mooradian & Meenrajan, 2009).

The academic medical centers have also strategized about new sources of revenue and that their survival depends on their turning the tertiary-care institutions into integrated health-care systems by developing primary care networks. In this way, they are assured a flow of patients into the hospital, and they have the ability to develop teaching programs in outpatient settings for primary care physicians. This is a new venture for many of the centers. The centers are also looking for ways to capitalize on their research ventures. They are developing sophisticated offices of technology transfer to capture the revenues that can be generated as a result of the basic and applied research that is taking place.

Voluntary Hospitals

Nonprofit or voluntary hospitals make up the majority of hospitals. These hospitals serve an important economic function in the communities where they are located. Hospitals employed nearly 5.3 million people in 2007, and hospitals spent about $304 billion on goods and services from other businesses. According to reports by the American Hospital Association, each hospital job supports about two more jobs in the community, making it a key fixture and indicator of the community's economic health (AHA Resource Center, 2008).

Despite the name, community hospitals often find themselves working at cross purposes. There is pressure for all hospitals to behave like teaching hospitals and provide the most advanced diagnosis and treatment. The physicians on their staff are highly trained and want to practice specialized medicine. Patients expect to receive comprehensive services at their local hospital. This results in the unnecessary duplication of facilities and facilities that have poor outcomes because of their low utilization rates (Chassin, 2002).

Voluntary hospitals also experience pressure to serve as a community resource for a range of services such as alcoholism, substance abuse, and HIV/AIDS care that extend beyond tertiary care. Hospitals still serve a vital community function as they did when they were first opened in the late 1800s. As a result, communities are reticent to close hospitals regardless of their occupancy rates or financial status. The only way that they are being closed is when an outside buyer purchases a hospital and seeks to rationalize care or when a local community is no longer willing to subsidize a failing community institution.

Even excluding the academic medical centers, community hospitals are not a monolithic group, as not all hospitals have access to the same profitable patients and services. The community hospitals in the greatest difficulty are those located in minority, low-income neighborhoods. Their financial distress is not directly due to cost of care. It is due to their serving a large number of uninsured patients. Mount Sinai Hospital in Chicago is a good case study of this phenomenon (Abraham, 1993). Mount Sinai was built on the west side of the city in a working class Jewish neighborhood. When the Jewish community moved to the north side of the city, the hospital trustees chose not to follow its historic patient population but to continue serving its geographic community that had become a black low-income community. The hospital now functions like a public hospital. It serves those persons with no other options for care. It runs a large emergency department and does not have the financial base to subsidize services. Mount Sinai has managed to survive through affiliation with two different medical schools. Rather than allow the hospital to be closed because so many of its patients are uninsured or inadequately insured, Mount Sinai has put itself at the hub of a group of treating and teaching centers. Its fate is quite different than many other facilities located in low-income urban neighborhoods (Harrison & Sexton, 2004).

Rural Hospitals

Hospitals in rural areas were built as a result of the Hill-Burton legislation. In order to distribute funds equitably across the 50 states, money went into the construction of hospitals in communities of less than 10,000 persons. There are currently 2,000 rural hospitals, which is 40% of all nonfederal hospitals.

Rural hospitals are even more financially vulnerable than many of the inner-city community hospitals. These hospitals tend to be smaller, less than 50 beds, and cannot offer highly complex care. As a result, they have low-volume occupancy rates of less than 40%. There is a reduced demand for rural hospital beds because many medical procedures that might have been done in such a facility can now be done on an outpatient basis. More complex procedures require costly technology and high-volume use, neither of which can occur in a rural hospital. In addition, rural hospitals received a lower DRG rate than do urban hospitals, and they have increased bad debt because of poverty.

Although rural hospitals are at the greatest risk of closing, they also serve a vital community function, and there is a political notion that as the sole community resource for Medicare patients federal initiatives should be used to bolster these hospitals. The primary strategy is to diversify services and offer clinical and long-term care services (Succi et al., 1997).

Public Hospitals

The public hospital is the dumping grounds for patients and services. They serve the working poor, unemployed, those with inadequate insurance, undocumented immigrants, and Medicaid patients due to low reimbursement rates. Public hospitals also provide unprofitable services that are highly labor intensive (Horwitz, 2005). These are inpatient and outpatient services that combine medical and social services that many nonprofit hospitals find too costly to offer. In the 10 largest cities, public hospitals account for 11% of acute-care hospitals, but provide 20% of emergency visits and 27% of outpatient visits. These hospitals represent 32% of Level I trauma providers and 58% of beds for burn patients (National Association of Public Hospitals and Health Systems, 2009). Their debt is picked up by local government, but the tax base is not adequate in poorer communities to assure their survival. Local tax revenues have risen less quickly than hospital costs.

Although competition in the hospital sector has resulted in many voluntary hospitals absorbing Medicaid patients as their lengths of stay have declined and as some revenue per bed is better than none, there is a general belief that public hospitals serve a critical function in terms of access and maintenance of health status of those with no other recourse to care. A study of acute-care public hospitals between 1980 and 1996 found that public hospitals that were privatized tended to provide less uncompensated care than public hospitals that were not privatized (Desai et al., 2000). The public hospitals also serve a vital educational function by exposing medical students to a wider range of illnesses and injuries across a broader spectrum of the population. Their closure has limited the ability of these students to make a choice to serve the medically underserved simply by removing the opportunity to experience the challenge (Walker et al., 2008). The public hospitals will always be essential community providers and cannot be disregarded in any efforts to achieve healthcare reform.

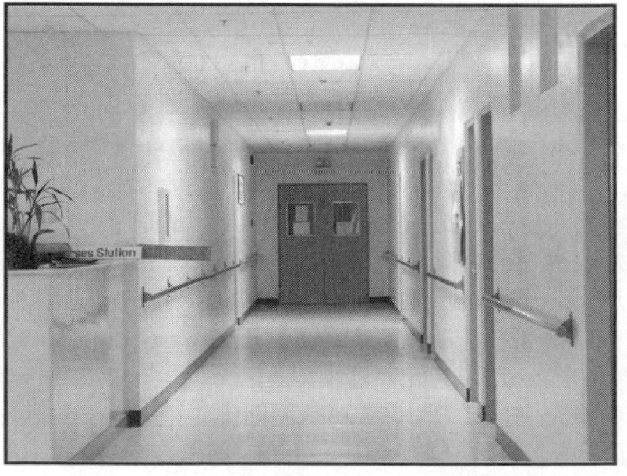

Proprietary Hospitals

The trajectory of for-profit or proprietary hospitals has been uneven moving up and down with the opportunity to make a profit. By the early 1980s, many health policy analysts feared that the for-profits would eventually overtake the voluntary hospitals as the primary source of care. As a result of government efforts to control reimbursement, the industry suffered major setbacks in the late 1980s and a broad based takeover never materialized (Seay & Vladeck, 1988). The for-profits made a comeback in the early 1990s with the ability to pick and choose what patients to serve and what services to provide. The ability to pick and choose patient and service mix permits for-profit hospitals to function in a profitably sustainable manner. They design staffing to maximize flexibility and are known to be careful in the purchase and use of supplies. This improves the cost side of their ledgers. Even more critical, they create incentives for physicians to refer to the hospital on the revenue side. This was the Columbia/HCA strategy (Klienke, 1998). Columbia/HCA moved aggressively into a market and developed tight referral networks.

In theory, for-profit hospitals should be more cost-effective and provide a higher quality of care than nonprofit hospitals. This has not been the case. The first research on the quality of for-profit hospitals showed that for-profit hospitals had higher average costs and charges and no differences in outcomes (Kuttner, 1996). Data on whether for-profit hospitals provide less uncompensated care and/or treat less complex patients than do nonprofits or public hospitals are mixed. A study of uncompensated care in California found the level of uncompensated care is related to levels of debt and cash flow, not to hospital ownership (Kim et al., 2009); however, a different service mix was found between for-profit and nonprofit hospitals. For-profit hospitals are more likely to provide open-heart surgery, a highly profitable service than are nonprofit or public hospitals (Horwitz, 2005). In a competitive market, the cherry picking of profitable patients or services is acceptable. Health care, however, is not a competitive market. If a for-profit is the only provider in a given area, then segments of the community have only limited access to critical services.

Healthcare Policy, Health Reform, and the Role of Hospitals

Hospitals remain at the center of the U.S. healthcare delivery system. Although many hospitals have formed alliances with physicians and other providers and many have merged into multihospital systems, the hospital sector remains as it was at the beginning of the 20th century, roughly 5,000 separate institutions that function independently.

Since the 1970s, health policy experts have documented the need for greater integration. For example, leaders of the well-regarded Dartmouth Atlas of Health Care offered their prescription for rational health reform in a 2009 article published in the *New England Journal of Medicine*. They recommend two strategies: fostering the growth of integrated systems and payment reform that supports greater integration. "Consensus is emerging that integrated delivery systems that provide strong support to clinicians and team-based care management for patients offer great promise for improving quality and lowering costs" (Fisher et al., 2009).

Few such reforms were incorporated into federal health reform legislation. The question is why not? Although there are a variety of possible explanations ranging from the difficulty of conceptualizing an effective method to simple ignorance, one fact might provide a clue—hospitals control about one third of the $2 trillion spent in the U.S. health system in 2008 (see Table 6-3). With such gigantic sums comes an enormous capacity to influence public policy. Although hospitals operate independently, they have banded together into a potent political force to defend that autonomy. According to the Center for Responsive Politics, hospitals and nursing homes employed 1,175 lobbyists who helped spend $78 million to influence health reform during 2009 (Center for Responsive Politics, 2009).

This is clearly a case where rational common interests and rational individual interests are in conflict. Our inability to transcend the conflict produces what Garret Harden in 1968 described as a "tragedy of commons" (p. 1244). The solution is simple to state and extraordinarily difficult to achieve—not to charge the stake holders with acting irresponsibly and demand better behavior but to change what is in their best interests to do.

References

Abraham, L. K. (1993). *Mama might be better off dead: The failure of health care in urban America*. Chicago: University of Chicago Press.

AHA Resource Center. (2008). *Fast facts on US hospitals.* Retrieved February 11, 2010, from http://www.aha.org/aha/resource-center/Statistics-and-Studies/fast-facts.html

American Hospital Association. (2002). *Hospital statistics* (2002 edition). Chicago: Health Forum LLC.

American Hospital Association. (2008). *AHA hospital statistics* (2008 edition). Chicago: Health Forum LLC.

Bazzoli, G. J., Brewster, L. R., Liu, G., & Kuo, S. (2003). Does U.S. hospital capacity need to be expanded? *Health Affairs, 22*(6), 40–54.

Berenson, R. A., Ginsburg, P. B., & May, J. H. (2007). Hospital-physicians relations: Cooperation, competition, or separation? *Health Affairs, 26*(1), w31–w43.

Berwick, D. M., Nolan, T. W., & Whittington, J. (2008). The triple aim: Care, health, and cost. *Health Affairs, 27*(3), 759–769.

Blumenthal, D., & Meyer, G. (1996). Academic health centers in a changing environment. *Health Affairs, 15*(2), 200–215.

Center for Responsive Politics. (2009). *Lobbying spending database hospitals/nursing homes, 2009.* Retrieved January 17, 2009, from http://www.opensecrets.org/lobby/indusclient.php?year=2009&lname=H02&id=

Chassin, M. (2002). Achieving and sustaining improved quality: Lessons from New York State and cardiac Surgery. *Health Affairs, 21*(4), 40–51.

Centers for Medicare and Medicaid Services (CMS). (2010). *Historic national health expenditure data.* Retrieved January 16, 2010, from http://www.cms.hhs.gov/NationalHealthExpendData/02_NationalHealthAccountsHistorical.asp

Cuellar, A. E., & Gertler, P. J. (2003). Trends in hospital consolidation: The formation of local systems. *Health Affairs, 22*(6), 77–87.

Cullen, K. A., Hall, M. J., & Golosinsky, A. (2009, January 28). Ambulatory surgery in the United States, 2006. *National Health Statistics Report, 11* (revised September 4, 2009). Retrieved January 17, 2010, from www.cdc.gov/nchs/data/nhsr/nhsr011.pdf

Desai, K., Lukas, C. V., & Young, G. (2000). Public hospitals: Privatization and uncompensated care. *Health Affairs, 19*(2), 167–172.

DiMaggio, P. J., & Powell, W. W. (1983). The iron cage revisited: Institutional isomorphism and collective rationality in organizational fields. *American Sociological Review, 48,* 147–160.

Duke, K. (1996). Hospitals in a changing health care system. *Health Affairs, 15*(2), 49–61.

Fisher, E. S., Wennberg, D. E., Stukel, T. A., & Gottlieb, D. J. (2004). Variations in the longitudinal efficiency of academic medical centers. *Health Affairs,* Web Exclusive. Var 19-Var 32.

Fisher, E. S., Bynum, J. P., & Skinner, J. S. (2009). Getting past denial: The high cost of health care in the United States. *New England Journal of Medicine, 360,* 849–852.

Gray, B. H., & Schlesinger, M. (2009). Charitable expectations of nonprofit hospitals: Lessons from Maryland. *Health Affairs, 28*(5), w809–w821.

Gruber, J. (2006). *The role of consumer copayments for health care: Lessons from the RAND health insurance experiment and beyond.* Prepared for the Kaiser Family Foundation. Retrieved January 14, 2010, from http://www.kff.org/insurance/upload/7566.pdf

Hardin, G. (1968). The tragedy of the commons. *Science, 162*(5364), 1243–1248. Retrieved February 11, 2010, from http://www.sciencemag.org/cgi/reprint/162/3859/1243.pdf

Harrison, J. P., & Sexton, C. (2004). The paradox of the not-for-profit hospital. *Health Care Management, 23*(3), 192–204. Retrieved January 17, 2010, from http://www.ncbi.nlm.nih.gov/pubmed/15457836?itool=EntrezSystem2.PEntrez.Pubmed.Pubmed_ResultsPanel.Pubmed_RVDocSum&ordinalpos=16

Horwitz, J. R. (2005). Making profits and providing care: Comparing nonprofit, for-profit, and government hospitals. *Health Affairs, 24*(3), 790–801.

Kaiser Family Foundation. (2009). Hospital beds per 1,000 population, 2007. Retrieved January 15, 2010, from http://www.statehealthfacts.org/comparemaptable.jsp?ind=382&cat=8&sort=a

Kim, T. H., Mccue, M. J., & Thompson, J. M. (2009). The relationship of financial and mission factors to the level of uncompensated care provided in California hospitals. *Journal of Healthcare Management, 54*(6), 383–401.

Klienke, J. D. (1998). Deconstructing the Columbia/HCA investigation. *Health Affairs, 17*(2), 7–26.

Kuttner, R. (1996). Columbia/HCA and the resurgence of the for-profit hospital business, Parts I and II. *New England Journal of Medicine, 335*(5), 362–367, and *335*(6), 446–451.

Law, S. (1986). Blue Cross: What went wrong? In P. Conrad & R. Kern (Eds.), *The Sociology of Health and Illness* (2nd ed.). New York: St. Martin's Press.

Lee, J. S., Berenson, R. A., Mayes, R., & Gauthier, A. K. (2003). Medicare payment policy: Does cost shifting matter? *Health Affairs,* Web Exclusive.

Luft, H. S. (1981). *Health maintenance organizations: Dimensions of performance*. New York: John Wiley and Sons.

Mitchell, J. M. (2007). Utilization changes associated with physician ownership of ambulatory surgery centers (ASCs). iHEA 2007 6th World Congress: Explorations in Health Economics Paper. Available from SSRN: http://ssrn.com/abstract=992622

Mooradian, A. D., & Meenrajan, S. (2009). The business of academic medicine is a business like no other: A perspective. *Health Care Management, 28*(4):344–350.

National Association of Public Hospitals and Health Systems. (2009). *America's safety net hospitals and health systems, 2007: Results of the NAPH annual hospital characteristics survey.* Retrieved January 17, 2010, from http://www.naph.org/Main-Menu-Category/Our-Work/Safety-Net-Financing/Characteristics-Report/Characteristics-2007.aspx

New York State Department of Health. (2009). *Hospital profile.* Retrieved January 14, 2010, from http://hospitals.nyhealth.gov/

Newcomer, R., Wood, J., & Sankar, A. (1985). Medicare prospective payment: anticipated effect on hospitals, other community agencies, and families. *Journal of Health Politics, Policy and Law, 10*(2), 275–282.

Robinson, J. C. (2002). Bond-market skepticism and stock-market exuberance in the hospital industry. *Health Affairs, 21*(1), 104–117.

Rosenberg, C. E. (1982). From almshouse to hospital: The shaping of Philadelphia General Hospital. *Milbank Memorial Fund Quarterly, 60*(1), 108–154.

Rosner, D. (1982). *A once charitable enterprise: Hospital and health care in Brooklyn and New York, 1885–1915*. Princeton: Princeton University Press.

Seay, J. D., & Vladeck, B. C. (1988). Mission matters. In J. D. Seay & B. C. Vladeck (Eds.), *In sickness and in health: The mission of voluntary health care institutions*. New York: McGraw Hill Books.

Starr, P. (1982). *The social transformation of American medicine*. New York: Basic Books.

Stevens, R. (1989). *In sickness and in wealth: American hospitals in the twentieth century*. New York: Basic Books.

Stoeckle, J. (1995). The citadel cannot hold: Technologies go outside the hospital, patients and doctors too. *Milbank Quarterly, 73*(1), 3–17.

Succi, M. J., Lee, S. Y., & Alexander, J. A. (1997). Effects of market position and competition on rural hospital closures. *Health Services Research, 31*(6), 679–699.

Tompkins, C. P., Altman, S. H., & Eilat, E. (2006). The precarious pricing system for hospital services. *Health Affairs, 25*(1), 45–56.

Walker, K. O., Calmes, D., Hanna, N., & Baker, R. (2008). The impact of public hospital closure on medical and residency education: Implications and recommendations. *Journal of the National Medical Association, 100*(12), 1377–1383.

Chapter 7

Long-Term Care

Emma Kontzamanis and Keville Fredrickson

OVERVIEW

In this chapter, the need for long-term care services is explained from the perspective of the explosive growth of the older population as well as the increase in disability and chronic illness in the general population. A definition of long-term care within the contexts of inpatient and community-based services is also explained. In the United States the focus of long-term care is on nursing homes. This will be discussed as well as alternatives to nursing home care which involve integrated services such as case management, social health maintenance organizations, and programs of all-inclusive care for elders. Solutions to the key issues affecting cost, quality, and access to long-term care services are proposed.

OBJECTIVES

- To discuss two reasons for the increasing need for long-term care
- To describe alternatives to nursing home care that provide comparable services
- To explain the benefits of integrated long-term care services
- To identify policy issues affecting cost, quality, and access to long-term care

KEY TERMS

- Case management
- Chronic care population
- Frail older population
- Home- and community-based services
- Integrated long-term care
- Long-term care reform
- Managed long-term care
- Nursing home services
- Program of All-Inclusive Care for the Elderly (PACE)
- Social health maintenance organization (SHMO)

The impact of medical advances and technology has generally increased the average lifespan of Americans. In addition, people of all ages are living longer with chronic conditions requiring a variety of long-term care services. The older population, in particular, and all other age groups living with chronic or disabling health conditions need long-term care services because these conditions require ongoing attention and have the potential to deteriorate over time. This chapter defines long-term care along the continuum of social to medical care systems, as well as discusses the need for long-term care services for older persons and other chronic care populations. Long-term care in nursing homes, alternatives to nursing homes, and the need for integrated services, such as case management, social health maintenance organizations (SHMOs) and Programs of All-Inclusive Care for the Elderly (PACE) are also discussed. In conclusion, the issues driving long-term care policy, specifically cost, quality, and access, are presented. The intent is to provide the reader with an overview of long-term care, including definition, types, and policy issues.

Long-Term Care Defined

The federal government defines long-term care as a variety of services that includes medical and nonmedical care to people who have chronic illness or disability. Long-term care helps to meet the health and personal needs of individuals over a period of months or years. Most long-term care assists people with activities of daily living, such as dressing, bathing, and toileting, and instrumental activities of daily living, such as housework, meal preparation, shopping, and money management. These are primarily low-tech services. These services are provided by paid professionals, paraprofessionals, unpaid family members, and other informal helpers to individuals who need assistance on a prolonged basis with personal care, household chores, and life management in order to minimize, restore, or compensate for the loss of physical, cognitive, and/or mental functioning (Kodner, 2004). Long-term care can also encompass highly complex medical services such as nursing care and are provided by trained professionals. Because of the range of services from health care to social service long-term care can be provided in one's home, in the community, in an assisted living facility, or in a nursing home (Centers for Medicaid and Medicare Services, 2007).

Who Needs Long-Term Care

Older Persons

National trends indicate that growing numbers of the older population will require long-term care services in residential facilities, at home, and in community-based settings. The need and demand for these services are driven by the higher incidence of chronic illness in the population, in general, and frailty in an aging population. The U.S. Census Bureau (2004) has projected that between 2000 and 2030 the population of those aged 65 and older will grow from 35 million to 71 million. The fastest growing segment of this age group is the 85 and older component. Census Bureau projections for this group for the same time period are estimated to increase by 126%. The numbers are staggering, going from 4.2 million to 9.6 million. The need for long-term care becomes even more apparent by comparing the census numbers to the findings of a 2005 Commonwealth Fund Survey indicating that people are living longer with chronic illnesses such as cancer, cardiovascular disease, and diabetes (Collins et al., 2005). In addition, older persons living with chronic disease many times require assistance with activities of daily living. This is a key determinant of frailty. Kaiser-Permanente's model for predicting the proportion of frail older persons in selected age groups shows a rate of 214 frail older persons per 1,000 population for those aged 80 to 84, 368 per 1,000 for those aged 85 to 89, and 563 per 1,000 for those aged 90 and older (Brody et al., 2002). These predictions compound the need for long-term care in the older population.

The U.S. Census Bureau (2008) projects that the racial and ethnic diversity of the older population will also undergo major changes. Minority groups will become a much larger percentage of the 90 and older population, growing from 14% in 2000 to nearly 50% in 2100. Among older persons, the Hispanic population is projected to be as large as all other minority groups combined by 2070. This change has major implications for chronic care service demands for several reasons. Age adjusted mortality rates of blacks are persistently higher than those of whites, whereas those of Hispanics and Asians/Pacific Islanders are lower than those of whites. There are also some striking racial and ethnic differences in the prevalence of chronic conditions. Blacks, for example, have higher rates of cerebrovascular disease, diabetes, obesity, and hypertension than whites, whereas Hispanics have

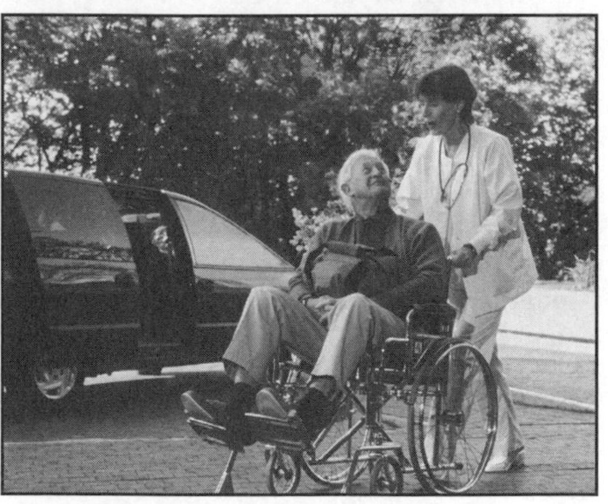

lower rates of some diseases, such as arthritis and hypertension, and higher rates of other diseases, such as diabetes, than whites have.

Furthermore, it is well known that service use and treatment practices differ across racial and ethnic groups (Smedley et al., 2003). Several explanations have been proposed, including one's attitude and belief patterns, preferences, and behavior, as well as providers' discriminatory behavior (Wolf, 2001).

Among the important manifestations of cultural differences across racial and ethnic groups are patterns of household and living arrangements, which in turn have consequences for informal care patterns and formal service use. In particular, minority older persons are much less likely than whites are to live alone (including with a spouse only) and much more likely to live with other family members (Wolf, 2001). Historically, minority older persons have been less likely than whites have been to reside in nursing homes, although recent findings suggest some reversal of that pattern. It is also the case that for home and community-based care, both the levels and mixture of service use by type differ by race (Wolf, 2001).

Currently, about 9 million people over the age of 65 years are receiving long-term care services.

Many are cared for at home by family and/or significant others, and many are in institutional settings. A U.S. Department of Health and Human Services (2008) study reports that people who reach 65 years old will likely have a 40% chance of entering a nursing home, and 10% of those entering will stay there 5 or more years. If nursing home care is not an option for this population because of economic issues or personal choice, community-based care is the alternative.

Other Chronic Care Populations

The need for long-term care services goes beyond the elderly. Almost 54 million Americans have a limitation or disability that is associated with a long-term physical, sensory, or cognitive condition that substantially limits one or more major life activities. The U.S. Department of Health and Human Services (2008) reports the prevalence of disability in the population has remained fairly consistent at 18% to 19% of the population. In addition, the 2001 census survey data indicate that the following percentages of any type of disability in the civilian noninstitutionalized population are 5.8% of those 5 to 15 years of age, 18.6% of those 16 to 64 years of age, and 41.9% of those 65 years of age and older.

The disability statistics on race, ethnicity, income, and education level further add to the need for long-term care services. According to the 2000 census for those 5 years of age and older, 24.3% of blacks, 24.3% of American Indians and Alaska Natives, 16.6% of Asians, and 21.7% of people of two or more races have a disability. Ethnicity data from the same source indicate 18.3% of white, non-Hispanic, or Latino and 20.9% of Hispanic or Latino of any race have a disability. The impact of socioeconomic status is another serious consideration when looking at the need for long-term care. The 1997 U.S. Census Bureau Report indicates the poverty rate among the 25- to 64-year-old population with no disability was 8% in contrast to 10% for people with a nonsevere disability and 28% for those with a severe disability. Additionally, 8.7 million people with disabilities are poor. This is a substantially higher proportion (17.6%) than was found among those aged 5 years and older without disabilities (10.6%). Education level data show the same pattern. People with disabilities are less likely to be highly educated than are people without disabilities: 22% of people with disabilities do not have their high school diploma, as opposed to the 8% of the population without disabilities. It is also less likely that people with disabilities will graduate from college (12%) than it is for people without disabilities (23%) (U.S. Department of Health and Human Services, 2008).

The population under the age of 65 years requiring long-term care is substantial and continues to validate the need for long-term care services in the United States. Defining the population as those needing assistance with activities of daily living and instrumental activities of daily living requires a look at the types of care currently available as well as current models and proposals for more effective and efficient types of long-term care.

Long-Term Care in Nursing Homes

Nursing homes are one of the major providers of long-term care. They are defined as residential facilities for people with chronic illness or disability, particularly older individuals who have mobility and eating problems. Other terms used for nursing home are convalescent home or long-term care facility (Center for Medicaid and Medicare Services, 2007). For individuals who are too frail or sick to live at home, nursing homes provide a permanent residence. The basic services provided to residents in nursing homes are room and board, 24 hour per day nursing care, pharmacy and diagnostic services, assistance with activities of daily living, activity programs, optometry, audiology, and dental services, physical and occupational therapy, and speech pathology services. In looking at the future of nursing homes in New York State, the Long Term Care Community Coalition (2008) found that the need for nursing home care may grow as New Yorkers get older, poorer, sicker and more disabled. Additionally, nursing homes will be called on to do more as the population becomes more racially and ethnically diverse and as some consumers may want a congregate setting with social interaction as an alternative to being isolated in their homes (p. 3).

There have been significant changes in nursing home care starting in the mid 1990s. In response to the financial pressures on hospitals to decrease length of stay and the decreased demand for long-term care beds due to other long-term care options, nursing homes began to play a more active role for people recovering from short term hospital stays (Dennison, 2008). Long-term care nursing home beds have been converted to subacute beds; however, the findings of the Long Term Care Community Coalition and the increase in those needing residential long-term care may necessitate a shift back to changing subacute beds to long-term care beds in New York and other states. Some of the issues that nursing homes face in addressing this potential change are shifting from meeting minimum regulatory standards to a culture of person-directed care, empowering direct-care workers to be more responsive to individual needs, and ensuring funding for appropriate care and physical plant (Long Term Care Community Coalition, 2007, 2008). The coalition proposes that promoting resident and worker satisfaction will help to facilitate the change needed to ensure that nursing home care is a viable option for those who want it.

Alternatives to Nursing Homes

There are many people who require nursing home care but prefer to stay in their own home or in alternative living arrangements with the help of family and friends, community services, and professional care agencies. Home services such as Meals on Wheels programs, friendly visitor and shopper services, and adult day care can facilitate individuals remaining at home. Moving into a nursing home may not be necessary for someone ill and disabled if he or she can receive community services from various agencies.

For individuals needing assistance with a small number of tasks, several housing options can be considered. Assisted living is a living situation in which some services are available to residents who basically live independently within a housing complex. Generally, assisted living residents pay a regular monthly rent and additional fees for services that they may require. Often assisted living includes dining facilities so residents do not have the pressure to shop and cook for themselves and may have the opportunity to engage with their neighbors over a meal. Board and care homes are group living arrangements designed to meet the needs of people who cannot live independently but do not need nursing home services. Most of these homes provide assistance with activities of daily living. Additionally, there are housing programs for the older population and disabled with low to moderate incomes subsidized by the federal and state government. Some of these residences provide assistance to residents who need help with some instrumental activities of daily living. In general, residents live independently in an apartment within a housing complex. Finally, continuing care retirement communities provide care based on residents' needs, ranging from independent living apartments to skilled nursing care in an affiliated nursing home. Residents move from one setting to another based on their needs but remain a part of their continuing care retirement community (Centers for Medicaid and Medicare Services, 2008).

For those individuals wanting to remain in their homes, long-term care community-based programs allow them to remain in the community with the assistance of formal caregivers, professional services, and supplemental support services. Programs such as New York State's Long Term Home Health Care Program allow individuals requiring nursing home care to remain at home with essential services that ensure their health and safety. Individuals of all ages, including children and people with AIDS, who require long-term care for chronic and disabling conditions can receive these services. Also known as "The Lombardi Program" or "Nursing Home without Walls," this program provides eligible patients an alternative to institutional care. Based on an individualized plan of care, a comprehensive package of coordinated services is designed to meet the specific needs of eligible patients in their homes. (The program serves chronically ill and disabled persons over the age of 18 years who have ongoing healthcare needs.) The hallmark of this program is case management by a registered nurse. An interdisciplinary team of healthcare professionals provides assessments, visits, and delivery of ongoing quality care in the home. Services include nursing care, physical, occupational, and speech language pathology, social work, personal care aides, adult day health care, transportation, personal emergency response system, nutrition, and audiology (New York State Department of Health, 2008).

In addition to the Long Term Home Health Care Program, the New York State Department of Health administers the Care at Home (CAH) Medicaid waiver program. Initiated in 1985, Care at Home is a Medicaid waiver program for children with disabilities. It is an alternative to institutionalization involving home and community-based services. A waiver program is a federally approved suspension of regular Medicaid rules to allow for a more cost-effective expenditure of Medicaid dollars. New York's CAH waivers suspend the eligibility rules for qualified children and provide access to Medicaid waiver services as well as necessary State Plan services (New York State Department of Health, 2007).

The Need for Integrated Long-Term Care Services

Individuals receiving long-term care need an array of services from various providers and sources. Integrating those services into a comprehensive package allows for monitoring the quality and quantity of service to ensure effective, efficient care to those who need it. Several integrated models of long-term care exist in the United States. Most of them have been tested in urban areas or with urban populations. Rural regions have both barriers and opportunities in implementing integrated long-term care. Although a full range of home and community-based long-term care services is available to meet the needs of individuals in urban areas, rural areas may be better equipped for cooperation among acute and long-term care providers. Managed care penetration and experience are limited in most rural regions. Models such as the Program of All-Inclusive Care for the Elderly (PACE), the Arizona long-term care system, the Carle Clinic demonstration as well as developments in several states for serving rural long-term care populations, integrate long-term care services across providers and funders (Beaulieu et al., 2001).

The cost and coordination of long-term care services are complex problems. Integrated long-term care has been proposed as one of the ways to address this (Kodner, 2004). Three approaches to integrated long-term care are presented next.

Case Management

According to the Case Management Society of America (2008), case management is a collaborative process of assessment, planning, facilitation, and advocacy for options and services to meet an individual's health needs through communication and available resources to promote quality cost-effective outcomes. Case management is an area of practice within a profession, such as nursing or social work. Its underlying premise is that when an individual reaches the optimum level of wellness and functional capability, everyone benefits: the individuals being served, their support systems, the healthcare delivery systems, and the various reimbursement sources. Case management serves as a means for achieving client wellness and autonomy through advocacy, communication, education, identification of service resources, and service facilitation. The case manager helps to identify appropriate providers and facilities throughout the continuum of services, while ensuring that available resources are being used in a timely and cost-effective manner in order to obtain optimum value for both the client and the reimbursement source. Case management services are best offered in a climate that allows direct communication between the case manager, the client, and appropriate service personnel in order to optimize the outcome for all concerned.

One model for case management services is managed long-term care (MLTC). This program assists people who are chronically ill or have disabilities that require health and long-term care services to stay in their homes and communities as long as possible. The MLTC plan arranges and pays for a large selection of health and social services and provides choice and flexibility in obtaining needed services from one place. The MLTC model provides an array of services and is designed to reduce the costs of long-term care by making clinical and nonmedical services available to frail older and disabled populations in a home or community setting rather than in an institution. The availability of a range of services minimizes the use of high-cost institutional resources and makes services available in settings more satisfactory for consumers and their families. MLTC differs from other models of noninstitutional long-term service delivery because it places a greater emphasis on care coordination as well as reimbursement methods designed to contain cost growth. It provides a coherent system of long-term care services, care coordination, and social supports. The MLTC plan services and operations are developed around patient requirements and preferences. Plans arrange for a wide range of clinical services, backed by support services, such as transportation, personal care, and care management. All services required by enrollees are coordinated through the plans' care managers who serve as a central point of contact for all providers (Novello, 2004).

Social Health Maintenance Organization

A social managed care plan or social health maintenance organization (SHMO) is a model that provides the full range of Medicare benefits offered by standard managed care plan's plus services, which include care coordination, prescription drug benefits, chronic care benefits covering short-term nursing home care, a full range of home- and community-based services such as homemaker, personal care services, adult day care, respite care, and medical transportation. Eyeglasses, hearing aids, and dental benefits may also be included. The full range of medical benefits offered by standard managed care plans plus chronic care services is provided to members. There are currently four SHMOs in the United States: Kaiser-Permanante, Portland, Oregon; SCAN, Long Beach, California; Elderplan, Brooklyn, New York; and Health Plan of Nevada, Las Vegas, Nevada. All enrollees must be 65 years of age or older and have Medicare Parts A and B in addition to other geographic and medical criteria (Center for Medicare and Medicaid Services, 2008). There are four basic elements of the SHMO model: a sponsoring agency merges acute and chronic care into a single system; the SHMO services a membership of both disabled and able-bodied older persons; the SHMO is paid on a prepaid capitation basis; and the SHMO bears responsibility for service costs. Because Medicare and private insurance cover only a very small part of long-term care, SHMOs attempt to extend the managed care acute-care financing and delivery model to include chronic care management and services supported by the Robert Wood Johnson Foundation (Stone, 2000).

Program of All-Inclusive Care for the Elderly

The Program of All-Inclusive Care for the Elderly (PACE) provides comprehensive medical and social services at an adult day health center, home, and/or inpatient facilities. Older people who meet their state's standard for nursing home care can choose this comprehensive service package that allows them to stay at home while receiving services rather than being institutionalized. A team of doctors, nurses, and other health professionals assess participant needs, develop care plans, and deliver all services that are integrated into a complete healthcare plan. PACE is available only in states that have chosen to offer PACE under Medicaid. Enrollees must be at least 55 years of age, live in the PACE service area, be screened by a team of doctors, nurses, and other health professionals as meeting that state's nursing home level of care, and at the time of enrollment, be able to live safely in the community. PACE offers and manages all of the medical, social, and rehabilitative services needed to preserve or restore their independence, to remain in their homes and communities, and to maintain their quality of life. Services are available 24 hours a day, 7 days a week, and 365 days a year. PACE teams include primary care physicians and nurses; physical, occupational, and recreational therapists; social workers; personal care attendants; dieticians; and drivers (Centers for Medicaid and Medicare Services, 2008).

In order to provide accessible, cost-effective, quality long-term care to those who need it, comprehensive healthcare policy needs to be established and promoted in the United States. Healthcare professionals can and should be the driving force behind the development and implementation of long-term care policy. Knowledge of the current system, including its strengths and weaknesses, as well as knowledge of the issues affecting long-term care policy is important and essential for healthcare professionals to be aware of as they advocate for change in the system and become influential in the policy process.

Problems Driving Policy: Cost, Quality, and Access

Cost, access, and quality are highly intertwined. If costs are high, a person may not be able to afford services. If costs are low, quality may suffer. The Centers for Medicaid and Medicare Services is the U.S. federal agency administering Medicaid and Medicare benefits to the population. People receiving social security benefits, either from retirement or disability, are entitled to Medicare. Medicare pays for long-term care in only the most minimum of ways such as nursing home care post-hospitalization. It also offers limited access to long-term care through either PACE or SHMO. On the other hand, Medicaid is the primary payer for long-term care but is available only to certain low-income individuals and families who fit into an eligibility group that is recognized by federal and state law. Each state sets its own guidelines regarding Medicaid (Centers for Medicaid and Medicare Services, 2008). Those who need long-term care and are not eligible for Medicaid can pay privately for that care. This may be done directly or through the purchase of long-term care insurance. Both of these options are expensive and may not be affordable to those who need it.

Because of the extraordinary costs that can be associated with long-term care, there is a growing effort to encourage the purchase of long-term care insurance. An innovative long-term care insurance program, the New York State Partnership for Long Term Care (NYSP), offers full asset protection in exchange for mandatory insurance

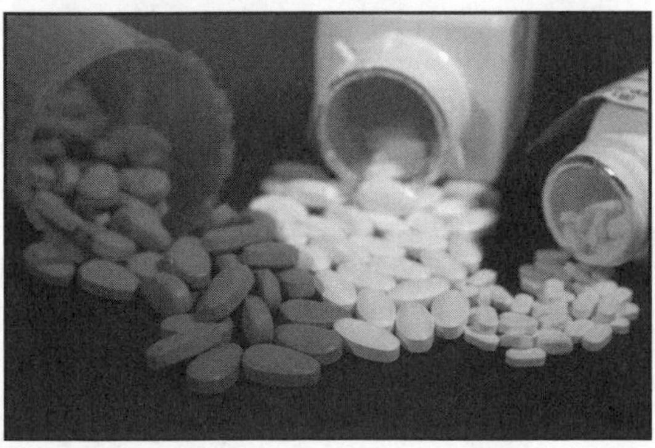

for nursing home and home care. Implemented in 1993, the NYSP combines long-term care insurance and Medicaid Extended Coverage. Its purpose is to help New Yorkers financially prepare for the possibility of needing nursing home care, home care, or assisted living services. The program allows New Yorkers to protect some or all of their assets, depending on the insurance plan purchased, if their long-term care needs extend beyond the period covered by their private insurance policy. Individuals who purchase NYSP insurance from the insurers participating in the program use the benefits according to the conditions of the program and can apply for New York State Medicaid Extended Coverage. Unlike regular Medicaid, Medicaid Extended Coverage allows one to protect some or all of their assets. The NYSP was created to help New Yorkers finance long-term care without impoverishing themselves or signing over their life savings, with the accompanying loss of dignity. The program has also reduced New York's Medicaid long-term care expenditure by over $9 billion in 2003 (Robert Wood Johnson Foundation, 2006).

Despite such efforts, there is a recognition that the cost of long-term care services means that families do not adequately plan for a service they will most likely need later in their life. Genworth Financial, Inc., a Fortune 500 financial institution, convened a national symposium of noted experts from the healthcare industry, seniors' organizations, government, and academia on Capitol Hill to discuss the future of long-term care in America. It also released the results of a new poll on the importance of long-term care in the 2008 elections. Representatives from organizations such as the American Association of Retired Persons, the American Association for Homes Services for the Aging, the American Health Care Association, the Alzheimer's Association, and the National Alliance of Caregivers participated in an exchange of ideas and solutions aimed at addressing the looming crisis America faces amid rising long-term care costs and a lack of sufficient planning at the national, state, and individual levels. According to the bipartisan national survey, nearly 7 in 10 Americans have not made any plans for their own, a spouse's, or another relative's long-term care needs; nevertheless, over half of those surveyed have had a loved one who needed some form of long-term care. The polling also showed that Americans are willing to bear part of the responsibility to develop a national long-term care program, whether through tax incentives for the purchase of private long-term care insurance or through a universal healthcare initiative that includes long-term care coverage. Sixty percent of voters surveyed supported new taxes or payroll deductions to subsidize a long-term care program. Sixty-eight percent of those who supported new taxes or payroll deductions also indicated a willingness to pay between $25 monthly and upward of $50 per month (Genworth Financial, 2007). These results speak to the importance of establishing affordable, effective long-term care policy in the United States.

The increasing gap between cost and quality of healthcare in the United States is evident. One of the reasons contributing to this problem is the lack of communication among institutions, providers, insurers, payers, and patients. Operating in silos contributes to increased cost and decreased quality, particularly in long-term care. This disconnect prevents the collection and analysis of information that can provide evidence to guide decisions about best practices and patient outcomes. Establishing a national information technology infrastructure can help close the gap between cost and quality. Care planning tools, point of care systems, personal health systems, data and knowledge sharing services, standard terminologies and decision support systems are the essential elements necessary for an information technology infrastructure. Privacy standards established in the 1990s have provided the foundation for patient confidentiality in the age of technology. Federal programs to increase adoption of health (information technology) have been instituted in the first 5 years of the 21st century. Rapid movement to adopt and implement the essential elements of a national healthcare information technology infrastructure can facilitate closing the cost and quality gap.

Other issues in the quality of long-term care have been identified by the Institute of Medicine, who examined the quality of care for those in nursing homes and other long-term care settings from mid 1997 to early 2001. Their findings indicate a lack of core quality measures that apply across long-term care settings and services to nursing homes, home care, assisted living facilities, and board and care home. There remains a continuation of serious problems in long-term care despite some improvements in quality of care resulting from the Omnibus Budget Reconciliation Act of 1987 (OBRA'87). The federal government's action plan to reform long-term care means serious deficiencies are being addressed by the implementation of programs to assess and enforce basic standards of quality in long-term care (Wunderlich & Kohler, 2001). In May 2005, however, the administrator for the Centers for Medicaid and Medicare Services formed the Policy Council, whose first priority was to develop a plan for long-term care reform (Centers for Medicaid and Medicare Services, 2006). The Policy Council has developed a set of long-term care reform activities to build on provisions in the Deficit Reduction Act of 2005, which has provisions that also target long-term care reform. The council's principles for long-term care reform are the cornerstone for improving the current system and achieving the vision of centering the system around the needs of the individual rather than around the settings where care is delivered. It is important to list them here, as they address the issues of cost, quality, and access to long-term care. The principles are as follows: (1) increase consumer choice and control for older individuals, persons with disabilities and chronic illnesses of any age, their family members, and caregivers and ensure access to an appropriate array of institutional and home- and community-based long-term care supports; (2) reverse the institutional bias in long-term care services and increase the flexibility for states; (3) enhance quality measurement to enable the provision of high-quality long-term care in the setting most appropriate for an individual's needs and improve quality and oversight in each setting and across settings; (4) reduce costs and promote payment mechanisms that support and reward better performance; (5) encourage personal planning for long-term care support needs among individuals and their family members and caregivers, including greater use and awareness of private sources of funding; (6) support administration efforts to pursue tax law changes for asset accumulation and long-term care tax clarifications to provide for private funding for long-term care needs; (7) improve coordination of long-term care and postacute services, as well as related funding streams; and (8) use enhanced health information technology better to inform beneficiary choices, clinical decisions, payment, and care coordination functions (pp. 2–3).

The vision of the Centers for Medicaid and Medicare Services expressed in the foregoing principles is a person-centered long-term care system of the future. The goals of the system are to optimize choice and independence; to be served by an adequate workforce; to be transparent, encouraging personal responsibility; to provide coordinated, high-quality care; to be financially sustainable; and to use health information technology (p. 3). Reform of the current long-term care system will provide an effective and efficient structure to address the increasing numbers of individuals needing these services.

Conclusion

Long-term care is an essential component of healthcare in the United States. The increasing need for these services is evidenced by the growing numbers of older, disabled, and chronically ill individuals of all ages. Nursing homes and other types of residential care facilities as well as home- and community-based programs provide long-term care services. Problems of cost, quality, and access are key determinants of healthcare policy that healthcare professionals must be aware of in order to advocate for the changes necessary to improve the system. The importance of understanding and engaging in the economic, political, and policy issues around long-term care are essential for healthcare professionals.

References

Beaulieu, J., Rowles, G. D., & Kuder, L. (2001). Current research in rural models of integrated long-term care. *Journal of Applied Gerontology, 20*(4), 379–385.

Brody, K. K., Johnson, R. E., Ried, D. L., Carder, P. C., & Perrin, N. (2002). A comparison of two methods for identifying frail medicare-aged persons. *Journal of American Geriatrics Society, 50*(3), 562–569.

Case Management Society of America. (2008). *Definition of case management.* Retrieved November 2, 2008, from http://www.cmsa.org/ABOUTUS/DefinitionofCaseManagement/tabid/104/Default.aspx

Centers for Medicaid and Medicare Services. (2006). *Policy council document: Long-term care reform plan.* Retrieved January 26, 2010, from http://www.cms.hhs.gov/medicaidgeninfo/downloads/ltcreformplan2006.pdf

Centers for Medicaid and Medicare Services. (2007). *Definitions of long-term care options.* Retrieved October 23, 2008, from http://www.medicare.gov/LongTermCare/static/Home.asp

Centers for Medicaid and Medicare Services. (2008). *Alternatives to nursing home care.* Retrieved October 23, 2008, from http://www.medicare.gov/LongTermCare/Static/HomeCare.asp?dest=NAV|Types|Types|HomeCare#TabTop

Collins, S. R., Davis, K., Schoen, C., Doty, M. M., How, S. K., & Holmgren, A. L. (2005). *Will you still need me? The health and financial security of older Americans.* The Commonwealth Fund. Retrieved October 23, 2008, from http://www.commonwealthfund.org/publications/publications_show.htm?doc_id=282096

Dennison, T. H. (2008). *Changes in nursing home care, 1996–2005: New York State Medicaid Institute at United Hospital Fund.* New York: United Hospital Fund.

Genworth Financial. (2007). *The future of long term care in America.* Retrieved November 1, 2008, from http://www.genworth.com/content/etc/medialib/genworth/us/en/pdfs/ltc_book_pdfs.Par.41959.File.dat/LTC%20Book%20-online%20version.pdf

Kodner, D. L. (2004). Following the logic of long-term care: toward an independent, but integrated sector. *International Journal of Integrated Care, 4* (online).

Long Term Care Community Coalition. (2008). *The future of nursing homes in New York State: Results of two roundtable discussions.* Retrieved February 11, 2010, from http://www.nursinghome411.org/documents/LTCCCRoundtableReportFinalJuly08_000.pdf

New York State Department of Health. (2007). *Medicaid care at home waivers participant survey.* Retrieved November 8, 2008, from http://www.health.state.ny.us/facilities/long_term_care/docs/2007_survey_summary.pdf

New York State Department of Health. (2008). *Consumer guide to community based long term care.* Retrieved November 1, 2008, from http://www.health.state.ny.us/health_care/managed_care/mltc/pdf/mltc_inter_rep.pdf

Novello, A. C. (2004). *New York State managed long-term care interim report (report to the governor and the legislature).* New York: New York State Department of Health.

Robert Wood Johnson Foundation. (2006). *Program to promote long-term care insurance for the elderly.* New York State Partnership for Long-Term Care. Retrieved November 1, 2008, from http://www.nyspltc.org

Smedley, B. D., Stith, A. Y., & Nelson, A. R. (2003). *Unequal treatment: Confronting racial and ethnic disparities in health care.* Washington, DC: National Academies Press.

Stone, R. L. (2000). *Long-term care for the disabled elderly: Current policy, emerging trends and implications for the 21st century.* Retrieved January 26, 2010, from http://www.milbank.org/sea/jan2000/trends.html

U.S. Census Bureau. (2001). *Projections of the total resident population by five-year age groups, race, and Hispanic origin with special age categories: Middle series, 1999 to 2100.* Table NP–T4. Retrieved October 23, 2008, from http://www.census.gov/population/www/projections/natproj2000.html

U.S. Census Bureau. (2004). *U.S. interim projections by age, sex, race, and Hispanic origin 2000–2050.* Table 1A. Retrieved October 23, 2008, from http://www.census.gov/population/www/projections/usinterimproj

U.S. Census Bureau. (1997). *Disability.* Retrieved January 26, 2010, from http://factfinder.census.gov/jsp/saff/SAFFInfo.jsp?_pageId=tp4_disability

U.S. Department of Health and Human Services. (2008). *Office on disability fact sheet.* Retrieved November 2, 2008, from http://www.dhhs.gov/od/about/fact_sheets/prevalenceandimpact.html

Wolf, D. A. (2001). Population change: Friend or foe of the chronic care system? *Health Affairs, 20*(6), 28–42.

Wunderlich, G. S., & Kohler, P. O. (Eds.). (2001). *Improving the quality of long-term care.* Washington, DC: National Academies Press.

Chapter 8

Mental and Behavioral Health: Clinical and Policy Impact on Mental Health Trends

Kunsook Bernstein and Joseph Saladino

OVERVIEW

This chapter introduces the concepts of mental and behavioral health and the provision of mental and behavioral health services, including political, quality, financial, and consumer advocacy. It explains how mental and behavioral health is defined based on the current research trends and studies and how treatment services have been transformed through public policy, research, consumer advocacy, and evolving payer–provider relationships. Finally, this chapter addresses the impact of cost, access, quality, and issues driving the mental healthcare delivery system.

OBJECTIVES

- To define mental and behavioral health and disorders
- To review global and national mental and behavioral health policy
- To discuss the trends of mental and behavioral healthcare delivery system
- To discuss the current payment issues of and access to mental and behavioral health services
- To discuss the issues driving mental and behavioral healthcare policy

KEY TERMS

- ❑ Behavioral health professionals
- ❑ Behavioral healthcare delivery system
- ❑ Carve-out
- ❑ Consumer advocacy
- ❑ Health policy
- ❑ Managed behavioral health care

(continues)

- ❑ Mental and behavioral health and illnesses
- ❑ Mental health policy
- ❑ Parity
- ❑ Patient-centered care
- ❑ Policy makers
- ❑ Recovery-oriented care
- ❑ Serious persistent mental illnesses
- ❑ Transformation

Mental and Behavioral Health Policy

The *Mental Health: A Report to the Surgeon General-Executive Summary* (U.S. Department of Health and Human Services, 1999) provides an up-to-date review of scientific advances in the study of mental health and mental illnesses that affect at least one in five Americans. In this report, mental and behavioral disorders are clearly defined. First, mental health is defined as a state of successful performance of mental function, resulting in productive activities, fulfilling relationships with other people, and the ability to adapt to change and to cope with adversity. Mental health is indispensable to personal well-being, family and interpersonal relationships, and contribution to community or society. It is easy to overlook the value of mental health until problems surface. Yet from early childhood until death, mental health is the springboard of thinking and communication skills, learning, emotional growth, resilience, and self-esteem. Second, mental illness is the term that refers collectively to all diagnosable mental disorders. Mental disorders are health conditions that are characterized by alterations in thinking, mood, or behavior (or some combination thereof) associated with distress and/or impaired functioning (U.S. Department of Health and Human Services, 1999). Considering health and illness as points along a continuum helps one appreciate that neither state exists in pure isolation from the other (Cline, 2003). Mental health is fundamental to and necessary for a healthy life, and mental disorders are real health conditions with enormous consequences for individuals, families, communities, and nations (U.S. Department of Health and Human Services, 1999).

In the era of growing concern about patient safety and quality of care in the United States, various groups—healthcare delivery services, educational institutions, policy makers, health professionals, and consumer advocates—have been challenged to address the current policy of mental healthcare delivery systems.

Mental and Behavioral Health Policy in the United States

A series of publications (Institute of Medicine, 2001, 2005; President's New Freedom Commission on Mental Health, 2003; U.S. Department of Health and Human Services, 2005; Adams & Boscarino, 2005; Daniels & Adams, 2004, 2006) addressed improving the quality of mental health care.

First, the report by the Institute of Medicine's (2001) delineated six primary aims for general healthcare delivery and stated that quality care should be patient centered, equitable, effective, timely, efficient, and safe. The second policy report of President's New Freedom Commission (2003) addressed the fragmentation and gaps in care of mental health delivery systems and more specifically targeted issues of the following: children with severe emotional disturbances and adults with serious mental illness, high unemployment and disability for people with serious mental illness, a lack of care for older adults, and a lack of a national priority for suicide prevention. The commission recommended six primary change goals; it envisioned that a public mental health system to be

- Consumer and family driven
- Mental health being essential to overall health
- Elimination of disparities in mental health
- Early mental health intervention and prevention
- Mental healthcare excellence and research
- Technology and informatics implementation to mental health system

These recommendations were consistent with Institute of Medicine's six primary aims but were more specific to mental health service. The third report of the Federal Action Agenda (U.S. Department of Health and Human Services, 2005) was generated in response to the recommendations of the New Freedom Commission. The Federal Action Agenda focused on systems transformation by articulating the delineation of a transformation process of the mental health system. Finally, added to the first Institute of Medicine's quality chasm compendium was Improving the Quality of Health Care for Mental and Substance-Use Conditions (Institute of Medicine, 2005). In this report, the convened expert panel concluded that there were serious problems in the U.S. service delivery systems for the treatment of mental and substance-use conditions in both the public and private sectors. The Institute of Medicine (2005) report provided a structured set of recommendations and a blueprint for improvement in the behavioral health specialty sector. This was ground breaking in its effort to link the mental and substance use care in the public and private sectors and also address the issues of integration with primary care (Daniels & Adams, 2006).

Adams and Boscarino (2005) and Daniels and Adams (2004, 2006) addressed improving the quality of mental health care. Daniels and Adams (2006) presented the second monograph based on the consolidated findings and recommendations of four key policy reports, as listed here:

- Institute of Medicine's Quality Chasm
- President's New Freedom Commission report
- Substance Abuse and Mental Health Services Administration's (SAMHSA) Federal Action Agenda
- Institute of Medicine's Improving the Quality of Health Care for Mental and Substance-Use Conditions

Assimilating these reports, the second monograph (Daniels & Adams, 2006) was generated and built a consensus framework and the tools required to develop a more coherent, coordinated, and effective national response for systems transformation to reflect the concerns and responsibilities of all stakeholders. Embedded in these reports is an agreement on the imperative for change as well as the priority and direction of change. Ultimately, the goal of all stakeholders was to reduce health disparities and embed quality, safety, evidence-based practice, interprofessional practice, and cultural competence as essential dimensions of consumer-focused 21st century mental healthcare delivery and professional practice.

Global Mental Health Policy

The World Health Organization's (WHO) *Mental Health Atlas 2005* reported an increase in countries with a mental health policy, mental health legislation, and a therapeutic drug policy or essential drug list. Also, more countries are providing community mental health services and disability benefits in some form, and there was an increase in the number of mental health professionals in the world, with the greatest increase noted in the number of psychologists and social workers. Their report also included the following components of a mental health policy to be standardized globally: advocacy, promotion, prevention, treatment, and rehabilitation (WHO, 2005b).

The WHO MIND Project (WHO, 2007a) developed global mental health improvements, targeting concrete changes in people's daily lives. The project reported an overall summary of the worldwide mental health issues that mental and neurological disorders (such as depression, schizophrenia, epilepsy, and substance abuse) can cause. The immense suffering for those affected amplifies people's vulnerability and can lead individuals into a life of poverty. Despite the worldwide availability of cost-effective treatments, the vast majority of people are left without access to the treatment they need. Instead of getting the help and support they require to lead productive lives, many people are subject to stigma, discrimination, and human rights violations and are denied the basic life opportunities given to other citizens.

Also, mental illness emerged from the Global Burden of Disease study (WHO, 2005a) as a surprisingly significant contributor to the burden of disease. The measure of calculating disease burden in this study, called disability adjusted life years, allowed a comparison of the burden of disease across many different disease conditions (see Table 8-1). Disability adjusted life years account for lost years of healthy life, regardless of whether the years were lost to premature death or disability. The disability component of this measure is weighted for severity of the disability. For example, major depression is equivalent in burden to blindness or paraplegia, whereas active psychosis seen in schizophrenia is equal in disability burden to quadriplegia (Murray & Lopez, 1996).

Following the identification of mental health and illness issues at the global level, the WHO (2007b) developed an overview of a mental health policy and plan development process to meet the current global mental health needs and then to address type of care, supervision, and rehabilitation of mental patients outside the hospital by mental healthcare workers based in the community. In order to achieve this, countries need to put in place human rights–oriented mental health policies, strategic plans, and laws to ensure that effective treatment, prevention, and promotion programs are made available to all people who need them (WHO, 2007a).

Other mental health concerns need to be addressed; these include the social integration of the most vulnerable and disorder-prone groups of population, such as refugees, people affected by natural and man-made disasters, indigenous people, and minorities. Special populations also include people who need special care, such as the older persons and children.

Both national and international reports on mental and behavioral health and illness services share the need for change of mental health policy aiming to achieve the common goals of consumer-focused 21st century mental healthcare delivery and professional practice. Those are to reduce health disparities through consumer advocacy and mental health promotion and to embed quality, safety, evidence-based practice, interprofessional practice, and cultural competence to enhance mental illness prevention, treatment, and rehabilitation.

The Need for Change: Transformation of Concepts of Mental Health and Illness and Mental Healthcare Delivery

President George W. Bush's New Freedom Commission issued its report on the state of the mental health delivery system for publicly funded care in this country in 2003. The commission found that the mental healthcare delivery system was fragmented and in disarray, leading to un-

Table 8-1 DISEASE BURDEN BY SELECTED ILLNESS CATEGORIES IN ESTABLISHED MARKET ECONOMIES, 1990

	Percentage of Total Disability-Adjusted Life Years*
All cardiovascular conditions	18.6
All mental illness[†]	15.4
All malignant diseases (cancer)	15.0
All respiratory conditions	4.8
All alcohol use	4.7
All infectious and parasitic diseases	2.8
All drug use	1.5

* The disability-adjusted life year is a measure that expresses years of life lost to premature death and years lived with a disability of specified severity and duration (Murray & Lopez, 1996).

† The disease burden associated with mental illness includes suicide.

necessary and costly disability, homelessness, school failure, and incarceration (President's New Freedom Commission, 2003). The Institute of Medicine (2005) reported a similar report stating that a broad range of stereotypes, stigma, and discrimination impair the quality of mental health care. The outcomes of these public attitudes toward mental illness are shown in a number of ways: a lessening of patients' ability to manage their illnesses and achieve recovery, encouraging nontherapeutic clinician attitudes, behaviors that limit self-care management of these conditions, and fostering discriminatory public policies that create barriers to recovery (Institute of Medicine, 2005).

The culture of mental healthcare needs to shift from one that is driven by professionals to one that is a consumer-led, recovery-oriented, and community-based self-care model. Berwick (2002) wrote a user guide for the Institute of Medicine's quality chasm report that presented needed changes at the four levels of mental health services: the experience of patients, the functioning of small units of care delivery (or "microsystems"), the functioning of the organizations that house or otherwise support microsystems, and the environment of policy, payment, regulation, and accreditation. Often policy, payment, regulation, and accreditation shape the behavior, interests, and opportunities of the organizations. Berwick claims that patients' experiences should be the fundamental driving source of the definition of "quality."

Consumer-Led Mental Health Care

The concept of consumer-led or patient-driven care is based on the philosophy of phenomenology, which accepts experience as it exists in the consciousness of the individual. To implement this concept to transform the current mental healthcare delivery system, mental healthcare providers need to understand patient/consumers' experience of living with mental and behavioral disorder and support their own decision making and treatment preferences. Additionally, mental health organizations need to use illness self-management practices by involving patients/families in design, administration, and delivery of services. In a transformed system, the role of the provider/clinician shifts away from being an authority figure to an advocate for each patient's decision-making consistent with the individual and family's culture and preferences and coordinated within resources of the healthcare delivery system and the community at large (Daniels & Adams, 2006). Overall, person-centered consumer-led mental health care can be achieved in a number of ways: through the strong voice of consumers and their families, consumer advocacy organizations, the use of peer-support programs in facilitating recovery-oriented treatment modality, and community-based self-care model with support of case management. Then patient/consumer can be empowered by building self-management over his or her treatment and recovery from mental and behavioral disorders, and patient-driven mental health care can be feasible.

Recovery-Oriented Mental Health Care

Recovery has now been widely discussed within the mental health field for nearly 2 decades, and many people have put forward definitions, including those that are philosophical, those based on grounded theory from lived experience, and those involving operational definitions that shaped practices and research studies (Onken et al., 2007). The concept of mental health recovery is philosophically and conceptually a shift from the traditional view of mental illness as an incurable and devastating illness. Recovery embodies the concept that people with mental disorders are consumers of healthcare services taking charge of their own health and well-being. This is a transformation of shedding the traditional physician-driven mental health care to implementing the new concept of patient/consumer-driven care as addressed earlier, and policy is a way to achieve success in transforming mental and behavioral health care.

Recovery involves the constant interweaving of the elements of one's life context (such as psychosocial, cultural, spiritual, and economic experiences) and the meanings attributed to these as they occur (Davidson & Strauss, 1995).

The SAMHSA of U.S. Department of Health and Human Services issued in 2006 a consensus statement on mental health recovery (U.S. Department of Health and Human Services, 2006). In the report, the 10 fundamental components of recovery were included: (1) self-direction, (2) individualized and person centered, (3) empowerment, (4) holistic, (5) nonlinear, (6) strengths based, (7) peer support, (8) respect, (9) responsibility, and (10) hope (SAMHSA, 2006). The first three components of self-direction, individualized and person centered, and empowerment are consistent with the general term "patient-centered care concept." The next three components of holistic, nonlinear, and strengths based are targeting mental health professionals to understand the complexity of individuals' life context and shift from the professional-driven traditional health care to patient-centered care. The last three components of peer support, respect, and responsibility are placing the primary focus on patients/consumers to lead their own life, including the mental health care. The last component of hope is a theme in recovery-oriented mental health care, which is differentiated from the notion of "mental illness is incurable" from the past.

Community-Based Self-Care Model

Finally, the community-based self-care model is based on the concept that individuals with severe mental disorders prefer and do better in community settings. One of the challenges to this concept is residual stereotypes that face those with mental illness. Specifically, these include impaired decision making, dangerousness, the notion that drug dependence is solely volitional, the wrongful application of coercion, and the resulting stigma and discrimination by healthcare providers that can be evidenced in public policy (Institute of Medicine, 2005).

However, studies of decision-making capacity among those seeking treatment for mental illness find significant variability in these abilities. Decision-making capacity is more affected by cognitive ability than psychotic symptoms, and it can be improved with interventions (Institute of Medicine, 2005); therefore, it is inappropriate to conclude assumptions about decision-making capacity based on a diagnosis of mental illnesses. The concept of self-care management is base on the notion that a patient is the source of control and customized care must be developed based on his or her needs and values. Patient's active involvement in the self-management of their own illness is central to improving his or her ability to lead a quality life.

U.S. data from the Vermont Longitudinal Research Project (begun in the mid 1950s) offered some dramatic evidence that individuals with severe mental illness who were provided with a range of comprehensive services could live in the community. The results of this experiment indicated that two thirds "could be maintained in the community if sufficient transitional facilities and adequate aftercare was provided." Similar longitudinal studies in the United States, Switzerland, and Germany came to similar conclusions. A variety of other mental health service demonstration projects supported by private foundations and Federal agencies (e.g., the Robert Wood Johnson Foundation, National Institute of Mental Health, the Agency for Health Care Research and Quality, and Community Mental Health Services) have confirmed the effectiveness of a system that provides employment opportunities, supportive housing, social supports, treatment of individuals with both mental illness and substance abuse diagnosis, and the diversion of persons with mental illnesses from jails into integrated treatment facilities. That individuals with severe mental disorders prefer and do better in community settings is clear. Access to economic resources (particularly vocational rehabilitation) and empowerment provide a feeling of mastery rather than a sense of dependency (Goldman, 1998; Harding, 1994; Rosenfield, 1992).

Meeting the comprehensive needs of consumers with long-term mental illnesses in community settings requires provision and coordination of a variety of mental health and social services (Turner-Crowson, 1992), as well as effective interactions between these resources and the families and significant others associated with the consumer (Intagliata, 1982). The organizational ability of local mental health service centers to mobilize and coordinate effectively the mentally ill individual's care among various service systems determines effective service delivery to patients. There are both theoretical and pragmatic questions about how formal care systems and primary groups cooperate to solve mutual problems without interfering with each other.

The earliest of the Federal Community Mental Health Acts, which led to the construction of community mental centers, required states to provide plans of how they would create catchment areas and then structured services for all catchment areas in order to qualify for the grants (Beigel, 1982). Throughout the history of community mental health center funding, states were required to complete a variety of planning mechanisms, many of which included public comment, and to include appropriate providers and later consumers and family members in the planning process. This basic model was adopted by many states in their community mental health legislation in the 1960s and early 1970s.

The Provision of Behavioral Health Services

Comprehensive and collaborative service delivery of mental health care is essential to reduce fragmentation within and across mental health, substance abuse, and general healthcare systems. There are several components to be considered in mental healthcare services, including mental health providers, mental health settings where the services are provided, and the content of mental health clinical and nonclinical services.

Mental Healthcare Providers

WHO's *Mental Health Atlas 2005* reported the international mental health and illness surveys' comparison data between 2001 and 2005 targeting the availability of mental health resources within different countries. The report indicated no substantial changes in availability of mental health resources between the data collected in 2001 with that updated in 2004; however, there were marked differences in the availability of mental health resources, particularly between high- and low-income countries. The report also revealed that there was a significant relationship between the presence of primary care activities in mental health and the number of psychiatrists and the number of psychiatric nurses. Primary care treatment facilities for mental disorders also showed a significant relationship with the number of health professionals, psychiatric nurses, psychologists, and social workers. Additionally, mental health in primary care is considered to be the provision of basic preventive and curative mental health at the first level of the healthcare system (WHO, 2005b). Usually this means that care is provided by a nonspecialist who can refer complex cases to a more specialized mental health professional.

Although a large number of countries have reported mental health as an integral part of primary care, the actual implementation of this at ground level is highly uneven. Often the facilities are restricted to particular areas where specific projects are in place and do not extend to the entire country. Treatment facilities for severe mental disorders in primary care settings across different countries also vary greatly. More information is required about the different personnel involved in the primary care of psychiatric patients. Whereas in some countries primary care is essentially provided by medical assistants, nurses, or other primary care workers, in other countries, it is provided by primary care doctors. Training also varies across countries. Although some have regular and more comprehensive programs for different types of personnel, others do not. Some countries might not have reported having regular training facilities for primary care workers because the latter may have been trained in mental health before their job placements or there may be local facilities for training (WHO, 2005b).

Mental Health Professional

A mental health professional is a specialist who has essential knowledge and skills in identification, prevention, and care of mental disorders and treatments. Table 8-2 presents the global mental health and related professionals by each discipline per 100,000 population (WHO, 2007a).

Table 8-2 clearly documents the lower levels of availability of all mental healthcare professionals. Psychiatric nurses are the most plentiful providers, and social workers working in mental health are the least among mental health professionals. Table 8-3 presents the U.S. data of six major mental health professionals for specified years. There are no significant differences in data representing the time period 2002–2004; one can assume that the data among the disciplines are comparable. In this report, social

Table 8-2 MENTAL HEALTH AND RELATED PROFESSIONALS PER 100,000 POPULATION IN THE WORLD

Professionals	Mean	Median	Standard Deviation
Psychiatrists	4.15	1.2	6.07
Psychiatric Nurses	12.97	2.0	26.17
Neurologists	2.13	0.3	3.74
Neurosurgeons	0.58	0.2	1.26
Psychologists working in mental health	7.35	0.6	18.1
Social workers working in mental health	1.58	0.4	44.96

Source: Data from World Health Organization, 2005b.

workers and counselors are the most plentiful providers, followed by psychologists and psychiatrists. Advanced practice psychiatric nurses are the smallest population among mental health professionals. The data do not include psychiatric nurses and only report advanced practice psychiatric nurses who are registered nurses with advanced academic and clinical experiences. Approximately 80,000 psychiatric nurses are employees of hospitals and agencies providing mental health services (Manderscheid & Henderson, 2000).

Figure 8-1 presents comparison data of the distribution of full-time professional, administrative, and other patient care staff in mental health organization between the years 1972 and 2000 in the United States. Overall, the data indicate that there was a significant increase of professional staff working in mental health organizations, but also there was a decrease of professional staff in other mental health organizations outside of hospital settings and residential treatment centers. The most impressive increase of professional staff is in Veterans Administration (VA) medical centers, which jump approximately 40% from 1972 to 2002.

Mental Health Service Settings

The full range of comprehensive mental health services to support an individual suffering with mental disorders is inclusive of all relevant clinical and nonclinical care aimed at reducing the impact of mental disorders and improving the quality of life of the person. Clinical care involves direct-person care, including assessment, diagnosis, treatment, evaluation, plan of care, and rehabilitation from mental illnesses. Depending on the acuity of an individual's mental illness, the level of care is determined by using one or more of the following: in-patient hospitalization, a partial hospital program, an intensive outpatient program, an outpatient program, a mental health rehabilitation program, a residential program, and a community mental health program.

Hospitals and Residential Treatment Centers

There are approximately 1.84 million psychiatric beds in the world, and 68.6% of them are in mental hospitals. In 2002, Americans had 10.3% of their total psychiatric beds in settings other than mental or general hospitals (see Table 8-4).

Table 8-3 PERCENTAGE OF CLINICALLY TRAINED MENTAL HEALTH PERSONNEL INVOLVED IN EACH TYPE OF WORK ACTIVITY, BY DISCIPLINE, FOR SPECIFIED YEARS[1]

	Discipline and Year							
Type of Work	Psychiatry 2002	Psychology[3] 2004	Social Work[4] 2004	Adv. Practice Psychiatric Nurses[10] 2003	Counseling[5] 2004	Marriage/ Family Therapy[6] 2004	Psycho-Social Rehab. 1994	School Psychology 2000[7]
(N)	(1,070)[2]	(51,354)	(103,128)	(7,759)	(100,533)	50,158	N/A	N/A
Patient care/ direct services	94.3	89.4	61.2	80.7	73.4	98.9	96.1	82.5
Research	20.0	24.5	0.3	1.3	0.4	N/A	N/A	2.0
Teaching	N/A	38.9	2.69	1.7	10.8	24.0	N/A	5.2
Administration[8]	85.4	34.4	13.4	3.7	7.9	18.7	10.1	4.3
Other activities[9]	85.1	39.4	8.8	12.6	7.5	36.5	N/A	6.0

[1] Percentages will not sum to 100 because clinically trained mental health personnel can be involved in more than one type of work activity.

[2] Respondents to the 2004 APA NSPP who are currently active in psychiatry (N = 1,095); data have been weighted. Note: 25 psychiatrists had missing information on type of work activity.

[3] Source: 2000 American Psychological Association Directory compiled by APA Research Office. Because 35,768 members did not specify work activities, percentages are based on the 25,298 members who responded and applied to the estimated number of clinically active psychologists in 2004.

[4] Source: National Association of Social Workers (NASW) PRN survey, 2004, which requested the principal role in the primary area of practice; thus, data are not comparable to other disciplines.

[5] Estimates are based on the 2000 National Study of the Professional Counselor, with growth rate taken from National Certified Counselor data.

[6] Estimates are based on 2004 national survey of clinical members of the American Association for Marriage and Family Therapy (AAMFT), which asked for primary and secondary job function.

[7] Data are from Thomas (2000) and replace earlier data.

[8] Includes staff supervision.

[9] Mainly consultation as other activity.

[10] Data are based on the total number of PMH-APRNs board certified by the American Nurses Credentialing Center (ANCC) as of October 2003, including clinical nurse specialists (adult and child) and psychiatric nurse practitioners (family and adult). Missing data are excluded.

Source: Manderscheid & Berry, 2004, p. 267.

Although the number of mental health organizations providing 24-hour services (hospital inpatient and residential treatment) increased significantly over the 32-year period, the number of psychiatric beds provided by these organizations decreased by more than half, from

Figure 8-1 Percent distribution of full-time professional, administrative, and other patient care staff in mental health organizations: United States, 1972 and 2000.

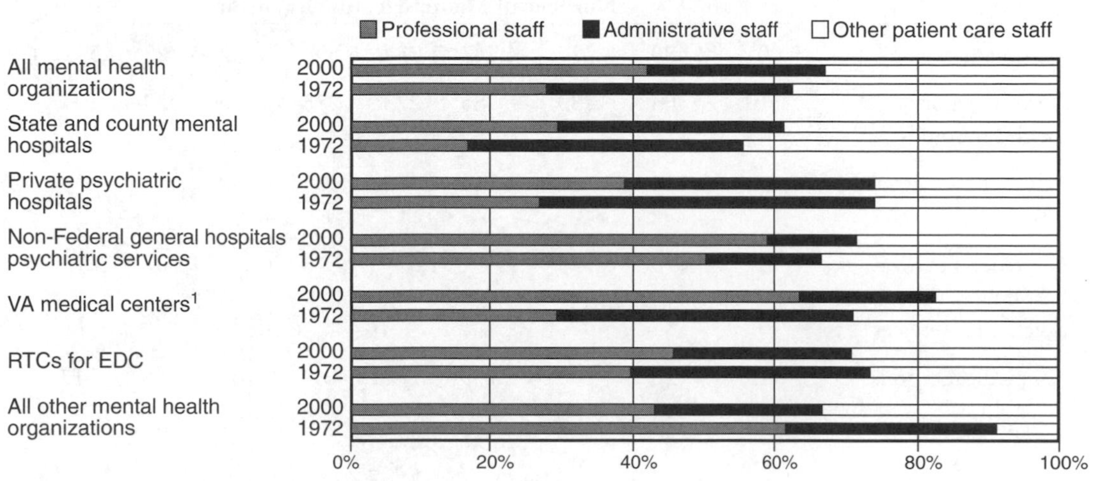

[1]Staffing for 2000 is based on 1998 estimates.

Source: Manderscheid and Berry, 2004, p. 212.

524,878 in 1970 to 211,199 in 2002 (SAMHSA, 2004). The corresponding bed rates per 100,000 the civilian population dropped proportionately more in the same period, from 264 to 73. Beds in state mental hospitals accounted for most of this precipitous drop, with their number representing only 27% of all psychiatric beds in 2002, compared with almost 80% in 1970 (see Figure 8-2).

Trends in bed occupancy for specific organization types (Table 8-4) indicate that the rates for private psychiatric hospitals, nonfederal general hospitals with separate psychiatric services, residential treatment centers, and "all other mental health organizations" increased substantially between 1970 and 1990, with the greatest growth occurring between 1980 to 1990. Bed rates for nonfederal general hospitals remained stable throughout the 1990s but declined substantially between 1998 and 2002. In addition, bed rates for private psychiatric hospitals declined, although they remained above the rates for 1980 and earlier. The rate for residential treatment centers was nearly flat from 1970 to 2002, whereas the rate for state mental hospitals and VA psychiatric organizations decreased substantially (SAMHSA, 2004).

Community-Based Mental Healthcare Settings

WHO's (2007a) survey of community-based mental healthcare facilities includes adult day care centers, therapeutic and supervised residential services, crisis residential services, sheltered homes, clubhouses, community mental health services for children and adolescents or older persons, agricultural psychiatric rehabilitation villages, and so forth. Comprehensive community

Table 8-4 NUMBER OF MENTAL HEALTH ORGANIZATIONS, BY TYPE OF ORGANIZATION: UNITED STATES, SELECTED YEARS, 1970–2002*

Type of Organization	1970	1976	1980	1986	1990	1992	1994	1998	2000	2002
	Number of Mental Health Organizations									
All organizations	3,005	3,480	3,727	4,747	5,284	5,498	5,392	5,722	4,541	4,301
State and county mental hospitals	310	303	280	285	273	273	256	229	223	222
Private psychiatric hospitals	150	182	184	314	462	475	430	348	269	253
Nonfederal general hospitals with separate psychiatric services	797	870	923	1,351	1,674	1,616	1,612	1,707	1,373	1,285
VA medical centers	115	126	136	139	141	162	161	145	142	140
Federally funded community mental health centers	196	517	691	—	—	—	—	—	—	—
Residential treatment centers for emotionally disturbed children	261	331	368	437	501	497	459	461	475	508
All other mental health organizations	1,176	1,151	1,145	2,221	2,233	2,475	2,474	2,832	2,059	1,893

Note: Published and unpublished inventory data from the Survey and Analysis Branch, Division of State and Community Systems Development, Center for Mental Health Services.

*Some organizations were reclassified as a result of changes in reporting procedures and definitions. For 1979–1980, comparable data were not available for certain organization types and data for either an earlier or a later period were substituted. These factors influence the comparability of 1980–1998 data with those of earlier years.

Source: Manderscheid and Berry, 2004, p. 202.

care facilities, including the majority of those mentioned previously, are found only in the high-income countries. U.S. federally funded community mental health centers and residential treatment centers for emotionally disturbed children are listed on Table 8-4, but data after 1980 are not listed for the federally funded community mental health center. The type of organization listed as all other mental health organizations on Table 8-4 includes freestanding psychiatric outpatient clinics, partial care organizations, and multiservice mental health organizations.

Mental Health Services

The description of mental health services is delineated to three major components: therapeutic drug treatment, psychotherapeutic intervention, and case management.

Figure 8-2 Percent distribution of 24-hour hospital and residential treatment beds, by type of mental health organization: United States, selected years, 1970–2002.

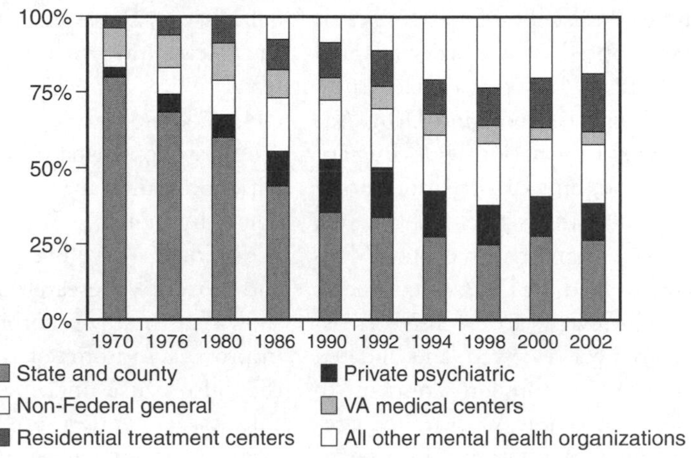

Source: Manderscheid and Berry, 2004, p. 201.

Therapeutic Drug Policy and Treatment

The current interest in exploring the neurobiology of mental illness is based on the assumption that there is a link between biology and behavior. A paradigm shift occurred as research renewed the emphasis on the neurobiological basis of mental illness and addiction. As more efficacious psychotropic medications with fewer side effects were developed, psychopharmacology assumed a more central role in psychiatric treatment. Specialists evolved to encompass the expanding biopsychosocial perspective, and the competences required for practice were kept congruent with emerging science (American Nurses Association, 2007). In recent years, the studies of mental disorders have been greatly enriched by the convergence of research interests by psychiatrists, biologists, and neuroscientists who are more sophisticated in their biochemical understanding. These studies have provided an evolving certainty that mental disorders such as schizophrenia, mood disorders, anxiety disorders, obsessive compulsive disorder, and addictive disorders are all results from specific biochemical, neuroanatomical, or genetic processes (Frisch & Frisch, 2006).

Therapeutic Drug Policy

WHO (2007a) defined therapeutic drug policy as a written commitment, endorsed by the Minister of Health or the Cabinet, to ensure accessibility and availability of essential therapeutic drugs. It contains measures for regulating the selection, purchase, procurement, distribution, and use of essential and appropriate drugs, including those for mental and neurological disorders. It can also specify the number and types of drugs to be made available by health workers at each level of the health service according to the functions of the workers and the conditions that they are required to treat. Under the national policy, drugs may be supplied free of charge to all or selected groups. An essential list of drugs means the officially approved list of essential drugs that the country has adopted. It is usually adapted from the WHO Model List of Essential Drugs. In the United States, the Food and Drug Administration monitors the nation-wide drug approvals, including ongoing quality monitoring and evaluation of each drug's risks and benefits. For the past 3 years, a consortium of state Medicaid agencies has funded the Drug Effectiveness Review Project. The reviews are extensive, transparent, extensively peer reviewed, and updated annually. The federal government in response to the Medicare Modernization Act initiated a series of drug class reviews to inform multiple intermediaries better through the Medicare part D drug benefit (Carey, Williams, Melvin, Lodham, & Goodman, 2007).

Therapeutic Drug Treatment and Intervention

The historical perspective of antipsychotic drugs started with the phenothiazine derivative chlorpromazine, which was the first of the conventional antipsychotics to be synthesized in the early 1950s. Its success in treating patients with schizophrenia was reported in 1952. The clinical introduction of chlorpromazine was quickly followed by the introduction of other phenothiazines (e.g., perphenazine and fluphenazine) and then other structurally distinct compounds such as haloperidol and pimozide. Clozapine, the first of atypical antipsychotic, was approved in 1990 by the U.S. Food and Drug Administration for treatment-resistant schizophrenic patients. The last decade has heralded the development of a number of new atypical antipsychotics, including risperidone, olanzapine, quetiapine, ziprasidone, and aripiprazole. Each of these atypical antipsychotics provides unique choices when deciding on a treatment that will deliver the efficacy while minimizing the potential for side effects (such as weight gain, diabetes, metabolic and cardiovascular issues, and sexual dysfunction) so that patients can stay with treatment over the long term.

In addition to antipsychotic medications, other psychopharmacotherapeutic agents such as antidepressants, antianxiety agents, mood stabilizers, hypnotics, stimulants, and other therapeutic drugs have been available for clinicians and patients. Research and clinical evidences show that these psychotherapeutic drugs help to improve symptoms of the mental illness, but they also cause undesirable adverse reactions; thus, patients often stop taking them and then experience the recurrence of symptoms of the illness. Medication noncompliance or nonadherence has been a major issue in therapeutic drug treatment for individuals suffering from mental disorders. The common scenario of therapeutic drug treatment presents a gap between a prescriber and a patient in the traditional approach: a physician prescribes a medication; either a pharmacist or a nurse dispenses the prescribed medication, and the patient takes it. In this model, the physician dictates and the patient becomes a recipient of the treatment. Currently in the United States, physicians, nurse practitioners, and physician assistants—and in some states psychologists—are allowed to prescribe, and each state sets a standard of these professional disciplines' practice guideline.

The recovery-oriented mental health program is aimed at activating both clients and mental health practitioners to participate in shared decision making for treatments, including psychotropic medications (Deegan, 2007). Traditional notions of compliance with medical authority do not adequately capture the challenges involved in the recovery process. Shared decision making is a person-centered alternative to traditional notions of medical compliance and is consistent with psychiatric rehabilitation's emphasis on the centrality of client choice in service provision (Anthony & Liberman, 1994). People with psychiatric disabilities need support to resolve decisional conflict regarding the use of psychiatric medications (Kisely, Campbell, & Preston, 2005).

Psychotherapeutic Intervention

Psychotherapy is a treatment modality that is based on a trusting relationship between a patient and a therapist. The overall goals of individual psychotherapy are to empower the patient to experience more satisfying relationships, to have increased self-esteem and self-worth, to feel integrated with self-chosen work activities, and to find a greater meaning in life (Cline, 2003). Sigmund Freud (1856–1939) who pioneered psychoanalysis revolutionized psychiatry by developing a systematic theoretical framework of human mind. Freud's influence in the early 20th century and the development of psychoanalytic theory led to the emergence of psychotherapy delivered in office settings as an acceptable form of treatment; however, this form of treatment was most often available only to those who could afford to pay privately and most often focused on persons with neuroses. Nonetheless, psychoanalytic/psychodynamic psychotherapy practices in the mid 20th century were challenged as biological treatment, especially the use of psychosurgery (lobotomy), electroshock treatment, and the introduction of phenothiazines in the treatment of psychoses. The traditional psychopharmacological agencies, however, some of which are still in use today, are associated with numerous side effects that can and do diminish the quality of life for those with mental disorders (Salzer et al., 2000). In addition to individual psychotherapy, there are other therapeutic approaches such as group therapy, family therapy, addiction-specific treatment modalities, and child- and adolescent-specific therapies.

Case Management

In the 1970s, the first community support program introduced the concept of the case manger, a person to coordinate the various functions that address the various need of the patient with mental illness living in the community with the intention to reduce the frequency of hospitalization. Ideally, case management enables the patient and the primary group to access the formal service system by facilitating contact between a variety of service systems and the patient. Mental health, human service, welfare, and medical service organizations constitute the potential sources of formal support for the patient residing in a community. The role of formal organization is to ensure the availability of housing, economic support, and psychiatric and medical treatment to sustain the consumer. Community-based mental health care of patients is predicated on the assumption that the community will provide social and tangible support to ensure the continued optimal functioning of the patient. The ideal of community placement presumes the immersion of the patient into the social structure of the family and community, connecting the patient to supports that enable the consumer to thrive in the community (Fox, Blank, Kane, & Hargrove, 1994).

Kanter (1989) characterized participation in all aspects of the patient's community life as the unifying principle of case management. Other principles include (1) continuity of care, (2) the use of the case management relationship, (3) titrating support and structure, (4) flexibility, and (5) facilitating the consumer's resourcefulness. Kanter emphasized the case manager's responsibility for linking with family and social networks of clients in order to enhance and develop consumer resourcefulness. Several investigators have reported that the extent of consumers' support networks and the frequency of the case manager's contact with family, neighbors, and friends of consumers was related to the decreased case manager/client contacts, decreased hospitalization, and increased community stability (Harris & Bergman, 1988; Albert, Becker, McCrone, & Thornicroft, 1998).

Our review begins with a discussion of global and national mental health policies, the need to change the fundamental concepts of mental health care and delivery, existing availabilities of mental health services and practitioners, and provision of mental health services. This is followed by finance, regulation, accreditation, and organization of services, including parity, legislation, managed care, and systems interventions.

Financing Mental Healthcare and Its Relation to Access and Treatment Issues

Financing Mental Healthcare Services

In order to appreciate fully issues related to access and the delivery of behavioral health care, it is critical to appreciate the complex and evolving methods of financing care from the private, public, local, and federal perspectives, as there have been significant shifts in funding sources over the past 50 years. Future access to care, outcomes, and quality improvements will be influenced by emerging decisions in regard to funding. Providers and consumers have often been in positions of reacting to the consequences of these decisions as opposed to influencing their formulation.

The consistent increases in healthcare costs and the burden placed on payers (private and public) will continue to drive efforts to provide care in the most cost-efficient manner available. Projections indicate that healthcare spending will reach 20% of the gross domestic product by 2015. In order to meet consumer expectations and finance those expenditures, private and public payers will need to prioritize areas for spending and reduce cost while increasing efficacy and efficiency (Hartman, Smith, Heffler, & Freeland, 2006). It is hoped that a historical overview of funding trends will assist advocates for the mentally ill to appreciate fully key stakeholder concerns and goals in determining policies and their subsequent impact on access to safe and effective treatment. The challenge is to align incentives for consumers, providers, payers, and regulators in a continuous effort to reach recovery for all in a fiscally sound environment.

Post World War II Era-Shift From Institutional to Community-Based Care

Before the 1960s, people with severe mental illnesses were primarily treated in large state-sponsored mental health institutions or small numbers of private psychiatric hospitals. Access to private hospitals was significantly limited because the cost as health insurance was not widespread. The majority of families were forced to care for their mentally ill members at home or to seek state assistance. Many of those patients who were able to afford private care eventually entered the state system when faced with the need for chronic hospitalization. In reality, there was a significant disparity in access to care and quality based on the availability of personal economic resources (Mechanic, 1989). The lack of effective treatments for serious mental illnesses such as psychotic and mood disorders as well as organic-based illnesses such as Huntington's Chorea and dementias resulted in a custodial level of care in state hospitals. Persons with less serious disorders (neurosis) and adequate resources were able to access a small number of psychiatrists who provide outpatient therapy (psychoanalysis). Those without sufficient economic resources went without professional treatment for less serious yet disabling illnesses.

The 1950s witnessed the start of a shift from state mental institutions to community-based care. The National Mental Health Act of 1946 provided federal funding to expand and create outpatient mental health centers. This shift was in response to an increased acceptance of the effectiveness of outpatient community-based treatment during and after World War II, the expansion of psychiatrists in the community using psychodynamic interventions, and the belief that early community-based interventions could prevent the later development of more serious mental illnesses (Grob, 2001). Improvements in treatment because of the development of lithium, first-generation antipsychotic medications (chlorpromazine, 1952), and tricyclic antidepressant medications (early 1960s) provided the clinical improvements to discharge patients to the community. In 1955, there were 560,000 patients in state psychiatric hospitals throughout the United States. By 1996, deinstitutionalization had reduced the national state hospital census to 77,000 patients (SAMHSA, 2003). The emergence of the civil rights movement and President Johnson's efforts to create the "Great Society" were social and political factors converging with state government attempts to place patients in less restrictive environments as well as to reduce the burdensome cost of chronic custodial care. The passage of legislation, which established Medicare and Medicaid, provided funding in the form of Supplemental Social Security Income during the 1960s. Many chronically mentally ill aged patients were transferred from state psychiatric hospitals to community-based nursing homes, as these patients could now access Medicaid to pay for nursing home care. This influenced the acceleration in the expansion of the nursing home industry and again shifted funding from the states to the federal government (Grob, 2001). In 1965, the Community Mental Health Center Act Amendments (P.L. 91-211) provided federal funding for mental health services in low-income communities as well as for children and those with substance abuse disorders. Although there appeared to be consensus among providers, professionals, patients, and families to move care into the community as well as the addition of increased federal responsibility in line with states' incentive to reduce cost by discharging inpatients to the community, the outcomes very often fell short of the high expectations.

In addition to the problems resulting from the shift of institutional to community care, there remained significant barriers to affordable care as private and public funding placed limits on care in the form of annual or lifetime number of inpatient hospital days and outpatient visits as well as individual co-pays and deductibles. These attempts to limit costs remain far more extensive for mental health care than comparable limits for medical care (Mental Health America, 2006), and thus, the issue of parity between mental health care and medical care continues to be debated.

Another outcome of 30 years of deinstitutionalization and the failure of the Community Mental Health Centers Act to provide adequate services was the dramatic increase in the number of chronic homeless people with mental illness and or substance use disorders. Of the estimated 200,000 chronically homeless persons, it is estimated that 40% suffer with substance use disorders and 20% have serious mental illness (SAMSHA, 2003). Many patients discharged from state psychiatric hospitals were placed in single room occupancy apartments but never connected to adequate follow-up treatment. Many of these persons were then displaced during the period of urban renewal when real estate owners were able to rent these properties to higher income people. Faced without stable housing or access to psychiatric treatment, many former patients cycled among shelters, prisons, and acute-care hospital emergency rooms. Unlike many of the chronically mentally ill aged patients who were discharged to nursing homes, many of these patients were younger and at greater risk for substance abuse disorders. This combination resulted in several high-profiled incidents of violence by mentally ill persons. It can be speculated that the increased presence of serious and persistently mentally ill and or substance abusing individuals reinforced the stigma of mental illness in society, which further hampered attempts to house patients in local community settings. In addition, several high-profile murders by persons suffering psychotic disorders further inflamed community outcry for government action, which is discussed in the chapter. The Stewart B. McKinney Homeless Assistance Act 1987 (P.L. 100-77) was the first federal legislation to address the problem of homelessness in a comprehensive manner for people with mental illness and substance use disorders. In 1992, the report *Outcasts on Main Street* was released; it further delineated a national strategy for reducing homelessness and improving access to psychiatric treatment (SAMSHA, 2003).

Barriers to Accessing Care

Funding for community mental health centers did not meet demand, and many serious and persistently mentally ill persons were left in the community without adequate supervision or effective coordination of care while many nursing homes lacked adequate psychiatric services to effectively treat the influx of patients discharged from state psychiatric hospitals (Grob, 2001). Although the combined efforts of advocacy groups, providers, civil rights, and social activists resulted in dramatic increases in federal spending, a lack of coordination and integration of services reduced the effectiveness and efficiency of care. Despite these problems, a number of studies indicate that with sufficient support in the areas of housing, vocational rehabilitation, social support, and integrated mental health and substance abuse treatment seriously and persistently mentally ill individuals could be effectively treated in the community (Grob, 2001).

In addition to the barriers faced by the homeless and substance-dependent persons, there has been increasing concern regarding those persons with developmental disabilities accessing effective mental health care. The expected lifespan of persons with mental retardation, autism, and other developmental disabilities continues to expand, placing them at higher lifetime risk for also acquiring a mental illness. They have also faced the effects of stigma in their attempts to access all aspects of health care and mental health care in particular. The clinical presentation of the developmental disabilities can understandably complicate the ability to identify separate underlying mental illness. Similar to those with "dual diagnosis" of substance abuse and mental illness, they are dually diagnosed with developmental disabilities and mental illness and face similar barriers. The developmentally disabled population has also seen a shift from state-managed and -funded institutions to community-based care. This has often led to fragmentation in care, as specialty providers are neither equipped nor willing to treat patients who they consider out of their scope of practice (Fisher, 2004). Many of these patients receive Medicaid, which reimburses individual providers at much lower rates than private insurers, which further raises barriers to care. Policies that support enhanced training for mental health providers and reasonable rates of reimbursement may improve the availability and quality of their care.

Mental Health Care Costs: Private Sector and Managed Behavioral Health Care

Private insurance expanded during the 1970s in response to continued public advocacy. The National Alliance for the Mentally Ill established in 1979 (Howe & Howe, 1987) and President Carter's Commission on Mental Health established in 1977 (Mulligan, 2003) were examples of efforts to place greater scrutiny on the needs of the mentally ill. The decade of the 1980s experienced acceleration in the number of specialty psychiatric hospitals and specialty programs such as child and adolescent units (Frank & Garfield, 2007). Many of these hospitals and programs were for profit and were reimbursed by fee-for-service contracts, which created incentives for expansion. For example, providers were paid for each service performed. Increasing the number of services, treatments, and tests increased the level of reimbursement. Between 1980 and 1990 the number of specialty psychiatric hospital beds more than doubled (Frank & Garfield, 2007). The increased availability of fee for service reimbursement to providers may have influenced care itself, such as the common practice of "28-day programs" for substance abuse treatment, which assumed a standard length of stay for all patients as opposed to individually evaluated and determined care.

In response to rising costs, payers (employers and insurers) sought to minimize "unnecessary" care as defined by payers and reduce liability. Most private insurance policies established an annual limit of 30 inpatient days as well as a limit on annual outpatient visits and increased co-pays by the insured. For example, many patients are responsible for 50% of outpatient care (co-pays), which far exceeds the average co-pay for general medical care, which is often a $10 or $20 co-pay. It is estimated that private funding for mental health services increased by 10.7% annually from 1986 to 1989, but funding for medical services rose by 15.1%; nevertheless, employers focused greater emphasis on controlling increasing expenditures for mental health care (Mark et al., 2007). Speculation as to the disparity in attempts to control costs between mental health and medical insurance coverage may include society's continued stigmatization of mental illness as well as questions as to its biological versus behavioral etiology.

Managed Behavioral Healthcare "Carve-Outs"

In response to soaring expenses by the private sector, the concept of the managed behavioral healthcare industry was developed. It was based on the belief that specialization, appropriate utilization, and care management protocols could reduce unnecessary and inefficient care while improving quality by steering patients to providers who met established clinical outcomes (Frank & Garfield, 2007). By the mid 1990s, over 170 million people were covered by managed behavioral health organizations (MBHO), which provide behavioral health care through "carve-out" arrangements. This system of insurance coverage separated behavioral healthcare coverage from medical care coverage by subcontracting or "carving out" management and sometimes financial risk (Frank & Garfield, 2007). The rationale for this approach was based on the belief that specialty organizations familiar with mental illness, treatment strategies, and effective providers could more efficiently manage the care and cost associated with behavioral healthcare. Employer purchased health plans would contract with MBHO, or employers could purchase services directly from MBHOs. Carve-outs differed in their structure as some managed administrative tasks and utilization review only, whereas others included provider networks. Their provider agreements were sometimes based on capitated rates in which a provider was paid an annual set fee for each "covered life" in the contract. The provider was responsible for delivering required treatment and accepted the risk for the cost of such care. Other providers accepted discounted fee-for-service contracts in order to remain in the network and receive referrals from the MBHO. This system for purchasing treatment by employers through insurance companies using MBHOs allowed for greater scrutiny and control of services by using efficient providers, increasing competition, and ultimately managing costs; however, many consumers and providers were concerned that incentives to reduce cost were the priority, as access to care was reduced and fragmentation between medical and behavioral healthcare increased (Frank & Garfield, 2007). Some providers withdrew from MBHO networks in response to what were considered burdensome administrative requirements, inadequate fees, and inappropriate control of care by the MBHO. Consumers were then faced with the decision to pay increased out-of-pocket expenses to remain with their provider or transfer to an unknown in network provider in order to avoid the increased expenses. Questions were raised as to the quality of care provided by MBHOs and the negative aspects of increased administrative costs required in order to manage care. Despite these concerns, managed care organizations using carve-outs have expanded as state Medicaid systems have also begun to administer benefits through managed care organizations (MCOs). Inpatient lengths of stay have declined as treatment continues to shift to outpatient care.

A review of the literature by Frank and Garfield (2007) reveals that "although not perfect, carve-outs have been instrumental in addressing long- standing challenges in utilization, access, and cost of behavioral healthcare." As the use of managed care by the private and public sectors expands, future research and advocacy may need to scrutinize access, consumer satisfaction, treatment outcomes, and cost savings further.

Psychotropic Medication Use and Financing

One of the most significant changes in the delivery and funding for mental healthcare has been the dramatic increase in the number and use of medications to treat psychiatric illnesses. In 1986, retail prescription medications accounted for 7% of all expenditures for mental health care; by 2003, it had increased to 23% of all expenditures. Prescription medication costs grew annually by 14.9% during the period from 1986 to 2003. This represented the leading growth rate for all types of mental health services (SAMHSA, 2007). Insurance companies have expanded prescription drug coverage over the past 30 years while placing greater emphasis on their therapeutic use by providers through concurrent authorization and utilization review practices. Coverage for medications, including psychotropic medications, has been traditionally covered within the medical component of health insurance plans as opposed to mental healthcare carve-outs; therefore, MBHOs have the incentive to promote the utilization of medications because they are effective and at no cost to the MBHOs. These increases may also be a result of greater research by the pharmaceutical industry, resulting in new and more effective classifications of medications to treat mood disorders and psychosis such as the selective serotonin reuptake inhibitors (SSRIs) and serotonin norepinephrine reuptake inhibitors (SNRIs) and second-generation antipsychotics previously discussed. In addition, pharmaceutical companies developed the new marketing strategies that advertise medications directly to the consumer (Frank et al., 2005). These combined practices in the face of dramatically increased usage rates of psychotropic prescriptions, especially to children and adolescents, have raised questions about their medical justification. Although the public appears to embrace the use of medications for medical disorders that were not commonly treated in the past, such as erectile dysfunction, there appears to be some skepticism when prescribing medications to children and adolescents for attention deficit hyperactivity disorder and bipolar disorder as opposed to greater emphasis on psychosocial interventions, which are more costly (Frank et al., 2005). Inpatient length of stays dropped as providers used more psychopharmacological options to stabilize patients and discharge them to outpatient care, resulting in reduced cost (Mark et al., 2007); however, the dramatic increase in costs for medications and increased co-pays to reduce insurer liability created barriers to purchasing psychiatric medications. Many providers were placed in the position of prescribing newly developed medications with fewer side effects that may be cost prohibitive for the patient and thus a greater risk of non-adherence or less expensive older medication with more significant side-effect profiles. In response to the overall increase in medication costs, the federal government passed Medicare Part D, which went into effect in 2006 to assist older citizens in purchasing needed medications. There was significant concern within Congress that providing prescription drug coverage would dramatically increase costs to the federal government and adversely affect a rapidly growing deficit. In an effort to manage drug costs, many Medicare and Medicaid recipients were enrolled in managed care plans, which negotiated contracts with pharmaceutical benefit managers. Pharmaceutical benefit managers developed formularies, which limited access to the most cost-effective medications in an effort to reduce costs. Despite these efforts, medication costs continue to present a barrier to necessary health care in general and mental healthcare specifically. Future advocacy will need to focus on enhancing access to the most effective medications available.

Parity for Mental Healthcare Financing

The issue of parity refers to the historical practice by insurers to establish and maintain different policies for providing mental health care as opposed to medical care. As previously mentioned, co-pays and deductibles were established to minimize unnecessary or inappropriate utilization of health care while annual or lifetime limits on coverage capped insurer liability for catastrophic illness. In general, insurers have placed higher co-pays and deductibles as well as lower lifetime limits on policies for mental health coverage as compared with medical coverage. This has created barriers to persons seeking mental health care.

The federal government recognized the danger of such disparity and enacted the Mental Health Parity Act of 1996, which outlawed disparity in health coverage; however, the law had many stipulations such as pertaining only to employers that offered mental health insurance coverage for at least 50 employees or more and excluded self-insured employers. This limited the actual impact of the law. Since 1996, many states have enacted their own parity laws, but many exceptions persist limiting their effectiveness. Concern that parity would result in dramatic increases in insurance premiums appears to have blocked attempts to enact full parity laws. The RAND Health Insurance Experiment completed in the 1970s supported those concerns (Barry et al., 2006), but recent studies of parity coverage since 1996 have indicated that those concerns have not been realized. The proliferation of managed care and carve-out plans appears to have minimized premium increases (Buchmueller et al., 2007). According to Mental Health America's position statement on the federal government's responsibility in assuring parity, the cost of not providing parity in health coverage and thus not effectively treating mental illness results is a far greater cost to employers and the tax payers than providing coverage (Mental Health America, 2006). Despite these findings, there remained resistance to effective parity legislation.

In 2007, the Senate passed the Mental Health Parity Act of 2007 S.558, and in 2008, the House passed its own version. In October 2008 President Bush signed into law P.L. 110-343 which included the parity legislation. This law went into effect in 2009 and expanded the 1996 law requiring parity in regard to treatment and financial limitations. However, final regulations detailing the specific rules have not been released. In light of the financial recession of 2009–2010 and contentious national healthcare debate, there may be attempts to limit the law's effect by holding down costs. Efforts to overcome the stigma of mental illness and substance abuse disorders and to convince payers (public and private) in the ethical as well as cost-effective rationales to provide effective treatment without financial barriers to all persons will need to continue into the foreseeable future. Increasing costs and consumer demand as a result of an aging population more dependent on government-financed health care will maintain the pressure to reduce funding to those areas that are perceived to be inefficient or low on the tax payer priority scale. The influence of the mental health constituency, which has grown dramatically over the past 30 years, cannot be maintained without persistent action.

Quality Improvement in Mental Health Care

Efforts to improve the quality of mental health care originate in the belief that quality results in improved outcomes, which allow persons with mental illness to recover, thereby participating in the workforce and reducing the long-term cost of health care; however, the delivery of quality mental health care has been compromised because of fragmented systems, funding cuts intended to reduce short-term expenditures, and the failure to implement evidenced-based treatments. In order to participate actively in the quality debate, it is suggested that interested providers maintain an awareness of various strategies identified by critical stakeholders.

In 2006, the National Alliance for the Mentally Ill released *Grading the States: A Report on America's Healthcare System for Serious Mental Illness*. The report focused on an evaluation of state mental health authorities using an extensive questionnaire that resulted in a grading of all 48 states that participated in the survey. The final report used a letter grading system (A = excellent to F = failure), resulting in an overall grade of "D" for the performance of state mental health authorities, which was consistent with the President's New Freedom Commission on Mental Health (2003). The National Alliance for the Mentally Ill's report supported the call for an integrated healthcare delivery system based on the concept of recovery. In regard to funding, the report was very clear: "There is increasing awareness that short-term savings accrued through cuts in public mental health funding lead to increased long-term public costs associated with hospitalizations, incarcerations, and other costly consequences of a lack of treatment" (National Alliance for the Mentally Ill, 2006). Ten elements were identified as necessary to create "high-quality mental health systems" (http:/nami.org).

- Comprehensive services and support
- Integrated systems
- Sufficient funding
- Consumer and family driven systems
- Safe and respectful treatment environments
- Accessible information for consumers and family members
- Access to acute care and long term treatment
- Cultural competence
- Health promotion and mortality reduction
- Adequate mental health workforce

The Joint Commission, the National Association of State Mental Health Program Directors, the National Association of Psychiatric Health Systems, and the National Research Institute, Inc. collaborated to develop five test measures leading to eventual implementation of a core performance measures for hospital-based inpatient psychiatric services. Such cooperation among various stakeholders supports the accelerating trend to require continuous quality improvements as opposed to standards compliance. The initial core measures include the following (The Joint Commission, 2010):

- Assessment of violence risk, substance abuse disorder, trauma, and patient strengths completed
- Hours of restraint use
- Hours of seclusion use
- Patients discharged on multiple antipsychotic medications
- Discharge assessment and aftercare recommendations, which are sent to next level of care providers on discharge

An emerging debate is the extent to which payment to providers should be based on performance and outcomes. Although it is widely accepted that aligning financial rewards to outcomes has the potential to improve quality, reliably tested systems have not been identified (The Joint Commission, 2010). The Joint Commission has therefore identified 10 Principles for the Construct of Pay-for-Performance Programs in order to ensure that "unintended consequences" of such programs will be avoided (The Joint Commission, 2010). A prerequisite to managing quality data is the implementation of a national electronic health record infrastructure, which has been referenced in the previously cited President's New Freedom Commission, NAMI, and Joint Commission reports. How the private sector will be able to finance the infrastructure remains a question that will require monitoring, advocacy, and active government intervention.

Future Issues Driving Policy

Many of the challenges previously discussed, including overcoming stigma, obtaining funding parity, enhanced coordination of care, and expanding the use of technology, will continue to set the agenda for stakeholders and advocates for persons with mental illness and substance-dependence disorders. One of the emerging clinical research issues that may have a great influence on future policy is the expanding use of neuroscience to define and treat mental illness. In the report *The New Frontier: Neuroscience Advancements & their Impact on Nonprofit Behavioral Healthcare Providers*, Aron and Zimmer (2006) identify five advancements that may have "important and direct impact on nonprofit behavioral healthcare."

- Genotyping—diagnosis of mental disorders
- Deep brain stimulation—increase treatment effectiveness
- Improved pharmaceuticals
- Brain imaging technology—identify most effective treatments and patient response
- Psychotherapy combined with cognitive enhancing medications

In order to use these advances effectively, providers will need to acquire knowledge and new skills necessary to either provide these advanced services or refer clients to those organizations that have the capability. Participating in research such as clinical trials can help in acquiring the needed skills and contribute to the body of research that will lead to evidence-based treatment strategies (Aron & Zimmer, 2006). As advances in neuroscience are realized, the issues of cost, access, and funding parity will once again call for action by informed advocates.

References

Adams, R. E., & Boscarino, J. A. (2005). Differences in mental health outcomes among whites, African Americans, and Hispanics following a community disaster. *Psychiatry, 68*(3), 250–265.

Albert, M., Becker, T., McCrone, P., & Thornicroft, G. (1998). Social networks and mental health service utilization: A literature review. *International Journal of Social Psychiatry, 44*(4), 248–266.

American Nurses Association. (2007). *Psychiatric-mental health nursing: Scope and standards of practice.* Silver Spring, MD: Author.

American Psychiatric Association. (2000a). *Diagnostic and statistical manual of mental disorders* (4th ed.). Arlington, VA: Author.

Anthony, W. A., & Liberman, R. P. (1994). The practice of psychiatric rehabilitation: Historical, conceptual, and research base. In L. Spaniol, M. A. Brown, L. Blankertz, D. Burnham, J. Dincin, K. Furlong-Norman, et al. (Eds.), *An introduction to psychiatric rehabilitation.* Linthicum, MD: The International Association of Psychosocial Rehabilitation Services.

Aron, L. Y., & Zimmer, C. (2006). *The new frontier: neuroscience advancements and their impact on nonprofit behavioral health care providers*. Milwaukee, WI: Alliance for Children and Families.

Barry, C. L., & Busch, S. H. (2006). Do parity laws reduce the financial burden on families of children with mental health care needs? *Health Services Research, 42*(3), 1061–1079.

Beigel, A. (1982). Community mental health centers: A look ahead. *Hospital Community Psychiatry, 33*, 741–745.

Berwick, D. (2002). A user's manual for the IOM's "Quality Chasm" report. *Health Affairs*, *21*(3), 80–90.

Buchmueller, T., Cooper, P. F., Jacobson, M., & Zuvekas, S. H. (2007). Parity for whom? Exemptions and the extent of state mental health parity legislation. *Health Affairs, 26*(4), 483–487.

Carey, T. S., Williams, J. W., Melvin, C., Lodham, J., & Goodman, F. (2007). Comparing medication treatments in mental health: Drug class reviews and policy challenge. *Psychiatric Services, 58*(6), 746–748.

Cline, J. L. (2003). Collaborative care of individuals. In W. Mohr (Ed.), *Psychiatric mental health nursing* (6th ed., pp. 171–188). Philadelphia: Lippincott Williams & Wilkins.

Daniels, A., & Adams, N. (2004). *From policy to service: A quality vision for behavioral health: Using the quality chasm and New Freedom Commission Reports as a framework for change.* Albuquerque, NM: American College of Mental Health Administration.

Daniels, A., & Adams, N. (2006). *From study to action: A strategic plan for transformation of mental health care.* Albuquerque, NM: American College of Mental Health Administration.

Davidson, L., & Strauss, S. (1995). Beyond the biopsychosocial model: Integrating disorder, health, and recovery. *Psychiatry, 58,* 44–55.

Deegan, P. E. (2007). The lived experience of using psychiatric medication in the recovery process and a shared decision-making program to support it. *Psychiatric Rehabilitation Journal, 31*(1), 62–69.

Fisher, K. (2004). Health disparities and mental retardation. *Journal of Nursing Scholarship. 36*(1), 48–53.

Fox, J. C., Blank, M. B., Kane, C. F., & Hargrove, D. S. (1994). Balance theory as a model for coordinating delivery of rural mental health services. *Applied and Preventive Psychology*, *3*(2), 121–129.

Frank, R. G., Conti, R. M., & Goldman, H. H. (2005). Mental health policy and psychotropic drugs. *The Milbank Quarterly*, *83*(2), 271–298.

Frank, R. G., & Garfield, F. L. (2007). Managed behavioral health care carve-outs: Past performance and future prospects. *The Annual Review of Public Health, 28,* 303–320.

Frisch, N. C., & Frisch, L. E. (2006). *Psychiatric mental health nursing* (3rd ed.). New York: Thomson Delmar Learning.

Goldman, H. H. (1998). Deinstitutionalization and community care: Social welfare policy as mental health policy. *Harvard Review of Psychiatry, 6,* 219–222.

Grob, G. N. (2001). Mental health policy in 20th-century America. In R. W. Manderscheid & M.J. Henderson (Eds.), *Mental Health United States 2000.* Washington, DC: U.S. Government Printing Office.

Harding, C. M. (1994). An examination of the complexities in the measurement of recovery in severe psychiatric disorders. In R. Ancili (Ed.), *Exploring the Spectrum of Psychosis* (pp. 153–169). New York: Wiley.

Harris, M., & Bergman, H. C. (1988). Misconceptions about the use of case management services by the chronically mentally ill: A utilization analysis. *Hospital and Community Psychiatry, 39,* 1276–1280.

Hartman, M., Smith, C., Heffler, S., & Freeland, M. (2006). Monitoring health spending increases: Incremental budget analyses reveal challenging tradeoffs. *Health Care Financing Review, 28*(1).

Howe, C. W., & Howe, J. W. (1987). The national alliance for the mentally ill: History and ideology. *New Directions for Mental Health Services, 34,* 22–33.

Institute of Medicine. (2001). *Crossing the quality chasm: A new health system for the 21st century.* Washington, DC: National Academies Press.

Institute of Medicine. (2005). *Committee on crossing the quality chasm: Adaptation to mental health and addictive disorders, board on health care services. Improving the quality of health care for mental and substance-use conditions.* Wash ington, DC: National Academies Press.

Intagliata, J. (1982). Improving the quality of community care for the chronically mentally disabled: The role of case management. *Schizophrenia Bulletin, 8,* 655–674.

Kanter, J. (1989). Clinical case management: Definition, principles, components. *Hospital & Community Psychiatry, 40,* 361.

Kisely, S., Campbell, L. A., & Preston, N. (2005). Compulsory community and involuntary outpatient treatment for people with severe mental disorders. Cochrane Database of Systematic Reviews 4, 2005.

Manderscheid, R. W., & Berry, J. T. (2004). *Mental health, United States, 2004.* Rockville, MD: U.S. Department of Health and Human Services, Substance Abuse and Mental Health Services Administration, Center for Mental Health Services.

Manderscheid, R. W., & Henderson, M. J. (2000). *Mental health, United States, 2000.* Rockville, MD: U.S. Department of Health and Human Services, Substance Abuse and Mental Health Services Administration, Center for Mental Health Services. Retrieved from http://mentalhealth.samhsa.gov/publications/allpubs/SMA01-3537/default.asp

Mark, T. L., Levit, K. R., Buck, J. A., Coffey, R. M., & Vandivort-Warren, R. (2007). Mental health treatment expenditure trends, 1986–2003. *Psychiatric Services, 58*(8), 1041–1048.

Mechanic, D. (1989). *Mental health and social policy* (3rd ed.). Upper Saddle River, NJ: Prentice Hall.

Mental Health America. (2006). *Position statement 14: The federal government's responsibilities for mental health services.* Retrieved January 12, 2010, from http://www.mentalhealthamerica.net/go/position-statements/14

Mulligan, K. (2003). Carter Commission legacy still reaping benefits. *Psychiatric News, 38*(5), 14.

Murray, C. J. L., & Lopez, A. D. (1996). *The Global Burden of Disease.* Geneva: World Health Organization.

National Alliance for the Mentally Ill. (2006). *Grading the States: A report on America's healthcare system for serious mental illness.* Retrieved January 12, 2010, from nami.org/gtstemplate.cfm?section=grading_the_states&template=ContentManagement/ContentDisplay.cfm&ContentID=31064

Onken, S. J., Craig, C. M., Ridgway, P, Ralph, R. O., & Cook, J. A. (2007). An analysis of the definitions and elements of recovery: A review of the literature. *Psychiatric Rehabilitation Journal, 31*(1), 9–22.

President's New Freedom Commission on Mental Health. (2003, July). *Achieving the promise: Transforming mental health in America: Final report.* Rockville, MD: U.S. Department of Health and Human Services. Retrieved from http://www.mentalhealthcommission.gov/reports/FinalReport/toc.html

Rosenfield, S. (1992). Factors contributing to the subjective quality of life of the chronically mentally ill. *Journal of Health and Social Behavior, 33*(4), 299–315.

Salzer, M. S., Blank, M., Rothbard, A., & Hadley, T. (2000). Adult mental health services in the 21st century. In R. W. Manderscheid M. J. Hunderson (Eds.), *Mental Health, United States 2000.* Rockville, MD: U.S. Department of Health and Human Services, Substance Abuse and Mental Health Services Administration, Center for Mental Health Services. Retrieved from http://mentalhealth.samhsa.gov/publications/allpubs/SMA01-3537/default.asp

Substance Abuse Mental Health Services Administration. (2003). *Blueprint for change: Ending chronic homelessness for persons with serious mental illness and co-occurring substance use disorders.* DHS.Pub.No.SMA-04-3870. Rockville, MD: Author.

The Joint Commission. (2010). *Hospital based inpatient psychiatric services (HBIPS) core measure set.* Retrieved February 11, 2010, from http://www.jointcommission.org/PerformanceMeasurement/PerformanceMeasurement/Hospital+Based+Inpatient+Psychiatric+Services.htm

Thomas, A. (2000). *Report to the National Association of School Psychologists' delegate assembly on the State demographic survey.* Bethesda, MD: National Association of School Psychologists.

Turner-Crowson, J. (1992). Long term strategies for system change: The US community support programme. *Journal of Mental Health, 1*(1), 90–92.

U.S. Department of Health and Human Services. (1999). *Mental health: A report to the Surgeon General—Executive summary*. Rockville, MD: Author.

U.S. Department of Health and Human Services. (2005). Substance Abuse and Mental Health Services (SAMHSA). Transforming mental health care in America. The federal action agenda: First steps. Retrieved from http://www.samhsa.gov/Federalactionagenda/NFC_TOC.aspx

U.S. Department of Health and Human Services. (2006). The Substance Abuse and Mental Health Services Administration (SAMHSA) issues consensus statement on mental health recovery, 2006 press release. Retrieved February 2008 from www.mentalhealth.samhsa.gov

World Health Organization. (2005a). *The global burden of disease: 2004 update.* Retrieved January 12, 2010, from http://www.who.int/healthinfo/global_burden_disease/2004_report_update/en/print.html

World Health Organization. (2005b). *Mental health atlas 2005. Mental health: Evidence and Research Department of Mental Health and Substance Abuse.* Geneva: Author.

World Health Organization. (2007a). Mental health Improvements for Nations Development: The WHO MIND Project. Geneva: Author. Retrieved February 2008 from http://www.who.int/mental_health/policy/en

World Health Organization. (2007b). Monitoring and evaluation of mental health policies and plan: Mental health policy and service guidance package. Geneva: Author.

Chapter 9

Public Health Policy: Promotion, Prevention, and Protection

Mary Mincer Hansen and Mary Jones

OVERVIEW

Public health touches everyone's life every day. Healthy children are better learners. Healthy workers are more productive. Healthy countries are more prosperous and peaceful. Doctor Margaret Chan (2008a), Director of the World Health Organization (WHO), eloquently states that "health care is a critical contributor to social cohesion. Social cohesion is the best protection against social unrest . . . (and) healthy human capital is the foundation of economic productivity." Her point is further explicated by a statement from WHO (2008b): "The prevention of illness and the promotion of health through the delivery of efficient and effective public health services lie at the core of society's ability to create a virtuous circle of better health, more productive citizens and affordable health care." Public health has impacted the history of the United States in many ways. One of the more notable contributions being that the average life span of Americans was increased by 25 years because of public health initiatives during the last century (Centers for Disease Control and Prevention [CDC], 1999). Given its undisputed contribution to our nation and the world, it is stunning to realize that the United States annually spends more than $1.7 trillion in health care but less than 4 cents of every dollar is spent on prevention and public health (Lambrew, 2007). This resource disparity is directly related to the lack of a strong public health voice in health policy development and advocacy.

This chapter defines public health in the context of its history and service components. Service delivery in the areas of health prevention, promotion, and protection is delineated. Factors transforming global and national public health service delivery, including a focus on wellness, chronic and infectious diseases, environmental assets and threats, health inequity, and emergency preparedness are discussed. An analysis of the priority issues of accreditation, globalization, media, economics, and workforce that are shaping the future of public health is presented. This chapter concludes with a discussion of the skills and strategies integral for public health advocacy and policy formulation.

OBJECTIVES

- To define public health in terms of history
- To outline public health service delivery within the framework of health prevention, promotion, and protection
- To delineate the factors influencing public health's capacity to provide services
- To discuss the issues shaping the future of public health
- To explicate the skills needed to shape public health advocacy and policy formulation

KEY TERMS

- ❑ Accreditation
- ❑ Advocacy
- ❑ Chronic disease
- ❑ Economics
- ❑ Emergency response
- ❑ Globalization
- ❑ Health inequity
- ❑ Health prevention
- ❑ Health promotion
- ❑ Health protection
- ❑ Infectious disease
- ❑ Media
- ❑ Policy
- ❑ Politics
- ❑ Population
- ❑ Public health
- ❑ Wellness
- ❑ Workforce

Historical Underpinnings of Public Health

Precisely defining public health is difficult. From its origins in ancient times to the mid 19th century when the first formal governmental health departments were established in the United States and into the 21st century, public health has evolved over a number of landmark eras in history. Table 9-1 provides an overview of these eras, the paradigms associated with each era, analytical approaches, and actions used during that time and initiatives that continue to be a critical part of public health practice (Awofeso, 2004).

The earliest landmark era in public health dates from ancient times to the 1830s. This era began with health protection that addressed disease prevention by enforcing regulation of human behavior through social structures. For example, this included enforcement of spiritual practices or customs imposed by ruling elites. Quarantine and some environmental protection laws were used. The next era was sanitation control, which surfaced in the 1840s through the 1870s, and addressed unsanitary environmental conditions that would cause disease. Community approaches were used through implementation of minimum standards for sewage, drainage, and refuse disposal, leading the way for potable water and early sanitation programs. This landmark time was the foundation from which the public health legal framework and disease surveillance and epidemiology methodology evolved.

Contagion control or the germ theory marked the next landmark era in public health history, dating from 1880 to the 1930s. The central theme of this era was the "demonstration of infectious origins of disease," which focused on the presence of disease-causing microorganisms, their hosts, and modes of transmission. These discoveries led to vaccinations, improved water filtration, and more standardized disease outbreak control strategies. Evidence-based public health practice came to light during this time. From the 1940s through the 1960s, the preventative medicine era emerged, focusing on the prevention and cure of diseases in high-risk populations. These included the treatment of communicable diseases and interventions directed at disease vectors. This moved public health program planning toward high-risk population groups and created an environment for gaining a better understanding of the pathogenesis of communicable and noncommunicable diseases.

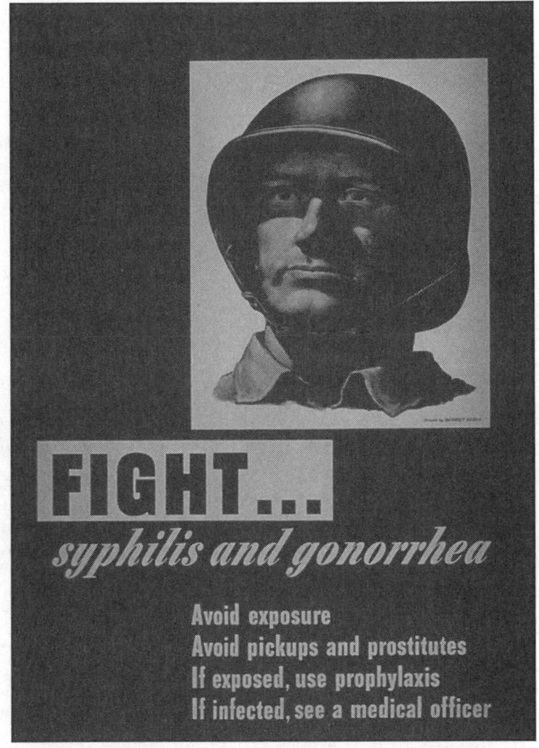

Primary health care was the priority in the 1970s and 1980s, giving rise to a focus on the community. This meant that effective health care was geared toward the community, for the community, and by the community. Although preventative health care was at the forefront, emphasis was also placed on equity, accessibility, and the social determinants of health such as poverty and education. This led to a more global approach to public health and closer linkages between health promotion and disease prevention. Multicultural health emerged, healthy city initiatives grew, and community participation in public health surfaced. Early in the 1990s the era of health promotion and advocacy for health became the focus. This created supportive environments for impacting optimal health at the community level. Behavioral, social, and environmental changes could be made as a result of education, economic, and political actions. This assisted individuals and the community in strengthening actions toward optimal health (Awofeso, 2004).

The 21st century ushered in another era in public health. In the first few years of this century, the terrorist attacks on the United States in 2001 and subsequent anthrax-laden letters sent through the U.S. Postal Service, Severe Acute Respiratory Syndrome (SARS) in 2003, and the threat of another pandemic demonstrated how the world is changing in terms of vulnerability to public health threats. Concerns about the United States public health system's preparedness for epidemics and disasters have been elevated. According to a WHO (2007a) report, SARS confirmed fears generated by the bioterrorism threat that a

Table 9-1 SIX ERAS IN THE EVOLUTION OF PUBLIC HEALTH

Public Health Era	Dominant Paradigm	Analytic Approaches	Action Frameworks	Legacies Incorporated into Contemporary Public Health
1. Health Protection (antiquity–1830s)	Diseases may be prevented by enforced regulation of human behavior, mediated through societies' social structures.	Interpretation/promulgation of religious and cultural rules that are thought by the ruling elites to protect the health of the individual and the community	Enforcement of spiritual practices, community taboos, customs, and quarantine	Quarantine of illegal migrants; enforcement of some environmental protection laws; aspects of spirituality in prevention and coping with disease; some occupational and transport safety laws
2. Miasma Control (1840s–1870s)	Addressing unsanitary environmental conditions may prevent diseases.	Demonstration that poor health and epidemics resulted directly from unsanitary physical and social environments	Centralized action to improve environmental sanitation; public health legislation relating to minimum standards for drainage, sewage, and refuse disposal	Aspects of Healthy Cities initiatives; potable water and sanitation programs; legal framework for implementing public health activities; foundations of modern epidemiology and surveillance
3. Contagion Control (1880s–1930s)	Germ Theory is a positivist approach to demonstration of infectious origins of diseases.	Demonstration of the presence of disease-causing microorganisms in infected media, their isolation, and experimental transmission	Interruption of disease transmission through improved water filtration processes, vaccination, standardized disease outbreak control measures	Evidence-based public health practice; ethical vaccination practices; foundations for international cooperation in health; foundations for modern chemotherapy
4. Preventive Medicine (1940s–1960s)	Improvements in public health through focus on	Definition of, and interventions aimed at, main avenues for disease	Environmental interventions directed at disease vectors	Focus on "high-risk groups" in the planning and implementation of public health such

	the prevention and cure of diseases in "high-risk groups"	transmission. Medical dominance, with focus on treatment of communicable diseases and primary care of "special populations" (e.g., pregnant women and factory workers)	identification and use of "useful" microbes; enhanced medical care for "high-risk groups"; foundations of modern clinical pathology	as mosquitoes; programs; improved understanding of the pathogenesis of communicable and noncommunicable diseases
5. Primary Health Care (1970s–1980s)	Health for All: effective health care geared toward the community, for the community, and by the community	Largely preventive health care approach, underpinned by emphasis on equity, community participation, accessibility of services, and social determinants of health	Emphasis on global cooperation and peace; adapting health services to countries and communities; links between health care and socioeconomic development; intersectoral cooperation in health promotion and disease prevention; equity in health care	Concepts underpinning multicultural health and Healthy Cities initiatives, health inequalities, and community participation in health promotion activities
6. Health Promotion (1990s–present)	Advocacy for health; enabling individuals and communities to attain optimal health	Individuals and communities may be assisted by educational, economic, and political actions to increase control over, and improve, their health through attitudinal, behavioral, social, and environmental changes	Encapsulated by the key action areas of the Ottawa Charter: build healthy public policy; create supportive environments; strengthen community action; develop personal skills; and reorient health services	Encapsulated by the key action areas of the Ottawa Charter: build healthy public policy; create supportive environments; strengthen community action; develop personal skills; and reorient health services

Source: Table 1 from Awofeso, N. (2004). What's new about the new public health? *Am J Public Health, 94*(5), 705–709. Used with permission of the author.

new or unfamiliar pathogen would have profound national and international implications for global public health security.

Organization of Public Health Services

Public health cannot be completely defined without a discussion of its infrastructure. One of the earliest designers of governmental public health infrastructure can be traced back to Lemuel Shattuck (1850) in his *Report of the Sanitary Commission of Massachusetts*. From the time the report was written, several decades had passed before state and local public health agencies began to form. By 1900, health departments existed in nearly all states, and the first county-based health department was formed in 1911 (Turnock & Barnes, 2006). As state and local public health agencies began to form, serving different population sizes and addressing diverse health issues, the structure, governance, and statutory frameworks of these agencies varied depending on health needs.

Governmental public health is intrinsically a network of local, state, and federal agencies that are collectively responsible for health promotion and protection and disease prevention. These agencies provide basic community services, including collecting vital statistics, prevention services, and the promotion of health education and healthy life styles. In addition, these services include ensuring clean drinking water, sanitation, and prevention and control of diseases. The focus of traditional public health practice occurs at the community level and is aimed at the population. The practice must allow for flexibility in order to deal with specific community health needs, which vary from jurisdiction to jurisdiction (Institute of Medicine [IOM], 1988).

Public health is primarily the responsibility of the state. Although primary responsibility belongs to the state, a majority of public health services are provided at the local level. Thousands of local, state, and federal agencies participate in public health practice and are governed independently by varying degrees of authority. The U.S. public health agencies are products of federalism—a system of government in which power is distributed between a central authority and the constituent units. The agencies are regulated by the orders of boards at the local level, governors at the state level, and primarily secretaries at the federal level.

Governance of public health practice is driven by administrative and bureaucratic realities, meaning that programs are influenced and shaped by their political context. It is a culmination of science and politics coming together in the public arena and being influenced by political forces. The translation of turning plans into action requires a great deal of perseverance and negotiating skill. If successful, it comes with varying degrees of support in terms of funding and infrastructure. As political alliances rise and fall, so does public health. In essence, public health is not defined by what the profession is capable of doing; instead, it is driven by the decisions made by a political system within a jurisdiction (IOM, 1988).

The shaping of public health occurs as a result of the health problems needing to be addressed in a particular community and by the political system within which it functions. It is at that local level that an understanding of how programs should function and what resources are necessary to address particular health needs are realized. It is at the state level that resource acquisition, coordination, and evaluation occur. It is at the federal level that coordination of national public health initiatives takes place, state and local governmental public health is supported, and a national vision is articulated. This vision is captured by the IOM's definition of the public health system (1988): "A complex network of individuals and organizations that, when working together, can represent 'what we as society do collectively to assure the conditions in which people can be healthy.'"

Service Delivery

Based on the 1988 IOM report the *Essential Public Health Services*, ideas about service delivery were developed in 1994 (see Table 9-2). This broad framework is used across the nation by public health leaders to articulate what public health does. Based on this framework, basic service delivery includes preventing epidemics and the spread of disease, protecting against environmental hazards, preventing injuries, promoting healthy behaviors, and addressing public health emergencies.

Preventing epidemics and the spread of disease encompasses surveillance and investigation to determine the etiology, virulence, and communicability of actual and potential sources of disease. Based on these data, public health practitioners design, implement, and evaluate control strategies to prevent, reduce, or eliminate infectious disease. The SARS epidemic in 2003 confirmed the need to ensure that the nation's public health system has the capacity to prevent, detect, respond to, and manage outbreaks of infectious disease.

Protecting against environmental hazards involves assessing both the natural and built environments to determine health risk factors. Programs and activities focus on mitigating the effects of harmful substances and structures that endanger individuals and populations. This involves monitoring environmental risk factors and enforcing regulation. Examples of activities include ensuring food safety, conducting housing inspections, and monitoring air and water quality. More recently, environmental health includes exploring links between community design and public health. This expanded role is geared toward protecting against and preventing injury and disease by improving where we live, work, shop, and play (Heishman & Dannenberg, 2008).

Preventing injuries encompasses activities that facilitate the prevention, reduction, or elimination of intentional or unintentional injuries. This involves studying how, when, and why injuries occur; designing new strategies to prevent injuries; and educating the public about evidence-based prevention strategies. The goal is to keep people safe from injury and violence with a reduction in disabilities, death, and medical expenses across all life stages (CDC, 2006a).

Services that promote healthy behaviors include activities that prevent and reduce illness and disease. These activities support and incentivize individuals and communities to develop healthy behaviors. The result is increased wellness and quality of life with a decrease in chronic disease, premature mortality, and disease burden.

Addressing public health emergencies includes activities to prepare the public health system to respond to public health threats, emergencies, and disasters and to assist in the recovery process. In order to address these threats, the public health system must have adequate capacity and capability to reduce morbidity and mortality from infectious diseases either naturally occurring or intentionally introduced. Coordination of prevention and response activities, along with strong linkages among multiple partners, is integral in public health preparedness.

Throughout history, the context of public health practice has been transformed a number of times and continues to be transformed today given the demographic change in age and diversity of the population, globalization, the explosion in technology, and national security. Each period of transformation is the result of changing health threats to our nation that either add new responsibilities to public health or change

Table 9-2 TEN ESSENTIAL PUBLIC HEALTH SERVICES

1. Monitor health status to identify community health problems.
2. Diagnose and investigate health problems and health hazards in the community.
3. Inform, educate, and empower people about health issues.
4. Mobilize community partnerships to identify and solve health problems.
5. Develop policies and plans that support individual and community health efforts.
6. Enforce laws and regulations that protect health and ensure safety.
7. Link people to needed personal health services and assure the provision of health care when unavailable.
8. Assure a competent public health and personal healthcare workforce.
9. Evaluate effectiveness, accessibility, and quality of personal and population-based health services.
10. Research for new insights and innovative solutions to health problems.

Source: Centers for Disease Control and Prevention, 1994.

its focus in order to ensure optimal health for the population. One of the earliest public health actions (quarantine) in protecting health is still used, and many of the legacies left by each public health era continue today. Thus, precisely defining public health remains problematic; however, three key themes continue to surface and have survived the test of time toward defining public health: promotion, prevention, and protection. These themes are the cornerstones of public health and public health practice.

Factors Transforming Global and National Public Health Service Delivery

Public health is a complex mosaic of programs that focus on the interconnected roles of protecting and promoting health and preventing illness in populations. This complexity has been amplified by rapidly changing factors that are transforming public health practice and service delivery: a focus on wellness, increased incidence of chronic disease, actual and potential emergence, re-emergence of lethal infectious diseases, population-focused programs to address health inequities, the increased role of public health in assisting with disasters, and the myriad environmental factors influencing health.

Wellness and Chronic Disease

Wellness is optimal health for individuals and groups. Wellness focuses on realizing maximum potential of the individual physically, psychologically, spiritually, and socioeconomically. When wellness is realized, it creates the additional benefit of healthy individuals being able to participate fully in their roles as members of families and the community (Smith et al., 2006).

The major threats to achieving wellness for the United States at the beginning of the 21st century are chronic and preventable diseases, which account for the majority of mortality, morbidity, and healthcare costs. Cardiovascular disease, cancer, chronic obstructive pulmonary disease, and diabetes account for two thirds of all deaths in the United States (CDC, 2004). More than half of all Americans live with one or more chronic disease (DeVol et al., 2007).

Risk factors that the majority of chronic diseases have in common include excess caloric intake, physical inactivity, and tobacco use. These are lifestyle choices, and therefore, the chronic diseases attributable to them are considered preventable by risk factor modification (Office of the Surgeon General, 2001). The need for risk factor modification is amplified further by the fact that our country has the highest rate of preventable disease of the industrialized nations (Nolte & McKee, 2008).

Approximately 24% of Americans were obese in 2005 compared with 15% in 1995 (CDC, 2006b). The implications of this statistic are staggering. One study postulates that a 20-year-old obese man could experience a 17% reduction in life expectancy (Fontaine et al., 2003). Our children's life spans may be shorter than their parents for the first time in a hundred years (Olshansky et al., 2005). In addition, obese children are at risk for a range of physical and mental problems that may negatively impact school performance (Dietz, 1998).

Obesity contributes to 75% of hypertension cases (American Obesity Association, 2008). Statistics show that approximately 90% of middle-aged Americans will develop hypertension, with almost 70% of these individuals failing to achieve adequate blood pressure control (American Heart Association, 2003).

One of the most prevalent chronic diseases related to obesity is diabetes. More than 20 million American adults have type 2 diabetes. An additional 54 million are prediabetic, and 2 million of those are adolescents (Cowie et al., 2009). Approximately 20% of cancer in women and 15%

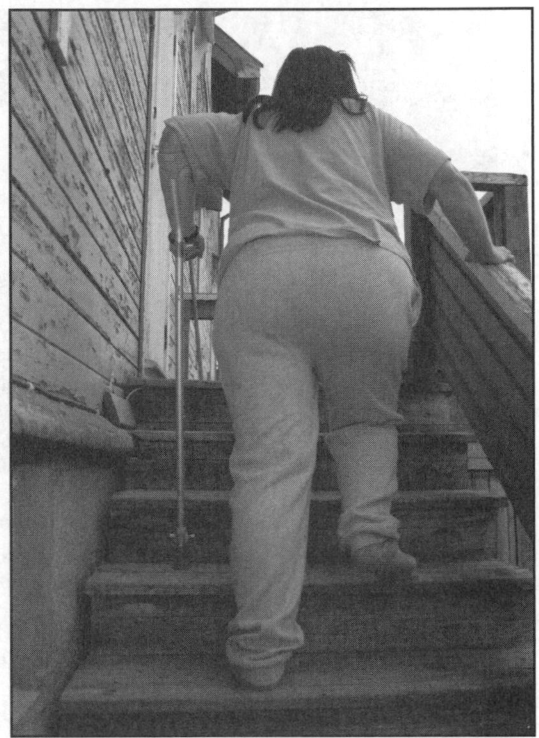

of cancer in men can be attributed to obesity (CDC, 2004). These statistics emphasize the health impact on the population created by the obesity epidemic and the important role of public health.

Another health behavior that contributes to chronic disease is tobacco use, use which is the cause of nearly 5 million deaths per year (WHO, 2008c). It is the leading preventable cause of death in the United States. Smoking and secondhand smoke kill approximately 440,000 people in the United States annually (Armour et al., 2005). It is one of the major risk factors for coronary heart disease. This is significant because coronary heart disease is the leading cause of death in the United States (CDC, 1993).

The U.S. public health system has attempted to deal with the epidemic of chronic and preventable diseases by using a national consensus process

to develop an agenda for improving the health of Americans and promoting wellness. Through this process, a document entitled *Healthy People 2010* was created. The two goals of Healthy People 2010 are (1) to increase life expectancy and improve quality of life and (2) to eliminate health inequities (Keppel et al., 2007). In order to measure progress toward a healthier nation, Healthy People 2010 has identified 10 leading health indicators that will be used to monitor progress in improving the health of our nation: physical activity, overweight and obesity, tobacco use, substance abuse, responsible sexual behavior, mental health, injury and violence, environmental quality, immunization, and access to care. A complete copy of the Healthy People 2010 plan can be found at http://www.healthypeople.gov.

This discussion has documented that chronic diseases are among the most preventable health problems facing our nation. Evidence-based interventions for risk-factor modification can prevent or delay much of the burden while mitigating the devastating consequences. This is accomplished by implementing public health initiatives that promote both healthy behavior choices and community policies and practices that create a culture of wellness (CDC, 2004).

Infectious Disease

The public health system came into existence as the first line of defense against infectious disease. Investment in this system waned with the advent of effective pharmaceuticals and the belief that we had conquered infectious disease as a threat to human health; however, over the past 40 years, 39 new infectious diseases have been discovered, among which are some that drug therapy has been unable to cure. The most deadly of these include HIV/AIDS, Ebola, and SARS (The Millennium Project, 2009). Another disease that has become a serious threat to health is hepatitis C. An estimated 4.1 million Americans have been infected, with 3.2 million suffering chronically (CDC, 2005).

A further complication of infectious diseases is that illnesses previously identified and responsive to medical therapy such as tuberculosis have mutated and developed drug resistance, making them harder to treat. Drug resistance makes the infection less responsive to current therapies and more difficult to treat (WHO, 2007a). Influenza is another disease that has proven to be difficult to both treat and prevent. The United States public health surveillance systems find that seasonal flu results in 200,000 hospitalizations and kills an average of 36,000 Americans yearly (CDC, 2008a).

One of the most deadly and debilitating diseases worldwide has been HIV/AIDS, with 33 million people living with HIV and approximately 7,500 new infections occurring daily. In the United States, an estimated 1.1 million people are infected with HIV. Of serious concern is the projection that approximately one in five persons living with HIV in the United States is unaware that he or she is infected and may be unknowingly transmitting the virus to others (CDC, 2008b).

Our rapidly changing world has led to challenges in implementing public health strategies to contain infectious disease spread. For example, "Airlines now carry more than 2 billion passengers a year, making it possible for any [infectious] diseases they may have to pass from one country to another in a matter of hours" (WHO, 2007a). Globalization will contribute to the rapid spread of the next influenza pandemic. A severe pandemic is projected to "result in 90 million Americans becoming sick, 2.2 million deaths, and the second worst U.S. economic recession since World War II" (Trust for America's Health [TFAH], 2007, p. 6).

Another challenge has been the recent phenomenon of some people refusing immunizations. Six years after the original 2000 target date for the worldwide eradication of polio, the disease persists in countries where the virus is endemic, and new outbreaks are occurring in previously polio-free areas. Public health workers are finding that socioeconomic factors are hindering attainment of complete global obliteration. An example is the suspension of polio vaccination programs in Nigeria in 2003 and 2004 because of a rumor that the vaccine would cause infertility and infection with HIV (Pallansch & Sandhu, 2006).

Environmental

Our environment is both friend and foe. The National Academy of Sciences estimates that 25% of developmental diseases, such as cerebral palsy, autism, and mental retardation, are caused by environmental factors acting alone or together with genetic risk factors. The WHO (2006) estimates that 13 million deaths annually are due to preventable environmental causes.

The WHO sounded a warning on the dangers of ignoring environmental hazards in their recent report on global public health security. The report stated that an inadequate investment in public health, resulting from a false sense of security that vector diseases were eradicated, led to control programs being discontinued and a reduction in training and employment of specialists in the 1980s. The result being that within the following 20 years many important vector-borne diseases, including dengue hemorrhagic fever and malaria, emerged into new areas or reemerged in areas where the diseases were previously controlled (WHO, 2007b).

Indoor and outdoor air pollution is estimated to be responsible for nearly 5% of the global burden of disease. Childhood asthma in the United States has more than doubled over the last 2 decades, and this rise has been linked to indoor and outdoor air quality. The WHO estimates that about 40% of lower respiratory infections occurring in developing countries are related to environmental conditions. In addition, poor air quality is related to the incidence and severity of heart and lung diseases, allergies, and several types of cancers (National Center for Environmental Health: Office of Global Health).

Environmental factors contribute to higher incidence of chronic disease. Research shows that over 50% of American adults do not get enough physical activity to provide health benefits. There has been a marked decline in children walking or biking to school, 13% today compared with 66% in 1974. This can be directly related to the fact that the United States has the lowest prevalence of walking and biking among developed countries. Research also demonstrates that living in sprawling counties like the United States contributes to individuals walking less, weighing more, and having a higher prevalence of hypertension than those living in compact counties.

The environment can also be a positive force for health. The design and development of communities can promote physical activity and act as a public health intervention to promote wellness. One example of doing this is the concept of healthy places. Healthy Places, also known as Smart Growth or New Urbanism, builds physical activity into daily life by creating walk-able, mixed-use communities. Healthy Places takes into account multiple factors that impact health including transportation, land use planning, housing, school siting, public safety, and access to goods and services. The goals of Healthy Places are as follows (Association of State and Territorial Health Officials [ASTHO], 2006):

- Create safe and walk-able communities
- Create a range of housing opportunities and choices
- Provide a variety of transportation choices
- Develop mixed land uses
- Preserve green space

This discussion has demonstrated that our environment is both an asset and a threat. Improving our environment whether it is in the home, workplace, or community is integral to a healthy future for all citizens of the world.

Inequity

Public health is viewed as a safety net for those individuals without access to health care, the majority of whom are from low-income and minority groups having higher exposure to health threats such as violence and environmental hazards. The combination of these factors contributes to decreased health outcomes and increased strain on the safety net (TFAH, 2008a).

Consequences of inequities are illuminated by the following statistical examples. Rates of death from heart disease for black adults were 29% higher than their white counterparts in 2000. Similarly, death rates from stroke were 40% higher (Office of Minority Health & Health Disparities, 2008). Black males are more than twice as likely to die of prostate cancer (Pfizer Facts). Another alarming statistic is that black, American Indian, and Puerto Rican infants have higher death rates than white infants (Office of Minority Health & Health Disparities, 2004).

It is not only ethnic inequity that leads to poor health. Individuals in lower income levels have fewer opportunities to access health care and make healthy choices. There is limited access to nutritious, affordable foods in low-income areas because of fewer and smaller grocery stores in the community. Individuals in these areas often pay more for fresh fruits and vegetables if they are even available for purchase (TFAH, 2008a). This is also an important environmental issue because there is a correlation between the presence of grocery stores and lower rates of obesity, with higher rates of obesity related to the presence of convenience stores (Morland et al., 2006). A lack of health insurance is also a risk factor for poor health. Thirteen percent of white Americans are uninsured—that figure nearly doubles to 22% among blacks, and nearly triples to 36% among Latinos (Kaiser State Health Facts, 2007).

Emergency Preparedness

Preparedness is a relatively new role for public health. After the September 11, 2001, terrorist attacks, the federal government has invested more than $6 billion to improve public health emergency preparedness (Cohen et al., 2004); however, sustained investment needs to be a priority. Having the system and resources to prepare for and respond to such epidemics as SARS, which infected more than 8,000 people and left 774 dead, is the essence of public health preparedness (TFAH, 2008d).

Our ability to respond effectively to public health emergencies also has economic implications. It is estimated that SARS cost our world 30 to 50 billion dollars in terms of lives lost, quarantines, and lost tourism dollars (Aldrich & Newcomb, 2005).

Public health is a critical partner in emergency response. During 2007, there were 63 federally declared disasters, with health agencies responding to almost all of them (Federal Emergency Management Agency, 2008). At the state level, almost 90% of state public health agencies were involved in a response that required activation of their incident command system or involvement in a statewide multidepartment emergency operations center (ASTHO, 2008a).

The public health system plays a critical role in all types of emergencies. Terrorism, natural disasters, infectious disease, environmental hazards, infrastructure failures, and food-borne outbreaks all require that public health coordinates the protection and provision of health care for large numbers of people (ASTHO, 2008a).

Issues Shaping the Future of Public Health

Accreditation

Many accreditation programs have been developed as a result of internal or external pressure to improve the quality and value of services provided by an industry, whether public or private. In addition, accreditation seeks to strengthen the viability and competitive position of the agency or organization. Today there are a number of accreditation programs that address health and public service organizations, including medical care providers, insurers, education, and public safety to name a few. Within the United States healthcare system, accreditation programs have emerged to provide consumers, employees, and other stakeholders with assurance of complying with a basic set of service delivery standards. Public health agencies, however, "remain one of the few organizational components of the U.S. health and social service system that have yet to develop an accreditation program tailored to their specific scope of activities" (Mays, 2004, p. 4).

In a white paper prepared for the Robert Wood Johnson Foundation (RWJF), several important policy considerations were identified from other service industries that deserve consideration for public health accreditation, including the following (Mays, 2004):

- The potential for promoting improvements in service deliver, operations, and outcomes
- Costs being weighed against the potential benefits to determine feasibility and value
- Costs being distributed and financed equitably to ensure that they do not preclude participation by organizations that could benefit the greatest
- Strong incentives for seeking and maintaining accreditation are essential to the viability and success of the program
- Governance for the accreditation program should include representation from multiple stakeholders engaged in the field of practice
- Accreditation programs, which should be driven by evidence-based practice and focus on performance standards that are linked to service outcomes

A national accreditation program for public health is inevitable. Many momentous initiatives have set the stage for accreditation and modernizing public health and public health practice. Two landmark reports by the IOM—*The Future of Public Health* in 1988, indicating that the governmental public health infrastructure was in disarray, and in 2003 a second report, *The Future of the Public's Health in the 21st Century*, focusing on several broad themes, including population health, determinants of health, strengthening the public health infrastructure, partnerships, accountability, evidenced-based practice, and communication—have been critical in this work. Both reports prompted movement by policy makers, public health agencies, and educational institutions toward greater awareness, investments, and accountability in public health practice.

The 1988 report planted the seed for the development of the IOM's *Essential Public Health Services* (1994) (National Public Health Performance Standards Program) as a method to identify and describe better the activities used to promote health and prevent disease (Table 9-2). Essential public health services were the precursor to the development of national public health performance standards to improve the quality of public health practice and the performance of the public health system. Another ground breaking activity, *Exploring Accreditation Project*, a partnership coordinated by the ASTHO and the National Association of County and City Health Officials, including the American Public Health Association and the National Association of Local Boards of Health, released final recommendations for a Voluntary National Accreditation Program for State and Local Public Health Departments (CDC, 2008c).

In May of 2007, a national Public Health Accreditation Board was formed through funding support from the CDC and the RWJF. The goal of the voluntary national accreditation program is to improve and protect the health of the public by advancing the quality and performance of state and local public health departments (RWJF, 2006–2007).

Through consensus, a proposed model for a voluntary national accreditation program for state and local health departments has been developed. This model addresses feasibility, cost, structure of the program, and desirability. Feasibility includes existing building blocks of current state programs, a cadre of existing and evolving best practices, and interest of funders and potential applicants. Cost is addressed in the model by applicant fees, governmental support, and private grants. The accreditation program is structured according to national standards, proven evaluation processes, specific financing and incentive plans, and a negotiated governance structure. Desirability encompasses improving quality, performance, accountability, and credibility, as well as recognizing excellence and increasing the visibility of public health (RWJF, 2006–2007).

Several states have developed and implemented accreditation programs while monitoring the ongoing evolution of a national accreditation program. If a national accreditation program is implemented and accomplishes what it is intended to do, the public can be assured that basic public health services are equitably and consistently available regardless of location. Ultimately, however, success will be dependent on sustained policy maker and constituent support and financial commitment.

Accreditation may hold strong potential for improving public health; however, it should not be viewed as a single solution. Meaningful and sustained improvements in public health capacity and service delivery require a systems approach to improvement through workforce education, performance evaluation, quality improvement, professional certification and licensure, system financing, leadership development, and public and policy maker engagement.

Globalization

The amazing advancements in travel and technology have led to international interconnectedness that influences the health of individual citizens in ways never before seen in the history of humankind. The WHO serves as the hub for data and policy in this new world of globalized health problems. According to the WHO, global health is defined by Lee (2003) as the transnational impacts of globalization upon the health of persons that is beyond the control of individual nations.

The WHO delineate major effects of globalization on health as the "inequities caused by patterns of international trade and investment, the effects of global climate change, the vulnerability of refugee populations, the marketing of harmful products by transnational corporations and the transmission of diseases resulting from travel between countries" (Smith et al., 2006, p. 3). Although these threats have global consequences, they must be dealt with simultaneously at the international, national, state, and local level. This requires partnering and priority setting by and among all levels of the public health and healthcare systems (Smith et al., 2006).

Collaboration, however, can be elusive. Without changing human behavior and value systems, sustained change at the global level is unattainable. Global public health strategies require the cooperation of individuals, populations, political leaders, the military, and policy makers working in conjunction with public health professionals to institute sustainable change.

A major issue of globalization is public health security. This refers to the need to protect the world from natural, accidental, or intentional biological, chemical, and radiological agents that threaten human health. A recent WHO report delineates some of the factors controlled by humankind that are contributing to the threats against public health security. These factors include inadequate investment in public health, a false sense of security with a reduction in acute infectious disease outbreaks, policy changes that undermine evidence-based public health interventions such as mandatory immunizations, conflicts that lead to the displacement of individuals to unsanitary and impoverished living conditions, and inadequate animal husbandry and food processing practices that endanger a healthy food supply (WHO, 2007a).

A recent WHO report entitled *A Safer Future: Global Public Health Security in the 21st Century* offers key recommendations to secure the highest level of global public health security. These include cooperation in global surveillance and disease outbreak alert and response, transparency in sharing information and technologies; joint research on samples of disease causing organisms, joint efforts to build a strong public health infrastructure in all countries that includes training, emergency preparedness capacity, and prevention strategies; and improved cross-sector collaboration by governmental agencies within and across (WHO, 2007b).

"Given today's universal vulnerability to these threats, better security calls for global solidarity," said Dr. Margaret Chan, Director-General of WHO. "International public health security is both a collective aspiration and a mutual responsibility. The new watchwords are diplomacy, cooperation, transparency and preparedness" (World Health Organization, 2007b).

A recurring theme in discussions of global health is the importance of strong political advocacy. At the Sixth Global Conference on Health Promotion in Bangkok, this was a major focus. The participants came together and reiterated the need for political advocacy, investment in strategies and infrastructure that address the determinants of health, regulatory interventions, and building health promotion capacity and partnerships. They stressed that these strategies were essential in addressing the challenges posed by globalization (WHO, 2005).

Media

The role of media in public health is pervasive. The Internet, television, radio, newspapers, and magazines are often the most influential sources of information about health. The flow of information has become interactive in that the media presents scientific information and government policies to the public while providing a real-time venue for the public to express their concerns (WHO, 2002). Public health media can be either reactive or proactive. During an acute public health event such as SARS, public health must respond to media-driven requests for information.

According to a study by the Nuffield Trust, the media can either heighten levels of anxiety or provide reassurance at times of acute public health events. Authorities such as governments may use the mass media but can seldom keep control of the information delivered. They have to strike a difficult balance between saying too much and saying too little: One course of action may cause an overreaction; the other may seem complacent (McInnes, 2005).

They also have to be aware that lack of information creates a vacuum that the media will fill. Thus, it behooves public health professionals to respond quickly, conveying competence and control of the situation.

During an acute public health situation, the media can be a valuable public health partner. The use of the web to collect data, communicate findings, and collaboratively plan interventions can facilitate a rapid, comprehensive, and effective response that can reduce morbidity and mortality. Electronic and print media can be used to inform the public about ways they can protect themselves, their family, and their community and mitigate the consequences of the incident. For example, in the case of a food-borne disease outbreak, the public can provide information about the incidence of illness and can be instructed on how to avoid exposure based on the findings of the epidemiological investigation.

The media is also critical to disease prevention and health promotion activities. One example was offered by Lambrew (2007), who recommends a national Wellness Trust and argues that a major component would be electronic infrastructure that includes both an electronic prevention record system similar to the electronic medical record and online options for prevention, control, and community resources (Lambrew, 2007). A second example is the CDC's National Center for Health Marketing. The Center director's inaugural blog entry includes a quote from legendary newsman Daniel Shorr, "If you do not exist in the media, for all practical purposes you do not exist" (Bernhardt, 2006). The CDC now has its own MySpace page, using this electronic social networking tool to dialogue with other health sites. Their presence on Internet social networking sites is based on the belief that this venue has incredible potential to "protect health when accurate and relevant information is shared between trusted peers to support positive and healthy decision-making" (Bernhardt, 2006).

These innovative technologies have also impacted global public health. Internet-based health information is now being accessed by the most socially isolated communities and populations. "Any serious consideration of public health populations must thus be cognizant of the role of the media in both representing and constructing [public health] problems and policies." The reality, however, is that public health often has to fight to make sure that their voice is heard by the media (Bunton & Crawshaw, 2006).

Economics

Economics influences the future of public health in two major ways. Public health has a critical role in controlling and reducing healthcare costs; however, the funding of public health is woefully inadequate, thus jeopardizing its capacity and capability to meet the needs of society as well as reduce healthcare costs.

"The skyrocketing costs of health care threaten to bankrupt American businesses" (TFAH, 2008c, p. 13). It is clear that we must implement public health strategies to promote healthy lifestyles and manage chronic illnesses to reverse this economic crisis.

The most prevalent chronic diseases are costing our country more than $1 trillion every year. Some projections predict that this figure could reach $6 trillion by the middle of this century. Failure to reduce these costs threatens the capacity to provide universal health insurance and adequate health care for a rapidly aging population (DeVol et al., 2007).

Older persons are particularly prone to chronic illness. The Kaiser Family Foundation estimated that 87% of Medicare beneficiaries have at least one chronic illness. Another study concluded that most all of the spending growth in Medicare over the past 15 years was related to caring for individuals with multiple chronic conditions (Thorpe & Howard, 2006).

Affordable, accessible health care is only one aspect of the economic consequences of chronic disease. Other indirect consequences include the financial drain of chronically ill workers utilizing sick days; presenteeism, where workers come to work, but have sub-par productivity; and the loss of productivity of caregivers who must miss work to care for chronically ill family members. The combined cost of these indirect factors was estimated at approximately $1 trillion in 2003.

DeVol et al. (2007) analyzed the economic factors associated with chronic disease-reduction strategies. The researchers found that modest reductions in avoidable factors such as unhealthy behavior, environmental risks, and lack of early detection and innovative treatment would lead to 40 million fewer cases of illness. This translates into a gain of over $1 trillion annually in labor supply and efficiency by 2023. The analysis also compared this best case scenario to one in which costs would be incurred under the status quo and found a 27% reduction in total economic impact. These authors further postulated that this projection was low because it did not take into account the ability to redirect these savings into education and training for future generations.

The exponential increase in the incidence of chronic disease is costing lives, quality of life, and prosperity. It is up to the public health workforce to take the lead in advocating for an increased proportion of healthcare spending to be directed toward the promotion of specific health behaviors that will reduce smoking, obesity, and substance abuse. A reduction in these unhealthy behaviors would yield a significant return on investment (DeVol et al., 2007).

Public health cannot take the lead without adequate capacity. According to the TFAH, there is currently a $20 billion annual deficit in spending on public health (TFAH, 2008b). This deficit prevents public health from adequately fulfilling its core responsibilities of:

- Monitoring health status and health problems
- Enforcing public health laws
- Mobilizing community partnerships
- Developing policy related to individual and community health strategies
- Assuring an adequate and competent public and healthcare workforce

- Linking individuals to health programs
- Evaluating population based health services
- Researching innovative evidenced-based approaches to health promotion and protection and disease prevention

To meet these responsibilities, the TFAH report recommends that the current federal, state, and local public health spending of approximately $35 billion per year ($120 per person) should be increased to $55 to $60 billion annually (approximately $187 per person) (TFAH, 2008b).

Workforce

Adequate funding is only one component of assuring a strong public health system. The workforce in public health is facing critical challenges, namely a steep decline in numbers and resources. These challenges will undermine the ability of a dedicated workforce to protect the public's health. Underserved areas will not have the health services they need. Communities will be ill prepared to deal with disasters, and the public will not have the information needed to protect themselves from an emerging infectious disease, such as pandemic flu or mumps (Perlino, 2006).

The ASTHO (2008b) has compiled some startling statistics that delineate this problem:

- Since 1988, the ratio of public health workers per 100,000 Americans has decreased by 39% while their responsibilities have increased.
- Retirement rates are projected at 56% in some public health agencies by 2012.
- Vacancy rates are up to 25% in some public health agencies.
- In some parts of the country, workforce turnover rates reach 29%.
- The average age of a public health worker in state government is 47 years.
- In 2006, approximately 6,800 individuals graduated from an accredited school of public health. Most took jobs in the private sector.

The most severe shortages are found in the areas of epidemiology, nursing, laboratory science, and environmental health (Perlino, 2006). Nursing is the largest professional group of the public health workforce, with an average age of 49 years. Seventy-eight percent of state public health laboratories report difficulty recruiting and retaining bioterrorism preparedness staff. Additionally, environmental health graduates have dropped 50% since 1998 (ASTHA, 2008b).

Recruiting, training, and retaining the public health workforce is complicated, and there is not one typical career path. The field encompasses a range of specialties. The IOM (2001) points out that public health professionals "receive their education and training in a wide range of disciplines and in diverse academic settings, including schools of public health, medicine, nursing, dentistry, social work, allied health professions, pharmacy, law, public administration, veterinary medicine, engineering, environmental sciences, biology, microbiology, and journalism."

Barriers that have been identified as causative factors to the public health workforce shortage include budget shortfalls, resulting in noncompetitive wages, a lack of an understanding regarding the opportunities of a public health career, and bureaucracy. The ASTHO (2008b) has identified ways to address these barriers:

- Facilitate a broader awareness of the public health workforce crisis
- Advocate for additional resources
- Foster research to address public workforce challenges
- Improve marketing of public health careers

- Forge public–private partnerships to ensure a strong public health workforce

Public Health Advocacy and Policy Formulation

In order to address the myriad of challenges facing public health, it is imperative that health professionals have the knowledge, skills, and competencies required to influence public policy. This will require adopting new approaches to engage the public, communities, business, and policy makers collectively. Success depends on a well-informed public and a valuing of individual, community, and global health. It also requires a culture that views the public health system as an essential component of the well being of the world. This means that policy makers must commit to an increased and sustained investment in public health in order to address effectively the complex health challenges facing this nation in the 21st century (Benjamin, 2006).

The current healthcare system focuses on curing and treating disease and places less value on health promotion and protection and disease prevention. Research has found that prevention is effective in both economic savings and healthy outcomes; however, "a common focus on creating broader access to preventive programs and services continues to fail to get real traction. Because of this, public health advocates now argue that it is time to balance the investment with a greater emphasis on prevention" (Benjamin, 2006, p. 1040).

To transform the paradigm to one in which public health is viewed as the foundation for a vibrant society, health professionals must effectively engage each stakeholder group in policy development, advocacy, and implementation. A strong case must be made regarding the value of public health as a partner in shaping healthy communities and that healthy communities provide tangible benefits for all stakeholders.

A model that can be used by public health professionals to engage partners is megacommunity. The impetus for the development of this model was the authors' experiences in dealing with complex global challenges in the areas of security, economics, health, and safety. These challenges are within public health's sphere of responsibility and influence, having biological, cultural, and geopolitical roots. Because of the complexity of these challenges, "multisector, multilateral, collaborative and innovative solutions" are required (Gerencser et al., 2008, p. 10).

Megacommunity is based on the idea that communities of organizations need to act as vehicles for change. These communities "come together across national, organizational, and sector boundaries to reach goals they cannot achieve alone" (Gerencser et al., 2008, p. 28). The model identifies business, government, and civil society as the three power sectors that must work together to address complex mutual problems. Each sector brings their sphere of influence to the table. The resultant dynamic tension leads to excitement and energy that fosters sustained strategy formulation and leads to transnational solutions necessary in this age of globalization. One caveat the authors have is that sustainable strategy must not compromise future generation's ability to meet their needs. This is consistent with public health's mission to promote and protect the health of the population by enforcing clean air and water regulations and promoting healthy lifestyles to reduce societal economic burden.

Megacommunities may also have a significant effect on globalization. The author's definition of globalization is the interdependence of human activity that is enabled by innovative types of technology, communication, and financial interrelationships. An example of a public health policy that exemplifies this is the preparation for pandemic influenza. Technologies such as real-time disease reporting by healthcare providers to public health and emergency alerting systems are now in place. Multisector and multidisciplinary information sharing regarding issues such as novel infectious diseases and suspicious agents have been developed through a megacommunity approach. Public–private partnerships exist where all three sectors integrate resources and expertise to enhance the response to public health emergencies and disasters (Gerencser et al., 2008).

In order to use megacommunities effectively to influence public health policy, it is necessary to build network capital through negotiated relationships and shared control over processes and goal attainment. Recent successful efforts to ban smoking in public places are an example of building network capitol. Megacommunities of associations, business, and government successfully lobbied state policy makers to enact smoke free legislation. This was directly related to years of relationship building, joint strategy formulation, and problem solving.

Public health policy advocacy involves many of the basic tenets of a megacommunity. The first tenet is that, in order to influence from a position of strength, it is necessary to convince partners that the proposed policy will be a win–win situation. Another tenet is that you must understand the needs of the constituents affected by the policy in order to provide the information needed to either support or remain neutral during the political process. Cultural sensitivity is a megacommunity tenet that stresses avoiding stereotyping to navigate successfully political, economic, and social changes that can sabotage your advocacy efforts (Gerencser et al., 2008).

Another megacommunity tenet is continuous environmental scanning. This is done to forecast and anticipate opportunities for and potential barriers to effective policy formulation. Success is inexorably tied to timing and adapting to current events (Gerencser et al., 2008).

In this information age, the megacommunity tenet of transparency is critical to policy success. This transparency is also important in developing trust, another Megacommunity tenet. As Steven Covey (2006) discusses, trust can create immeasurable success and prosperity in all dimensions of our lives. After trust is broken, partners frequently become adversaries, making policy acceptance extremely difficult (Gerencser et al., 2008).

The foundation of an effective megacommunity is based on four guiding principles. These principles are inherent in public health policy formulation and advocacy. These principles are as follows (Gerencser et al., 2008):

- Respect the autonomy and opinions of all partners
- Share a commitment to continuous communication, engagement, and resource sharing
- Be dedicated to taking action
- Embrace conflict and practice effective conflict resolution

The health problems this nation and the world are facing are complex. Public health is charged with planning, acting, and evaluating strategies to address these problems. The idea of megacommunities is an innovative 21st century model that can be used to solve these complex problems by facilitating effective policy formulation and advocacy.

References

Aldrich, S., & Newcomb, J. (2005). *Thinking ahead: Anticipating early impacts of an avian influenza pandemic.* Cambridge, MA: Bio Economic Research Associates.

American Heart Association. (2003). *Heart disease and stroke statistics: 2003 update*. Dallas, Texas: Author.

American Obesity Association. (2008). *AOA fact sheets.* Retrieved December 31, 2008, from http://obesity1.tempdomainname.com/subs/fastfacts/Health_Effects.shtml

Armour, B. S., Woollery, T., Malarcher, A., Pechacek, T. F., & Husten, C. (2005). Annual smoking-attributable mortality, years of potential life lost, and productivity losses—United States, 1997–2001. *Morbidity and Mortality Weekly Report, 54*(25), 625–628.

Association of State and Territorial Health Officials. (2006). *The built environment, physical activity, and health* (fact sheet). Retrieved February 12, 2010, from http://www.govinstitute.org/policyguide/pdfs/health.pdf

Association of State and Territorial Health Officials. (2008a). *States of preparedness: Health agency progress.* Arlington, VA: Author. Retrieved February 12, 2010, from http://www.astho.org/WorkArea/DownloadAsset.aspx?id=674

Association of State and Territorial Health Officials. (2008b). *2007 State public health: workforce survey results.* Arlington, VA: Author. Retreived February 12, 2010, from http://www.astho.org/WorkArea/DownloadAsset.aspx?id=500

Awofeso, N. (2004). What's new about the "new public health"? *American Journal of Public Health, 94*(5), 705–709.

Benjamin, G. C. (2006). Putting the public in public health: New approaches. *Health Affairs, 25*(4), 1040–1043.

Bernhardt, J. (2006). *Director's blog: Health marketing musings.* Retrieved December 30, 2008, from http://www.cdc.gov/healthmarketing/blog_071306.htm

Bunton, R., & Crawshaw, P. (2006). Representing public health. *Critical Public Health, 16*(1), 1–4.

Centers for Disease Control and Prevention. (1993). Ciga rette smoking-attributable mortality and years of potential life lost—United States, 1990. *Morbidity and Mortality Weekly Report, 42*(33), 645–649.

Centers for Disease Control and Prevention. (1994). *10 Essential public health services.* Retrieved December 31, 2008, from http://www.cdc.gov/od/ocphp/nphpsp/essentialphservices.htm

Centers for Disease Control and Prevention. (1999). Ten great public health achievements—United States, 1900–1999. *Morbidity and Mortality Weekly Report, 48*(12), 241–243.

Centers for Disease Control and Prevention. (2004). *The burden of chronic diseases and their risk factors: National and state perspectives 2004* (No. 2008). Atlanta, GA: U.S. Department of Health and Human Services.

Centers for Disease Control and Prevention. (2005). *Hepatitis C fact sheet.* Retrieved February 12, 2010, from http://www.doh.wa.gov/cfh/Hepatitis/Documents/cfact.pdf

Centers for Disease Control and Prevention. (2006a). *CDC injury fact book*. Atlanta, GA: Author.

Centers for Disease Control and Prevention. (2006b). State specific prevalence of obesity among adults: United States,2005. *Morbidity and Mortality Weekly Report, 55*(36), 985–988.

Centers for Disease Control and Prevention. (2008a). *Key facts about seasonal influenza (flu).* Retrieved February 12, 2010, from http://www.cdc.gov/Flu/keyfacts.htm

Centers for Disease Control and Prevention. (2008b). *Celebrate life: World AIDS day 2008.* Retrieved December 18, 2008, from http://www.cdc.gov/Features/WorldAidsDay

Centers for Disease Control and Prevention. (2008c). *National public health performance standards program: Overview.* Retrieved August 7, 2009, from http://www.cdc.gov/od/ocphp/nphpsp/overview.htm

Cohen, H. W., Gould, R. M., & Sidel, V. W. (2004). The pitfalls of bioterrorism preparedness: The anthrax and smallpox experiences. *Am J Public Health, 94*(10), 1667–1671.

Covey, S. (2006). *The speed of trust: The one thing that changes everything.* New York: Free Press.

Cowie, C. C., Rust, K. F., Ford, E. S., Eberhardt, M. S., Byrd-Holt, D. D., Li, C., et al. (2009). A full accounting of diabetes and prediabetes in the U.S. population, 1988–1994 and 2005–2006. *Diabetes Care., 32*(2), 287–294.

DeVol, R., Bedroussian, A., Charuworn, A., Chatterjee, A., Kim, I. K., Kim, S., et al. (2007). *An unhealthy America: The economic burden of chronic disease.* Santa Monica, CA: Milken Institute.

Dietz, W. H. (1998). Childhood weight affects adult morbidity and mortality. *The Journal of Nutrition, 128*(2 Suppl), 411S–414S.

Federal Emergency Management Agency. (2008). *Annual major disaster declarations totals.* Retrieved December 18, 2008, from http://www.fema.gov/news/disaster_totals_annual.fema

Fontaine, K. R., Redden, D. T., Wang, C., Westfall, A. O., & Allison, D. B. (2003). Years of life lost due to obesity. *Journal of the American Medical Association, 289*(2), 187–193.

Gerencser, M., Van Lee, R., Napolitano, F., & Kelly, C. (2008). *Megacommunities: How leaders of government, business and non-profits can tackle today's global challenges together*. New York: Palgrave Macmillan.

Heishman, H., & Dannenberg, A. L. (2008). Influencing the environment in your built community. *Journal of Environmental Health, 70*(4), 66–67.

Institute of Medicine, Committee for the study of the Future of Public Health. (1988). *The future of public health.* Washington, DC: National Academy Press.

Institute of Medicine. (2001). *Who will keep the public healthy? educating public health professionals for the 21st century.* Washington, DC: The National Academies Press.

Kaiser State Health Facts. (2007). *United states: Health coverage & uninsured.* Retrieved January 1, 2009, from http://www.statehealthfacts.org/profileind.jsp?sub=40&rgn=1&cat=3

Keppel, K., Bilheimer, L., & Gurley, L. (2007). Improving population health and reducing health care disparities. *Health Affairs (Project Hope), 26*(5), 1281–1292.

Lambrew, J. M. (2007). *A wellness trust to prioritize disease prevention* (discussion paper). The Hamilton Project. Retrieved February 12, 2010, from www3.brookings.edu/views/papers/200704lambrew.pdf

Lee, K. (2003). *Globalization and health: An introduction.* New York: Palgrave Macmillan.

Mays, G. P. (2004). *Can accreditation work in public health? Lessons from other service industries.* Working Paper Prepared for the Robert Wood Johnson Foundation, November 30, 2004.

McInnes, C. (2005). Health, security and the risk society. *The Nuffield Trust.* Retrieved February 12, 2010, from http://www.nuffieldtrust.org.uk/ecomm/files/HSecrisksoc.pdf

Morland, K., Diez Roux, A. V., & Wing, S. (2006). Supermarkets, other food stores, and obesity: The atherosclerosis risk in communities study. *American Journal of Preventive Medicine, 30*(4), 333–339.

National Center for Environmental Health: Office of Global Health—Programs—Air Pollution/CDC. Retrieved August 5, 2009, from http://www.cdc.gov/nceh/globalhealth/projects/airpollution.htm

National Public Health Performance Standards Program. *National public health performance standards program frequently asked questions.* Retrieved December 17, 2008, from http://www.cdc.gov/od/ocphp/nphpsp/PDF/FAQ.pdf

Nolte, E., & McKee, C. M. (2008). Measuring the health of nations: Updating an earlier analysis. *Health Affairs, 27*(1), 58–71.

Office of Minority Health & Health Disparities. (2004). *Highlight 4/04 national minority health month.* Retrieved January 1, 2009, Retrieved from, http://www.cdc.gov/omhd/Highlights/2004/HApr04.htm

Office of Minority Health and Health Disparities. (2008). *Disease burden and risk factors.* Retrieved December 18, 2009, from http://www.cdc.gov/omhd/AMH/dbrf.htm

Office of the Surgeon General. (2001). *The Surgeon General's call to action to prevent and decrease overweight and obesity.* Rockville, MD: U.S. Department of Health and Human Services.

Olshansky, S., Jay, D. J., Passaro, R. C., Hershow, J. L., Carnes, B. A., Brody, J., et al. (2005). A potential decline in life expectancy in the United States in the 21st century. *New England Journal of Medicine, 352*(11), 1138–1145.

Pallansch, M. A., & Sandhu, H. S. (2006). The eradication of polio—progress and challenges. *The New England Journal of Medicine, 355*(24), 2508–2511.

Perlino, C. M. (September, 2006). The public health workforce shortage: Left unchecked, will we be protected? Washington, DC: American Public Health Association. Retrieved February 12, 2010, from http://www.apha.org/NR/rdonlyres/597828BF-9924-4B94-8821-135F665E9D45/0/PublicHealthWorkforceIssueBrief.pdf

Pfizer Facts. *Racial differences in cancer: A comparison of black and white adults in the United States.* Retrieved August 9, 2009, from http://media.pfizer.com/files/products/Racial_Differences_in_Cancer.pdf

Public health and environment. Retrieved January 1, 2009, from http://www.who.int/phe/en

Robert Wood Johnson Foundation. (2006–2007). *Exploring accreditation: Final recommendations for a voluntary national accreditation program for state and local public health departments.* Retrieved February 12, 2010, from http://www.rwjf.org/files/research/explore_accreditation.pdf

Shattuck, L. (1850). *Report of the sanitary commission of Massachusetts 1850* (No. 37). Boston: Dutton & Wentworth. Retrieved July 28, 2008, from http://www.deltaomega.org/shattuck.pdf

Smith, B. J., Tang, K. C., & Nutbeam, D. (2006). *WHO health promotion glossary: New terms.* Retrieved July 31, 2009, from http://www.who.int/healthpromotion/about/HP%20Glossay%20in%20HPI.pdf

The Millennium Project. (2009). *State of the future 2009.* Retrieved August 5, 2009, from http://www.millennium-project.org/millennium/SOF2009-English.pdf

Thorpe, K., & Howard, D. (2006). The rise in spending among Medicare beneficiaries: the role of chronic disease prevalence and changes in treatment intensity. *Health Affairs, 25*(5), 378–388.

Trust for America's Health. (2007). *Pandemic flu and the potential for U.S. economic recession.* Retrieved August 7, 2009, from http://healthyamericans.org/reports/flurecession/FluRecession.pdf

Trust for America's Health. (2008a). *A healthier America: 10 top priorities for prevention.* Retrieved August 9, 2009, from http://healthyamericans.org/assets/files/10ThingsBook.pdf

Trust for America's Health. (2008b). *F as in fat 2008.* Retrieved December 18, 2008, from http://healthyamericans.org/reports/obesity2008

Trust for America's Health. (2008c). *Blueprint for a healthier America.* Retrieved December 18, 2008, from http://healthyamericans.org/assets/files/Blueprint.pdf

Trust for America's Health. (2008d). *Ready or Not? Preparing for potential health emergencies and bioterrorism attacks.* Retrieved December 18, 2008, from http://healthyamericans.org/reports/bioterror08

Turnock, B. J., & Barnes, P. A. (2006). *Director's blog: Health marketing musings.* Retrieved December 30, 2008, from http://www.cdc.gov/healthmarketing/blog_071306.htm

World Health Organization. (2002). *The world health report 2002.* Geneva: Author.

World Health Organization. (2005). *The Bangkok charter for health promotion in a globalized world* (11 August 2005). Retrieved July 30, 2009 from, http://www.who.int/healthpromotion/conferences/6gchp/bangkok_charter/en/index.html

World Health Organization. (2006). *Preventing disease through healthy environments: Towards an estimate of the environmental burden of disease.* Retrieved December 15, 2008, from http://www.searo.who.int/en/Section316/Section503/Section2141_11776.htm

World Health Organization. (2007a). *International spread of disease threatens public health security.* Retrieved December 18, 2008, from http://www.who.int/mediacentre/news/releases/2007/pr44/en/index.html

World Health Organization. (2007b). *The World Health Report 2007: A safer future: Global public health security in the 21st century.* Retrieved July 30, 2009 from http://www.who.int/whr/2007/whr07_en.pdf

World Health Organization. (2008a). *Impact of the global financial and economic crisis on health.* Retrieved February 12, 2010, from http://www.who.int/mediacentre/news/statements/2008/s12/en

World Health Organization. (2008b). *WHO regional office for Europe: Public health services.* Retrieved February 12, 2010, from http://www.euro.who.int/publichealth

CASE STUDY

Policy Tools for Helping People at Risk for or Living with Cancer

Alison P. Smith, BA, BSN, RN

The bad news is that the lifetime probability of developing cancer is one in every two men and one in every three women (National Cancer Institute, 2005). Cancer remains the second most common cause of death by disease, claiming the lives of more than half a million people per year (American Cancer Society, 2007). As the population ages, cancer rates are expected to increase (U.S. Cancer Statistics Working Group, 2003). Disparities in health outcomes persist among minority populations (Agency for Healthcare Research and Quality. 2008).

The good news is that for the first time since 1999 the incidence and mortality rates for all cancers combined decreased for both men and women. Similarly, death rates decreased, on average, 1.8% per year from 2002 through 2005 (CDC, 2005a). The 5-year cancer survival rate has risen to 64% for adults (CDC, 2005b).

The hope is that nearly one third of cancer deaths are preventable. Health policy is a powerful and evidence-based tool for preventing, detecting early, and successfully treating cancer. Although not all of these policy levers are currently being put to their fullest use, the discussion here provides an overview of how and where policy at the federal, state, and local level can effect outcomes for people at risk for and living with cancer. These examples span the continuum of cancer research and care. These examples encompass policy vehicles such as the creation, expansion, and appropriation of funding for programs and services; taxation for users and tax credits for developers; and incentives for or restrictions on personal behavior.

Cancer Prevention

Smoking is the number one cause of preventable cancer deaths (CDC, 2005). Although smoking rates have dropped in recent years, the CDC reported that in 2004 approximately 20.9% of U.S. adults were current smokers. Although health education has proven somewhat effective in reducing tobacco use, other policy interventions have been more directly linked to healthy behaviors, namely, smoke-free air ordinances, tobacco taxation, and provision of evidence-based smoking-cessation services.

Today, males are twice as likely to die from lung cancer in Kentucky as they are in California (Figure 9-1), or as Tim Byers, MD, MPH, University of Colorado, put it, "Children face wildly different prospects in terms of mortality based solely upon the chance of their geo-political place of birth." Since 1986, California has pursued a coordinated,

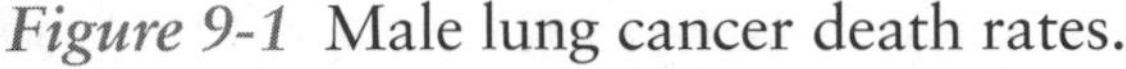

Figure 9-1 Male lung cancer death rates.

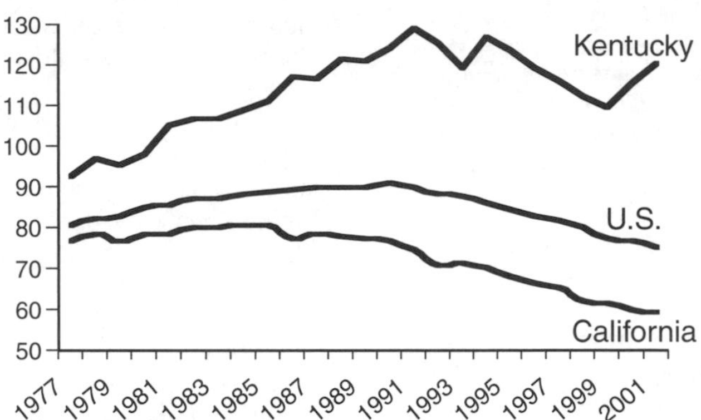

aggressive, multipronged approach to reduce tobacco use through education, user taxation, and clean-air legislation. By applying evidence-based policy and practice intervention from tobacco research, California has realized a steady decline in tobacco use and in deaths caused by lung cancer as well as healthcare cost savings.

In 2006, the Surgeon General Richard Carmona published a report on second-hand smoke that accelerated the adoption of smoke-free air ordinances across the country. As of April 2008, 24 states have passed smoke-free laws that cover restaurants and bars. Hundreds of cities and counties across the country have also taken action in some form. These ordinances not only protect nonsmokers from the deleterious effects of smoke, but they support smokers in their efforts to quit. Of note, smoke-free policies do not have an adverse economic impact on the hospitality industry—a counter argument commonly posed by opponents of smoke-free laws.

Tobacco taxation at the federal and state level has also proved effective in reducing smoking (Husten, 2008). Adults and particularly youth are sensitive to price increases (Chaloupka et al., 2002). For adults, a 10% price increase decreases consumption by 4% and increases cessation by 1.5% (Task Force on Community Preventive Services, 2005).

Finally, policies driving tobacco cessation services are an important component of cancer prevention (Husten, 2008). Seventy percent of smokers want to quit, and more than 40% try to quit each year; however, most tobacco users do not use treatments shown to be effective when trying to quit (Fiore et al., 2008). Access to cessation services can be provided through private and public policy decisions (e.g., employer insurance benefits, publicly funded health insurance plans like Medicare and Medicaid). In addition, publicly funded quit lines are available in the United States through a national network via 1-800-QUIT NOW (Husten, 2008). This network routes callers to their state's quit line service, which is funded by the state and/or the CDC. Coverage for nicotine replacement therapy also varies by state (North American Quitline Consortium, 2010).

Other cancer-preventing policies are currently being tested, evaluated, and debated. With the link between colon and other cancers with obesity, a variety of polices targeting obesity reduction are being debated, including "fat taxes" for unhealthy foods, mirroring tobacco taxes, mandatory calorie reductions in public school lunch programs or increased physical activity requirements, and food content bans such as the New York City Board of Health's action to ban artificial trans fats in restaurants. Similarly, the discovery and approval of vaccines to prevent human papilloma virus (HPV), a common cause of cervical cancer, has stimulated more discussion on policy opportunities to prevent cancer. Just as the hepatitis vaccination policies mandate immunization for school entrance, mandatory HPV vaccination is also being debated (Wells, 2008).

Cancer Screening and Early Detection

Scientific discovery is rapidly evolving to achieve better screening and earlier detection of cancer through advances of the fields of radiology imaging, pathology, genetics, and others. As screening and early detection methods become perfected and Food and Drug Administration approved, the U.S. Preventive Services Taskforce (USPSTF) evaluates and grades the evidence supporting the wide spread use of these methods. The USPSTF was first convened by the U.S. Public Health Service in 1984 and, since 1998, is sponsored by the Agency for Healthcare Research and Quality. This independent panel of experts in prevention and primary care rigorously reviews "impartial assessments of the scientific evidence for the effectiveness of a broad range of clinical preventive services, including screening, counseling, and preventive medications" (Agency for Healthcare Research and Quality, 2008). The USPSTF recommendations routinely trigger changes in Medicare and Medicaid, which routinely trigger changes in private insurance coverage benefits. In this example, access to cancer screening and early detection is significantly affected by the role of a federal agency influencing public and private health policy decisions.

In addition to effecting standards of coverage and care, federal and state public health policy has also been put in place to administer screening and early detection programs. In the case of cervical and breast cancer, the federal government funds public health programs such as the National Breast and Cervical Cancer Early Detection Program through the CDC. States also play a role in administering these programs through local and state health departments. Federal and state policy makers determine the scope of such programs the degree to which they are funded (Wells, 2008).

Other states have pursued cancer-specific program policies. Using Arizona tobacco tax revenues authorized through Proposition 303, the state funds the AZ Well Woman HealthCheck Program aimed to improve the early detection of breast cancer. Through Amendment 35, a portion of Colorado's tobacco excise taxes are directed through the Department of Public Health and Environment to fund programs that raise awareness and provide screening for breast, cervical, and colorectal cancer. Similarly, Wyoming passed in 2007 a Cancer Control Act that funded the creation of a the Wyoming Colorectal Cancer Early Detection Program in hopes of addressing the state's second leading cause of cancer death, colon cancer (C-Change, 2007).

Cancer Treatment

The Institute of Medicine (IOM) report "Care Without Coverage: Too Little, Too Late" states that uninsured patients get about one half the health care of insured patients and, consequently, die sooner than insured patients, largely because of delayed diagnoses (IOM, 2002). Another IOM report, "Ensuring Quality Cancer Care," cites concerns about lapses in care that can lower the chances of survival and can compromise the quality of life of cancer patients (IOM, 2004). The number of uninsured and underinsured Americans coupled with the high and rising costs of cancer treatment makes access to health services through private or public health insurance essential. In fact, half of personal bankruptcies are attributed to illness and medical bills (Himmelstein et al., 2005). Without insurance, some individuals choose not to be screened, delay screening, or refuse treatment do to financial constraints. Federal healthcare reforms have the potential to change cancer outcomes dramatically by providing better access to screening, early detection, and treatment services.

At a point when patients and their families are facing the challenge of cancer, they must navigate an extremely complex healthcare system. As the 2001 President's Cancer Panel (PCP, 2001) report "Voices of a Broken System: Real People, Real Problems" stated, many patients "must fight their way into and through a dysfunctional system even as they struggle to save their very lives." The often-devastating personal hardships of the cancer experience were noted in the 2004 PCP report "Living Beyond Cancer: Finding a New Balance: Medical, Psychosocial, Insurance, Employment and Educational Issues." Patient navigation in cancer care refers to individualized assistance offered to patients, families, and caregivers to help overcome healthcare system barriers and facilitate timely access to quality medical and psychosocial care, from prediagnosis through all phases of the cancer experience. Cancer patient navigation services can and should take on different forms in different communities. In 2005, the H.R. 1812 Patient Navigator Outreach and Chronic Disease Prevention Act was signed into law authorizing appropriations for the Department of Health and Human Services to award grants to programs designed to facilitate access to health services. Limited appropriations have restricted the impact of this act.

In 2004, Delaware was the first state to provide treatment for qualified individuals who do not have health insurance and who are not eligible for Medicaid. The Delaware Cancer Treatment Program helps to pay for cancer treatment for a period of 1 year for Delaware residents between the ages of 0 and 64 years who have been diagnosed with cancer on or after July 1, 2004, were a resident of Delaware at the time of diagnosis, have no comprehensive health insurance, and have a household income that meets qualification guidelines, which are 650% of the Federal Poverty Level (e.g., the income for a family of four must be less than $122,525) (C-Change, 2007).

Cancer Research

Continuing to research aspects of cancer prevention, early detection, treatment, and quality of life issues remains a top scientific and policy priority for the cancer community. Although research is carried out by academic institutions and pharmaceutical and biotech companies, the NCI drives a significant portion of cancer research within its walls and through its grant programs to NCI-designated cancer centers and others. The effects of advocacy and policy actions are illustrated in this recent chain of events. In 1998, cancer patients, survivors, caregivers, scientists, and advocates marched on the National Mall in Washington, DC to renew the Nation's commitment to fighting cancer. Congress responded by doubling the National Institute of Health budget for the following 5 years beginning in fiscal year 1999. The NCI budget was increased by 80% over this period. The direct result of this funding infusion was a 30% increase in R01 grant dollars to individual investigators. University researchers and administrators responded by becoming more involved in cancer research and investing more heavily in their scientific programs and facilities (Niederhuber, 2007).

Enabling the promise of cancer research through policy actions extends beyond funding the NCI. For example, chemoprevention, the development of agents to prevent or halt cancer, is an emerging field that faces several major systemic barriers currently delaying progress in research and development. Specifically, the limited life of patents, the uncertainty of reimbursement, and an uncharted clinical trial design and regulatory approval process deter scientific and financial investment in this area. In order to recoup investment in drug development, pharmaceutical companies require patent and intellectual property protection and data exclusivity. In the case of chemopreventive drugs, which take far longer to evaluate their efficacy and safety, extended protection/exclusivity or other tax incentives would likely stimulate investment in this field (Grabowski & Moe, 2008). Similarly, federal policy actions to value and cover preventive therapies would reduce the uncertainty of agents being paid for by Medicare, Medicaid, and other private payers once they are developed (C-Change, 2008). Additional legislative encouragement and agency level action by the Food and Drug Administration to define further the procedures for evaluating agents developed using biomarkers and other new scientific techniques would accelerate the research process.

Other Key Policy Issues

The ability to fight cancer depends on the health of the cancer workforce. A critical shortage of cancer specialists threatens the nation's ability to provide cancer care across the continuum from prevention to survivorship. Nearly all of the professional disciplines who play a role in the delivery of comprehensive cancer services are experiencing a shortage, including physicians, nurses, social workers, pharmacists, public health workers, researchers, scientists, technologists, and cancer registrars (American Public Health Association, 2007; American Society for Therapeutic and Radiation Oncology, 2004; American Society for Clinical Oncology, 2007; Buerhaus, 2006; Oncology Nursing Society, 2005; National Association of Social Workers, 2006; National Cancer Registrars Association, 2006). For example, the demand for oncologists is expected to exceed supply by 25% to 30% by 2020 (ASCO, 2008). Advocacy efforts to attract students; better fund scholarships, education, and training; and improve or adapt reimbursement mechanisms are underway to bolster the field. Without a healthy workforce, achievement of any national goals to improve cancer research, prevention, and care will be difficult.

Policy Landscape

The policy landscape for affecting the hope of people at risk for and living with cancer is vast. These examples demonstrate a variety of ways in which funding, restrictions or allowances, and programs at the federal, state, and local level can affect some aspect of the cancer problem. Because cancer is more than one disease, affects so many people, and relies on so many interconnected systems to be prevented and treated, the policy challenges are equally complex; however, the growing body of evidence-based policy and practice outcomes offers another source of hope for fighting cancer.

References

Agency for Healthcare Research and Quality. (2008). *2007 National Healthcare Disparities Report.* Rockville, MD: U.S. Department of Health and Human Services, Agency for Healthcare Research and Quality; February 2008. AHRQ Pub. No. 08-0041.

American Cancer Society. (2007). *Cancer facts & figures 2007.* Atlanta, GA: Author.

American Public Health Association. (2007). *Strengthening the public health workforce.* Retrieved February 10, 2007, from http://www.apha.org/NR/rdonlyres/0E0166BC-2D70-4352-9FC1-98DF8520861E/0/PublicHealthWorkforceFactSheet.pdf

American Society for Clincal Oncology and Association of American Medical Colleges. (2007, March). *Forecasting the supply of and demand for oncologists: A report to the American Society of Clinical Oncology from the AAMC Center for Workforce Studies.* Retrieved December 8, Downloads/Cancer%20Research/Oncology%20Workforce%20%Report%20FINAL.pdf

American Society for Therapeutic and Radiation Oncology. (2004). Grants, internet helping improve oncology workforce shortage. *Cancer/Oncology News.* Retrieved August 28, 2004, from http://www.medicalnewstoday.com/medicalnews.php?newsid=12598

Buerhaus, P., Donelan, K., Ulrich, B. T., Norman, L., & Dittus, R. (2006). State of the registered nurse workforce in the United States. *Nursing Economic$, 24*(1), 6–12.

Campaign for Tobacco-Free Kids. (2009). A decade of broken promises: The 1998 state tobacco settlement ten years later. Retrieved November 18, 2008, from http://www.tobaccofreekids.org/reports/settlements/2009/fullreport.pdf

C-Change. (2007). Increasing access to cancer care: A guide for comprehensive cancer control coalition action. Washington, DC: Author.

C-Change. (2008). Considering reimbursement for cancer preventive agents. Washington, DC: Author.

Centers for Disease Control and Prevention. (2005a). Annual smoking attributable mortality, years of potential life lost, and productivity losses—United States, 1997–2001. *MMWR, 54*(25), 625–628.

Centers for Disease Control and Prevention. (2005b). *Morbidity and Mortality Weekly Report, 53,* 528.

Chaloupka, F. J., et al. (2002). Tax, price and cigarette smoking: evidence from the tobacco documents and implications for tobacco company marketing strategies. *Tobacco Control, 11,* i62–i72.

Fiore, M. C., & Jaén, C. R. (2008). A clinical blueprint to accelerate the elimination of tobacco use. *Journal of the American Medical Association, 299*(17), 2083–2085.

Grabowski, H., & Moe, J. (2008). Impact of economic, regulatory, and patent policies on innovation in cancer chemoprevention. *AACR's Cancer Prevention Research, 1*(2), 84–90.

Himmelstein, D. U., Warren, E., Thorne, D., & Woolhandler, S. (2005). Illness and injury as contributors to bankruptcy. *Health Affairs.* Retrieved February 12, 2010, from http://content.healthaffairs.org/cgi/reprint/hlthaff.w5.63v1

Husten, C. G. (2008, October). Tobacco use: Ending the epidemic. *MedSurg Nursing, 17*(5), 345–354.

Institute of Medicine, Board on Health Care Services. (2002). *Care without coverage: Too little, too late.* Washington, DC: National Academy of Sciences.

Institute of Medicine. (2004, January). *Ensuring quality cancer care.* Washington, DC: National Academy of Sciences.

Jemal, A., Thun, M. J., Ries, L. A. G., Howe, H. L., Weir, H. K., Center, M. M., et al. (2008). Annual report to the nation on the status of cancer 1975–2005, featuring trends in lung cancer, tobacco use, and tobacco control. *Journal of the National Cancer Institute.* Retrieved February 12, 2010, from http://jnci.oxfordjournals.org/cgi/content/full/djn389v1

National Association of Social Workers, Center for Workforce Studies. (2006). *Assuring the sufficiency of a frontline workforce: A national study of licensed social workers executive summary.* Washington, DC: Author.

National Cancer Institute. (2005). *DevCan: Probability of Developing or Dying of Cancer Software*, Version 6.0 Statistical Research and Applications Branch. Retrieved December 8, 2008, from http://srab.cancer.gov/devcan

North American Quitline Consortium. *Quitline facts.* Retrieved January 19, 2010, from http://www.naquitline.org/?page=quitlinefacts

National Cancer Registrars Association. (2006, June). *Frontline workers Workforce analysis study of the cancer registry field.* San Francisco, CA: University of California at San Francisco Center for Health Professions.

Niederhuber, J. (2007). Perspectives in cancer research: A look inside the National Cancer Institute Budget process: Implications for 2007 and beyond. *Cancer Research, 67,* 856–862.

Oncology Nursing Society. (2005, March). *The impact of the national nursing shortage on quality cancer care—ONS position.* Pittsburgh, PA: Author.

President's Cancer Panel. (2001, September). *Voices of a broken system: Real people, real problems, 2000–2001.* Bethesda, MD: National Cancer Institute, National Institute of Health.

President's Cancer Panel. (2004, May). Living beyond cancer: Finding a new balance, 2003–2004. Bethesda, MD: National Cancer Institute, National Institute of Health.

Task Force on Community Preventive Services. (2005). Tobacco. In S. Zaza, P. A. Briss, K. W. Harris (Eds.), *The Guide to Community Preventive Services: What Works to Promote Health?* (pp. 3–79). Atlanta, GA: Oxford University Press.

U.S. Cancer Statistics Working Group. Department of Health and Human Services, Centers for Disease Control and Prevention and National Cancer Institute. (2003). *United States cancer statistics: 2000 incidence.* Atlanta, GA: Author.

Wells, S. (2008). Cervical cancer: An overview with suggested practice and policy goals. *MedSurg Nursing, 17*(1), 43–50.

Section IV

Healthcare Finance: Understanding the Role of Markets in Government

Chapter 10

Healthcare Costs: Follow the Money!

Jonathan Engel

OVERVIEW

Financing the U.S. healthcare system requires a complex patchwork of public and private third-party payers, as well as cash payments made by consumers for co-pays, deductibles, out-of-network treatment, and uncovered drugs and services. Providers and manufacturers are aware of inconsistencies in reimbursement and tend to position their goods and services so as to optimize revenue. This has led to an expensive and cumbersome system of health care, overly reliant on specialist providers, imaging technology, surgical procedures, and new drugs. Efforts to change reimbursement will always be imperfect because of fundamental economic inefficiencies in the provision of health care.

OBJECTIVES

- To understand the flow of funds within the healthcare system
- To discuss economic inefficiencies in the production and provision of health services within the framework of a rational market model
- To learn more about inflationary pressures on the health system
- To understand the historical development of third-party payment
- To discuss both failed and successful efforts to rectify abuses and inefficiencies implicit in a system of third-party payment
- To know more about the critical role of Medicare and Medicaid in paying for health care
- To understand the fundamental ways in which managed care attempts to rein in costs and rationalize healthcare delivery
- To learn about the essential nature of risk within an insurance framework and areas in which health insurance is inconsistent with risk distribution

KEY TERMS

- ❑ Community rating
- ❑ Economic inefficiency
- ❑ Fee-for-service
- ❑ Gatekeeper
- ❑ Health maintenance organization
- ❑ Indemnity
- ❑ Individual rating
- ❑ Insurance
- ❑ Managed care
- ❑ Medicaid
- ❑ Medicare
- ❑ Point of service plan
- ❑ Preferred provider organization
- ❑ Risk pool

National Health Spending

United States spending on health care now totals over $6,000 per capita for an aggregate expenditure of nearly $2 trillion, or some 15% of gross domestic product (GDP). This compares with just under $5,000 per capita in Germany and Canada (the next highest two) and about $3,000 per capita in the United Kingdom (about the lowest in the industrialized world). Canada and Germany devote about 12% of their GDP to healthcare spending, whereas in the United Kingdom, it hovers at around 7.5% (Center for Healthcare Research and Transformation, 2009). Although the United Kingdom actually posts a worse health profile than does the United States (lower life expectancy, higher infant mortality controlling for recent immigrants), most nations spending above 9% of GDP do as well or better than we do. Sweden and Japan, for example, have infant mortality rates hovering around 3 per 1,000 live births, whereas we come in near 7 per 1,000 (United Nations Department of Economic and Social Affairs, 2007). Thus, by any meaningful measure of national health profile, we are spending substantially more money, both in per capita expenditures and in percentage of GDP, to achieve results no better, and often worse, than do other industrialized countries.

What do we have to show for our efforts? In some areas, we clearly lead the world and can rightly boast that our greater investment has produced superior results. The United States leads the world by a large margin in the success of its biomedical research efforts (both laboratory and clinical), and its training programs in the surgical and medical specialties are still considered unparalleled. The same cannot really be said for our primary care and general practice residencies. Although these training programs clearly maintain high standards, other nations have developed greater expertise than we in treating patients in more psychologically and socially sensitive ways and in reducing the numbers of invasive surgical procedures used by the population. One interesting statistic is that although U.S. citizens stay in the hospital far fewer days each year than do Europeans (7 days vs. close to 30 in some countries), we spend far more money each day that we are in a hospital (WHO Statistical Information System, 2009). For Americans, hospitals, and to some degree physicians' offices and clinics, are sites to receive intensive medical and surgical intervention. Other nations view the purpose of their healthcare infrastructure as one of more general care giving. To this day, the German health system will pay for nearly a week's stay at a spa each year for German citizens. The best we can get out of our managed care plans is a modest discount on our sports club membership fees. It is not quite the same thing.

Our health system is expensive for a number of reasons. First, we train more specialists in relationship to primary care physicians than do other countries, meaning that the system has to absorb both the cost of the extra training as well as the cost of the extra consultations with specialists that their greater number induces. (Health economists have long been aware of the phenomenon of "induced demand," in which the mere presence of greater numbers of doctors prompts greater use of their services [Iversen, 2004].) Only about 30% of recent medical school graduates go on for training in primary care (which means general practice, family practice, pediatrics, internal medicine, and sometimes gynecology [Mutha et al., 1997]). In contrast, most nations push nearly 80% of their medical school graduates into primary care and limit spots in specialty residency programs through national and regional regulations.

Second, we have overcapacity in our system. We have overbuilt our hospitals to the point that we have national vacancy rates in hospital beds of nearly 30% (National Center for Health Statistics, 2006). The costs of these beds are borne up front and then later distributed through patient billings over the 10- or 15-year depreciation period of the goods. Although they are functioning, these rooms induce demand insofar as their owners are interested in filling them and using them to recoup their purchase costs quickly.

Third, we invest huge amounts of money in novel equipment for diagnosis, treatment, surgery, and convalescence, whose cost must again be built into ordinary billings. Health economist Henry Aaron believes that this is probably the single greatest cost driver in our system (Aaron, 1991). Unless you are a jet fighter pilot, you will probably never be as close to sophisticated machinery as when you are admitted to even a modest community hospital. Such developments as artificial skin and organs, genetically engineered drugs, and magnetic resonance imagers give testament to our world-class research and engineering capability but cost a great deal without substantially adding to the general health of the population. Americans have gotten used to the noninvasive diagnosis and treatment of painful joints, arthritic spines, and inflamed tendons, even though very few patients would be willing to pay for these treatments if faced with an actual bill for services.

Why are Americans willing to spend so much on health care? In part, this is because the cost is largely hidden. The value of a family insurance policy is between $12,000 and $15,000 per year, yet few employees ask themselves if they are willing to take a $15,000 pay cut for health care. Most employees seem to view health insurance as a nonnegotiable portion of their compensation, assuming that if it disappeared their salary would not rise concomitantly. This is simply untrue. Even during the tight labor markets from 1995 to 2008, medical plans became decidedly less generous, as employers demanded that workers pay a greater portion of the cost. This is likely to continue in this era of high unemployment. Why cannot an employer simply give workers the choice of receiving a salary bonus or health insurance? The answer is that no insurance company would sell such a policy. Given the choice, healthy workers would opt out of the insurance plan, leaving only sick and expensive workers in. Because health insurance works on the principle of risk distribution, such a situation is simply not viable for a competitive insurance industry.

One question we might ask is whether we as a nation should commit ourselves to guaranteeing a certain level of health coverage. The United States is almost unique among industrialized countries for having a significant portion of its population uninsured—most other nations implemented either a state health insurance plan or a state health plan (in which the government owns the doctors and hospitals outright) gradually between about 1910 and 1950. America has considered proposals periodically (in the 1940s, the 1960s, and 1993, to name a few instances), but each time has rejected them in favor of a privately funded employer-based system. We did pass a limited form of national health insurance for our senior citizens (in the form of Medicare) in 1965, which has been popular with our citizens, but all efforts to extend this system down to those who are not older have failed. Presently, the nation is divided about the idea of national health insurance, but people do seem to favor more government regulation on the activities of managed care companies. Various types of incremental reforms have been enacted since the Clinton health plan debacle of 1993, including the 1998 balanced budget amendment, which reduced Medicare payments to hospitals, and the 1997 Health Insurance Portability and Accountability Act (HIPAA), which in theory guaranteed that if you left a job with health insurance, you could not be prevented from continuing that policy, regardless of medical history (U.S. Department of Labor, Employee Benefits Security Administration, 2004). (In fact, the HIPAA has not achieved its ultimate goal. All that happens if you do have a chronic condition is that the insurance company raises the premiums to almost unaffordable levels. Congress forgot to put price controls into the legislation.) The most recent expansion of Medicare was the 2004 prescription drug coverage. Its ability to assure access to prescription drugs in terms of costs is also debatable (Hoadley, Cubanski, Hargrave, Summer, & Neuman, 2009).

The issue of whether people have a right to health care has been hotly debated for decades. Clearly such a right is not enshrined in our constitution, yet many people feel that it belongs with the "penumbral" rights of privacy, housing, and dignified employment. Other countries clearly feel that it is unseemly for a portion of the population to be walking around unable to see a doctor. In fact, very few Americans are closed out from the doctor's office or from the local hospital. A patient in need of basic medical care in this country can get it regardless of ability to pay, be it through community clinics, public hospital emergency rooms, state-level uncompensated care programs, and the like. The issue with poor care in this country probably has more to do with the chaos, discontinuity, and the accompanying degradation that results from seeking charity care. In this country, if you do not have private health insurance or Medicaid you are definitely a second-class (or perhaps third-class) citizen after you enter the medical care system. In other countries, the difference between medical care for the poor and the middle class is less pronounced.

Medical care is a public good that needs to be guaranteed, insofar that certain diseases are infectious and impact the community. Given this, we have a vested interest in seeing our neighbors inoculated against whooping cough and diphtheria, as well as making sure that they have access to a public sewer and public garbage pickup. Back when infectious diseases were still a major health hazard (before antibiotics), the public was much more supportive of public health interventions including school nurses, community clinics, and community inoculations. Now that infectious disease seems to pose much less of a threat (outside of AIDS), we are more likely to assume that our neighbors are responsible for their own states of health.

In a more abstract sense, medical care is a public good, as most people deem it morally unacceptable to live in a community where people die (or at least suffer avoidable health consequences) for lack of access to basic medical care.

Most people do not consider a society unjust when rich people can buy fancier cars than poor people, but most do take profound difference with a society in which rich children receive smallpox and polio vaccinations and poor children do not. We have continually rewritten Medicaid regulations in this country to ensure that children, at the very minimum, are universally covered, as well as pregnant women, the permanently disabled, the older population, and the severely injured (Engel, 2006). We also guarantee coverage for U.S. military veterans, civil servants, and Native Americans. In fact, the only people who are really not guaranteed coverage in this country are young able-bodied men, who are assumed to be able to either hold down a job that will come with health benefits or pay for their own coverage. In fact, many men (some 30 million) do not have coverage, and evidence suggests that many of these really cannot afford to pay for either a private insurance policy or to pay for medical expenses out-of-pocket. Childless women, as well as illegal immigrants, who have been thrown off of Temporary Assistance for Needy Families (TANF) (the current name for the U.S. welfare program) are finding themselves in a similar situation.

We might ask whether 15% of the GDP is too much to spend on health care. After all, we do not consider it a problem when a young Wall Street trader spends 80% of his income on a new Porsche. We assume that the individual is capable of allocating his resources to optimize his own utility. Why should people not be able to spend their money on buying as much health care as they wish? The answer is, in part, that people are spending the government's money (which is to say, our money) on health care, but the larger problem is that health care does not follow some of the most basic laws of economics that we use to produce and distribute goods. In this chapter we will consider the application of basic economic principles to the supply and demand for health services. We will then consider how physicians and hospitals respond to these economic incentives. In the last sections, we will consider health insurance as a means to protect individuals from risk and the advantages and disadvantages of several forms of insurance including managed care, Medicaid, and Medicare.

Supply and Demand

Classical economics presupposes a smooth and continuous demand curve and supply curve for normal goods or service. A demand curve shows the relationship between the price of a good and the quantity an individual demands of it (or how much society overall demands of it). For normal goods, as the price goes down, the demand goes up, although this is more easily observable at high prices then at low prices. Also, as the quantity goes up, the individual requires a greater and greater price drop to induce him to buy more. This suggests that as an individual accrues greater and greater numbers of an object (or units of service) he or she values the last object less and less and thus requires a greater and greater diminution of price to induce him or her to buy one more.

Consider, for example, cans of tuna. At full price, you would like to buy three cans. When you see that they are on sale, you buy five or six. Once, when there was an unbelievable sale, you actually bought eight. How low would the price have to go to induce you to buy 10 cans, or 20? Even if the tuna was only a penny a can, you would still limit yourself to maybe 100. At a certain point, the cost of storing the tuna or concern about spoilage makes you value an additional can of tuna at even less than a penny. In fact, at some point, the tuna might actually begin to have negative value, as you might be willing to pay someone to haul it away.

This idea that you value the last item less and less as your total quantity goes up is known as "diminishing marginal utility." What this means is that a dollar is not always a dollar. If you are broke and you find a $10 bill, it is a small fortune. If you make a good salary, it is a nice windfall, but it will not change your way of life. If you are quite wealthy, it becomes nearly valueless. If you look at an extreme example of this, Bill Gates (current worth around $40 billion) regularly loses or gains 4 or 5 billion dollars in a given day, depending on the price fluctuation of Microsoft stock. For most of us, winning a $4 billion lottery prize would profoundly change our lives. For Mr. Gates, it is hardly noticeable.

On the supply side, producers exhibit the behavior in the law of supply, which says that as the price goes up, they are willing to supply more of a particular good—whether through working longer hours, investing more capital in an enterprise, or expanding a business. We see this demonstrated every day in the fact that people who earn the highest hourly wages (doctors, lawyers, investment bankers, corporate chiefs) also tend to work the longest hours (90-hour work weeks are not uncommon for partners in investment banks). You might suppose that someone who is earning $600 an hour might choose to work only 100 hours per year and thus bring home a tidy salary of $60,000 while having most of her hours free. In fact, however, he or she does just the opposite and works exceptionally long hours. Why? People do not look at how much money they need in a year to support a certain lifestyle and then stop when they hit that number. Rather, people evaluate the alternatives for each hour of their time and then choose their activity accordingly. If you can earn $600 per hour, each hour you are not working is costing you $600. Thus, taking a morning off to see your child in the school play costs you almost $2,000. Would you be willing to spend $2,000 to see your child in the school play? You might, or you might not. The empirical evidence suggests that most people who can earn that much money choose to skip the play.

When all is operating as it should, a market for a particular good or service *clears* at the most efficient point. The clearing point (which is graphically where the supply line intersects the demand line) is a stasis to which the market returns. If producers produce more than that quantity, either the price will have to go down to move the goods or they will go into storage as surplus. Because it costs money to store goods (cost of the storage facility, tied up capital, etc.), companies will slow production. In contrast, if demand goes up, a shortage is created, at which point the prices go up. Because the price is now higher, more producers want to jump in to take advantage of the high prices, at which point the quantity will increase and the price will slowly drift back to the clearing point. In absence of information blockages, regulatory issues, externalities, or artificial transaction costs, a market optimizes efficiency at the clearing point. At the clearing point, the most people in society are receiving the greatest happiness, or utility, as possible. At any other quantity or price, the sum total utility of society is diminished.

Two very important concepts in determining the clearing point are *marginal benefit* and *marginal cost*. The marginal benefit is the benefit that accrues on acquiring the last widget, or the last can of tuna. As already discussed, each successive widget gives less and less benefit to the consumer until utility drops to zero, or possibly less than zero. Marginal cost is the cost of producing the last widget, or can of tuna. The marginal cost is almost always much less than the average cost. For example, in a busy delicatessen, the cost of making one more pastrami sandwich is the cost of the pastrami, the cost of two slices of bread, a little mustard, about 30 seconds of a worker's time, and a pickle—probably less than $1.00. In contrast, the marginal cost of making the first pastrami sandwich would include opening a deli, hiring help, buying furniture, getting phone and electric hookups, getting contracts for meat and bread with a supplier, and all the other things that go into starting a new restaurant. Total cost of going from 0 pastrami sandwiches to 1 pastrami sandwich is about $500,000.

Some businesses have much lower startup costs and higher marginal costs. For example, for someone in the private tutoring business, the marginal cost of the 30th hour of service is the value of his or her time, plus maybe a clean shirt; however, the marginal cost of the first hour of service is also just the cost of time, plus the cost of a printing up a few flyers, maybe some business cards, and a new pad of paper.

Hospital care, incidentally, resembles the deli. After the hospital is built and equipped and nurses hired, the marginal cost of caring for one more patient is relatively low—a few Tylenol, and a certain percentage of a nurse's time. The marginal cost of caring for the first patients, however, is several millions of dollars (the cost of building and equipping the hospital). Building the hospital is by far the most expensive part of the enterprise, which is why it is very difficult to cut costs in a hospital after it is built and equipped. You have already spent the bulk of the money; the best you can do now is lay off staff and cut back on supplies, but these are not the high cost items that go into the cost of services.

From an insurer's perspective, however, marginal costs are bizarre. The marginal cost of providing coverage for one more patient could be only a few dollars per year for a healthy young person with few medical problems and no medication needs to millions of dollars per year for a severely disabled preemie or someone in intensive care on life support. Because insurance companies tend to charge about the same premium for both patients, they have a huge incentive to avoid people who have a high probability of ending up on life support. This wild volatility in costs is one of the things that makes the economics of healthcare provision so interesting.

From a consumer's side, marginal benefit is also extremely volatile, depending on his or her own state of health. For a relatively healthy person, the benefit of an additional physical exam, or Pap smear, or dental cleaning, is nearly nil, and economic theory posits that he or she would be willing to pay almost nothing for them. On the other hand, the marginal benefit of a procedure becomes near infinite in a life or death situation. To a healthy person, a course of penicillin is worthless. To a person sick with pneumonia, however, a course of penicillin could be worth millions, as there is a good chance that the person would die without it. Not surprisingly, a fear of price gauging is one of the reasons patients insist on a professional, rather than an entrepreneurial medical sector.

These strange fluctuations in marginal cost and benefit of medical services and goods explain some of the difficulties in creating an efficient market in health care. Add to this a huge information gap between supplier (doctor) and consumer (patient) and you have a recipe for gross overutilization and underefficiency, which we have today. Further complicating the scenario is the difficulty in matching marginal costs of producing more health care to marginal benefits of consuming it.

Physicians

Economic rules also fall apart in the most basic transactions between patients and physician. For one, there is an enormous information gap between doctor and patient. Although the Internet has allowed many patients to educate themselves better about the nature and treatment of their conditions, nearly all patients go to a doctor seeking first a diagnosis and second a treatment plan. Because the doctor simply knows more than the patient about the patient's health (often much more), the patient essentially throws himself or herself on the mercy of the doctor in hope that the physician will be honest, competent, and fair concerning pricing.

Second, because every diseased body is slightly different and every patient has a unique medical history, there is always a degree of uncertainty regarding the outcome of a physician–patient interaction. As a result, no doctor can, in good faith, offer a "guarantee" concerning a successful surgery or recovery from trauma or flu. This fundamental uncertainty, coupled with the inability of the physicians to simply replace the defective service (as might be expected to happen in the event you are unhappy with your house painter, for example), creates a requirement that the patient reimburse the physician not for a guaranteed product or outcome, but rather for making a good faith effort. Consider how unusual this arrangement is in economic life. Can you imagine taking your car to a mechanic and paying him for his best efforts, regardless of his ability to fix your car? More likely, if he could not fix the problem, you would not pay him, or at least you would withhold part of his fee. Oncologists, for obvious reasons, cannot work this way. You pay them for granting you access to their accumulated wisdom, skill, and judgment, and then you both pray for the best.

Third, because demand for medical services fluctuates wildly depending on whether you are sick, the patient–doctor relationship invites price gouging. Imagine that you arrive at the local emergency room hemorrhaging wildly from injuries suffered in a car crash, and before the emergency room physician starts the blood transfusion, he tells you that this relatively simply procedure will cost you $50,000. You are not really in a position to argue. Incidentally, locksmiths face a similar situation when they are called out late at night to get someone into their house to which they have forgotten the key. Ordinarily, the services of a locksmith are worth only $20 to $30, but at 2:00 in the morning on a freezing cold night when you are locked out of your apartment, those same services might be worth $150 to you. Locksmiths know this and elevate their price accordingly. Notice, however, that they usually demand payment up front, in cash. After they have got your door opened for you, they have lost their leverage.

For these reasons—information asymmetry, uncertainty of outcome, and opportunity for price gouging—physicians professionalized at an early stage (Stevens, 1998). What does it mean to be a professional? Before the word became diluted in modern corporate speak, it meant that a group of people in a certain trade or business agreed to hold themselves to certain standards of behavior beyond simply savvy business skills. Professions create ethical standards for themselves, police themselves, and license themselves. Both professionals and clients benefit from professionalization. The profession grants itself some degree of protection from outside competition (only those who have met certain entrance standards are allowed to practice) while the customers (patients) can rest assured that the licensed professional will not take advantage of their ignorance or need. If a member of the profession refuses to abide by these standards of conduct, he or she is (or is supposed to be) punished by the profession, possibly stripped of his or her license, and generally ostracized.

Professionalization is the way in which mature economies compensate for market flaws in certain kinds of services. If you think of the traditional professions—law, medicine, accounting, architecture, engineering—there is always an information asymmetry inherent in the transaction and the opportunity for the professional to cheat the client, were he or she not pledged to certain ethical standards of conduct. As electrical work and mechanical work have become more complex and often beyond the ken of weekend homebodies, these trades too have professionalized. Walk into your local mechanic and you will probably see a diploma on the wall from some automotive institute or a certificate from Volvo saying that the mechanic is a licensed Volvo air-conditioner repairman. This is because most weekend fix-it types are no longer able to fix their own car air-conditioning systems (or their car electrical systems for that matter) and thus are no longer able to discern whether the mechanic has done the job correctly. We all rely on licensure and professional standards to guarantee some level of quality in these types of interactions.

Physicians limit their supply through the use of two closely related mechanisms: licensure and schooling. You cannot practice medicine in this country without being licensed by the state, and you cannot get licensed by the state without having graduated from 1 of 125 medical schools approved by the American Association of Medical Colleges (American Association of Medical Colleges, 2009). Alternatively, you can go to certain foreign medical schools, but before you can practice in the United States, you need to complete a U.S. residency, which in turn must be approved by a medical specialty group. In short, practicing medicine in the United States requires an almost slavish adherence to a rather exhaustive training regimen, taking anywhere from 8 to 13 years beyond college, to which access is stringently controlled by the profession at every turn. There are advantages and disadvantages. Physicians benefit from restricting entrance to the profession because the restriction artificially drives up prices (physicians are among the best paid professionals in the country). On the other hand, for those wishing to enter the profession, the process may seem exhausting. It is no wonder that the physician assistant programs have become so popular in recent years—it is a route by which interested people can enter clinical practice legally while circumventing much of the medical licensing restrictions (U.S. Department of Labor, Bureau of Labor Statistics, 2009).

Patients benefit from the system as they are guaranteed extraordinarily high level skills in their doctors. Walk into virtually any licensed physician's office in the country, and unless that particular doctor has a hidden drug or alcohol problem, you are almost guaranteed a level of competence and expertise that exceeds that available in most of the world. On the other hand, we pay a steep price for all of this expertise and training in the high fees that our physicians charge us. In most countries, medicine is not a particularly high-paying vocation, and medical care is within the reach of most middle-class members of a society (when a middle class exists) (World Salaries, 2008). In this country, many middle-class workers would have a difficult time paying their medical bills for anything but routine preventive care. Even a minor surgical procedure, such as a hysterectomy or appendectomy, can run into the thousands of dollars. In other countries, this simply is not so.

Unfortunately, this situation is getting worse rather than better. Although we are seeing greater numbers of young physicians entering primary care specialties, we are also seeing greater number of physicians taking postresidency fellowships to get certified in subspecialties to increase their qualifications further and thus inflate their market worth. For all of the talk of the deflationary consequences of managed care, most physicians in the United States are making more money today (in constant dollars) than they were a decade ago (Allied Physicians Salary Survey, 2006). Although there are certain specialties in which this is not the case (notably anesthesiology, radiology, and ophthalmology), most doctors have found ways to make up in volume and expanded purviews what they lost in billings. Doctors have slanted their practices toward the most lucrative of procedures available to them, have increased the volume of patients they see, and have learned to leverage their expertise through inflated support staffs and physician extenders (nurse practitioners, dental hygienists, physician assistants). What this suggests is that doctors, despite their allegiance to a professional code of ethics, are economically rational and within the bounds of acceptable medical practice will skew their time toward the most lucrative patients, procedures, locations, and specialties.

One of the great challenges of constructing fair physician compensation assignments is in rewarding the cogitative components of medical practice. The value of an internist, to a large degree, lies in what the internist knows and in the way in which information and past experience is used to arrive at diagnoses, prognoses, and regimens. Unfortunately, it is almost impossible to reward someone for simply sitting and thinking (Hsiao et al., 1992). Patients will not tolerate it, and insurers fear that they are being cheated. Rather, doctors (like all professionals) are rewarded for what they produce or do. This same conundrum exists in other professions as well. Architects are paid for the plans they draft and not the time they spend thinking about the project, despite the fact that much of the drafting has become rote and mechanical and farmed off to drafting assistants who do it on computers. Lawyers, who offer little beyond their knowledge of the law, get around this problem by charging for their services by the hour, rather than by the result. Academics are rewarded for the volume of material they publish, rather than the quality of thought that goes into the material, leading to a plethora of mediocre journal articles and academic monographs that are rarely read and rarely cited.

Insurance companies (led by Medicare) have tried to adjust physician compensation toward thought and diagnosis and away from procedure over the past decade and have been partly successful. Internists, pediatricians, and psychiatrists did see their compensation rise moderately in relationship to surgeons in the early 1990s using a compensation algorithm known as the Resource Based Relative Value Scale (Hsiao et al., 1992. Nonetheless, surgeons' salaries continue to be more than double those of internists, and the surgical subspecialties double again (Allied Physicians Salary Survey, 2006). An experienced heart surgeon in a major metropolitan area can earn over a half million dollars today, whereas the pediatrician next door may earn no more than $120,000. Incidentally, surgical compensation tends to be high because the results are so immediately measurable. Ask someone with chronic, intense lower back pain how he or she felt the day after corrective back surgery, and he or she tends to sing the surgeon's praises in almost religious tones. Now ask a long-term depressive how he or she feels about his or her psychotherapist and you will get a much more measured response. Both professionals are smart, hard working, highly trained, and ethical, but one produces an immediate and measurable result, whereas the other produces modest change over an extended period. Compensation favors the one producing the fireworks. (Incidentally, most labor economists theorize that this is why teachers' salaries, in nearly all countries, are low compared with the level of skill and training required to enter the profession—the results of a second grade teacher's efforts are not really discernible until 2 decades later, and even then are hard to separate from the results of the other teachers' efforts.)

One of the great breakthroughs of managed care has been capitation payment—that is, paying the doctor up front to keep the patient healthy, regardless of how much work this entails. By reversing incentives, doctors are encouraged to practice efficient, preventive medicine, and refrain from hospitalizing and referring out. Initially managed care was supposed to totally capitate patients—that is, the primary care doctor would have to pay the specialist and hospital bills when they arose—but this was quickly discerned to be untenable for any but enormous physician groups. Unfortunately, capitation has failed in many ways. Doctors do not seem to be emphasizing prevention (it turns out that going to the gym and eating your broccoli just does not make that big a difference in your medical bills, and quitting smoking actually increases lifetime medical bills because you live longer), and recent studies have shown that the gate-keeping function seems to do more to annoy and antagonize patients than it does to actually keep them away from specialists. Moreover, primary care doctors have become expert at processing patients through their examining rooms at startling speed, further antagonizing patients (although not particularly jeopardizing their health). Capitation has kept patients out of hospitals (which accounts for the nearly flat healthcare inflation in the early 1990s), but it has failed to keep patients away from expensive prescription medications and medical devices. As is usually the case, the only mechanisms that reliably keep people from seeing the doctor more and demanding more medicine and devices is forcing them to pay for it. New drug formularies and co-pays, in which patients have to pay up to $50 for expensive brand-name drugs, are the most recent response to this type of inflation.

Physicians have also responded to managed care by agglomerating into ever larger groups. Although partnerships of two or three doctors had been the standard, physician groups of 50, 70, or 100 doctors are not uncommon today in heavily populated areas. The intent here is twofold: to distribute overhead and support-staff costs over larger numbers of doctors and to create a monopoly, or near monopoly, of a certain type of practice in an area, thus creating better bargaining leverage with managed care plans. If a neurology group has cornered the market on neurology for all of northern New Jersey, then any managed care plan wishing to offer neurology services (which is nonnegotiable) must use them and pay their price. Fortunately for managed care plans, physician groups of this size frequently split, and doctors have demonstrated themselves to be terrible businessmen and negotiators. One mark of this is their unwillingness to pay adequately for the top-flight management that such a group needs. It is not unusual for a medical group with annual revenues in the $20 to $30 million range to be paying its executive director (its CEO, as it were) under $100,000. As is often the case, you get what you pay for.

Hospitals

The modern hospital is a relatively recent creation (Stevens, 1999). Although buildings dedicated to the care of the sick have existed since the Middle Ages, these institutions were little more than glorified alms houses for the unaffiliated and widowed to convalesce in. Medical care was scant, equipment nonexistent, and nursing care more spiritual than clinical. It was not until the 1930s (and really not until the 1950s) that hospitals became the technologically sophisticated emporiums of surgery, intensive care, and postoperative care that they are today. Despite the fact that hospitals are highly competitive budget-driven institutions, the majority remains loyal to their nonprofit community origins; few have applied for for-profit status over the past decade, and most continue to provide enormous amounts of care to the poor whether reimbursed through Medicaid or written off as uncompensated care.

Hospitals in the United States today can be divided up into nonprofit, for-profit, and government owned. Government owned hospitals are often called "public" hospitals and tend to be owned by either municipalities or counties. States own almost no hospitals (outside of psychiatric institutions), and the federal government's role in hospital ownership is limited to military hospitals. Nonprofit hospitals, which constitute the majority of hospitals in the country, including most academic medical centers and nearly all of the most prestigious tertiary-care hospitals, are sometimes known as "community" hospitals, and are sometimes called "private" hospitals. Keep in mind that both nonprofit hospitals and for-profit hospitals are private. For-profit hospitals are largely limited to mid-sized hospitals in the south and a few national chains. Although their ranks were expanding in the late 1980s and early 1990s, they are now on the decline. It is almost impossible to turn a profit in the hospital business in the present healthcare environment unless you specialize in a few cash-backed procedures (Perkins, 2010).

Private (nonprofit) hospitals were almost all established by sectarian ethnic or religious groups in the late 19th and early 20th century, and their names often give strong hints as to their origins. Hospitals with names such as Swedish, Beth Israel, Lutheran, Presbyterian, Jewish, St. Luke's, St. Mark's, and St. Michael's abound and give testament to the community spirit of the immigrant groups that founded them. Nearly all hospitals that are named after a city, state, or county—New York Hospital, Pennsylvania Hospital, Massachusetts General Hospital, Montgomery County Community Hospital, Washington Hospital Center, and so forth—are actually private hospitals (the exception is Cook County Hospital which is Chicago's large public hospital). More confusing is the fact that although most people think of the role of public hospitals as caring for the poor, most poor patients seek care at private hospitals where their bills are paid for by Medicaid. Public hospitals, in fact, spend most of their resources today caring for illegal immigrants and working class people who cannot afford private insurance but are too wealthy too qualify for Medicaid. Public hospitals also often have first-rate emergency rooms and trauma units (because their mission is to care for the community and they are located near epicenters of violent crime in inner cities). As a result, their emergency rooms often double as the local primary care physician for nearby poor populations.

All hospitals, public and private, are required to accept any patient requiring critical care who shows up at their door if they take Medicare, and because virtually every hospital in the country takes Medicare, this means that if you are bleeding to death, you cannot be turned away by a hospital, no matter how wealthy and exclusive it may be. Thus, most private hospitals today will stabilize critical care patients and quickly transfer them to a public hospital if they lack adequate insurance coverage. This phenomenon of "dumping" is relatively recent and reflects the fact that as managed care has negotiated tighter contracts with private hospitals in the past decade, these hospitals have been left with fewer discretionary funds to use for indigent care (Koetting, 1989). The days of generous cost-shifting from private insurers to the uninsured are over.

Private hospitals receive operating revenues from private insurance (35%), Medicare (45%), Medicaid (10%), self-pays (5%), and philanthropy (5%) (American Hospital Association, 2009). The balance of these numbers fluctuates a good deal. Small rural hospitals tend to have much higher rates of Medicare reimbursement, whereas inner-city academic medical centers may find that their Medicaid revenues approach 70% of the total income. In contrast, a pediatric and maternity hospital in a wealthy suburb may have close to 100% privately insured patients.

Private insurance these days means predominantly managed care contracts. Managed care organizations (MCOs) with large local market share will either bargain up front for heavily discounted rates, which they will indemnify the hospital for (sometimes 60% off of book value), or they will simply purchase blocks of hospital services up front knowing that on average their subscribers' hospital usage will come out close to the predicted rate. In an effort to negotiate more evenly with the payers, hospitals have resorted to the same strategy, as have physicians—aggregating and merging themselves into networks and systems to try to achieve monopoly power in a particular area. Unfortunately, since the United States has nearly 30% more hospital beds than it currently needs, it is very difficult for a hospital system to absorb enough of the excess capacity in the system to achieve negotiating parity. The mergers have created certain economies of scale in terms of inventory pricing and administrative streamlining, but in the grand race between managed care and hospitals, the payers are probably coming out ahead.

Hospitals spend their operating funds on personnel, supplies, and capital depreciation (and debt service). The personnel, somewhat counter to common knowledge, is everybody but the doctors, although certain physicians such as anesthesiologists, emergency room doctors, and pathologists may have exclusive contracts with a hospital. (Doctors, who make up the "medical staff" of a hospital, do not actually work for the hospital. They are private practitioners who are granted admitting privileges to the hospital.) The one exception is the "house staff" in those hospitals that have residency programs. These young medical residents provide emergency and critical care for poor patients and backup care to the medical staff. The central component of a hospital's personnel is really the nursing staff. Although the nursing work force has been augmented in recent years by all sorts of ancillary therapists, nutritionists, social workers, lactation consultants, rehab specialists, and the like, it is the line nurses who in many ways define the major value that a hospital adds to the healthcare system. They carry the weight of a hospital's reputation, and it is their responsiveness to physicians' orders that makes a hospital able to attract competitive, well-reputed physicians to its medical staff. Other personnel worthy of note are the support staff that includes administrators, orderlies and aides, and dietary and maintenance staff. In some hospitals services such as maintenance are purchased from outside vendors.

The supplies (as well as utilities) include both medical and nonmedical inventory, and both are crucial to a hospital's contribution to the healthcare product. Nonmedical supplies would include linens (huge!), food, televisions, furniture, office equipment, and the like. Medical equipment ranges from tongue depressors to sophisticated imaging and operating room equipment and is the other great resource (after nurses) that makes hospitals uniquely situated to add value to the medical transaction. Some healthcare analysts go as far as suggesting that a hospital's primary value is in serving as a community depository of biomedical equipment, and certainly, the remarkable acceleration in investment into new equipment has fueled much of the cost explosion in health care over the past 2 decades. American hospitals are, by world standards, overequipped, with multiple hospitals in a given area competing to outdo each other in a medical arms race of cutting-edge positron emission tomography scans, magnetic resonance imaging machines, catheter laboratories, and renovated operating rooms (Morris, 2005). The advantage of this race is the total absence of queuing in hospital services in this country. The downside lies in our paying nearly double per capita for healthcare services as the rest of the world, with no measurable advantage in longevity, infant mortality, or quality of life.

The fact that a portion of a hospital's operating budget goes to servicing debt is a strikingly new phenomenon and could not really exist before the inauguration of Medicare in 1965. Previous to that year, when hospitals wished to raise money for capital expansion (a new wing, a new building, or a major new piece of equipment), they went to their boards and to the larger philanthropic community. With Medicare, however, hospitals could issue bonds to purchase new buildings and then build the cost of debt service into their current operating costs and bill the balance back to the government. Because private insurance companies nearly always followed the lead set by the government, private insurance billings soon reflected the increased costs of a debt-financed plant.

This development was unusual not because it was a new approach to financing (nearly all for-profit companies carry at least part of their capital burden in debt) but because it was new to the hospital sector. Previously, hospitals were seen, first and foremost, as philanthropic institutions, existing by the grace of the community to serve all who arrived, moneyed or not. With debt financing, hospitals began to look more like for-profit companies. No longer beholden to their donors, they could function more professionally, and the beginnings of a professional management layer can be traced to this era. These days, it is not clear why many hospitals retain their nonprofit (and thus tax-exempt) status when they donate little charitable care to their communities and take scant roles in medical education and public outreach. A few studies have shown that nonprofit hospitals produce slightly better patient outcomes than for-profits, but this is probably because they are being artificially subsidized by the government through tax exemption (McClellan & Staiger, 1999).

Further complicating this scenario is Medicaid, which is the name for the 50 state health care programs for low income persons regulated (and subsidized) by the federal government. Medicaid programs were brought into existence at the same time as Medicare, with the idea of making public hospitals obsolete. Unfortunately, Medicaid reimbursement rates quickly fell far behind private insurance and Medicare reimbursement, and thus, public hospitals found a new niche in the 1970s and 1980s of caring for Medicaid patients who would be turned away from private hospitals. Ironically, Medicaid reimbursement became more attractive to private hospitals as managed care contracts began to drive down occupancy rates in the early 1990s, and private hospitals began to woo Medicaid patients away from public hospitals (Biles & Abrams, 1998). Medicaid recipients have obviously benefited from this situation, as they can now routinely seek care at private hospitals, but public hospitals have been devastated financially as they have lost large chunks of their revenue and been forced to turn to state and municipal funds to bail them out so that they can continue to function.

This discussion of debt financing makes clear that hospitals loosely distinguish between capital and operating costs. As a result, they tend to have rather loose rules in allocating indirect costs. One of the great problems with hospital financial planning is that nearly all costs in a hospital are indirect (outside of tongue depressors and Tylenol). It takes a huge amount of money to open a hospital's doors, but once they are open, the marginal cost of an additional patient is nearly trivial. Nursing, therapy, and equipment needs to be allocated to various patients, and often the system for doing so is no more scientific than measuring the square footage of floor space of a particular unit and allocating a portion of the nursing staffs costs accordingly. When generous indemnity plans paid bills unquestioningly, such ambiguous accounting practices allowed hospitals to freely shift money from wealthy, better insured patients to poor and uninsured ones and thus remain true to their founding charitable missions. As managed care has dried up the "give" in the system, the loose accounting protocols have made it difficult for hospitals to get a handle on their own costs. This kind of ambiguity can be seen in the failure of many merged hospital systems to achieve financial health. In the late 1980s, hospitals enthusiastically began to merge, assuming that as in the manufacturing sectors great economies of scale could be realized from larger institutions. This simply was not true. Big hospitals have nearly identical costs, per bed, as small hospitals because within a narrow range nurse–patient ratios and equipment–patient ratios are fixed. While hospitals can achieve some economies of scale in the kitchen and in nonmedical inventory, for the most part, these are not the major cost drivers in the hospital system. In this sense, health care is similar to education, despite it being a more complex product. If you are running an elementary school, you need one teacher for every 20 children, regardless of whether the school has 50 students or 500 students. Even at the administrative level, there are few economies of scale, as the need for assistant principals grows with institution size. The same is true with hospitals. There may be savings in such areas as supplies but the costs of merging often far exceed the savings.

One solution to holding down hospital costs has been for the government to step in and tell hospitals what they can and cannot build or buy. Most countries do heavily regulate hospital building, at a national or provincial level, with a global budget over which the many hospitals can fight. In the United States, these types of "Certificate of Need" (CON) regulations proliferated in the 1970s and 1980s and did succeed in moderately limiting bed expansion (Stevens, 1999). However, hospitals usually managed to game the system and build what they wished to anyway, with the added costs incurred of going through the bureaucracies and offices that oversaw the CON processes. CON regulations are on the decline, as the deflationary pressures of managed care have largely superseded their function. Many smaller, financially distressed community hospitals have closed in the past decade, and most hospital building these days is for ambulatory care satellite clinics and ambulatory same-day surgical centers that should reduce costs in the system. Certainly Americans are spending fewer days in the hospital, but each day in them is more expensive than ever.

A more theoretical approach to hospital cost containment is to treat the hospital not as a community institution but rather as a job shop for doctors and charge the doctors for their use of the facility. Just as a rock band has to pay for recording studio time (with all of the accompanying sound engineer professionals) if they wish to produce their product, so might doctors pay for operating room time or postoperative time or intensive care time if they deem such services necessary to treating their patients. The doctors would, of course, build these costs into their bills, but such a system would acknowledge the reality that a hospital's true customers are its medical staff, and not its patients. Players in the health system—government regulators, physicians, and hospital administrators—are generally not considering this approach, so it probably will not come to pass. Such a system would force the primary "purchasers" of hospital care—the medical staff—to be more cost-conscious as they utilize hospital services, knowing that any savings they accrue could either be passed back to their patients or retained as profit.

Risk and Insurance

Healthcare financing in the United States is conducted almost entirely through third-party agents; that is, most people pay a third-party (usually called a health insurer, an MCO, a health maintenance organization [HMO], preferred provider organization [PPO], or a carrier) monthly premiums (either out of pocket, or as part of their compensation package from an employer), which in turns pays healthcare providers, be they doctors, hospitals, diagnostic labs, or pharmacies. Payment arrangement may be through indemnity (retroactive payment for expenses incurred), capitation (up front payment for estimated average costs), or some combination thereof. Third-party payers often purchase services in bulk from hospitals, pharmacy chains, and large physicians groups, allowing them to negotiate better terms on behalf of their subscribers. The system promotes overuse from an economic standpoint as a result of irresponsible utilization on the part of patients or overprovision on the part of providers. It is imperfect, frustrating, expensive, and pervasive. It is also probably fundamentally flawed.

Health insurance, which is a relatively new idea, is modeled on the idea of general insurance, which is quite old, despite the fact that medical care does not fit the criteria of an insurable product. Insurance relies on four basic assumptions: (1) low annual premiums, (2) unpredictable chance of adverse outcomes, (3) a low chance of adverse outcomes, and (4) intolerably high costs in the event of an undesirable outcome. An insurance product that nicely meets these basic criteria is homeowner's insurance. The chance of your house burning down is very low; few people will ever experience it. The cost of a house burning down is intolerably high except for the very wealthiest people. For most middle- or even upper middle-class Americans, the loss of a house would mean financial doom. The cost of the insurance premium is surprisingly low. Most Americans can insure a home and its contents worth upward of a quarter of a million dollars for less than $500 per year. Finally, it is almost impossible to predict whose house will burn down with any degree of certainty. As a result, virtually all American homeowners carry insurance, even those with no mortgage to pay off. In fact, if you found out that an acquaintance had not insured his house and belongings, you might think that he or she was a bit nuts!

Health insurance is actually two products rolled into one: prepaid medical care and insurance against a catastrophic medical event. Catastrophic coverage is a reasonable product. Few of us can predict at a young age who will require a $100,000 liver transplant or a million dollars in critical care after a horrible accident. The premium for such coverage (to insure only events which produce medical costs of over $5000, say) is relatively inexpensive, and the cost of one of these events would be catastrophic for most Americans. In contrast, prepaid medical care, which consumes the bulk of our health insurance premiums, makes no sense as an insurable product. Regular medical costs are highly predictable, constant, and affordable for most families. Furthermore, costs are not equally distributed. Older people and people with chronic sicknesses and disabilities spend consistently much more each year on regular medical costs than do young healthy people. If we could each buy a separate catastrophic policy (often called "major medical," which kicks in only after an annual deductible of several thousand dollars), few young people would voluntarily purchase a comprehensive policy. The 27-year-old accountant would just earmark $1,000 or so each year for a checkup, dental cleaning, some prescription drugs, and maybe a Pap smear. In fact, self-employed young people tend to do just this. The reason most of the rest of us do not do this is that we are not given a choice. Our employment carries with it comprehensive health insurance as part of the benefits package, and we receive no bonus for refusing the health coverage.

The problem with using a third-party payer to pay medical costs is that it leads to much higher system utilization and oftentimes economic waste. In appealing to a third party to cover medical bills, Americans (and most everybody else in the industrialized world) make themselves utterly insensitive to the price/utility quotient that governs all economic transactions. This means that they routinely purchase services and goods for themselves in the healthcare sector that cost more than the utility they provide, creating a net loss for society. Think about the way you eat when you travel on expense account. You tend to go to nicer restaurants than you might otherwise go to and to order more expensive entrees than usual. In short, you spend more money on dinner than you would if it were your own money. This is not because you do not have enough money to eat this way on your own; it is because when you spend your own money, you weigh the alternative ways in which you can spend your own money and decide that the same $100 spent on something else (groceries, heating oil, clothes) will bring you more pleasure than spending it on a nice meal out. In short, you maximize the total utility that your money can bring to you.

Purchasing health care with health insurance is like eating out on expense account. It is not that the $900 MRI does not bring you utility; it is just that the same $900 spent in other ways might bring you more utility. The difference between the utility brought to you by the medical service or good and the potential utility brought to you if you spent the money optimally is a loss for society. You do not feel it in your own pocket, but society feels it as money spent to produce goods and services that do not bring as much utility (or wealth creation) as money spent to produce alternative goods. We are having expensive goods and services foisted on us by a system that is insensitive to our own utility valuations.

How much loss does this system create? Nobody knows for sure, as we do not have a particularly good control group, but we have a few isolated pieces of evidence that the loss is substantial. For example, we know that primary care physician visits drop precipitously (as much as 40%) in an HMO when the co-payment goes from $0 to $10, suggesting that 40% of the time patients do not value their visit to a general practitioner or internist at even as much as $10 (Cherkin, Grothaus, & Wagner, 1989). When you consider that the cost of producing such a visit (in physician time, support staff, equipment amortization, rent, and administration) could easily run $100, you can see that society is losing $90 or more in nearly half of the primary care visits in the country. Similarly, we know that patients seeking certain sorts of services that are not covered (or are covered incompletely) by most health plans, such as cosmetic surgery, dental work, psychotherapy, Lasik surgery, and fertility treatments, are highly price sensitive and will shop around at length to find a cheaper provider. Although many Americans claim that they want the "best care money can buy" for themselves and their loved ones, this seems to be true only when the money is not their own. When the money is their own, Americans approach the purchase of health services with the same penny-pinching zeal they display at Wal-mart, Target, Costco, and CVS. The difficulty, however, of relying on a model of economic utility to guide the purchase of health services is that the choice to forgo a doctor's visit because of cost undermines the benefits of early detection and treatment of certain diseases.

Other losses are associated with third-party payment as well. Simply administering the system uses nearly one fifth of our entire healthcare budget annually, due to the Byzantine forms, rules, and regulations that each provider must comply with to win reimbursement for services rendered. Most private physicians today have nearly one full-time staff member per doctor to do nothing but billing work, at a cost of $45,000 per year in salary and benefits. Doctors report spending large portions of their time arguing with managed care companies, utilization oversight professionals, and hospital bursars on behalf of their patients. Furthermore, as managed care pushes people toward certain providers and away from others, we incur losses in utility from suboptimal market flexibility. The system as it stands today is distorted, cumbersome, frustrating to use, and frustrating to work in. It is not a system any of us would design from scratch.

Third-party payment has its uses. Catastrophic medical insurance is a very sensible product and, with the federal government covering everybody over 65 through Medicare, a relatively cheap one. It is possible to purchase a high-deductible major medical policy for as little as $70 per month if you are young and healthy versus the $250 you would spend on a basic managed care plan if it were comprehensive. Unfortunately, few employers offer such an option. A different option is a flexible health savings account, that some employers offer (Dicken, 2008). This plan allows you to place money in a special account, tax free, to spend on health purchases and is usually used in conjunction with a catastrophic plan. For a variety of reasons, these plans have not been popular, most likely because individuals have to guess how much money to set aside, and if this money is not spent on health services the individual forfeits that income.

Managed Care

Managed care is the general term for any sort of oversight in the process by which patients receive either funding for their medical care or the funded care in and of itself. Managed care, as a concept, is as old as the industrial health plans from the 1920s. Over the past 80 years it has periodically received increased interest, as when the Kaiser plans were founded in the 1930s, and when the Puget Sound health plans, HIP of New York, and GHA (Washington) were founded in the 1940s and 1950s. Starting around 1980 the federal government began to take a greater interest in the concept, mostly in hope of holding down healthcare costs, which were rising at rather frightening speeds. Companies began to be required to offer at least one managed care option, and Medicare began to offer a managed care choice for reduced co-payments in the early 1980s.

The modern age of managed care really begins in the mid 1990s; however, when in the aftermath of the failed Clinton health bill, employers began to heavily push their employees into managed care plans in an effort to reduce healthcare costs. At the beginning of the 1990s, fewer than 15% of all Americans covered with third-party coverage were being "managed," and 85% were receiving indemnity care; by the end of that decade, those percentages had exactly switched. Today, almost all covered Americans receive their health insurance in some sort of managed care package. It has become prohibitively expensive to purchase traditional indemnity insurance, and few people (and even fewer companies) do so. Effectively, managed care is health insurance today.

Managed care works through one or more of several mechanisms as follows:

1. *Capitation:* In a capitated system, MCOs pay the provider (either the physician or the hospital) a set amount each month for each covered patient. Most patients in any given month will require no care, but a few will require a great deal of care. Capitation provides an incentive to the provider to provide as little care as possible, in the most efficient manner possible, as there is no compensation for providing superfluous care. Contrast this with indemnity insurance in which the provider has an incentive to provide as much care as possible, regardless of its redundancy. Many providers work on partial capitation in which basic services are capitated, but specialty referrals are indemnified, or on a system of reinsurance in which costs of patients who require extraordinary amounts of care are indemnified by a secondary insurer. Initially, capitation was seen as a panacea, but health payment specialists quickly realized that individual physicians and small partnerships could not bear the risk of a few catastrophic patients. Today, only very large physician groups and certain types of specialists (such as obstetricians) work on full capitation; the others are reinsured or work on partial capitation.
2. *Utilization review (UR):* Utilization review refers to the use of a second professional (often a nurse practitioner) to oversee some of the decision making of the primary provider. The utilization reviewer is employed by the MCO and must give her permission for certain types of referrals, elective procedures, hospitalizations, and nearly all surgeries. UR is effective in holding down costs but tends to antagonize physicians (who resent the time spent in seeking review). In most MCOs that employ UR, physicians are given license to refer for most common problems and only seek review for major procedures, tests, and hospitalizations.
3. *Gatekeeping:* Primary care providers, who can be either an internist, pediatrician, general practitioner, family practitioner, or sometimes a gynecologist, are used as gatekeepers by the MCO as they screen all patient concerns and complaints before access to specialty care is granted. Gatekeeping has become ubiquitous but is a relatively new idea in the United States. Before the 1990s most insured individuals in the United States could see any specialist on their own volition and have the visit indemnified, regardless of the medical need of the visit. Gatekeeping has been remarkably successful in holding down costs, as specialty care is one of the greatest single cost drivers in the healthcare system. Unfortunately, gatekeeping is probably the single component of managed care that Americans find most odious, and the majority of Americans now choose a managed care plan (such as a PPO or point of service [POS] plan), that allows them some latitude in avoiding the gatekeeper. Gatekeepers work on capitation with extra indemnity for hospital rounds and certain procedures (pediatricians tend to be more heavily indemnified, as they have to see their patients so frequently). Not surprisingly, gatekeeping and capitation have created substantial incentives for primary care providers to be highly efficient with their time, and as a result they have tended to hire more office help (including clinical help) so they can increase the volume of patients they see each day and thus keep their

incomes up. It is not unusual for each full-time primary care provider to employ five or more clinical and clerical staff.

4. *Bulk purchasing of hospital services:* MCOs have responded to hospitalization, which is the largest cost driver in the U.S. healthcare system, by both negotiating substantially reduced hospitalization rates for their members (often half of the published rates for certain diagnosis-related groups) as well as by purchasing "covered days" up front for their entire local patient population. This latter technique, which is essentially a modified capitation arrangement, creates the same incentives for volume and efficiency in the hospitals as it does for the physician practice. Hospitals have responded by merging and creating networks so that they can control a larger portion of the local hospital market and thus bargain more forcefully on indemnity and capitation rates.
5. *Preferred provider networks:* MCOs sign up doctors selectively who are willing to treat their members at reduced fees and then offer members a financial incentive to see these doctors (usually by waving the copayment). Doctors are willing to join the networks out of fear that exclusion from the networks will hinder their ability to develop a healthy practice. While patients are concerned that the doctors on the networks are of lower quality, this is probably not the case, as competing MCOs wish to demonstrate that each includes certain numbers of board-certified specialists or subspecialists. Essentially, a network that registered only sub-par doctors would probably fail to satisfy large numbers of patients, who would demand that their employer switch to an alternate MCO. In fact, physician quality in the networks is rarely a cause of concern for patients; far more frequent are complaints about physician location. The single biggest complaint is the absence from a network of a physician with whom a patient has a pre-existing relationship. This is not so much a quality issue as an aesthetic one. Few patients, after all, have the wherewithal to assess objectively the quality of their own physicians.
6. *Ambulatory care:* MCOs try as hard as they can to keep patients out of hospitals, as hospitals are the most expensive venue in which to receive care. Consequently, MCOs have pushed patients to receive certain sorts of diagnostic and surgical procedures in outpatient settings, either in physicians' offices or in ambulatory surgical centers. This phenomenon is not so much a managed care strategy as a response of providers to managed care constraints. A hospital, working on capitation or a negotiated contract, has an incentive to provide its services as inexpensively as possible and thus may choose to build a free-standing surgical center in an effort to move patients through more quickly and efficiently. The hospital receives the same payment for a given procedure regardless of the costs it incurs, and thus, its most effective competitive strategy is to reduce its own costs.

These six strategies, usually used in some combination, collectively make up managed care. Capitation was initially the great hope of managed care planners, but it was flawed in placing too much financial risk on small providers and groups. UR was effective but antagonized the clinical professions. Gatekeeping worked too, but tended to antagonize the patients. In fact, all of these strategies work to hold down costs, but each has drawbacks. Most MCOs use some combination of the six.

MCOs take on one of several types: HMOs, PPOs, and POS plans. HMOs can be of three types: staff and group, network, or independent practice associations. The staff model HMO is notable in that it is the most highly "managed" of all and was the original template for all managed care. In this arrangement, doctors are all full-time employees of the plan, and patients simply pay a monthly membership fee that covers all services. Disadvantages are the high cost of putting the plan together in the first place and the inability of patients to go outside the plan. The first HMOs used a staff model. These are now rare but they tend to be the cheapest way in which to deliver quality health care because of gatekeeping and the fixed nature of costs that are not affected by the use of services.

Group and network HMOs contract with physicians who work for multiple plans, sometimes as solo practitioners, sometimes as part of a larger physician group. The physicians are paid on partial capitation, with indemnity for specialty referrals. Patients are assigned a primary care provider who serves as a gatekeeper (and may incur penalties if overly zealous on the referrals!) and may not go out of network. Large groups sometimes work for the HMO on full capitation, if they have adequate specialists in-house to handle the bulk of their own referral needs.

An independent practice association (IPA) is a close cousin to a network HMO in which the doctors themselves bear risk through a shared arrangement—drawing down indemnity for all services from a joint fund but equally bearing the risk that the fund may run out before the end of the year while they are still obligated to provide coverage to the patients.

HMOs are the cheapest form of managed care arrangement, but also the most constraining for patients. In response to patient dissatisfaction (and tight labor markets), many employers offer to put their employees into a PPO for an additional monthly fee. The PPO also has a network of physicians who agree to contract on an indemnified basis with the PPO for reduced reimbursement rates; however, the patient may go out of network if he or she is willing to pay a 30% (sometimes 40%) co-payment. The strongest allure of PPOs for patients, beyond providing them the ability to go out of network, is the end of the gatekeeper; patients may see any specialist on the roster without a referral. Reducing this added barrier seems to bring patients enormous satisfaction, and recent studies indicate that it does not seem to promote substantial overutilization.

Point of service plans (POSs) are part HMO and part PPO. If patients elect to stay in network, they must use their primary care physician, obtain a referral, and use a network specialist. If they do this, there is no (or minimal) co-payment. If patients elect to go out of network, they can dispense with the gatekeeper, but must pay a 30% or 40% co-payment. POS plans are attractive to MCOs because they can realize cost savings through the HMO function while granting patients the choice associated with a PPO.

Many patients worry that their doctors have a financial incentive to withhold care, or to withhold referrals, but in fact, most primary care providers find that they realize savings by referring, as long as they do not exceed basic standards set by the MCO.

Managed care or the system of private health insurance is evolving from tight staff model HMOs to loose PPOs, but is not going away. In addition to the models described, there are a variety of other arrangements, such as physician hospital organizations (PHOs), and various sorts of networks, but all combine in some manner or other the tools of networks, gatekeeping, negotiated hospital rates, and utilization oversight. If there is any revolt against the phenomenon, it is in the turn to cash medicine (either out of pocket, or aided by a medical savings account), not in a return to fee-for-service indemnity insurance. We are groping our way toward a highly diversified payment system in which patients receive insurance along a continuum of choice and cost, from HMO to POS to PPO to fee-for-service to medical savings accounts, to cash. Poorer, younger, or healthier patients will choose from the left-hand side of the list. Whereas older, sicker, or richer patients might like to choose from the right, that choice is constrained by their ability to pay and is often reserved for richer patients. The distinction will be not so much one of quality, but of convenience and freedom, with the freer and less constraining plans costing more in either monthly premiums or in out-of-pocket co-payments and expenses.

Medicaid

Medicaid is not one program but rather fifty separate state health insurance programs. The fifty programs were established by the states in the aftermath of the federal Medicaid legislation (passed in 1965 as an amendment to the Social Security Act), which provided matching federal funds for health services to all states that established a Medicaid program that met certain federal guidelines (Engel, 2006). In general, the programs had to provide comprehensive hospital and physician services, prescription drugs, eyeglasses, and emergency room care to all women and children who lived under a certain poverty threshold. The programs were required to care for the same population, which qualified for Aid to Families with Dependent Children, more commonly known as welfare. Since its creation in 1965, federal legislation has sought to expand care for children, pregnant women, and others who previously fell through the cracks.

In addition to caring for poor people, Medicaid also pays for medical care for permanently disabled workers, for patients with end-stage renal disease (dialysis treatment), for blind persons, and for long-term (nursing home) care for older patients who fall below the poverty line. Medical care for impoverished older populations is provided through Medicare, but nursing home care is provided through Medicaid once they have expended their Medicare benefits. Although Medicaid is perceived by the public to be poor-people's medicine, nearly 40% of all Medicaid disbursements go to caring for these other categories of patients, and indeed, these categories have been the fastest growing part of Medicaid since disabilities were more broadly defined under the Americans with Disabilities Act.

The 50 different state programs reimburse at different levels, with the programs of the poorest states (Mississippi, Alabama, and Arkansas) spending less than half as much per patient as those of the wealthiest and most generous states (New York and California) (American Academy of Pediatrics, 2008). These discrepancies are partially accounted for by differing costs of medical and hospital care in the different states, but not entirely. In general, New York's Medicaid program is viewed as the most generous program in the country, providing the highest quality medical care, prompting some conservative New York voters to suggest that this might be a fruitful area for budget cutting.

Medicaid reimbursement rates (nationally) quickly fell below the "customary and prevailing" rates paid by Medicare and private insurers, making these patients unattractive to most private hospitals and doctors. As a result, for most of the program's history, Medicaid patients have been shunted to public and municipal hospitals and have had access to only a limited selection of doctors—disproportionately graduates of foreign medical schools. In addition, the original Medicaid formularies did not pay for regular check-ups, meaning that many beneficiaries had no regular physician and relied instead on the local hospital emergency room for routine care. This pattern of care led most analysts to describe the U.S. health system as being two tiered, with private high-quality doctors and hospitals for privately insured patients and public hospitals and lower quality physicians for Medicaid patients. Such a description is not entirely accurate, however. Many municipal hospitals, although overcrowded and unattractive, provide first-rate surgical and critical care, and many have excellent emergency rooms. Efforts have also been made to create primary care practices within these settings. Despite these efforts, public hospitals are losing Medicaid patients to private hospitals for reasons explained earlier and this is creating a budget crisis as they historically depended on these patients to augment their revenues.

Medicaid is often the single largest line item on a state budget, and governors across the country have pondered ways to reduce its ever-increasing magnitude. In the past 15 years, many states have begun to move their Medicaid patients into managed care programs in an effort to save money. The programs have actually been among the most successful in the history of managed care. Under these programs, Medicaid patients have been assigned regular primary care providers for the first time and are now receiving the type of consistent and preventive care that private patients have long enjoyed. Primary care providers who chiefly see Medicaid patients report that their incomes are actually rising. This is not so with specialists, however. To make money from Medicaid patients, MCOs have whittled specialty care reimbursement down to meager levels; specialists report that Medicaid reimbursement is 10% what private MCOs pay for the same procedures, and the arduous task of preapproval for any specialty procedure further deters them from seeking these patients. Some specialists have stopped seeing Medicaid patients altogether, whereas others threaten to do so.

One of the oddities of Medicaid is that its inception created the strange American syndrome of the uninsured working class. In our country, the people who receive the worst medical care are not the poor and older populations (for they have Medicaid and Medicare) but rather those working people just above the poverty line who do not receive insurance from their employers and are unable to purchase it out of pocket. These people rely on public hospitals, cash payments for doctors' bills, alternative healers, and over-the-counter treatments. They tend to avoid doctors whenever possible and as a result exacerbate conditions that could be more easily treated if diagnosed earlier. Currently, some 45 million Americans fall into this group; their lack of care represents one of the greatest domestic challenges to our nation.

Medicare

Anyone over 65 in this country is eligible for Medicare Part A (free hospital insurance) and Medicare Part B (low cost physician insurance), and nearly 100% of the elderly enroll. However, there are gaps in what is covered by Medicare, and over 90% enroll in some sort of additional health plan as well to cover the high deductibles and co-pays in the Medicare program (which can total up to $2,500 per year) as well as the cost of prescription drugs that are covered only partially by Medicare Part D. This additional coverage is sometimes obtained through Medicaid (for the older poor), but most of the time by buying a private insurance product offered by commercial insurers known as "Medigap" coverage (Medigap is frequently covered by an employer for an active employee or by a pension plan for a retiree) (U.S. Department of Health and Human Services, 2008).

Medicare is wildly popular and is considered politically untouchable because of the lobbying strength of the American Association of Retired Persons (AARP). Medicare insures almost all of its beneficiaries through indemnity plans (making it an anachronism in today's managed care environment) and has fought vigorously, albeit unsuccessfully, to hold costs down. The Medicare program is the largest single purchaser of health care in the country. The program purchases almost a third of all healthcare services and goods in the country, and it is the single greatest driver of inflation in the healthcare economy. Medicare sets the standard for reimbursement which the private sector follows. It was Medicare that created hospital payments based on diagnosis-related groups, and physician payments based on resource-based relative value scales, and it is Medicare that sets prevailing rates for hospital services and physician care.

Older persons cannot be integrated into commercial programs because (1) they tend to be unemployed, and most private insurance programs are funded through employment; and (2) they are actuarially off the charts. The older population simply incurs more medical expenses than do the young; nearly 50% of all medical costs are incurred in the last years of life, and the majority of chronic afflictions afflict those over 65 years. Thus, older persons could probably never be integrated into a commercial, profit-driven insurance system, yet our sense of national fealty compels us to make provisions for their care. Of course, older persons respond to third-party coverage in the same manner as does everybody else—by overusing it—and for older persons, there is a particularly pernicious aspect of the equation in that they tend to value their time at next to nothing (as they do not work) and thus do not mind waiting in a doctor's office. The comprehensive Medigap policies have only exacerbated the situation, as they have removed the co-payments, deductibles, and hesitation fees, which can be highly effective in preventing patients from frivolously obtaining medical care. As a result, we routinely purchase expensive and sophisticated treatment for the very old in this country (bypass surgery on 90 year olds is not unheard of, and hip replacement for 80 year olds is relatively common), which contributes to our very high per capita health costs. Congress considered forcing all older persons into managed care programs about 15 years ago; however, Senator Bob Dole led a floor fight to prevent the legislation. There is a managed care option called Medicare Advantage plans. It was hypothesized that these would be less costly than Medicare fee-for-service, but this was not the case. Thus, today Medicare remains the last bastion of fee-for-service care.

Conclusion

Clearly, financing America's healthcare system is a complex and often counterintuitive enterprise. The industry defies basic laws of economics. Most consumers do not actually pay for their care; most payers do not actually have to market their products to the end state patients, and most providers must prenegotiate reimbursement rates with different payers, creating different pricing scales depending on who is paying the bills. Although elements of these complications can be found in other industries, no other industry has all of these complicating elements. Furthermore, the landscape changes constantly as the state governments rebudget their Medicaid program, as the federal government reconsiders comprehensive health reform, and as new managed care products evolve and wane to the consternation of consumers. Employers must decide yearly how much of the cost of employee benefits they will pass on to the employees, whereas retirees must choose between a dizzying array of Medigap and prescription drug plans. A number of good pamphlets are available to help consumers navigate these waters, but no one pamphlet or information source can possibly explain them all.

Based on economic theory, a strong argument can be made that medical care probably cannot be rationalized until most Americans start paying for it out of pocket. Only then will doctors stop seeking extra training (realizing that few patients will be willing or able to compensate them for their training investment); learn to prescribe lower cost medications, diagnostic tests, and procedures; and learn to market themselves to working class folk. Who knows—just as Sam Walton discovered that you can make a fortune selling low-cost items to moderate income individuals, if you price them right and move them through at high volume, so may some business-savvy doctor discover that the real money in medicine is in delivering flu shots, Pap smears, and throat cultures to the masses at $10 a pop. Economic theory suggests this will not happen as long as someone else pays our bills, but then economic theory does not fully explain the dynamics of the healthcare market.

References

Aaron, H. (1991). *Serious and unstable condition*. Washington, DC: Brookings.

Allied Physicians Salary Survey. (2006). Retrieved February 13, 2010, from http://www.allied-physicians.com/salary_surveys/physician-salaries.htm

American Academy of Pediatrics. (2008). *Medicaid reimbursement survey, 2007/08*. Elk Grove Village, IL: Author.

American Association of Medical Colleges. (2010). *Medical school*. Retrieved January 25, 2010, from http://www.aamc.org/medicalschools.htm

American Hospital Association. (2009). *Trendwatch chartbook: Trends affecting hospitals and health systems.* Chapter 4: Trends in hospital financing. Retrieved February 13, 2010, from http://www.aha.org/aha/research-and-trends/chartbook/ch4.html

Biles, B., & Abrams, M. (1998). The double bind: Challenges to safety net and teaching hospitals. *Journal of Urban Health, 75*(1), 17–21.

Center for Healthcare Research and Transformation. (2009). *CHRT issue brief*. Ann Arbor, MI: Author.

Cherkin, D., Grothaus, L., & Wagner, E. H. (1989). The effect of office visit copayments on utilization in a health maintenance organization. *Medical Care, 27*(7), 669–679.

Dicken, D. (2008). *Health savings accounts: participation increased and was more common among individuals with higher incomes.* Retrieved February 13, 2010, from http://www.gao.gov/new.items/d08474r.pdf

Engel, J. (2006). *Poor people's medicine*. Durham, NC: Duke University Press.

Hoadley, J., Cubanski, J., Hargrave, E., Summer, L., & Neuman, T. (2009). *Part D plan availability in 2010 and key changes since 2006.* Menlo Park, CA: Henry Kaiser Family Foundation. Retrieved February 13, 2010, from http://www.kff.org/medicare/upload/7986.pdf

Hsiao, W. C., Braun, P., Becker, E. R., Dunn, D. L., Kelly, N. L., & Yntema, D. L. (1990). *Managing reimbursement in the 1990s*. New York: McGraw-Hill.

Hsiao, W. C., Braun, P., Dunn, D. L., Becker, E. R., Yntema, D., Verrilli, D. K., et al. (1992). An overview of the development and refinement of the RBRVS: The foundation for reform of U.S. physician payment. *Medical Care Supplement, 30*(11), NS1–NS12.

Iversen, T. (2004). The effects of a patient shortage on general practitioners' future income and list of patients. *Journal of Health Economics, 23*(4), J673–J694.

Koetting, M. J. (1989). Correctly defining and assessing the causes of hospital dumping. *American Journal of Public Health, 79*(6), 780.

McClellan, M., & Staiger, D. (1999). Comparing hospital quality at for-profit and not-for-profit hospitals. *NBER Working Papers Series no. 7324*. Retrieved February 13, 2010, from http://www.nber.org/papers/w7324

Morris, C. (2005). The economics of health care. *Commonweal, 132*(7), 12–17.

Mutha, S., Takayama, J., & O'Neil, E. H. (1997). Insights into medical students' career choices based on third and fourth-year students' focus-group discussions. *Academic Medicine, 72,* 635–640.

National Center for Health Statistics. (2006). *Hospitals, beds, and occupancy rates, by types of ownership and size of hospitals, 1975–2004*. Washington, DC: Government Printing Office.

Perkins, B. B. (2010). Designing high-cost medicine. *American Journal of Public Health, 100*(2), 223–233.

Stevens, R. (1998). *American medicine and the public interest*. Berkeley, CA: University of California Press.

Stevens, R. (1999). *In sickness and in wealth*. Baltimore, MD: Johns Hopkins University Press.

United Nations Department of Economic and Social Affairs, Population Division. (2007). *World population prospects: The 2006 revision*. New York: Author.

U.S. Department of Health and Human Services, Center for Medicare and Medicaid Services. (2008). *Medigap (supplemental insurance) policies.* Retrieved February 13, 2010, from http://www.medicare.gov/medigap/Default.asp

U.S. Department of Labor, Employee Benefits Security Administration. (2004). *HIPAA fact sheet.* Retrieved February 13, 2010, from http://www.dol.gov/ebsa/newsroom/fshipaa.html

U.S. Department of Labor, Bureau of Labor Statistics. *Occupational Outlook Handbook, 2010–11 Edition. Physician assistants.* Retrieved February 13, 2010, from http://www.bls.gov/oco/ocos081.htm#outlook

WHO Statistical Information System. (2009). Retrieved February 13, 2010, from http://www.who.int/whosis/en

World Salaries. (2008). *International average salary income comparison: General physician salaries: International comparison.* Retrieved February 13, 2010, from http://www.worldsalaries.org/generalphysician.shtml

Chapter 11

The History of Health Insurance in the United States

Leah Curtin
and
Franklin A. Shaffer

OVERVIEW

This chapter provides an overview of the growth of the insurance within the healthcare industry. The major trends and merits of public and private insurance are described. The major stakeholders are presented with their role in the evolution of healthcare insurance including the government at the state and federal level, insurance companies, employers and the consumer. The major features of various insurance plans are described. An overview of the major features and aims of healthcare reform is presented as well as a look towards the future relative to existing political influence.

OBJECTIVES

- To describe the evolution of the insurance industry in the healthcare sector
- To identify the role of the stakeholders such as federal and state government, employers, and private insurance companies in the evolution of healthcare insurance
- To analyze the various types of insurance accompanied with their major features
- To explain role and choice relative to the type of insurance selected by an individual
- To analyze the nurse's role as an advocate and its important impact on healthcare insurance and the voice for the consumer

KEY TERMS

- ❑ Benefits
- ❑ Blue Cross and Blue Shield
- ❑ Civilian Health & Medical Program for Uniformed Services (CHAMPUS)

(continues)

- ❑ Consolidated Omnibus Budget Reconciliation Act (COBRA)
- ❑ Disability insurance
- ❑ Employees Retirement Income and Security Act (ERISA)
- ❑ Employer coverage
- ❑ Government regulation
- ❑ Health Information Technology for Economic and Clinical Health Act (HITECH)
- ❑ Health insurance
- ❑ Health Insurance Portability and Accountability Act (HIPAA)
- ❑ Healthcare reform
- ❑ History of healthcare reimbursement
- ❑ Managed care
- ❑ Market economics
- ❑ Medicaid
- ❑ Medicare
- ❑ Private coverage

The rudimentary state of medical technology before 1920 had one thing going for it: Most people had very low medical expenditures because there was not much on which to spend any money. A 1918 Bureau of Labor Statistics survey of 211 families living in Columbus, Ohio, found that the chief cost associated with illness was not the cost of medical care, but rather the fact that sick people could not work and did not get paid (Starr, 1982). A 1919 State of Illinois study reported that lost wages because of sickness were four times larger than the medical expenditures associated with treating the illness (State of Illinois, 1919). As a result, most people felt they did not need health insurance. Instead, households purchased "sickness" insurance—similar to today's "disability" insurance—to provide income replacement in the event of illness.

Thus, health insurance in the United States is a relatively new phenomenon. The first *individual* insurance plans to cover accidents or illness began during the Civil War (1861–1865). These offered coverage against accidents related to travel by rail or steamboat. The plans did, however, pave the way for more comprehensive coverage of all illnesses and injuries. The first *group* policy giving comprehensive benefits was offered by Massachusetts Health Insurance of Boston in 1847. Insurance companies issued the first individual disability and illness policies in about 1890. The first employer-sponsored group disability policy was issued in 1911 (Scofea, 1994).

The precursor to modern group health insurance plan was formed in 1929. A group of teachers in Dallas, Texas contracted with Baylor Hospital for room, board, and medical services in exchange for a monthly fee (Starr, 1982). As the demand for hospital care increased in the 1920s, this new payment innovation revolutionized the market for health insurance. The Baylor Plan provided 21 days of hospitalization for a fixed $6.00 payment. Among other things, Baylor Hospital embraced the plan as it helped ensure that people paid their bills. Prepaid hospital service plans grew over the course of the Great Depression. Prepaid hospital care was mutually advantageous for subscribers and hospitals: The prepaid plans enabled (healthy) consumers to afford hospital care. They also benefited hospitals by providing them with a way to earn income during a time of falling hospital revenue.

The demand for health insurance increased with advances in medical technology and as government policies encouraged the popularity of health insurance as a form of employee compensation. In 1932, the nonprofit Blue Cross was the first to offer group health plans (Reed, 1947). The American Hospital Association designed the Blue Cross guidelines so as to reduce price competition among hospitals. Prepayment plans seeking the Blue Cross designation had to provide subscribers with free choice of physician and hospital given a requirement that eliminated single-hospital plans from consideration. Blue Cross plans benefited from special state-level enabling legislation allowing them to act as nonprofit corporations and enjoy tax-exempt status. They were also free from the usual insurance regulations. Originally, this exemption was provided because Blue Cross made benefits available to low-income individuals. Without the enabling legislation, Blue Cross plans would have had to organize under the laws for insurance companies. As for-profit companies, the plans would have had to meet reserve requirements to ensure their solvency. Organizing as commercial insurance companies meant that they either had to meet reserve requirements or be subject to assessment liability. Given that most plans had limited financial resources available to them; they would not have been able to meet the requirements.

The commercial insurance companies were initially reluctant to offer health insurance. They feared that they would not be able to overcome problems relating to adverse selection so that offering health insurance would not be profitable. The success of Blue Cross and later Blue Shield showed how easily adverse selection problems could be overcome by focusing on providing health insurance only to groups of employed workers. This allowed commercial insurance companies to avoid those most likely to become ill because they insured only relatively young, healthy people. The success of private health insurance was always based on avoiding adverse selection. (Adverse selection is a disproportionately large number of sicker persons enrolled in a health plan.) Over the years, the techniques for doing so improved. Insurance companies avoided insuring the older population, disabled persons, and those at high risk to illness until eventually they were covered by governmental plans.

Several large life insurance companies entered the health insurance market in the 1930s and 1940s as the popularity of health insurance increased. These plans were not beholden to the hospitals like Blue Cross and Blue Shield. They were organized as indemnity plans meaning that cash payments were made for covered healthcare services. Individuals received the fixed payment and were responsible for the bill. These employee benefit plans gained popularity during World War II and into the late 1940s and 1950s. Strong unions bargained for better benefit packages, including tax-free, employer-sponsored health insurance. Wartime (1939–1945) wage freezes imposed by the government actually accelerated the spread of group health plans. Unable by law to attract workers by paying more, employers instead improved their benefit packages, adding health care.

Government Coverage (Public Insurance Programs)

Government programs to cover healthcare costs began to expand during the 1950s (federal matching for welfare recipients and the Veteran's Administration) and 1960s (Medicare and Medicaid). Disability benefits were included in social security coverage for the first time in 1954. The political atmosphere become favorable toward nationalized health insurance proposals after John F. Kennedy was elected to office in 1960, especially when the Democrats won a majority in Congress in 1964. Following Kennedy's assassination, Lyndon Johnson led the movement to pass Medicare and Medicaid. In 1965, Medicare passed with bipartisan support (70 House Republicans joined 237 House Democrats and in the Senate 13 Republicans joined 57

Democrats). Wilburn Cohen, Secretary of Health, Education, and Welfare under Johnson, is widely considered to be the architect of Medicare (U.S. Department of Health and Human Services, n.d.). It is a federal program with uniform standards that consisted of two parts: Part A is the hospital insurance program that the aged are automatically enrolled in on reaching age 65; Part B provides supplemental medical insurance, or subsidized insurance for physicians' services. One broadly held misconception is that Medicare provides free coverage for all Americans over the age of 65 years. This is not entirely true. To be eligible for Medicare, one must have worked and paid the Medicare tax for at least 10 years, and then one must pay the monthly premium for Part B.

Ironically, although the American Medical Association vigorously opposed Medicare, calling it socialized medicine, physicians and hospitals stood to benefit tremendously. They would both receive payment for services that were previously considered bad debt or charity. Fearing that physicians would refuse to treat Medicare patients, the government agreed to reimburse physicians according to their usual, customary, and reasonable rate. In addition, doctors could continue to bill patients directly so that the patients rather than the doctors had to deal with Medicare for reimbursement. Funding for Medicare comes from payroll taxes, income taxes, trust fund interest, and enrollee premiums for Part B. Medicare has grown from serving 19.1 million recipients in 1966 to 44.1 million in 2008, and projections are that it will cover over 70 million retirees by 2020 (Kaiser Family Foundation, 2009).

Part A of the Medicare benefit program covers hospital stays of at least 72 hours. It also will pay for limited stays in a nursing home, provided that the nursing home care is related to the hospital stay, the patient requires skilled nursing supervision in lieu of rehabilitation, and the Medicare benefit received in the nursing home is skilled rather than routine. Part A coverage is usually free, having been paid for by the beneficiary's periodic payroll tax deductions.

Part B of the Medicare benefit package is optional and offers medical insurance. It covers some of the medical providers and services not covered by Part A. Part B Medicare benefit can include a doctor's visit, a laboratory test, an X-ray, a flu vaccination, and certain outpatient procedures, to name a few. The Part B Medicare benefit is not free. Instead, the person must choose whether to pay for Part B when notice of Medicare benefit eligibility is received at the age of 65 years. In 2008, the Part B monthly premium was $96.40 (and more for seniors with higher incomes) (Kaiser Family Foundation, 2009).

In 1997, Part C of the Medicare Benefit system gave Medicare members the option to receive their care through private insurance plans. These private plans were in place of the Part A/Part B coverage of the original Medicare benefit plan. Regulations for these private plans were modified in 2003, and they became known as Medicare Advantage, or MA, plans (http://www.ms.hhs.gov).

The Part D Medicare benefit became effective on January 1, 2006. Anyone eligible for Parts A or B was automatically eligible to participate in the Part D prescription drug plan. Part D is confusing and complicated. In 2008, the standard benefit requires payment of a $275 deductible. The beneficiary then pays 25% of the cost of a covered Part D prescription drug up to an initial coverage limit of $2,510. Once the initial coverage limit is reached, the beneficiary is subject to another deductible, known officially as the Coverage Gap, but referred to more commonly as the "donut hole," in which they must pay the full cost of medicine. When total out-of-pocket expenses on formulary drugs for the year, including the deductible and initial coinsurance, reach $4,050 (now $4,350 in 2009), the beneficiary then reaches catastrophic coverage, in which he or she pays $2.25 for a generic or preferred drug and $5.65 for other drugs, or 5% coinsurance, whichever is greater. The $4,050 amount is calculated on a yearly basis, and a beneficiary who amasses $4,050 in out-of-pocket costs by December 31 of one year will start his or her deductible anew on January 1 (Kaiser Family Foundation, 2009). Most low-income subsidy patients are exempt from all or part of the donut hole and the deductible. This defined standard benefit is not the most common benefit offered by Part D plans for other beneficiaries. For further information on Medicare and all of its complexities, you are referred to visit Medicare's excellent and extremely informative Web site at www.medicare.gov.

The other major health insurance program that is offered as a partnership between the federal and state governments is Medicaid. Medicaid was passed at the same time as the Medicare legislation. It is an entitlement program that originally provided healthcare services to welfare recipients including the aged, blind and disabled. As currently designed, the federal government sets broad guidelines for the program in terms of eligibility and services, and states have discretion over implementation. The costs are primarily covered by the federal government. In 2008 Medicaid served 58 million persons and cost $319 billion dollars (Kaiser Family Foundation, 2010).

Medicaid eligibility covers two groups. Mandatory groups covered by the program include most persons who receive federally assisted income maintenance, low-income families and children who meet eligibility requirements for AFCD as of 1996, SSI recipients, low income pregnant women and children, recipients of adoption and foster care services and certain Medicare beneficiaries. Optional groups are populations that the states may include in the program. There is tremendous flexibility. For example, states have the option to cover distinct populations such as AIDS patients.

Medicaid is a comprehensive program because the population served by Medicaid is sickest and least able to pay. Every state must provide 10 basic health services: inpatient, outpatient hospital services, physician services, rural health clinics, other laboratory and X-ray, skilled nursing facility and home health for individuals 21 and over, EPSDT for individuals under 21, family planning, and nurse midwives. There are an additional 33 optional services that states may choose to provide including prescription drugs, dental, and optical. Nursing home and home health care fall under optional services under this category. As a result, Medicaid is best described as 50 different programs. The federal government matches state healthcare spending between 50% and 83% of costs based on the average per capita income in each state (Kaiser Family Foundation,

2010). States have tremendous discretion to specify income cut-off for eligibility and payment levels for services which impacts the cost of the program (Kaiser Family Foundation, 2010).

Medicaid serves three distinct populations. It is most clearly associated with the services provided to children. In fiscal year 2006, children accounted for 50% of Medicaid beneficiaries but only 19% of costs. The elderly for whom Medicaid pays long-term care services and Medicare Part B premiums for qualified individuals were 10% of beneficiaries and accounted for 24% of costs. Last, Medicaid is the primary source of healthcare coverage for the disabled. They comprise 15% of beneficiaries and 41% of costs (Kaiser Family Foundation, 2010). This is the fastest growing part of Medicaid in terms of numbers and costs.

In addition to Medicare and Medicaid, the federal government has extended health benefits to children through the SCHIP program that was created in 1997. This program allocated $40 billion over 10 years to expand child health insurance coverage. States could provide services using their Medicaid programs; they could develop separate plans that could limit benefit packages or require cost sharing; or they could develop plans with elements of both. States set eligibility guidelines for the program but could offer health insurance to children up to 19 who were not already insured (GovTrack, 2007).

The federal government's role extends over many areas of health care, including the Food and Drug Administration, Centers for Disease Control, and National Institutes of Health (the nation's research agency), for the public's benefit. The federal government not only provides insurance through the Medicare and Medicaid Programs, but it also serves as an employer and offers its own insurance through the Federal Employees Health Benefits Program. The government also covers the Department of Defense, ensuring that the active and retired service personnel receive their healthcare coverage. Also, the Department of Veterans Affairs covers civilian, current, and retired personnel's health care. The arm of the federal government extends beyond Medicare, even though Medicare is its largest public insurance. In 2008, national health spending was estimated to reach $2.4 trillion (Centers for Medicare and Medicaid Services, n.d.). The total public share of this amount, including state, federal, and local, was estimated at $1,108 trillion, or 46% of all national health spending. The federal share alone, through Medicare, Medicaid, and other programs and entities, was $810.6 billion, or 33.75% of the total national health spending. If tax subsidies that encourage provisions of health coverage and health care are added in, the total governmental share comes close to three fifths (60%) of all U.S. health spending (Centers for Medicare and Medicaid Services, n.d.).

Large Employer Coverage

Most private health coverage in the United States is employment based. Employer-sponsored health insurance originally was paid for by businesses on behalf of their employees as part of an employee benefit package. Today, the employer typically makes a substantial contribution toward the cost of coverage. In 2008, the average employee contribution was 16% of the cost of single coverage and 27% of the cost of family coverage. These percentages have been stable since 1999. Health benefits provided by employers are also tax favored. Employees can make contributions to health spending accounts on a pretax basis if the employer offers the benefits through a section 125 cafeteria plan. Although large companies are more likely to offer retiree health benefits than small firms, the percentage of large firms offering these benefits fell from 66% in 1988 to 34% in 2002 (Thomasson, 2002).

Employers are reticent to continue paying for retiree benefits because the costs for employer-paid health insurance are rising rapidly. Since 2001, premiums for family coverage have increased 78%, whereas wages have risen 19% and inflation has risen 17%, according to a 2007 study by the Kaiser Family Foundation. Employer costs generally have risen significantly per hour worked and vary significantly. In particular, average employer costs for health benefits vary by firm size and occupation. The percentage of total compensation devoted to health benefits has been rising since the 1960s. Average premiums, including both the employer and employee portions, were $4,704 for single coverage and $12,680 for family coverage in 2008.

Small Employer Group Coverage

According to a 2007 study, about 59% of employers at small firms (3 to 199 workers) in the United States provide employee health insurance; however, the percentage of small firms offering coverage has been dropping steadily since 1999 (Claxton et al., 2007). The study notes that cost remains the main reason cited by small firms who do not offer health benefits. Small firms that are new are less likely to offer coverage than ones that have been in existence for a number of years. For example, using 2005 data for firms with fewer than 10 employees, 43% of those that had been in existence at least 20 years offered coverage, but only 24% of those that had been in existence less than 5 years did. The rates from year to year are volatile and appear to be higher for newer, small businesses.

The types of coverage available to small employers are similar to those offered by large firms, but small businesses do not have the same options for financing their benefit plans. In particular, self-insuring the benefits is not a practical option for most small employers. A RAND Corporation study published in April 2008 found that the cost of healthcare coverage places a greater burden on small firms, as a percentage of payrolls, than on larger firms. A study published by the American Enterprise Institute in August 2008 examined the effect of state benefit mandates on self-employed individuals and found that the larger the number of mandates in a state, the lower the probability that a self-employed person will be a significant employment generator (Eibner, 2008).

Beneficiary cost sharing is, on average, higher among small firms than large firms. For the last 30 years, health policy has been characterized by increasing cost sharing with beneficiaries

(deductibles, co-payments) and increasing determination to reduce usage of health benefits. This policy was supported by a surprisingly small number of studies on moral hazard, which have exerted a disproportionate influence on the thinking of policy makers (Nyman, 2003). The term *moral hazard* is defined as the additional healthcare coverage that consumers purchase when they are insured. With the advent of this theory, health insurance was transformed from a solution into a problem. Under this theory, insurance was socially valuable only if one could substantially curb the behavior of the insured. Otherwise, health insurance promoted overuse of health resources and contributed substantially to the growth in medical inflation. Managed care was born partially in response to this belief. Managed care is considered the systematic integration and coordination of the financing and delivery of health care performed by health plans that try to provide their members who are at least partly at risk for the cost of care.

When small group plans are medically underwritten, employees are asked to provide health information about themselves and their covered family members when they apply for coverage. When determining rates, insurance companies use the medical information on these applications. Sometimes they will request additional information from an applicant's physician or ask the applicant for clarification.

States regulate small group premium rates, typically by placing limits on the premium variation allowable between groups (rate bands). Insurers price to recover their costs over their entire book of small group businesses while abiding by state rating rules. Over time, the effect of initial underwriting "wears off" as the cost of a group regresses toward the mean. Recent claim experience—whether better or worse than average—is a strong predictor of future costs in the near term, but the average health status of a particular small employer group tends to regress over time toward that of an average group. Insurance brokers play a significant role in helping small employers find health insurance, particularly in more competitive markets. Average small group commissions range from 2% to 8% of premiums (Nyman, 2003). Brokers provide services beyond insurance sales, such as assisting with employee enrollment and helping to resolve benefits issues.

Health Insurance Regulation

Health insurance is regulated by both state and federal governments primarily to protect the public. The state is responsible for regulating the business or operations of insurance carriers. The federal government regulates the companies that cross individual state borders to ensure that they act in a similar and consistent manner. In 1945, the McCarran-Ferguson Act gave states the authority to govern the standards and oversee the business of insurance companies (Fernandez, 2005). The state requires that insurance carriers, with the exception of self-insured companies, be licensed by the state in order to conduct their business. The state also requires that companies provide certain benefits as stipulated by that state's regulations. Federal regulations focus more on ensuring that the right people get the right benefits (especially at-risk populations, including the poor and others). The three most notable federal laws regulating health insurance are the Employee Retirement Income and Security Act, the Consolidated Omnibus Budget Reconciliation Act, and HIPAA.

The Employee Retirement Income and Security Act (ERISA) was passed in 1974 in an effort to protect the retirement benefits of the public at large. ERISA has had a profound impact on health insurance as it supersedes state laws related to benefit plans (Kaiser Family Foundation, 2002). Therefore, companies that self insure as opposed to companies that purchase health insurance plans are exempt from state insurance regulation. Since the passage of ERISA, the number of employees covered by self insured plans increased to over 50%. This means there can be both federal and state regulation of health insurance in a given state. The question regarding exemption is whether or not weak state laws are being preempted by stronger federal law. Self insured plans tend to be less comprehensive than plans regulated by state insurance agencies. This impacts services such as prenatal care, well child care, and coverage of alternative medical providers such as chiropractors. In addition, self insured plans are not as expensive as companies do not pay premium taxes to state risk pools or reserves. Last, are problems sited in areas like the appeals process. The only remedy available to a covered person who has been denied benefits or dropped from coverage altogether is to seek an order from a federal judge (no jury trial is permitted) directing the plan (in actuality the insurance company that underwrites and administers it) to pay for "medically necessary" care. If a person dies before the case can be heard, however, the claim dies with him or her, as ERISA provides no remedy for injury or wrongful death caused by the withholding of care (Hall, 1994).

Even if benefits are improperly denied, the insurance company cannot be sued for any resulting injury or wrongful death. Many persons included among the 47 million people presently without healthcare coverage in the United States are former ERISA "subscribers" (insurance plan beneficiaries) who have been denied benefits—usually on grounds that the prescribed care is not medically necessary or is "experimental" or the beneficiary has been dropped from coverage, perhaps because he or she lost his or her job because of the very illness for which care was denied (Hall, 1994).

Another federal law is the Consolidated Omnibus Budget Reconciliation Act better known as COBRA which was passed in 1985 (Shaffer, 1986) . COBRA applies to job-based plans with 20 or more employees. It allows workers the right to temporarily remain in their company's group health plan even if they lose their job or their dependent status. The protection offered by COBRA is important because group coverage cannot discriminate based on health status while individual coverage can. If an individual is sick and about to lose his or her job, COBRA assures the availability of coverage. The cost of coverage, however, discourages most persons from applying for coverage because there is no requirement that employers pay a portion of the premium.

The other federal statute governing the insurance industry is the Health Insurance Portability and Accountability Act (HIPAA). It was passed in 1996 and addressed employees' concerns over their inability to take their insurance from one employer to another (Fernandez, 2005, p. 7). HIPAA also limited the plan's ability to deny coverage for preexisting medical conditions to 5 years. HIPAA also protects the confidentiality of personal as well as business information. Recently, HIPAA's reach was expanded by the Health Information Technology for Economic and Clinical Health Act (HITECH) provisions of the American Recovery and Reinvestment Act which made important changes in privacy regulation in an effort to protect the confidentiality of the information housed in electronic records (Centers for Medicare and Medicaid Services, 2010). HITECH is a regulatory response to the data-mining efforts of many insurance companies as they seek to reduce their exposure to the effects of adverse selection. HIPAA and HITECH regulations require that practicing healthcare professionals protect the confidentiality of personal records of patients just like the insurance industry is obliged to protect the personal information of its enrollees and potential enrollees, regardless of the settings or the industry confidentiality of personal information.

Managed Care in the 1990s

Health insurance underwent major changes starting in the early 1990s, with the defeat of the Clinton Health Plan. The American public "chose" by default market-based reform as that strategy most likely to yield the highest quality service for the lowest cost. Universal coverage, indeed even provision of essential services to those in greatest need, was considered political "pie in the sky." The health insurance industry rapidly developed managed care products to replace its indemnity plans. Managed care never promised the American people universal coverage or even affordable health insurance coverage for all. Rather, it promised its investors a respectable return on investment and its beneficiaries the fulfillment of its contractual obligations: nothing more and nothing less. It did suggest that competition would control costs and increase quality. Managed care is an insurance or delivery mechanism that includes: limitation on the number of providers serving a covered population, either through direct ownership or employment, or through selective contracting or through some combination of these elements; adherence by providers to utilization management controls; incentives for patients to use only the providers designated by the managed care plan; some degree of financial risk for providers, ranging from HMOs that assume the full risk for the cost of care to contractual arrangements under which carriers and providers share risk (Center for Studying Health System Change, 1997).

Managed care demonstrates that health insurance is more than protection against risk. It is a highly profitable business. Market economics demands the adoption of strategies that optimize profit through gaining competitive advantage. Competitive edge is determined by meeting the demands of one's customers (i.e., the ones who buy your products/services). Today, that customer is almost always business or government, and their chief demand is for lower prices. These customers are fostering competition among health plans that, in turn, seek providers who underbid one another. Historically, the first managed care organizations (called health maintenance organizations) were nonprofit. They delivered services to clearly defined populations such as city employees (Health Insurance Plan in New York City), or cooperative members (Group Health in Puget Sound), or ship workers (Kaiser Permanente in California) (Center for Studying Health System Change, 1997). With federal incentives to expand this model, insurance companies developed managed care plans. These managed care organizations (MCOs), now dominate the market (Center for Studying Health System Change, 1997). The entry of for-profit insurance companies led to competition among health plans for members which was evidenced by mergers and hostile takeovers as MCOs sought greater market share and thus greater bargaining power with both their customers (business and government) and clients (healthcare providers) (Eckholm, 1994). The larger the MCO and the greater its market share in a given region, the tougher the strategies for controlling costs and the tighter is the squeeze on local providers. Managed care strategies, which exclude high-risk patients, limit access to high-cost care, and reward low-cost providers, encourage hospitals and health networks to

- Adopt economies of scale (form chains, expand established product lines, create group purchasing arrangements)

- Increase their market share (arrange mergers and acquisitions, bid aggressively for managed care contracts, purchase physician practices)
- Increase the efficiency of service delivery (develop outpatient services, streamline management, standardize care plans)
- Control costs (close unprofitable institutions and services, increase productivity through restructuring and re-engineering jobs, hire and incentivize physicians to encourage frugal decision-making)

Individual providers (physicians, in particular) responded to the pressures brought by both managed care entities and institutional providers by organizing large multispecialty group practices that gave them leverage in bargaining with local and even national health networks and managed care entities. Many have formed their own "managed care products" called individual practice associations; still others have bought stock in or received stock options as part of their agreements with existing publicly traded MCOs. Many physicians have become employees of hospitals and health networks and MCOs, often incentivized through profit sharing.

To put the matter succinctly, health insurance organizations (private and governmental) and the strategies they adopted and providers of all types (for-profit, nonprofit, personal, and institutional) and the strategies that they employ are more a function of market-based economics than of "managed care." The drive for profit, which is the sine qua non of the marketplace, is ipso facto a disincentive to ensuring high-risk populations (McCormick, 1998).

Employer coverage and age-dependent coverage virtually guarantee plan switching, which discourages long-term accountability because members do not stay in a plan over their lifetimes. Indeed, in the case of Medicare Advantage Plans (Part C), enrollees are almost encouraged to change plans when they are dissatisfied. As a result, (managed care) plan managers have no incentive to provide preventive care and may be tempted to ration access to care. Enrollees, on the other hand, have little incentive to take "lifetime benefit limits" seriously and make careful choices about the use of their benefit over the long haul.

Health Insurance in the Twenty-First Century

Since its initial uptake in the 1990s, there has been tremendous resistance to managed care. Patients resent their loss of choice. Physicians resisted the loss of autonomy that resulted from tightly structured managed care plans. Employers had difficulty controlling costs following the initial savings. The government found it difficult to develop managed care systems in either the Medicare or Medicaid systems. What has evolved are hybrid forms of organization that represent a loosening of the managed care model. MCOs now offer a range of products including indemnified products. For example, an enrollee can see a panel physician and only make a copayment for services or an enrollee can go out-of-network and be reimbursed a fixed amount for the service. What has become more popular than MCOs are Point-of-Service Plans that have no gate keeping and Preferred Provider Organizations that offer discounted fee-for-service in a limited panel.

Consumer–driven plans are a relatively new insurance model, but many persons assume it will grow. They represent a fundamental shift in the provision of health insurance. The insurance industry understood the managed care mandate as constraining costs by modifying physician practice patterns. In contrast, the industry is redefining its mission as designing benefit packages to encourage cost conscious choices by consumers. By making consumers responsible for more of the purchasing decisions these plans transfer risk to individuals who will control demand for services. Existing health insurance products do not expose enrollees to financial risk. The lack of risk exposure leads enrollees to pay little attention to whether they genuinely need a health service before using it. This leads to extensive overuse and misuse of services and thus ever increasing costs. The solution is to put consumers at risk and provide them with extensive information and support to make wise decisions. The two components of consumer-driven plans are high deductibles and health savings accounts. High deductible for an individual are minimally $1,000 but may be much higher. Expenses subject to the deductible are covered by health savings accounts to which employers and employees have contributed. Recognizing that many persons will avoid preventive care if they have to pay out-of-pocket, these services are sometimes exempt from the deductible.

Problems and More Problems

The history of health insurance can also be understood as a history of expanding access to health care. This was the intent of the Baylor Plan, Blue Cross and Blue Shield, commercial health insurance, and Medicare and Medicaid. In 1993, President Bill Clinton presented to Congress a healthcare reform plan that guaranteed health insurance for all Americans. Fueled by well-funded opposition from the health insurance industry, the bill was soundly defeated, allegedly for its high cost and complexity. Despite various federal efforts such as the 1996 Mental Health Parity Act that required some employers to offer health plans with psychiatric benefits, or the Health Insurance Portability and Accountability Act whose purpose was to protect individuals from losing their health insurance when they changed jobs or became self-employed or the SCHIP program, the government has not ensured the overall quality or comprehensiveness of insurance offered by employers.

In 2007, more than 45 million people in the United States (15.3% of the population) were without health insurance for at least part of the year (Kaiser Family Foundation, 2010). The percentage of the non-older population who are uninsured has been steadily increasing since the year 2000. Among the uninsured population, some 37 million were employment-age adults (ages 18 to 64 years) and more than 27 million worked at least part time. About 38% of the uninsured live in households with incomes over $50,000. According to the U.S. Census Bureau (2007), nearly 36 million of the uninsured are legal U.S. citizens. Another 9.7 million are noncitizens, but the Census Bureau does not distinguish in its estimate between legal noncitizens and illegal immigrants (U.S. Census Bureau, 2007). It has been estimated that nearly one fifth of the uninsured population is able to afford insurance; almost one quarter is eligible for public coverage, and the remaining 56% need financial assistance (8.9% of all Americans). An estimated 5 million of those without health insurance are considered "uninsurable" because of pre-existing conditions (Kaiser Family Foundation, 2010).

A report published by the Kaiser Family Foundation in April 2008 found that the economic downturn of 2008 placed a significant strain on state Medicaid and SCHIP programs. The authors estimated that a 1% increase in the unemployment rates increased Medicaid and SCHIP enrollment by 1 million and increased the number uninsured by 1.1 million. State spending on Medicaid and SCHIP increased by $1.4 billion (total spending on these programs increased by $3.4 billion). This increased spending occurs at the same time state government revenues are declining. During the last downturn, the Jobs and Growth Tax Relief Reconciliation Act of 2003 included federal assistance to states, which helped states avoid tightening their Medicaid and SCHIP eligibility rules. The authors concluded that Congress should consider similar relief for the current economic downturn.

Many health professionals, tend to look at an aging society from the standpoint of its health; however, few of us consider the social, political, and clinical impact of a rapidly growing, heavily entitled cohort of aging people—the Baby Boomers—who already are characterized by political activism. Now this voting block, all 79 million, is more united than ever: rich or poor, educated or illiterate, of all races and of both parties and genders, over concerns surrounding entitlements, including Medicare.

2009 Insurance Reform Efforts

Once again, healthcare reform is on the table and Congress is considering how to expand access to health insurance. The value of health insurance is not difficult to establish. It helps restore both physical health for a person when he has an accident, experiences a heart attack, or discovers a cancer. The benefits of health insurance in these circumstances underlie the public support for policies that subsidize health insurance or extend publicly provided health insurance to a large portion of Americans who are otherwise uninsured. Obama's health plan is currently stalled in Congress, but the complexity of making health care widely available was seen in the range of options considered by the House and Senate during 2009.

On June 19, 2009, the House Tri-Committee released a draft bill on health reform that included a public plan financed by premiums (American Nurses Association, 2010).

This bill initially reimbursed healthcare providers using Medicare's lower rates. The triggered responses were predictable, including those voiced from the American Medical Association, the health insurance industry, and House Republicans: (1) Doctors and hospitals say that a public plan that forces them to accept lower payments (Medicare rates) would shrink their incomes dramatically; (2) Insurance companies say that a public plan would have built-in advantages—that would allow it to "take over" the insurance market; (3) Republicans worry that a public plan would amount to a "government takeover" of health care that would cost untold trillions. In response, the House Republicans proposed individual tax breaks for buying health insurance and "pools" for states and small business to get lower cost healthcare plans. They also proposed increasing incentives for people to build health savings accounts, allowing dependent children to stay on parents' policies until the age of 25 years and encouraging employers to reward employees for improved health. This, of course, assumes that the uninsured/underinsured have the money to save, get tax refunds, and so forth.

On June 19, 2009, the Senate Finance Committee leaked a 10-page draft that contains the following four alternatives:

1. A Medicare-based plan in which providers would be paid the same rates as from Medicare. Premiums would be the lowest of any model, but government costs would be the highest.
2. A self-sustaining plan in which premiums would cover the cost of claims. Patients would pay more than under the Medicare model but less than for private insurance.
3. A triggered plan in which the "public plan" would kick in only if private insurers did not sufficiently expand coverage and lower costs to certain mandated levels at some as yet unspecified future date.
4. Regional co-ops that would be owned and operated by states/regions and that would collect premiums and provide coverage (keeping the federal government out of it).

In September of 2009, the Senate's "Bi-Partisan" Health Reform Plan was released (American Nurses Association, 2010). This effort, led by Senator Max Baucus, was supposed to construct a bipartisan plan. The Democratic chairman of the Senate Finance Committee (Baucus) eliminated the public option entirely and kept the insurance mandates, but to date, no Republicans are willing to vote for his bill. The public health insurance option as defined in both the Senate HELP bill and the House bill (H.R. 3200) was not a far-left liberal proposal. A far-left liberal proposal would actually have been a single-payer plan. The public option is a program that initially had broad based support.

If the Senate bill is enacted as is, citizens would have to buy a private insurance policy or

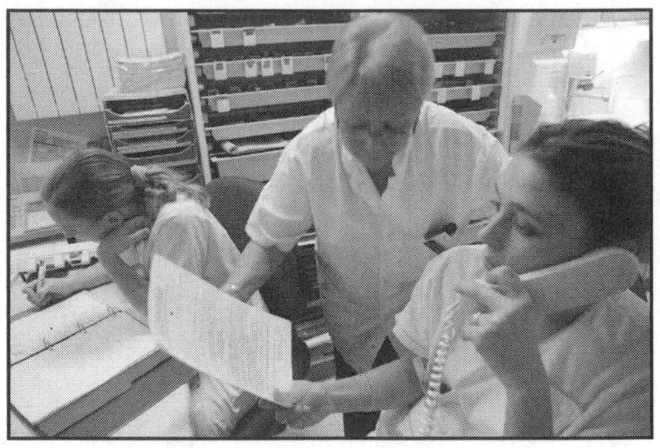

be penalized by the federal government. Thus, individuals would be forced to purchase insurance from the same companies that have refused to cover pre-existing conditions, canceled policies if someone does get sick, denied claims, or refused to pay for life-saving procedures. Penalties for failing to get insurance would start at $750 a year for individuals and $1,500 for families. Households making more than three times the federal poverty level—about $66,000 for a family of four—would face the maximum fine: $3,800 for families and $950 for individuals.

2009 began with a Democratic Administration that was determined to reform health care. To achieve health reform, lawmakers must stifle their reluctance to impose mandates and some form of taxation. But such action comes in the face of powerful lobbyists for the insurance and pharmaceutical companies who are fighting to protect their constituents' profits. Even the American Medical Association, although favoring reform, is not supportive of any plan that will cut physician reimbursement. So far, the hospital industry is the only one making any concessions. In August 2009, the hospital industry pledged to contribute $155 billion in Medicare and Medicaid savings in the next decade. But their support is not enough to move what is now a stalemated situation.

Nursing and Healthcare Reform: A Progressive Experience

Nursing, as articulated by its professional associations, has been deeply committed to addressing the inequities of the current healthcare system. Since the early 1980s, nursing organizations, particularly the American Nurses Association (ANA), have participated in representing, as well as informing, the profession at state and national levels on healthcare reform and organized nursing's agenda for healthcare reform (American Nurses Association, 2010). The ANA supported the Clinton Healthcare Plan and has been extremely involved at all levels with the Obama administration's current effort to reform "health insurance" in this country.

The American Nurses Association developed *Nursing's Agenda for Health Care Reform* when Clinton was president, and over 70 nursing organizations signed it (American Nurses Association, 1991). Its essential elements are providing access to care, ensuring universality of coverage, shifting resources more toward primary care, involving consumers in the decision process, and emphasizing quality. Clinton's major domestic agenda was to pass the Health Security Act. Clinton included nurses in task forces and coalitions with consumers and the business community as well as in the review process developing the Health Security Act. It is generally accepted that the Clinton plan was too complex to pass, but media and market forces were more influential in its defeat than any other single factor.

Since the Clinton era, nursing has become increasingly more visible as well as more vocal in positioning nurses within the policy formulation and implementation arena. This can be attributed to two major factors: first, the endorsement of a presidential candidate, and second, the success gained with obtaining reimbursement for advanced practice nurses. Certainly their endorsement of Barack Obama as a presidential candidate in 2008 brought nursing to the forefront of the public within the nation as well as around the world. Nursing indeed was highly visible during the Obama campaign and even more so after his election.

President Obama made it clear from the beginning that his domestic agenda would have healthcare reform as a major priority and that nursing was part of the solution. Senator Ted Kennedy was another strong proponent of nursing, and he too helped move nursing's agenda to the federal level. *Nursing's Agenda for Health Care Reform*, with some minor adjustments, continues to be the nursing platform. The agenda has also served to some degree to solidify nursing and nurses across specialties and area of practice settings.

Aspects of nursing's agenda were also addressed in several of the recent Institute of Medicine's research studies that addressed quality and safety as well as staffing and workforce preparation, Another factor that may have added to nursing's visibility is the American Nurses Credentialing Center's Magnet Recognition Program, which was recently included in The Joint Commission's accreditation processes (American

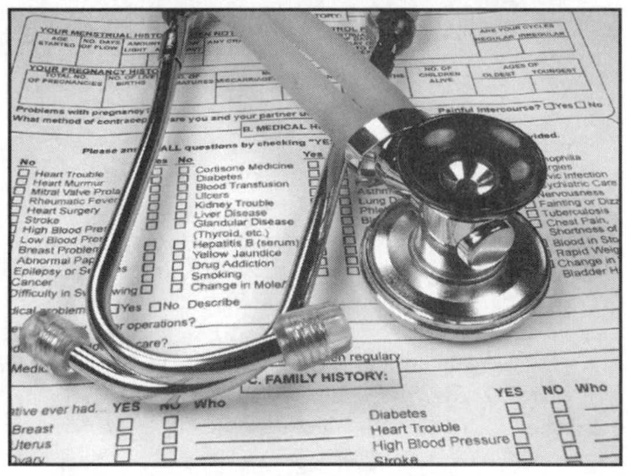

Nurses Credentialing Center, 2010). Thus, it is gratifying that H.R. 3200, to provide affordable, quality health care for all Americans and reduce the growth in healthcare spending, and for other purposes, goes further than any recent legislative initiative in recognizing nursing and its contribution to solving the "health insurance crisis" in this nation. The findings from the recent Gallup Survey, the first of its kind, *Nursing Leadership from Bedside to Boardroom: Opinion Leader's Perceptions,* conducted on behalf of Robert Wood Johnson Foundation, found that opinion leaders from diverse roles and industries believed that nurses have the expertise, knowledge and ability to influence health reform (Robert Wood Johnson Foundation, 2010a). "Nurses are highly trusted sources of healthcare information, but as we look to reform our health system, our nation is not taking advantage of all that nurses have to offer," said Risa Lavizzo-Mourey, MD, MBA, president and CEO of the Robert Wood Johnson Foundation. "This survey shows that opinion leaders recognize that we are squandering opportunities to learn from nurses and implement their ideas. We must build on the widespread trust of nurses' expertise as an essential component in leading and implementing reform" (Robert Wood Johnson Foundation, 2010b).

References

American Nurses Association. (1991). *Nursing's agenda for health care reform* [Brochure]. Washington, DC: Author.

American Nurses Credentialing Center. (2010). *ANCC Magnet recognition program.* Retrieved September 10, 2009, from http://www.nursecredentialing.org/Magnet.aspx

American Nurses Association. (2010). Health system reform. Retrieved February 12, 2010 from http://www.nursingworld.org/MainMenuCategories/HealthcareandPolicyIssues/HealthSystemReform.aspx

Annas, G. (1995). The market vs. medicine. *New England Journal of Medicine, 332,* 745–748.

Blecher, M. B. (1998). Burned on the street. *Hospitals and Health Networks, 72*(5), 22–26.

Center for Studying Health System Change. (1997). The trajectory of managed care. *Issues Brief, 9,* 1.

Centers for Medicaid and Medicare Services. (2010). *CMS information related to the Economic Recovery Act of 2009: Health information technology.* Retrieved February 16, 2010, from http://www.cms.hhs.gov/Recovery/11_HealthIT.asp

Centers for Medicaid and Medicare Services. (n.d.). *Research, statistics, and data systems.* Retrieved February 10, 2010, from http://cms.hhs.gov/home/rsds.asp

Claxton, G., Gabel, J., DiJulio, B., Pickreign, J., Whitmore, H., Finder, B., et al. (2007). Health benefits in 2007: Premium increases fall to an eight-year low, while offer rates and enrollment remain stable. *Health Affairs*, 26(5), 1407–1416.

Davis, M. M., & Rorem, C. R. (1932). *The crisis in hospital finance and other studies in hospital economics*. Chicago: University of Chicago Press.

Eckholm, E. (1994, December 18). The healing process . . . A special report: While Congress remains silent health care transforms itself. *The New York Times,* p. A11.

Eibner, C. (2008). *Economic burden of providing health insurance: How much worse are small firms.* Santa Monica, CA: Kauffman-RAND Institute for Entrepreneurship Public Policy, RAND Corporation. Retrieved February 16, 2010, from http://www.rand.org/pubs/technical_reports/2008/RAND_TR559.pdf

Emery, G., & Emery, J. C. H. (1999). *A young man's benefit: The independent order of odd fellows and sickness insurance in the United States and Canada*. Montreal, Québec: McGill-Queen's University Press.

Fernandez, B. (2005). *Health insurance: A primer.* Washington, DC: Congressional Research Service.

Flexner, A. (1910). *Medical education in the United States and Canada*. New York: Carnegie Foundation for the Advancement of Teaching.

Hall, M. A. (1994). Disclosing rationing decisions: A reply to Paul S. Applebaum. *Milbank Quarterly, 72,* 645.

Henderson, J. W. (2002). *Health economics and policy* (2nd ed.). Cincinnati, OH: South-Western.

Kaiser Family Foundation. (2007). *The Medicare Part D coverage gap: Costs and consequences in 2007*. Retrieved September 20, 2009, from http://www.kff.org/medicare/7811.cfm

Kaiser Family Foundation. (2009). *Kaiser fast facts.* Retrieved September 20, 2009 from http://facts.kff.org

Kaiser Family Foundation. (2010). *State health facts.* Retrieved February 8, 2010, from http://www.statehealthfacts.org/mfs.jsp?rgn=2&rgn=1&x=9&y=10

Kaiser Family Foundation and Health Research and Educational Trust. (2002). *Kaiser/HRET survey of employer-*

sponsored health benefits, 2002. Retrieved February 12, 2010, from http://www.kaisernetwork.org/health_cast/uploaded_files/ACF4D95.pdf

McCormick, R. (1998). The end of Catholic hospitals? *America, 179*(1), 5–12.

Madden, J. M. (2008). Cost-related medication nonadherence and spending on basic needs following implementation of Medicare Part D. *Journal of the American Medical Association*, *299*(16), 1922–1928.

Marmor, T. R. (2000). *The politics of Medicare* (2nd ed.). New York: Aldine de Gruyter.

Newhouse, J. P., Manning, W. G., Duan, N., Morris, C. N., Keeler, E. B., Leibowitz, A., et al. (1987). The findings of the Rand Health Insurance Experiment—a response to Welch et al. *Medical Care, 25,* 157–179.

Numbers, R. L. (1978). Almost persuaded: American physicians and compulsory health insurance, 1912–1920. Baltimore, MD: Johns Hopkins University Press.

Nyman, J. A. (2003). *The theory of demand for health insurance.* Stanford, CA: Stanford University Press.

Reed, L. S. (1947). *Blue Cross and medical service plans.* Washington, DC: U.S. Public Health Service.

Robert Wood Johnson Foundation. (2010a). *Nursing leadership from bedside to boardroom: Opinion leaders' perceptions.* Retrieved February 10, 2010 from http://www.rwjf.org/pr/product.jsp?id=54350

Robert Wood Johnson Foundation. (2010b). *Opinion leaders say nurses should have more influence on health systems and services.* Retrieved February 16, 2010, from http://www.rwjf.org/healthreform/product.jsp?id=55091

Scofea, L. A. (1994, March). The development and growth of employer-provided health insurance. *Monthly Labor Review, 117,* 1–10.

Shaffer, F. A. (1986). *Patient and purse strings.* New York: National League for Nursing.

Starr, P. (1982). *The social transformation of American medicine: The rise of a sovereign profession and the making of a vast industry.* New York: Basic Books, Inc.

State of Illinois. (1919). *Report of the health insurance commission of the state of Illinois.* Springfield, IL: Illinois State Journal Co. Retrieved September 20, 2009, from http://openlibrary.org/works/OL10306882W/Report_of_the_health_Insurance_Commision_of_state_of_Illnois

Thomasson, M. A. (2002, July). From sickness to health: The twentieth-century development of U.S. health insurance. *Explorations in Economic History, 39,* 233–253.

U.S. Census Bureau. (2007). *Health insurance coverage: 2007.* Retrieved February 16, 2010, from http://www.census.gov/hhes/www/hlthins/hlthin07.html

U.S. Congress. Medicare, Medicaid, and SCHIP Extension Act of 2007, S.2499-110th (2007). Retrieved February 11, 2001, from http://www.govtrack.us/congress/bill.xpd?bill=s110-2499&tab=summary

U.S. Department of Health and Human Services. (n.d.). *Medicare.gov.* Retrieved February 16, 2010, from http://www.medicare.gov

CASE STUDY

Public Mores and the "Business of Health Care"

Leah Curtin and Franklin A. Shaffer

The "business of health service delivery" is at odds with long-held and highly cherished public perceptions of health care as a humanitarian service—a resource for individuals and communities in times of need. Case law as well as generally accepted codes of professional ethics support this assumption. Thus, one of the most pervasive and significant problems that providers face vis-à-vis managed care involves public expectations that access to the providers' services will be determined by an individual's need rather than a contractual arrangement between two business entities (or between a business entity and the government). Moreover, the public assumes that once access is gained, treatment is determined by professional assessments of services needed to correct (or at least ameliorate) the patient's medical condition when, in fact, treatment options often are influenced by an intricately worded list of limited benefits and exclusions.

So pervasive is the influence of the market ethos that business language and metaphors have replaced those of medicine among health administrators, physicians, and even nurses (Annas, 1995):

> *The market metaphor leads us to think about medicine in already familiar ways: emphasis is placed on efficiency, profit maximization, customer satisfaction, the ability to pay, planning, entrepreneurship, and competitive models. The ideology of medicine is replaced by the ideology of the marketplace. Trust is replaced by* caveat emptor. *There is no place for the poor and uninsured in the metaphor of the market. Business ethics supplant medical ethics as the practice of medicine becomes corporate. Nonprofit medical*

organizations tend to be corrupted by adopting the values of their for-profit competitors. A management degree becomes at least as important as a medical degree. Public institutions, which by definition cannot compete in the for-profit arena, risk demise, second-class status, or simply privatization.

This language gap—and the distance it connotes between the person who is a patient and the person who is the professional—becomes ever more apparent as the language of managed care evolves. It is the language of a coldly complex business, which confuses patient and professional alike almost as thoroughly as it changes the climate within which they receive and give care (California Medical Association, 1996). The power of language to alter attitudes is unchallenged: This in and of itself is a serious issue for all healthcare professionals (who now are called "providers"). At the very least, changes in language and metaphors presage a change in culture: the collective manifestations of a collective value system.

The social and political aspects of the current situation are defined in terms of the national debate over the economic nature of healthcare services: Are they social goods to be distributed equitably, or are they commodities to be bought and sold in an open market? Although most Americans tend to think of health care as a service necessary for personal well-being, they also tend to support a capitalist ideology that treats health services like any other commodity. Even if healthcare services are commodities, the only valid reference point for evaluating them needs not be the market place. It is possible to conceptualize a compromise. That is, health service delivery's primary purpose need not be solely the generation of wealth (secondary to customer satisfaction, of course)—it could be similar to that of the nation's utility, education, and transportation systems. Their primary function is to support the nation's activities and only secondarily to generate wealth. Public access is protected by law and provided by tax monies, and their quality is both a benefit and a concern for all. In all of these sectors, one can find both not-for-profit and for-profit service providers—some publicly traded, and others not.

If access to healthcare services is in the public's best interests—and few would argue in the contrary—should their provision remain primarily in the private sector? Government has been contracting with the private sector for provision of health services for many years (Medicare and Medicaid) and in recent years has dismantled much of its own delivery system (public health hospitals, the Veteran's Administration, Civilian Health & Medical Program for Uniformed Services [CHAMPUS, a healthcare plan for military dependents and retirees operated by the DoD]). One might question if this is appropriate in view of the unprofitability of many of the most essential services: control of infectious diseases, immunizations, health screening, care of the chronically ill, indigent care, neonatal intensive care, trauma centers for the severely injured, chronic psychiatric care, and so forth. In terms of the competition inherent in a market-based system, is it appropriate for government to contract with low-cost providers who do not subsidize research, who do not educate health professionals, and who do not provide indigent care and/or other costly social burdens? Is it fair to make public hospitals and teaching hospitals and health networks compete for contracts with agencies that have no social duty to absorb the costs of teaching, researching, or caring for the poor?

The California Medical Association reported that California's seven top for-profit managed care organizations (HMOs) spent an average of 74% of premiums on patient care in 1995, whereas their nonprofit counterparts California Kaiser and Group

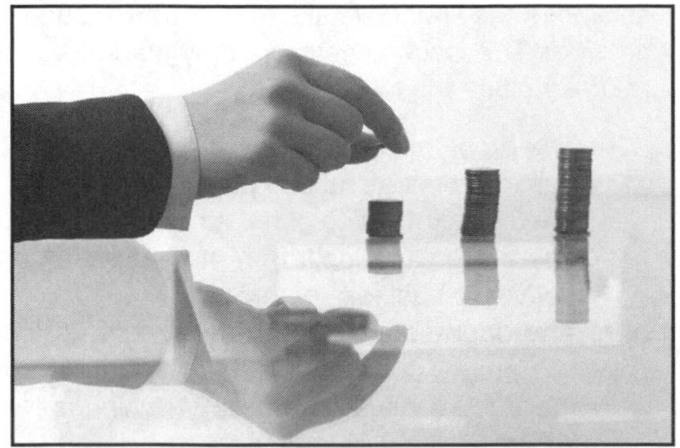

Health of Puget Sound spent 98% and 94%, respectively (Langley, 1998). Few publicly traded health organizations (whether they are managed care entities or for-profit hospital chains) subsidize either education or research, and very few provide indigent care—while they commonly eliminate their unprofitable "product lines." For example, CNN reported on July 7, 1998, that several for-profit HMOs have pulled out of their Medicaid contracts because of unacceptable medical-loss ratios, and this when the nation's 130 public hospitals are in crisis; they have been forced to cut or even eliminate some services entirely, and many will soon be forced to close, despite the disproportionate share funds they receive. *The New York Times* (April 7, 1996) predicted that "cash poor public hospitals and private hospitals serving large numbers of uninsured or those on Medicaid" will most likely be forced to close their doors in the next few years.

This is not to say that nonprofit institutions necessarily do provide unprofitable care: The Daughters of Charity closed all of their inner-city (unprofitable) hospitals while sitting on $2 billion in liquid cash reserves (Warren, 1999). As a people, we are somewhat hypocritical in our attitudes toward for-profit medicine. We complain about for-profit MCOs, but most of us have been quite comfortable with for-profit insurance companies. We resent the profits made by publicly traded managed care and hospital corporations, but we accept with equanimity the profits made by pharmaceutical firms and medical equipment companies. We are alarmed about the growing influence of for-profit hospitals and accept with equanimity, the prevalence, indeed the dominance of, for-profit nursing homes. Is the problem defined in terms of tax status (for-profit *versus* not-for-profit), or is the problem *profiteering* under either tax status? Is the problem far more fundamental—one that pits our ideals against one another: the ideal of care for the sick as a work of charity and the ideal of entrepreneurial capitalism as a function of rugged individualism?

Professional Ethics as a "Provider" Issue

It is perhaps only human to think that the problems faced by one's own generation are unique to it. In some rare cases, this may be so, but in almost anything that has to do with money, there truly is nothing new under the sun. In fact, *The Encyclopedia of Bioethics* devotes considerable space to money, medicine, and conflicts of interest, and the British Medical Association in its 1974 document *Medical Ethics* succinctly summarized the wisdom of the ages on this subject: "A general ethical principle is that a doctor should not associate himself with commerce in such a way as to let it influence, or appear to influence, his attitude toward the treatment of his patients" (Hall, 1994).

Few would disagree, but what is unique about contemporary managed care in the United States is its institutionalization of conflict of interest. For example, Hall contends that managed care plans should be permitted to give physicians financial incentives for rationing resources, even though he stipulates that the incentives should be "reasonable" and that plan participants should be informed of them. Most likely, Hall's argument is based on his previous contention that people who make informed decisions to purchase less expensive health insurance waive their right to be informed of particular decisions not to treat them (Burton, 1998).

Although there is little doubt that the cumulative financial impact of fee-for-service medicine is staggering, few before have suggested that we give physicians and nurse practitioners financial incentives not to treat people. The cumulative impact of common MCO strategies (paying a reduced fee-for-service tied to year-end profit sharing) is just coming to light. A study by the nation's largest managed care company, United HealthCare Corporation, found that many of their doctors routinely fail to prescribe essential drugs and diagnostic tests (Burton, 1998).

Paying healthcare professionals for improving systems, piloting innovative approaches to care delivery, researching less invasive diagnostics and therapeutics, and even doing something really revolutionary such as engaging in prevention and health promotion might save money. "Incentivizing" professionals does not save money; it merely shifts it around (Blecher, 1998). Paying caregivers to ration care at the bedside more than implies that professionals will make clinical decisions based on personal gain rather than on patient need—it relies on it.

Advocacy Versus Stewardship?

If, in fact, many care decisions in the past were based *less* on improving the patient's health than on increasing the provider's wealth leading to massive overutilization, it seems reasonable to assume that creating financial incentives for professionals not to do things for patients will result in equally enormous underutilization—but not necessarily savings. Cost per case has been going up every year, and managed care premiums are going up (even operating revenues among the nation's top HMOs went up an average of 22% last year) (Aaron, 2004), whereas access among the insured and uninsured alike has been going down and public programs such as Medicaid are under financial duress. Critics claim that incentivizing professionals not to treat will lead to a situation in which the money that would have been spent on care will end up in the provider's pocket rather than the public's purse appears to be justified.

Now, in an interesting move, some bioethicians are suggesting that the advocacy model of professional ethics be modified to reflect contemporary circumstances. The primary ethical obligation of the professional would move from patient advocacy to responsible stewardship of society's resources, thus legitimizing the subordination of the patient's best interests to what, in a market-driven economy, amounts to the providers' profit!

Managed Care's Issues

To summarize, the many issues managed care poses for providers and health networks are crystallized in the moral problems occasioned by its shifting of the financial risks of care from insurer to provider. The issues occasioned by market-based reform include the following:

- The problems presented by clashes between public expectations and payer restrictions
- The corporatization of health service delivery and the cultural shift from humanitarian endeavor to business enterprise
- The depersonalization of treatment as time and money constraints stretch resources and the culture rewards efficient "business-like" behavior
- The underfunding of care for the poor and uninsured, even as these populations grow
- The restructuring of care and re-engineering of healthcare roles as the emphasis shifts from quality of care to conservation of resources
- Rapid mergers of both health plans and institutional providers with all the turmoil that represents as rules change, services are eliminated, and support services are minimized to save money
- The unhealthy competition inherent in market-based reform that posits profit-taking and market-share as the measures of successful performance
- The undermining of the professional ethic of advocacy
- The use of incentives that pander to greed and self-interest

The costs of sophisticated technologies and the ongoing care of increasingly fragile patients have pulled many other elements into what previously were considered "privileged" professional interactions. The fact that very few citizens indeed could pay out of their own pockets for the treatment and ongoing care they might need led to social involvement (few people remember that both widespread health insurance and public programs are relatively recent phenomena); however, whether in tax dollars or insurance premiums, other people's money is being spent on the patient's care. Clearly, those "other people" never intended to give either the patient or the professional open-ended access to their collective pocketbooks. Just what form their involvement ought to take is being tested as "managed care" attempts to control the costs. What limits are acceptable to providers: lower profit margins? Quality controls? Acceptable risk levels? What are acceptable limits for patients: restricted choice? Restricted mobility? Restricted access to high tech? What about the general public: decreased access to high tech? Higher taxes? Underserved populations? Abandonment of the sick/poor?

Which "techniques" are acceptable, and which are not: risk sharing with providers? Financial incentives for decision makers? Rationing access? Imposing behavioral parameters? The issues posed by market-based managed care cannot be adequately addressed merely in terms of social resources, nor will answers be found in subordinating human rights to practical materialism. Negotiating ethical guidelines for the "safe" handling of such problems to the good of individuals and of society requires a revitalization of the "old" values: the old commitment to master craftsmanship and altruism, the old emphasis on patient advocacy and human rights. These old values, however, must be applied with the "new" knowledge of lifestyle choices (and thus personal responsibility), likely outcomes (and thus reasonable options), and the limits of success (and thus fair redeployment of health resources) (see Appendix B: Glossary of Managed Care Terminology).

Case Study References

Aaron, H. J. (2004, January 15). The good, the bad and the ugly. *The Washington Spectator, 30.*

Annas, G. (1995). The market vs. medicine. *New England Journal of Medicine, 332,* 745–748.

Blecher, M. B. (1998). Burned on the street. *Hospitals and Health Networks, 72*(5), 22–26.

Burton, T. M. (1998, July 8). United HealthCare Corp finds drugs, tests are often underutilized. *The Wall Street Journal,* p. A1.

California Medical Association. (1996). *Knox-Keene health plan expenditures summary: Fiscal year 1994–1995.* San Francisco, CA: California Medical Association.

Center for Studying Health System Change. (1997). The trajectory of managed care. *Issues Brief, 9,* 1.

Hall, M. A. (1994). Disclosing rationing decisions: A reply to Paul S. Applebaum. *Milbank Quarterly, 72,* 645.

Langley, M. (1998, January 7). Nuns zeal for profits... *The Wall Street Journal,* p. A1.

Rosenthal, E. (1996, April 7). Groups predict New York hospital closings. *New York Times,* A11. Retrieved on February 9, 2010, from http://www.nytimes.com/1996/04/07/nyregion/groups-predict-new –york-hospitals-closings.html?pageswanted=1

Warren, T. (Ed.). (1999). The history of bioethics. *The Encyclopedia of Bioethics.* London: MacMillan.

CASE STUDY

The Advocacy Imperative

Elizabeth Summy

The role of advocacy by organizations has evolved dramatically from the early days when friends would share opinions and resources. Today, advocacy—the act of arguing on behalf of a particular issue, idea, person, or animal—is a highly sophisticated practice and a multimillion dollar enterprise. It exists in many forms: grassroots, the act of engaging those with similar interests around a specific action or agenda; grass tops, the act of teaching those with similar interest (i.e., nurses) about organizing themselves and their message to enhance effectiveness; and net roots, the act/practice of taking an advocacy agenda to and through the Internet in order to spread the message and engage participation through online dialogue and influence. The proliferation of social networking sites is revolutionizing the way people connect. Hospital CEOs are blogging to link the executive suite with the OR suite. Surgeons are "tweeting" from the operating room, and their patients are posting stories about their recovery on Facebook. These are truly unprecedented times.

Although the Internet has flattened the world, just because someone says (or writes) so, does not make it so. In advocacy, influence is predicated on credibility. To be credible one has to have the experience and perspective to explain the facts and tell the stories that provide context to the situation. In healthcare settings, clinicians have tremendous influence among peers, administration, and patients. How and when they choose to use their influence is both learned (through clinical training) and observed (influenced by the culture of an organization). Likewise, institutional providers have influence shaping the context in which clinicians provide care.

With health care emerging as one of the most important national issues, how to address our healthcare challenges will dominate the Congressional agenda and that of state legislatures, to a certain degree, in the upcoming years. It will also be the driver of advocacy agendas for the organizations that represent the providers and consumers of health care. In this case, examples of advocacy related to hospitals will be given from an organization that takes a system perspective and from engaged practitioners who take are concerned with the provision of care.

The American Hospital Association: Advocacy for System Change

For organizations, influence is "peddled" in many different ways. One of the most important is associations that represent a constituency with a shared mission. The role of advocacy by such associations has grown dramatically as the stakes for resources, prestige, and influence have grown. The members of these associations count on them to track issues that may impact their profession or the industry in which they work. Likewise the associations count on their members as being among their greatest assets. The credibility of a nurse talking with a legislator about how a particular bill will impact his or her work is very powerful. When that same nurse speaks on behalf of thousands of nurses and thousands of healthcare organizations, the voice is magnified. Understanding the environment and representing the interests of the people served are at the core of advocacy.

The American Hospital Association (AHA) is one of the oldest representative organizations in the health care sector. Organized in 1898, by a small group of hospital "superintendents" (the original terms for hospital directors) the AHA was initially a venue for the group to share among its members information and gather new ideas. While many groups are formally organized and recognized for their efforts on behalf of hospitals, the AHA is the largest. The AHA membership includes 5,717 hospitals, health systems, and postacute care organizations. It represents the majority of the nation's hospitals (public, private, not-for-profit, and special).

For nearly 115 years, the AHA has been a leader or contributor for a number of key activities that have shaped the healthcare field and hospital environment. Since the 1930s when the AHA played a key role in the organization of hospital insurance through Blue Cross, to the 1960s when the AHA's support was critical to the passage of Medicare to the present discussion of health care reform, the AHA has been at the fore of most key changes in the financing and delivery of care. Many think of the AHA as an influential lobby, which it is, but it is also a convener of conversations and content. It has played a variety of roles over the years in the identification of practices to improve hospital care and delivery through dialogue, advocacy, and dissemination of best practices. A "society of healthy communities where individuals reach their highest potential for health" is the vision behind the work of professional staff in Washington, DC and Chicago. Staff in Washington is focused on policy, communications, and partnerships to advance the interests of hospitals before Congress and the Executive Branch. The Chicago presence, lesser known but no less significant, focuses on serving members, both institutional and personal, through education, research, and publishing. The hospital advocacy agenda is really a cycle of activities that span a continuum from practice to legislation back to practice.

Advocacy is the strong voice that the AHA lends to the field. At the core of any advocacy activity is the desire to shape legislation and regulation the implementation of which affects the operations of an organization that provides feedback to inform policy and, ultimately, influences legislative and regulation. To illustrate, the AHA advocacy agenda focuses on legislation (i.e., reauthorization of the Children's Health Insurance Program) or regulation (i.e., Schedule H implementation). After passed or implemented, the AHA prepares the field for implementation through education, tools, and resources. It stays close to the field through conversations and gathers feedback to identify and inform other conversations about policy. These insights from the field are synthesized and embedded in the policy, which is used to influence the legislative or regulatory landscape, and the cycle starts all over again. The AHA represents a strong future through work on long-term system reform. It builds stronger, more efficient, and more effective acute care delivery through performance improvement activities.

Nurses Transforming Care at the Bedside: Advocacy for Quality Care

Another approach to improving the delivery of care can be seen in the project, Transforming Care at the Bedside (TCAB) is a joint effort by the Robert Wood Johnson Foundation and the Institute for Healthcare Improvement. Begun in 2001, it is a deliberate effort to engage nurses at the bedside in improving the quality of care that they deliver. The approach is intended to address the many serious problems in health care that were identified in the Institute of Medicine report "Crossing the Quality Chasm."

At its core, TCAB is about transformation, innovation, and engagement—of nurses, patients and families, and healthcare leadership. The principles for engagement are rooted in the science of high reliability, which calls on organizations to actively "seek to know what they don't know." Organizations must place a priority on learning, communication, and systems thinking. This means tracking small failures, resistance to oversimplification, sensitivity to operations, capacity for resilience, and deference to expertise, even as it shifts in the organization (Weick & Sutcliffe, 2007). Highly reliable organizations know that they are vulnerable to failures, but they work hard and smart to avoid failure while preparing for it so that they can minimize the impact.

Since inception, the TCAB has relied on the nurses and staff closest to the process to redesign the work to reduce waste. By reducing waste, nurses are able to spend more time at the bedside. Comprised of nurses, TCAB teams focus on three things: (1) generating innovative ideas to improve the safety and reliability of care, increase patient-centeredness of care, and shift staff effort from work of low value to patients to work of high value; (2) focusing on building effective care teams; and (3) developing systems that enhance the timeliness, reliability, and efficiency of delivering quality care (Robert Wood Johnson Foundation and the Institute for Healthcare Improvement, 2005).

TCAB is just one example that highlights the influence of nurses and their contributions to the success of a hospital. Numerous associations represent the professional interests of the nursing profession. These concepts of quality must also become integrated into the agenda of large membership organizations like the AHA. At their formation, all associations were created to share and gather ideas from others about their professional interests. Associations affirm the notion that the influence of many is more powerful than the interest of one. It is in that collection of ideas and perspectives that change can take root. It is important for nurses to embrace the notion that they can "lead where they are."

The Future of Advocacy for Acute Care Delivery/Hospitals

In a 2008, the Joint Commission issued a report containing guiding principles and actions for hospitals of the future in meeting care delivery challenges. The report recommended action in five core areas: economic viability (i.e., need to align performance and payment systems to meet quality and efficiency related goals), technology (i.e., make the business case and provide sustainable funding to support the widespread adoption of health information technology, patient-centered care (i.e., make adoption of patient-centered care values a priority for improving patient safety and patient and staff satisfaction), staffing (i.e., develop professional knowledge and skills necessary in a more complex healthcare environment), and hospital design (i.e., improve safety with evidence-based design principles and design flexibility in to the building to accommodate advances in medicine and technology) (The Joint Commission, 2008).

We are at the crossroads of decisions that we have never had to make before. The growth in healthcare costs cannot be sustained. In the history of health care, fundamental change has come about because of consumer demand (access), environmental factors (post-WWII recovery and the current recession), or financial incentives (both market and government driven). The shape of these decisions requires advocacy on the part of those who best understand what is required to provide to provide quality care to patients in a context that can be sustained.

References

The Joint Commission. (2008, November). *Healthcare at the crossroads: Guiding principles for the development of the hospital of the future.* Retrieved from http://www.aramarkhealthcare.com/RelatedFiles/JC_Hosptal_Future.pdf

Robert Wood Johnson Foundation and the Institute for Healthcare Improvement. (2005). *A new era in nursing: Transforming care at the bedside.* Retrieved from http://www.rwjf.org/pr/product.jsp?id=15704&topicid=1252

Weick, K., & Sutcliffe, K. (2007). *Managing the unexpected: Resilient performance in the age of uncertainty.* New York: John Wiley and Sons.

Section V

Drivers

Chapter 12

Advancing the Use of Technology in the Organization and Delivery of Health Care

Diane J. Skiba and Donna Dulong

OVERVIEW

This chapter describes a grassroots initiative that harnessed the intellectual and social capital of numerous professional specialty organizations in nursing to advance an informatics agenda. This example illustrates how social and intellectual capital can be used to create a critical mass and influence policy decisions. A case study using nursing education stakeholder organizations illustrates the policy implications of this grassroots initiative. The chapter concludes with some strategies for success that can be applied to other initiatives.

OBJECTIVES

- To distinguish between the terms social and intellectual capital
- To articulate the TIGER vision
- To identify how intellectual and social capital were influential in advancing an informatics agenda
- To outline strategies for success to influence policy development

KEY TERMS

- ❑ Grassroots organizing
- ❑ Informatics
- ❑ Intellectual capital
- ❑ Social capital
- ❑ Technology Informatics Guiding Education Reform (TIGER)

The notion of harnessing intellectual and social capital is not new. These concepts repeatedly appear in literature about organizations, business development, leadership, community development, and social policy. The goal of this chapter is to explicate how a grassroots effort, the Technology Informatics Guiding Education Reform (2007) (TIGER) Initiative, harnessed the social and intellectual capital of professional nursing organizations to unify the voice of nursing and move forward an informatics agenda. The informatics agenda was to prepare the current and future nursing workforce with the necessary knowledge and skills to work in an ever-increasing informatics intensive and consumer-centric healthcare environment.

It is important to first define and explicate the principles that underlie intellectual and social capital. In the past, human, physical and financial resources were most often mentioned as value assets of any organization. These resources were tangible and seemingly easy to manage, but as we enter a more knowledge-driven society with more complexity, other forms of capital are surfacing as valuable assets in an organization (Landry et al., 2000). One such asset is intellectual capital. It is defined as "the collective knowledge of individuals in an organization or society. This knowledge can be used to produce wealth, multiply output of physical assets, gain competitive advantage, and/or to enhance value of other types of capital. Intellectual capital includes customer capital, human capital, intellectual property, and structural capital" (BusinessDictionary.com, 2010).

Organizations that value intellectual capital recognize that individuals need to be cultivated to develop continuously their knowledge and share that knowledge not internally but externally to the larger discipline or community. The sharing of knowledge benefits not only the community but also the individual organization (Nahapiet & Ghoshal, 1998).

It is important to harness intellectual capital for the benefit of society. This is where the concept of social capital comes into play. "Social scientists have used the concept of social capital to highlight the pivotal nature of relationships" (DiCicco-Bloom et al., 2007, p. 13). Social capital was initially used to understand how social relations impacted the growth and survival of communities and cities (Putnam, 2000). More recently, the concept is being applied to smaller collectives of individuals or organizations; "social capital consists of the stock of active connections among people; the trust, mutual understanding and shared values and behaviors that bind the members of human networks and communities and make cooperative action possible" (Cohen & Prusak, 2001). They go on to describe "social networks as incubators of collaboration, especially voluntary collaboration that does not rely on external incentives to spur it on" (Skiba & Dulong, 2008, p. 16).

Perhaps the best way to explain the importance of both intellectual and social capital is to understand that both are new currency of modern times. Organizations thrive when the two function well together. "The new currency of the Internet Age isn't simply intellectual capital; it's *social capital*—the collective value of the people we know and what we'll do for each other. When social connections are strong and numerous there's more trust, reciprocity, information flow, collective action, and even happiness" (Baker, 2000, cited in Kouzes & Posner, 2003, p. 71).

Catalyst for the TIGER Initiative

The field of healthcare informatics and the use of clinical systems have quietly been in existence since the early 1970s. Clinical information systems were being developed and implemented in a variety of healthcare facilities throughout the world. In 1976, Dr. Judith Ronald (1979) at the State University of New York in Buffalo offered the first course on computers in nursing. Over the next decade, several schools of nursing followed suit and offered such classes. In the early 1980s, the importance of health informatics was recognized by the profession, and there was a call for all nurses to have computer literacy skills (Ronald, 1983; Ronald & Skiba, 1987; Skiba, 1983). In that same decade, the first graduate programs in nursing informatics were started (Romano & Heller, 1990), along with the growing acceptance of the term informatics in the healthcare community. What followed was the continued development of informatics as a specialty and numerous studies identifying informatics competencies for nurses (Staggers et al., 2001). These studies identified the lack of integration of informatics into the education and clinical practices of nurses. They called on educators to include these competencies in the curriculum (McNeil et al., 2003; Thompson & Skiba, 2008). Despite these early efforts, there is still relatively little emphasis on informatics in nursing education. The intellectual capital or individual knowledge from a growing informatics community to explicate the need for informatics competencies for all nurses existed, but there was not the critical mass or social capital to push this agenda forward. Thus, work continued over the next 30 years with little recognition by the larger healthcare community and the nursing profession in particular.

At the turn of the new century, a set of driving forces converged, serving as a major catalyst for the informatics agenda. The idea that all healthcare professionals must have necessary "21st century knowledge and skills for practice in a complex, emerging technologically sophisticated, consumer-centric, global environment" (Warren & Connors, 2007, p. 58) began to emerge. The top two driving forces were the Institute of Medicine (IOM) reports and the creation of the Office of the National Coordinator of Health Information Technology and its federal mandate *The Decade of Health Information Technology.*

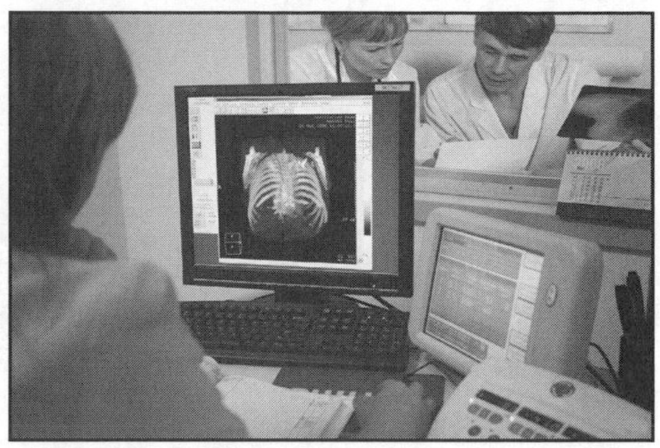

IOM

Since 2000, the IOM consistently highlighted the use of health information technologies as one solution for insuring safe and quality health care. Various reports have called on the healthcare delivery system to implement the effective use of health information technologies. Starting with the IOM's report, *To Err Is Human* (Kohn et al., 2000), the use of appropriate technologies was one recommended solution to reduce errors and ensure patient safety. As a follow-up, *Patient Safety, Achieving a New Standard of Care* (Aspden et al., 2004) spoke to the establishment of a national health information infrastructure and the use of electronic health records (EHRs) as a prerequisite to achieving patient safety as a standard of care. According to the report, "a national health information infrastructure is needed (1) to provide immediate access to complete patient information and decision support tools for clinicians and their patients and (2) to capture patient safety information as a by-product of care and use this information to design even safer delivery systems" (Aspden et al., 2004, p. 45). In addition, the report recommended "a secure platform for the exchange of patient information across healthcare settings, and data standards to make that information understandable to all users" (Aspden et al., 2004, p. 7).

In *Crossing the Quality Chasm* (IOM, 2001), there was general consensus that the current healthcare system was in need of massive reform. It stated throughout the report that in order to achieve this reform, healthcare systems must demonstrate their "effective use of information technologies to automate clinical information and make it readily accessible to patients and all members of the care team" (IOM, 2001 p. 12). Another recommendation was that healthcare systems needed an "improved information infrastructure to establish effective and timely communication among clinicians and between patients and clinicians" (IOM, 2001, p. 12). This report highlighted not only to the need for electronic health records but also the use of communication tools and personal health records to foster communication between patients and clinicians.

Perhaps the most compelling report for educators was the *Health Professions Education: A Bridge to Quality*. This report recommended the following goal: "All health professionals should be educated to deliver patient-centered care as members of an interdisciplinary team, emphasizing evidence-based practice, quality improvement approaches and informatics" (Greiner & Knebel, 2003, p. 3). To achieve this goal, all healthcare professionals must have the following five core competencies: provide patient-centered care, work in interdisciplinary teams, employ evidence-based practice, apply quality improvement, and use informatics. In this report, informatics tools were considered essential for communication, management of information and knowledge, mitigation of error, and support for decision making and healthcare interventions. In reality, an informatics infrastructure is a necessary prerequisite to achieve the four core competencies of evidence-based practice, quality improvement, patient-centered care, and team work.

These reports, individually and collectively, served to raise healthcare professionals and the public's awareness of the value of health information technology. The report focusing on the education of healthcare professionals caught the attention of healthcare institutions, academia, state boards of nursing, professional organizations, and foundations that grant monies specifically to health care. One foundation in particular, Robert Wood Johnson, funded an initiative in 2005 called the Quality and Safety Education for Nurses that developed knowledge, skills, and attitude competencies for prelicensure nursing students (Cronenwett et al., 2007.

Decade of Health Information Technology

Another driving force was the creation of the Office of the National Coordinator of Health In-

formation Technology in 2004. Through an executive order, President Bush created this office to address the use of health information technology as part of healthcare reform. The former Secretary of Health and Human Services Tommy Thompson stated, "We have reached a tipping point as far as technology is concerned. I think, finally, healthcare technology has arrived. We are reaching that critical mass where people are now starting to focus on the fact that technology is actually here for the practice of medicine." He went on to say, "Virtually every other sector of the economy is charging ahead into the 21st century, it's time for health care to catch up." To achieve this, an agenda was set to establish the Decade of Health Information Technology. The agenda included a strategic plan that set four major goals to be accomplished by 2014. These goals included the following:

- Inform clinicians by encouraging the widespread adoption of EHRs
- Interconnect clinicians so that data and information can be more easily shared
- Personalize care through the use of personal health records and telehealth
- Improve public health through accessible information

These strategic goals focused primarily on adoption of technologies by physicians. The acknowledgment of other healthcare professionals and the importance that health informatics to their practice appeared to be limited if any.

TIGER: The Grassroots Effort

Several leaders in informatics and nursing attended the Department of Health and Human Services kickoff conference for the Office of the National Coordinator of Health Information Technology. It appeared that nurses almost 3 million strong and the largest percentage of

healthcare professionals in a healthcare labor force were not considered an integral part of the Office of the National Coordinator of Health Information Technology's strategic plan. Thus, the birth of the TIGER Initiative occurred on July 21, 2004. As Warren and Connors (2007, p. 58) stated, TIGER was created in response to "nursing not being on the radar screen when the Decade of Health Information Technology was released in 2004." This grassroots effort's initial vision was to ensure that nursing was at the table as health information technologies were integrated into the healthcare delivery system.

The initial grassroots leaders surveyed their social networks to determine who should attend an initial meeting. The first official TIGER meeting was held in January of 2005 at John Hopkins University School of Nursing. This meeting, initiated by Dr. Marion Ball, brought together informatics professionals from academia, health care organizations, and industry to determine TIGER's next steps. At this meeting, Dr. Angela McBride remarked that although the informatics community had many accomplishments, it was an insular community that had not reached out to the larger nursing community whose interests could be easily brought into alignment. This remark planted the seed: If nursing was to be represented, it was necessary to bring together a critical mass to influence policy decisions. The informatics agenda would have to include the power of nursing and represent the 3 million nurses. TIGER needed to include not only these professional nursing organizations but needed to harness the power of their social network to move the agenda.

An invitation summit was selected as the mechanism to coalesce the professional nursing community. The summit was designed to bring together leaders from professional nursing organizations and their social capital—the nurses who were members of these specialty organizations. The summit would create a sense of urgency and call on the leadership of these professional organizations to ensure a common goal: that all nurses are able to provide safe, effective, and patient-centered care to all. This common goal served as the foundation for the preparation of nurses to use health information technology tools in the provision of safe, effective, and patient-centered care.

The TIGER leaders solicited the support of the IOM to ensure that the summit would garner the attention of healthcare policy makers. TIGER wanted the results of the summit to be the next publication in the IOM series on transforming health. TIGER wanted to use IOM's national and international stature as an influential organization to support nursing work to transform patient care through the use of health information technology. Although a successful proposal was approved by the IOM, funds were not secured within their timeframe. This was a setback as the momentum for TIGER was growing. A fund raising committee raised monies to host an invitational summit at the end of October in 2006. There were 26 sponsors that contributed funds, and grants were received from the Agency for HealthCare Research & Quality, Robert Wood Johnson, and the National Library of Medicine. (For a complete listing of sponsors, go to http://www.tigersummit.com/Sponsors.html.) The results of the summit, however, were not going to be published in the IOM's series of healthcare reports.

The TIGER Summit

The invitational summit was held at the end of October in 2006. Over 100 participants attended the 2-day event held at the Uniformed Health Services University in Bethesda, Maryland. The members of Nursing Organization Alliance served as an initial list of invitees. The summit invited elected leaders (chair, president, or their designees) or executive directors of other professional nursing organizations, elected leaders of the health informatics and nursing informatics specialty organizations, representatives from key federal agencies (Veteran's Administration, Military, and Division of Nursing, Health Services Resources Administration), and industry and related organizations (National Library of Medicine, the American Dietetics Association). The invitations were governed by one rule—there needed to be more nursing leaders than informatics professionals in attendance.

The range of nursing organizations represented at the conference was impressive. It included the 39 specialty organizations represented by the American Academy of Nursing, various nurse practitioner organizations, and leaders from medical surgical nursing, critical care, neuroscience, nurse anesthetists, nurse executives, long-term care nurse administrators, perianesthesia and perioperative nurses, women's health, oncology, clinical nurse specialists, infusion, forensic, emergency room, vascular, and insurance nursing specialty organizations. The National League for Nursing, the American Association of Colleges of Nursing, the American Nursing Association, the National Council of State Boards of Nursing, and Sigma Theta Tau were also represented. More than one leader commented that this was a historic meeting in which so many leaders from nursing were gathered to craft an agenda. (For a complete listing of participants, go to http://www.tigersummit.com/Summit_Attendees.html.)

External facilitators from Bonfire Communications were hired to conduct open-space facilitation that included small and large group dialogues, graphic recording of all decisions, and the use of audience response technologies to reach group consensus.

Structured learning experiences were used to create a shared knowledge base and to prepare everyone for interactive group sessions to create the vision and action plans. The structured learning experiences included a gallery walk and presentation of case studies of innovative work in practice and education. The gallery walk is an inquiry-directed learning experience in which small groups reviewed state-of-the-art demonstrations of health information technology.

Throughout the 2-day summit, consensus was reached on a vision, a 3- and 10-year action plan. To support the vision, seven key foci were identified within the healthcare ecosystem. These key "pillars" are both interdependent and essential for creating an environment that will enable nurses to use informatics to provide safer, higher quality care. They included the following: communication and collaboration, leadership and management, education, information design, information technology, culture, and policy. During the summit, participants engaged in conversation around these pillars with certain underlying assumptions in place: (1) The "practice" of nurses is in reference to "point of care" services that nurses provide across the continuum of care (home, hospital, ambulatory, long-term care, etc.), and (2) the "education" of nurses is in reference to all nursing preparation (all degree preparation and specific role preparation [e.g., advance practice nurses]). (For more information about the pillars, go to http://www.tigersummit.com/Pillars.html.)

At the end, each leader was asked to identify action plan goals that could be accomplished by their particular organization. Each leader signed the Commitment Wall, acknowledging their pledge to share the work of this summit and to promote that the TIGER action plans be incorporated into their organization's strategic goals.

The intent was to build on the intellectual capital of the various organizations, and to mobilize the social capital in order to develop a vision and action plan and ensure collectively that nurses were prepared for the decade of health information technology. The overall mission was to strengthen the voice of nursing in this transformation of the healthcare delivery system. The plan was then to use the social networks of these specialty organizations to disseminate the work of the TIGER Summit and to harness the social capital of the professional organizations to advance an informatics agenda. This was no longer just an agenda being espoused by informatics professionals but one that was supported by the profession of nursing. The first step to achieving a critical mass was accomplished.

The TIGER SUMMIT Report

The work of the summit was widely disseminated in its report *Evidence and Informatics Transforming Nursing: 3-Year Action Steps toward a 10-Year Vision*. The TIGER vision is to enable nurses to use informatics tools, principles, theories, and practices to make healthcare safer, more effective, efficient, patient centered, timely, and equitable by interweaving enabling technologies transparently into nursing practice and education, making information technology the stethoscope for the 21st century. (For more information about the vision, go to http://www.tigersummit.com/Vision.html.)

The expected outcomes were to establish guidelines for organizations to follow as they integrate informatics knowledge, skills, and abilities into academic and practice settings and set an agenda whereby the nursing organizations specify what they plan to do to bridge the quality chasm via information technology strategies. The TIGER Initiative "aims to enable practicing nurses and nursing students to fully engage in the unfolding digital era of health care. The purpose of the initiative is to identify information/ knowledge management best practices and effective technology capabilities for nurses. TIGER's goal is to create and disseminate local and global action plans that can be duplicated within the nursing and other multidisciplinary healthcare education and practice settings" (The TIGER Initiative: Evidence and Informatics Transforming Nursing: 3-Year Action Steps toward a 10-Year Vision, 2007).

The report not only described the summit, but set forth a series of recommendations for various audiences: professional nursing organizations, nursing education, information technology vendors, government and policy makers, healthcare delivery organization, health information management professionals, and health sciences librarians. (These recommendations and action plans are available at http://www.tigersummit.com/Action_Plan.html.)

TIGER: Moving from Grassroots Organizing to Action

Six months after the summit, phase II of TIGER was initiated. In this phase, TIGER needed to better leverage the work of the professional organizations. To accomplish this leverage, nine collaboratives were created to address the recommendations. These nine TIGER collaboratives were work groups organized from the participating TIGER organizations to complete the TIGER Summit recommended activities. Each collaborative was assigned co-leaders, including one from the nursing and one from the informatics community. To best illustrate the continued use of intellectual and social capital to move the informatics agenda, the Education Collaborative will be used as an example. Dr. Mary Anne Rizzolo from the National League for Nursing and Diane Skiba, University of Colorado Denver College of Nursing Health Care Informatics Coordinator, served as co-chairs of the Education Collaborative. (To read more about the work of other collaboratives established as a result of the TIGER Summit, go to http://www.tigersummit.com/Home_Page.html.)

Faculty Development and Education Collaborative Case Study

One of the pillars important to the overall vision of TIGER was education. During the TIGER Summit, a vision statement was created and approved for the education pillar. The vision statement is to create "collaborative learning communities that maximize the possibilities of technology toward knowledge development and dissemination, driving rapid deployment and implementation of best practices." In addition, the key actions related to the education pillar were voted on and prioritized. The key actions were as follows:

- Reform the nursing curriculum through integration of information technology, information literacy, and informatics and the infusion of technologies for learning (65%).
- Seek funding to develop and implement learning innovations, foster faculty development, and ensure necessary infrastructure (41%).
- Identify, model, and implement collaborative partnerships among public and private academic, service, and industry enterprises (40%).
- Increase faculty acceptance of technology through education and training, incentives, and necessary supports (38%).

- Convene a national group to develop strategies for the recruitment, retention, and training of current and future workforces in informatics education, practice, and research (37%).

As you can see, there was strong support for the first key action. To achieve these key actions, the TIGER Report specifically established the following recommendations for academic institutions (The TIGER Initiative: Evidence and Informatics Transforming Nursing: 3-Year Action Steps toward a 10-Year Vision, 2007):

1. Adopt informatics competencies for all levels of nursing education (undergraduate/graduate) and practice (generalist/specialist).
2. Encourage faculty to participate in faculty development program in informatics.
3. Develop a school task force /committee to examine the integration of informatics throughout the curriculum.
4. Encourage the Health Services Resources Administration Division of Nursing to continue and expand its support for informatics specialty programs and faculty development.
5. Measure baseline and changes in informatics knowledge among nursing educators and students and among the full range of clinicians seeking continuing education.
6. Collaborate with industry and service partners to support faculty creativity in the design, acceptance, and adoption of informatics technology.
7. Develop strategies to recruit, retain, and train current and future nurses in the areas of informatics education, practice, and research.

The TIGER Summit put together a list of recommendations for action steps that could be achieved within the next 3 years and would help to bring about the TIGER vision. To address specifically the education pillar and its recommendations, a Faculty Development and Education Collaborative was formed. This collaborative would solicit volunteers from the academic professional organizations and the academic community. The Education and Faculty Development Collaborative Team was formed to identify innovative academic educational programs that are preparing the nursing work force to use technology and information systems better to provide safer, more effective, more efficient, and patient-centered care. TIGER as an entity would provide the infrastructure necessary to allow this collaborative to work as a team, including monthly conference calls, tools to create educational web and audio conferences, editorial and publishing support, and assistance with opportunities to present these topics at national conferences.

To guide the Faculty Development and Education Collaborative, the following objectives were formulated:

1. Use the informatics competencies, theories, research, and practice examples throughout nursing curriculums.
2. Create programs and resources to develop faculty with informatics knowledge, skill, and ability and measure the baseline and changes in informatics knowledge among nurse educators and nursing students.
3. Develop a task force to examine the integration of informatics throughout the curriculum.
4. Develop strategies to recruit, retain, and train current and future nurses in the areas of informatics education, practice, and research.
5. Improve and expand existing nursing/clinical/health informatics education programs.

6. Encourage the existing Health Services Resources Administration Division of Nursing to continue and expand its support for informatics specialty programs and faculty development.
7. Encourage foundations to start programs that provide funding for curriculum development, research, and practice in nursing informatics and information technology adoption.
8. Collaborate with industry and service partners to support faculty creativity in the adoption of informatics technology and offer informatics tools within the curriculum.

To address these objectives, several smaller workgroups were formed. Many of these groups were established within existing organizations as a way to advance the informatics agenda within the policy making sphere of the organization. The workgroups were as follows: State Boards of Nursing, the National League for Nursing, the American Association of Colleges of Nursing, State Initiatives, the National Organization for Associate Degree Nursing, the Health Services Resources Administration Faculty Development Initiative, and other specialty organizations. These work groups maximized the intellectual capital of the members and also used their social capital to garner feedback and disseminate ideas. Figure 12-1 shows a sampling of the workgroup accomplishments.

The National League for Nursing workgroup, for example, is within the National League for Nursing task group structure to move the informatics agenda. The workgroup surveyed faculty and deans to assess their integration of informatics in the nursing curriculum (Thompson & Skiba, 2008). They were also very involved in surveying the literature and starting work to create a toolkit for faculty to learn more about informatics integration into the nursing curriculum. Perhaps the most significant accomplishment was the release of the National League for Nursing's Position Statement. This statement, *Preparing the Next Generation of Nurses to Practice in a Technology-Rich Environment: An Informatics Agenda*, echoes TIGER's message and delineated specific recommendations for faculty, administrators of nursing educational programs, and the National League for Nursing itself. The position statement is being quoted and used by a variety of nursing professionals to ensure that nursing education as well as staff development begins to prepare nurses to practice in the current and emerging healthcare delivery system. (To read the position statement, go to http://www.nln.org/aboutnln/PositionStatements/index.htm.)

The American Association of Colleges of Nursing were drawn into the work of TIGER through an invitation to a presummit event and were exposed to the gallery walk. The purpose was to garner their support and to make them aware of emerging technologies being used by nurses in practice. This exposure and involvement in TIGER, as well as other factors, catalyzed their decisions to include informatics in the essentials documents of both the doctoral and baccalaureate levels of education.

The State Initiatives workgroup was comprised of members from various states who met to examine how various nursing education infrastructures could be useful to move the informatics agenda. In North Carolina, the State Board of Nursing in collaboration with schools of nursing was pushing the incorporation of the IOM's five core competencies that includes informatics to be an integral component of prelicensure nursing education. In Minnesota, a Minnesota TIGER was instituted to promote the informatics agenda. In Massachusetts and California, both states had successful initiatives focused on the use simulation as an educational technology to facil-

Figure 12-1 A sampling of TIGER workgroup accomplishments.

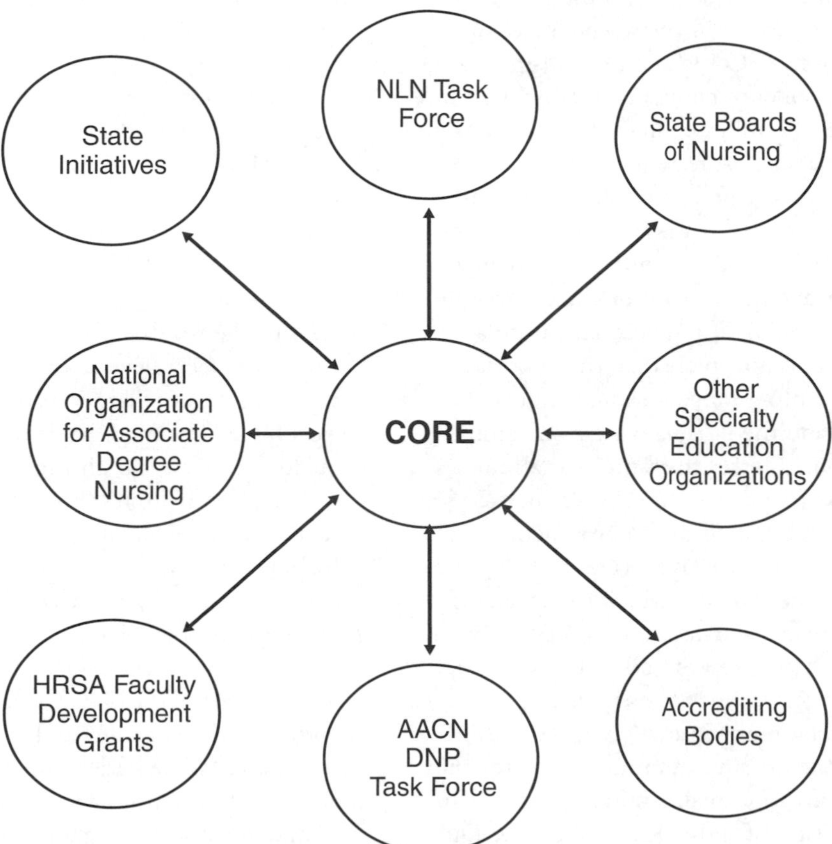

itate nursing education. Given the success of their state initiatives, a ready-made infrastructure existed to tackle the broader informatics agenda.

The Faculty Development and Education Collaborative sponsored two webinars that highlighted approaches to incorporating informatics into the nursing curriculum and creative partnerships to provide nursing students with access to electronic documentation and EHR systems. In the first webinar, several hundred faculty members attended to hear how three different schools (University of Iowa, Indiana University, and Vanderbilt University) addressed the incorporation of informatics into the nursing curriculum. In the second webinar, three different partnerships demonstrated how schools were able to connect to partners and provide their students with access to clinical documentation and EHR systems. At Maricopa Community College, the nursing department partnered with the computer science department to create an electronic documentation system for their associate degree nursing students. At Ball State University, the School of Nursing, in partnership with a local hospital, Ball Memorial Hospital, was able to provide students with access to their EHR system in the school's learning laboratory. The last was a partnership between University of Kansas and Cerner Corporation. In this partnership, the school of nursing was instrumental in redesigning the EHR system to mimic the workflow of a baccalaureate student.

These are just a few examples of how this TIGER grassroots effort was able to capitalize on the intellectual capital from numerous organizations and academic institutions and leverage their social capital to promote an informatics agenda. There is now more than the informatics community calling for educational reform. The informatics and the nursing education community have joined forces to ensure that all nurses are prepared to practice in an ever-increasing technology-rich healthcare environment. "The success of the TIGER Initiative will depend largely upon the extent to which the social capital of the broader nursing community is leveraged. The shared values and rules for social conduct expressed in personal relationships, trust, and a common sense of 'civic' responsibility within the nursing community creates the 'common voice' and makes nursing more than just a collection of individuals" (Skiba & Dulong, 2008, p. 16).

Strategies for Success

Throughout the work of TIGER, several strategies promoted the success of this initiative. These strategies for success can serve as a guide for others that want to harness the power of intellectual and social capital to influence policy decisions.

1. Clearly identify the beneficiary of the policy. In the case of the TIGER Initiative, the beneficiary was the entire nursing workforce. Historically, nursing informatics specialists have been pursuing better education for nurses in selected areas related to technology and informatics, but this message and agenda had to reach the entire nursing population, not just the nursing informatics specialists. Because the beneficiary of the TIGER Initiative represented the largest sector of the healthcare workforce, it was a policy that could affect millions of constituents and was therefore significant for policy makers. In addition, if successful, the results of the TIGER Initiative could be relevant to all healthcare clinicians, an even larger sector of the U.S. workforce. The magnitude of the impact made it easier to reach high-level policy makers, as the relevance to their constituents was articulated.
2. Include stakeholders from all areas that are potentially impacted by the policy. This includes the beneficiaries. Their buy-in from the start of the effort will be critical to the success of the policy, as it will be important to demonstrate to the policy makers that all stakeholders are represented. For the TIGER Initiative, it was difficult to find one nursing organization that was truly representative of the needs of all nursing professionals. Historically, nurses participate in professional organizations that are linked to their specialty practice (e.g., nurse executives, perioperative, perianesthesia, critical care, emergency department, med-surg, clinical nurse specialists, and oncology). Each of these different nursing specialties represented different intellectual and social capital. In organizing the TIGER summit, it was critical to have representation from all of the nursing specialty organizations. In addition, each of these organizations represented the oppor-

tunity to reach as many as 50,000 additional nurses within their respective membership. The TIGER Initiative was a grassroots effort with minimal funding. Thus, the best way to impact the largest group of nurses was to include a high-level representative (president or officer) from each of the nursing professional organizations and ask for a commitment to take the shared vision back to their respective organizations. The vision ultimately represented all nursing stakeholders. By including them in the development of the vision and action plan the credibility of the agenda was established within their respective organizations.

3. Involve experts in the development of the policy. This is the only way to accelerate the development of a policy, and you want to use the best advice available in developing a plan. Eventually, policy makers call on experts to evaluate the quality of the policy, and thus, it is important that you know the state of knowledge in the field from the start. In the TIGER Collaborative teams, it was critical to pair nursing specialty experts with nursing informatics experts to develop a message and action plan that resonated with the specialty organization members. To help establish criteria for the nursing education accrediting agencies, it was critical to work within the organizations to help achieve their strategic goals as well.
4. Establish the common mission/goal and values. This is why the stakeholders become and remain engaged. Focus on an issue that reaches the most people in terms of the way they conceptualize the field and that has emotional meaning to these stakeholders. In the case of the TIGER Initiative, it was clear that health care needed to be reformed using a framework of information technology, but it was essential for nursing to be at the table helping to design the new healthcare system. The common values that helped cement broad nursing support was the desire to create a patient-centered, quality, and safe healthcare delivery system that better supported nursing activities. The threat of this reform occurring without nursing at the table is the reason that the issue became so urgent for nursing leaders to become involved. Define the issue in a way that the participants easily understand it. The expected outcome of the TIGER Initiative was to raise awareness within the entire nursing community of the need for all nurses and nursing students to obtain a minimum set of competencies related to computer literacy, information literacy, and information management skills. The approach was multifaceted, targeting reform of the educational system, practice requirements, and improvement of technologies to meet the nursing requirements for safer, higher quality, patient-centered delivery of health care.
5. Create a sense of urgency. It is impossible to mobilize people quickly to support your policy if you do not have a burning need to act. With the TIGER Initiative, the urgency was created by the threat of the healthcare information technology infrastructure being designed without adequate nursing input. Nurses emotionally connected with this threat, as most have had some form of technology or system forced on them without the opportunity to influence the decision. The President established the timeline when demanding that health care will be delivered with EHRs by the year 2014 and creating a Federal

Agency (the Office of the National Coordinator) to develop the plan.

6. Be very clear about "the ask." It is critical to be specific about your desired outcome. Use the "SMART" rule to develop your policy: The intended outcome should be *S*pecific, *M*easurable, *A*ctionable, *R*ealistic, and *T*imely. The outcome should be defined in terms of recommended actions. It is extremely critical that the policy is realistic and within the targeted policy maker's area of influence; otherwise, your efforts will be ineffective. It is also important that your interactions are within the timeframe that the policy maker needs to act. For example, if you are looking at developing a funding policy, be sure to be aware of the budget cycle and when the policy maker is taking input from the public for the budget to be part of that process. It was critical for the American Association of Colleges of Nursing to influence the development of their "Essentials for Baccalaureate Education" while it was being reviewed in 2008. The "essentials" are only updated every few years, and thus, the TIGER Initiative had to work while the opportunity was available. Often there is a defined timeline for "public comments," and you want to be prepared to provide input during these critical review cycles.
7. Align your recommended policy with the larger, strategic picture. For example, the TIGER Initiative was aligned with the IOM recommendations and the Federal Office of the National Coordinator's strategic plan from its inception. Policy makers look favorably on opportunities to build on previous work, and the context of the policy fitting into larger strategic initiatives gives you the opportunity to link onto their efforts. It also will allow you to gain the support of the related initiatives.
8. Develop a dissemination plan for your policy in order to gain larger support. In the case of the TIGER Initiative, the plan was for each participating organization to commit to bring the work back to their respective organizations and develop their own action plan to be completed within 3 years. Over the past 2 years, representatives of TIGER have presented their plan and results at over a hundred conferences and meetings nationally, regionally, and even internationally.

References

Aspden, P., Corrigan, J., Wolcott, J., & Erickson, S. (Eds.), for Committee on Data Standards for Patient Safety, Institute of Medicine. (2004). *Patient safety: Achieving a new standard of care.* Washington, DC: National Academies Press.

BusinessDictionary.com. (2010). *Intellectual capital.* Retrieved February 13, 2010, from http://www.businessdictionary.com/definition/intellectual-capital.html

Cohen, D., & Prusak, L. (2001). *In good company: How social capital makes organizations work.* Cambridge, MA: Harvard Business School Press.

Cronenwett, L., Sherwood, G., Barnsteiner, J., Disch, J., Johnson, J., Mitchell, P., Sullivan, D., & Warren, J. (2007). Quality and safety education for nurses. *Nursing Outlook, 55*(3),122–131.

DiCicco-Bloom, B., Frederickson, K., O'Malley, D., Shaw, E., Crosson, J., & Looney, J. (2007). Developing a model of social capital: Relationships in Primary Care. *Advances in Nursing Science, 30*(3), 13–24.

Greiner, A., & Knebel, E. (Eds.). (2003). *Health professions education: A bridge to quality.* Washington, DC: National Academies Press.

Institute of Medicine. (2001). *Crossing the quality chasm: A new health system for the 21st century.* Washington, DC: National Academies Press.

Kohn, L. T., Corrigan, J. M., & Donaldson, M. S. (Eds.). (2000). *To err is human: Building a safer health system.* Washington, DC: National Academies Press.

Kouzes, J. M., & Posner, B. Z. (2003). *Academic administrator's guide to exemplary leadership.* San Francisco: Jossey-Bass.

Landry, R., Amara, N., & Lamari, M. (2000). Does social capital determine innovation? To what extent? Fourth International Conference on Technology Policy and Innovation. Retrieved February 13, 2010, from http://kuuc.chair.ulaval.ca/francais/pdf/apropos/publication5.pdf

McNeil, B. J., Elfrink, V. L., Bickford, C. J., Pierce, S. T., Beyea, S. C., Averill, C., & Klappenbach, C. (2003). Nursing information technology knowledge, skills, and preparation of student nurses, nursing faculty, and clinicians: A U.S. survey. *Journal of Nursing Education, 42*(8), 341–349.

Nahapiet, J., & Ghoshal, S. (1998). Social capital, intellectual capital, and the organizational advantage. *Academy of Management Review, 23*(2), 212–266.

Putnam, R. (2000). *Bowling alone: The collapse and revival of American community*. New York: Simon & Schuster.

Romano, C., & Heller, B. (1990). Nursing informatics: A model curriculum for an emerging role. *Nurse Educator, 15*(2), 16–19.

Ronald, J. S. (1979). Computers in undergraduate nursing education: A report of an experimental introductory course. *Journal of Nursing Education, 18*(9), 4–9.

Ronald, J. S. (1983). Guidelines for computer literacy curriculum in a school of nursing. *Journal of the New York State Nurses Association, 14*(1), 12–18.

Ronald, J., & Skiba, D. (1987). *Guidelines for basic computer education in nursing*. New York: National League for Nursing.

Skiba, D. J. (1983). Computer literacy: The challenge of the 80s. *Journal of the New York State Nurses Association, 14*(1), 6–11.

Skiba, D., & Dulong, D. (2008). Using TIGER vision to move your agenda forward. *Nursing Management, 39*(3), 14, 16.

Staggers, N., Gassert, C. A., & Curran, C. (2001). Informatics competencies for nurses at four levels of practice. *Journal of Nursing Education, 40*(7), 303–316.

Technology Informatics Guiding Education Reform. (2007). *The TIGER Initiative: Evidence and informatics transforming nursing: 3-year action steps toward a 10-year vision.* Retrieved February 13, 2010, from http://www.tigersummit.com/uploads/TIGERInitiative_Report2007_Color.pdf

Thompson, B., & Skiba, D. J. (2008). Highlights from the National League for Nursing Survey of Informatics in the nursing curriculum. *Nursing Education Perspectives, 29*(5), 312–316.

Warren, J., & Connors, H. (2007). Health information technology can and will transform nursing education. *Nursing Outlook, 55*(1), 58–60.

CASE STUDY

Web 2.0, Healthcare Policy and Community Health Activism

Jessie Daniels

The emergence of Web 2.0 is perhaps the most dramatic and significant shift in information and communication technologies since John Snow's map making. John Snow, sometimes referred to as "the father of" public health, helped end a cholera epidemic in London in the 19th century through the innovative use of maps to display visually his theory for what was causing the epidemic (Johnson, 2006). Snow's maps persuaded the policy makers of his day to close the water pumps that were causing the cholera epidemic. Early in the 20th century, Jacob Riis, reporter and reformer, used the recently developed technology of "flash photography" to cast light on the darkest corners of the lives New York City's impoverished, mostly immigrant, communities (Pascal, 2005). Riis' photographs influenced a young New York politician by the name of Theodore Roosevelt to implement public health laws that improved the city's health and are still in place today. In the early part of the 21st century, a tremendous and growing number of citizen reformers gather online everyday at a number of blogs to raise their collective voice and proactively influence their government in a collectivity known as "Netroots," which now includes progressive organizations and politicians who use new media technologies to communicate with their constituents (About Netroots Nation, 2010). These new media technologies have also begun to reshape healthcare policy and community health activism. New technologies of participatory digital media such as Twitter, Facebook, and YouTube make it easier than at any other time for many people to create their own media and distribute it to many other people. This many-to-many model of distribution marks an innovative new approach to communication built on social networks (Wellman, 2001). The radically "bottom-up" quality of many-to-many distribution stands in stark contrast to earlier top-down models of communication in which a very few people set policy agendas for the many. In the case that follows, the meaning of

Web 2.0 and a number of forms of Web 2.0 as they relate to community healthcare policy and health-related activism will be explored.

What Is Web 2.0?

The term Web 2.0 (pronounced: web two point oh) came into wide use after the inaugural O'Reilly Media Web 2.0 conference in 2004 (O'Reilly, 2005). Web 2.0 refers to a range of web-based Internet practices based on information sharing, social networks, and collaboration rather than the one-way communication style of "brochure" Web sites that characterized the early era of the Internet. The key idea with the concept of Web 2.0 is that people are using the Internet to connect with other people through their old face-to-face networks and through newly formed online networks. To clarify, Web 2.0 does not refer to a new form of technology but rather a new way that everyday people (sometimes called "end-users") and developers (sometimes called "programmers") make use of that technology.

In order to convey the conceptual shift in Web 2.0, people will often talk about specific contrasting examples to illustrate the shift, such as Britannica Online versus Wikipedia. Britannica Online is an electronic version of the print version of the encyclopedia that was written by experts and professional writers, edited by a staff of editors who served as gatekeepers, and sold to reader consumers by door-to-door sales staff. Wikipedia, in contrast, is an online encyclopedia that anyone can edit. It relies on content from both readers and contributors. Wikipedia is also free. The collaborative knowledge community that works to contribute to Wikipedia and to stop vandalism and incorrect information has sometimes been referred to as an example of the wisdom of crowds, or the notion that "we" is smarter than "me." This example of Britannica Online—an online version of a print-based source, published by a for-profit publishing company, intended for one-way distribution of information—and Wikipedia—a collaborative, information sharing project made possible almost entirely by volunteers who are geographically dispersed—captures the essence of the shift in emphasis from the initial incarnations of the Internet to the realization of Web 2.0.

Web 2.0 concepts have led to the development and evolution of web culture communities and hosted services, such as social-networking sites, video-sharing sites, wikis, blogs, and folksonomies (or, "tagging"). These collaborative, information-sharing Internet practices have broad social implications (DiMaggio et al., 2001). In the sections that follow, particular implications of Web 2.0 for healthcare policy and community health activism are explored.

Healthcare Policy and Web 2.0

In November, 2008 as President-Elect Barack Obama's transition team prepared to take office, they took an unprecedented step in the use of Web 2.0 to inform their health policy agenda. In keeping with Obama's goals of a transparent and engaged governance, the incoming administration asked the public to participate in a discussion about health care on their Web site. Over a few days, thousands of people commented on questions drafted by the Obama Health Policy Team. Some people answered the initial question, but others engaged with one another debating and developing new ideas and approaches to healthcare reform. Members of the Health Policy Team, including former Senator Tom Daschle, read through these comments over the Thanksgiving holiday weekend. The suggestions from the public included a range of ideas from basic public health (e.g., focus on prevention to lower costs of chronic diseases) to relatively left-of-center suggestions such as a proposed "health corps" similar to the Peace Corps, where people would volunteer for 2 years of service in health-related fields. Then Daschle and Lauren Aronson (another member of the Health Policy Team) responded in an online video in which they read aloud a number of the comments and vowed to incorporate some of these ideas into the new health policy of the Obama administration. New forms of communication that are based on the many-to-many style of distribution (rather than the top-down, one-to-many style) are making conversations possible now that either did not exist or were very unlikely in the past. As anyone knows who has read any the literature on the mystification of medical (and scientific) knowledge, this is a pretty dramatic shift in the way we conceptualize community health and the ways we affect change in health policy.

Stakeholders in healthcare policy, such as medical personnel and administrators, are also adopting Web 2.0 technologies in innovative ways. Healthcare blogs ("blog" is short for "web log") are Web sites that feature frequent updates by one or more authors, often in the format of a daily diary, written and published by health personnel and administrators about their healthcare settings. These blogs are rewriting the rules of healthcare policy. Paul Levy's blog is a good example. In August 2007, Levy, chief executive of Beth Israel Deaconess Medical Center, began writing an Internet blog called "Running a Hospital," which is about the inner workings of an academic medical center. Since then, he has broken a few unwritten rules. In a recent entry on his Web site and two previous ones, Levy, saying patients have a right to know, posted the percentage of Beth Israel Deaconess patients who get infections each month from intravenous tubing inserted by staff, known as central-line infections, which can cause serious harm and even death. (The hospital's rate has fluctuated, but five or six patients got infections in August, whereas none did in January, he said.) He challenged other hospitals to publicize their infection rates, a step that is also being pushed nationally by patient advocates, including Consumers Union, the nonprofit publisher of Consumer Reports. The Globe asked several other Boston teaching hospitals if they would release their monthly central line infection rates, which they have collected internally for years. They all said no, at least for now, but added that they expect to in the near future. Levy's initiative has some legislators talking about passing laws to require hospitals to publicize the kinds of information that Levy is pushing on his blog (Kowalczyk, 2007).

Health Wonk Review (http://www.healthwonkreview.com/mt) is a valuable Web 2.0 resource for those interested in healthcare policy, as it features a biweekly compendium of the best of the health policy blogs. More than two dozen individual bloggers contribute on a variety of healthcare policy-related themes, including health business, healthcare law, Medicaid, disease management, healthcare infrastructure, insurance, technology, and managed care. Each blogger contributes his or her best recent blog postings, and those posts are compiled into a digest. Participating bloggers find it a useful way to network and share ideas, and stakeholders in healthcare policy can find the latest information on a variety of issues.

Whereas healthcare policy was once the domain of a limited field of experts setting the agenda for the rest of us, the rise of user-generated content signals a radical departure from this approach. The emergence of user-generated content means that millions of people are now logging on to contribute information about healthcare policy. This dramatic shift marks the rise of what some have called "Health 2.0" (2007). Whatever one calls it, what seems clear is that new information technologies that rely on user-generated content (known collectively as Web 2.0) are shifting the discussion of healthcare policy from a top-down model to one in which a wide range of people from a broad array of backgrounds can and do come together in a more dynamic, interactive space in which information is continually requested, consumed, and reinterpreted (Giustini, 2006), and this paradigm shift from top down to bottom up encompasses far more than just healthcare policy; Web 2.0 technologies are also driving a profound transformation in community health activism.

Community Health Activism and Web 2.0

Activists want to create change involving a variety of issues and have taken up the use of new media technologies and strategies that characterize Web 2.0. These new activists are called "cyberactivists" (McCaughey & Ayers, 2003). In the pre-Internet era, activists made use of existing technology to mobilize supporters through the use of "phone trees." One person would call 10 others, and each of those 10 would call 10 others, and so on. In the digital era, cyberactivists use Web 2.0 to accomplish a number of kinds of goals, including public representation of their cause through an online presence, information distribution to and solidarity with other cyberactivists, outreach to potential new supporters, fundraising and direct action (Costanza-Chock, 2003). With Web 2.0 technologies, social networks that are already in place can be amplified when combined with online networks, asynchronous communication, and always-on connectivity. Taken together, these features mean that there is tremendous potential to leverage of Web 2.0 to advocate for change. To accomplish these goals, cyberactivists use a range of digital tools that are in a fairly constant state of change.

E-mail was one of the first Web-based advocacy tools. For example, cyberactivist Irene Weiser from upstate New York effectively used an e-mail campaign to save the Violence Against Women Act, which provides funding for domestic violence programs and was set to expire in 2000. She created a Web site (www.stopfamilyviolence.org) and sent out letters to friends, colleagues, and family. Within 2 months, she built an e-mail list of 36,000 subscribers who helped send 164,000 e-mail messages to Congress. In October 2000, the Senate reauthorized the act unanimously, after a House vote of 371–1. President Clinton signed legislation into law on October 28, 2000, doubling the funding for the program.

Although e-mail may be an effective advocacy tool at times (Geser, 2001), e-mail is increasingly being eclipsed by a range of new applications that draw their effectiveness from the social networking and collaborative information sharing typical of Web 2.0. These new tools for cyberactivism include blogs, social networking sites, Internet-enabled mobile phones, SMS, digital photo and video, wikis, and collaborative knowledge networks.

A "blog" which can be used as a noun (e.g., Did you read Janet's blog?) or a verb (e.g., Jamal is going to blog about the conference) is typically maintained by an individual, although there are a growing number of group blogs in which several individuals make regular contributions to a single blog. The conventional format for blogs is that each entry, or "post," is displayed in reverse-chronological order, with the most recent post appearing first. Blogs include three key features: (1) text, (2) hyperlinks (links to other blogs, news reports, or other web-based resources), and (3) images (either digital photos or videos). Each blog combines these three elements in uniquely different ways. One of the earliest and longest running blogs began in 1993, when Dr. Glen Barry began his *Forest Protection Blog* (http://forests.org/blog/) as part of his PhD project and as a way to campaign for forest protection. Barry's blog has been on the web continuously since 1995, making it the web's first and longest continuously running environmental blog. By the end of the 1990s, there were a few hundred blogs, and today there are literally millions; this explosion in the popularity of blogs was at least partially driven by new blogging tools that made daily updates as easy as writing in a word-processing program. In an effort to make their own work easier, early bloggers built tools, such as Blogger.com and Diaryland.com, which allow anyone, even with very little technical skill, to create and maintain a blog (Jensen, 2003).

Most blogs in the blogging universe, called the "blogosphere," are more attuned to personal life experiences and less focused on political activism (Lenhart & Fox, 2006). A 2006 random sample telephone survey conducted by the Pew Internet and American Life Project found that the American blogosphere dominated by those who use their blogs as personal journals. When asked to choose just one topic that they blog about, 37% of bloggers responded that "my life and experiences" are their primary focus. Politics and government ran a very distant second, with 11% of bloggers citing issues of public life as the main subject of their blog. Entertainment-themed topics were the next most popular category of blog, with 7% of bloggers, followed by sports (6%), general news and current events (5%), business technology (4%), religion, spirituality or faith (2%), a specific health problem or illness (comprising 2% of bloggers). Of interest here is the 2% that blog about a "specific . . . health problem or illness." Although this is a comparatively small percentage of the total blogosphere, this 2% still constitutes a vast universe of health blogs. A conservative estimate would place the number of health blogs in the hundreds of thousands, and a less conservative estimate would be upward of 5 million; these blogs are consulted by an estimated 60 million users in the United States, according to research conducted in 2008 (Manhattan Research, 2008). Although the majority of blogs are focused on personal life experiences, people's lives are often profoundly shaped by experiences of disease or illness so that blogs that were once exclusively focused on the blogger's dating life may change course when that person is diagnosed with breast cancer. It is also the case that some bloggers may focus part of their blog on their personal experience of disease or illness, yet may not devote the entirety of every post to that topic. Although most blogs are maintained by individuals who are affected by a particular health condition, some health-related blogs are sponsored by traditional newspapers and others by community activist organizations.

Health blogs written by patients (and families of patients) cover a wide range of diseases and health conditions. For example, there are blogs about asthma (www.theasthmamom.com), autism (www.autism-hub.co.uk), diabetes (www.diabetesmine.com), prostate health (prostate-help.blogs.com), infertility (lovelifeandinfertility.blogspot.com), and rheumatoid arthritis (www.anaudlife.com). A number of health-themed blogs focus on the experience of cancer (e.g., The Assertive Cancer Patient, www.assertivepatient.com). The feelings of many patient bloggers are summed up in the description the "e-Patient Dave" (patientdave.blogspot.com), who writes this about his experience with patient blogging:

> *In 2007, supported by an extraordinary team of family, friends, and medical staff, I stomped the snot out of a nasty cancer that was on its way to killing me. I've since learned that the way I did it has a lot in common with the advice of the "e-patients" movement, so I've changed my blogger name from Patient Dave to e-Patient Dave.*

Here, "e-Patient Dave" characterizes his active engagement in his own wellness, much of it through blogging, as part of an "e-patients movement." Although not all patient bloggers describe their participation in terms of a social movement, there is a widely shared sense that there is something uniquely different about approaching medical care in the digital age as a patient blogger.

Jen McCabe Gorman, who blogs at Health Management Rx (healthmgmtrx.blogspot.com), captures the central feature of what's exciting and innovative about Web 2.0 as it relates to health in this passage:

> *Like this year's presidential election, social media and networking sites are breaking down some siloed barriers in the healthcare strata. On Twitter [Twitter is a microblogging platform], I chat with docs, nurses, med students, marketers, health executives, entrepreneurs, analysts, etc. Would I ever have the opportunity to find and initiate conversations in the brick-and-mortar delivery world with such a diverse group? Not bloody likely.*

The opportunity to engage directly with a range of medical providers and a variety of stakeholders in the healthcare field that were once "siloed" or cordoned off behind walls, both literal and figurative, that separated experts from patients is a key dimension of Web 2.0 that patient bloggers find appealing. In addition, the opportunity to engage in these interactions in an asynchronous and decentralized platform unbounded by the constraints of office visits and payment schedules compounds this appeal.

Health-focused blogs sponsored by activist organizations encompass a wide range of health issues, including, for example, the magazine *POZ* created by, for, and about the HIV-positive community, has created a new and innovative approach to publishing online with its roster HIV Blogs, including one by the Editor-in-Chief, Regan Hofmann. More and more CEOs, editors, and other top-level management types are creating their own blogs (or having someone else write a blog that has their name on it), and it is good to see this takeoff in a health-related field; however, the well-intentioned folks at *POZ* have made the classic public health (and beyond) blunder of not including enough voices (or in this instance blogs) by people of color. Given the increasing impact of HIV on communities of color and particularly women in those communities, it is shocking that of the HIV blogs listed at *POZ* none is by a black woman.

Community-based cyberactivists also use blogging for social justice. When the men accused of murdering Gwen Araujo, a woman they beat, bound, and strangled after they discovered that she was biologically male, went to trial, Andy Shie Kee Wong, the Development Director of Community United Against Violence, decided to use a blog to document the trial. Volunteers, including the Community United Against Violence Speaker's Bureau

Program Director, Connie Champagne, followed the trial's proceedings and recounted them on the blog. They recorded the defendants' testimonies word for word and filled in the blanks for readers who may not have understood the subtleties of the proceedings.

Because many of the Community United Against Violence's volunteer bloggers were more knowledgeable about issues such as the transphobic tactics that were being used by the lawyers, they were able to address many issues that the mainstream media missed. The blog also kept people informed during the second trial, when media coverage had diminished, and eventually drew attention to the trial when the blog got news coverage. (For more information, read Susan Tenby's story, "Blogging for Justice: The Gwen Araujo Murder," and listen to her interview with the Community United Against Violence's Andy Shie Kee Wong.)

Virtual Community and Social Networking Sites

Virtual communities extend the potential of activism beyond what can be accomplished on a blog and are an important source of support for people dealing with sudden illness or chronic disease. Howard Rheingold, a leading thinker about the social implications of the Internet, popularized the term *Virtual Community* back in 1993 with his book by the same name that chronicled his experiences at The Well, an early online community (Rheingold, 1993). Rheingold writes that virtual communities form "when people carry on public discussions long enough, with sufficient human feeling, to form webs of personal relationships" (p. 3). In terms of the technologies involved, early virtual communities used the Bulletin Board system of UNIX, and today, most typically involve some kind of discussion board software that organizes text-based comments either by theme (in a "threaded" discussion) or by time (in a chronological discussion).

One recent development in virtual community includes video-based discussions (e.g., www.seesmic.com), in which members record themselves talking into a digital video camera and then upload those to the web. Others watch and listen to those recordings, make their own and upload them, and have conversations that are video and audio based rather than text based. Although this will certainly become more popular in the near future, at the moment, the majority of virtual communities are still exclusively text based.

Virtual communities emphasize reciprocity among members and depend on social interaction and exchange between users online. Early on in the emergence of virtual communities, people began to look online for information and support around specific diseases and health-conditions that affected them personally or someone in their immediate family. Numerous research studies indicate that seeking information and support online has positive impact regardless of the illness or health condition. Kalichman (2002a, 2002b) and Kalichman et al. (2003) found a positive association between health-related Internet use among people living with HIV/AIDS and greater HIV disease knowledge, active coping, and social support. Fogel (2003a, 2003b) found that among women cancer patients, those who sought information and support online reported greater overall, appraisal, and tangible social support using standardized psychological measures and across racial/ethnic differences. Pitts' study of women's participation in virtual communities for women with breast cancer suggests that women seek out Internet spaces where they can explore and reaffirm the bodily selves in the presence of illness, surgery, recovery, and loss (Daniels, 2009).

The development of Web 2.0 has meant increased participation and media attention on virtual communities, most frequently in social networking sites (SNSs) such as Facebook and MySpace. The impact that SNSs will have on health is still emerging, but there are some intriguing early examples of the advantage of social networking sites may hold for community health activism. For instance, people are using the incredibly popular social networking site Facebook to gather support for their favorite causes, many of these health focused. One report that has received attention from the mainstream press is that of "Baby Bethany." Bethany Dawson is a baby born with gastroschisis, a severe birth defect that causes the intestines to develop on the outside of the body; as a result, Bethany is in need of a bowel and liver transplant. In an effort to find a suitable organ donor, Bethany's parents went online and created a Facebook group, "Help Save My

Daughter Bethany." Within weeks, the Dawson's group had 30,000 members (Neil, 2008). At the time of this writing, her parents are still searching for a suitable donor, the large and quick response to their plea posted to Facebook assures them that they will get the word out to many more people than would have been possible without the SNS.

The promise of online community and SNS for community health activism has captured the attention of major funders in the both health and cyberactivism, including the Robert Wood Johnson Foundation (www.rwjf.org) and the Benton Foundation (www.benton.org). In a unique joint venture between Robert Wood Johnson and Benton, in 2007, the two foundations launched New Routes to Community Health (www.newroutes.org). New Routes, a Madison, Wisconsin-based initiative, is an attempt to bring the power of a social networking site to bear on improving the health of immigrants. New Routes does this through immigrant-created media and by funding other immigrant-led collaborations across the United States. In each of these efforts, immigrants have worked to create locally focused media and outreach campaigns that speak directly to immigrants' health concerns in their area.

New businesses focusing on and based on the principles of virtual communities and social networking sites have also begun to emerge. For example, in 2007, Keith Schorsch launched Trusera, a health-focused business built on a social networking site that attempts to build virtual communities in which users can learn from one another's experiences and seek out knowledgeable advice (Harris, 2008). As part of the branding at Trusera, the site features the founder's own experience as the impetus for starting the business:

> *Keith Schorsch was diagnosed with Lyme Disease after he was bitten by a tick on the East Coast. After seeing 11 doctors, he had plenty of expert opinions. He found lots of information online. What he didn't have was honest, credible insight from real people. People who could share their personal stories and offer relevant and useful health information. People who'd been there. Inspired by the possibilities, Keith began work on Trusera in 2007.*

The founding narrative about Trusera's origins relies on a central notion about Web 2.0 and health: that there is a sea change happening in which people are increasingly going online to become more informed about health. In order to become profitable, businesses such as Trusera typically rely on two strategies: (1) creating a revenue stream from advertisers hoping to attract the attention of users that visit the site for free or (2) charging users a fee for "premium" content that is otherwise locked behind a pay-wall. Whether virtual communities will prove to be a successful business model in the longer term remains to be seen; nevertheless, as more Americans go online, more rely on the Internet for important health information.

A 2006 study found that fully 58% of those surveyed reported that the Internet was crucial or important during a loved one's recent health crisis (Madden & Fox, 2006). A majority of those said that the single most important source of information was something they found online. The reality that so many Americans are consulting online sources first for information about health raises important questions about health and Internet literacy and about unequal access to technology.

Health and Internet literacy means understanding basic health information online. Health literacy refers to the ability to understand basic concepts related to health; Internet literacy refers to the ability to understand the basic skills of navigation and understanding when using search engines to find information online. Health and Internet literacy can be a tricky proposition for a number of reasons. First, when people without a medical background use a search engine as a diagnostic tool, it is very easy for such online searches to escalate concerns, a phenomenon known as "cyberchondria" (White & Horvitz, 2008). In a large-scale, longitudinal, log-based study of how people search for medical information online, supported by a large-scale survey of 515 individuals' health-related search experiences, researchers White and Hovritz found that escalation of anxiety about symptomology is influenced by the amount and distribution of medical content viewed by users, the presence of escalatory terminology in pages visited, and a user's predisposition to escalate versus to seek more reasonable explanations for ailments. We also demonstrate the persistence of postsession anxiety after escalations and the effect that such anxieties can have on interrupting user's activities across multiple sessions.

Conclusion

Much has changed since the days of John Snow, when closing one water pump could effectively end a cholera epidemic. Noted scholar Henry Jenkins argues that Web 2.0 is driving the emergence of a new culture characterized as "innovative, converged, everyday, networked, global and unequal" (Jenkins, 2007). Whether you subscribe to Jenkins' view that a new culture is emerging, it seems clear from the examples discussed in this case that Web 2.0 is changing the way we approach healthcare policy and community health activism. The distributed knowledge networks and communication model of Web 2.0 that relies on many-to-many strategies rather than top-down mechanisms have created a paradigm shift in thinking about healthcare policy and community health activism.

The kinds of challenges we face in the 21st century are both depressingly similar to and dramatically different from those that John Snow faced in the 19th century or Jacob Riis confronted in the early 20th century. The tools we have today may help improve the public's health. Public health leaders of the next generation will have to change the tools they use to incorporate new, participatory digital media, in order to address different public health needs of our world.

References

About Netroots Nation. (2010). Retrieved January 31, 2010, from http://netrootsnation.org/about

Costanza-Chock, S. (2003). Mapping the repertoire of electronic contention. In A. Opel & D. Pompper (Eds.), *Representing resistance: Media, civil disobedience and the global justice movement.* New York: Greenwood Press.

Daniels, J. (2009). Cyberfeminism. *Women's Study Quarterly, 37*(1 & 2), 101–124.

DiMaggio, P., Hargittai, E., Neuman, W. R., & Robinson, J. P. (2001). The social implications of the Internet. *Annual Review of Sociology, 27,* 207–236.

Fogel, J. (2003a). Internet use for cancer information among racial/ethnic populations and low literacy groups. *Cancer Control, 10*(5), 45–51.

Fogel, J. (2003b). Racial/ethnic differences and potential psychological benefits in use of Internet by women with breast cancer. *Psycho-Oncology, 12*(2), 107–117.

Geser, H. (2001, March). On the functions and consequences of the Internet for social movements and voluntary associations. Sociology in Switzerland, Online Publications. Retrieved February 13. 2010, from http://socio.ch/movpar/t_hgeser3a.htm

Giustini, D. (2006). How Web 2.0 is changing medicine. *British Medical Journal, 333,* 1283–1284. Retrieved February 13, 2010, from http://www.bmj.com/cgi/content/extract/333/7582/1283

Health 2.0. (2007, September 6). *The Economist.* Retrieved February 13, 2010, from http://www.economist.com/printedition/displaystory.cfm?story_id=9719054

Jenkins, H. (2007). White paper, for the John D. and Catherine T. MacArthur Series on Digital Media and Learning. Retrieved February 13, 2010, from http://www.digitallearning.macfound.org

Jensen, M. (2003, September/October). A brief history of weblogs. *Columbia Journalism Review, 5.* Retrieved February 13, 2010, from http://cjrarchives.org/issues/2003/5/blog-jensen.asp

Johnson, S. (2006). *Ghost map: The story of London's most terrifying epidemic—and how it changed science, cities, and the modern world.* New York: Riverhead Books.

Kalichman, S. C. (2002a). Internet use among people living with HIV/AIDS: Association of Health Information, Health behaviors and Health status. *AIDS Education and Prevention, 14*(1), 51–61.

Kalichman, S. C. (2002b, August). Closing the digital divide in HIV/AIDS care: Development of a theory-based intervention to increase Internet access. *AIDS Care, 14*(4), 523–537.

Kalichman, S. C., Benotsch, E. G., Weinhardt, L., Austin, J., Luke, W., & Cherry, C. (2003). Health-related Internet use, coping, social support, and health indicators in people living with HIV/AIDS: Preliminary results from a community survey. *Health Psychology, 22*(1), 111–116.

Kowalczyk, L. (2007, February 23). Blog tests hospital leaders' patience: Beth-Israel CEO jabs competitors. *The Boston Globe.* Retrieved February 13, 2010, from http://www.boston.com/yourlife/health/diseases/articles/2007/02/23/blog_tests_hospital_leaders_patience

Lenhart, A., & Fox, S. (2006). *Bloggers: A portrait of the Internet's new storytellers.* Washington, DC: Report, Pew Internet & American Life Project.

Madden, M., & Fox, S. (2006). *Finding answers online in sickness and in health.* Washington, DC: Pew Internet & American Life Project.

Manhattan Research. (2008). *Cybercitizen health*. Retrieved February 13, 2010, from http://www.manhattanresearch.com/cch

McCaughey, M., & Ayers, M. D. (Ed.). (2003). *Cyberactivism: Online activism in theory and practice*. New York: Routledge.

Harris, L. (2008). Online medical advice goes social. Retrieved February 13, 2010, from http://www.technologyreview.com/Biztech/20908/?a=f

Neil, B. (2008, June 24). "Facebook tot with 30,000 friends . . . and a year to live." *The Daily Mirror*. Retrieved February 13, 2010, from http://www.mirror.co.uk/news/top-stories/2008/06/24/facebook-tot-with-30-000-friends-and-a-year-to-live-89520-20619038

O'Reilly, T. (2005). What is Web 2.0: Design patterns and business models for the next generation of software. Retrieved November 1, 2008, from http://www.oreillynet.com/pub/a/oreilly/tim/news/2005/09/30/what-is-web-20.html?page=1

Pascal, J. B. (2005). *Jacob Riis: Reporter and reformer.* New York: Oxford University Press.

Rheingold, H. (1993). *Virtual community.* Boston: Addison-Wesley Longman.

Wellman, B. (2001). Computer networks as social networks. *Science, 293,* 2031–2034.

White, R. W., & Horvitz, E. (2008, November). Cyberchondria: Studies of the escalation of medical concerns in web search. *Microsoft Research Report*. Retrieved from http://research.microsoft.com/apps/pubs/default.aspx?id=76529

Chapter 13

Healthcare Quality

Donna Middaugh

OVERVIEW

This chapter presents an overview of human error, error theory, and the application of these concepts to healthcare delivery. Error measurement tools and injury prevention models are applied to healthcare settings. Public reporting systems and regulatory agency requirements are analyzed in conjunction with nursing performance measures. Research and its impact on quality care are explored, as measures used by regulating agencies are often research driven.

OBJECTIVES

- To explain common theories of error as they relate to patient care
- To apply effective error management techniques from aviation and industry to healthcare delivery
- To identify examples of quality care initiatives that are cost driven
- To discuss the role of quality care mandates from regulating agencies
- To describe the impact of research on quality care

KEY TERMS

- ❑ Active error
- ❑ Adverse event
- ❑ Aviation
- ❑ Braden Scale
- ❑ Centers for Medicare and Medicaid
- ❑ Code of silence
- ❑ Critical access hospital
- ❑ Error theory

(continues)

- ❑ Healthgrades
- ❑ Human error
- ❑ Latent error
- ❑ Morse Fall Scale
- ❑ National Database of Quality Nursing Indicators
- ❑ Negligence
- ❑ Norton Scale
- ❑ Nursing
- ❑ Patient safety
- ❑ Quality
- ❑ Quality care
- ❑ Quality check
- ❑ Quality improvement
- ❑ Quality indicators
- ❑ Risk assessment

Quality Care and Public Policy

Above all, do no harm (Hippocratic Oath).

The public belief and trust in the healthcare system was shaken in 1999 when the Institute of Medicine (IOM) reported that between 44,000 and 98,000 Americans die each year as a result of medical errors (Kohn et al., 2000). The November 1999 report of the IOM, published in the book entitled *To Err is Human: Building a Safer Health System*, alerted healthcare institutions and professionals to the true scope of the quality problem (Kohn et al., 2000). Errors occur in every healthcare delivery setting: clinics, physicians' offices, pharmacies, homes, and nursing homes, as well as hospitals.

Every day, Americans expect to receive high-quality health care to maintain or restore their health. Unfortunately, every day, thousands of Americans do not receive quality health care and are injured or die in the course of treatment. For example, a hospital study conducted in New York State found that 3.7% of patients experienced adverse events: 12.6% of these events led to death, and 2.6% led to permanent disability. One fourth of the events resulted from negligence (AHRQ, 2002). A Harvard study reported in 2003 that one fourth of patients with health problems in five countries declare that they have suffered from a medical or prescription error in the past 2 years. A minimum of 750 persons were surveyed in the United States, Canada, the United Kingdom, New Zealand, and Australia. Twenty-eight percent of those surveyed in the United States reported errors—the highest of all countries studied. The United Kingdom was the lowest, with 18%. This study suggests that the most significant risks to patients appear to occur when they are treated by multiple healthcare professionals. At least 25% of all those surveyed reported having duplicate tests performed but received conflicting information from different doctors (Dorschner, 2003).

The IOM released its staggering report on medical errors over 10 years ago. This report estimated that the United States loses more patient lives to safety incidents every 6 months than it did in the entire Vietnam War (Kohn et al.,

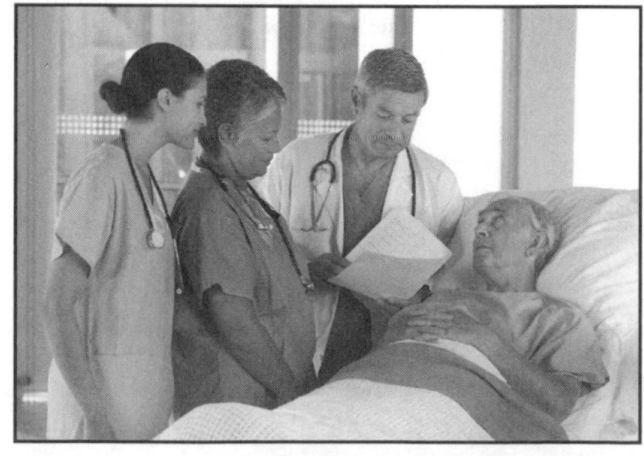

2000). Statistics indicate that more deaths occur in the United States each year from medical errors than from motor vehicle accidents, breast cancer, or AIDS. Put in other terms, medical errors, if documented by the Centers for Disease Control and Prevention, would rank as the sixth leading cause of death in the United States (HealthGrades, Inc., 2005).

The IOM has estimated that more than 7,000 patients die each year in hospitals alone because of medication errors, and other reports have estimated that 100,000 hospital deaths occur each year because of adverse drug reactions (Kohn et al., 2000). These studies focused only on hospitalized patients. When one considers the billions of medications that are prescribed at clinics and physician offices and taken home, it is staggering to think of the scope of possible error. All medication mistakes may be preventable.

HealthGrades' Second Annual Patient Safety in American Hospitals Report released in May 2005 reported that error-reduction efforts have had a positive impact on public perception; however, hundreds of thousands of Medicare beneficiaries continue to experience adverse medical events each year. In fact, adverse patient safety events increased from 1995 to 2003 (HealthGrades, Inc., 2005). Since the IOM report, healthcare providers, the public, and federal and state governments have been seeking facts and answers as to why these errors are so prevalent.

Human Error

Errors can occur in all phases of healthcare delivery. Diagnostic errors can occur with improper testing, misread or misinterpreted laboratory results, or failure to act on the results. During patient treatment, technical errors can result in the inaccurate preparation or delivery of treatments. Treatment can be delayed, missed, or performed incorrectly, for example. A medical error might mean that the healthcare provider chose an inappropriate method of care or that the provider chose the right course of care but carried it out incorrectly (Nordenberg, 2000). Medical errors are not purposeful or reckless actions that are intended to harm a patient (Liang, 2001), and errors do not always result in harm. Adverse events, on the other hand, do imply harm to an individual.

Throughout the literature, the term error is used to denote a mistake, close call, near miss, or active or latent error. Active errors occur at the level of the front-line provider—for example, administering the wrong medication. Active errors are limited in time and space, and thus, they are easier to measure. Latent errors involve system defects, such as faulty maintenance on equipment, poor design, or inadequate staffing. Latent errors are more difficult to measure because they occur over greater periods of time and space and because they may exist for a long period before they lead to an error or adverse event (Thomas & Petersen, 2003).

Error Theory

Human error has been studied extensively by Professor James Reason (2000), who identified two approaches to the problem of human error: the person approach and the system approach. A person approach concentrates on the unsafe acts of individuals, which usually result in blame for forgetfulness, inattention, or moral weakness. A systems approach focuses on the conditions under which the person works and assumes that humans are fallible and errors are to be expected. Errors are then viewed as consequences rather than causes.

The person approach has been the tradition in medicine, blaming someone for having made an unsafe choice of behavior (Reason, 2000). Shame and blame have been the method traditionally used by the medical profession to reduce medical error. This person approach shames an individual into believing that his or her error denotes lack of professionalism and incompetence. It does not recognize the systems-based nature of successful error reduction (Liang, 2001).

The culture of blame seems to be reinforced throughout the education and training of physicians. Clinicians are led to believe that errors are caused by carelessness. This, combined with the public and media's quick-to-blame mentality, results in fear of both making a mistake and being caught (Weinberg, 2002). There are experts who argue that in complex environments that undergo constant change, such as our healthcare environment, complete elimination of all error will never be possible (Ebright et al., 2004).

Reason's "theory of error" has been used by airlines, railroads, nuclear power plants, financial management companies, and the military (Wachter & Shojania, 2004). Reason's research led him to develop a model of system accidents. High-technology systems, such as health care, have many defensive layers. These can include technological barriers (alarms, automatic shutdowns, etc.), people (surgeons, nurses, etc.), and procedures or administrative controls. The function of these layers is to protect victims and assets from hazards. In an ideal world, each defensive layer would be solid and intact.

Reason (2000) emphasizes that by nature there are always weaknesses or holes in these layers, making them similar to Swiss cheese. He calls this a Swiss Cheese Model for latent errors. Each slice of cheese represents a safety defense or system, which can have either small holes or large holes. Each hole allows errors to penetrate—thus, the larger the hole, the more errors that get through the defense.

Reason (2000) argues that when these holes in the cheese align, a number of slips can occur so that an error finally reaches the patient. The presence of holes in one layer does not normally cause an adverse event, but these holes are constantly opening and shutting. This allows mistakes or errors to slip through, hopefully to be caught by the next layer. Adverse events can happen only when the holes in many layers momentarily line up to permit a trajectory of accident opportunity, which brings the hazards into contact with victims (Reason, 2000). These holes arise because of active failures or latent conditions described. This suggests the need for a systems perspective toward patient safety.

Byers and White (2004) discuss three major approaches to the causes of medical errors. The first is Reason's (2000) concept of the Swiss Cheese Model, just described. The second is related to the visibility of the actions of the practitioner. There are many visible and invisible factors involved in any single error. Usually, however, only the final action receives the blame or attention, although a true systems analysis must look at all those involved in the process leading up to the error. Finally, Byers and White noted that too often a simplified analysis is undertaken after an error occurs because of hindsight bias. It is easy to look back and determine that a different course of action should have been taken, but this is not easily accomplished during complex patient care situations (Byers & White, 2004).

Error Management

Reason (2000) believes that error management has two dimensions: limiting the occurrence of dangerous errors and creating systems that are better able to tolerate errors and contain their damaging effects. He argues that there are high-reliability organizations that operate in hazardous conditions yet have few adverse events. He proposes that systems in health care should be modeled after these high reliability organizations, such as the U.S. Navy nuclear aircraft carriers, nuclear power plants, and air traffic control centers (Reason, 2000).

These organizations anticipate the worst and equip themselves to deal with the worst at all levels. This literally means asking individuals in these systems to remain chronically uneasy, yet the culture of these high reliability organizations provides their employees with the reminders and tools to help them remember to be afraid. They have created a culture that makes their system as robust as practicable in the face of both human and operational hazards. Characteristics that allow high-reliability organizations to accomplish this include the following (Reason, 2000):

- Being internally dynamic, complex, and interactive
- Performing exacting tasks under time pressure
- Carrying out demanding activities with low incident rates
- Managing complex, demanding technologies so as to avoid major failures
- Maintaining the capacity to meet periods of peak demand

Error Settings

The use of outpatient settings, including physician offices, has risen dramatically in the last 2 decades, from 202 million visits in 1980 to 521 million visits in 2000 (Landro, 2002). Healthcare reform efforts have primarily focused on studies that have linked deadly errors to hospital settings; however, experts say that patients can face equal or greater risks in doctors' offices and outpatient settings (Landro, 2002). These errors can occur during routine visits or during outpatient surgery procedures. Very little data exist from malpractice insurers, medical societies, or federal researchers to document the scope of this problem.

The California Academy of Family Physicians has identified key sources of errors in primary care and provided recommendations for family physicians to reduce the risk of errors and adverse outcomes in primary care practice settings (California Academy of Family Physicians, 2002). They note that errors are inevitable and expected, and thus, healthcare delivery systems must be designed to prevent and absorb errors. They also believe strongly that a culture must be created that supports error reporting and that blame and punishment will not correct the problem.

The California Academy of Physicians has also reported a study that analyzed 330 errors made by 50 family physicians over the course of 1 year. These errors fell into the following categories (California Academy of Family Physicians, 2002):

- Communication problems (staff/patients)—24%
- Discontinuity of care—20%
- Lab results—19%
- Missing values or charting—13%
- Clinical mistake with knowledge/skill—8%
- Prescribing errors—8%
- Other—8%

Interestingly, this list conflicts with the common beliefs that medical errors are synonymous with prescriptions for medications and that errors are clinical errors made by bad practitioners. In this study, prescribing medications and clinical judgment errors accounted for only 16% of the total errors. The study found that errors were largely the result of latent conditions or system properties rather than active failure on a practitioner's part (California Academy of Family Physicians, 2002).

Woods and Doan-Johnson (2002) developed a taxonomy of nursing errors with prevention as the goal. To achieve this goal, they identified eight categories of errors, all of which include system, individual, and practice contributions. It is unclear whether the advisory panel studied subjects who were from all levels of nurses, including registered nurses and nurse practitioners; however, the eight categories of nursing errors can be applied to all levels of nursing practice. The categories are (Woods & Doan-Johnson, 2002) as follows:

1. Lack of attentiveness
2. Lack of agency/fiduciary concern
3. Inappropriate judgment
4. Medication errors
5. Lack of intervention on the patient's behalf
6. Lack of prevention
7. Missed or mistaken patient orders
8. Documentation errors

A lack of attentiveness can be caused by system level problems such as understaffing or fluctuations in patient acuity, and a lack of attentiveness often translates into lack of monitoring. Patient safety depends on attentiveness to both predictable and unpredictable conditions.

Agency concern is defined as the moral agency of the nurse or his or her trustworthiness in working for the patient/family's best interest. Moral agency is lacking when nurses do not advocate for the best interests of their client. Failing to question an order, failing to call a physician for consultation, or failing to heed a patient or family request for assistance and breach of confidentiality are all examples of lack of fiduciary concern. These can all contribute to causing harm to the patient.

The Practice Breakdown Research Advisory Panel identified various types of inappropriate judgment, including insufficient evaluation, faulty logic, flawed intervention, and inappropriate delegation. Interestingly, the panel also acknowledged a subclass of inadequate assessment, which occurred when nurses in the study did not understand or recognize the implications of the signs and symptoms they identified in their patient assessments (Woods & Doan-Johnson, 2002).

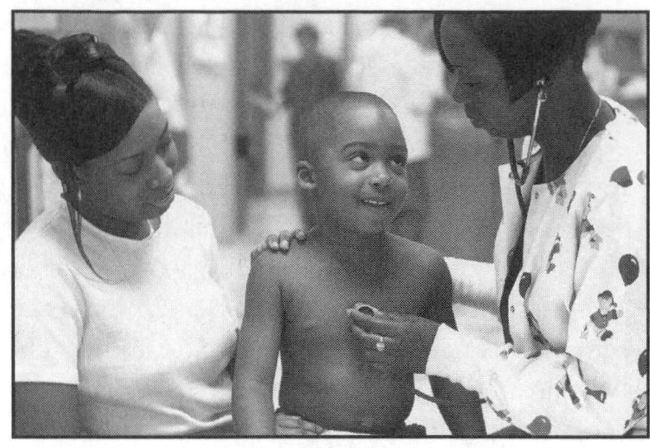

The Advisory Panel (Woods & Doan-Johnson, 2002) identified six types of medication errors in their study population:

1. Missed doses of medications
2. Wrong administration time
3. Delivery of too much intravenous medications or delivery too fast
4. Wrong route of medication delivery
5. Wrong medications delivered to wrong patient

Eight of the nine cases of medication errors found that the patient died as a direct result of the nurse's action. Because medication errors can encompass a wide range of causes and categories, the root cause and practice responsibility for the error must be analyzed on an individual basis.

Intriguingly, four of the panel's cases involved death of a patient related to lack of attentiveness or failure to intervene on the patient's behalf by the nurse. These involved a combination of situations in which patient signs and symptoms of postoperative bleeding, pregnancy-induced hypertension, acute cardiovascular accident, high blood glucose levels, or dehydration were missed or the nurse failed to obtain assistance in an acute situation (Woods & Doan-Johnson, 2002).

Prevention of patient complications, threats to patient safety and error are essential to good nursing care. Breaches of infection control, failure to prevent complications of immobility, and failure to prevent harm from environmental causes were all identified by the panel as present in their study sample (Woods & Doan-Johnson, 2002).

The category of missed or mistaken patient orders included all instances when nurses carried out orders that were inappropriate or misread or misunderstood orders, resulting in patient harm. As with medication errors, this type of error necessitates in-depth investigation of each specific incident to categorize the root cause correctly.

Finally, documentation errors in this study included charting procedures or medications before they were completed or administered to the patient and failure to chart observations of the patient (Woods & Doan-Johnson, 2002). These resulted in serious harm to patients by masking a patient's true condition, causing a medication error, or generally failing to communicate vital information to other healthcare providers. Wood and Doan-Johnson's study attempted to develop a guide for statistically analyzing nursing errors.

Medical Errors and Aviation

Research on the factors that cause human error has been in existence since the 1940s. Some of the early studies involved aviation. The 1999 IOM report noted that the number of Americans who die each year as a result of medical errors is the equivalent of more than 230 full jumbo jets crashing each year (Kohn et al., 2000). The aviation and nuclear power industries learned long ago not to rely on human perfection to prevent accidents. These industries have implemented sound risk-management techniques, such as training, rules, and high standards to aid their systems (Spath, 1999). Experts have tried to assure the public that the United States healthcare system is safe, despite the IOM statistics; however, compared with the complex aviation industry, the healthcare system is not safe. Nordenberg (2000) reports that a person would have to fly nonstop for 438 years before expecting to be involved in a deadly airplane crash. This places health care at least 10 years behind aviation in safeguarding consumers (Nordenberg, 2000).

Helmreich and Davies (2004), through the Human Factors Research Project at the University of Texas at Austin, have identified multiple similarities in the struggle for safety in the healthcare and aviation industries. They point out that safety must be the primary goal in both, but cost drives decisions. Also, there are multiple sources of serious threats to safety in both industries, although both have become safer because of technological innovations (Helmreich & Davies, 2004).

Aircraft accidents are infrequent, but when they occur, they often involve a massive loss of life and therefore naturally gain world attention. Aviation accidents immediately stimulate an enormous, exhaustive investigation into the causes and remedial action necessary. Adverse events in health care, on the other hand, involve individual patients and seldom receive even local, let alone national publicity. There is no standardized method of investigation or remedial action (Helmreich, 2000).

Errors can result from (Helmreich, 2000) the following:

- Psychological limitations
- Physiological limitations
- Fatigue
- Heavy workload
- Cognitive overload

- Fear
- Poor interpersonal communications
- Imperfect information processing
- Flawed decision making

These factors are present among workers in both aviation and health care, but the aviation industry is doing something right to maintain the low incidence of disasters, whereas the healthcare industry continues to have a high accident rate.

Rivers et al. (2003) looked at whether the safety techniques used in aviation could be applied to the healthcare delivery system. To test this idea, an aviation training team implemented 12 hours of error-reducing skills training for operating room personnel. The findings revealed a significant effect on the behaviors of operating room staff. Specific error-reducing behaviors included more effective, efficient communication among team members, a 50% decrease in surgical count errors, early identification of potential red flags, standardized checklists and protocols, fewer delays in procedures, and savings in time and resources for the operating room as a whole (Rivers et al., 2003).

Error Management in Healthcare Settings

Preventable adverse events can occur in any healthcare setting despite the best intentions. The National Quality Forum and the Agency for Healthcare Research and Quality (AHRQ) together have identified 30 safe practices that evidence shows can work to reduce or even prevent adverse events (AHRQ, 2005). These 30 practices have been endorsed by the National Quality Forum, which is comprised of 215 of the Nation's leading healthcare providers, purchasers, and consumer organizations. All healthcare practitioners and organizations are strongly urged to adopt these practices to reduce the risk of harm to patients. The 30 practices are grouped under five major categories, listed below (AHRQ, 2005):

1. Creating a culture of safety
2. Matching healthcare needs with services delivery capability
3. Facilitating information transfer and clear communication
4. Providing specific settings or processes of care
5. Increasing safe medication use

All of the 30 recommended safe practices can be used by physicians and nurses. Of particular relevance to nurses are the safe practices that relate to communication with other healthcare providers and with patients and thorough regular evaluation and monitoring of clients for change in health status or risk of complications.

Strategies for Error Management

The American Society of Anesthesiologists was one of the first groups to adopt specific error-reduction strategies. Their clinical practice guidelines and system improvements have significantly reduced anesthesia-related mortality (Spath, 1999). The risk management error-reduction strategies listed here have been successfully applied in numerous industries, and Spath (1999) suggests that these system and task redesigns could serve as the basis for improving quality in healthcare delivery as well (Spath, 1999).

- Improve information access: Information should be readily available to all who need it.
- Reduce reliance on memory: Checklists, computerized decision aids, and protocols can minimize the need for reliance on human memory.
- Error-proof processes: Critical tasks should be structured so that errors cannot be made.

- Standardize tasks: Tasks are to be done in a standardized process.
- Reduce the number of hand-offs: Processes and procedures should be restructured to minimize the number of people who are involved in transferring materials, information, people, instructions, or supplies.

The California Academy of Family Physicians proposes that a wide-ranging approach must be taken to reduce errors in health care. Their research has led them to suggest the following error-reduction methods (California Academy of Family Physicians, 2002):

1. Pay more and hire great staff. Hire those who have a positive attitude and good communication and teamwork skills. Check references carefully and have a thorough orientation and training program.
2. Invest in new technologies. Use technologies that will enhance communication with staff and patients, prescription writing, e-mail, messaging, and electronic medical records.
3. Simplify and standardize. Have an office-wide formulary with standardized prescription-writing standards. Spread authority and accountability in the office to enable checks and balances. Use office flow sheets and check lists. Reward staff for identifying an actual or potential mistake. Create processes for patient and lab follow-up, and follow principles of evidence-based medicine.
4. Listen to the patients. Collect data on patient satisfaction. Ask patients what they need and design services to meet these needs.
5. Create a culture of healthcare safety. Always look for weak links. Take ownership for safety and establish a clear chain of command. Empower and incentivize staff to report errors, and minimize the punishment of those who commit errors. Keep policies and procedures up to date. Inservice all staff regarding error identification.

Error Measurement Tools

The abundance of scientific articles and news accounts of medical errors and adverse events have stimulated great efforts and research geared toward identification, measurement, and management of errors and adverse events (Kohn et al., 2000). Thomas and Petersen (2003) offer a conceptual model for measuring latent errors, active errors, and adverse events. They identify the following methods to measure errors and adverse events (Thomas & Petersen, 2003):

1. Morbidity and mortality conferences and autopsy
2. Error reporting systems
3. Administrative data analysis
4. Chart review
5. Electronic medical record
6. Observation of patient care
7. Clinical surveillance
8. Malpractice claims analysis

Their research has documented that morbidity and mortality (M and M) conferences' ability to improve care is unproven, although there is strong belief in the effectiveness of such conferences, especially when combined with autopsy; however, this method of detecting errors and adverse events is the weakest form of study design. Error reporting systems can provide details about the latent errors that lead to active errors and adverse events, but used alone, they are not a reliable measure because of the underreporting of errors. Administrative or billing data are sometimes used to measure errors and adverse events; however, these data may be incomplete and subject to bias.

Chart reviews have served as the foundation for research into errors and adverse events; however, Thomas and Petersen (2003) found this method to be fraught with limitations, including low reliability and incomplete documentation in medical records. The method may be strengthened if it is combined with provider reporting. Electronic medical record review uses computers to search electronic documentation for errors and adverse events that may not be detected by traditional chart review. Thomas and Petersen (2003) suggest that as hospital computerized systems become more sophisticated this will become an accurate and precise method for measuring errors and adverse events.

Observation or videotaping of patient care has been effective in measuring active errors; however, this method is limited by the need to protect confidentiality. It is time intensive. Hindsight bias may be present, and the method focuses on the provider instead of the system of care delivery. Clinical surveillance is identified by Thomas and Petersen (2003) as the most precise and accurate method of measuring adverse events; however, this is an active, costly, prospective surveillance method that focuses on specific events in a specific time and place, and thus, it may provide less information on latent errors.

Medical malpractice claims analysis is a strong method of identifying latent errors, and it has led to important patient safety standards; however, claims may be highly selected cases from which it is difficult to generalize. Thomas and Petersen (2003) suggest that a comprehensive monitoring system for patient safety should include combinations of all these measurement tools. They recommend using incident reporting, morbidity and mortality (M and M) conferences with autopsies, and malpractice claims analysis as the strongest tools for latent error identification. Direct observation is recommended for active error detection and clinical surveillance for adverse event recognition (Thomas & Petersen, 2003).

National Error Reduction Efforts

The Code of Silence

A serious question is why the statistics of the IOM were such a shock to people. Part of the answer is that fear of being sued suppresses discussion of medical errors. If procedures are done with the best intentions and skill, yet something does not turn out the way it was supposed to, the doctor often still has to compensate the patient with a huge settlement. The culture is that physicians are going to lose no matter what they do, and thus, that keeps physicians closed among themselves (Nordenberg, 2000).

All professional codes of conduct require that breaches of professional behavior by colleagues be reported to the profession or appropriate licensing body. This is to ensure that there will be some form of investigation and discipline for conduct or service below standards. Williams (2004) notes that there is a deadly conspiracy of silence in health care today. This "silent negligence" is a marriage between a conspiracy to remain silent and negligence that is witnessed (Williams, 2004). Healthcare providers who witness negligent care share in the guilt if they refuse to speak out about it. Williams (2004) describes today's health environment as having no system of professional accountability, which reinforces physicians' suspicion that the need for a conspiracy of silence far outweighs the demand for ethical behavior. By definition, professionals self-regulate their practice, which requires a protective system for the society they serve. This concept is not unique to physicians. It is essential for all professionals, including advanced practice nurses. Self-regulation allows for mutual obligations, shared between healthcare providers and society.

State departments of transportation routinely gather data on vehicle accidents. Other professions systematically investigate and publicize findings about problems that impose a danger to the public; nevertheless, there are no laws that require healthcare professionals to compile and share data on their mistakes—an action which would make healthcare safer (Monk, 2002). Hospitals frequently take part in national error prevention or alert programs and have their own internal safety programs; however, information is often not shared or publicized regarding equipment malfunctions or personnel errors.

In 2002, a major newspaper in South Carolina reported that about 30 of the lawyers who specialized in suing doctors, nurses, and hospitals had won more than $57 million that year in settlements and verdicts for those killed or injured by medical negligence (Monk, 2002). On interview, these malpractice lawyers stated that they turned down dozens of cases for each suit they accepted. They only accepted cases with strong evidence and expected doctors and their insurance companies to fight hard when sued. One factor causing patients to sue is the fact that hospitals and doctors rarely volunteer information about errors. One attorney told the newspaper that it was easier to win malpractice cases if they went to trial because of the increasingly business-like atmosphere in medical care. The attorney added that when relationships between medical providers and patients are abrupt, questions unanswered, and time not spent, people were driven to sue (Monk, 2002).

The newspaper also reported that secrecy about medical errors is common and facts about medical mistakes are often concealed (Monk, 2002). The State reported that doctors and hospitals regularly made secret payouts to victims of medical mistakes and that hospitals did not always tell patients or families about mistakes that injured or killed. Although courts are routinely open in South Carolina, hundreds of secret settlements are made in courthouses involving hospitals, doctors, and nurses (Monk, 2002). Other states, such as Florida, mandate that court settlements must be open and part of the public record. Some argue that confidentiality encourages quick resolution of lawsuits, whereas others argue that confidentiality conceals information essential to the public about their healthcare providers.

Sorry Works! Coalition

The Sorry Works! Coalition began in 2005 and has over 1,500 members, comprised mostly of doctors, insurers, lawyers, and patient advocates (Wojcieszak et al., 2006). This organization advocates that full disclosure and apologies for medical errors are a "middle-ground solution" to the medical malpractice crisis. It is surmised that apologies for bad outcomes, adverse events, or medical errors, combined with upfront compensation, help to reduce anger of patients and families. The healthcare providers apologize to the patient/family, admit fault, provide an explanation of what happened and how the hospital will fix the procedures so that the error is not repeated, and make a fair offer of upfront compensation (Wojcieszak et al., 2006). This approach is taken only after a root-cause analysis shows that the standard of care was not met. This, in turn, will hopefully lead to a reduction in medical malpractice lawsuits and associated defense litigation expenses.

If the standard of care was met or there was no medical error or negligence, the providers still meet with the patient/family and their attorney(s) and explain what happened, apologize, and offer empathy. They do not admit fault or provide compensation or offer to settle any claim. These protocols are based on a disclosure program developed at the Veteran's Administration Hospital in Lexington, Kentucky (Wojcieszak et al., 2006). It is expected that this approach will spread to all healthcare organizations committed to creating a culture of safety and quality.

Reporting of Medical Errors

In January 2005, the Bush Administration commissioned experts to study medical malpractice litigation. The experts concluded that the public needs to be protected against substandard physician practices, and policing medical treatment would decrease the number of malpractice lawsuits. Additionally, it has been suggested that risk management efforts must be emphasized: including mandatory reporting of medical errors, helping physicians invest in health information technologies, and requiring physicians to study medical malpractice prevention techniques as part of their licensing requirements (Insurance Information Institute Inc., 2005).

Liability systems need to be in place to compensate those who have been negligently harmed, to penalize those who are negligent, and to deter negligence. A Congressional Joint Economic Committee Study headed by Jim Saxton (R-NJ) in 2003 analyzed the current medical malpractice system and found that the system does none of these things (Joint Economic Committee, 2003). Victims of negligence are not appropriately compensated, and the current system does not effectively deter negligent acts. In fact, the liability system may actually increase the number of errors and impede efforts to improve patient safety (IOM, 2001). In addition, the current liability system imposes tremendous costs on the American public that ultimately result in increased numbers of uninsured. The Joint Economic Committee (2003) concluded that reform of the current system could:

- Save on healthcare spending
- Reduce unnecessary treatments that are done out of fear of being sued
- Assist in identifying and reducing medical errors
- Help stop the mass exodus of physicians from high-litigation specialties
- Improve access to health care
- Increase the number of insured Americans
- Produce up to $19.5 billion in savings for the federal government

Injury Prevention Model

The IOM's report *To Err Is Human: Building a Safer Health System* focused attention on medical errors (Kohn et al., 2000). Patient safety may also be approached by focusing on the injury itself. Error-oriented approaches tend to include mistakes that do not harm patients, such as near-misses, whereas injury-oriented approaches include only mistakes that result in patient harm. This harm can result from either a therapeutic or diagnostic intervention. Harm and error are not always linked, as some errors do not result in injury.

The injury-oriented approach may therefore be more productive and provide more reliable data (Layde et al., 2002). Error-oriented studies can identify situations that might have led to patient injury, but Layde et al. (2002) are not convinced that the type of errors that do not harm patients are similar to the errors that do. Unfortunately, there is no shortage of patient injuries caused by error or otherwise. If studies target errors alone, they may focus on only a relatively small subset of medical injuries, missing the majority. It is also much easier to determine medical injury than medical error.

All healthcare providers must weigh the benefits of their proposed interventions against the risk of harm to the patient. Injury prevention models have been used successfully to reduce the incidence of patient falls, burns, and so forth. Focusing on patient injury, rather than error, facilitates implementation of an injury prevention model. The scientific foundation of this model is the belief that injuries are not accidents or random events, but are damage that results from predictable and preventable events (Layde et al., 2002). These events are thought to occur in particular patterns—that is, a chain of events leads to the injury. The injury prevention model seeks out the weakest link in the chain of causation. It takes into account the fact that breaking any link in the chain may prevent the injury.

Focusing on injury rather than on negligence has the advantage of recognizing crucial postinjury and rehabilitation care needs, which will improve patient outcomes. Furthermore, concentration on patient injuries can avoid many personal, institutional, and operational barriers to identifying errors. It also emphasizes preventability rather than culpability, which is consistent with patient safety goals (Layde et al., 2002).

National Patient Safety Goals

A few years ago, through the AHRQ, the federal government adopted the term *patient safety* (Kohn et al., 2000). Patient safety endeavors are crucial components of quality improvement and risk management activities in healthcare institutions. The Joint Commission has developed a set of National Patient Safety Goals (NPSGs) to help organizations address explicit areas of patient safety. Beginning January 1, 2003, all healthcare organizations accredited by The Joint Commission were required to demonstrate how they met the first six Joint Commission NPSGs (The Joint Commission, 2003). In 2009, The Joint Commission revised and expanded the NPSGs. The NPSGs have been identified for the following specific healthcare arenas (The Joint Commission, 2009):

1. Ambulatory health care
2. Behavioral health care
3. Critical access hospitals
4. Disease-specific care
5. Home care
6. Hospital
7. Laboratory
8. Long-term care and medicaid/medicare certification-based long-term care
9. Office-based surgery

There are currently ten NPSGs required for U.S. hospitals. These 10 goals focus on problems in healthcare safety in hospital settings and how to solve them.

The 2009 Hospital NPSGs are as follows (The Joint Commission, 2009):

1. Identify patients correctly
2. Improve staff communication
3. Use medicines safely
4. Prevent infection
5. Check patient medicines
6. Prevent patients from falling
7. Help patients to be involved in their care
8. Identify patient safety risks
9. Watch patients closely for changes in their health and respond quickly if they need help.
10. Prevent errors in surgery

In addition to comprehensive guidelines for each NPSG, The Joint Commission (2009) offers additional resources as follows:

- Medication reconciliation NPSG to be reviewed and refined
- 2009 FAQs about the NPSGs and the Universal Protocol
- Facts about the NPSGs
- A 2009 NPSG PowerPoint presentation

- Request for review of an alternative approach to an NPSG requirement
- Easy-to-read versions of the 2009 NPSGs for the public

Patient Safety in Critical Access Hospitals

The Critical Access Hospital Program was created by the 1997 federal Balanced Budget Act as a safety net device to assure Medicare beneficiaries access to healthcare services in rural areas. It was designed to allow more flexible staffing options relative to community need, simplify billing methods, and create incentives to develop local integrated health delivery systems, including acute, primary, emergency, and long-term care (Washington State Department of Health, 2009).

Casey et al. (2004) conducted a national survey of 474 critical access hospitals (CAHs) to identify their top patient safety priorities and their familiarity with and implementation of the Joint Commission NPSGs, limitations and supports for implementation of safety interventions, and efforts directed at medication safety. Results indicated that medication safety and prevention of patient falls were the most frequent categories of CAH safety initiatives. Sixty-three percent were familiar with The Joint Commission patient safety goals, and 55% to 88% had implemented strategies to achieve the goals in some manner. At least 50% of the CAH's reported limitations of financial, staff, and technological resources. Sixty-three percent had a pharmacist on site for less than 40 hours per week, and half used software to aid with medication dosing.

The authors concluded that CAHs are implementing some patient safety activities and are aware of national goals; however, more than half report severe limitations to full implementation, and pharmacy/medication safety efforts are still lacking (Casey et al., 2004).

Public Quality Reporting Systems

Since the IOM reports, there have been considerable attempts to hold healthcare providers accountable for the quality of care. To accomplish this, an abundance of national policies, performance measurement tools, and public and private reporting mechanisms have been put into place. The effort to hold healthcare providers accountable has come in response to lagging performance, mounting healthcare costs, and misaligned reimbursement systems (Kurtzman & Jennings, 2008).

Centers for Medicare & Medicaid Services

HOSPITAL COMPARE

In 2005, Hospital Compare was begun through a combined effort with Centers for Medicare & Medicaid Services (CMS), the American Hospital Association, the American Association of Medical Colleges, and the Federation of American Hospitals. To date, it is one of the largest volunteer hospital public reporting systems for short-term acute-care hospitals. Hospital Compare is a consumer-based Web site that provides information on how well hospitals provide recommended care to their patients that experienced congestive heart failure, heart attack, pneumonia, or surgery. In 2008, data from the Hospital CAHPS survey was added to provide a standardized method for measuring patient perspectives on their hospital care (CMS, 2009). Approximately 90% of the facilities that report their scores are acute-care hospitals, and the remaining 10% are CAHs (Laschober et al., 2007).

CMS REPORTING HOSPITAL QUALITY DATA FOR ANNUAL PAYMENT UPDATE

The CMS also collects 30 quality measures as part of its Reporting Hospital Quality Data for

Annual Payment Update program. This program requires hospitals to submit data for specific quality measures for health conditions that are common among people with Medicare and that typically result in hospitalization. The initiative is designed to furnish consumers with quality of care information to make more informed decisions about their health care. It is also designed to encourage clinicians and hospitals to improve the quality of inpatient care provided to all patients. Hospitals that do not participate in the Reporting Hospital Quality Data for Annual Payment Update initiative or that do not meet the reporting requirements are subject to a 2% reduction in their Medicare Annual Payment Update for the upcoming fiscal year (U.S. Department of Health and Human Services, 2008).

Preventable Complications

The CMS is now withholding payment for preventable complications of care (Pronovost et al., 2008). The preventable complications include those that are nurse sensitive and hospital acquired, including pressure ulcers, falls with injuries, and nosocomial infections. For example, nursing homes will no longer receive insurance reimbursement from Medicare for treatment provided to patients with hospital-acquired (iatrogenic) stage 3 pressure ulcers. A community-acquired pressure ulcer that a patient comes in to the hospital with, that is not documented on admission, and/or within the timeframe required by hospital policy is then considered hospital acquired (iatrogenic). Nurses must assess the patient's skin with the same attention as the patient's respiratory and cardiac status. This new Medicare standard essentially mandates that registered nurses admitting patients conduct a thorough skin assessment and document appropriately. After the initial skin assessment is completed by the registered nurse, it is incumbent on the physician to order appropriate treatments specific to the pressure ulcer stage and thus reduce the risk of advancement of a stage 1 pressure ulcer to a stage 3 pressure ulcer. Although pressure ulcers are widely viewed as a result of poor nursing care, it is actually the collaborative effort of the multidisciplinary healthcare team responsible for the patient or lack thereof.

AHRQ

The AHRQ is the health services research division of the U.S. Department of Health and Human Services. It works in conjunction with the biomedical research mission of the National Institutes of Health. The AHRQ research endeavors center around the following:

- Quality improvement and patient safety
- Outcomes and effectiveness of care
- Clinical practice and technology assessment
- Healthcare organization and delivery systems
- Primary care (including preventive services)
- Healthcare costs and sources of payment

In other words, this includes how people get access to health care, how much that care costs, and what happens to the patients during this care. The ultimate goal is to improve patient safety. At this printing, Congress has appropriated over $372 million for the 2009 fiscal year for AHRQ (Research America, 2009).

Patient Safety Indicators

A key research area for AHRQ has been the nursing workforce and patient care environment, linking healthcare staffing and workflow design to medical errors (Clancy et al., 2005). The AHRQ continues to develop patient safety indicators, which are tools to help healthcare agencies to identify potential adverse events occurring during hospitalization. Failure to rescue is one of the AHRQ patient safety indicators that has garnered much attention and research. Failure to rescue is measured by comparing the number of patients who die after surgery when they develop a postoperative complication with the number of patients who survive these complications and are discharged (Simpson, 2004). These postoperative complications may include sepsis, acute renal failure, cardiac arrest, pneumonia, hemorrhage, or thrombosis/embolus. Although the concept of failure to rescue a patient is not new, research by the AHRQ has suggested that it is a sensitive indicator of both the quality and quantity of nursing care (Simpson, 2004).

The Joint Commission

Quality Check

In 1996, The Joint Commission launched a directory of Joint Commission-accredited organizations and performance reports entitled Quality Check. This all-inclusive guide includes performance results on measures for common treatment areas, accreditation decisions, compliance with NPSGs, and Magnet status. In 2007, Quality Check was expanded to include organizations that are not Joint Commission accredited (Kurtzman et al., 2008).

Speak Up Campaign

The Joint Commission initiated a new national "Speak Up" campaign in January 2005, and this program urges Americans to take an active role in avoiding medication errors at the doctor's office, pharmacy, hospital, or clinic. The acronym "SPEAK UP" stands for (Hill, 2005):

- Speak up if you have questions or do not understand
- Pay attention to the care you are receiving
- Educate yourself about your diagnosis and tests
- Ask a trusted family member or friend to be your advocate
- Know what medications you take and why
- Use a hospital or clinic that has been evaluated for its quality
- Participate in all decisions about your treatment

Brochures and posters entitled "Things You Can Do to Prevent Medication Mistakes" were mailed to the nation's Fortune 1000 companies because The Joint Commission believes that employers have a crucial role in developing informed healthcare consumers among their employees.

Hospital Rating Systems

HealthGrades

HealthGrades, founded in 1999, is a private healthcare rating organization that is publically traded on NASDAQ. They provide profiles and independent ratings of hospitals and nursing homes to physicians, consumers, corporations, and insurance companies (HealthGrades.com, 2009). In their annual reports, HealthGrades identifies the top 5% of hospitals in terms of mortality and complication rates across 26 procedures and diagnoses. These top hospitals receive the designation of Distinguished Hospitals for Clinical Excellence by HealthGrades. In 2009, a study of Medicare patients found that 152,666 lives may have been saved and 11,772 major complications avoided during the 3 years studied had the quality of care at all hospitals matched the level of those in the top 5% (HealthGrades, Inc., 2009).

America's Best Hospitals

In 1990, the *U.S. News & World Report* magazine initiated an annual appraisal of U.S. hospitals.

Table 13-1 Red Flag Alerts for Patient Safety

Healthcare practitioners today must be educated and alert to "red flags" in their patient care. When a red flag is identified, appropriate action should be taken to remedy the situation. Specific red flags, as identified by Kavaler and Spiegel (2003), include the following:

- Poor treatment results
- A lack of follow-up care
- Repetitious problems
- Equipment malfunctioning
- Dissatisfied patients and/or family members
- Poor staff/patient relations
- Intimidated patients
- Poorly maintained medical records
- A lack of policies or procedures
- Excessive volume of patients
- Acting outside the scope of practice
- Personality conflicts
- Performance of a procedure without needed supervision

The patient who truly needs outstanding care is the target of the annual *U.S. News* "Best Hospitals" rankings. Hospitals are judged, not in routine procedures, but in difficult cases across 16 specialties. Twelve of the 16 specialty rankings are driven largely by hard data; in four others, ranking is based on 3 years of nominations by specialists surveyed. To be considered at all for the 12 data-driven specialties, a hospital had to meet at least one of three requirements: membership in the Council of Teaching Hospitals, affiliation with a medical school, or availability of at least 6 of 13 key technologies such as robotic surgery. In 2008, nearly two thirds of all hospitals failed this first test, and only 170 of 5,453 hospitals scored high enough to appear in any of the specialty rankings (Camarow, 2008).

National Database of Nursing Quality Indicators

The National Database of Nursing Quality Indicators (NDNQI) is a repository for nursing-sensitive indicators developed by the American Nurses Association and managed by the University of Kansas School of Nursing. More than 1,200 hospitals across the United States participate, volunteering unit-level data on structure, process, and outcome measures quarterly (Kurtzman et al., 2008). The NDNQI nursing-sensitive indicators are designed to be a sign of the structure, process, and outcomes of nursing care. Structure is indicated by the availability of nursing staff, skill level of nurses, and the education and certification of nursing staff. Process indicators measure the assessment, intervention of patient care, and registered nurse job satisfaction. Outcomes measured for nursing sensitivity are those that improve if there is a greater quantity or quality of nursing care. These might include patient falls, intravenous infiltrations, pressure ulcers, and so forth (American Nurses Association, 2009). Recently, the NDNQI has worked in conjunction with the National Quality Forum and The Joint Commission, using their nursing-sensitive indicators.

Conclusion

This chapter has focused on the tremendous impact the IOM studies have had on quality efforts to reduce errors in health care. Theories of error and error management are explored, along with numerous resulting national healthcare initiatives and mandates. Healthcare providers must be committed to developing a culture of safety where errors are accepted as inevitable, but members of the healthcare team are ever vigilant and committed to the prevention of error. This new culture of safety includes support and counseling for those who make mistakes and open communication of errors and safety issues (see Table 13-1).

References

Agency for Healthcare Research and Quality. (2002). *Improving health care quality. Fact sheet* (Agency for Healthcare Quality and Research Publication Number 02-P032, September, 2002. ed., Vol. 2003). Rockville, MD: Agency for Healthcare Research and Quality.

Agency for Healthcare Research and Quality. (2005). *30 safe practices for better health care.* Agency for Healthcare Research and Quality Publication No. 05-P007. Retrieved April 2, 2005, from www.ahrq.gov/qual/nqfpract.htm

American Nurses Association. (2009). *Nursing sensitive indicators.* Retrieved on March 15, 2009, from http://www.nursingworld.org/MainMenuCategories/ThePracticeofProfessionalNursing/PatientSafetyQuality/NDNQI/NDNQI_1/NursingSensitiveIndicators.aspx

Byers, J. F., & White, S. V. (2004). *Patient safety: Principles and practice.* New York: Springer Publishing Company.

California Academy of Family Physicians. (2002). *Diagnosing and treating medical errors in family practice.* Retrieved April 2, 2005, from www.familydocs.org/positions.html

Camarow, A. (2008). A Look Inside the Hospital Rankings: How 170 out of 5,453 centers made the cut. *U.S. News & World Report.* Posted July 10, 2008. Retrieved March 15, 2009, from http://health.usnews.com/articles/health/best-hospitals/2008/07/10/a-look-inside-the-hospital-rankings.html

Casey, M., Moscovice, I., & Klingner, J. (2004). *Quality improvement activities in critical access hospitals: Results of the 2004 National CAH Survey. (Briefing Paper No. 2).* Minneapolis, MN: Flex Monitoring Team. Retrieved February 13, 2010, from http://www.flexmonitoring.org/documents/Briefing Paper2_QI. pdf

Centers for Medicare & Medicaid Services. (2009). *Hospital compare.* Retrieved on March 15, 2009 from http://www.cms.hhs.gov/HospitalQualiatyInits/11_HospitalCompare.asp

Clancy, C. M., Farquhar, M. B., & Collins Sharp, B. A. (2005). Patient safety in nursing practice. *Journal of Nursing Care Quality 20*(3), 193–197.

Dorschner, J. (2003, May 6). Study finds healthcare error prone. *The Miami Herald.* Retrieved May 9, 2003, from http://www.miami.com/mld/miamiherald/5793074.htm

Ebright, P., Urder, L., Patterson, E., & Chalko, B. (2004). Themes surrounding novice nurse near-miss and adverse-event situations. *Journal of Nursing Administration, 34*(11), 531–538.

HealthGrades.com. (2009). *About us.* Retrieved March 15, 2009 from http://www.healthgrades.com/about-us

HealthGrades, Inc. (2005). *Health grades second annual patient safety in American hospitals report.* Retrieved May 5, 2005, from http://www.healthgrades.com/media/DMS/pdf/PatientSafetyInAmericanHospitalsReportFINAL42905Post.pdf

HealthGrades Inc. (2009). *Top hospitals have 27% lower mortality: annual health grades study.* January 27, 2009. Retrieved March 15, 2009, from http://www.healthgrades.com/media/dms/pdf/DHPCERRelease2008.pdf

Helmreich, R. L. (2000). On error management: Lessons from aviation. *British Medical Journal, 320*, 781–785.

Helmreich, R. L., & Davies, J. L. (2004). Culture, threat, and error: Lessons from aviation. *Canadian Journal of Anesthesia, 51*(6), R1–R4.

Hill, C. D. (2005). *Speak up: New national campaign offers Americans tips to prevent medication mistakes.* Retrieved February 22, 2005, from http://www.jcaho.org

Institute of Medicine. (2001). *Crossing the quality chasm: A new health system for the 21st century*. Washington: National Academy Press.

Insurance Information Institute Inc. (2005, February). *Medical malpractice.* Retrieved March 1, 2005, from http://www.iii.org/media/hottopics/insurance/medicalmal/

Joint Economic Committee. (2003). *Liability for medical malpractice: Issues and evidence*. Washington, DC: United States Congress.

Kavaler, F., & Spiegel, A. D. (2003). *Risk management in health care institutions: A strategic approach* (2nd ed.). Sudbury, MA: Jones and Bartlett Publishers.

Kohn, L. T., Corrigan, J. M., & Donaldson, M. S. (Eds.). (2000). *To err is human: Building a safer health system*. Washington, DC: National Academy Press.

Kurtzman, E. T., Dawson, E. M., & Johnson, J. E. (2008). The current state of nursing performance measurement, public reporting, and value-based purchasing. *Policy, Politics, & Nursing Practice, 9*(3), 181–191.

Kurtzman, E. T., & Jennings, B. M. (2008). Trends in transparency: Nursing performance measurement and reporting. *Journal of Nursing Administration, 38*(7/8), 349–354.

Kwong, E., Pang, S., Wong, T., Ho, J., Shao-ling, X., & Li-Jun, T. (2005). Predicting pressure ulcer risk with the modified Braden, Braden, and Norton scales in acute care hospitals in Mainland China. *Applied Nursing Research, 18,* 122–128.

Landro, L. (2002, August 29). Deadly errors dog procedures at doctors' offices and clinics. *The Wall Street Journal,* p. D3.

Laschober, M., Maxfield, M., Felt-Lisk, S., & Miranda, D. J. (2007). Hospital response to public reporting of quality indicators. *Health Care Financing Review, 28*(3), 61–76.

Layde, P. M., Cortes, L. M., Teret, S. P., Brasel, K. J., Kuhn, E. M., Mercy, J. A., et al. (2002). Patient safety efforts should focus on medical injuries. *JAMA, 287*(15), 1993–1997.

Liang, B. A. (2001). The adverse event of unaddressed medical error: Identifying and filling the holes in the health-care and legal systems. *J Law Med Ethics, 29*(3–4), 346–368.

Monk, J. (2002, June 16). Medical mistakes kept secret. *The State,* pp. A1, A6–A7.

Nordenberg, T. (2000, September–October). Make no mistake: Medical errors can be deadly serious. FDA Consumer Magazine. Retrieved January 27, 2004, from http://www.fda.gov/fdac/features/2000/500_err.html

Pronovost, P. J., Goeschel, C. A., & Wachter, R. M. (2008). The wisdom and justice of not paying for preventable complications. *The New England Journal of Medicine, 299*(18), 2197–2199.

Research America. (2009). Investment in research. Retrieved March 15, 2009 from http://www.researchamerica.org/investment_issue

Reason, J. (2000). Human error: Models and management. *British Medical Journal, 320*, 768–770.

Rivers, R. M., Swain, D., & Nixon, W. R. (2003). Using aviation safety measures to enhance patient outcomes. *Association of Operating Room Nurses Journal, 77,* 158–162.

Simpson, K. R. (2004). Failure to rescue: Implications for evaluating quality of care during labor and birth. *Journal of Perinatal Neonatal Nursing, 19*(1), 24–34.

Spath, P. L. (Ed.). (1999). *Error reduction in health care: A systems approach to improving patient safety*. San Francisco: Jossey-Bass, A Wiley Company.

The Joint Commission. (2003, January). Special report! 2003 JCAHO national patient safety goals: Practical strategies and helpful solutions for meeting these goals. *Joint Commission Perspectives on Patient Safety, 3*(1). Retrieved October 1, 2004, from www.jointcommission.org

The Joint Commission. (2009). 2009 National patient safety goals. Retrieved May 25, 2009, from http://www.jointcommission.org/PatientSafety/NationalPatientSafetyGoals/

Thomas, E. J., & Petersen, L. A. (2003). Measuring errors and adverse events in health care. *J Gen Intern Med, 18*(1), 61–67.

U.S. Department of Health & Human Services, Centers for Medicare & Medicaid Services. (2008, December 31). *Fact sheet: CMS updates the National Hospital Quality Measure Acute Myocardial Infarction Set for Discharges as of April 1, 2009.*

Wachter, R. M., & Shojania, K. G. (2004). *Internal bleeding: The truth behind America's terrifying epidemic of medical mistakes* (1st ed.). New York City: Rugged Land, LLC.

Washington State Department of Health. (2009). Rural health programs: What is a critical access hospital? Retrieved on March 15, 2009, from http://www.doh.wa.gov/hsqa/ocrh/CAH/cah399.html

Weinberg, J. K. (2002). Medical error and patient safety: Understanding cultures in conflict. *Law & Policy, 24*(2), 93–113.

Williams, I. E. (2004). *First, do no harm: The cure for medical malpractice*. Mount Pleasant: Corinthian Books.

Wojcieszak, D., Banja, J., & Houk, C. (2006). Forum: The Sorry Works! Coalition: making the case for full disclosure. *Joint Commission Journal on Quality and Patient Safety, 32*(6), 344–350.

Woods, A., & Doan-Johnson, S. (2002). Executive summary: Toward a taxonomy of nursing practice errors. *Nursing Management, 33*(10), 45–48.

CASE STUDY

Patient Risk Assessment Tools

Helen Werner

Patient Falls—Morse Fall Scale

Fall incidence and subsequent injuries are also of great importance as nursing quality indicators. The Morse Fall Scale is not always an accurate assessment of fall risk according to the guidelines developed by Morse (2009); therefore, the predictive value is indeterminate. A study conducted in Australia by McFarlane-Kolb (2004) found that the Morse Falls Scale, in combination with other risk factors, more accurately reflected fall risk among older persons admitted to an acute surgical unit. Major tranquilizer use and male gender were the most significant predictors of fall risk in this population. The Morse Fall Scale can be easily modified to include additional risk factors that are more accurate predictors of fall risk for the indigenous population. This is important in terms of guidelines that are developed by the hospital, which may be formulated based on the calculated fall risk may be inaccurate for the particular population being served. If a patient is identified to be at risk for falls, a more in-depth assessment is needed to determine the causative factors, especially those that are treatable.

Several fall-risk assessment tools were evaluated for validity by Ang et al. (2007). The Morse Fall Scale, St. Thomas Risk Assessment Tool in the Falling Elderly Inpatients, and Heindrich II Fall Risk Model were all validated in interrater reliability and validity studies; however, only the Heindrich II Fall Risk Model had a higher level of specificity (61.5%) than the Morse Fall Scale (48.3%). The Morse Fall Scale is the gold standard for fall-risk assessment in the United States; however, if nurses demonstrate difficulty scoring a patient's fall risk accurately, it may be necessary to consider piloting the use of another scale that may be more user friendly.

Patient Skin Assessment Tools

It is not uncommon for clinicians to shorten or modify risk assessments, like the Braden Scale, according to Braden and Maklebust (2005). This reduces the likelihood that a skin assessment will be predictive of pressure ulcer development during a hospitalization. The explanation is rather simple. The complete tool was tested for validity and reliability. Even minor changes can impact the accuracy of the scale. Research has been conducted by Bergquist (2001) testing modified Braden Scales and subsets to determine the extent of accuracy for predicting patients at greater risk of developing pressure ulcers. Bergquist found that the summative score rather than any subset of the Braden was most predictive of pressure ulcer risk for older persons receiving home health care; however, researchers in China (Kwong et al., 2005) found a modified Braden Scale more predictive for pressure ulcer prediction, with the addition of skin and body build for height and the exclusion of nutrition, which was a surprising finding. One explanation offered by the researchers was that the focus of oral intake and protein only does not accurately represent patients' nutritional status. It may also be necessary to explore modifications of the Braden Scale based on cultural differences.

Assessment tools such as the Braden Scale may not be as accurate as nurses' judgment. A study conducted by Lewicki et al. (2000) for cardiac surgery patients found that the sensitivity of the Braden Scale was 40% and its specificity was 70% compared with nurses' judgment, which was found to be a sensitivity of 49% and a specificity of 73%. Additionally, the researchers recommended that the cutoff score that has been 16 or less is more applicable to long-term care than acute care and may need to vary for each postoperative day.

The NDNQI accepts data from hospitals using other scales for skin assessment that the participating hospital is using. Data using the Norton Scale are also acceptable and, in fact, are noted on the data collection tool that the designated NDNQI site coordinator must use to enter data. Unfortunately, there is no way to determine whether the calculated score using the Braden Scale/Norton Scale published on the NDNQI Web site for the participating hospitals is based on use of the complete Braden Scale/Norton Scale or a modified version that had been previously tested for validity and reliability. The accuracy of this data is of great importance to the participating hospitals, as individual units are able to compare themselves to similar types of participating NDNQI units across the country. The collection and entry of data for quality improvement as a participating hospital in NDNQI is deemed necessary to attain Magnet Certification.

References

Ang, N. K. E., Mordiffi, S. Z., Wong, H. B., Devi, K., & Evans, D. (2007). Evaluation of three fall-risk assessment tools in an acute care setting. *Journal of Advanced Nursing, 60*(4), 427–435.

Bergquist, S. (2001). Subscales, subscores, or summative score: Evaluating the contribution of Braden scale items for predicting pressure ulcer risk in older adults receiving home health care. *Journal of Wound, Ostomy and Continence Nurses Society, 28,* 279–289.

Braden, B., & Maklebust, J. (2005). Preventing pressure ulcers with the Braden Scale. *American Journal of Nursing, 105*(6), 70–72.

Kwong, E., Pang, S., Wong, T., Ho, J., Shao-ling, X., & Li-Jun, T. (2005). Predicting pressure ulcer risk with the modified Braden, Braden, and Norton scales in acute care hospitals in Mainland China. *Applied Nursing Research, 18,* 122–128.

Lewicki, L. J., Mion, L. C., & Secic, M. (2000). Sensitivity and specificity of the Braden scale in the cardiac surgical population. *Journal of Wound, Ostomy and Continence Nurses Society, 27,* 36–41.

McFarlane-Kolb, H. (2004). Falls risk assessment, multitargeted interventions and the impact on hospital falls. *International Journal of Nursing Practice, 10,* 199–206.

Morse, J. M. (2009). *Preventing patient falls*, 2nd ed. New York: Springer Publishing.

Health Services Research

Chapter 14

Donna M. Nickitas, Keville Frederickson, and Jonathan Small

OVERVIEW

Predicting and responding to the healthcare demands of the 21st century will require resources from many fronts. Interdisciplinary partnerships will be needed to coordinate healthcare needs, to develop models for future needs, to determine appropriate resources, and to measure quality outcomes with respect to cost.

Because health services research is centrally focused on the ability to build knowledge and generate the evidence needed to craft the delivery of high-quality, cost-efficient health care, it will be the heuristic that leads to informed answers. This type of research provides the facts for improving how, when, and where health care is to be delivered; however, determining what criteria constitute "good" research is critical. If the research evidence is valid and reliable, then it has the potential to direct health policy that is innovative and fair, and that has a high level of cost benefit. For the peak and best use of resources, healthcare practices and delivery systems must be tracked and analyzed to determine improvement, progress over time, and most importantly factors that affect both quality and cost.

OBJECTIVES

- To understand the formal definition of health services research
- To determine factors that contribute to research that can serve as the foundation for health policy decisions
- To describe methods and strategies for health services research
- To explain how performance measurement and reporting systems are currently used
- To recognize how performance measurement data influence health policy decisions on process improvements that lead to improved quality and patient safety

(continues)

- To describe how to motivate and include all of the key stakeholders in health services research and improvement activities
- To identify ways to stay on top of new developments in health services research
- To overcome barriers to health services research and reporting

KEY TERMS

- ❏ Agency for Healthcare Research and Quality (AHRQ)
- ❏ Care coordination
- ❏ Centers for Medicare & Medicaid Services (CMS)
- ❏ Chronic illness
- ❏ Evidence-based practice
- ❏ Health Care Financing Administration
- ❏ Health disparity
- ❏ Health inequality
- ❏ Health policy meta-analysis
- ❏ Health services research
- ❏ Large data sets
- ❏ Process-of-care measures
- ❏ Quality indicators
- ❏ Quality measurement and improvement

Definition

Health services research is the multidisciplinary field of scientific investigation that studies how social factors, financing systems, organizational structures and processes, health technologies, politics, and personal behaviors affect access to health care and ultimately our health and well-being. The definition of health services research is constantly evolving and has been defined differently by a variety of experts and organizations; however, the most comprehensive definition is one by the Agency for Healthcare Research and Quality (AHRQ). It defines health services research as the analysis of how people get access to health care, how much care costs, and what happens to patients as a result of this care. The main goals of health services research are to identify the most effective ways to organize, manage, finance, and deliver high-quality care, reduce medical errors, and improve patient safety (AHRQ, 2007). Its research domains are individuals, families, organizations, institutions, communities, and populations. To effectively reshape the U.S. healthcare system to focus on objective evidence and outcomes rather than physician preference as the basis for treatment decisions, healthcare clinicians must recognize the importance of evidence-based practice (EBP) to guide healthcare delivery and the movement toward patient-centered care for many of the improvements in healthcare quality and efficiency. Rousseau (2006) describes evidence-based practice as a paradigm for making decisions that integrate the best available research evidence with decision-maker expertise and client/customer preferences to guide practice toward more desirable results. For evidence-based practice to make a difference in client outcome, it must include care coordination as well.

Care coordination ensures that client's needs and preferences are understood and that those needs and preferences are shared between clinicians, clients, and families as the client moves from one healthcare arena to another. As the number of healthcare clinicians and treatments involved in a patient's care has increased, the coordination of care has become more challenging. Less attention is being paid to the care that patients receive as they move from one setting to another (Naylor, 2006). In fact, a recent analysis of Medicare beneficiaries discharged from hospitals with a diagnosis of heart failure showed a 27% readmission rate within 30 days, a 39% readmission within 60 days, and almost 50% within 90 days (Jencks et al., 2009). Research has shown that care must be well coordinated to avoid waste, overuse, underuse, or misuse of prescribed medications and conflicting plans of care (Bodenheimer, 2008). Care coordination has a significant impact on health status and an effect on quality of life, especially for hospitalized older adults (Naylor & Keating, 2008). Older adults who experience several changes related to their care settings are at higher risks for adverse outcomes because of the numerous health issues that persist beyond hospital discharge (Naylor, 2004).

Care coordination becomes an even more important issue given the increasing number of persons with chronic health conditions. Bodenheimer (2008) suggests that clients with chronic health conditions may see up to 16 different physicians a year. When patients receive care from multiple providers, they are at greater risk for fragmented care because of communication breakdown, which often results in poor handoffs (Coleman & Berenson, 2004; Krizner, 2009; Naylor & Keating, 2008). As life expectancy increases so will chronic illnesses. In 2000, 125 million people in the United States were living with at least one chronic illness, a number that is expected to grow to 157 million by 2020. The number of individuals with multiple chronic conditions is expected to reach 81 million by 2020 (Bodenheimer, 2008). As individuals with chronic illness attempt to navigate the complex healthcare system and transition from one care setting to another, they will be unprepared or unable to manage their care. Again, incomplete or inaccurate transfer of information, poor communication, and a lack of appropriate follow-up care can lead to confusion and poor outcomes, including often preventable hospital readmissions and emergency department visits.

The Institute of Medicine has identified care coordination as a priority for national action because of its great importance to improve care (Adams & Corrigan, 2003). In May 2006, the National Quality Forum (NQF) endorsed a definition and framework for care coordination. NQF has defined care coordination as a "function that helps ensure that the patient's needs and preferences for health services and information sharing across people, functions, and sites are met over time" (National Quality Forum, 2009b). This framework includes five key dimensions: healthcare "home"; proactive plan of care and follow-up; communication; information systems; and transitions or hand-offs. These represent essential components and subcomponents for which performance measures are developed if care coordination is to be comprehensively measured and improved (see Table 14-1).

In 2008, the National Priority Partnership made care coordination one of six national priorities and has committed to working toward the following goals (National Quality Forum, 2009b):

- Improve care and achieve quality by facilitating and carefully considering feedback from all patients regarding coordination of their care
- Improve communication around medication information; work to reduce 30-day readmission rates
- Work to reduce preventable emergency department visits by 50%

Table 14-1 FRAMEWORK FOR CARE COORDINATION

1. Healthcare "home"—a source of usual care selected by the patient (such as a large or small medical group, a single practitioner, a community health center, or a hospital outpatient clinic). The medical home functions as the central point for coordinating care around the patient's needs and preferences.
2. Proactive plan of care and follow-up—an established and current care plan that anticipates routine needs and actively tracks up-to-date progress toward patient goals.
3. Communication—available to all team members, including patients and family—shared plan of care. All medical home team members work within the same plan of care and are measurably co-accountable for their contributions to the shared plan and achieving the patient's goals.
4. Information systems—the use of standardized, integrated electronic information systems with functionalities essential to care coordination is available to all providers and patients. Important characteristics include seamless interoperability; an evidence-based plan of care management; efficient and effective integration of patient information, laboratory, imaging, referrals, medications, social and community services, and self-management support; patient registries and population-based data, especially those promoted by local, state, and federal public health agencies; support for quality improvement and safety; case/disease management; decision support tools; and provider alerts and patient reminders.
5. Transitions or "hand-offs"—transitions between settings of care are a special case because currently they are fraught with numerous mishaps that can make care uncoordinated, disconnected, and unsafe. Some care processes during transition deserve particular attention:
   - Medication reconciliation
   - Follow-up tests and services
   - Changes in plan of care
   - Involvement of team during hospitalization, nursing home stay and so forth
   - Communications with persons who do not speak English well or at all

Using Research for Changes in Health Services

Health services research attempts to focus on practices that have strong evidence that they are effective in reducing the likelihood of harming a patient, are generalizable (i.e., they may be applied in multiple clinical care settings and/or for multiple types of patients), are likely to have a significant benefit to patient safety if fully implemented, and are usable by consumers, purchasers, providers, and researchers.

The evidence emerging from health services research is predominantly centered on quality measurement and improvement. These findings from quality and performance measures have historical roots within the American healthcare system dating back to the early 1900s. In 1910, Ernest Codman, MD, became one of the first healthcare professionals to propose a quality method system when he introduced what was known as the end-result system of hospital standardization. Codman learned to track every patient to measure the effectiveness of his or her treatment. Later, Codman created the minimum standard for hospitals to help diminish and eliminate substandard care. Only 13% of 692 hospitals initially met the minimum standard of care (Anderson & Schulke, 2008).

Efforts to improve or quality-control healthcare delivery were impacted by the quality movement. This movement which began in the industrial sector is identified with W. Edwards Deming and Joseph M. Juran. Deming is considered the pioneer in the quality management movement. As an advocate for quality, he identified that 80% to 85% of problems are system related with the rest of 15% to 20% associated with human error or worker produced. He advocated and adopted principles of management that encouraged organizations to increase quality while simultaneously reducing costs (by reducing waste, rework, staff attrition, and litigation while increasing customer loyalty). The key, as suggested by Deming, is to practice continual improvement and to think of manufacturing as a system, not as bits and pieces.

Juran's philosophy of quality is focused on three premises: quality planning, quality control, and quality improvement. This quality trilogy (planning, improvement, and control) seeks to define quality as fitness to serve, correct service the first time to meet customer's need and freedom from deficiencies (Anderson & Schulke, 2008). Before 1966, improvements in healthcare quality focused primarily on structure and included such activities as evaluating staffing levels, facility attributes, licensing, and accreditation. With the quality management work of Avedis Donabedian, the concept of quality management expanded to include the evaluation of processes and outcomes. This three-pronged approach (structure, process, and outcomes) launched the development of standards of care and clinical guidelines used by healthcare organizations today. In fact, it is the Donabedian model that drives the IOM in performance measurement with their six aims of quality, including: safe, effective, patient-centered, timely, efficient and equitable (IOM, 2006). Implementation of IOM guidelines by healthcare organizations support the creation of a mission and vision, development of a quality management plan, support for quality, use of evidence-based clinical practice, and utilization management. Studies and reports are available at the IOM Web site, http://www.iom.edu/CMS/8089.aspx.

Public reporting on measurement and outcomes by hospitals is relatively new. The Health Care Financing Administration (now renamed the Centers for Medicare & Medicaid Services [CMS]) was the first to attempt to measure and publicly report hospital outcomes that were reported from 1986 to 1993. The Health Care Financing Administration was forced to withdraw its mortality measures because of the widespread criticism it received from hospital administrators. In 2006, CMS reintroduced outcomes reporting with risk-adjusted mortality rates for heart failure and heart attack. The process-of-care measure shows how often hospitals give recommended treatments known to get the best results for patients with certain medical conditions or surgical procedures. This is one way to compare the quality of care that hospitals give.

The precursors of today's process-of-care quality measures began with the development of a modest set of Medicare quality indicators under the supervision of officials at the Health Standards and Quality Bureau. Indicators reflected a perceived need to acknowledge that the available data focused on care processes and could not capture or describe most of the factors influencing patient outcomes. In addition, quality indicators were developed for self-assessment and internal use by providers, avoiding much of the political pushback associated with public reporting. The indicators themselves were constructed by expert consensus among leading clinicians, based on the strong scientific foundation of large-scale clinical studies such as the Physicians' Health Study—a January 1988 study affirming that aspirin therapy prevents heart attack—and the

August 1988 Second International Study of Infarct Survival, which showed that aspirin therapy reduced heart attack mortality by 23% at a cost of $13 per life saved (Krumholz et al., 1995). Studies showed that about a quarter of patients who appeared to be candidates for aspirin treatment were not receiving it.

In 1999, the Joint Commission on Accreditation of Healthcare Organizations (now simply The Joint Commission) began to develop a set of core measures for hospitals, announcing its measure sets 2 years later. The measures for heart attack, heart failure, and pneumonia were nearly identical to those in nationwide use for 5 years by the Medicare program, but varied slightly in their specifications. The Joint Commission added measures addressing pregnancy and related conditions, extending the reach of quality measures to a large, new population beyond the older and disabled. With two similar public and private measurement systems for care of older persons operating side by side, providers asked for the compromise of a common set of measurement specifications, but it took 2 years of negotiations to produce a single nationally standardized set of 10 core measures in 2002. Agreement on these core measures lessened inefficiencies in hospital data gathering and reporting and coincided with the launch of the public–private Hospital Quality Alliance that called on hospitals to report publicly their performance using the new unified measure set. The core measures were formally adopted by act of Congress in 2003 as the basis for a reimbursement incentive for voluntary performance reporting. Subsequent legislation has repeatedly expanded both the measure set and the extent of the incentive for hospital reporting. All of the Hospital Quality Measures used by The Joint Commission and the CMS are endorsed by the NQF. These measures are also used for the "Hospital Quality Alliance: Improving Care through Information," a voluntary public reporting initiative led by the American Hospital Association, the Federation of American Hospitals, and the Association of American Medical Colleges. This initiative is supported by The Joint Commission, the CMS, the NQF, the AHRQ, the American Federation of Labor and Congress of Industrial Organizations, and the AARP (formerly American Association of Retired Persons). Hospital quality measures and other core measure data are part of the priority focus process that is used by The Joint Commission to help focus onsite survey activities. These data are also publicly reported on The Joint Commission's Quality Check Web site (www.qualitycheck.org). The public availability of performance measurement data facilitates user comparisons of hospital performance and permits comparisons against overall national rates.

Evidence Based Practice

One source of health services research is EBP. This approach to patient care stresses decision making, which is based not only on the available evidence but also on patient characteristics, situations, and preferences. It recognizes that care is individualized and ever changing and involves uncertainties and probabilities. EBP develops individualized guidelines of best practices to inform the improvement of whatever professional task is at hand. EBP is a philosophical approach that is in opposition to tradition. EBP began in 1971 when Professor Archie Cochrane scolded medical practitioners for their approach to care by saying that only health care based on research evidence should be reimbursed (Cochrane, 1971). At the same time, he contended that the only research that should be conducted and used would be the randomized controlled trial (RCT). The RCT is the highest level of research that includes randomization (all participants have an equal chance for assignment to the control and the experimental groups) at all levels of the research design, control, and intervention groups and represents an experimental design for a quantitative study. The key elements for using EBP are to determine the clinical problem or situation requirements, the level of EBP to be used, and how the outcome or evaluation of the intervention will be measured. Levels of EBP range from the RCT to perceptions of factors that influence treatment success by experts.

One of the most powerful approaches in determining factors that affect health and the effect of policy on health is a meta-analysis. A meta-analysis is a type of research in which the results of multiple studies are combined and analyzed to synthesize and summarize the results. In this way, one statistical outcome is produced to indicate the effectiveness of such things as a treatment outcome or factors that place populations at risk for an illness or disease. In order to conduct a meta-analysis, the terminology and definitions need to be systematic and have common meanings. For example, in attempting to present research data on health disparities, there were at least five different definitions of the criteria that constitute a health disparity. As a result, when synthesizing data on health disparities, it is difficult to know which studies to include as well as the frame of reference used to establish the definition.

Systems to stratify evidence by quality have been developed, such as this one by the U.S. Preventive Services Task Force for ranking evidence about the effectiveness of treatments or screening (Melnyk et al., 2005):

- Level I: evidence obtained from at least one properly designed RCT.
- Level II-1: evidence obtained from well-designed controlled trials without randomization.
- Level II-2: evidence obtained from well-designed cohort or case-control analytic studies, preferably from more than one center or research group.
- Level II-3: evidence obtained from multiple time series with or without the intervention. Dramatic results in uncontrolled trials might also be regarded as this type of evidence.
- Level III: opinions of respected authorities, based on clinical experience, descriptive studies, or reports of expert committees.

Exemplar of EBP from a Private Organization: The Cochrane Library

The Cochrane Library consists of reviews of research that are evaluated independently using rigorous criteria for evaluating research that is necessary for making informed decisions about practice by healthcare providers. This is an outstanding repository of seven databases with information that is categorized in many ways, including relevance for specific professions such as nursing, physical therapy, and medicine as well as according to illnesses, body systems, and health promotion/disease prevention. The databases also include research evidence related to patient safety issues, financial and economic reports, and assessment of technology and methodology for conducting EBP. Overall, there are almost 750,000 records related to EBP. By searching for "health policy," 60 entries were returned with titles such as "Policy interventions implemented through sporting organizations for promoting healthy behavior change," "Pharmaceutical policies: effects of cap and co-payment on rational drug use," and "Methods of consumer involvement in developing healthcare policy and research, clinical practice guidelines and patient information material." In summary, the Cochrane Library is an excellent source for research related to health and health services policy. The research is evaluated using high standards and reported in a way that can be applied to interventions by healthcare providers as well as used to guide and direct policy.

FEDERAL EXEMPLAR: AGENCY OF HEALTH CARE RESEARCH AND QUALITY

AHRQ is the lead Federal agency charged with supporting research designed to improve the quality of health care, reduce its cost, address patient safety and medical errors, and broaden access to essential services. AHRQ sponsors and conducts research that provides evidence-based information on healthcare outcomes; quality; and cost, use, and access. The information helps healthcare decision makers—patients and clinicians, health system leaders, and policy makers—to make more informed decisions and improve the quality of healthcare services.

One category of research supported by AHRQ is the Evidence-Based Practice Program. Twelve five-year contracts have been awarded to institutions in the United States and Canada to serve as EBP centers. The EBP centers develop evidence reports and technology assessments based on rigorous, comprehensive syntheses and analyses of relevant scientific literature, emphasizing explicit and detailed documentation of methods, rationale, and assumptions (http://www.ahrq.gov;/2009). Their publications are organized in three categories:

- Evidence reports/technology assessments
- Evidence reports/technology assessment summaries
- Technical reviews and summaries

Beginning in 1999, the first EBP report was published. This first report presented the evidence on systematic review of the literature regarding the diagnosis of sleep apnea (which is identified now as "out of date") and the most recent, number 177, published February 2009 on the topic of complementary and alternative medicine in back pain utilization. The standards for these publications are very specific.

EBP AND SOCIAL POLICY

There are increasing demands for social policy and other decisions related to programs run by government and non-government organizations (NGOs) to be based on sound evidence as to their effectiveness. This has seen an increased emphasis on the use of a wide range of evaluation approaches directed at obtaining evidence about social programs of all types. A research collaboration called the Campbell Collaboration has been set up in the social policy area to provide evidence for evidence-based social policy decision making. This collaboration follows the approach pioneered by the Cochrane Collaboration in the health sciences (Cochrane, 1971). Using an evidence-based approach to social policy has a number of advantages because it has the potential to decrease the tendency to run programs that are socially acceptable (e.g., drug education in schools) but that often prove to be ineffective when evaluated (Frederickson, 2007).

Quality of Care and Equality of Care

A primary area for health services research has been the quality of care provided by healthcare agencies. Healthcare providers are held accountable for the care that is rendered to the public through many mechanisms. Quality of care is evaluated by accrediting agencies, the federal government health-related programs, and the insurance companies. The Institute of Medicine defines quality as "the degree to which health services for individuals and populations increase the likelihood of desired health outcomes and are consistent with current professional knowledge." Attributes of patient care include improved safety, improved outcomes, and improved satisfaction.

In addition, standards for quality care are a priority for determining equality in health care. For example, in a large data set analysis of three states—California, Florida and New York—it was found that blacks were not afforded the same level of treatment for a myocardial infarction as non-Hispanic whites (Bennett, 2004).

One landmark study conducted by the RAND corporation (McGlynn et al., 2003) in collaboration with the Community Quality Index (a collateral study of the Community Tracking Study) determined the extent to which 439 indicators of quality of care were implemented for 30 acute and chronic illnesses and also included evidence of preventive care. In addition, participants were sampled in 12 large metropolitan areas throughout the United States to determine the extent to which recommended standards of medical care were actually implemented. Through a health history interview and an examination of health records, patient health assessments and interventions were analyzed.

The indicators of quality of care used parts of the RAND Quality Assessment Tools system. The leading causes of illness, death, and seeking health care for different age groups formed the basis for selecting the conditions to be studied, as well as preventive strategies for each of the study conditions. For example, the condition of hypertension had 27 medical care indicators and included interventions such as lifestyle modification for patients with mild hypertension and pharmacotherapy for uncontrolled mild hypertension.

The RAND study serves as an exemplar of health services research because the study exceeded most criteria for quality and reliable research. Beginning with sampling, the study included representative cities throughout the United States, accounting for geographic diversity. Reliability of the data was implemented through the use of two approaches for data collection. Participant interviews were conducted as well as the examination of their health records to corroborate interview data.

Health Disparity

Although there is no universal agreement on a definition of health disparities, the term is generally used to refer to gaps in health care along racial, ethnic, and socioeconomic lines. Health disparities do not encompass all variations in health or health care but, rather, specifically the experience in which less fortunate populations systematically experience worse health or increased health risks than more privileged communities (Braveman, 2006). As defined by The Health Resources and Services Administration, health disparities are "population-specific differences in the presence of disease, health outcomes or access to health care" (Goldberg et al., 2004).

In measuring health inequality, the most common method has been to take more and less advantaged social groups and compare the two. To determine where a social group is situated, socioeconomic advantages are often determined by educational achievement, employment characteristics, income/expenditures, net worth, health insurance, or geographical location. In the United States, because health inequality is most often associated with racial and ethnic differences, health disparities have long been measured by comparing minority groups with whites or non-Hispanic/Latino whites (Braveman, 2006).

The problem with measuring health inequality is the variations in defining terms such as health inequality, health disparities, and racial and ethnic disparities in health care. For research to be useful, a clear identification must be made of what makes a group of people quantifiably measurable against another social group. In order to do so, a proposed definition to guide measurement must be presented that encompasses the significance of social standing as well as comparisons made between groups with different social status. A more concise definition for health disparity than the one presented here might be this: Health disparities are possibly preventable discrepancies in health among groups of people who are more and less privileged socially—differences that systematically place communally less fortunate populations at additional inconvenience on health. This definition succeeds in identifying target populations for comparison and includes both similar and dissimilar social ranks (Braveman, 2006).

When measuring or defining health disparity/inequality, the certain conditions that produce illnesses in one population might not have the same effect in other populations. In addition, the course of an illness or disease differs between a person or a group with full health insurance as compared with those without a similar social safety net. The patient who does not have access to or has limited access to necessary treatment could be forced to pay for their treatments out of pocket, thus forcing them and their family into a state of poverty, bringing on even more lethal health consequences (Fiscella et al., 2000).

Although the term health disparity is used often in the field of public health, there remain many different attitudes on what the term actually means. Based on different dictionary definitions and long-held personal beliefs, these differences have continued to cause problems when surveying research over a wide spectrum. There is, however, no disagreement about what health disparity/inequality ultimately reflects—a problem that needs immediate attention and fixing.

Recognizing the Influence of Culture

Outcomes that either measure health disparities or factors that contribute to health disparities use criteria that are often culture bound. The work of Gilligan (1982) first identified the gender bias of instruments used to measure ethical development. Her work focused on the male orientation that was inherent in both the development and norming of Kohlberg and Lickona's instrument on Moral Development (1976). Gilligan's work represented an early acknowledgment that an important factor in measurement is the conceptual perspective of the instrument as well as the population of origin for instrument development and testing. The focus with health disparities and health policy is directed toward the outcomes and effects of measurement across cultures. For example, to measure health beliefs among Mexican immigrants, or blacks, the psychometric properties will differ according to the specific ethnic group or race, particularly when the instrument was developed and validated on white Americans. For example, Fillenbaum et al. (1990) examined seven cognitive screening or neuropsychological tests in relation to clinical diagnosis. The authors reported that most measures, when adjusted for race and education, had lower specificities for blacks than for whites. They suggested that most measures were culturally or educationally biased. Similarly, Teresi (2001) reviewed studies of Differential Item Functioning and item bias in the direct cognitive assessment measures with respect to race/ethnicity and education. Specifically, item performance varied across groups that differ in terms of education, ethnicity, and race (Jones & Gallo, 2002).

Another factor that influences the value of outcome measures is the validity and reliability of translations. Instruments that have been rated as highly reliable and valid may not be so, once translated. One example is the Mini-Mental State Exam (Teresi et al., 1995), which includes a question about certainty of a fact, stating "no ifs, ands, or buts." This item was more easily understood by Hispanics than by non-Hispanics because the translation into Spanish and the cultural context were more easily understood (Teresi, 2001). As a result, a Hispanic client may be identified as cognitively more coherent than he is, meaning that the Hispanic client would be less likely to receive treatment for confusion or dementia than the one who is non-Hispanic. Research that is based on instruments that have been translated is prone to findings that reflect differences based on subgroups such as race, ethnicity, education, or socioeconomic status.

Another bias that may occur emanates from cultural, ethnic, or differences in backgrounds when research methods include interviewers or raters. In this instance, the evaluators may identify cues that are not culturally congruent, or the evaluator may transmit cues that have very different meanings cross-culturally. van Ryn and Burke (2000) examined the impact of physicians' perceptions and beliefs on patient diagnosis and treatment. They reported that physicians (mainly white) were more likely to rate white patients as more educated and more rational than black patients even after controlling for patient's actual educational level. Although this finding can be simply explained by adherence to stereotypical beliefs that are inherently discriminatory, communication barriers such as differences in the patient's use of language when referring to symptoms or symptom expression and/or interpretation of health-related behavior could possibly influence physicians' ratings across racial groups.

In summary, research that is used to formulate health policies related to health disparities must take into account variables that may have affected outcome such as cultural/racial/ethnic biases in the development and norming of the instrument, translational inconsistencies, and interviewer bias. These inherent differences may account for differences and inconsistencies in diagnoses, treatment, and outcomes.

Chronic Illness

Encompassing a wide range of diseases, chronic refers to all disorders that are long lasting or recurrent. The term is used to specifically describe the track of a disease or its rate of inception and advance. Defined by the U.S. National Center for Health Statistics, a chronic disease is one lasting 3 months or more. Along with being identified by how long they last, chronic illnesses are also most often characterized by an inability to be cured with medication or prevented by vaccine. Each year, millions of Americans suffer through the negative effects of living with chronic illnesses; 133 million people, or almost half of all Americans, live with a chronic condition. That number is projected to increase by more than one percent per year by 2030, resulting in an estimated chronically ill population of 171 million.

Almost half of all people with chronic illness have multiple conditions. As a result, many managed care and integrated delivery systems have taken a great interest in correcting the many deficiencies in current management of diseases such as diabetes, heart disease, depression, asthma, and others (Wagner et al., 1996).

Those deficiencies include the following:

- Rushed practitioners not following established practice guidelines
- A lack of care coordination
- A lack of active follow-up to ensure the best outcomes
- Patients inadequately trained to manage their illnesses

Overcoming these deficiencies will require nothing less than a transformation of health care, from a system that is essentially reactive—responding mainly when a person is sick to one that is proactive and focused on keeping a person as healthy as possible (Wagner et al., 1996).

One approach to chronic illness based on research is the Chronic Care Model (CCM). This model focuses on information and strategies for the management of chronic illnesses and originated from a synthesis of scientific literature undertaken by The MacColl Institute for Healthcare Innovation in the early 1990s. The Robert Wood Johnson Foundation funded further work on the model, which included an extensive review by an advisory panel of experts and was then compared with the features of leading chronic illness management programs across the United States. In 1998, the model was again revised, and the Robert Wood Johnson Foundation incorporated the model as the basis for their program Improving Chronic Illness Care. This center offers research, practice, and dissemination guidelines as well as protocols for quality improvement. The value of the CCM is the utilization of EBP to evaluate current research and incorporate cutting-edge outcomes into the model. These have been identified as the Breakthrough Series Collaborative, which serves as the approach for quality improvement (http://www.improvingchroniccare.org/index.php?p=The_Chronic_Care_Model&s=2). According to the Improving Chronic Illness Care, a chronic condition is any condition that requires ongoing adjustments by the affected person and interactions with the healthcare system.

To speed the transition, Improving Chronic Illness Care created the Chronic Care Model, which summarizes the basic elements for improving care in health systems at the community, organization, practice, and patient levels.

Considering the serious nature of these illnesses, it is alarming to find that numerous reports on medical care have consistently found major holes in the course and result of chronic illness treatment. Whether the patients surveyed were receiving managed care or not, major deficiencies were found. According to evidence, patients suffering from chronic illnesses are often given limited help from their insurance providers as they struggle to keep up basic function and quality of life while managing their diseases. This limited care is sometimes caused, for example, by a doctor's failure to recognize their patient's level of understanding about their condition, ability to function, or their perception of self-management. A deficiency of such things can ultimately lead to a lack of useful care and the want for restorative, supportive, and instructive services. Although managed care continues to grow, at the core it remains a system that persists in delivering subpar treatment for the chronically unwell, threatening the integrity of the entire system.

Although many factors play a role in determining the lack of care a patient is going to receive, most often it is the acute care orientation of medical practice. This approach to medical care severely limits the ability of medical caregivers to adequately fulfill the quantifiable and self-coping requirements of chronically ill patients. Most medical practices are designed and trained to respond to acute medical disorders, which creates a method of diagnosing and treating based on patient initiated visits and goals. These quick meetings, usually lasting in the range of 15 minutes, target the relieving of symptoms rather than evaluation and recovery of purpose. Often physicians are untrained and too overloaded to take up the task of organizing care, advising, and following up treatment.

Conclusion

This chapter provides an introduction into health services research as a multidisciplinary field of scientific investigation that examines how social factors, financing systems, organizational structures and processes, health technologies, and per-

Figure 14-1 Model for improvement of chronic illness care.

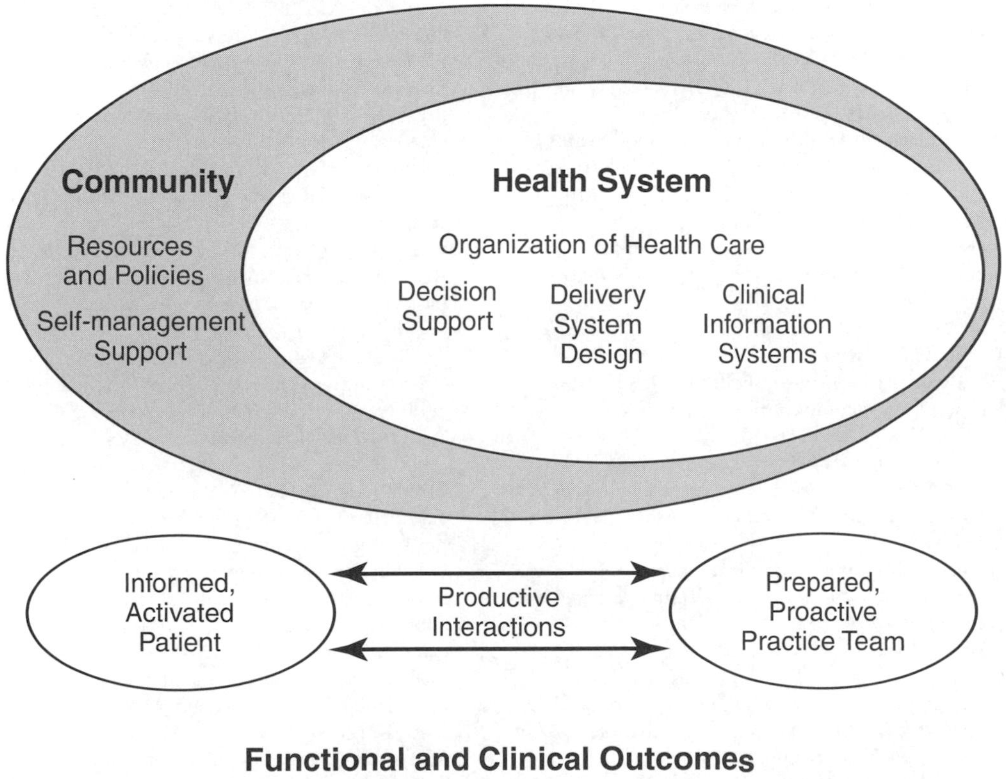

Community

Resources and Policies

Self-management Support

Health System

Organization of Health Care

Decision Support

Delivery System Design

Clinical Information Systems

Informed, Activated Patient

Productive Interactions

Prepared, Proactive Practice Team

Functional and Clinical Outcomes

Source: Wagner, E. H. (1998). Chronic disease management: What will it take to improve care for chronic illness? *Eff Clin Pract, 1,* 2–4. Used with permission of the American College of Physicians.

sonal behaviors affect access to health care, the quality and cost of health care, and quantity and quality of life. The focus of research studies in health services are often centered on research issues that examine outcomes of the individual, family, organizational, institutional, community, and population level. For example health service research will seek to examine how people get access to health care, how much care costs, and what happens to patients as a result of this care.

While the primary goal of health services research is to identify the most effective ways to organize, manage, finance, and deliver high quality care; reduce medical errors; and improve patient safety. Health services research is grounded in theory and exists to perform research that can be applied by physicians, nurses, health managers and administrators, and other health professionals and stakeholders who make decisions or deliver care in the healthcare system. Finally, the findings and products that result from health services research can be used to improve the design of healthcare benefits, develop new policies to optimize the way health care is financed and paid for, facilitate access to healthcare services, and improve patient outcomes.

References

Adams, K., & Corrigan, J. (2003). *Priority areas for national action: transforming health care. Committee on identifying priority areas for quality improvement.* Board on Health Services, and Institute of Medicine. Washington, DC: The National Academies Press.

AHRQ, Agency for Healthcare Research and Quality. (2007). National Healthcare Quality & Disparities Report. Retrieved February 13, 2010, from http://www.ahrq.gov/qual/qrdr07.htm

Anderson, K. M., & Schulke, K. (2008). Linking public accountability to quality improvement. *Health & Hospital Network, 82*(11), 60–61.

Ashton, C. M., Haidet, P., Paterniti, D. A., Collins, T. C., Gordon, H. S., & O'Malley, K. (2003). Racial and ethnic disparities in the use of health services: bias, preferences, or poor communication? *Journal of General Internal Medicine, 18,* 146–152.

Bennett, K. (2004). *Individual hospital effects upon the measurement of racial disparities in the treatment of myocardial infarction.* Doctoral Dissertation, University of South Carolina.

Bodenheimer, T. (2008). Coordinating care: A perilous journey through the health care system. *New England Journal of Medicine, 358,* 1064–1071.

Braveman, P. (2006). Health disparities and health equity. *Annual Review of Public Health, 27,* 167–194.

Calkins, E., Boult, C., Wagner, E. H., & Pacala, J. (1999). *New ways to care for older people: Building systems based on evidence.* New York: Springer.

Cochrane, A. L. (1989). *Effectiveness and efficiency random reflections on health services* (Memoir Club Publications). New York: B M J Books.

Cochrane, A. L. (1971). *Effectiveness and Efficiency: Random Reflections of Health Services* (2nd ed.), London: Nuffield Provincial Hospitals Trust.

Coleman, E. A., & Berenson, R. A. (2004). Improving patient care. Lost in transition: Challenges and opportunities for improving the quality of transitional care. *Annals of Internal Medicine, 141*(7), 533–536.

Department of Health Services. (2009). *What is health services research?* Retrieved April 20, 2009, from http://depts.washington.edu/hserv/hs-research-definitions

Fillenbaum, G., Heyman, A., Williams, K., Prosnitz, B., & Burchett, B. J. (1990). Sensitivity and specificity of standardized screens of cognitive impairment and dementia among elderly black and white community residents. *Clinical Epidemiology, 43*(7), 651–660.

Fiscella, K., Franks, P., Gold, M. R., & Clancy, C. M. (2000). Inequality in quality. *Journal of the American Medical Association, 283,* 2579–2584.

Frederickson, K. (2007). Evidence-based practice: A reliable source to access interventions for youth risk behavior. *Research and Theory for Nursing Practice: An International Journal, 21*(3), 149–152.

Gilligan, C. (1982). *In a different voice.* Cambridge, Massachusetts: Harvard University Press.

Goldberg, J., Hayes, W., & Huntley, J. (2004, November). *Understanding health disparities.* Health Policy Institute of Ohio.

Jencks, S. F., Williams, M. V., & Coleman, E. A. (2009). Rehospitalizations among patients in the Medicare fee-for-service program. *New England Journal of Medicine, 360*(14), 1418–1428.

Jones, R. N., & Gallo, J. J. (2002). Education and sex differences in the Mini Mental State Examination: Effects of differential item functioning. *Journal of Gerontology Series B—Psychological Sciences and Social Sciences, 37,* P548–P558.

Kenny, S. J., Smith, P. J., Goldschmid, M. G., Newman, J. M., Herman, W. H. (1993). Survey of physician practice behaviors related to diabetes mellitus in the U.S. Physician adherence to consensus recommendations. *Diabetes Care, 16,* 1507–1510.

Kohlberg, L., & Lickona, R. (Ed.). (1976). *Moral stages and moralization: The cognitive-developmental approach. Moral development and behavior: Theory, research and social issues.* Holt, NY: Rinehart and Winston.

Krizner, K. (2009). Transitional care lacking in elderly. Managed healthcare executive e-news. Retrieved May 4, 2009, from http://managedhealthcareexecutive.modernmedicine.com/mhe/News+Analysis/Transitional-care-lacking-in-elderly/ArticleStandard/Article/detail/574706

Krumholz, H. M., Seeman, T. E., Merrill, S. S., Mendes de Leon, C. F., Vaccarino, V., Silverman, D. I., et al. (1995). Lack of association between cholesterol and coronary heart disease mortality and morbidity and all-cause mortality in persons older than 70 years. *Journal of the American Medical Association, 272*(17), 1335–1340.

McGlynn, E. A., Asch, S. M., Adams, J., Keesey, J., Hicks, J., DeCristofaro, A., & Kerr, E. A. (2003). The quality of health care delivered to adults in the United States. *New England Journal of Medicine, 348*(26), 2635–2645.

Melnyk, B. M. (2005). *Evidence-based practice in nursing & healthcare a guide to best practice.* Philadelphia: Lippincott Williams & Wilkins.

Naylor, M. D. (2004). Transitional care for older adults: a cost effective model. *LDI Issue Brief, 9*(6). Retrieved May 4, 2009, from http://www.commonwealthfund.org/usr_doc/LDI_issuebrief_Naylor.pdf

Naylor, M. D. (2006). Transitional care: A critical dimension of the home healthcare quality agenda. *Journal for Healthcare Quality: Promoting Excellence in Healthcare, 28*(1), 48–54.

Naylor, M. D., & Keating, S. A. (2008). Transitional care: moving patients from one setting to another. *American Journal of Nursing, 108*(9), 58–63.

National Quality Forum. (2009a). *NQF-endorsed definition and framework for measuring care coordination.* Retrieved April 2009, from http://www.qualityforum.org/pdf/ambulatory/txCareCoordination%20defandframe08-02-06.pdf

National Quality Forum. (2009b). *Endorsing preferred practices and performance measures for measuring and reporting care coordination.* Retrieved February 13, 2010, from http://www.qualityforum.org/projects/ongoing/care-coordination

Partnership for Solutions, Johns Hopkins University, for the Robert Wood Johnson Foundation. (2004). Chronic conditions: Making the case for ongoing care. Baltimore, MD: University of Maryland.

Perrin, J. M., Homer, C. J., Berwick, D. M., Woolf, A. D., Freeman, J. L., & Wennberg, J. E. (1989). Variations in rates of hospitalization of children in three urban communities. *New England Journal of Medicine, 320,* 1183–1187.

Raines, J. C. (2008). *Evidence-based practice in school mental health.* New York: Oxford University Press.

Ramirez, M., Ford, M., Steward, A., & Teresi, J. (2005). Measurement issues in health disparities research. *Health Services Research,* 40(5 Pt 2), 1640–1657.

Rousseau, D. M. (2006). Is there such a thing as 'evidence-based management'? *Academy of Management Review, 31,* 256–269.

Stockwell, D. H., Madhavan, S., Cohen, H., Gibson, G., & Alderman, M. H. (1994). The determinants of hypertension awareness, treatment, and control in an insured population. *American Journal of Public Health, 84,* 1768–1774.

Teresi, J. A. (2001). Statistical methods for examination of differential item functioning (DIF) with applications to cross cultural measurement of functional, physical and mental health. *Journal of Mental Health and Aging, 7,* 31–40.

Teresi, J. A., Golden, R. R., Cross, P., Gurland, B., Kleinman, M., & Wilder, D. (1995). Item bias in cognitive screening measures: Comparisons of elderly white, Afro-American, Hispanic and high and low education subgroups. *Journal of Clinical Epidemiology, 48,* 173–183.

van Ryn, M., & Burke, J. (2000). The effect of patient race and socio-economic status on physicians' perceptions of patients. *Social Science & Medicine, 50*(6), 813–828.

Wagner, E. H., Austin, B. T., & Von Korff, M. (2001). Improving outcomes in chronic illness. *Managed Care Quarterly, 4*(2), 12–25.

Wagner, E. H., Austin, B. T., & Von Korff, M. (1996). Organizing care for patients with chronic illness. *Milbank Quarterly, 74,* 511–544.

Wagner, E. H. (1998). Chronic disease management: What will it take to improve care for chronic illness? *Eff Clin Pract, 1,* 2–4.

Wagner, E. H., Austin, B. T., Davis, C., Hindmarsh, M., Schaefer, J., & Bonomi, A. (2001). Improving chronic illness care: Translating evidence into action. *Health Aff (Millwood), 20,* 64–78.

CASE STUDY

Influence of Politics on Health Care Policy and Research

Carol F. Roye

In recent years, many barriers have been put in the way of women who simply want to obtain reproductive health care. These barriers are politically and ideologically driven. They have nothing to do with optimum health care. In fact, they often stand in the way of good health care. As I write, at the end of 2008, we have been living with increasing politicization of science and healthcare policy, to the detriment of patient well-being. This is not the first historical era when health care has been adversely impacted by politics, but it is certainly the worst that I have experienced.

A main concern for me was the Global Gag Rule. In 1984, President Reagan had implemented a policy at a world population meeting in Mexico City. Formally called the Mexico City Policy, the rule is often referred to as the Gag Rule because, in essence, the policy gags family planning providers. The Gag Rule is a ban on U.S. family planning aid—including shipments of free condoms and contraceptives—to foreign nongovernmental organizations and clinics that even mention the term abortion or advocate legalizing abortion in their country. In 1992, when Bill Clinton was elected, I felt tremendous relief because I knew patients and women around the world would benefit. We were not disappointed. President Clinton rescinded the Gag Rule, but President George W. Bush reinstated it on his first full day in office.

As a result, many clinics in underresourced countries have foregone U.S. aid. They gave up shipments of contraceptives, including condoms, which could have been used to curb the spread of HIV/AIDS and to prevent unwanted pregnancies. Many poor women around the world had come to depend on those shipments for family planning. The result of the Gag Rule has been, no doubt, more unwanted pregnancies, which leads to higher maternal and infant mortality and likely more cases of HIV/AIDS.

I was very acutely aware of the danger of the Gag Rule, as I had worked under what was essentially a domestic Gag Rule in the late 1980s. Between 1988 and 1993, Title X legislation prohibited doctors and nurses from providing information about abortion, even if the patient requested it. Although this domestic gag rule was not enforced nationwide, it was in effect in certain Title X funded clinics, including the inner-city clinic in New York City where I was a nurse practitioner.

Many of my patients were teen mothers. Sometimes they came to see me with a second unwanted pregnancy. When I asked representatives of the federal government who came to our clinic what I could tell a tearful, frightened 16-year-old who asked about abortion, I was told to say that it is "outside the purview of what I can discuss." Essentially, I was being told by representatives of the federal government that I would have to withhold information from my patients. I was not even supposed to refer pregnant patients to a prenatal clinic where a doctor or nurse might mention abortion as an option.

It was a good day for women's health when President Clinton rescinded the Gag Rule. Unfortunately, it was reinstated in January 2001 and has been in place ever since. Many professionals expect that President Obama will rescind the Gag Rule (Roye, 2009).

President Obama will have more health policy issues than the Gag Rule to contend with. President Bush left a parting jab at women's health. On December 18, 2008, just 1 month before the end of the Bush Administration, the Department of Health and Human Services introduced a regulation that was purportedly aimed at protecting workers with moral objections to abortion. The rule says that healthcare workers cannot be discriminated against for refusing to participate in procedures to which they object; however, the rule is so broad that the list of procedures can essentially be limitless, including provision of family planning or even vaccinations for that matter. Similarly, the definition of healthcare worker is so broad that it can include all workers and volunteers in a medical setting, including people who do not provide health care, such as janitors. The regulation went into effect 30 days after December 18, just a few days short of the Obama inauguration. Thus, if a woman goes to a federally funded clinic and requests contraception and the janitor objects to contraception and does not want to clean a facility where contraception is dispensed, his or her objections must be upheld, and the patient is denied care (Berger, 2009). Furthermore, there are already regulations that protect health workers' rights not to violate their religious beliefs.

The impact of this imposition of ideology on health policy is felt in the aggregate, as described previously here. Of course, it also has very personal ramifications for patients.

For example, recently I was sitting at the desk in my exam room in a large pediatric practice in a low-income neighborhood in New York City. The next patient to come in, Jasmine S., was an 18-year-old college freshman. She and her boyfriend had begun having intercourse. She told me that he is her first sexual partner. They use a condom most of the time, but she knows that she is at risk for pregnancy. After I examined her, we chatted about the birth control methods that are currently available. She decided that the vaginal ring would work best for her. I prescribed the ring and urged her to continue using condoms. I told her how to use both methods, and the important role of each in assuring her reproductive health.

Two weeks later, Jasmine came in for a scheduled appointment, to review the results of the laboratory tests we had done. When I asked her how she liked the ring, she told me she could not get it.

The pharmacist had written something on the back of the prescription. She handed it to me, and I saw that he had written "P/A." Not knowing what that meant, I called the pharmacist. He told me that she needed a prior authorization from her insurance company, and I thought I had heard incorrectly. Yes, we needed a prior authorization when my 6-month-old granddaughter needed neurosurgery and my 8-year-old daughter needed eye surgery. But is prior authorization to get the ring necessary? I called her insurance company, Fidelis, a Medicaid HMO in New York. The agent asked me whether the patient needed the ring for contraception or some other reason. I told her that I did not want to discuss the patient's private information with her. Indeed, that would have been violating the patient's confidentiality. She responded that without such information the patient could not get the medication.

Even with that information, the patient could not get the medication. I could have said that the patient has very irregular periods and I want to regulate them with the ring; however, I chose to be honest and, with Jasmine's permission, told the woman on the phone that it was for contraception. Fidelis is a Catholic company and therefore does not pay for contraception. The patient never asked to be put in a Catholic HMO. She was just assigned to that insurance plan. The Fidelis agent told me that another company pays for contraception for Fidelis patients. I spent a half hour on the phone with the other company. It was a long and difficult road to take to get a simple prescription. It was trying even for me, and I know how to navigate the healthcare system. Jasmine would probably never have gotten her contraception if I had not intervened. The barriers would have been insurmountable. Jasmine was not the only one of my patients to have difficulty filling her birth control prescription because of Fidelis.

Now, think about the plight of another patient, Marianna. She is typical of many of the patients I see. Marianna is 12 years old. She had her first period 6 months ago. This month her period has lasted for over 4 weeks and is still not going away. She comes into the clinic, and we check her for anemia. Her hemoglobin is 10.2. Marianna is anemic—no surprise given the fact that she has been bleeding for 4 weeks. How can we treat her? Of course, I will prescribe iron tablets for her, but that is a band aid. We need to stop the bleeding. There is really only one way to stop the bleeding. She needs to take birth control pills. I give Marianna and her mother the prescriptions and sent them out. They are smiling, relieved to know that the bleeding can be stopped.

When they get to the pharmacy, however, the pharmacist wrote P/A on the back of the prescription because Marianna has Fidelis insurance. Perhaps he just refused to give her the birth control pills because he does not believe in contraception and is horrified at the thought that this 12-year-old needs birth control—and her mother is letting her use it. He will not give her the contraception, although he does give her the iron. Marianna's mother has to get to work and cannot afford to take any more time. She will not have a day off for 2 more weeks. Thus, Marianna continues to take her iron, and she continues to bleed; hopefully she will be okay until she can come back to the clinic.

The standards of good health care do not change every 4 to 8 years; however, health policy can change dramatically according to the theology or ideology of the presidential administration. As a result, Americans' health can be jeopardized or enhanced at the whim of the prevailing political winds.

The same holds true on a state-by-state basis, depending on the politics of the state. In New York State, for example, a teenager can obtain an abortion without parental knowledge or consent. The regulation is written that way so that teens are not afraid to seek health care when confronted by an unwanted pregnancy. In other states, however, things are quite different. In 34 states, teens must obtain parental consent. In some states, such as Mississippi, for example, consent of both parents is required. In Mississippi, there is only one clinic where women can obtain an abortion. Thus, women—adolescent or adult—who do not have the wherewithal to travel cannot get an abortion. Are they turning to back alley abortionists? Are they trying to do their own abortions—perhaps with information gleaned on the internet? Possibly. We do not know for sure.

Political winds and whims affect community health and individual health, to be sure; however, it does not stop there. Politics also affects health research. Research sets the stage for healthcare advances in the future; however, over the last 8 years, research into certain politically controversial topics such as HIV prevention in adolescents has been thwarted. For example, during the Clinton administration, I was awarded a grant by the National Institutes of Health to study the effectiveness of a program to promote condom use by sexually active teenage girls who were using hormonal contraception such as birth control pills.

While conducting that study, the Clinton administration ended and that of George W. Bush began. I read in the newspapers about something that was being called "the hit list," which listed several hundred federally funded studies that were considered morally questionable by a group on the far right of the political spectrum. The Traditional Values Coalition took credit for it. Sure that my study was not on the list, I still checked the list on the Internet. I was deeply offended to see my name and my study on the list. The list described my study and then said, in what was clearly meant to be an indictment, that the study promotes condom use. I was, of course, promoting condom use, not sexual activity. My program was aimed at reducing risk for sexually active girls who were at high risk for contracting HIV and other sexually transmitted infections. I knew that Nancy Reagan's "just say no" campaign was not going to prevent infections or pregnancy in this population. As it turns out, the "hit list" was the beginning of the end for my program of research (Roye, 2008). It seems likely that under the Obama Administration scientific inquiry into issues dealing with such "touchy" subjects as sexuality will again return to the United States.

My experience was not at all unique. Scientists whose research came under scrutiny as part of the "hit list" were surveyed and interviewed about the effect that experience had on their research. Most agreed that the controversy had a "chilling effect" on their research. The scientists also reported that they removed certain words from the title of their abstracts, such as anal sex, needle exchange, and harm reduction. Some researchers altered their research programs to be more politically correct, for example, deciding not to study adolescent sexual health. Others decided not to study certain stigmatized groups. The authors of the study concluded that politics can shape what scientists decide to study (Kempner, 2008).

As one of the "hit list" scientists, I expect that politics will have a minimal, if any, influence on scientific research in the near future. I presume that grant proposals will once more be judged solely on merit. In fact, I am planning a proposal investigating understudied areas of adolescent sexual health.

It is important for healthcare providers to understand the influence that politics can have on health care—in the aggregate, for individual patients and for health research. We must be vigilant about advocating for untarnished science and evidence.

References

Berger, M. E. (2009). *New health regulation permits "conscience" exceptions.* Retrieved January 6, 2009, from http://www.sltrib.com/faith/ci_11296447

Kempner, J. (2008). The chilling effect: How do researchers react to controversy? *PLoS Medicine, 5*(11), e222.

Roye, C. (2009). *Global Gag Rule must not be domesticated.* Retrieved January 6, 2009, from http://www.womensenews.org/article.cfm/dyn/aid/3648

Roye, C. (2008). Politics and nursing science: Not always a healthy combination. *Nursing Science Quarterly, 21,* 13–17.

Chapter 15

Conclusion: A Policy Toolkit for Healthcare Providers and Activists

Roby Robertson and Donna Middaugh

OVERVIEW

What is the role of the healthcare professional in the political process? Given the range of issues addressed in this book, where does the political process begin and end? This healthcare policy book is centered on the notion that all healthcare providers require a fundamental understanding of the healthcare system that is not limited to the knowledge required to practice their discipline. No longer can healthcare professionals be prepared solely for clinical practice, but they must ready themselves to deal with the economic, political, and policy dimensions of health care because the services they provide are the outcome of these dynamics.

OBJECTIVES

- To define the role of the healthcare professional in policy advocacy and politics
- To describe processes for becoming a policy advocate within one's own organization and beyond
- To recognize the difference between expertise and internal and external advocacy in relation to stakeholders
- To apply the concepts of health policy to case study vignettes
- To develop one's own toolkit for becoming a health policy advocate

KEY TERMS

- ❑ Advocacy
- ❑ Constituent
- ❑ Expertise
- ❑ External stakeholder

(continues)

- ❑ Internal stakeholder
- ❑ Politics
- ❑ Power
- ❑ Stakeholder

This book offers an interdisciplinary approach to understanding healthcare practice and policy. Professional nurses and other allied health practitioners must have a seat at the policy table, but they must also understand the perspectives of their colleagues; therefore, we have used contributors from outside of nursing, including allied health professionals, activists, politicians, economists, and policy analysts who understand the forces of health care in America, to frame this textbook. The rationale behind an interdisciplinary approach is that no one person has the right solution to the challenges confronting health care in America. These challenges include high costs, limited access, medical errors, variable quality, administrative inefficiencies, and a lack of coordination.

It is not surprising that the healthcare system is under serious stress and that a host of actors both within and beyond the system have myriad solutions to the problem. This chapter suggests that politics is both necessary and critical to making changes, whether we are discussing system level reforms (e.g., national health insurance reform) or a local hospital improving health data access (e.g., electronic medical records). This textbook offers current and future healthcare practitioners who are committed to reducing health disparities and achieving healthcare equality insight into how clinical practice is derived from regulations and laws that are based on public policy and politics.

This book provides an overview of the essential elements that drive health policy in the United States. Within these pages, the reader has been given the following:

- A compelling rationale for engaging in health policy issues
- A thorough review of the healthcare delivery labor force
- An appreciation of the role of markets and government in the system of healthcare finance
- A description of how power, markets, and government affect healthcare organizations and the delivery of care
- Insight into key drivers of the organization of healthcare services, namely technology, quality, and research

This final chapter provides healthcare practitioners a toolkit or a working model of how to "do" policy advocacy within and beyond our organizational lines. This chapter answers these questions: "What is the health professional's role in policy advocacy and politics?" "What are the major distinctions in affecting policy through the two primary areas addressed in this book?" This chapter examines two broad components of policy change—the influence and power of stakeholders/constituencies and the power of expertise. These arenas overlap; of course, here we examine them separately to portray their specific roles more accurately.

What then is the healthcare practitioner's role in the political process? Where does that process take place? Many traditional views define the political process as external only, primarily defined at the policy-making levels of government or boards and commissions; therefore, the argument follows that professionals below senior-level decision makers are primarily reactive; that is, they respond to proposals from up the line and/or must calculate how to implement the changes that others have imposed on them.

In public administration, this has traditionally been defined as a politics/administration dichotomy; that is, political decisions are made by higher ups, and the administrator finds a way to carry out those decisions. In public administration and related policy fields, however, that dichotomy is no more because in actual decision-making and in the practicalities of day-to-day management, interactions at all levels of the organization are necessary to the practice of management/policy formulation and implementation. The administrators are trying to influence policy outcomes like those in the policy arena. And practitioners should do the same.

There is also another reason why practitioners must develop a political/policy toolkit. Politics and policy making are not a function only of the external environment of the organization. In fact, the most sophisticated and nuanced elements of such a policy/political role can be found also in the *internal environment* of the organization. Again, practitioners can play a role influencing these outcomes.

Imagine the following scenario. Your senior executive pulls you aside one day and says, "Do you know that proposal you've wanted to push forward about how we reallocate the staff here in the organization? Well, why don't you put together the budget, a time line, and what we need to do to move this forward in the next budget cycle?" You have been anxious to do so for some time, and you stay in the office every evening putting together the proposal (with fancy pie charts, a time line, personnel requirements, etc.), and you turn it in to your executive.

A week goes by and then two and then three. You are getting anxious; to do some of the time line issues you would need to get rolling soon, but you've heard nothing. You mention it to the executive and she nods, looks solemn, and asks you back into the office. She sits on the edge of the desk (not behind the desk, not a good sign) and pulls out your proposal. You can see it has been marked up with lots of red marks throughout. The executive shakes her head and says, "Well it really is a great idea; it really is the way to go in the future, but I ran it up the line, and well, you know, 'politics got in the way.' It's just not going to fly!" She hands back your proposal. You return to your office and open the file cabinet of other projects that didn't get off the ground, and you think, politics!

Well? Why didn't it fly? What could have happened? Senior managers did not like the proposal? It competed with other proposed changes that could "fly." What kept yours from flying? Perhaps it was because you had not accounted for the politics of your own organization. Politics exist at the organizational level, not just at the policy-making level, and you sat back and allowed others to make the decision. Thus, our approach in this chapter is to suggest that the politics of the environment are both external and internal.

We suggest that the key to gaining more effective use of the policy environment, both inside and outside the organization, is to understand more effectively the *power* that one has to effect change. Unlike many analyses of power that are often based on the individual, our approach is to examine the organizational power that exists for the practitioner/advocate. We examine that power through two broad arenas—the power of stakeholder relationships and the power of expertise.

Figure 15-1 is a simple heuristic about power. This simple pyramid has been widely used in political science and policy fields for years. Power can be seen in the levels of the pyramid, with the narrowest (and thus the weakest type of power) at the top of the pyramid and becoming broader with more effective types of power moving down the pyramid. *Force* we all understand. The power to make others do things by forcing them to do so is obvious, from the actual use of force (including weapons) through the more common use of force in an organization which is the power of the organization to enforce rules, standards, and practices. *Influence* is more nuanced, but its role is also obvious—does the organization have the capacity to convince others that they should support or acquiesce to the organization's decision? There are many reasons why an organization may be able to influence a decision. Possibly the organization has shown in the past the capacity to be successful; maybe it is because the organization has demonstrated knowledge or connections to accomplish the tasks required. Nevertheless, the organization must convince others that its decisions are good. Finally, the broadest and most critical part of the power pyramid is *authority*. At the core of a lot of political theory about the state is authority—the acceptance of the organization to decide and the acceptance by others of its decisions without serious question. Expertise is one form of authority. We tend to accept the recommendations of those who are expert in a field.

One example of how all three elements of the power triangle work is driving your car late at night and stopping at a red light with nobody around. There you sit because a light bulb with a red cover over it is "on"! Now, that is power! Do you recognize why you stopped? Did you have to be convinced (well, maybe you think for a second that lights regulate traffic, but it is the middle of the night and there are no cars

Figure 15-1 Power pyramid.

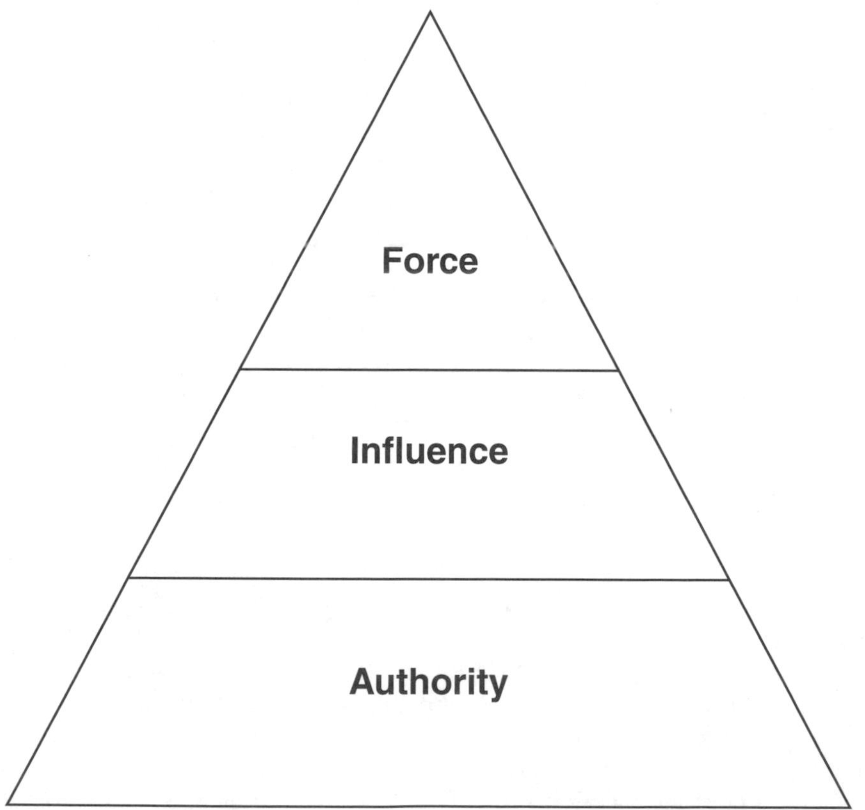

around!)? Do you run the light? Not right away because you first look around to see whether there is a police car around! Now, all three elements are in play, and you stopped at the light in the first place because? It turned red, and you stop at red lights!

Thus, how do we understand our power in organizations? Obviously, there are multiple elements in this—from the regulatory environment, the level of federalism, the growth of the state, and so forth. Here we summarize around two broad elements that undergird the organization's power: stakeholders and expertise. We are going to distinguish between internal and external power (power within the organization and beyond) (see Figure 15-2).

Stakeholder Power

For many in the healthcare arena, stakeholder power seems the most obvious political tool: A simple "who do you know, who is on our side" model of developing policy change is obvious. Too often, however, our approach is to simply add up the influentials on "our side" and on the "other side." The stakeholder list becomes a list of names, rather than a list of the nature of power relationships. Well, if it is just numbers, then

Figure 15-2 Focus and locus of organizational power.

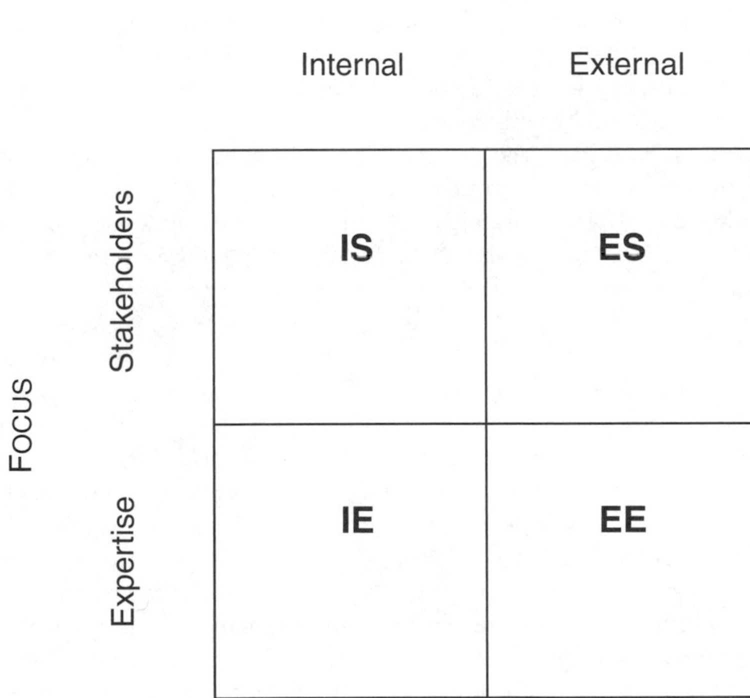

any policy supported by a greater number of individuals or organizations should prevail. Under those conditions, we would suggest that a national health system that is effective for the poor would be the easiest to pass, but somehow one knows that organizations representing low-income groups have less influence than those representing higher income groups. Right? So, it cannot be just numbers!

Thus, stakeholder analysis is tied to the network of stakeholders and which sets of stakeholders are closer to your organization and which are more distant. This close/distant issue is often defined in terms of natural and face-to-face relationships: ideally, what groups deal with your agency and/or policy arena on a routine and constant basis and what groups deal with your organization on a more limited basis. Thus, the classic stakeholder map often has concentric circles of groups and organizations closer and further away from the organization based on the level of interdependence and organizational closeness (Fottler et al., 1989). If you represent a Veterans' hospital, for example, members of veterans' organizations, such as the American Legion or Veterans of Foreign Wars, are more central to your organization, but if you are working from a children's hospital, that organizational tie is irrelevant. Thus, understanding how central other stakeholders are to the organization may be the first part of a stakeholder analysis (Figure 15-3).

To understand stakeholder power for an organization, however, one must define it in terms of *organized* stakeholders. When working with various healthcare organizations, we often hear stakeholders described in individual terms (e.g., patients or customers), but the key is to recognize the importance of having stakeholders who are organized and have well-defined structures. For example, "veterans" is a vague definition for a set of stakeholders, but American Legion or Veterans of Foreign Wars are two critical organized groups who represent veterans.

What if there is no organized set of stakeholders? The first question might be this: Why is that true? It might be that the stakeholders in the external environment that your organization deals with are too amorphous to be defined. In James Q. Wilson's (1989) terminology, you may represent a majoritarian organization that has no discernible set of constituents or stakeholders other than the public. If that is the case, stakeholder power will be more limited for your organization.

However, we have found that many organizations have developed stakeholder groups over time (often for nonpolitical reasons), which generates some level of influence. One of our favorite examples comes from outside the healthcare arena—police departments. If one thinks about natural constituents or stakeholders, then police departments' most obvious stakeholders are those who commit crimes—not sure how to build a stakeholder group there! Over time, police departments have developed a host of support organizations, including neighborhood watch groups. The reason for their creation is not to influence political decisions about police departments, but strong neighborhood watch groups (organized across a city) can become a critical secondary stakeholder group for a police department. Who organized those neighborhood watches? Generally, police departments took the lead in doing so and the neighborhood watch groups typically support what is being proposed by the police department.

The example of a children's hospital is appropriate here. One might argue that on a day-to-day basis, the constituents of such a hospital are the patients. They are children, but maybe we would include the parents. What about parent groups? Well, generally, they have limited interest in being stakeholders of the hospital; in

Figure 15-3 Simplified stakeholder map.

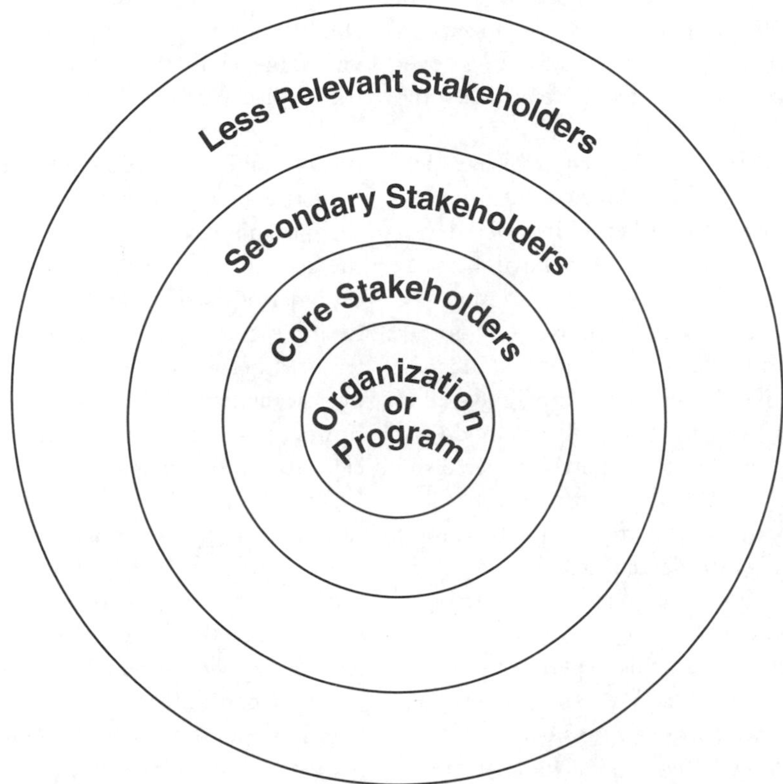

fact, they want to get their children well and leave the hospital. What about children suffering from a chronic illness or a long-term disease such as cancer? Most such hospitals have developed parent and children groups to get together from time to time to support each other (and to provide additional information to the hospital and to other patients and their families about coping with the illness). If the hospital's outreach department has helped organize the group so that it sets officers and meeting dates, then the group is now organized! Is it the same as a veterans' organization? Clearly not, but it would be wise to include such a group in any efforts to advocate for policy changes (inside and beyond the hospital).

Expertise

What is expert power in an organization? Some would define it in terms of knowledge acquisition and professionalism. Thus, an expert organization would have a high proportion of highly educated professionals, defined by advanced education, licensure, professional norms and ethical standards, and a lifetime of continuing education. The healthcare arena has a clear advantage here. The various professions within any existing healthcare arena are often complex, and they have specialized education, training, and licensure at virtually every level of professional delivery of services. Such professionalized organizations often begin with a noticeable advantage over other organizations in which there is little or no professionalized work force.

Thus, any definition of organizational expertise must begin with the nature of the expertise of the organization and whether it is well developed and professionalized and of the highest educational standards; however, one must be careful about defining this power simply as a set of acquired educational/professional standards. In the end, it is a bit like our traffic light—all of the diplomas, certificates, and licensure do not necessarily mean that the expertise is perceived as powerful. Similar to the number of stakeholders not being as important as the proximity of stakeholders to the decision makers, not all experts carry equal weight when it comes to organizational decisions.

What is the key to this expertise? It is the perception of others that the expertise is legitimate. Many healthcare professionals blunder here because they believe that achievement of a variety of graduate/professional degrees leads automatically to support of their expertise. To put it in simple terms, many occupations (especially in the healthcare arena) are licensed, certified, and with advanced education but thus do not have equal expertise power. Why? Maybe because the public or the broader political/policy environment does not differentiate the various specializations, or the expertise of the profession is recognized strongly only by the profession itself. The best example today is the widespread public agreement about the need for more nurses. How does that translate generally? Does the public differentiate well between LPN, RN, diploma, AD, BSN, MSN, NP, CRNA, CNS, or advanced practice nurses? No! Why not? Does the public see the difference between a general practitioner in medicine and a specialist in oncology? Yes! What is the difference here? We would suggest that the public has become convinced (generally through well-defined efforts by the medical establishment) that there are differences in behavior in the various medical specializations and that some of them have more expertise power because the public perceives them as more expert. Why is that not as true in the field of nursing? We suggest that part of the explanation is that the nursing profession has been reluctant to emphasize publically the differences between the various areas of nursing professionalism. We would suggest that this limits the political capacity of the various specializations to garner separate political support.

Thus, building expertise power in an organizational setting must also include addressing some important issues, not the least of which is the belief that the expertise of the particular set of professionals is desired by others in the policy environment. Internally, in a hospital, for example, when policy is being made about how practices are implemented, changed, evolved, or reorganized, is the profession you represent at the table in the discussion? If not, why not?

Thus, as we develop the toolkit for expert power, we must ask a critical question: "Who believes this expertise is valued and should be represented in the decision making process (both within and beyond the organization)?"

Toolkit Case Studies

The case studies included in this toolkit chapter are designed to aid the reader in understanding the politics of organizational power. They are divided based on four categories: external stakeholder, internal stakeholder, external expertise, and internal expertise. Each of these real-life case studies illustrates how health professionals have applied the tools as highlighted within this chapter. The case study authors have included references for the reader's use, when applicable. To guide your comprehension and application of the toolkit, the authors have included several thought provoking questions at the end of each case study. Readers are encouraged to critically analyze the political methods and power used in each case study, exploring the stakeholders and type of expertise involved. The questions following each case study are helpful for group discussion, as well as individual analysis. This chapter concludes with one additional case study that has not had any sort of political result to date, and readers are asked to analyze that case in terms of how one might build the necessary political stakeholder and expert power.

External Expert Power

The first two cases presented here are doubtless well known to readers, but what may not be well known is the history of the development of policy in these areas. As you examine these two case studies, remember that their purpose is to show the role of expertise in affecting policy.

CASE STUDY

Margaret Sanger as Nurse and Public Health Advocate

Ellen Chesler

"No Gods, No Masters," the rallying cry of the Industrial Workers of the World, was her personal and political manifesto. Emma Goldman and Bill Haywood, Mabel Dodge, and John Reed were among her earliest mentors and comrades. Allied with labor organizers and bohemians, Margaret Sanger first emerged on the American scene in those halcyon days at the turn of the 20th century when the country seemed wide open with possibility, before world war, revolution, and repression provided a more sober reality.

She organized pickets and protests and pageants in the hope of achieving wholesale economic and social justice. What began as a callow faith in revolution quickly gave way to a more concrete agenda for reform. Working as a visiting nurse on New York's Lower East Side, she watched a young patient die tragically from the complications of a then-all-too-common illegal abortion and vowed to abandon palliative work and devote herself instead to single-minded pursuit of reproductive autonomy for women.

Sanger proudly claimed personal freedom for women. She also insisted that the price women pay for equality should not be the sacrifice of personal fulfillment. Following in the footsteps of a generation of suffragists and social welfare activists who had forgone marriage in order to gain professional stature and public influence, she became the standard bearer of a less ascetic breed, intent on balancing work and family obligations.

The hardest challenge in writing this history for modern audiences, for whom these claims have become routine, is to explain how absolutely destabilizing they seemed in Sanger's time. Even with so much lingering animus toward women's rights today, it is hard to remember that reproduction was once considered a woman's principal purpose, and motherhood, her primary role—that women were assumed to have no need for identities or rights independent of those they enjoyed by virtue of their relationships to men—and that this principle was central to the long-enduring opposition they have faced in seeking rights to work, to inheritance and property, to suffrage, and most especially to control of their own bodies.

Sanger needed broader arguments. By practicing birth control, women would not just serve themselves, she countered. They would also lower birthrates, alter the balance of supply and demand for labor, alleviate poverty, and thereby achieve the aspirations of workers without the social upheaval of class warfare. Not the dictates of Karl Marx, but the refusal of women to bear children indiscriminately would alter the course of history, a proposition ever resonant today as state socialism becomes an artifact of history, while family planning, although still contested, endures with palpable consequences worldwide.

In 1917, Sanger went to jail for distributing contraceptive pessaries to immigrant women from a makeshift clinic in a tenement storefront in the Brownsville section of Brooklyn. Classic elements of modernization, including urbanization, industrialization, and secularization, were already driving down the nation's birthrate as a result of private contraceptive arrangements and a healthy underground trade in condoms, douches, and various contraptions. Sanger's contribution was to demand services for the poor that were available to the middle class. Her heresy, if you will, was in bringing the issue of sexual and reproductive freedom out in the open and claiming it as a woman's right. She staged her arrest deliberately to challenge New York's already anachronistic obscenity laws—the legacy of the notorious Anthony Comstock, whose evangelical fervor had captured Victorian politics, in a manner eerily reminiscent of our time—and led to the adoption by the federal government and the states of broad criminal sanctions on sexual speech and commerce, including all materials related to contraception and abortion. Zealous protector of traditional values and "savior" of vulnerable single women, Comstock had himself authorized as a special agent of the U.S. Post Office, with the power to undertake searches and make arrests. He died of pneumonia in 1915, after repeated confrontations with Sanger and her supporters that generated widespread publicity and sympathy for her cause, transforming it from a radical gesture to a cause célèbre.

Direct action tactics served Sanger well, but legal appeal of her clinic conviction also established a medical exception to New York's Comstock Law. Doctors—although not nurses, as she originally intended—were granted the right to prescribe contraception for health purposes, and under that constraint, she built the modern family planning movement with independent, free-standing facilities as the model for distribution of services, a development that occurred largely in spite of leaders of the medical profession, who remained shy of the subject for many years and did not formally endorse birth control until 1937, well after its scientific and social efficacy was demonstrated.

By then, Sanger and Hannah Stone, the medical director of her New York clinic, had also achieved another legal breakthrough. They prevailed in a 1936 federal appellate court decision in New York that licensed physicians to import contraceptive materials and use the federal mails for their transport. The ruling effectively realized years of failed efforts to achieve legislative reform in Congress, although it did formally override prohibitions that remained in several states until the historic ruling in *Griswold* with its claim of a constitutional doctrine of privacy, later extended so controversially to abortion in *Roe v. Wade*.

Sanger had long since jettisoned political ideology for a more reasoned confidence in the ability of education and science to shape human conduct and in the possibility of reform through bold public health initiatives. Her most prominent mentor through this passage was H.G. Wells, the renowned British man of letters and influence, who foresaw the development of states that would mix free markets with centralized planning for social welfare. Both became tribunes for the rational, scientific control of the world's population and its resources, with Wells giving Sanger international credibility and enhancing her stature.

With hard work and determination, she was able to mobilize men of influence in business, labor, academia, and the emerging professions. No less critical to her success was her decision to invest in the collective potential of women, many of whom had been oriented to activism by the suffrage movement and were eager for a new cause after finally winning the vote in 1920. She also lobbied the churches, convincing the clerical establishments of the progressive Protestant and Jewish denominations of the virtue of lifting sexuality and reproduction from the shroud of myth and mystery to which traditional faiths had long consigned them. She even won a concession from the hierarchy of the American Catholic Church, which overruled the Vatican and endorsed natural family planning, or the so-called rhythm method, as a way of countering the secular birth control movement and reasserting religious authority over values and behavior.

With an uncanny feel for the power of well-communicated ideas in a democracy, Sanger moved beyond women's rights to put forth powerful public health and social welfare claims for birth control. She proved herself a savvy public relations strategist and an adept grass-roots organizer. Through the 1920s and 1930s, she wrote best-selling books, published a widely read journal, crisscrossed the country, and circled the globe, giving lectures and holding conferences that attracted great interest and drove even more publicity. She built a thriving voluntary movement to conduct national and state-level legislative lobbying and advocacy work and to work in communities on the ground, sustaining affiliate organizations that organized and operated pioneering women's health clinics. Offering a range of medical and mental health services in reasonably sympathetic environments, many of these facilities became laboratories for her idealism.

Yet the birth control movement stalled during the long years of the Great Depression and World War II, stymied by the increasing cost and complexity of reaching those most in need and overwhelmed by the barrage of opposition it engendered. The issue remained mired in moral and religious controversy, even as its leadership determinedly embraced a centrist politics and a sanitized message. When hard times encouraged attention to collective needs over individual rights and when the New Deal legitimized public responsibility for economic and social welfare, Sanger cannily replaced the "birth control" moniker with the more socially resonant content of "family planning." Both were terms she invented and popularized after consulting allies and friends. These strategies of accommodation, however, did nothing to stop officials of the National Catholic Welfare Conference and other opponents from making the most scandalous accusations that birth control was killing babies, waging war on poor families, even causing the depression itself by slowing population growth and lowering consumer demand, a proposition that some economists of the day also endorsed.

Having enjoyed Eleanor Roosevelt's enthusiastic support and personal friendship in New York, Sanger went to Washington in the 1930s hoping that Congress would overturn the Comstock law and legalize contraceptive practice as a first step to her long-term goal of transferring responsibility and accountability for services from small, privately funded clinics to public health programs with appropriate resources and scale; however, she failed to anticipate that the success of the Roosevelt's would depend on a delicate balancing of the votes of conservative urban Catholics in the north and rural, fundamentalist Protestants in the south. There would be no invitations to tea at the White House and no government support, at least until Franklin was safely ensconced in a third term.

What is more, the ever-fragile alliance Sanger built with the country's elites itself became a liability. Sanger resigned from the American Birth Control League she had founded, severing official ties with others in the movement who boldly advanced contraception as a means of slowing birthrates among the poor. Her own politics had long tended to the left, and she became an enthusiastic New Dealer. She offered family planning not as a panacea but as a piece of a broader package of health and social welfare policies that would also provide economic and social safety nets. She framed poverty as a matter of differential access to resources, including contraception, not as the immutable consequence of low inherent ability or bad character, a view held by many conservatives. She spoke out against immigration restrictions, held advanced views on race, and enjoyed enthusiastic support for her work from W.E.B. Dubois, from many others in the progressive black community, and eventually from Mrs. Roosevelt, whose commitments to civil rights were well known.

Like other well-intended social reformers of her day, Sanger also endorsed eugenics, the then ubiquitous and popular movement that addressed the manner in which biological factors affect human, health, intelligence, and opportunity. She took away from Darwinism the essentially optimistic lesson that man's common descent in the animal kingdom makes us all capable of improvement, if only we apply the right tools. Believing that ability and talent should replace birthright and social status as the standard of mobility in a democratic society, she endorsed intelligence testing, an enduring legacy of this era, and she did not repudiate the infamous Supreme Court decision of 1929 in *Buck v. Bell* that mandated compulsory sterilization on grounds of feeble-mindedness. She also supported the payment of bonuses to women who volunteered for sterilization because they wanted no more children.

These compromised views placed her squarely in the intellectual mainstream of her time and in the good company of many progressives who shared these beliefs. Still, her failure to consider the validity of standard assessments of aptitude or the fundamental rights questions inherent in these procedures has left her vulnerable in hindsight to attacks of insensitivity and bigotry. The family planning movement at home and abroad has long been burdened by the charges that it fostered prejudice, even as it delivered welcome services and relief from unwanted childbirth to women in need.

Embittered by these controversies and disenchanted with the country's increasing pronatalism after World War II, Sanger turned her attentions abroad. In 1952, she founded the International Planned Parenthood Federation, with headquarters in London, as an umbrella for the national family planning associations that remain today in almost every country in the world.

By the time of her death in 1966, the cause for which she defiantly broke the law had achieved international stature. Although still a magnet for controversy, she was widely eulogized as one of the great emancipators of her time. She lived to see the United States Supreme Court provide constitutional protection to the use of contraceptives in *Griswold v. Connecticut.* She watched Lyndon Johnson incorporate family planning into America's social welfare and foreign policy programs, fulfilling her singular vision of how to advance opportunity and prosperity, not to speak of human happiness, at home and abroad. A team of doctors and scientists she had long encouraged marketed the oral anovulant birth control pill, and a resurgent feminist movement gave new resonance to her original claim that women have a fundamental right to control their own bodies.

In the years since, however, further controversy has surrounded the practices of what developed as often alarmist global population control efforts that adopted rigid demographic targets and imposed harsh, unwelcome, and culturally insensitive technologies on women. Population policy makers and service providers have been fairly criticized for abusing rights by ignoring or downplaying the risks of providing costly technologies where health services are inadequate to cope with potential complications and where failure rates have been high, even though these products are medically benign when properly administered.

In 1994, the United Nations International Conference on Population and Development in Cairo created a framework for state responsibility to ensure programs allowing women to make free and informed decisions about family planning, but also obligating access to comprehensive, reproductive health services of high quality, including birth control. The benefit of effective family planning to the well-being of individuals, families, and communities was officially acknowledged, despite continued resistance from the Vatican and some conservative Islamic states. Population and development professionals, however, also committed to a doctrine that weds policies and practices to improvements in women's status—to education, economic opportunity, and basic civil rights for women subject to culturally sanctioned discrimination and violence—just as Margaret Sanger first envisioned.

Hundreds of millions of women and men around the world today freely practice some method of contraception, with increasing reliance again on condoms, in light of the epidemic spread of HIV-AIDS and other sexually transmitted infections. This represents a sixfold increase since rates of population growth peaked in the 1960s.

Still, half the world's population today—nearly 3 billion people—are under the age of 25 years. Problems associated with widespread poverty, food insecurity, and environmental degradation are widespread. There remains considerable unmet need for family planning and tragically insufficient funding for research on new methods and for new programming to meet ever-increasing demand. Funding for both population and development programs has slowed dramatically, as other needs compete for funds and as concern now spreads instead about an aging and shrinking population in many countries in the global north and south where birthrates have declined sharply. The cycles of history repeat themselves.

Case Study Questions

At what points did the science of birth control precede any change in policy/practice in this area? Why do you think that was the case? Why was the expertise of effective birth control not widely shared, and why did it take the medical establishment so long to endorse policy change in this area? Clearly, the women's movement was part of the opening of change in this area, but how did it contribute to the creation of knowledge? What happened to the policy of birth control after the American Medical Association supported it in the 1930s? Why did it take another 30 years for birth control to be widely available to women in America? Have there been changes in recent years in the broader environment that are analogous to the early adoption of birth control programs (e.g., RU 487 or the "morning after" pill)? Have these changes increased or limited access to birth control? Think through the acceptance of the expertise in this area and the ways in which it has contributed (or limited) the change in policy in this environment and the ways in which it has not been taken into account. Can you illustrate how expertise is still about perception, both within professional fields as well as in the broader public?

CASE STUDY

The Centers for Disease Control's 2006 Recommendations on Screening for HIV Infection

Kathleen M. Nokes

HIV is the virus that causes AIDS. Because this diagnosis is consistent with severe immune depression, a person can be infected with HIV for many years before AIDS develops (Centers for Disease Control [CDC], 2007). Except for newborns, all persons who test positive for the antibody to the HIV are diagnosed with HIV infection. Antibody testing is cheaper than direct viral testing for genetic evidence of HIV. HIV antibody testing first became available in 1985 and was primarily used to increase the safety of the blood supply; by 1987, the United States Public Health Service issued guidelines making counseling and testing a priority as a prevention strategy. Extensive guidelines structured the counseling session before persons agreed to consent to HIV testing, and it was emphasized that infected persons needed to avoid transmitting the virus and at-risk persons needed to adopt behaviors to decrease their risk. In 1993, the CDC recommended voluntary testing for hospitalized patients as well as outpatients in acute-care hospitals and emergency departments. Hospitals with high incidence rates were encouraged to adopt a policy of offering voluntary HIV counseling and testing routinely to all patients aged 15 to 54 years (CDC, 2006). The CDC focused on screening pregnant women and did not turn their attention back to hospitalized patients again until 10 years later, in 2003. Over that period, HIV infection transitioned from a terminal to chronic illness because of the development of effective strategies to control the infection and immune damage caused by HIV.

HIV infection is a stigmatizing condition. In order to encourage persons to learn their HIV status, extensive confidentiality laws were enacted that required that persons *choose* when and if they will be screened for HIV infection. Written informed consent was mandated in some states, including New York State, so that persons would be aware that their blood was being tested for HIV infection. When persons learned that they were HIV positive, not only were they concerned about their physical health, but there were consequences impacting relationships, personal safety, and economics as well as mental health. Because HIV infection can persist for years before significant symptoms are manifested, many persons chose to avoid the stress of learning their HIV status and continued in their day-to-day activities. Because HIV is transmitted from one person to another, there is also a sense of betrayal and anger that an intimate interaction resulted in danger, reflecting a lack of caring.

By 2003, the CDC acknowledged that hospitalized patients were not being routinely offered voluntary screening and cited lack of reimbursement for HIV screening, inadequate time for healthcare providers to conduct risk assessments and adequate counseling, and lack of explicit information about HIV prevalence as reasons for the low screening rates. After extensive consultation with key stakeholders, the CDC issued the *Revised Recommendations for HIV Testing of Adults, Adolescents, and Pregnant Women in Health-care Settings* in 2006. This case study examines components of these recommendations from a policy perspective. This policy analysis focuses on the two sections of the recommendations related to screening for HIV infection and consent and pretest information for nonpregnant women. To quote from page 7 of the *Morbidity and Mortality Weekly Report* of September 22, 2006:

> *In all health-care settings, screening for HIV infection should be performed routinely for all patients aged 13-64 years. Healthcare providers should initiate screening unless prevalence of undiagnosed HIV infection in their patients has been documented to be less than 0.1%.*

In 1993, the CDC recommended screening persons aged 15 to 54 years, compared with the 2006 recommendation of ages 13 to 64 years. The lower age limit of 13 reflects the pediatric classification of AIDS, in which it is believed that infection occurred perinatally from the HIV infected mother to the fetus and/or infant. The decision to establish any upper age limit for routine screening in healthcare facilities, however, seems arbitrary. Of course, although it can be clearly established by looking at the 2006 prevalence data that while the highest percentage (22%) of persons living with AIDS were aged 40 to 44 (CDC, 2008), the number of persons older than age 64 diagnosed with HIV/AIDS increased only from 570 to 618 between the years 2003 and 2006 (CDC, 2008, Table 1) or less than 1% of the cases diagnosed in those years.

Nevertheless, the underlying rationale of the CDC for the 2006 recommendation is that approximately one quarter of the persons infected with HIV are unaware of their infection and therefore are not accessing treatment or engaging in preventing the spread of HIV infection. With any arbitrary upper age limit for routine HIV screening in healthcare facilities, we will never know the number of older persons who are living with HIV/AIDS. An argument for creating an upper age limit might be to avoid the cost associated with widespread HIV screening in very low-incidence populations, but the second part of the screening recommendations addresses this by instituting routine screening only in prevalence areas of more than 1%. New York has the highest prevalence case rate for adults with HIV infection (not AIDS) in the United States (261.7 per 100,000) (CDC, 2008, p. 8), and most of those New York cases live in New York City.

New York City reports the age category of 60 years or older and 8% of all the persons living with HIV or AIDS in NYC as of December 31, 2006, were in that age category compared with 24.5% of persons aged 50 to 59 years. From the time of HIV infection to the development of AIDS, as many as 10 to 12 years can elapse. There is thus every possibility that the numbers of cases of older persons are underreported, especially in an area with an established epidemic and high prevalence; nevertheless, the policy makers in New York are mirroring CDC recommendations to provide routine screening for persons only up to age 64 years. If the purpose of routine screening is to uncover persons who do not know they are HIV infected, then one wonders why an upper age limit for routine screening was recommended and implemented in high-incidence areas such as New York City.

The Federal Older Americans Act, amended in 2006, states that

> *The Congress hereby finds and declares that, in keeping with the traditional American concept of the inherent dignity of the individual in our democratic society, the older people of our Nation are entitled to . . . (2) The best possible physical and mental health which science can make available and without regard to economic status.*

Is the CDC policy of establishing an upper age limit on the public health recommendation for routine HIV screening an example of ageism and a deviation from the promises of the Older Americans Act?

The second component of the 2006 revised recommendations relates to consent and pretest counseling. Specifically, the recommendation states this:

> *Screening after notifying the patient that an HIV test will be performed unless the patient declines (opt-out screening) is recommended in all health-care settings. Specific signed consent for HIV testing should not be required. General informed consent for medical care should be considered sufficient to encompass informed consent for HIV testing.*

The assumption underlying this policy is that a competent person is seeking the services of a healthcare provider, and those services include screening for HIV infection. An opt-out option has been defined by CDC as

Performing HIV screening after notifying the patient that 1) the test will be performed and 2) the patient may elect to decline or defer testing. Assent is inferred unless the patient declines testing.

The American Cancer Society (2008) provides an explanation of the difference between implicit and written consent. They explain that all medical care requires the patient's consent, but in cases with low risk, such as having a blood test, a simple consent is adequate. They go on to say that in cases in which there are larger possible risks, written consent is necessary. The amount of blood needed for the HIV screening is easily included in the tubes of blood routinely drawn during a visit to a healthcare facility and the amount of time that the person drawing the blood takes to fill one more tube is negligible since access has already been attained.

The CDC recommendation supports that drawing blood for HIV is a low-risk procedure and simple consent is sufficient; however, the identification of an opt-out option recognizes that this screening requires special consideration. Persons are not given an opt-out option for other screening tests such as syphilis or hereditary issues such as sickle cell or other anemia. After admission into healthcare facilities, persons sign general consent forms and then explicit consent forms for specific procedures such as surgery. In the past, HIV screening has been handled as requiring an explicit consent form. With this new recommendation, HIV screening will be transferred to the general consent for medical treatment standard. Thus, why is an opt-out option being made available? If HIV is not a special case, why are persons being alerted that they can choose not to have this specific test? If HIV is a special case, what is the rationale? Could it be that, as cited by the CDC in 2003, healthcare providers do not want to spend the time doing the necessary counseling before the testing.

If healthcare providers do not want to take the time to counsel persons about HIV infection, will they be competent to handle newly diagnosed persons with HIV infection? Some persons will be surprised and perhaps devastated at learning that they are infected. By identifying the 25% of the cases that the CDC believes are infected and unaware, will networks of knowledgeable and sensitive healthcare providers also be identified? Will more resources be made available to stage and treat these newly diagnosed persons with HIV/AIDS? Does this public health policy focus on the needs of the group and harm the individual?

Because one of the reasons for the removal of a written consent is that healthcare providers do not have the time to counsel persons before testing for HIV, alternate methods of counseling could be developed. Persons could complete a simple true/false quiz while waiting to see the healthcare provider that addresses the key components of HIV counseling such as safer sex recommendations, the fact that HIV is a treatable condition, and that blood will be routinely tested for HIV but that clients can decline this testing. All clients would be required to complete five to six true/false questions in a format similar to that used in providing information about their health insurance. Clients would be able to review their answers with the healthcare provider and be more aware of their opt-out option, and healthcare providers would not need to spend excessive time in counseling. In situations in which computer access is available, these quizzes could be taken online and the responses made part of the client's electronic health record.

Policies related to HIV infection are often influenced more by politics and economics than public health considerations. Healthcare providers should not assume that new policies are based on sound practices but, rather, explore the motivation behind these policies, especially in situations in which marginalized populations are particularly impacted by the health issue. Healthcare providers should be vocal in their feedback about the proposed policy and provide clinical insights that might be helpful for legislators as they create laws.

Case Study Questions

In this second case, there are some very specific changes in hospital policy dealing with HIV. What are they? In what ways is the adoption and/or acceptance of those policies tied to expertise power? In the change in policy about HIV screening, what was the role of expertise, both within and beyond the medical community? How was expert knowledge balanced against our broader understanding of HIV throughout society? The expertise on these issues preceded the change in policy: what does that tell us about expertise and power?

Case Study References

American Cancer Society. (2008). *Making treatment decisions.* Retrieved May 11, 2008, from http://www.cancer.org/docroot/ETO/content/ETO_1_2X_Informed_Consent.asp

Centers for Disease Control and Prevention. (2006). Revised recommendations for HIV testing of adults, adolescents, and pregnant women in health-care settings. *Morbidity and Mortality Weekly Report, 55*(RR-14), 1–17.

Centers for Disease Control and Prevention. (2007). *Living with HIV/AIDS.* Retrieved May 11, 2008, from http://www.cdc.gov/hiv/resources/brochures/livingwithhiv.htm#q2

Centers for Disease Control and Prevention. (2008). *HIV/AIDS surveillance report, 2006.* Retrieved February 16, 2010, from http://www.cdc.gov/hiv/topics/surveillance/resources/reports

Older Americans Act Amendments of 2006. Title I—Declaration of Objectives; Definitions. Declaration of Objectives for Older Americans. Section 101. Retrieved May 11, 2008, from http://www.aoa.gov/AoARoot/AoA_Programs/OAA/oaa_full.asp

CASE STUDY

External Stakeholder Power: Successful Efforts to Pass Advanced Practice Nurse Legislation

Claudia J. Beverly

The Arkansas State Legislature meets every other year to conduct the business of the state. In the year preceding the legislative session, the Policy Committee of the Arkansas Nurses Association (ArNA) examines the healthcare needs of the state and designs a strategic health policy plan for nursing that will be introduced in the upcoming session. The work is always initiated with a clear understanding of the needs of the citizens of the State of Arkansas. In this rural state, 69 of the 75 counties are medically underserved. The poverty level is one of the worst in the country. The health statistics of Arkansans are in the bottom four states. and several counties do not have a single primary care provider. Given the many healthcare challenges facing the state, nursing is in a key position to address these needs and is expected to do so by society.

In the early 1990s, the ArNA, which represents all nurses in Arkansas, concluded that advanced practice nurses were best prepared to address the primary healthcare needs of Arkansans. At that time, however, there was no standardization or clear regulation for this level of nurse other than national certification and the registered nurse (RN) license that is basic for all levels of registered nurses.

The ArNA's first attempt to address the primary healthcare needs of the citizens was in 1993. Their attempt to pass legislation that would allow prescriptive authority by advanced practice nurses failed. After this failure, the ArNA, with the assistance of its lobbyist, began to develop legislation to be introduced in the 1995 legislative session to provide a mechanism for advanced practice nurses to practice to the extent to which they were academically prepared. Additionally, a mechanism whereby society could be assured of safe practice by all providers needed to be in place.

The process began when a legislator from a rural area where the need was greatest introduced a "study bill." This study bill provided the opportunity for the ArNA to educate legislators about advanced practice nursing and how this type of nurse could address the healthcare needs of Arkansans. The study bill was assigned to the Interim Public Health, Welfare and Labor Committee of both the House of Representatives and the Senate. Several public hearings were held by the committee, and various groups and individuals both in support and in opposition were given the opportunity to voice their opinions.

During the hearings, there were opportunities to provide correct information supported by the literature. Clarification of the proposed legislation was also always on the agenda. At one point, concern was raised about the use of the term "collaboration with medicine," as some persons preferred to use "supervision" or a definition that would limit the practice to one being supervised. The task force initiated a process to define the term collaboration. A review of the literature showed that collaboration had already been defined in the seventies by both medicine and nursing. Armed with that information and definitions given by other sources, the task force reported their findings at the next hearing and the definition jointly developed by medicine, and nursing was incorporated in the proposed legislation.

Process for Success

The leadership of the ArNA understood the monumental task and the many challenges and barriers to addressing the healthcare needs of Arkansans. The association decided that appointing a special task force to lead its efforts was the best strategy. This strategy provided a mechanism for focusing on this issue while ensuring that the health policy committee would continue to focus on broader policy issues.

The association selected a chair, included the chair in selection of the members by ArNA leadership, and established the first meeting. As the process evolved, two co-chairs, a secretary, and a treasurer were named. The task force was representative of nursing broadly and included members of the Arkansas State Board of Nursing, master's prepared advanced practice nurses (midwives, certified registered nurse anesthetists, nurse practitioners, and clinical nurse specialists), registered nurses, faculty from schools of nursing preparing advanced practice nurses, and representatives from other nursing organizations. The task force met every other week during the first 6 months of the 2-year preparatory period and then weekly for the remaining year and a half.

The first order of business was to develop a strategic plan that included establishing a vision, mission, goals and objectives, strategies, and a time line. The vision was critical as a means of keeping task force members focused on the vast needs of Arkansans, particularly those in rural areas. The vision statement also served to keep the broader ArNA membership focused. A literature search on advanced practice nursing and health policy issues was conducted, and articles were distributed to all task force members. The assumption was that all of the members needed information to expand their current knowledge. Subcommittees were developed based on goals and objectives and the operational needs of the task force. Chairs were assigned for each subcommittee, and thus began the 2-year journey.

The American Nurses Association played a vital role in the process. The legal department was available to assemble and provide information, offer guidance, and identify potential barriers and challenges. The support provided by the ANA was pivotal to our success.

The work of the task force focused on external and internal strategies. External strategies focused on stakeholders, which included the Arkansas Medical Society and the Arkansas Medical Board and the Pharmacy Association. Understanding the views of our colleagues in other disciplines and identifying the opposition to our plans were critical to our success. Many meetings focused on educating those disciplines about the legislation we were seeking. Often this was a balancing act, providing the right information, but not too much of our strategy while attempting to keep our "enemy" close to us. We valued the process of negotiation and participated in many opportunities to negotiate with colleagues.

Throughout this process, the ArNA did have a "line in the sand," defined as the point at which there was no negotiation. Our line in the sand included regulations of advanced practice nurses by the Arkansas State Board of Nursing and reimbursement paid directly to the nurses. These two points were never resolved until a vote on the legislation occurred.

The good news is that the APN legislation passed successfully in 1995. The legislation was successful in that the criteria for an APN to be licensed in the State of Arkansas were written by nursing, APNs were to be regulated by nursing, and the legislation acknowledged national certification and educational requirements. Prescriptive authority was granted, and selected scheduled drugs could be ordered by an APN. Reimbursement to APNs was lost at the last minute. For APNs practicing in the field of geriatrics, Medicare passed reimbursement regulations in 1997. Medicaid reimburses geriatric nurse practitioners according to national guidelines. Reimbursement is critical to meeting Arkansans' needs and is a topic that is continuing to be discussed.

Many individuals participated in this successful campaign. A clear vision, legislation based on evidence and current literature, a comprehensive strategic plan, education of all parties, including those in opposition and those in support, and well-informed legislators were critical to success. Probably the most critical message in health policy legislation is to focus on the needs of the citizenry and what nursing needs to contribute.

Case Study Questions

We suspect that most nursing professionals can expand on this case; however, the key question is what is the nature of the building of a stakeholder network here? Who were the critical "first" players in this movement and why? As the network expanded, which other professional groups were involved? Why those? Do you see why some professions were the logical next parts of the coalition for adopting change? Who was most likely to oppose advanced practice nursing? Obviously, you do not include likely opponents in the initial development of the network of stakeholders, but why is that? How did the coalition eventually succeed through this inclusive network? What would you have done differently in a different practice arena? What does this case study tell you about building stakeholders for advancing practice? What would you need to do to apply this policy to advancing roles in your healthcare setting?

CASE STUDY

Internal Expertise Power: The Politics of Moving to an Electrical Medical Record

Pamela Trevino

Making significant change in an institution is a long and tedious process. It is essential to get support and buy in from all levels of the organization and often requires fancy footwork. For example, moving to an electronic medical record is a substantial process change for all who use it, and even small portions of the change can be daunting.

After learning the benefits and safety of bedside medication verification (BMV) using barcode technology, an executive safety committee at a 310-bed hospital decided to implement the technology and an electronic medication administration record. In the earliest stages of development, an executive-level committee included representatives from the following divisions: medicine (physicians), pharmacy, and nursing. They discussed the theoretical and technological needs for the system to work within an existing technological framework and began evaluating systems.

As the executives began to evaluate the use of the system, it was decided that a front-line bedside staff member needed to be part of the decision making body, as the changes would directly affect those at the bedside. A nurse from an elite team trained to work in every hospital area was chosen to join the committee for her referent power, credibility, and knowledge of multiple hospital areas. Although the nurse was unsure about the necessity of the change, she joined the committee to represent the interests of the bedside staff. In the first weeks on the committee, the nurse was presented with the literature and evidence related to the increased safety of the barcode technology and asked to compare the new technology to the current standard of practice. As the bedside nurse became immersed in the literature, evaluated the current process, and was included in site visits, she became a strong advocate for the safety of the new technology.

As the process continued, a product was purchased, and the implementation process began. Interdisciplinary subcommittees, including all of the disciplines either affected or with a stake in the process, were formed to discuss the ways the system would change current practice. Medicine, nursing, pharmacy, respiratory therapy, information technology, quality management, billing, discharge planning, and fiscal administration were involved in building the system to meet all of the institution's needs, discuss the change in practice, and make policy and procedural changes.

To combat resistance to the product and related changes in process, the system was designed to look as much like the current paper forms as possible. A "BMV Fair" was held in which all front-line respiratory and nursing staff could see and use the technology prior to the official education and implementation. Staff members were encouraged to give feedback on the product, ways to improve the process, and their personal opinions of the technology. The system was then evaluated and changed to accommodate staff preferences where possible, to help remove barriers to acceptance, although the system was still not popular among front-line staff.

The "BMV Fair" also brought to the forefront the lack of basic computer skills in some members of the team. A basic computer competency was developed for all front-line staff members, and classes were offered for those team members who did possess basic computer skills. Staff members were advised early that they would be expected to be able to use the system, and they would not be allowed to work if they could not use the computer-based medication system.

With the move to computer-based charting, computers needed to be available at every bedside. Because of the diversity of the hospital, all units were asked to determine whether they would like mounted computers in every room or computers on wheels (COWs) that could be moved throughout a unit. Because patient rooms are fairly busy, all of the units decided on COWs because of their mobility and flexibility. Each unit was able to borrow several different models and "test drive" them in their area. Nurses were encouraged to give their feedback and suggestions to the purchasing team, and then to decide on a COW. Interestingly, all of the units chose the same COW, which then could be maintained in a central location by information technology personnel.

As the go-live dates approached, training was developed and taught by a member of the information technology staff with a nursing background and by the original bedside nurse on the committee. The bedside nurse shared her initial hesitancy to adopt the system as well as her change to advocacy. Because the institution had a culture geared toward patient safety, front-line staff were told that the process would feel clumsy and take longer initially than current practice but in the end would be safer for the patient. The education highlighted those things that had been added into the system for the convenience of the front-line staff, such as customized computers on wheels, the system "extras" that would save time and effort, and area-specific ways to incorporate the system into everyday practice. Because the hospital chose a staggered roll out, education for each area was held in the 2 weeks before the go-live date. Area-specific questions and concerns were anticipated and addressed with each class.

Within 30 minutes of going live, the system caught the first medication error. Initially, the staff member believed that the system was not working correctly but then learned that the system was correct and that he was attempting to give the wrong medication. This initial user became a strong advocate for the system, and without giving specifics, the information was shared with each subsequent group during their education to show the validity of the system. As more units began using the system, more events occurred, and the information was shared with all the staff members in the hospital. A centralized e-mail account was set up to allow staff to share successes, suggest improvements, and ask questions and feel they were part of the ongoing process.

The implementation was surprisingly smooth, and the system has become part of the culture of the hospital. There are still several committees related to different aspects of the system that meet on a regular basis to address issues that were not foreseeable during the original implementation; however, through careful planning, politics, and change agents, the implementation and enculturation have been a definite success.

Case Study Questions

Based on what you just read, what is the expertise being developed here? What is the challenge to others accepting this expertise? What is it in this case that indicates acceptance of the expertise? What were challenges? What role does process play in making changes such as these? Is there a danger that electronic records will define the questions rather than those involved in direct care?

CASE STUDY

Expanding Newborn Screening in Arkansas

Ralph Vogel

Advances in technology have created great advances in how we can provide services to families and their children. A prime example of this is the expansion of newborn screening, which has dramatically increased the number and type of genetic conditions that can be detected immediately after birth. Historically, most states have screened for hemoglobinopathies (like sickle cell anemia), thyroid, phenylketonuria, and galactosemia. These conditions, along with newborn hearing screening, were relatively easy to assess at a cost effective rate. With advanced laboratory and computer technology, we can now add multiple genetic conditions that are identified during a single run. In 2004, the March of Dimes proposed expanding the genetic conditions for which newborns are screened to their "List of 29," including several enzyme deficiency conditions and cystic fibrosis. The cost of the limited newborn screening was approximately $15 per newborn, and this would rise to about $90 with the expanded list. Insurance companies would cover the cost of adding the additional conditions. The value of newborn screening is in identifying genetic conditions early and implementing treatment plans from birth. Over the life span, this greatly reduces the morbidity and mortality associated with later diagnosis. With some conditions, the care can be as simple as a dietary change that is implemented from birth. Early diagnosis also allows for genetic counseling with families about the risk that additional children will have the condition.

Many states adopted this recommendation quickly, although the process has been slower in others. In Arkansas, a committee, titled the Arkansas Genetics Health Advisory Committee (formerly Service), has existed for several years. Their mission is to monitor health care related to genetics in the state. This diverse committee includes several members of the Arkansas Department of Health (ADH) involved in the newborn screening program administration and laboratory testing, the physicians from Arkansas Children's Hospital genetic clinic, and interested parties that either work in the area of genetics or are parents of children with genetic conditions.

The main purpose of the committee has been to coordinate care and to try to educate the public about genetic conditions and screening for newborns. The ADH receives samples from about 95% of the newborns in the state and does screening at their central location in Little Rock. When an infant is identified with a newborn genetic condition, the ADH then notifies the community hospital and the assigned pediatrician, who does the counseling with the family and develops a plan for care and follow-up.

Expanding the screening program to the existing March of Dimes List of 29 created several problems. The committee, however, felt strongly that it should take an advocacy role to address these concerns. The first problem was the cost of increased screening. Although most of the individual cost for each child could be absorbed by insurance or Medicaid reimbursement, as in other states, the initial financial support would need to be provided by the state. The ADH had no provision for increasing funding but estimated that the increased cost would be as follows:

- Two million dollars for equipment and supplies
- The addition of at least two more laboratory technicians to do the increased testing
- The addition of at least one more public health nurse to coordinate the increased number of identified genetic cases
- Training for new and current personnel on the new equipment
- Personnel time to develop and coordinate the expansion of the program
- Development of an education program to make parents and professionals aware of the changes

Overall, the estimated cost for startup was approximately $3 million, some of which could be recouped after billing for the tests was established.

The committee and ADH decided that we would outline a plan for expansion with estimated costs and submit it to the director of the ADH, Dr. Faye Bozeman. With his approval, we would then approach legislators and ask for the needed funding to be included in the upcoming budget. Because the state legislature for Arkansas only convened every 2 years, it would be critical to move forward over the next 6 months. We prepared a letter to Dr. Bozeman that the committee approved on a Friday with the intention of mailing it on the following Monday. On the next day, Saturday, Dr. Bozeman was killed in an accident on his farm; therefore, we were in a quandary about who should receive the letter and whose approval would be needed in the ADH. Over the next 6 months, there was an interim head who was thrust into the position and did not want to approve anything at this level of expense. Basically, we were on hold until a permanent director was named. After about 3 months, we decided to take another tack and develop a plan to seek legislative approval for funding and then approach the new ADH director after the person was named. We developed a list of legislators to contact and identified members of the committee who had worked with the legislators in the past and could approach them.

By this time, we were 2 months from the legislature convening and knew that once it convened nothing new would be introduced; therefore, we had to get support before their convening. We approached some legislators and received tacit support, but none was willing to introduce a new bill or request funding at this time without a permanent head of ADH. We had lost the opportunity for funding until the next legislative session in 2 years.

The committee decided to continue to seek support from the legislators and ADH with the idea of gaining funding in 2 years. Meanwhile, we began to look at other states and what newborn screenings they were currently doing to make sure that politicians were aware of national standards. We had identified that Arkansas was one of the last five states to not expand newborn screening, and all of the surrounding states in the region had incorporated all or a large part of the March of Dimes List of 29. Making legislators aware of this became one of our goals, and once they realized that the states surrounding Arkansas were already doing expanded screening of newborns, they were more receptive to our plan.

After we started to discuss funding with legislators during the legislative session, they seemed willing to support newborn screening; however, then we had a surprise: They stated that it did not require any special legislation or special funding. They stated that the ADH could expand newborn screening without their approval because this was already within their realm of responsibility. Funding could be obtained by submitting a budget request to cover the cost of expansion.

The interim head of ADH was willing to support this since the head of the newborn screening section, was on our committee. By fall, we had the budget expansion approved and support for newborn screening expansion. The decision was then made to target July 1, 2008, as the date for starting the expanded program.

After we knew that the finances and political support were confirmed, we developed a timeline that involved acquisition of the equipment, training for ADH staff, an education program for the public, and a plan for making community hospitals and professional healthcare providers aware of the expansion. At this point, the ADH contacted members of the media that it had worked with in the past and developed a plan for public information advertisements to be run on television and radio. These began running in early May, 2 months before the July 1 start date. Because the media members had worked with ADH in the past, it was much easier to develop the advertisements. Print media advertisements were also started, and the local chapter of the March of Dimes provided funding and brochures that were distributed to OB/GYN physicians in the state to make expectant mothers aware of the testing to be done on their newborns. One of the members of the committee also wrote an article that appeared in the March issue of the *Arkansas State Board of Nursing Update* magazine, which is distributed to 40,000 healthcare providers in the state.

In July, the expanded screening was begun, and it has been continued with a relatively smooth transition, largely because of the preparation of the ADH staff in the laboratory and the outreach nurses. Because of the public awareness campaign, there has been little voiced concern from parents, and there seems to be an awareness of the value of the expanded screening.

Lessons learned from the process are these:

- Preparation is the key to a smooth transition.
- Know exactly what is required to proceed and who needs to approve new or expanded plans of action. If we had approached the legislature first to find out what they wanted, we could have saved time.
- Plan for the unexpected. We could not have anticipated Dr. Bozeman's death, but it did cause about a 6-month delay.
- Educate everyone who is going to be involved. This includes administrators, healthcare providers, laboratory staff, parents, and professionals in the communities impacted.
- Discuss with the media exactly what they need and use their expertise in terms of length of announcements and the best ways to distribute information.

Although the entire process took over 2 years, in the end, the transition has been very smooth, and few problems have been identified at any level. Having a diverse group on the committee was a strength because different members had different perspectives. This gave us much greater ability to anticipate problems and coordinate care, and in the end, the program in place will benefit newborns in Arkansas for years to come.

Case Study Questions

This case is a good example of how the stakeholders adapted as the intended policy change moved from internal adoption of policy to legislation back to internal adoption of policy within an existing organization. Can you see how the nature of the stakeholders defined for a legislative change is different from stakeholders for an adaptation of existing policy? The initial group involved in this process was established primarily as an informational group but changed to one advocating change. How did the group evolve to influence policy differently? If the initial group had been more broadly defined at the start, would it have made the same mistake about requiring legislative change to adopt the policy? Why or why not?

Final Case Study

This final case study is presented to stimulate the reader's political thinking. We encourage you to read the case carefully and then consider how you would go about creating an environment for policy change.

CASE STUDY

Workplace Violence

Steven L. Baumann and Eileen Levy

In the wake of the terrorist attack of September 11, 2001, and a series of tragic school shootings, workplace violence has gained national attention in the United States. Although nurses and other healthcare workers are generally well educated and regularly reminded to practice good hand washing and infection control, there is little attention given to the potential for violence in hospitals and other healthcare settings, even though it is common and can have devastating long-term consequences (Department of Health and Human Services, 2002; U.S. Department of Labor, 2004). According to Love and Morrison (2003), nurses who sustain injuries from patient assaults, in addition to suffering psychological trauma, are often out of work for periods of time, have financial problems, show decreased work productivity, make more errors at work, and report a decreased desire to remain a nurse. In addition to these problems, nurses who have been assaulted report feeling less able to provide appropriate care to their patients (Farrell et al., 2006) and are reluctant to make formal complaints (Love & Morrison, 2003). As was the case with needle stick injuries in the past, many organizations do not openly discuss organizational problems that increase the risk for violence, nor do they adequately prepare for episodes of violence, leaving nurses more likely to blame themselves for its occurrence.

The National Institute for Occupational Safety and Health (NIOSH), the same organization that requires hospitals to be attentive to infection control strategies and proper handling of hazardous materials, also provides clear definitions and guidelines to reduce the potential for violence in the workplace. According NIOSH, workplace violence includes acts of physical violence or threats of violence directed toward people on duty or at work (Department of Health and Human Services, 2002). NIOSH has recognized employer responsibilities in mitigating workplace violence and assisting employees who are victims (Love & Morrison, 2003). The U.S. government has required employers to provide safe workplaces since 1970 (U.S. Department of Labor, 2004). These federal guidelines call for hospitals and other organizations to incorporate written programs to assure job safety and security into the overall safety and health program for their facilities. Violence prevention, they suggest, needs to have administrative commitment and employee involvement.

This case study is of a moderate-sized, nonprofit community hospital in the New York Metropolitan area. As in many parts of the United States, this hospital and the communities it serves are becoming increasingly crowded and diverse. In this environment of change and tension, the hospital is a meeting place of people, many not by choice but in crisis, bringing together dramatically different histories, backgrounds, educational attainment, and cultures. The hospital and its clinics have become increasingly stressful, unpredictable, and at times hostile places. For example, the use of hospitals as holding tanks for acutely disturbed and violent individuals, the release of mentally ill persons from public hospitals without adequate outpatient programs and follow-up services, and the accessibility of handguns and drugs in communities all contribute to hospital and community violence. A failure of leadership at various levels, as well as inadequate reimbursement from payers, has contributed to violence that can occur on its premises.

The case study hospital, like most in the United States, has dramatically reduced the number of public psychiatric beds. Many of these former psychiatric patients have to rely on outpatient mental health services supported by community hospitals with a limited number of beds on one or two psychiatric units. In addition, the case study hospital reduced inpatient and outpatient addiction services. New research suggests that actively psychotic patients with schizophrenia and patients with schizophrenia who had a premorbid conduct problem or exposure to violence are more likely to be violent than less acutely ill patients and those without substance abuse or antisocial personality co-morbidity (Swanson et al., 2008). Nevertheless, it is a mistake to consider persons with mental illness or substance abuse as the only individuals who can become agitated or violent in healthcare settings. It is also shortsighted to solely blame any single policy, such as the deinstitutionalization of the chronically mentally ill, for workplace violence in the United States.

At the same time that the case study hospital has cut beds and programs for persons in distress, the case study hospital has a clear mission/vision/value statement that puts professional nurses in leadership positions and has taken steps to address workplace violence. It has made efforts to reduce violence in high-risk areas, such as the emergency department and psychiatric unit by restricting access to these areas, using surveillance equipment, panic buttons, and a strict requirement for all staff to wear identification, as other hospitals have. Community hospitals, like the one in this case study, however, often do not provide the kind of ongoing self-defense and violence prevention education and training that many psychiatric hospitals provide. In addition, all hospitals should have a task force and regularly meeting committee consisting of management, human resources/employee relations, employee assistance program staff, security and the office of chief counsel with the sole purpose of developing policies and procedures to prevent and address workplace violence.

Following The Joint Commission's (2008) lead, the case study hospital and nursing administration have hospital wide discussions and training on "behaviors that undermine a culture of safety." In addition, the hospital requires workplace violence risk assessment, hazard prevention and control, and safety and health training, as well as careful record keeping and program evaluation (U.S. Department of Labor, 2004). Hospitals need to keep in mind the malpractice crisis in this country. The move to put patients first does not turn over control of the hospital to patients or their families. Indeed, to understand Friedman (2007) correctly, in order to put patients' health and satisfaction first, the hospital needs effective leadership at the top and from its professional nurses. To prevent violence in the workplace, nurses need to strive to be as authentic in their patient contact as possible and to avoid detached impersonal interactions (Carlsson et al., 2006). The case study hospital provides considerable avenues of reward for individual nurses and other staff members to advance themselves and stand out as innovative, which helps mitigate the tendency for workers to "herd," to use Friedman's (2007) term—that is to say, to avoid developing themselves and improving the institution for the sake of togetherness with selected coworkers.

The case study hospital does provide a psychiatric nurse practitioner on staff and onsite one day a week as an employee assistance provider. Having this person onsite provides an opportunity for hospital staff to have counseling to become less reactive to emotionally intense environments, as recommended by Friedman (2007). Healthcare organizations also need to provide referral information such as employee assistance program or clinicians experienced in trauma care for employees who may exhibit more serious and persistent reactions to perceived violence and aggression (Bernstein & Saladino, 2007). Nurses and nursing organizations should become more familiar with national guidelines and recommendations and persuade their hospitals to adopt and implement them. The process for nurses is to focus more on taking responsibility for their own condition, practice self-regulation, and have a wide repertory of responses to stressful situations. Although this does not guarantee that violence will be avoided, it does make it less likely to happen and makes nurses better able to keep it in perspective. Friedman (2007) described this as being able to turn down the dial or volume. Nurses need to be just as effective in managing "toxic" emotional environments, as in handling toxic chemicals and infections. Nurses' interpersonal effectiveness is increased when they look for and support strengths in others. Postincident debriefing helps transform the experience into a team building and learning opportunity. Leaders should involve all staff and review events, including what precedes and follows an incident.

Case Study Conclusion

A community hospital in the New York metropolitan area is presented as a case study of an organization struggling to carry out its mission in a way that facilitates the growth and well-being of its employees. The hospital is experiencing different pulls. On the one hand it has had to cut back on essential programs. On the other hand, the nurses and the central leadership in the hospital need to work together to avoid quick-fix solutions and suffer the failure of nerve that Friedman (2007) talked about. The busy hospital environment in a changing society is stressful and at times a hostile and violent one. Nurses need to be effective leaders to help protect the integrity of the hospital as an organization—that is to say maintain its self-definition. They can best do this by becoming as self-defined as they can and by consistently implementing federal guidelines to prevent and manage workplace violence.

Case Study Questions

In this last case you have a need for policy change—which we suspect is a need in many healthcare organizations—the need for workplace violence policies. Here is our challenge to the reader. Can you take our two components, both an internal and external role, and define what needs to be done to accomplish this policy change? We suggest that you define the work in terms of your most likely environment, whether a psychiatric facility or a hospital or clinic. How would you go about creating an environment for policy change here?

Some core questions should guide you. First, what key stakeholders are in the initial stakeholder group (i.e., those most likely to feel the strongest need for the policy)? Are they organized around various professional lines within your organization? How do you begin to create a networked shared view among these stakeholders? As you begin to broaden the network, which groups should be brought into the discussion? Let us give you an example: The human resource specialists in your organization will need to be involved at some point in creating a policy about the elimination/reduction of workplace violence. Should they, however, be in your initial set of stakeholders? Why or why not?

Now . . . the more difficult question: What is the expertise needed to make such a policy change? What are the kind of facts (someone has to gather the data in a systematic way), that need to be gathered? Are we discussing violence between patients and those providing medical services, or are we also talking about violence between fellow professionals within the organization? What kind of violence/danger are we discussing here—physical or verbal violence or both? What about safety issues (including other types of danger to employees and patients)? Would you agree that an emergency room might see these questions a bit differently from those handling financial claims (although both have real needs here)? How do you build expert power here? Who shares it, and who might be expert in defining these issues over time?

Case Study References

Bernstein, K. S., & Saladino, J. P. (2007). Clinical assessment and management of psychiatric patients' violent and aggressive behaviors in general hospital. *Medsurg Nursing, 16,* 301–309.

Carlsson, G., Dahlberg, K., Ekcbergh, M., & Dahlberg, H. (2006). Patients longing for authentic personal care: A phenomenological study of violent encounters in psychiatric settings. *Issues in Mental Health Nursing, 27,* 287–305.

Department of Health and Human Services. (2002). *Violence: Occupational hazards in hospitals.* Centers for Disease Control and Prevention/National Institute for Occupational Safety and Health. Document # 2002-101. Cincinnati, OH: National Institute for Occupational Safety and Health.

Farrell, G. A., Bobrowski, C., & Bobrowski, P. (2006). Scoping workplace aggression in nursing: findings from an Australian study. *Journal of Advanced Nursing, 55,* 778–787.

Friedman, E. H. (2007). *A failure of nerve: Leadership in the age of the quick fix.* New York: Seabury (originally published in 1999).

Love, C. C., & Morrison, E. (2003). American Academy of Nursing expert panel on violence policy recommendation on workplace violence (adopted 2002). *Issues in Mental Health Nursing, 24,* 599–604.

Swanson, J. W., Van Dorn, R. A., Swartz, M. S., Smith, M., Elbogen, E. B., & Monahan, J. (2008). Alternative Pathways to Violence in Persons with Schizophrenia. *The Role of Childhood Antisocial Behavior, 32*(3), 228–240.

The Joint Commission. (July, 2008). Behaviors that undermine a culture of safety. Retrieved February 2, 2009, from http://www.jointcommission.org/SentinelEventAlert/sea_40.htm

U.S. Department of Labor. (2004). *Guidelines for preventing workplace violence for health care & social service workers* (OSHA 3148-01R). Washington, DC: Occupational Safety and Health Administration.

Chapter Conclusion

This book on politics and policy requires an understanding of how to build support and adapt to change. If we are to be effective advocates, we must be responsive to broader societal needs. Building support is not done simply by presenting the facts. This toolkit is designed to help readers know what it takes in a political environment to build a case and adapt when necessary. A huge mistake in advocacy is to simply believe that the facts are on our side, and if we just continue to list the facts, everyone will believe! In reality, values and political issues are at the core of successful change. Our tasks as political advocates for change are to:

1. Believe we can convince others to adapt
2. Adapt ourselves to handle broader political value issues
3. Learn to mobilize our expert power as one of the largest group of stakeholders in the healthcare field

Chapter References

Fottler, M. D., Blair, J. D., Whitehead, C. J., Laus, M. D., & Savage, G. T. (1989). Assessing key stakeholders: Who matters to hospitals and why? *Hospitals and Health Services Administration, 34*(4), 525–546.

Wilson, J. Q. (1989). *Bureaucracy: What government agencies do and why they do it.* New York: Basic Books.

Appendix A

Web Resources

Compiled by Lametria Wafford

Section I Introduction

Healthcare Policy and Research Groups

Agency for Healthcare Research and Quality
http://www.ahrq.gov

Center for Studying Health System Change
http://www.hschange.com

Centers for Disease Control and Prevention
http://www.cdc.gov

Gerontological Society of America
http://www.geron.org

Kaiser Family Foundation
http://www.kff.org

National Institutes of Health
http://www.nih.gov

Robert Wood Johnson Foundation
http://www.rwjf.org

The Commonwealth Fund
http://www.commonwealthfund.org

United States National Library of Medicine
http://www.nlm.nih.gov

World Health Organization
http://www.who.int/en

Representative Consumer Advocacy Groups

American Association of Retired Persons
http://www.aarp.org

American Cancer Society
http://www.cancer.org

American Heart Association
http://www.americanheart.org

Families USA
http://www.familiesusa.org

Leukemia & Lymphoma Society
http://www.leukemia-lymphoma.org

Multiple Sclerosis Society
http://www.nationalmssociety.org

National Alliance on Mental Illness
http://www.nami.org

National Association for the Advancement of Colored People
http://www.naacp.org

National Council of La Raza
http://www.nclr.org

National Mental Health Association
http://www.nmha.org

National Organization for Women
http://www.now.org

Section II The Health Labor Force: Understanding the Distribution of Power and Influence

Representative Professional Healthcare Associations

American Association of Ambulatory Care Nursing
http://www.aaacn.org

American Association of Nurse Executives
http://www.aone.org

American College of Health Care Administrators
http://www.achca.org

American College of Healthcare Executives
http://www.ache.org

American Medical Association
http://www.ama-assn.org

American Medical Informatics Association
https://www.amia.org

American Nurses Association
http://www.nursingworld.org

American Psychiatric Association
http://www.psych.org

American Psychological Association
http://www.apa.org

American Public Health Association
http://www.apha.org

National Association of State Mental Health Program Directors
http://www.nasmhpd.org

Section III Healthcare Providers: Understanding How Power, Markets, and Government Impact the Organization and Delivery of Care

Representative Provider Organizations

American Association of Medical Colleges
http://www.aamc.org

American Academy of Nursing
http://www.aannet.org

American Health Care Association
http://www.ahca.org

American Association of Colleges of Nursing
http://www.aacn.nche.edu

American Hospital Association
http://www.aha.org

American Association of Homes and Services for the Aging
http://www.aahsa.org

Association of State and Territorial Health Officials
http://www.astho.org

Federation of American Hospitals
http://www.fah.org

National Association of Community Health Centers
http://www.nachc.org

National Association of Public Hospitals and Health Systems
http://www.naph.org

National League of Nursing
http://www.nln.org

Section IV Healthcare Finance: Understanding the Role of Markets in Government

America's Health Insurance Plans
http://www.ahip.org

Association of Maternal & Child Health Programs
http://www.amchp.org

Blue Cross and Blue Shield Association
http://www.bcbs.com

Centers for Medicare and Medicaid Services
http://www.cms.hhs.gov

Healthcare Financial Management Association
http://www.hfma.org

Medical Group Management Association
http://www.mgma.com

Medicaid
http://www.cms.hhs.gov/home/medicaid.asp

Medicare
http://www.cms.hhs.gov/home/medicare.asp

National Council of State Boards of Nursing
http://www.ncsbn.org

US Department of Health and Human Services
http://www.hhs.gov

Section V Drivers

Health Care Quality Organizations

American Health Quality Association
http://www.ahqa.org

Institute for Healthcare Improvement
http://www.ihi.org

Institute of Medicine of the National Academies
http://www.iom.edu

The Joint Commission
http://www.jointcommission.org

The Leapfrog Group
http://www.leapfroggroup.org

National Association for Healthcare Quality
http://www.nahq.org

National Committee for Quality Assurance
http://www.ncqa.org

National Health Quality Forum
http://www.qualityforum.org

Technology Informatics Guiding Educational Reform
http://www.tigersummit.com

Health Policy Journals

American Journal of Public Health
http://ajph.aphapublications.org

Health Affairs
http://www.healthaffairs.org

Health Care Financing Review
http://www.cms.hhs.gov/healthcarefinancingreview

Health Care Management Review
http://journals.lww.com/hcmrjournal/pages/default.aspx

Inquiry
http://www.inquiryjournal.org

Journal of the American Medical Association
http://jama.ama-assn.org

Journal of Health Economics
http://www.elsevier.com/wps/find/journaldescription.cws_home/505560/description

Journal of Health Politics, Policy and Law
http://jhppl.dukejournals.org

Journal of Public Health Policy
http://www.palgrave-journals.com/jphp/index.html

Medscape
http://www.medscape.com

Milbank Quarterly
http://www.milbank.org/quarterly.html

New England Journal of Medicine
http://www.nejm.org

Nursing Economic$: The Journal for Health Care Leaders
http://www.nursingeconomics.net

Policy, Politics, & Nursing Practice
http://ppn.sagepub.com

The Gerontologist
http://www.geron.org/Publications/The%20Gerontologist

Appendix B

Glossary of Managed Care Terminology

The language of managed care is alien to many providers and almost all consumers. An abbreviated glossary of terms compiled by Paul Grimaldi and published in *Nursing Management* (October 1996 and August 1997 issues) follows. Managed care's growth has expanded the terms used to describe how the nation purchases, delivers, and finances health care. This glossary defines commonly used terms. Readers are cautioned that experts may not agree universally with every definition presented here.

Adjusted average per capita cost (AAPCC)—the average monthly amount that Medicare spends to provide health services to Medicare beneficiaries in a fee-for-service environment. Medicare's capitation rates presently equal 95% of the projected AAPCC, adjusted for a beneficiary's age and other factors. For each county in the nation, there are four AAPCCs: one each for Part A and Part B of Medicare for aged and disabled persons, and one statewide rate for beneficiaries with end-stage renal disease.

Adjusted community rate (ACR)—the average monthly cost that a health maintenance organization (HMO) expects to incur in serving Medicare beneficiaries. The ACR equals the plan-wide average cost adjusted for higher utilization levels by Medicare beneficiaries.

Adverse selection—occurs when a disproportionately large number of sicker persons enroll in a health plan and the capitation rate or premium is not adjusted for their greater medical needs. Such a selection process is adverse or unfavorable to the health plan's financial soundness.

Any willing provider—any healthcare provider who is willing to abide by a health plan's terms and conditions, including its fee schedules. Any willing provider laws require a health plan to accept all willing providers or specific types of specialists or allied healthcare professionals.

Capitation—a fixed dollar amount that a health plan or provider is paid to furnish specific kinds of medical services that an insured person needs, regardless of the volume of care needed. The dollar amount ordinarily depends on the person's age and gender.

Carve out—a health benefit (perhaps mental health care or dental care) that is removed from a larger benefit package and contracted separately to a specialized managed care organization.

Case management—the coordination and integration of health services for patients with complex or extraordinarily costly medical problems, such as acquired immunodeficiency syndrome, spinal cord injury and premature birth. Case managers, typically registered nurses or clinical social workers, strive to ensure that patients have timely access to high quality, coordinated cost-effective medical care. A primary care physician ordinarily approves specialty care before it is provided.

Choices demonstrations—a project that the Health Care Financing Administration (HCFA) is sponsoring to increase the types of health plans available to Medicare beneficiaries. The HCFA plans to sign risk contracts with 22 managed care plans (e.g., preferred provider organizations and provider sponsored organizations) that do not meet current HMO contracting requirements to test their ability to attract and serve Medicare beneficiaries.

Closed panel model—a managed health plan that contracts with physicians on an exclusive basis. The physicians are not allowed to contract with other health plans.

Community rating method—an actuarial method for establishing a managed health plan's capitation rates. Under pure community rating, all members in the health plan's service area are charged the same capitation rate.

Competitive bidding—a method that relies on price competition to establish the fee schedules, capitation rates or other amounts paid for health care. For example, companies that wish to provide clinical laboratory services or durable medical equipment to Medicare beneficiaries could be asked to bid for the business. Medicare could base its fee schedule on the lowest bid or an average of the lowest bids. Similarly, Medicare could use competitive bidding to establish capitation rates paid to HMOs.

Competitive medical plan (CMP)—a managed health plan that qualifies for a Medicare risk contract without meeting some of the requirements required to qualify as a health maintenance organization. It is somewhat easier for a health plan to qualify as a CMP than as an HMO.

Consumer Assessment of Health Plans Study (CAHPS)—the name of the consumer satisfaction survey that the Agency for Health Care Policy and Research (AHCPR) is developing for Medicare beneficiaries enrolled in an HMO. The survey is administered annually; it contains about 60 questions, five of which address advice that smokers have received from the plan to quit smoking. The AHCPR also is developing a similar survey for a health plan's Medicaid members.

Deselection—the process by which a provider's participation in a managed health plan's network is terminated.

Direct access—a health plan member may visit a specialist without first having to obtain a referral from that primary care physician. Members are allowed to self-refer to a specialist for certain types of services, perhaps at an additional out-of-pocket cost or higher premium.

Direct contract HMO model—an HMO that contracts with physicians individually rather than through an intermediary (an independent practice association) or group practice.

Direct contracting—a provider agrees to care for a group of persons by contracting directly with an employer or other third-party payer rather than through an HMO or other intermediary.

Disenrollment—the process by which a person's membership in a managed health plan is terminated. A member may disenroll voluntarily, perhaps to join another managed health plan or to return to fee-for-service medicine. A health plan may decide to disenroll a member involuntarily if premiums are not paid for a lengthy time.

Downstream risk—insurance risk that has been shifted from one entity to another entity further removed from the original transaction, for example, a health plan that signs a capitation contract with an employer assumes insurance risk. If the health plan subsequently subcontracts with different provider groups, some or all of the risk is said to flow downstream to the providers.

Dual eligibility—a situation in which a person is entitled to receive healthcare benefits under two insurance programs. Dual eligibility most frequently refers to aged or disabled persons who are eligible for both Medicare and Medicaid benefits.

Employee Retirement Income Security Act of 1974 (ERISA)—one provision of this federal retirement law limits the ability of state governments to regulate self-funded or self-insured employer health plans. The ERISA plans are thus able to avoid paying premium taxes and do not have to cover health services that states require other health plans to cover. Lower taxes and greater freedom to design health benefits help to explain why nearly all large employers have established self-insured health plans.

Encounter data—the demographic, clinical, financial and insurance information that a managed care plan uses to make decisions on benefits and potential candidates.

Exclusive provider organization (EPO)—a preferred provider organization that requires its members to receive health care exclusively from its provider network. Members usually are liable for out-of-plan utilization, except for emergency care.

External quality review organization (EQRO)—an entity that reviews the quality of care provided to Medicaid patients. The entity is not part of or is external to the Medicaid agency. Formerly, the entity was referred to as a peer-review organization.

Federally qualified HMO—a health maintenance organization that meets federal requirements specified in Title XIII of the public Health Service Act. This act addresses an HMO's organizational structure, health service areas, provider contracts, marketing strategies, information systems, quality improvement activities, and grievance and appeal systems. An HMO must be federally qualified to become a Medicare risk contractor.

Fifty-Fifty (50-50) composition—a federal rule that requires at least one-half of a Medicare-contracting HMO's members to have private health insurance and not be eligible for Medicare or Medicaid. This *rule* is intended to safeguard the quality of an HMO's care on the assumption that a person with private insurance will not remain in a plan with substandard care.

Foundation for Accountability (FACCT)—a non-profit organization composed of consumer, purchaser, and government representatives working to develop patient-oriented outcome measures for managed care plans. The FACCT currently is the leading alternative to HEDIS performance measures.

Group model HMO—an HMO that contracts with a large physician practice to provide medical care to its members. The group may contract exclusively with and be partly owned by the health maintenance organization.

Health maintenance organization (HMO)—a managed health plan that offers or arranges for health care to be provided to its members.

Health of seniors measure—one of the Effectiveness of Care measures in HEDIS 3.0. This measure reports the percentage of aged Medicare beneficiaries in a risk HMO whose self-reported physical and mental health status has improved, worsened or stayed the same over a 2-year period. The measure is based on a random sample of a risk HMO's aged Medicare members.

Health plan employer data and information set (HEDIS)—a series of data elements that enable interested parties to calculate and compare numerous performance measures for HMOs. HEDIS data are collected by the National Committee for Quality Assurance, a nonprofit organization that accredits HMOs that meet its quality-of-care standards. Version has about 60 performance measures for such areas as quality, access, utilization and finances.

HEDIS 3.0—the third version of the Health Plan Employer Information and Data Set consists of over 70 "reporting" measures that indicate the rating an HMO attained in the following eight areas: effectiveness of care, access and availability of care, satisfaction with the experience of care, health plan stability, use of services, cost of care, informed healthcare choices and health plan descriptive information. Health plans must use the same definitions and procedures to collect HEDIS measures for their commercial, Medicare and Medicaid members.

Hold harmless—a provision in a healthcare contract that shields a member from being charged by an in-plan provider if the health plan is unable to pay for a service the provider delivered.

Independent practice association (IPA) model HMO—an HMO that contracts with numerous small independent group and solo practices through the intermediary (i.e., independent practice association) that represents them. Physicians maintain their individual practices and negotiate as a group with payers. The physicians may be compensated on a capitated or fee-for-service basis.

Managed behavioral health organization (MBHO)—a managed care organization that specializes in mental health care, which may be defined to include substance abuse services. An MBHO may contract directly with a payer to provide this single benefit or may subcontract with another MCO for the mental health component of a comprehensive health benefit package.

Managed care—the systematic integration and coordination of the financing and delivery of health care. These activities are performed by health plans that try to provide their members with prepaid access to high quality care at relatively low cost and usually are at least partly at risk for the cost of care. The health plans may rely on physician gatekeepers and prior authorization mechanisms to minimize unnecessary or inappropriate utilization.

Managed indemnity plan—a health plan that reimburses providers on a fee-for-service basis but relies on preadmission certification, continued-stay review, second surgical opinion and other utilization management techniques to minimize unnecessary spending. Utilization management is broader than exists under a typical indemnity plan.

Management services organization (MSO)—an entity that performs claims processing, enrollment, marketing and other management services for a health plan.

Medicaid and Medicare Common Date Initiative (McData)—a program sponsored by the HCFA to establish a minimum set of encounter data elements for managed care plans, and to coordinate data issues related to managed care. Information about encounters between providers and patients include demographic data, diagnosis and procedure codes, dates and number of services, provider name and specialty and costs.

Medical loss ratio—the proportion of an HMO's premium revenue that is spent on or "lost to" medical care. The American Association of Health Plans estimates that the national medical loss (or health expense) ratio was about 87% in 1993. The ratio generally increased with the health plan's age, reaching almost 94% for HMOs treating patients before 1973.

Medicare cost contracts—contracts between a fed qualified HMO and the HCFA that allows the HMO to be reimbursed the reasonable cost of care provided to Medicare members but no more than the AAPCC.

Medicare risk contracts—contracts between a federally qualified HMO and the HCFA that requires the HMO to provide all medically necessary Medicare benefits to any Medicare beneficiary who joins the HMO in exchange for a monthly capitated payment. The payment amount depends on several factors, including the beneficiary's age, gender and Medicaid eligibility status.

Network model HMO—an HMO that contracts with several large single or multi-specialty physician groups to provide medical care to its members.

Open enrollment period—a designated period, perhaps 1 or 2 months a year, during which a health plan's current members may switch health plans and non-members may apply for membership. State law may require a health plan to accept all applicants.

Open panel model—a managed health plan that contracts with physicians who render care in their own offices; physicians may contract with other health plans.

Partial risk—the sharing of the financial risk associated with providing specific health services. The risk may be spread among multiple parties, such as an MCO and its physicians and hospitals. In contrast, full risk means that one entity is financially liable for the total cost of rendering specific services. Coordinated affiliation, including the use of a common financial system and medical management strategies and other means can function to reduce risk.

Per member per month (PMPM)—the basis on which capitation rates ordinarily are quoted. For the contract period, which may span 1 year, the member is charged the same amount each month.

Per member per year (PMPY)—the basis on which managed health plans ordinarily express their members' annual utilization rates, e.g., four physician encounters per member per year. A related way to express utilization is in terms of the annual units of service provided per 1,000 members, such as 4,000 physician encounters per 1,000 members per year.

Physician gag rule—provision in a contract that a physician signs with a health plan that prohibits him or her from discussing treatment options with a patient and from criticizing the health plan (e.g., its utilization review policies). Many states have adopted laws prohibiting physician gag rules. Considerable controversy exists about the extent to which HMOs have tried to bar physicians from discussing treatment options with patients.

Physician-hospital organization (PHO)—an entity that integrates and coordinates the health services that a hospital and its medical staff have packaged together to contract with HMOs, employers and other payers. The entity may provide medical care, administrative services or both types of services. It usually is sponsored by the hospital and members of its medical staff, who ordinarily continue to maintain their individual practices.

Point-of-service (POS) HMO—a POS HMO allows members to go out-of-plan to receive certain services. The member makes the decision where to receive care at the time care is needed. The member usually pays an additional premium or co-payment for a POS option. The additional payment varies with the types of services covered by the option.

Point-of-service (POS) product—an insurance policy that allows a person to decide at the time service is needed whether to go out-of-plan for treatment. The option may extend to some, most, or all of the health services covered by the insurance policy. The individual pays an additional premium or cost-sharing amount for this option.

Preexisting condition—an illness that a person has a preset number of months before applying for health insurance. The illness could disqualify the person for health insurance or prevent him or her from obtaining coverage for treatment of medical problems related to the preexisting condition.

Preferred provider organization (PPO)—a managed health plan that uses its provider network to render care to employers and other groups in its provider network. The network usually is limited in size. Providers are paid discounted fees and usually are not at financial risk. Utilization review is used to manage patient care but the methods are not as rigorous as HMOs with risk-bearing primary care physicians serving as gatekeepers.

Primary care network (PCN)—a panel of physicians, nonphysician practitioners and health centers specializing in primary care services. Primary care physicians ordinarily are defined as family practitioners, general practitioners, internists and pediatricians. Sometimes the definition includes obstetricians/gynecologists for some (e.g., prenatal care) or all of their services.

Provider service organization (PSO)—a health plan owned, operated, governed and/or managed by one or more affiliated healthcare providers. The health plan may be a loose affiliation of providers or a highly structured organization.

Provider-sponsored network (PSN)—a single system or multiple affiliated providers that render a prescribed benefit package on a prepaid basis. The PSN may contract with payers or an MCO; it is at financial risk for the benefit package.

Quality compass—a national database that houses HEDIS performance measures for HMOs that voluntarily submit data to the National Committee for Quality Assurance (NCQA). This database also contains the ratings attained by other health plans that have undergone a NCQA accreditation survey. HMO performance measures and accreditation ratings can be linked together. Some of the information is accessible at NCQA's Web site.

Report card—a document that displays the scores a managed care plan attained in such matters as access, quality, utilization, and cost. State agencies, the media, employers, and even some health plans are publishing report cards to help consumers make informed choices about which plan to join.

Risk adjuster—a factor that is used to increase or decrease an average capitation rate to reflect a person's health status or expected utilization of services. A factor greater than one indicates a person with above-average healthcare needs (e.g., 20% greater for a factor of 1.2). A factor less than one indicates a person with below average needs.

Risk pool—an accounting fund that contains the withheld portions of providers' fees and capitation rates. Withheld amounts are at risk and are returned to the providers only if specific performance goals are met.

Risk-bearing entity—the health plan, provider group, or other entity that is financially responsible for providing a defined package of medically necessary health services to a group of persons in exchange for a fixed prepaid payment. The entity is liable or at risk for costs that exceed the payment amount.

Self-insured or self-funded employer—an employer who sets aside a sum of money to pay for the health care its employees receive. The employer therefore assumes the insurance risk associated with providing health care to its employees. Employers with healthy employees can save money by self-insuring.

Solvency reserves—the cash, securities and/or delivery (e.g., building and equipment) assets that a health plan sets aside to pay for health services its members receive if bankruptcy occurs. Cash and securities may be deposited in a bank specified by the state. Delivery assets may not be easily converted into cash without a substantial discount from their book value. Delivery assets' value may plummet after a health plan goes broke if the assets are of limited value outside a healthcare setting.

Staff model HMO—an HMO that relies on employee or staff physicians to provide most of the medical care its members need. The physicians are salaried and may receive bonuses annually if performance goals are met.

Stop loss—the dollar threshold at which the provider's financial liability for additional care is greatly reduced or eliminated. The threshold may apply to each member individually or to all members combined. The threshold commonly is expressed on an annual basis. Once it is reached, the provider may be liable for only a small portion of all remaining costs.

Substantial financial risk—a situation that exists when more than a preset percentage (for Medicare more than 25%) of a physician's or physician group's income is at risk for the cost of referral services. Concern exists that physicians might jeopardize the quality of care if they assume too much risk.

Super-IPA or super PHO model—several IPAs or PHOs that join forces to provide health care over a large geographic region.

Withhold—the dollar amount that an MCO deducts from a provider's fees. The withheld amount is set aside in a risk-sharing fund and is returned to the provider if certain preset goals are met.

Index

I

Photo Credits

Chapter 1

Page 8 Courtesy of Library of Congress, Prints & Photographs Division, [reproduction number ppmsca 09733]; **page 21 (top)** © Andresr/ShutterStock, Inc.; **page 21 (bottom)** © Samuel Perry/ShutterStock, Inc.

Chapter 2

Page 26 © Cerenzio/Dreamstime.com; **page 34** © Joel Shawn/ShutterStock, Inc.; **page 35** © Photos.com; **page 37 (left)** © Ryan McVay/Photodisc/Getty Images; **page 37 (right)** © Gualtiero Boffi/Dreamstime.com; **page 38** © Liv friis-larsen/ShutterStock, Inc.

Chapter 3

Page 58 © Claro Alindogan/Dreamstime.com; **page 61** © Photos.com

Chapter 4

Page 77 Courtesy of the National Library of Medicine; **page 83** © michaeljung/ShutterStock, Inc.; **page 91** © Carlos Arranz/ShutterStock, Inc.; **page 92** © Photos.com

Chapter 5

Page 110 (left) © Avava/ShutterStock, Inc.; **page 110 (right)** © aceshot1/ShutterStock, Inc.; **page 116** © Monkey Business Images/ShutterStock, Inc.

Chapter 6

Page 124 © Photos.com; **page 125** © Monkey Business Images/ShutterStock, Inc.; **page 130** © Photos.com; **page 134** © Monkey Business Images/ShutterStock, Inc.; **page 138** © Lorelyn Medina/ShutterStock, Inc.

Chapter 7

Page 145 (left) © Kentannenbaum/Dreamstime.com; **page 145 (right)** © thumb/ShutterStock, Inc.; **page 147** © Irina Shoyhet/Dreamstime.com; **page 151** © David Watkins/ShutterStock, Inc.

Chapter 9

Page 183 Courtesy of the National Library of Medicine; **page 189** © Inger Anne Hulbaekdal/ShutterStock, Inc.; **page 190** Courtesy of the California Tobacco Control Program

Chapter 11

Page 240 © VisualField/ShutterStock, Inc.; **page 243 (left)** © Dieter Henke/ShutterStock, Inc.; **page 243 (right)** © bhowe/ShutterStock, Inc.; **page 249** © Tony Freeman/PhotoEdit, Inc.; **page 250** © T & L/age fotostock; **page 251** © Chad McDermott/ShutterStock, Inc.; **page 254** © Kevin Lamarque/Reuters/Landov; **page 255** © Yellowj/ShutterStock, Inc.

Chapter 12

Page 265 © Kiselev Andrey Valerevich/ShutterStock, Inc.; **page 266** © Photos.com; **page 267** © John Wollwerth/ShutterStock, Inc.

Chapter 13

Page 288 © Smilla/Dreamstime.com; **page 292** © Creatas/Alamy Images; **page 306** © Andrew Gentry/ShutterStock, Inc.